The State of Families

The State of Families: Law, Policy, and the Meanings of Relationships collects essential readings on the family to examine the multiple forms of contemporary families, the many issues facing families, the policies that regulate families, and how families—and family life—have become politicized.

This text explores various dimensions of "the family" and uses a critical approach to understand the historical, cultural, and political constructions of the family. Each section takes different aspects of the family to highlight the intersection of individual experience, structures of inequality—including race, class, gender, sexuality, disability, and immigration—and state power. Readings, both original and reprinted from a wide range of experts in the field, show the multiple forms and meanings of family by delving into topics including the traditional ground of motherhood, childhood, and marriage, while also exploring cutting edge research into fatherhood, reproduction, child-free families, and welfare.

Taking an interdisciplinary approach to the family, *The State of Families* offers students in the social sciences and professionals working with families new ways to identify how social structure and institutional practice shape individual experience.

Jennifer A. Reich is Professor of Sociology at the University of Colorado Denver. She is the author of two award-winning books, *Fixing Families: Parents, Power, and the Child Welfare System* and *Calling the Shots: Why Parents Reject Vaccines*, and is a co-editor of the book *Reproduction and Society*. Her research examines how individuals and families weigh information and strategize their interactions with the state and service providers in the context of public policy, particularly as they relate to healthcare and welfare.

The State of Families

Law, Policy, and the Meanings of Relationships

Edited by Jennifer A. Reich

Routledge
Taylor & Francis Group

NEW YORK AND LONDON

First published 2021
by Routledge
52 Vanderbilt Avenue, New York, NY 10017

and by Routledge
2 Park Square, Milton Park, Abingdon, Oxon, OX14 4RN

Routledge is an imprint of the Taylor & Francis Group, an informa business

© 2021 Taylor & Francis

Library of Congress Cataloging-in-Publication Data
Names: Reich, Jennifer A., author.
Title: The state of families: law, policy, and the meanings of
relationships / edited by Jennifer Reich.
Description: New York, NY: Routledge Books, 2021. |
Includes bibliographical references and index.
Identifiers: LCCN 2020032018 (print) | LCCN 2020032019 (ebook) |
ISBN 9780367027728 (hbk) | ISBN 9780367027766 (pbk) |
ISBN 9780429397868 (ebk)
Subjects: LCSH: Families—United States. | Marriage—United States. |
Parent and child—United States.
Classification: LCC HQ536 .R4343 2021 (print) | LCC HQ536 (ebook) |
DDC 306.850973—dc23
LC record available at https://lccn.loc.gov/2020032018
LC ebook record available at https://lccn.loc.gov/2020032019

ISBN: 978-0-367-02772-8 (hbk)
ISBN: 978-0-367-02776-6 (pbk)
ISBN: 978-0-429-39786-8 (ebk)

Typeset in Joanna MT & Frutiger
by codeMantra

Every effort has been made to secure required permissions for all text, images, figures and diagrams reprinted in this volume.

The Publisher would like to acknowledge The Conversation for their generous permission to reuse articles from their website. The Conversation, which can be found online at theconversation.com, is a non-profit news site with a mission of democratizing knowledge by getting academic experts to write understandably about issues of public concern.

Contents

Acknowledgments

I owe a debt of gratitude to many. I am grateful to Anna Muraco, an early believer in this volume. She and her students at Loyola Marymount as well as my students at the University of Colorado Denver provided honest assessments of different selections and topics that led to these final chapters. Candan Duran-Aydintug offered advice and encouragement as I developed this book. Laura Carpenter, Jonathan Wynn, Rene Almeling, and Anna Muraco generously read chapters and offered feedback.

Dana Young, Mikayla Barr, and Leah Norland were excellent research assistants and helped to keep me and this project organized. Thanks to Sam Barbaro who imagined this book, and Tyler Bay, Charlotte Taylor, and the team at Taylor & Francis. Suggestions from anonymous reviewers on additional topics to include greatly strengthened the book.

In writing about family, I am especially thankful for my own. My family, immediate and extended, has been a vital source of strength and support for me. Jonas, Lilia, Harrison, and Dave tolerated some very long workdays and provided encouragement along the way, which made all the difference.

Thank you to the authors of the many amazing chapters in this book. Many of them helped to make it possible to include their work, which has made the book so much better.

Here's hoping we can all work to find ways to support everyone's families.

Notes on Contributors

Katie L. Acosta is Associate Professor of Sociology at Georgia State University.

Madina Agénor is the Gerald R. Gill Assistant Professor of Race, Culture, and Society in the Department of Community Health at Tufts University.

Michael K. Ault is Assistant Professor of Organizational Communication at Weber State University.

Maxine Baca Zinn is Professor Emeritus in the Department of Sociology at Michigan State University.

M. V. Lee Badgett is Professor of Economics at the University of Massachusetts Amherst and Williams Distinguished Scholar at UCLA's Williams Institute.

Beth Bailey is Foundation Distinguished Professor of History and Director of the Center for Military, War, and Society Studies at the University of Kansas.

Rana E. Barar is Senior Project Director at Advancing New Standards in Reproductive Health (ANSIRH) at the University of California, San Francisco.

Christina Barmon is Assistant Professor of Sociology at Central Connecticut University.

Amitrajeet A. Batabyal is the Arthur J. Gosnell Professor of Economics at the Rochester Institute of Technology.

Aggie Ebrahimi Bazaz is Assistant Professor of Film, Media, & Theatre at Georgia State University.

Alexis A. Bender is Assistant Professor of Medicine at Emory University.

Jacquelyn J. Benson is Associate Professor in Human Development and Family Science at the University of Missouri.

Dana Berkowitz is Associate Professor of Sociology and Women's and Gender Studies at Louisiana State University.

Amy Blackstone is Professor of Sociology at the University of Maine.

Sarah Bowen is Associate Professor of Sociology at North Carolina State University.

Joslyn Brenton is Associate Professor of Sociology at Ithaca College.

Jamie Budnick is an NICHD Postdoctoral Fellow at the Population Studies Center in the Institute for Social Research at the University of Michigan.

Elisabeth O. Burgess is Professor of Sociology and Director of the Gerontology Institute at Georgia State University.

Kate Cairns is Assistant Professor in the Department of Childhood Studies at Rutgers University-Camden.

Jessica Calarco is Associate Professor of Sociology at Indiana University.

Alma Carten was Associate Professor of Social Work at New York University until her retirement in 2017.

Colleen Cary is Assistant Professor at the Silberman School of Social Work at Hunter College, City University of New York.

Soon Kyu Choi is the Richard Taylor Public Policy Fellow and a Project Manager at the Williams Institute at the University of California Los Angeles.

Teresa M. Cooney is Professor of Sociology at the University of Colorado Denver.

Shelia R. Cotten is Professor in the Department of Media and Information at Michigan State University.

Gary Cross is Emeritus Professor of History at Penn State.

Danielle Czarnecki is a postdoctoral researcher at the Ohio Policy Evaluation Network at the University of Cincinnati.

Bella DePaulo is Project Scientist at the University of California, Santa Barbara.

Dawn Marie Dow is Associate Professor in the Department of Sociology at the University of Maryland, College Park.

Sinikka Elliott is Associate Professor of Sociology at the University of British Columbia.

Diana Greene Foster is Professor in the Department of Obstetrics, Gynecology & Reproductive Sciences at the University of California, San Francisco.

Angela Frederick is Assistant Professor of Sociology in the Department of Sociology & Anthropology at the University of Texas El Paso.

Joshua Gold is Professor of Educational Studies in the College of Education at the University of South Carolina.

Heather Honoré Goltz is Associate Professor of Social Work at the University of Houston-Downtown.

Heather Gould is Research Manager for the Turnaway Study at Advancing New Standards in Reproductive Health (ANSIRH) at the University of California, San Francisco.

Richard Gunderman is the Chancellor's Professor of Medicine, Liberal Arts, and Philanthropy at Indiana University.

Simon F. Haeder is Assistant Professor of Public Policy at Penn State.

Margaret A. Hagerman is Associate Professor of Sociology at Mississippi State University and Faculty Affiliate in both the African American Studies and Gender Studies programs.

Jens Hainmueller is Professor of Political Science at Stanford University.

Kieran Healy is Professor of Sociology at Duke University.

Josée Johnston is Professor of Sociology at the University of Toronto.

Matthew D. Johnson is Professor of Psychology at Binghamton University.

Tera R. Jordan is Associate Professor of Human Development and Family Studies at Iowa State University.

Vikki S. Katz is Associate Professor in the Department of Communication and affiliate graduate faculty in the Department of Sociology at Rutgers University.

Gayle Kaufman is the Nancy and Erwin Maddrey Professor of Sociology at Davidson College.

Eva Feder Kittay is Distinguished Professor of Philosophy at Stony Brook University.

Vicki Lens is Professor at the Silberman School of Social Work at Hunter College, City University of New York.

Krystale Littlejohn is Assistant Professor at the University of Oregon.

Meika Loe is Professor of Sociology and Women's Studies at Colgate University.

Gina Marie Longo is Assistant Professor of Sociology at Virginia Commonwealth University.

Tracey Loughran is Professor of History at the University of Essex.

Kate Luther is Associate Professor in the Department of Sociology at Pacific Lutheran University.

Norah MacKendrick is Associate Professor of Sociology at Rutgers University in New Jersey.

Tey Meadow is Associate Professor of Sociology at Columbia University.

Nara Milanich is Professor of History at Barnard College.

Lisa R. Miller is Assistant Professor of Sociology at Eckerd College.

Martha Minow is the 300th Anniversary University Professor of Law at Harvard University.

Mark Montgomery is Donald L. Wilson Professor of Enterprise and Leadership and Professor of Economics at Grinnell College.

Amanda Moras Associate Professor of Sociology at Sacred Heart University.

Carolyn M. Morell retired from the Department of Social Work at Niagara University.

Kristin Natalier is Associate Professor of Sociology at Flinders University.

Elizabeth Weber Ollen is a Licensed Clinical Psychologist at the UCLA Semel Institute for Neuroscience and Human Behavior.

Carla A. Pfeffer is Associate Professor of Sociology and Women's and Gender Studies at University of South Carolina.

Iris Chin Ponte is Director at the Henry Frost Children's Program Inc. and the President of Ponte and Chau Consulting in Belmont, MA.

Irene Powell is Professor of Economics at Grinnell College.

Christine M. Proulx is Associate Professor of the Department of Human Development & Family Science at the University of Missouri.

Nicholas Raine-Fenning is Reader/Associate Professor of Reproductive Medicine and Surgery at the Queen's Medical Centre at the University of Nottingham.

Jennifer M. Randles is Associate Professor of Sociology at California State University, Fresno.

Mark R. Rank is the Herbert S. Hadley Professor of Social Welfare at Washington University in St. Louis.

Jennifer A. Reich is Professor of Sociology at the University of Colorado Denver.

Maria Rodriguez is Associate Professor of Obstetrics and Gynecology in the School of Medicine at Oregon Health & Science University.

Diana Romero is Associate Professor of Community Health and Social Sciences at the City University of New York.

Barbara Katz Rothman is Professor of Sociology, Public Health, Disability Studies, and Women's Studies at the Graduate Center of the City University of New York.

Maura Ryan is Senior Lecturer in the Department of Sociology at Georgia State University.

Susan M. Shaw is Distinguished Professor Emerita of Sociology at the University of Waterloo.

Shailen Singh is Assistant Professor in the Department of Occupational, Workforce, & Leadership Studies at Texas State University.

Matthew Lee Smith is Associate Professor at the Center for Population Health and Aging in Texas A&M University.

Linley A. Snyder-Rivas is Instructor of Integrative Studies at Texas Tech University.

Rickie Solinger is an independent historian, curator, and lecturer.

Nicholas Syrett is Professor of Women, Gender, and Sexuality Studies at the University of Kansas.

Pauline H. Tesler is Director of the Integrative Law Institute at Commonweal and is owner of the firm Tesler & Sandmann.

Stacy Torres is Assistant Professor of Sociology in the Department of Social and Behavioral Sciences at the University of California, San Francisco.

Dawn E. Trussell is Associate Professor of Sport Management at Brock University.

Lynn H. Turner is Professor of Communication Studies at Marquette University.

Jean Twenge is Professor of Psychology at San Diego State University.

Jessica Valenti is a feminist author, columnist, and co-founder of the blog, *Feministing*.

Bobbi Van Gilder is Assistant Professor of Communication, Journalism & Media at Suffolk University.

Lisa Wade Associate Professor of Sociology and Gender and Sexuality Studies at Tulane University.

Suzanna Danuta Walters is Professor of Sociology and Professor and Director of Women's, Gender, and Sexuality Studies at Northeastern University.

Leslie Kim Wang is Associate Professor of Sociology at the University of Massachusetts Boston.

Shannon Weber is a writer, educator, and editorial and social media manager at the global digital media and education company The Body Is Not An Apology.

Richard West is Professor of Communication Studies at Emerson College.

Bianca D.M. Wilson is a Rabbi Barbara Zacky Senior Scholar of Public Policy of the Williams Institute at UCLA School of Law.

Lily Wolf is a medical student at the Indiana University School of Medicine.

SECTION I
Defining Families

WHAT IS THE FAMILY?

Most of the time when we think of the meanings of family, we think of the social and emotional experiences of family as they relate to us as individuals. Our sense of emotional, social, and material support is intimately woven into our sense of what family should mean. For good or bad, family comprises relationships that are more intimate, emotionally powerful, and enduring than other connections. Family relationships are long-lasting; from birth onward, and even when alienated from family members, we still speak of them as family. We participate in a wider number of activities with family members than with others—eating, sleeping, traveling, illness, fighting—and family members are most often with whom we shape milestones in our lives. And typically, we experience a wider range of emotions with family members than with anyone else—no one can make us more angry, happy, or can hurt us more than our family. Family relationships are indeed unique. Since family is so personal, it seems odd to think of family as also an institution regulated by law and policy.

This book aims to link the ways we experience family with the ways family is organized, defined, and governed as an institution that grants rights and responsibilities. Said differently, family life provides privileges but also creates obligations. Although we do not often recognize it, family members get dozens of benefits simply by being defined and recognized as family. Here are a few: the right to make medical decisions for family members, to automatically inherit property when a family member dies, to gain custody of children after divorce, to file joint tax returns, to access immigration processes, to decide how one's own children should be educated. At the same time, family life comes with obligations: to provide care to children, to pay child or spousal support, to support aging parents.

Of course, the rights and obligations of family are not absolute. Although parents have choices of how to educate and discipline their children, they must do so within legal requirements that mandate education or define excessive punishment as child abuse. Individuals may choose who to marry, but they do so within state laws that define who is eligible to marry, which may exclude some kinds of relationships. Legal action may result when family members fail to meet their obligations, including garnishing of wages to pay child support or social service intervention in the case of child or elder abuse or neglect. The selection of readings featured in this book aims to give some understanding not only of how families matter personally and interpersonally to the people in them, but also of how families matter to the community in ways that lead to legal regulation of them.

How Should Families Be Defined?

The formal definition of family includes those people who are related through blood (or genetic relationship), marriage, or adoption. This is clearly a fairly narrow definition and is the one used most often in law. However, when we think of who we define as family, we often think in terms of broader criteria. Family friends who are like uncles or aunts, roommates, and best friends who we define as our chosen family, our parents' long-term romantic partners who helped raise us. Ex-spouses who are still close friends. Foster siblings. Even pets. These definitions reflect a functional definition of family, which raises an obvious question: if we function like a family, are we not family? More generally, we might wonder, why can't any group that feels like family be recognized as a family?

Admittedly, it is difficult to come up with one definition of family as we see a growing diversity in family forms and relationships. That diversity could support the view that since family is personal, individuals should define for themselves who counts as family. However, because the family is not just a source of personal experience, but is also an institution that distributes privileges and obligations, definitions matter. There are good reasons we should make sure that our definition of family does not just recognize those who want rights, but also recognizes those who want to share responsibilities. For example, we have to decide who should be eligible for health benefits or survivor benefits that come with being a family member. Who should be presumed a decision maker when someone is incapacitated? Who should decide how children should be educated or with what religion they should grow up? The chapters by law professor Martha Minow and communication scholars Lynn Turner and Richard West take up these very questions.

Regulating the Family

Regulation of family life happens on multiple levels. In the United States, most questions of how to define and regulate the family have been left to the states. For example, states pass laws to dictate who can marry—including how old you must be or whether you can marry a cousin. The chapter by gender scholar Nicholas Syrett highlights the continuing presence of child marriage within US state law as an example. Laws about the process of adopting a child are state laws. The federal government may also regulate family life. Most commonly, Congress passes laws that set funding or policy priorities, including requirements for accessing public benefits or guiding states in their own legal processes. For example, in 1978, Congress passed the Indian Child Welfare Act, which established standards that agencies had to meet before children of Native American heritage could be adopted outside of tribal lands and to non-Native families. In 1997, Congress passed the Adoption and Safe Families Act, which set priorities for states and counties to increase the number of children adopted from foster care and gave states funding to meet these goals. In the past few decades, the federal government has taken a larger role in regulating family than it has in the past. Interstate child support enforcement, welfare reform, funding for abstinence-only sex education, marriage promotion education, and family medical leave are examples of federal laws that affect family life.

State laws must be compatible with federal law. They can go further than federal law but cannot contradict or undermine federal law. Federal courts may review state laws to make sure they do not violate the US constitution. Here is one example. In 1992, California passed a state law that said that people who move to California and apply for welfare benefits could only receive the amount of money they would have received in the state where they used to live for the first year they live in California. Since California at the time had the sixth highest level of public assistance benefits in the country, the state argued this change would save them $10.9 million in welfare benefits. Welfare recipients sued arguing this was discriminatory. The US Supreme Court reviewed this case and ruled that the US Constitution's Fourteenth Amendment protects the right to travel "by allowing citizens to move freely between states, securing the right to be treated equally in all states when visiting, and securing the rights of new citizens to be treated like long-time citizens of a state" (*Saenz v. Roe*). This state law violated rights guaranteed in the constitution and, thus, could not go into effect.

Family is also regulated in ways that are less obvious. The tax code—both state and federal—defines family and attaches benefits, including tax credits, depending on who is recognized as a member of the family. Building codes in cities or counties may identify certain neighborhoods as residential or as zoned for single-family homes, or may recognize age requirements for some communities, like ones built for seniors. Counties or cities might require that businesses in their territory provide benefits to unmarried domestic partners. These local laws must also not violate state or federal law and must be constitutional.

FAMILIES IN PUBLIC AND PRIVATE LIFE

Most people think of our family life as intensely personal. We also see decisions about family as an expression of our individualism. In fact, this view of family is supported by (and seemingly incompatible with) law and policy. Many of the legal decisions that have shaped family life reference the importance of allowing individuals to pursue their own interests and sense of personal reward. For example, in the 1967 US Supreme Court case of *Loving v Virginia*, in which the Supreme Court overturned a law that forbid marriage between individuals of different races, the majority decision explained, "The freedom to marry has long been recognized as one of the vital personal rights essential to the orderly pursuit of happiness by free men." (This case is discussed in more detail in Section III.) Similarly, the 2003 US Supreme Court decision of *Lawrence v Texas* struck down a Texas law that made it a crime for two persons of the same sex to engage in certain intimate sexual conduct. In that decision, the justices highlighted the importance of individual freedom. The decision explained, "Liberty presumes an autonomy of self that includes freedom of thought, belief, expression, and certain intimate conduct." We do not necessarily expect total freedoms, as we each face social pressures, family obligations, and cultural rules within our family—and the families we may join. However, individuality and personal liberty, that is the ability to exercise one's rights without limitation by the government, are key aspects of what we expect from family life.

As much as family is fundamental to our individual happiness (and sometimes misery), the family also holds benefits for the community beyond the individuals within those families. Where families live, how they treat their children, how they pay taxes, and what benefits they receive are all matters of public concern. While we must be free to exercise liberty, we are never isolated in those freedoms. Communities invest in families and families rely on the community for resources they could not otherwise obtain alone. For example, communities rely on families to produce and raise children who will become workers, service providers, and contributors to social security and other tax-based programs. We want children to be safe and raised well so our communities are safe, productive, and successful. In many less visible ways, communities and companies benefit from the unpaid labor that happens in households. Small daily acts to support household members—from laundering work clothes to cooking meals—all support workers who in turn support the economy.

Because we rely on families to make communities function, communities support families too. For example, communities fund schools, parks, recreation programs, healthcare, and social services. Even individuals who do not have children—or whose children are grown—benefit from the work other families do to raise children and are therefore asked to invest in community resources to benefit other families. For example, homeowners, even those without children, may pay property taxes to support schools. Taxes may support drug treatment programs for those who need them but cannot afford them. Perhaps no one in our family will use those programs, but we accept that our communities are better when those who want treatment can access it. We can think of other examples of similar investments, like in programs for the aging, health insurance for people who have disabilities, or subsidized preschool.

The relationship between families and communities is reciprocal. It would be difficult for individuals in families to accomplish all their goals without community support. Food safety, education, transportation, ramps on sidewalks for strollers or wheelchairs, and traffic lights are all public investments that help families achieve their goals. Some families need help from the state to access nutrition. Others rely on government agencies to inspect restaurants, which makes food safer. Families in turn can contribute to the workforce and the economy, and can more fully participate in making communities better.

POLITICIZING THE FAMILY

The family is both intensely personal and fundamentally public. The result is that the family is subject to political and social debates about what it should be and how it should function. The shapes and meanings of family are not fixed and have changed over time as a result of political, economic, and social pressures, as the chapter by Maxine Baca Zinn in this section and many others throughout the book show. Social change has also led to and resulted from declines in marriage rates, as Bella DePaulo points out in her chapter. The result is that many family forms, particularly those that violate forms seen as traditional, are portrayed as the result of individual choices and as causing other social problems. Claims about the decline of the family, family immorality, increasing rates of cohabitation, or too much or too little childbearing map on to existing systems of inequality. Accusations most often focus on those whose race, class, gender, ethnicity, immigration status, sexuality, or abilities have limited their access to power and resources in the community. Whether it is single parents, queer families, immigrant parents, mothers with disabilities, fathers who can't find work in rural communities, or couples choosing not to marry, we often hear claims that by existing as a family, these families cause societal problems. The result is often laws and policies that target certain families, particular family members, or certain behaviors in order to change or punish them. How the family is politicized tracks on to other systems of inequality.

If we agree that policies relating to family should work to improve the lives of family members, and, thus, our communities, we need to consider some core questions when examining laws. We should ask what has been identified as the problem, what are the proposed solutions, who is targeted by the proposed law or policy, and how will the proposal be implemented—and at what monetary and social cost? When laws and policies target those who are already the most vulnerable, and may deliberately or accidentally make their circumstances worse, community members need question whether they should be implemented.

OVERVIEW OF THIS BOOK

This book looks closely at the state of the family. I aim to take seriously the issues of how we define family, how we regulate family, and how the experiences of family reflect other systems of inequality. Each section provides a sample of readings that offer an opportunity to think about the different ways people experience family, feel recognized as family, and are regulated as family. The sections also highlight how family has changed over time.

Most of the chapters have been edited from their original form and some citations and discussions of related research that were in the original articles have been removed or abbreviated to make it possible to cover more topics. The citations to the original material are included in this book and readers with additional questions should look to those for more detail or background. The chapters here aim to provide a variety of perspectives to think about the multiple dimensions of the family. This section begins by delving into ways of thinking critically about how we define families and how families have changed over time. The next three sections look at formal and informal regulation of relationships, including dating and courtship, marriage and partnerships, and divorce and dissolutions. The following sections examine reproduction, adoption, families without children, and children in families to explore different family choices and configurations. The remaining sections look closely at motherhood, fatherhood, welfare policy, and aging. By thinking about the complexities of family life, we can begin to critically examine claims that are made about the family and can work toward ensuring our policies support families, which in turn will make our communities better.

1

The Challenge of Defining "Family"

Lynn H. Turner and Richard West

The family is a critically important social institution with huge implications for laypeople, policy makers, and scholars alike. Family comprises the first group to which a person belongs, and usually provides the most long-lasting group membership for individuals. In addition, in the United States, family is seen as a group that is qualitatively different from any other group to which a person belongs. The enduring bonds of obligation, the unique communication behaviors, the evolution through time, as well as the expectations for affection and support that characterize family set it apart from other groups. Further, the family's contributions to an individual's sense of identity and self-worth have long been noted, and as Olson, Baiocchi-Wagner, Kratzer, and Symonds (2012) comment, "…our families provide the glue that connects all the parts of our lives—for better and for worse" (p. 1). Clearly, family is a term signifying something of importance to people, and a term that is fraught with meaning. The question is: what does it mean?

When a term is as important to people as family is, then the process of defining it also becomes important. Yet, defining family often is a problem that bedevils policy makers, laypeople, and scholars alike. The task of defining family becomes critical as politicians try to develop laws and policies affecting families. The myriad laws related to family life have had a profound effect upon family members. Specific laws, including the Family and Medical Leave Act (FMLA) and the Patient Protection and Affordable Care Act (PPACA), continue to influence nearly every family today. More general policies, too, including those related to child custody, unemployment benefits, and earned income tax credits, also affect how policy contributes to the definition process. In many ways, these laws and policies comment on the definition of family either specifically as in the 2013 US Supreme Court decision allowing married same-sex couples to receive federal benefits, or by implication, as in the FMLA.

Many questions attend the task of defining family, including but not limited to: is a difference implied in saying "the family" as opposed to "family"? And, what might that difference mean? Do we see family as a refuge from outside trauma and a source of comfort and support in the face of life's stressors? Or do we imagine the family as a crucible for pain and conflict? Or is it both? Or neither? For that matter, when we invoke the concept of family, what people do we include? Are we speaking of people who share living space, who are related by blood, or those who, through some qualitative algorithm, feel like family to us? When we mention family, are we talking about those who raised us (our families-of-origin), those to whom we

Turner, Lynn H., and Richard West. "The challenge of defining 'family'." *The SAGE Handbook of Family Communication* (2015): 10–25.

were born (our families-of-procreation), those with whom we currently live, or some other configuration? Is anyone, or any entity, allowed to have the final say in defining family? If we privilege one family form over others, what does that mean about the forms we leave out of our definition?

DIFFICULTIES IN CREATING A DEFINITION OF FAMILY

The task of defining family may be complicated by the myriad choices currently affecting family structures. Relational choices, including cohabitation, divorce, and postdivorce friendships, have influenced the composition of the Western family. Reproductive technologies, including contraception, surrogacy, and in vitro fertilization, have provided both women and men with opportunities to plan how many children to have, whether to have children at all, or whether to involve others in the process of childbearing for the family. In addition, other technologies may affect who is a member of the family. For instance, online communication allows people to interact across geographic space, and this may have an effect on who is considered a family member. Grandparents, and other extended family members, may become more central to a family's functioning through their ability to Skype with and text their grandchildren. Technologically assisted communication also serves to maintain family ties. Social media such as Facebook, for example, have been used to seek reassurance from others and to alleviate loneliness for college students who have moved away from their families-of-origin. Yet, if such reassurance from family members has not been provided, what effect does this have upon the family? Are the college students beginning to be edged out of the definition?

Further, we cannot ignore the influence of the media on shaping the definition of family, because so many people in the United States base their ideas about family on mediated images. Television, talk radio, social media, newspapers, and popular press all remain instrumental teachers about what constitutes family. Watching *Modern Family*, for instance, gives the viewer some insights into a gay-father-headed household. Listening to Rush Limbaugh, a conservative talk show host, provides listeners with Limbaugh's views on the effects immigration has on families. Reading tweets from unmarried Hollywood couples who are recent parents sends messages about possibilities for parenting and family life.

Another complicating factor for understanding the definition of family concerns the economy. The financial ebbs and flows in the United States affect the family unit and even strike at people's conception of family. Some family members, because of job loss, reduced labor hours, or unemployment, are incapable of living alone. These members frequently return to their family-of-origin because they can no longer afford housing expenses. A man and his children may return to his parents' house because he can no longer sustain childcare costs. A daughter who could not get a job after college might decide to return to live with her single mother. A recently unemployed family member may have to take a job in a city 500 miles away, resulting in a change in the household's occupants, and, perhaps, in the definition of the family itself.

Culture is a critical factor in considering the meaning of family. From a demographic vantage point, the waves of immigrants who currently live in the United States have had a profound effect upon family definitions. Because immigrants arrive with various values related to family life (e.g., parenting, discipline, patterns of communication), it is increasingly difficult to establish a universal definition for family. For example, some immigrants arrive with a deep reverence for their elders, and households are established with this multigenerational configuration. Other immigrants arrive in the United States with few, if any, of their family members, thereby creating an entirely different family arrangement (e.g., families who are geographically separated or new families of volunteer members). And, deportation also necessarily affects housing insecurity and, in some cases, permanent family dissolution. Finally, it is relevant to point out that internal migration patterns may alter the emotional support of kin; external members of the family, therefore, may necessarily become part of the newly configured family type.

The cultural conversation about what and who should be included in the definition of family has been taking place for quite some time. Years ago, these dialogues may have been relegated to holiday dinners, where family members met, perhaps for the only time all year, and weighed in on social issues. [But] the reality is that many family members have no problem tackling difficult topics. Among those topics is family itself. Myriad areas related to family are rife for Thanksgiving Day banter around the table: same-sex marriage, caring for aging family members, divorce, and surrogate mothers among others. At first glance, such difficult dialogues may be viewed as simply vehicles for family members to exhibit strong opinions. Yet, these interactions may provide families with both clarity and confusion about what constitutes a family, the dynamics of family life, and the various arrangements and configurations related to family.

The numerous organic and cultural influences upon families today make it nearly impossible to construct a single unifying definition. As society changes and evolves, so, too, does our conception of family. Change has been a constant feature in our notions about the family. Despite the obvious difficulties of the task, researchers continue to work toward defining family in a variety of different ways. In the following section, we discuss some of these approaches.

THE CONCEPTUAL APPROACH

Many researchers have offered specific, relatively concise, conceptual definitions for the term family, perhaps beginning with Burgess's (1926) classic definition stating that the family consists of a unity of interacting personalities. Olson et al. (2012) profile ten examples of conceptual definitions for family. These include the following: "[t]he family is a social group characterized by common residence, economic cooperation, and reproduction. It includes adults of both sexes, at least two of whom maintain a socially approved sexual relationship, and one or more children, own or adopted, of the sexually cohabiting adults" (Murdock, 1949, p. 1, cited in Olson et al., p. 5); "[a] family is a set of relationships determined by biology, adoption, marriage, and in some societies, social designation, and existing even in the absence of contract or affective involvement, and in some cases, even after the death of certain members" (Bedford & Blieszner, 1997, p. 526, cited in Olson et al., p. 5); and "[a] social group of two or more persons, characterized by ongoing interdependence with long-term commitments that stem from blood, law, or affection" (Braithwaite & Baxter, 2006, p. 3, cited in Olson et al., p. 5).

Some researchers have distilled some of the common elements across these conceptual definitions to create some general perspectives for defining family. For instance, Koerner and Fitzpatrick argued that three perspectives describe the various conceptual definitions advanced by researchers. They noted that conceptual definitions based on the presence or absence of certain members (e.g., mothers, fathers, grandparents, and so forth) could be classified as structural definitions. Second, Koerner and Fitzpatrick noted that other definitions were predicated on the group accomplishing certain social and psychological tasks, and they labeled these functional definitions. Finally, they claimed that some definitions focused on the emotional ties formed in families as well as their evolutionary nature resulting in a shared past and the expectation of a common future. Koerner and Fitzpatrick called these transactional definitions.

THE LENS APPROACH

Floyd and his colleagues, Mikkelson and Judd (2006) argued that when scholars define family they usually do it by using one or more of three lenses: (1) a structural lens that focuses on biological relationships (they label this the biogenetic lens), (2) a legal lens that concentrates on relationships sanctioned by the laws of a given culture (a sociolegal lens), or (3) a functional lens that spotlights the roles that people play relative to one another and the extent to which people "feel and act like family" (p. 27) (called a role lens). The role lens highlights communication for being the connecting tissue that binds people into family, the sociolegal lens focuses on social behaviors that have been codified into laws that define family relationships, and the biogenetic lens turns away from social behaviors, and instead uses two criteria for determining the definition of family: (1) the extent to which a relationship is directly reproductive, at least potentially, and (2) whether or not people share genetic material. Although Floyd and his coauthors note that each lens has advantages as well as disadvantages for scholars, they especially commend the biogenetic lens. They observe that this lens is extremely useful for scholarship for at least two reasons. First, it is much easier for a researcher to find families to study using this lens compared to the others, and, second, the biogenetic lens allows researchers to be consistent in defining and recruiting families to study.

The Social Construction or Discourse-Dependence Approach

Another approach for defining family is often called social construction because it is grounded in the notion of how people *do* family, or how family members' behaviors construct a sense of "familiness." In a study of how children in England think about kinship, Mason and Tipper (2008) exemplify this approach. They say that creativity is a part of developing family, because kinship is not a given, but rather is shaped and molded "by people's own family negotiations and practices as well as through shifting public understandings and legal definitions of what is considered relatedness" (p. 441). Galvin (2006) acknowledges that all families are somewhat discourse-dependent, and by this she means that all families rely on communication behaviors to "talk family into being." Families use a variety of rituals, stories, pet names, and other communication behaviors to accomplish this task. However, Galvin observes that families who do not resemble one another physically, and, in fact, may not be biologically related to each other (such as European American parents who have adopted children from Korea, for instance) are the most discourse-dependent. Galvin asserts that these families talk their relationships into family status by naming, justifying, and defending them.

Laypeople's Definitions

Rather than propose a definition themselves, some researchers have been interested in how laypeople define family and how these definitions compare to scholars' definitions. For instance, Leslie Baxter and her colleagues (2009) found some consistency in their respondents' definitions with the biogenetic and sociolegal approaches to defining family. Yet, they also observed subtle signs in their data that laypeople were taking a more expansive approach to defining family than scholars, using those lenses, do. For example, the participants in their study revealed that the presence of frequent communication among members increased the likelihood that they would label the group a family regardless of their biological or legal status. In addition, the authors noted that there may be some reciprocity between scholars' and laypeople's definitions, such that "when the research community defines 'family' along traditional lines, this definition functions to marginalize our understanding of alternative family forms" (p. 186). This insight suggests that researchers have a greater role in the definitional struggle than they may have realized.

Gillis (1996) was interested in how laypeople *think* about family life. In examining this aspect of the definition, Gillis stated,

> …we all have two families, one that we live *with* and another we live *by*. We would like the two to be the same, but they are not. Too often the families we live with exhibit the kind of self-interested, competitive, divisive behavior that we have come to associate with the market economy and the public sphere. Often fragmented and impermanent, they are much less reliable than the imagined families we live by. The latter are never allowed to let us down. Constituted through myth, ritual, and image, they must be forever nurturing and protective, and we will go to any lengths to ensure that they are so, even if it means mystifying the realities of family life.
>
> (p. xv)

Stacey (1999) observed that the family of fables that Gillis refers to as the family we live *by* is more compelling than

> the messy, improvisational, patchwork bonds of postmodern family life … [and since these fabled families] function as pivotal elements in our distinctive national imagination, these symbolic families are also far more stable than any in which past generations ever dwelled.
>
> (p. 489)

These scholars argue that laypeople tend to idealize the family and overload it with impossible expectations because it is reassuring to think about the family as an institution of unconditional love and constant support, even when our own experiences may not conform to this definition.

Culture and Social Class

Researchers have also noted that the entire process of defining family must be filtered through the prism of culture and social class. For instance, Dill (2001) reminds us that many conceptual definitions of family are predicated on White, middle-class norms. Dill cautions that these definitions cannot extend universally because White, middle-class family norms depend upon different family arrangements from other classes and racial groups. For instance, White middle-class children could not have begun staying home longer in the nineteenth century, nor could their mothers have redirected their time to caring for them, without the labor of slaves and immigrants who provided cotton to the mills, cheap factory clothes, and household help. Thus, the new construction of childhood and motherhood that arose in the nineteenth century was not extended to slave and poor immigrant families.

Stewart (2007) asks the question: who is kin or what is family? But she specifically examines that question through African American family practices. She found, consistent with other research on the topic, that her respondents had an expansive definition for family, including extended members, as well as voluntary members or "fictive kin." Stewart also found, however, that socioeconomic status did mediate this result somewhat in that members of higher socioeconomic groups made a distinction between immediate and extended family, although they included them all in the definition. Members of lower socioeconomic groups did not make the same distinction.

Summary

Defining family is a complex task and the definition differs depending on which approach a researcher takes. The task is further complicated because of the wide range of diversity characterizing the contemporary US family. In examining the family in the twenty-first century, Bachman (2008) observes that it is "post-traditional" because "it does not adhere to one specific structural model: it is fluid, not static; inclusive, not exclusive; diverse, not monolithic" (p. 44). However, Bachman also notes that social support for such diversity is contested, lending support to our assertion about the struggle over defining family. Interestingly, however, Coontz (2005) argues that "the diversity in U.S. families today is probably no larger than in most periods in the past" (p. 78). Indeed, she states, "family variability" (p. 66) has been with us for centuries.

Conclusions

Our ideas of family are constantly changing and social issues compel us to continue renovating our definitions of family. Currently, our image of the family is affected by many changes, but these changes do not represent the disintegration of the American family. They are simply more reconstructions in the family's continual evolution. This evolution often provokes nostalgia. As Gillis (1996) observed, much changes in family life, but one constant is that each generation looks back at past families as being more stable and authentic than current families.

Yet, even if the term *family* resists a simple unchanging definition, it still remains a critically important construct for laypeople, policy makers, and scholars. As laypeople, we recognize a need for historical roots, a communal present, and a way to connect to our future and the future beyond our own lifetimes. It seems likely that these needs find satisfaction within the family context. Jane Smiley (1996) eloquently speaks about how these needs all came together for her at her grandmother's funeral. In the midst of the eulogies for her grandmother, Smiley's three-year-old son came to ask her a question. Smiley looked down at her young son in the context of the funeral and said,

> [h]e stood beside me, looking out at the group. I like to think that he was surveying his past, beginning to write his future, assembling the characters in his subconscious to live alongside the immediate, Freudian ones of Mom, Dad, and sisters, and I like to think that our voices, speaking of our grandmother entered him and lodged there, just at the boundary of conscious memory, ready to emerge when all of us are gone, and he is speaking to our unknown descendants.

(p. 247)

As long as family means something this powerful to laypeople, scholars will continue to be interested in studying the communication processes that go on within it and construct it. In so doing, researchers will have to grapple with the meaning for family. Our responsibility may not be to find the one true definition, however, but rather to carefully define family for purposes of our study and clearly communicate that definition for our readers. Further, it behooves us to acknowledge the diversity of family in people's lived experiences and be sure that diversity is reflected in communication research.

References

Bachman, M. K. (2008). Family values, feminism, and the post-traditional family. In D. G. Wiseman (Ed.), *The American family: Understanding its changing dynamics and place in society* (pp. 39–52). Springfield, IL: Charles C. Thomas Publisher, Ltd.

Baxter, L. A., Henauw, C., Huisman, D., Livesay, C. B., Norwood, K., Su, H., Wolf, B., & Young, B. (2009). Lay conceptions of "family": A replication and extension. *Journal of Family Communication, 9*(3), 170–189.

Bedford, V. H., & Blieszner, R. (1997). Personal relationships in later life families. In S. Duck (Ed.), *Handbook of personal relationships* (2nd ed., pp. 523–539). New York, NY: Wiley.

Braithwaite, D. O., & Baxter, L. A. (2006). *Engaging theories in family communication: Multiple perspectives.* Thousand Oaks, CA: Sage.

Burgess, E. W (1926). The family as a unity of interacting personalities. *The Family, 7,* 3–9.

Coontz, S. (2005). *Marriage, a history: How love conquered marriage.* London, UK: Viking.

Dill, B. T. (2001). Our mothers' grief: Racial-ethnic women and the maintenance of families. In M. L. Andersen & P. H. Collins (Eds.), *Race, class, and gender: An anthology,* 4th edition (pp. 268–289), Belmont, CA: Wadsworth.

Floyd, K., Mikkelson, A. C., & Judd, J. (2006). Defining the family through relationships. In L. H. Turner & R. West (Eds.), *The family communication sourcebook* (pp. 21–39). Thousand Oaks, CA: Sage.

Galvin, K. M. (2006). Diversity's impact on defining the family: Discourse-dependence and identity. In L. H. Turner & R. West (Eds.), *The family communication sourcebook* (pp. 3–19). Thousand Oaks, CA: Sage.

Gillis, J. R. (1996). *A world of their own making: Myth, ritual, and the quest for family values.* New York, NY: Basic Books.

Koerner, A., & Fitzpatrick, M. A. (2004). Communication in intact families. In A. Vangelisti (Ed.), *Handbook of family communication* (pp. 177–195). Mahwah, NJ: Lawrence Erlbaum.

Mason, J., & Tipper, B. (2008). Being related: How children define and create kinship. *Childhood, 15*(4), 441–460. doi: 10.1177/0907568208097201.

Murdock, G. P. (1949). *Social structure.* New York, NY: Macmillan.

Olson, L. N., Baiocchi-Wagner, E. A., Kratzer, J. M. W., & Symonds, S. E. (2012). *The dark side of family communication.* Cambridge, UK: Polity Press.

Smiley, J. (1996). Afterword: Gen-narration. In S. S. Fiffer & S. Fiffer (Eds.), *Family: American writers remember their own* (pp. 241–247). New York, NY: Pantheon Books.

Stacey, J. (1999). The family values fable. In S. Coontz (Ed.), *American families: A multicultural reader* (pp. 487–490). New York, NY: Routledge.

Stewart, P. (2007). Who is kin? Family definition and African American families. *Journal of Human Behavior in the Social Environment, 15*(2), 163–181. doi:10.1300/J137v15n02_10.

2

Redefining Families

Who's In and Who's Out?

Martha Minow

My remarks here are partly inspired by that distinguished scholar, Lily Tomlin. You see, I am going to discuss a series of worries, and no one is more acute or perceptive about worry than Lily Tomlin (and her collaborator, Jane Wagner). Lily Tomlin says she worries because *what* if the inventor of MUSAK thinks up something else. She says, "I worry about reflective flea collars. Oh, sure, drivers can see them glow in the dark, but so can the fleas." And "I worry if peanut oil comes from peanuts and olive oil comes from olives, where *does* baby oil come from?" "I worry no matter how cynical you become, it's never enough to keep up."[1]

I worry because I worked on a lawsuit recently presented to the highest court in New York. I'm not just worried about losing; I'm worried about the whole thing being in court in the first place.

The case is called *Alison D. v. Virginia M.*[2] The facts, briefly, are these: two unmarried people who lived together for several years decided to have a child. Because the two people are both women, they turned to artificial insemination. Virginia became pregnant and had a child; she agreed to raise the child together with her partner Alison and for two years they all lived together. Alison participated in the care of the child. Then, Alison and Virginia separated. The child remained with Virginia but spent regular weekly visits—overnight visits—with Alison for the next two years. The child also stayed in close contact with Alison's parents, known to the child as his grandparents. During this time, Alison continued to pay child support and mortgage payments to Virginia, but after two years had passed, Virginia started to place limits on such visits. When Virginia foreclosed all contact between Alison and the child, Alison went to court and sought a judicial declaration that she could continue her visits with the child.

I worry that this case should never have come to court. I worry that a judge could be so disapproving of the entire situation that the child will be taken away from both adults. I worry that we may see here the fulfillment of the lawyer's adage: hard cases make bad law.

I also worry that some of you will find the whole situation unacceptable, and I am not sure how to convince you that it's not. I will tell you about the argument I made in favor of a functional notion of family—and I will tell you about my worries about that argument.

Minow, Martha. "Redefining Families: Who's in and Who's Out." *University of Colorado Law Review* 62 (1991): 269.

A. Functional Family

I worry that neither you nor the courts will buy the argument that I and other lawyers working on the side of Alison have made: that it is not important here whether a group of people fit the formal legal definition of a family (created by marriage or adoption). Instead, what is important is whether the group of people function as a family: do they share affection and resources, think of one another as family members, and present themselves as such to neighbors and others?

The tension between official legal forms and functional families has created issues for centuries. The contrast between official, formal marriage and informal but still ultimately lawful marital unions is a good example. In medieval Europe, the practice of clandestine marriage, entered into with only the participation and knowledge of the two parties and without banns or public ceremony, persisted despite opposition by church and other leaders. Similarly, in places like the frontier in the early United States where people lived scattered from one another, the requisites of a formal marriage were often difficult to fulfill: finding a minister, recording the marriage officially. Therefore, many people—and many courts—concluded that a man and a woman could acquire the legal status of being married if they lived as husband and wife long enough to be functionally like a marriage.

Like most lawyers, I get nervous—I grow worried—when we start to imagine the law being whatever anyone says it is rather than what the rules say it is. But I am equally worried about preserving a set of legal rules that have little relationship to how people actually live. That's not law: that's ideology; that's the production of a set of beliefs used to distribute status and value rather than effectively guide behavior.

But unless we start to make family law connect with how people really live, the law is either largely irrelevant or merely ideology: merely statements of the kinds of human arrangements the lawmakers do and do not endorse. The gap between law and practice is especially pronounced in the face of revolutionary scientific and technological changes. With the wonders of modem technology—indeed, not even that modem—people can have children with the help of an absent and even anonymous sperm donor. With the wonders of modem technology, a doctor today implants an embryo made with the genetic material of two people into the womb of a third person. This is a feat not only of science but also of law, because this act also bypasses the usual legal rules of adoption.

And with the wonders of modem technology, I can dip into the database of thousands if not millions of court cases just by sitting at my computer. When I plug in the terms: nonparent within ten words of visitation, out pop a pile of cases. Some are like the Alison D. case, same-sex couples that have raised a child together. Many more are different family constellations: a boyfriend of the mother who lived with her and her children by another man; an aunt who cared for a child; a grandparent; a foster parent who cared for the child for years before the child returned to the biological parent. A related case involves a woman who belongs to the Navajo tribe; the tribe gave this woman custody of the three children of her cousin because the tribe concluded the children were neglected. When the woman applied for Aid for Families with Dependent Children (AFDC) benefits to support the children, she was denied on the ground that she did not fit the requisite definitions of kin used by the regulations in New Mexico.[3]

These cases are windows into the home lives of people who do not fit the legal definition of parent—but who may well have lived in the kinds of relationships we signify by saying "parent-and-child." Getting behind words, legal formalities, and even blood ties to see how people really live and who cares for whom I think should bear on the question, who should be treated like family?

The trial judge in the case of In re Alison D. did not think about things this way. Instead, that court reasoned that Alison is not a parent and thus cannot even be heard in her argument for visitation. The governing law only empowers the courts to hear petitions for visitation brought by parents. Alison is not a biological or adoptive parent, reasoned the court, so she cannot be heard. Case dismissed. And it is that dismissal we appealed. The majority on review agreed with the trial court.

I worry about court decisions like this one. The court assumed that it knew what a "parent" is—the notion that a parent must be biological or adoptive is not set out in the statute; the court supplied it on its own.

The court there was not irrational; the dictionary might provide some support. So might popular cultural images—so even might statistical predictions about the likelihood that people without a biological or adoptive tie take on parental roles. But I worry about all these things. Turning to the dictionary as if it gave answers about how people do or should live is simply submitting important social—and judicial—choices to another group of people, the people who write dictionaries. And those people are not too with it. It takes a long time for a new word to get in, or for an old word to reflect its current meanings. But most worrisome to me is the way a dictionary can be used to foreclose discussion, as in one case in which a judge rejected two women's argument that the clerk wrongly denied them a marriage license. The judge reasoned that the dictionary defines marriage as the union of a man and a woman, so these applicants themselves were to blame for their ineligibility for the license.[4] They could easily obtain licenses if they came in with the right kind of partners. End of discussion. I think that this "dictionary" approach is bad legal reasoning, whatever the result. If there are arguments for gay and lesbian marriage, the court should address them; if the court concludes that these issues belong in the legislature, the court should say that. Let's not, instead, simply open Webster's and shut the case.

A conscientious judge may seek empirical information, then, about actual family living patterns. Statistical predictions have their own problems, but if forced to use that form of argument, I bet we'd see an intriguing challenge to prevailing popular images of parent/child relationships and of families more generally. Perhaps this too reflects a lag in reconciling images with changing realities.

In the face of statistical complexity, how should lawyers make arguments on behalf of clients with real problems? As I worked with my colleagues on behalf of Alison, we asked, what if instead of dictionaries, or social images, or statistics, the judge could turn to a functional definition? What if the Court were to ask, is Alison someone who has filled the functions of a parent? Of course, then we need to define the functions of a parent. We could try one out, like, someone who has taken care of the child on a daily basis, is known to the child as a parent, and has provided love and financial support. Interestingly, kids themselves seem to identify who is a family based on who lives together and has daily contact.

It is not absolutely incredible that a court would turn to something like this. In fact, the very court that heard Alison D.'s case, the New York Court of Appeals (which happens to be New York's highest court), turned to a functional definition of family recently to resolve another case, called *Braschi v. Stahl Associates*.[5] The question in that case was whether a man could inherit a rent-controlled apartment after the death of his lover, whose name was on the lease. The governing law called for protecting family members after the death of the named tenant; it said that a landlord cannot evict "either the surviving spouse or some other member of the deceased tenant's family who has been living with the tenant"[6] after the tenant of record dies thereby letting the apartment go back on the market—and importantly—off rent control.

The court ruled that a homosexual man could claim membership in the family because of the "reality" of family life. The court found that these two men had emotional and financial commitments and interdependence: they lived together as a couple for over ten years. They also were known to other family members and neighbors as a couple; they exchanged bracelets to symbolize their relationship; they were faithful to one another. They had joint credit cards and safe deposit boxes.[7] They also had joint bank accounts. This is the one that amazes me: my sister's advice is that the secret to a happy marriage is separate checking accounts. The court here didn't make shared banking the key: it looked to the totality of the circumstances and found that these two men functioned like a family. Our hope was that this same reviewing court would adopt a functional approach to defining "parent" and give Alison simply the chance to be heard in her request for visitation. But we lost.

B. PROBLEMS WITH THE FUNCTIONAL APPROACH

I did not tell the New York Court of Appeals my worries about the functional approach. I saved them for you. First, a functional approach can be messy. That's law talk for unpredictable. Which factor or combination of factors ends up being enough? Isn't this simply a more direct invitation for judges to express their own ideas about what should count as a family? Decision-making in light of a list of varied factors is decision-making in light of discretion. That the results in a given case are unpredictable may be all that we can predict.

We could guide or limit that unpredictable discretion if we legislated more specific rules—and more specific rules could be drafted that still use the idea of a functional family. Already, different legislative rules rely on uniquely tailored definitions of family status for each possible legal purpose. I have some favorites: the immigration service's rule recognizing stepfamily relationships, but not if the marriage creating the step-relationship was itself a sham, and the tax law specifying that a family corporation can actually be formed through the joint efforts of several families. The problem is, if we proliferate specific and allegedly functional notions of family, domestic partnership, parent, and child for each distinctive social context, we will expose real people to enormously varied rules that create their own kind of unpredictability.

Perhaps the longest unit of time—other than when you are late and waiting for the elevator—is what we call "in the meantime." And we are here in the meantime until we answer these problems of unpredictability and inadequacy of generalized definitions. Certainly nothing in the meantime exists to help someone like Alison who is claiming parental status. I find myself returning to the functional approach—only to find new worries about it.

Besides its unpredictability, I have a second set of worries about a functional approach. Using a functional test rather than a formal, legal definition may open the system up to manipulation by people who want to take advantage of certain benefits from family status but not take on certain obligations or burdens. For example, if the legal consequences of being treated like a married couple are desirable because of benefits that accrue, we might get into another mess, such as the one depicted in the movie, "Green Card." There, a noncitizen and a citizen of this country marry and claim that theirs is a genuine marriage although it is really a sham, arranged solely to deceive the Immigration and Naturalization Service and designed to get advantageous immigration status for the noncitizen.

As the movie suggests, suspicion about such uses of marriage has led the Immigration and Naturalization Service to investigate whether asserted marriages are "real" or "sham" and produced massive invasions of the privacy of many people. By tolerating this kind of invasion, society may be jeopardizing the security of anyone's family relations. At the same time, without some kind of check, there is a genuine concern that some people can manipulate the system by arranging for a sham marriage and thereby leapfrog ahead of other immigrants waiting in line for the nation's approval. Flexible definitions, especially when chosen by their users, can be abused. Both that abuse and the likely bureaucratic response can hurt people.

Unpredictability and manipulability are a lot to worry about, and not just because they are tongue twisters. But I have two more worries. One I will mention only briefly: functional approaches have a suspicious pedigree. The first element to be suspicious of is that functionalists are themselves often quick to deny that there is a pedigree, or a history, to functional approaches; they like to think this is just truth or realism. A history of family sociology I have read emphasizes the connection between analyses of family functions and evolutionary thought, a notion of progressive development from the more primitive to the more civilized. It is this kind of intellectual work that also brought us Social Darwinism, eugenics, and programs of governmental intervention into and control over the lives of immigrants, racial minorities, and poor people. Perhaps put more gently, talk of functions has tended to be pushed by people with little sensitivity to cultural variation or to their own biases. But just because some functionalists did it badly does not seem to be enough of a reason to abandon this kind of analysis. Why not just try to do it better? Still, the failure to see one's own biases is a real risk in any approach to family law matters, and I feel cautioned by the history of functionalism.

My final worry is my biggest worry. My biggest worry is that even inclined as I am in the cases of *Alison D.* and *Braschi* to support functional definitions of parent and family, in other cases I have contrary intuitions. Now, I can handle inconsistency when I have to, and I know about hobgoblins and little minds. But this kind of inconsistency makes me think I have to think some more. And after reflecting about those instances where I favor less expansive, functional definitions, I think this: I favor functional definitions of families that expand beyond reference to biological or formal marriage or adoptive relationship because the people involved have chosen family-like roles. But I worry when the government assigns family-like status in order to punish people or deny them benefits for which they would otherwise be eligible. Thus I think there is an important difference between the expanded family chosen by its participants and the expanded family used by the government to achieve its own ends.

Let me give you some examples. These are contrasting situations that lead me at times to oppose expansive, functional definitions of family because the government is using those definitions for its own purposes. The Department of Housing and Urban Development adopted a regulation that allows the eviction—or forfeiture of subsidized housing eligibility—of any family member of an individual suspected of engaging in criminal drug-related or violent activity.[8] "Family" is treated quite expansively here and basically includes any member of the same household. Certainly it is important to try to assure safety in housing settings, but I worry that this expansive reading could permit the eviction of a child due to drug-related activities of one parent. I worry about the government using an expansive reading to evict a grandmother due to the drug-related activities of a grandchild.

Now, it is true that in other contexts, I would support an interpretation that would treat a grandmother as a member of a family. One such context is when the question is whether a grandmother living with her child and grandchildren forms a single family for purposes of satisfying a zoning restriction. Recognizing this as a family seems to match the traditional functions that the family serves. But treating the grandmother as "family" in an extended household in which another person is suspected of engaging in criminal activity seems largely punitive without cause or else predicated on an unrealistic view that the grandmother has the ability to prevent the criminal activity.

Another worrisome example arises when the state seeks to reduce its own obligation to pay financial benefits by finding someone else on whom to pin the financial responsibility—or on whom to blame the ineligibility decision. Until the Supreme Court rejected such a practice, the administrators of AFDC denied benefits to single mothers who were found to have paramours. This "man-in-the-house" rule was officially justified on the theory that the presence of another adult even occasionally in a household implied the availability of his income to support the children; it clearly was also used to express disapproval of the single mothers found to have lovers. The Supreme Court ultimately did reject this rule by relying on a strict and formal definition: the Court held that Congress specified the presence of another "parent" would make that income presumed available to the children, and a paramour is not a legal parent and has no legal duty to support the child.[9] Here, then, is an instance in which insistence on the narrow, formal definition of parent helped families avoid the state's effort to deny them public benefits.

States continue to try to assert family or family-like relationships in order to avoid or reduce public responsibility for a family's economic dependency. In one case, an agency drastically reduced the amount of food stamps available to a mother and two minor daughters because a disabled adult son lived in the household and received his own Supplemental Security Income Benefits, even though these benefits were deemed under the Social Security Act for his exclusive use.[10]

Sometimes even the presence of a sibling who receives child support can threaten a family's eligibility for public benefits. States often treat child support not as the entitlement of the child who receives it, but instead as income to the family household if that household applies for food stamps or welfare. The state governments clearly prefer this view because it will reduce the benefit awards or even make the household ineligible. But one consequence may be to make the absent father less inclined to pay the child support after learning it is going to people besides his child, including other children he did not father. And this could also impair his visiting relationship with the child. Another consequence may be to lead the mother to relinquish custody of this child in order to avoid the reduction of benefits for the rest of her household. In the face of considerable evidence about these negative effects, the Supreme Court nonetheless rejected a challenge to such an approach and approved the deeming of sibling income to the household in its application for public benefits.[11]

Similarly, the states routinely deny AFDC benefits to a person who refuses to name the father of her child and to someone who names as the father of her child someone excluded by a blood test.[12] Yet there may be many reasons why a woman would decline to name the father of her child—reasons that include seeking to protect herself against physical violence or other intrusion by that individual. An oddly different kind of threat can arise if an absent father makes one child support payment—for the government may then terminate the mother's public benefits even if the father never pays child support again. My objection is not to enforcing the child support obligation: it is to treating the absent parent as a member of the household that is applying for public benefits—the effects of this treatment may punish the individuals only to help the state.

There are punitive uses of family status underway even with narrow or traditional definitions of family, as with the Wisconsin law that terminates a parent's welfare benefits if the minor child is truant from school, or the California law that applies criminal penalties against a parent who fails to supervise a child—a law adopted specifically to try to reduce gang activity. Another example arises in the Medicaid rules that require a spouse to deplete all of her or his own assets before the ailing spouse may become eligible for public medical benefits. This last rule is prompting divorces simply to allow individuals to avoid losing all their goods while trying to assure care for an ailing wife or husband.

Again, my objection is not to the notion that being a family member entails obligations. Indeed, I may occupy a somewhat unusual position in that I favor what might be called a liberal approach to family membership but a strict view of family obligations. I would favor legal recognition of a wide variety of personal groupings and would urge the state to permit a range of voluntary, chosen relationships. I oppose state appropriation of these relationships to achieve governmental ends such as budget cutting. Yet I do not favor leaving the content of family obligations to the private choices of those individuals. I think people should be able to choose to enter family relationships, but not be free to rewrite the terms of those relationships.

The danger of an expansive, functional voluntarist view of family—in which people can pick and choose what kinds of family ties that they want to have—is that people will choose to walk out when it gets tough and to avoid responsibilities when it is no longer fun.[13] I am against this. I am interested in exploring ways to lead people to adhere to their obligations, to understand that life is not just about fun or self-interest. At the same time, I worry about governmental uses of relationships to serve governmental ends, like reducing governmental financial obligations. And I worry that by advocating expansive, functional definitions of family in some contexts, I may be fueling this kind of governmental control in others.

A vivid illustration of this dilemma arises as states debate how to treat stepparent relationships. In almost every state, stepparents who have not adopted the children do not have a financial support obligation nor indeed do they have legal rights to control the health, education, or religious training of the children of their spouses. This is especially important where the biological parent retains an involvement with the children. Functionally, however, in many contexts, stepparents *are* parents: they provide emotional and financial support and help to make the fast growing household type—the blended family. Moreover, some states do treat stepparent income as a factor in determining eligibility for public benefits, one of life's many inconsistencies. Should the law treat such stepparents as *in the family* and if so, for what purposes? Might such a conclusion deter some adults from being willing to join a new household—given obligations they already have to a prior family? Up until recently, stepfamily relationships, like friendships, were blessedly free of governmental regulation, free to develop however they would. If, however, we seek the benefits of governmental recognition for these relationships, what negative consequences could also follow?

C. CHILDREN'S INTERESTS

Perhaps we can resolve dilemmas raised by legal adoption of a functional definition of family by leaving it to the parties; let them choose: do you want to be a family for legal purposes? But the dangers of unpredictability and manipulability surely return with a vengeance in that scenario.

In part because of the tension between arguments for expansive family definitions and arguments for more restrictive ones, I felt in the case of *Alison D.* a need to search for an alternative approach. It is compatible with a functional approach but I think it adds an important difference. With my colleagues in law and in human development, I developed an argument that emphasizes not any particular definition of family, but instead the interests of the child. We defended the functional test as a way of achieving the child's interests—but those interests, above all, are what must take center stage. Neither the government's interests nor the interests of the adults supply the justification for regulating otherwise private and intimate concerns. The needs of vulnerable and developing children supply that justification.

Thus, in our brief, we argued that, based on psychological evidence and theories, children form strong attachments not only to one primary parenting figure, but to more than one caretaker if they have sustained contact in the home. From the child's point of view, the marital status, biological or nonbiological connection, and also the sexual orientation of such adults are irrelevant. Children form strong attachments without asking about such things; indeed, children form strong attachments before they even know what it is to ask about such things. Nonetheless, at very early ages, children perceive the differences between parents and others of significance in their lives. Based on a concern for the child's interests, we argued that the reviewing court should at least order a hearing to determine whether visits with Alison would indeed serve the child's needs. Our brief also argued that this psychological evidence supports a functional test for parenthood and that this evidence also helps to limit the number of people who could seek such visitation hearings.

Calling for inquiry into any person's interests is hardly an easy task; it may be even more difficult than deciding who should be treated as a parent or as a family member. But at least this inquiry is addressed to what matters most. If we are going to worry, let's worry about something that is worth it!

Notes

1 J. Wagner, *The Search for Intelligent Life in the Universe* 25 (1985), p. 26.
2 Alison D. v. Virginia M. Lexis 634 (N.Y. 1991).
3 Monte v. New Mexico Dep't of Human Services (N.M. Human Services Dep't Fair Hearings Bureau, June 22, 1990).
4 Jones v. Hallahan, 501 S.W.2d 588 (Ky. Ct. App. 1973).
5 74 N.Y.2d 206, 543 N.E.2d 44 (1989).
6 N.Y. City Rent and Eviction Regulations, 9 NYCRR § 2204.6(d) (1984).
7 Blanchard also gave Braschi power of attorney regarding medical, persona, and financial decisions, and named Braschi beneficiary of the life insurance policy and principal legatee of the estate.
8 Section 8 Certificate Program, Moderate Rehabilitation Program and Housing Voucher Program, 55 Fed. Reg. 28,538 (1990) (to be codified at 24 CFR Parts 882 and 887).
9 King v. Smith, 392 U.S. 309 (1968).
10 Moody v. Lung, No. 86 Civ. 3088 (SDNY, filed March 24, 1986).
11 Bowen v. Guillard, 483 U.S. 587 (1987).
12 Doston v. Duffy, 732 F. Supp. 857 (N.D. IL. 1988); French v. Mansour, 834 F.2d 115 (6th Cir. 1987).
13 I worry about parents abandoning their children, refusing to pay for college, and more troubling, refusing to pay for any child support.

3

Child Marriage Is Still Legal in the United States

Nicholas Syrett

The recent outrage over Alabama Republican Senate candidate Roy Moore allegedly targeting teenage girls for sex has elicited reports that some evangelical churches actually encourage teenage girls to date older men.

It seems unlikely that Moore was ever interested in marrying any of the women who have thus far accused him of unwanted sexual attention and assault. However, Moore is married to a woman 14 years his junior whom he first met when she was 15 and he was 29. These conversations about older men dating and marrying young girls have left many Americans surprised. The reality is that these practices are still around, as I learned in researching my recent book, *American Child Bride: A History of Minors and Marriage in the United States*.

MINORS AND MARRIAGE

Child marriage has a long and vibrant history in the United States. While activists have long urged legislators to raise the age of consent to marriage – and continue to do so – with parental consent it remains possible for minors to marry in every single state.

Though some boys do marry, the vast majority of marrying minors are girls. This has been the pattern throughout US history.

The minimum marriageable age in Alabama today is 16, though for most of the state's history girls could marry at 14 and boys at 17. Different minimum marriageable ages for girls and boys were common nationwide until the 1970s. While marriage as a minor is significantly less common today than it was in the early or mid-twentieth century – two periods with particularly high rates – it is certainly not a thing of the past. In the last 15 years, more than 207,000 minors have become legally wed in the United States, many marrying below the age of consent to sex in their states.

Data from the US Census show that the marriage of legal minors has always been more common in the South. This may be one reason – aside from liking his conservative politics – that voters in Alabama seem less disturbed by Roy Moore's targeting of teenage girls. Leigh Corfman claims Moore initiated sexual contact with her when she was 14 in 1979. Nothing in the law would have prevented the two from marrying if they'd had her parents' permission.

Syrett, Nicholas "Child Marriage Is Still Legal in the US." *The Conversation*, December 11, 2017.

Today southern states like Alabama, Kentucky and West Virginia have among the highest rates of minor marriage in the nation. They are also joined by Idaho and other rural states in the West. These states share high rates of poverty and are home to religious conservatives who often see marriage as the solution to teenage sex and premarital pregnancy. Some even condone marriage when it results from statutory rape. In many cases, district attorneys have been willing to waive prosecution if a girl's statutory rapist agrees to marry her and her parents are also supportive.

WHO ARE CHILD BRIDES?

Child marriage has long been portrayed as an issue in the developing world – especially in India and various nations in Africa and the Middle East. Americans are often surprised by its persistence right here at home. Many assume that it was a practice brought to the United States by immigrant populations, or one used in isolationist religious sects. Neither belief is borne out by the numbers.

Even at the height of immigration to the United States in the 1910s and 1920s, US-born white children of US-born parents were more likely to be married as minors than were immigrant girls of the first or second generation. US-born black girls were about one-and-a-half times more likely to be married than were white girls. In both cases, poor girls in rural states accounted for the numbers.

Opposition to child marriage in the United States also has a long history, dating back to the middle of the nineteenth century. Women's rights advocates like Elizabeth Oakes Smith and Elizabeth Cady Stanton called marrying as a minor "the great life-long mistake." They argued it deprived girls of the opportunity to develop into womanhood and some semblance of independence before they yoked their lives to a husband and began to bear children.

While the legal minimum marriageable age has gone up in almost all states since the nineteenth century, almost all states have exceptions built in that allow parents and/or judges to consent to the marriage of minors below the stated minimums, in some cases if they are pregnant, in others if they are already emancipated minors. This means that with judicial or parental consent, children as young as 10, 11 and 12 have been married in the United States in the last couple of decades. When exceptions are taken into consideration, 25 states actually do not have an absolute minimum marriageable age.

When activists have sought to eliminate those exceptions and ban marriage prior to age 18 outright, as they are attempting to do in about 10 states nationwide today, they have met with substantial pushback. Some religious conservatives worry that without access to marriage, pregnant girls might turn to abortion. Others simply place faith in the institution of marriage to establish a happy and financially secure household. This is despite the fact that studies have shown that marriage as a minor is much more likely to lead to divorce, to dropping out of high school, to spousal abuse and to mental and physical health problems.

Only when Americans are able to have more honest conversations about what marriage really looks like – as opposed to some idealized image of marital perfection – are we likely to see the abolition of child marriage in the United States.

4

Family, Feminism, and Race in America

Maxine Baca Zinn

Rapid social changes have often besieged families. Much of the contemporary crisis in American family life is related to larger socioeconomic changes. Upheavals in the social organization of work have created a massive influx of women into the labor force. At the same time, the removal of certain kinds of work has left millions of workers without jobs. Both kinds of change have affected the well-being of American families.

As debates about the context and consequences of family change reach heightened proportions, the racial ethnic composition of the United States is undergoing dramatic shifts. Massive waves of immigration from Latin America and Asia are posing difficult issues for a society that clings stubbornly to its self-image of the melting pot. Changes in fertility and immigration patterns are altering the distribution of Whites and people of color, and, at the same time, creating a nation of varied racial ethnic groups. In many cities and communities, Blacks, Hispanics, Asians, and Native Americans outnumber the White population. Their families are distinctive not only because of their ethnic heritage but because they reside in a society where racial stratification continues to shape family resources and structures in important ways. The changing demography of race in the United States presents compelling challenges to family sociology.

Questions about what is happening to families in the United States and how this country's racial order is being reshaped are seldom joined. Yet they are more closely related than either popular or scholarly discourse on these topics would suggest. The national discussion about the erosion of inner-city Black and Latino families has not been applied to our understanding of the family in general. Instead of marginalizing minority families as special cultural cases, it is time to bring race into the mainstream of our thinking about family life in America.

THE FEMINIST REVISION

Feminist challenges to traditional family theory have been accomplished by decomposing the family, that is, by breaking the family into constituent elements so that the underlying structures are exposed. In doing so, feminists have brought into relief three aspects of that structure: ideologies that serve to mystify women's experiences as wives and mothers, hierarchical divisions that generate conflict and struggle within families, and the multiple and dynamic interconnections between households and the larger political economy. An

Zinn, Maxine Baca. "Family, Feminism, and Race in America." *Gender & Society* 4, no. 1 (1990): 68–82.

understanding of family dynamics has been transformed by exposing gender as a fundamental category of social relations both within and outside the family.

First evolved as a critique of functionalism and its emphasis on roles, the crucial impact of feminist scholarship on family research has been to recast the family as a system of gender stratification. Because roles neglect the political underpinnings of the family, feminists have directed attention outside the family "to the social structures that shape experience and meaning, that give people a location in the social world, and that define and allocate economic and social rewards" (Hess and Ferree 1987, 11). Once feminist scholars made it clear that gender roles are not neutral ways of maintaining order in family and society but benefit some at the expense of others, virtually everything about the family looked different. Rather than viewing the family as a unit shaped only by affect or kinship, we now know that families are settings in which people with different activities and interests often come into conflict with one another.

Feminists have challenged the monolithic ideology of the family that elevated the contemporary nuclear family with a breadwinner husband and a full-time homemaker wife as the only legitimate family form. We now give equal weight to the varied family structures and experiences that are produced by the organization of the economy, the state, and other institutions. Some of these alternative family structures and living arrangements are nonmarital cohabitation, single-parent households, extended kinship units and expanded households, dual-worker families, commuter marriages, gay and lesbian households, and collectives.

REVISIONS IN RACE-RELATIONS SCHOLARSHIP

The model of the backward and culturally deviant minority family originated within the sociology of race relations in the United States and its then guiding framework of assimilation and modernization. The preoccupation in race relations with "traditional" and "modern" social forms fit well with family sociology's preoccupation with the nuclear family, its wage-earner father, and domestic-caretaker mothers. Minorities and others whose family patterns differed from the ideal were explained as cultural exceptions to the rule. Their slowness to acculturate and take on the normal patterns of family development left them behind as other families in American society modernized. They were peripheral to the standard family and viewed as problems because of their failure to adopt the family patterns of the mainstream.

The "social problems" origin of family studies in the nineteenth century also contributed to this perspective. Family study as a new field emerged out of a deep concern with the need to solve such problems as rising divorce rates and the effects of slavery and industrialization on the family. Social reforms of the times favored the modern family as a way of combating social problems, a belief that remains widely held in American society, if not in American family sociology.

Scholars of various disciplines have long refuted this culturally deviant model of family, arguing that alternative family patterns do not reflect deviance, deficiency, or disorganization and that alternative family patterns are related to but not responsible for the social location of minorities. Revisionist approaches have emphasized the structural conditions giving rise to varied family forms, rather than the other way around. Differences in family patterns have been reinterpreted as adaptations to the conditions of racial inequality and poverty, often as sources of survival and strength.

Assessing the Revisions

The family was an important starting point in the development of women's studies, Black studies, and Chicano studies. In each of these areas, study of the family represented a vital thread in the evolution of critical scholarship. Both bodies of scholarship locate family experience in societal arrangements that extend beyond the family and allocate social and economic rewards. Both begin with the assumption that families are social products and then proceed to study their interrelationships with other social structures. Just as feminist theories have reconceptualized the family along a gender axis of power and control, racial ethnic family scholarship has reconceptualized the family along the axis of race, also a system of power and control that shapes family life in crucial ways. Studying the intersection of gender, race, and class in minority families has enormously enhanced family scholarship. Now, in studying racial ethnic families, we routinely examine race and gender as interacting hierarchies of resources and rewards that condition material and subjective experiences within families. Interacting race, class, and gender ideologies have shaped prevailing models of minority families, appearing even in the culturally deviant explanations of racial ethnic families. As Collins (1989) explains, the new version of this argument is that because minority women and men do not follow dominant notions of masculinity and femininity, they are responsible for their subordinate class placement in society. As Bridenthal (1981) has put it:

> Black people have been called matriarchal (ruled by the mother) and Chicano families have been called patriarchal (ruled by the father). These supposedly opposite family structures and relationships have been blamed for the failure of many members of each group to rise to a higher socioeconomic level. In other words, black and Chicano families have been blamed for the effect of racial discrimination.
>
> (p. 85)

To be fair, feminist literature on the family does recognize the societal context of inequality that gives rise to distinctive family forms. Feminist rethinking of the family has dropped the cultural deviant perspective. But for the most part, it retains a cultural perspective. Most contemporary feminist thought takes great care to underscore class, race, and gender as fundamental categories of social organization, but when it comes to family patterns, race and ethnicity are used as elements of culture, not social structure. Descriptions of cultural diversity do not explain why families exhibit structural variations by race. While it is true that many family lifestyles are differentiated by ethnicity, structural patterns differ because social and economic conditions produce and may even require diverse family arrangements. Although the family nurtures ethnic culture, families are not the product of ethnic culture alone.

RACIAL INEQUALITY AND FAMILY LIFE

Social Location and Family Formation

In our quest to understand the structural sources of diversity in family life, we must examine all of the "socioeconomic and political arrangements and how they impinge on families" (Mullings 1986a, 13). Like class and gender hierarchies, racial stratification is a fundamental axis of American social structure. Racial stratification produces different opportunity structures that shape families in a variety of ways. Marriage patterns, gender relations, kinship networks, and other family characteristics result from the social location of families, that is, where they are situated in relation to societal institutions allocating resources.

Thinking about families in this way shifts the theoretical focus from cultural diversity or "ethnic lifestyles" of particular groups to race as a major element of hierarchical social relations that touches families throughout the social order (Omi and Winant 1986, 61). Racial stratification is a basic organizing principle in American society even though the forms of domination and discrimination have changed over time. Omi and Winant use the term "racial formation" to refer to the process by which social, economic, and political forces determine the content and import of racial categories and by which they are in turn shaped by racial meanings (1986, 61). As racial categories are formed and transformed over time, the meanings, practices, and institutions associated with race penetrate families throughout the society.

Social categories and groups subordinate in the racial hierarchy are often deprived of access to social institutions that offer supports for family life. Social categories and groups elevated in the racial hierarchy have different and better connections to institutions that can sustain families. Social location and its varied connection with social resources thus have profound consequences for family life.

If families are to be conceptualized in a way that relates them to social, historical, and material conditions, then racial stratification cannot be ignored. We are forced to abandon conventional notions that racial ethnic diversity is a cultural phenomenon best understood at the microstructural level. Instead of treating diversity as a given, or as a result of traditions alone, we must treat racial stratification as a macrostructural force situating families in ways requiring diverse arrangements. These macrostructural forces can be seen in two periods of economic upheaval in the United States—industrialization and the current shift from manufacture to information and services. In both of these transitions, the relationship between families and other institutions has been altered. Despite important differences, these economic transformations have produced new relations among individuals, families, and labor systems that have had profound effects on family development throughout American society. Industrialization and deindustrialization are not neutral transformations that touch families in uniform ways. Rather, they manifest themselves differently in their interaction with race and gender, and both periods of transition reveal racial patterning in family and household formation. The theme of historical variation has become increasingly accepted in family studies, but theories of the family have largely ignored the new knowledge about race, labor, and family formation.

Industrialization and Family Structure

The past two decades of historical research on the family have revealed that industrialization has had momentous consequences for American families because of massive changes in the way people made a living. The industrial revolution changed the nature of work performed, the allocation of work responsibilities, and the kind of pay, prestige, and power that resulted from various positions in the economy. The effect of industrialization on American family life was uneven. Instead of a linear pattern of change in which families moved steadily to a more modern level, the pattern of change was checkered. Labor force exploitation produced various kinds of family and household adaptations on the part of slaves, agricultural workers, and industrial workers.

Both class and race were basic to the relations of production in the United States in this period. Race was intertwined with class; populations from various parts of the world were brought into the labor force at different levels, and racial differences were utilized to rationalize exploitation of women and men. European ethnics were incorporated into low-wage industrial economies of the north, while Blacks, Latinos, Chinese, and Japanese filled labor needs in colonial labor systems of the economically backward regions of the west, southwest, and the south. These colonial labor systems, while different, created similar hardships for family life.

All these groups had to engage in a constant struggle for both immediate survival and long-term continuation of family and community, but women's and men's work and family patterns varied considerably within different racial labor structures, with fundamentally different social supports for family life. Thornton Dill (1988) has compared patterns of White families in nineteenth-century America with those of racial ethnics and identified important racial differences in the social supports for family life. She finds that greater importance was accorded Euro-American families by the wider society. As primary laborers in the reproduction and maintenance of family life, these women were acknowledged and accorded the privileges and protections deemed socially appropriate to their family roles. While this emphasis on family roles denied these women many rights and privileges and seriously constrained their individual growth and development, it also revealed public support for White women's family roles. Women's reproductive labor was viewed as an essential building block of the family. Combined with a view of the family as the cornerstone of the nation, this ideology produced experiences within the White dominant culture very different from those of racial ethnics (Dill 1988, 418). Because racial ethnic men were usually unable to earn a "family wage," their women had to engage in subsistence and income-producing activities both in and out of the household. In addition, they had to struggle to keep their families together in the face of outside forces that threatened the integrity of their households (Glenn 1987, 53–54).

During industrialization, class produced some similarities in the family experiences of racial ethnic women and those of White working-class immigrants. Working-class women during this period were often far removed from the domestic ideal. The cults of domesticity and true womanhood that proliferated during this period were ideals attained more frequently by those Euro-American women whose husbands were able to earn enough to support their families.

This ideal was not attainable by Blacks, Latinos, and Asian Americans, who were excluded from jobs open to White immigrants. For example, in most cities, the constraints that prevented Black men from earning a family wage forced Black married women into the labor market in much greater proportions than White immigrant women. By 1880, about 50 percent of Black women were in the labor force, compared with 15 percent of White women. Furthermore, the family system of the White working class was not subject to institutional assaults, such as forced separation, directed against Black, Latino, and Chinese families.

Racial ethnic women experienced the oppressions of a patriarchal society but were denied the protections and buffering of a patriarchal family. Their families suffered as a direct result of the labor systems in which they participated. Since they were a cheap and exploitable labor force, little attention was given to their family and community life except as it related to their economic productivity. Labor and not the existence or maintenance of families was the critical aspect of their role in building the nation. They were denied the social and structural supports necessary to make their families a vital element in the social order. Nevertheless, people take conditions that have been thrust upon them and out of them create a history and a future. Using cultural forms where possible and creating new forms where necessary, racial ethnics adapted their families to the larger social order. These adaptations were not exceptions to the rule; they were instead variations created by mainstream forces. One family type was not standard and the others peripheral. Different forms existed at the same time.

Once we recognize how racial stratification has affected family formation, we can understand why the idealized family was not a luxury shared by all. At the same time, we can see how some idealized family patterns were made possible because of the existence of alternative family forms and how all of these are products of the social and economic conditions of the times. Although Blacks, Mexicanos, and Asians were excluded from industrial work, all three groups helped build the agricultural and industrial base for subsequent industrial development. New ways of life and new family patterns sprang from industrialization. As Mullings (1986b) says, "It was the working class and enslaved men and women whose labor created the wealth that allowed the middle class and upper middle class domestic life styles to exist" (p. 50).

Deindustrialization and Families

Vast changes in the social organization of work are currently transforming the American family across class and race groups. Not only are women and men affected differently by the transformation of the economy from its manufacturing base to service and high technology, but women and men in different racial categories are experiencing distinctive changes in their relationship to the economy. This transformation is profoundly affecting families as it works with and through race and gender hierarchies.

In the current American economy, industrial jobs traditionally filled by men are being replaced with service jobs that are increasingly filled by women. Married White women are now entering the labor force at a rate that, until recently, was seen exclusively among women of color. The most visible consequences of the increased labor force participation among White women include declining fertility and changes in marriage patterns. American White women are delaying marriage and childbearing and having fewer children over their lifetimes, living alone or as heads of their own households—living with neither parents nor husbands. The new economy is reshaping families as it propels these women into the labor force.

The minority communities across America, families and households are also being reshaped through new patterns of work and gender roles. The high level of female-headed families among Blacks and Hispanics (especially Puerto Ricans) is the outgrowth of changes in the larger economy. The long-term decline in employment opportunities for men is the force most responsible for the growth of racial ethnic families headed by women. The shortage of Black men with the ability to support a family makes it necessary for many Black women to leave a marriage or forego marriage altogether. Adaptation to structural conditions leaves Black women disproportionately separated, divorced, and solely responsible for their children.

Families throughout American society are being reshaped by economic and industrial change: "The shifting economy produces and even demands diverse family forms—including for example, female headed households, extended kinship units, dual career couples, and lesbian collectives" (Gerstel and Gross 1987, 7). Families mainly headed by women have become permanent in all racial categories in America, with the disproportionate effects of change most visible among Blacks and Latinos. While the chief cause of the increase in female-headed households among Whites is the greater economic independence of White women, the longer delay of first marriage and the low rate of remarriage among Black women reflect the labor force problems of Black men. Thus, race creates different routes to female headship, but Whites, Blacks, and Latinos are all increasingly likely to end up in this family form.

CONCLUSION

Knowing that race creates certain patterns in the way families are located and embedded in different social environments, we should be able to theorize for all racial categories. Billingsley (1988) suggests that the study of Black families can generate important insights for White families: families may respond in a like manner when impacted by larger social forces. To the extent that White families and Black families experience similar pressures, they may respond in similar ways, including the adaptation of their family structures and other behaviors. With respect to single-parent families, teenage childbirth, working mothers, and a host of other behaviors, Black families serve as barometers of social change and as forerunners of adaptive patterns that will be progressively experienced by the more privileged sectors of American society.

While such insights are pertinent, they should not eclipse the ways in which racial meanings inform our perceptions of family diversity. As social and economic changes produce new family arrangements, alternatives—what is sometimes called "family pluralism"—are granted greater legitimacy. Yet many alternatives that appear new to middle-class White Americans are actually variant family patterns that have been traditional within Black and other minority communities for many generations. Presented as the new lifestyles of the mainstream, they are, in fact, the same lifestyles that have in the past been deemed pathological, deviant, or unacceptable when observed in Black families.

In much popular and scholarly thinking, alternatives are seen as inevitable changes, new ways of living that are part of an advanced society. In other words, they are conceptualized as products of the mainstream. Yet such alternatives, when associated with racial ethnic groups, are judged against a standard model and found to be deviant. Therefore, the notion of family pluralism does not correctly describe the family diversity of the past or the present. Pluralism implies that alternative family forms coexist within a society. In reality, racial meanings create a hierarchy in which some family forms are privileged and others are subordinated, even though they are both products of larger social forces.

REFERENCES

Billingsley, A. 1988. The impact of technology on Afro-American families. *Family Relations* 7: 420–425.

Bridenthal, R. 1981. The family tree: Contemporary patterns in the united. In *Household and kin*, edited by A. Swerdlow, R. Bridenthal, J. Kelly and P. Vine. Old Westbury, NY: Feminist Press.

Collins, P. Hill. 1989. A comparison of two works on Black family life. *Signs* 14: 875–884.

Dill, B. Thornton. 1988. Our mother's grief: Racial ethnic women and the maintenance of families. *Journal of Family History* 13: 415–431.

Gerstel, N. and H. E. Gross, eds. 1987. *Families and work.* Philadelphia, PA: Temple University Press.

Glenn, E. Nakano. 1987. Racial ethnic women's labor: The intersection of race, gender and class oppression. In *Hidden aspects of women's work*, edited by C. Bose, R. Feldberg, and N. Sokoloff. New York, NY: Praeger.

Hess, B. and M. M. Ferree. 1987. Introduction. In *Analyzing gender*, edited by B. Hess and M. M. Ferree. Newbury Park, CA: Sage.

Mullings, L 1986a. Anthropological perspectives on the Afro-American family. *American Journal of Social Psychiatry* 6: 11–16.

———. 1986b. Uneven development: Class, race and gender in the United States before 1900. In *Women's work*, edited by E. Leacock and H. I. Safa, and contributors. South Hadley: Bergin & Garvey.

Omi, M. and H. Winant. 1986. *Racial formation in the United States*. New York: Routledge & Kegan Paul.

5

More People than Ever Before Are Single – and That's a Good Thing

Bella DePaulo

The twenty-first century is the age of living single.

Today, the number of single adults in the USA – and many other nations around the world – is unprecedented. And the numbers don't just say people are staying single longer before settling down. More are staying single for life. A 2014 Pew Report estimates that by the time today's young adults reach the age of 50, about one in four of them will have never married.

The ascendancy of single living has left some in a panic. US News & World Report, for example, cautioned that Americans think the country's moral values are bad and getting worse, and one of the top reasons for their concern is the large number of people remaining single.

But instead of fretting, maybe we should celebrate.

I'm a social scientist, and I've spent the past two decades researching and writing about single people. I've found that the rise of single living is a boon to our cities and towns and communities, our relatives and friends and neighbors. This trend has the chance to redefine the traditional meaning – and confines – of home, family and community.

TIES THAT BIND

For years, communities across the country have been organized by clusters of nuclear families living in suburban homes. But there are some signs that this arrangement isn't working out so well.

These houses are often too isolating – too far from work and from one another. According to a national survey ongoing since 1974, Americans have never been less likely to be friends with their neighbors than they are now, with neighborliness lowest in the suburbs.

But studies have also shown that single people are bucking those trends. For example, they are more likely than married people to encourage, help and socialize with their friends and neighbors. They are also more likely to visit, support, advise and stay in touch with their siblings and parents.

DePaulo, Bella. "More People than Ever Before are Single – and That's a Good Thing." *The Conversation* April 23, 2017.

In fact, people who live alone are often the life of their cities and towns. They tend to participate in more civic groups and public events, enroll in more art and music classes, and go out to dinner more often than people who live with others. Single people, regardless of whether they live alone or with others, also volunteer more for social service organizations, educational groups, hospitals and organizations devoted to the arts than people who are married.

In contrast, when couples move in together or get married, they tend to become more insular, even if they don't have children.

BUILDING STRENGTH AND RESILIENCE

Unfortunately, single life continues to be stigmatized, with single people routinely stereotyped as less secure and more self-centered than married people. They're said to die sooner, alone and sad.

Yet studies of people who live alone typically find that most are doing just fine; they don't feel isolated, nor are they sad and lonely.

Reports of the early death of single people have also been greatly exaggerated, as have claims that marriage transforms miserable, sickly single people into happy and healthy spouses.

In some significant ways, it's the single people who are doing particularly well.

For example, people with more diversified relationship portfolios tend to be more satisfied with their lives. In contrast, the insularity of couples who move in together or get married can leave them vulnerable to poorer mental health.

Studies have shown that people who stay single develop more confidence in their own opinions and undergo more personal growth and development than people who marry. For example, they value meaningful work more than married people do. They may also have more opportunities to enjoy the solitude that many of them savor.

REDEFINING THE FAMILY AND HOME

Married people often put their spouse (and, for some, kids) at the center of their lives. That's what they're expected to do, and often it's also what they want to do.

But single people are expanding the traditional boundaries of family. The people they care about the most might include family in the traditional sense. But they'll also loop in friends, ex-partners and mentors. It's a bigger, more inclusive family of people who matter.

For many single people, single-family suburban homes aren't going to offer them the balance between sociability and solitude that they crave. They are instead finding or creating a variety of different lifespaces.

Sometimes you'll see twenty-first-century variations of traditional arrangements, like multi-generational households that allow for privacy and independence as well as social interaction. Others – and not just the very young – are living with their friends or other families of choice.

Those who cherish their alone time will often choose to live alone. Some have committed romantic relationships but choose to live in places of their own, a lifestyle of "living apart together."

Some of the most fascinating innovations are pursued by people who seek both solitude and easy sociability. These individuals might move into their own apartment, but it's in a building or neighborhood where friends and family are already living. They might buy a duplex with a close friend, or explore cohousing communities or pocket neighborhoods, which are communities of small homes clustered around shared spaces such as courtyards or gardens.

Single parents are also innovating. Single mothers, for example, can go to CoAbode to try to find other single mothers with whom they can share a home and a life. Other single people might want to raise children with the full support of another parent. Now they can look for a partner in parenting – with no expectations for romance or marriage – at websites such as Family by Design and Modamily.

As the potential for living a full and meaningful single life becomes more widely known, living single will become more of a genuine choice. And when living single is a real choice, then getting married will be, too. Fewer people will marry as a way of fleeing single life or simply doing what they are expected to do, and more will choose it because it's what they really want.

If current trends continue, successive generations will have unprecedented opportunities to pursue the life that suits them best, rather than the one that is prescribed.

SECTION II
Rules of Dating and Courtship

INTRODUCTION

Societies always have rituals about how pairings take place to form families. In the United States, these traditions have changed in myriad ways over time. I provide a brief overview to illustrate how norms have shifted. The readings here provide opportunities to think about how parents view their children's sexual behaviors and dating, how young people participate in dating rituals, and to examine hookup culture—on and off college campuses. In thinking about the historical evolution in norms, we can see how gender, class, race, and region matter.

Prior to the twentieth century, courtship, predominantly among white Americans, was a process in which one man and one woman would spend intentional time together to get to know each other with the expressed purpose of evaluating the other as a potential husband or wife. Most often, the young man and woman were members of the same community. The courting ritual usually took place within the woman's home in the presence of her family. Among the wealthy, "calling" became the custom. In this ritual, a young man showed up, presented his card announcing who he is to the servant who answered the door, and waited to be invited to come and sit with the eligible daughter. Working-class families did not necessarily require a card or have a servant, but the young couple would nonetheless visit in the young woman's home and would typically be supervised.

Between 1880 and 1920, the rituals of calling began to shift toward those of dating. This time period was one of dramatic change. The Progressive Era marks three interlocking phenomena: urbanization, industrialization, and immigration. The rise of manufacturing jobs in cities brought young people from rural communities and even other countries together in new urban spaces and created new social opportunities. Many working women lived in tenements with their relatives or rented rooms in boarding houses, which often had rules against male visitors and little space for visiting. The result was that young people began going out—to parks, dance halls, restaurants, arcades, theaters, bars—to meet. Rather than courting in the home with supervision, young men and women could gain privacy by socializing in public. These urban spaces allowed for socializing without supervision and a level of anonymity that did not exist in smaller communities. New commodities and markets emerged, including fashion, pornography, prostitution, and social spaces for interaction (D'Emilio and Freedman 1997). Nightclubs, drag shows, and other burlesque were all examples of the kinds of social spaces that emerged and that allowed for a more dynamic social scene where same-sex sexual encounters could happen as well.

The first use of the term "date" was in reference to a woman's date book and, according to writer Moira Weigel, appeared in 1896 in a newspaper column that offered middle-class readers a taste of working-class life. The freedom of dating also created social pressures on young women. They were expected to spend money on fashion, cosmetics, and some of the costs of going out. The promise was that dating could result in marriage and thus improve women's status. Young men, even from the same class background, were paid more than women. So dating also promised benefits of free food, drinks, and entertainment. Women who dated could take advantage of these benefits, but also had to manage their reputations. In fact, confusion about relationships between men who paid and women who accompanied them at times led to dating women being arrested for prostitution (Weigel 2017).

Under the dating system, women had more autonomy, but some historians suggest that women had certain advantages under the system of calling. Calling had particular rules—including the requirement that she consent to be called upon—and took place in women's homes, where a woman and her family may have had more control. Dating took place in public—arguably in men's spheres—and women had less control over situations. Under dating, men asked women out, but gender norms dictated that women were not able to claim that power in asking men out (Bailey 1989).

As the twentieth century progressed, a growing number of young people—both men and women—attended high school and college. As a result, a lower-stakes culture of social interaction developed. Dating was no longer expected to lead to marriage but was itself fun, sometimes competitive, and, as the chapter by historian Beth Bailey in this section suggests, a way to gain social status. Young people from privileged backgrounds danced, went to parties, and in many ways engaged in social life that sounds similar to college "hookup" culture today.

As we saw in the last section, family life changes in response to social, political, and economic shifts (see Chapter 4 by Baca Zinn in Section I). Dating for less privileged young people and those from communities of color responded to economic and legal pressures, as immigration policies changed the dating pools and at times pushed young people to balance multiple cultural pressures. Dating culture for predominantly white middle class and affluent young people shifted during and after World War II. With fewer men, women prioritized hanging on to the ones they had (Weigel 2017). Dating came to be seen—and represented in popular culture—as more wholesome and more focused on commitment.

Whether this was good or bad was controversial. Some adults continued to insist that young people would be better off for dating several people before settling down. In short, they were often encouraged to shop around. This market-based approach to future marriage was imagined to prevent regret (Whyte 1992). The more emotionally intense relationships typical in the 1950s seemed to place more sexual pressure on teenage girls who were expected to manage their boyfriend's sexual interest, though assumed to have none of their own. Without availability of reliable contraception, the result was soaring rates of teen pregnancy through the 1950s, for both married and unmarried teens (Ventura, Mathews and Hamilton 2001). Historian Ricki Solinger examines the adoption politics that arose in this time period in Section VI.

In subsequent decades, premarital sex became increasingly common. These changes in norms were supported by many cultural changes. The licensing of the birth control pill in 1964 created more opportunities for non-procreative sex. Anti-discrimination laws, including the Civil Rights Act of 1964, increased the number of women entering college and workplaces. Social movements for civil rights, women's rights, and gay rights also affected sexual culture. A Norms of remaining unattached reemerged.

In recent years, a great deal of attention has fallen onto what is referenced as "hookup culture," particularly on college campuses. The meanings of hooking up is somewhat (and intentionally) vague and used in different ways by different people. Generally, hooking up references "sexual contact between multiple individuals, all of whom claim no romantic intent" (Padgett and Wade 2019). Many researchers identify the beginnings of hookup culture and the decline of more formal dating on college campuses around the late 1980s and early 1990s. Increasingly, young people began delaying marriage, with average age of first marriage now around 28–30 years. Research suggests that students who hook up are more likely to be white men and women or Black men, middle or upper class, and non-church going (although religion alone does not predict hookup participation). Athletes and members of fraternities and sororities are more likely to report more hookups than their non-involved counterparts. Most hookups do not become relationships, but research suggests that most dating relationships do begin with hookups (Padgett and Wade 2019). The following chapters by Lisa Wade on hookup culture on college campuses and by Jamie Budnick about hookups off campus explore these issues Showing the stability of traditional gender norms of dating rituals, one recent study found that 88 percent of men initiated dates, and while on dates, men most often (63 percent) paid, with 36 percent of couples splitting the costs (Ford, England and Bearak 2015).

Individual behavior and adherence to norms of hookup and dating culture, like all courtship rituals, are evaluated by peers. These expected behaviors change over time as new economic, political, and structural forces provide new opportunities and invite new norms. For example, online dating, once seen as a sign of desperation, is used by 30 percent of American adults. This usage changes with age, with 48 percent of younger adults—age 18–29 years—having ever used a dating app or website compared with 38 percent of those 30–49 years old, and only 16 percent of those older than 50 years (Vogels 2020). Marking the change in norms, today a majority of adults (60 percent) see online dating as a good way to meet people – an increase since 2005 when only 44 percent of those in the same survey thought so. These shifts likely reflect larger generational changes in how adults describe themselves online for work, for college applications, and on social media. These norms reflect broader shifts in communication – issues explored in the chapter by Amitrajeet Batabyal.

Dating is often associated with young people. However, dating is increasingly a practice of older single people. In fact, while divorce rates in general are declining, they have doubled for those over the age of 50 years. Those over the age of 65 years are leading what has been dubbed the "grey divorce" trend. They are also breaking generational norms to stay together because of dissatisfaction with their relationships and a desire for richer intimate lives – issues explored in the upcoming chapter by Heather Honoré Goltz and Matthew Lee Smith. Even among older daters, there are norms and expectations.

In all eras, dating has been surveilled, evaluated, and often criticized by peers and parents alike. Adults often worry about their children's futures and see dating as intricately linked to their possibilities for success – issues examined in the chapter by Sinikka Elliott. Younger people develop new norms that are different than those from the prior generation, and are thus seen as inferior and sometimes even scary by that older generation. Yet it turns out that the strongest force in policing dating norms is peers. As journalist Alexandra Schwartz summarizes,

> The history of dating, then, is also the history of the surveillance of daters. As young people figured out how to conduct their private lives away from the supervision of parents, teachers, and chaperones, they took it upon themselves to do the supervising, creating and enforcing their own codes of behavior. They proved to be remarkably adept at it. No one, it turned out, regulates the sexual and romantic lives of young people as effectively as young people themselves.
>
> (Schwartz 2016)

The chapters in this section delve into these issues.

REFERENCES

Bailey, Beth L. 1989. From Front Porch to Back Seat: Courtship in Twentieth-Century America. Baltimore: Johns Hopkins University Press.

D'Emilio, John and Estelle B. Freedman. 1997. Intimate Matters: A History of Sexuality in America. Chicago: University of Chicago Press.

Ford, Jessie, Paula England and Jonathan Bearak. 2015. "The American College Hookup Scene: Findings from the Online College Social Life Survey." PowerPoint published in TRAILS: Teaching Resources and Innovations Library for Sociology. Washington, DC: American Sociological Association. http://trails.asanet.org.

Padgett, Joseph and Lisa Wade. 2019. "Hookup Culture and Higher Education." In The Routledge Handbook of Contemporary Feminism. Oren, Tasha, and Andrea Press, eds. New York: Routledge.

Schwartz, Alexandra. 2016. "Work It: Is Dating Worth the Effort?" *New Yorker*, May 16.

Ventura, Stephanie J., T.J. Mathews and Brady E. Hamilton. 2001. "Births to Teenagers in the United States, 1940–2000." Vol. 49. *National Vital Statistics Report*. Atlanta, GA: Centers for Disease Control and Prevention.

Vogels, Emily A. 2020. "10 Facts About Americans and Online Dating." *Pew Research*. https://www.pewresearch.org/fact-tank/2020/02/06/10-facts-about-americans-and-online-dating/.

Weigel, Moira. 2017. *Labor of Love: The Invention of Dating*. New York: Farrar, Straus and Giroux.

Whyte, Martin King. 1992. "Choosing Mates—the American Way." *Society* 29(3): 71–77.

6

From Front Porch to Back Seat

A History of the Date

Beth Bailey

One day, the 1920s story goes, a young man came to call upon a city girl. When he arrived, she had her hat on. The punch line is completely lost on twenty-first-century readers, but people at the time would have gotten it. He came on a "call," expecting to sit in her parlor, be served some refreshments, perhaps listen to her play the piano. She expected to go out on a date. He, it is fairly safe to surmise, ended up spending a fair amount of money fulfilling her expectations.

In fact, the unfortunate young man really should have known better. By 1924, when this story was current, "dating" had almost completely replaced "calling" in middle-class American culture. The term appeared in *The Ladies' Home Journal*, a bastion of middle-class respectability, several times in 1914—set off by quotation marks, but with no explanation of its meaning. One article, written in the then-exotic voice of a college sorority girl, began: one beautiful evening in the spring term, when I was a college girl of 18, the boy whom, because of his popularity in every phase of college life, I had been proud gradually to allow the monopoly of my "dates," took me unexpectedly into his arms. As he kissed me impetuously I was glad, from the bottom of my heart, for the training of that mother who had taught me to hold myself aloof from all personal familiarities of boys and men.[1]

Despite the sugarcoating provided by the tribute to motherhood and virtue, dating was a problematic new practice for the middle classes. Its origins were decidedly not respectable; they lay in the practices of "treating" and the sexual exchanges made by "charity girls." The very term "date" came from prostitution. While the urban working class and frankly sexual origins of dating were fairly quickly obscured, not only by such tributes to virtue but also by the increasingly common belief that young people began "going out" because automobiles made it possible, notions of exchange lingered. The same author who recorded the story about the frustrated caller and the woman in the hat made sense of dating this way: in dating, a man is responsible for all expenses. The woman contributes only her company. Of course, the man contributes his company also, but since he must "add money to balance the bargain," his company must be worth less than hers. Thus, according to this economic understanding, she is selling her company to him. Some men declared, flat out, that the exchange was not equitable, that men were operating at a loss. Others, of course, imagined ways to balance the equation: Man's Company + Money = Woman's Company +?

Bailey, Beth. "From Front Porch to Back Seat: A History of the Date." *OAH Magazine of History* 18, no. 4 (2004): 23–26.

Dating, which emerged from working-class urban culture, became a key ritual of youth culture in the 1920s and was unquestionably the dominant form of "courtship" by the beginning of World War II. Certainly not all American youth participated in the rituals of dating. But those who did not, whether by choice, exclusion, or ignorance of the dominant custom, often still felt the weight of a set of expectations that were enacted in high school peer cultures and even written into school curriculums. For the great majority of youth who did date, the highly personal emotions and experiences of dating were shaped, at least in part, through an increasingly powerful and far-reaching national culture that defined the conventions of dating and lent meaning and coherence to individual experience.

While dating remained "the way of American youth," in the words of one sociologist, it took radically different forms during its roughly 45-year heyday from the mid-1920s through the late 1960s. In the years before World War II, American youth prized a promiscuous popularity, demonstrating competitive success through the number and variety of dates they commanded. After the war, youth turned to "going steady," arguing that the system provided a measure of security from the pressures of the postwar world.

In the 1930s, a sociologist gave the competitive system a name: the dating and rating complex. His study of a college campus revealed that the system was based on notions of popularity. To be popular, men needed outward, material signs: an automobile, the right clothing, and money. Women's popularity depended on building and maintaining a reputation for popularity. They had to *be seen* with many popular men in the right places, indignantly turn down requests for dates made at the "last minute," which could be weeks in advance, and cultivate the impression that they were greatly in demand.[2] Thus, in *Mademoiselle's* 1938 college issue, a Smith College senior advised incoming freshmen to cultivate an "image of popularity." "During your first term," she wrote, get "home talent" to ply you with letters, telegrams, and invitations. College men will think, "She must be attractive if she can rate all that attention."[3] At Northwestern University in the 1920s, the competitive pressure was so intense that coeds made a pact not to date on certain nights of the week. That way they could find time to study, secure in the knowledge they were not losing out to others in the race for popularity by staying home.

The new conventions held sway well beyond the gates of colleges. The *Woman's Home Companion* explained the modern dating system—with no mention of college campuses—for its non-elite readers:

> No matter how pretty you may be, how smart your clothes—or your tongue—if you have no dates your rating is low.... The modern girl cultivates not one single suitor, but dates, lots of them.... Her aim is not a too obvious romance but general popularity.[4]

Writing to *Senior Scholastic*, a magazine for high school classrooms, a girl from Greensboro, North Carolina, summed it all up:

> Going steady with one date
> Is okay, if that's all you rate.[5]

Rating, dating, popularity, and competition: catchwords hammered home, reinforced from all sides until they seemed a natural vocabulary. You had to rate in order to date, to date in order to rate. By successfully maintaining this cycle, you became popular. To stay popular, you competed. In the 1930s and 1940s, this competition was enacted, most publicly, on the dance floor—whether in private dances, college formals, or high school parties. There, success was a dizzying popularity that kept girls whirling from escort to escort. One etiquette book advised young women to strive to become "once-arounders" who never completed a turn around the dance floor before another man "cut in" on her partner.[6] Dancing and cutting in were governed by strict protocol: the man had to ask the woman to dance and was responsible for her until she was taken over by another partner. On no account could he leave her stranded on the dance floor or alone on the sidelines. "Getting stuck" with a partner was taken quite seriously as a sign of social failure—even if it was with one's escort. Though a 1933 advice book told the story of a girl who, catching her partner waving a dollar bill behind her back as an inducement to cut in, offered, "Make it five and I'll go home,"[7] a more serious suggestion for handling the situation appeared in *Mademoiselle*: "Keep smiling if it kills you."[8]

By 1950, that system had almost completely disappeared. A girl in Green Bay, Wisconsin, reported that her parents were "astonished" when they discovered that she had not danced with anyone but her escort at the high school formal. "The truth was," she admitted, "that I wasn't aware that we were supposed to."[9] This 180-degree reversal signaled not simply a change in dancing etiquette but a complete transformation of the dating system. Definitions of social success as promiscuous popularity based on strenuous competition had given way to new definitions, which located success in the security of a dependable escort.

How did such an entrenched system change so quickly? It was in large part because of World War II. With virtually all physically fit men between the ages of 18 and 26 inducted into the military by 1943, a system already strained to provide multiple male escorts for every woman foundered. Though some women, near military bases, found an overabundance of men seeking companionship, in much of the nation the complaint was, in the words of the popular song, "There is no available male."

As war disrupted one pattern of courtship, it also changed priorities for many of the nation's youth. During the war, the rate at which Americans married jumped precipitously. That made sense—many young couples, facing an uncertain future, including the possibility the man might not survive the war, married in haste. Marriage rates also rose because the war revived the American economy; many couples had delayed marriage during the Depression, so there was a backlog of couples waiting to marry. But the high rate of marriages continued on well past the end of the war. And most strikingly, the average age at marriage plummeted. In 1939, the average age of marriage for women was 23.3. By 1959, fully 47 percent of brides married before they turned 19.

Before the war, when discussions of courtship centered on rating and dating, marriage had few cheerleaders. It is not that people did not intend to marry. They did. But marriage and the dating system were two quite different things. Dating was about competition within the peer culture of youth; marriage was the end, not the culmination, of participation in youth culture. By the time World War II drew to a close, however, American culture had begun celebrating marriage for youth. And the dating system was no longer a competitive struggle for popularity within youth culture, but instead preparation for an early marriage.

This new model had some unusual results. If girls were to marry at 18 and boys at 20, the preparation for marriage had to begin earlier than before. Experts told parents to help their children become datable, warning that a late start might doom their marriage prospects. Thirteen-year-olds who did not yet date were called "late daters"; magazines recommended formal sit-down birthday dinners and dances for ten-year-old boys and their dates. A 1961 study found that 40 percent of the fifth-graders in one middle-class Pennsylvania district were already dating.

In the prewar years, high school students had emulated the dating-rating system of their elders. As conventions changed for older youth, the younger group tried to keep up. As their slightly older peers married, younger teens developed a parallel convention: going steady. In earlier times, "keeping steady company" was understood as a step along the way to marriage. Going steady meant something quite different by the 1950s. Few steady couples really expected to marry one another—especially the 12-year olds—but, for the duration, they acted as if they were married. Going steady had become a sort of play marriage, a mimicry of the actual marriage of their older peers.

The new protocol of going steady was every bit as strict as the old protocol of rating and dating, with the form of going steady mirroring teenagers' concepts of young marriage. To go steady, the boy gave the girl some visible token—class ring, letter sweater, etc.—or they exchanged identical tokens, often gold or silver friendship rings worn on the third finger of the left hand. Customs varied locally, as Life magazine reported: in Birmingham, Michigan, the girl wore the boy's ID bracelet, but never his letter sweater. In rural Iowa, the couple wore matching corduroy "steady jackets," but in the far West, any couple wearing matching clothing was sure to be laughed at.

As long as they went steady, the boy had to call the girl a certain number of times a week and take her on a certain number of dates a week—both numbers were subject to local convention. Neither boy nor girl could date anyone else or pay too much attention to anyone of the opposite sex. While either could go out with friends of the same sex, each must always know where the other was and what he or she was doing. Going steady meant a guaranteed date, but it also meant that the girl had to help her boyfriend save up for big events by budgeting "their" money, even if it meant sitting home together. Going steady also implied, as parents quickly figured out, greater sexual intimacy—either more necking or "going further."

Despite the intense monogamy of such relationships, few saw going steady as a precursor to marriage. One study of 565 seniors in a suburban high school in the East found that 80 percent of them—or approximately 452 seniors—had gone or were going steady, but only 11 of them planned to marry their steadies.[10] In New Haven, Connecticut, girls wore "obit bracelets": each time they broke up with a boy they added a disc engraved with his name or initials to the chain. So temporary were such arrangements that a teen advice book from the mid-1950s suggested girls engrave a "Puppy Love Anklet" with "Going Steady" on one side and "Ready, Willing, 'n Waiting" on the other.[11]

Harmless as this system sounds today, especially compared to the rigors of rating and dating, going steady precipitated an intense generational battle. The key issue, predictably, was sex. A popular advice book for teenage girls argued that going steady inevitably led girls to heavy necking and thus to guilt for the rest of their lives. Better to date lots of strangers, the author insisted, than end up necking with a steady boyfriend.[12] Adults who advocated the old system as somehow sexually safer, however, had selective memories. The days of promiscuous popularity were also the days of "petting parties," and young people had worried endlessly about how "far" to go with a date. And who knew whether a stranger, parked on a dark road, would listen to a young woman's "firm but polite" NO?

Promiscuous dating and going steady held different dangers. Consent was the difference. A beleaguered system of sexual control based on the resolve of girls and young women to say no—at least to the final step of sexual intercourse—was further breaking down in the new system of going steady. As going steady was a simulated marriage, relationships could and did develop within its even short-term security, monogamy, and, sometimes, love. Parents thought it was easier for girls to say no to the rapid succession of boys who were, at some level, markers for popularity—even when the young men insisted, as one did in the pages of *Senior Scholastic*, that the $1.20 he spent on the date should entitle him to at least a little necking.[13] Adults were afraid it was harder for girls to say no to a steady.

In some ways parents were right, but it was youth themselves, not parental complaints, that would transform the dating system once again. By the late 1960s, the system of sexual exchange that underlay both dating systems was in tatters, undermined by a widespread sexual revolution. In the 1970s, many young people rejected the artificialities of dating, insisting that it was most important to get to know one another as *people*. And a great many women, recognizing the implied exchange in Man's Company + Money = Woman's Company +?, rejected that sort of bargain altogether for a variety of arrangements that did not suggest an equation in need of balancing. Since the early 1970s, no completely dominant national system of courtship has emerged, and the existing systems are not nearly so clear in their conventions and expectations as were the old systems of dating. Not always knowing "the rules" is undoubtedly harder than following the clear script of the traditional date, but those critics who are nostalgic for the good old days should first understand the complicated history of the date.

NOTES

1 "How Maya Girl Know?" LHJ, January 1914, 9. See also a letter to Mrs. Stickney Parks, "Girls' Affairs," LHJ, May 1914, 58.

2 Willard Waller, "The Rating and Dating Complex," *American Sociological Reviews* (1937): 727–734.

3 Mary Ellen Green, "Advice to Freshmen," *Mademoiselle*, August 1939, 8.

4 Anna Streese Richardson, "Dates in Christmas Socks," *Woman's Home Companion* (WHC), January 1940, 7.

5 "Jam Session," *Senior Scholastic* (SS), February 28–March 4, 1944, 32.

6 Elizabeth Eldridge, *Co-ediquette* (New York: E.P. Dutton &. Company, 1936), 203.

7 Alice Leone Moats, *No Nice Girl Swears* (New York: Alfred A. Knopf, 1933), 84–85.

8 Virginia Hanson, "Party-Girl—Princeton Style," *Mademoiselle*, May 1938, 46.

9 Jan London, "The Dateline: Every Dance with the Same Boy?" *Good Housekeeping* (GH), March 1955, 100.

10 Maureen Daly, ed., *Profile of Youth* (New York: J.B. Lippincott Co., 1949), 30.

11 Jan Landon, "The Date Line," GH, June 1957, 20; Landon, "The Date Line," GH, October 1954, 18; Beverly Brandow, *Date Data* (Dallas, TX: Banks Upshaw & Co., 1954), 100.

12 Helen Louise Crounse, *Joyce Jackson's Guide to Dating* (Englewood Cliffs, NJ: Prentice-Hall, 1957), 101.

13 Gay Head, "Boy Dates Girl Jam Session," SS, December 1943, 45.

7

What Meeting Your Spouse Online Has in Common with Arranged Marriage

Amitrajeet A. Batabyal

Most Americans who get married today believe they are choosing their own partners after falling in love with them. Arranged marriages, which remain common in some parts of the world, are a rarity here.

But while doing research about arranged marriages, I've made a surprising observation: these seemingly different kinds of matrimony may be beginning to converge.

Couples who ostensibly marry after spontaneously falling in love increasingly do that with some help from online dating services or after meeting through hookup apps. And modern arranged marriages – including my own – are becoming more like love marriages.

GOING STRONG IN INDIA

According to some estimates, more than half of the marriages taking place around the world each year are arranged. They are the norm in India, comprising at least 90 percent of all marriages.

The practice also remains relatively common elsewhere in South Asia, parts of Africa, the Middle East and East Asian countries like Japan and China.

I believe that most people in communities where arranged marriages predominate still feel that parents and other close relatives are qualified to select marriage partners. Some young Indians consider their parents as more objective than they are about this big decision and more adept at spotting compatibility.

In addition, arranged marriages help couples uphold cultural and religious traditions that have stood the test of time. Perhaps this explains why people in arranged marriages tend to get divorced less frequently.

Data comparing divorce rates within countries for arranged and love marriage are hard to come by. But in the US, between 40 and 50 percent of all marriages end in divorce. In India, the divorce rate for all marriages is about 1 percent and it's higher for love marriages than arranged ones there.

Batabyal, Amitrajeet A. "What Meeting Your Spouse Online Has in Common with Arranged Marriage." April 4, 2018.

To be sure, divorce is often frowned upon in nations and cultures where arranged marriages are common – making that metric a potentially unreliable way to assess marital bliss or the lack thereof. In addition, the US, Indian and other governments generally don't collect arranged marriage data.

NOT YOUR GRANDMA'S ARRANGED MARRIAGE

As a result of India's rising incomes, higher education levels and technological advances that ease communications, arranged marriage is changing there and among people of Indian heritage who live elsewhere. Young people who tie the knot that way have more power to choose their spouses and can even initiate the process instead of their parents.

In addition, the prevalence of matrimonial websites such as Shaadi (which means marriage in Hindi) and Jeevansathi (life partner in Hindi) empowers young Indians who reside in India or North America to become more self-reliant.

The internet, higher education levels, and cultural and economic globalization are also making single Indians freer to do their own searching for future spouses than their parents were. And some traditions that limit choices for single people, such as parents placing newspaper ads to announce eligibility and interest, are becoming less common.

Finally, when Indians reach a marriageable age – usually between 18 and 30 years old for women and between 22 and 40 for men – the ways these aspiring brides and grooms interact are beginning to resemble contemporary dating in the US. That's a big change from the rituals of the past, which typically involved a supervised meeting between the prospective bride and the groom and several meetings between their families.

ARRANGED MARRIAGE, AMERICAN-STYLE

Arranged marriage is stigmatized in the US, where parents are largely deemed ill-suited for the task of finding marriage partners for their children.

But, in my opinion, things are changing here for a reason. Online dating and matrimonial sites, such as eHarmony, OkCupid and The Right Stuff, are proliferating and becoming more accepted.

While these sites and apps don't use the word "arranged" in their branding, it's hard to deny that they do "arrange" for people to meet. In addition, the explicit criteria – online profiles, personality tests, questionnaires – that they use to match individuals resemble the implicit criteria parents and friends use to identify prospective spouses for arranged marriages.

An important difference is that third parties – dating websites and other matchmaking services or their staff – handle the "arranging" activities. eHarmony, for example, pre-screens candidates based on personality tests. OkCupid uses questionnaires to match people. Perfectmatch.com uses algorithms to match people, and The Right Stuff pairs people by profile.

Psychologist John Cacioppo of the University of Chicago recently did a study with several colleagues about internet dating and modern matrimony. They found that more than one-third of all American couples who got married between 2005 and 2012 met online. Marriages that began when couples met online were a little less likely to break up than those who didn't and those spouses were somewhat more satisfied with their marriages, the researchers determined.

In my view, all parents seeking to arrange a marriage for their sons and daughters do so with the best of intentions. They don't always get it right, but they frequently do. My own parents certainly did, 23 years ago, when I got married. And whether parents or computer algorithms make this connection, the ultimate goal is the same: to ensure a happy and long-lasting union.

8

What's So Cultural about Hookup Culture?

Lisa Wade

Arman was 7,000 miles from his family, one of the roughly million international students who were enrolled in US colleges last year. Dropped into the raucous first week of freshman year, he discovered a way of life that seemed intensely foreign, frightening, and enticing. "It's been a major shock," he wrote.

The behavior of some of his fellow students unnerved him. He watched them drink to excess, tell explicit sexual stories, flirt on the quad, and grind on the dance floor. He received assertive sexual signals from women. It was, Arman wrote, "beyond anything I have experienced back home."

By his second semester, Arman's religious beliefs had been shaken. He was deeply torn as to whether to participate in this new social scene. "Stuck," he wrote, "between a sexually conservative background and a relatively sexually open world." Should he "embrace, accept, and join in?" Or, he wondered, using the past tense like a Freudian slip, "remember who I was and deprive myself of the things I actually and truly want deep down inside?"

He struggled. "Always having to internally fight the desire to do sexual things with girls is not easy," he wrote. One night, he succumbed to temptation. He went to a party, drank, and kissed a girl on the dance floor. When the alcohol wore off, he was appalled at his behavior. "How much shame I have brought onto myself," he recalled with anguish.

A few months later, he would lose his virginity to a girl he barely knew. His feelings about it were deeply ambivalent. "I felt more free and unbounded," he confessed, "but at the same time, guilt beyond imagination."

For my book, *American Hookup: The New Culture of Sex on Campus*, I followed 101 college students through a semester of their first year. They submitted weekly journal entries, writing about sex and dating on campus however they wished. In total, the students wrote over 1,500 single-spaced pages and a million words. I dovetailed their stories with 21 follow-up interviews, quantitative data from the Online College Social Life Survey, academic literature, hundreds of essays written by students for college newspapers, and 24 visits to campuses around the country.

Arman was an outlier. Very few students are strongly motivated to abstain from sex altogether, but it's typical for students to report mixed feelings about the opportunity to have casual sex. Thirty-six of the

101 students I studied reported being simultaneously attracted to and repelled by hookup culture upon arrival at college, compared to 34 who opted out entirely, 23 who opted in with enthusiasm, and eight who sustained monogamous relationships.

For students like Arman, who are unsure of whether they want to participate, hookup culture has a way of tipping the scales. Its logic makes both abstaining from sex and a preference for sex in committed relationships difficult to justify, and its integration into the workings of higher education makes hooking up hard to avoid.

The Logic of Hookup Culture

Hooking up is immanently defensible in hookup culture. Students believe, or believe that their peers believe, that virginity is passé and monogamy prudish; that college is a time to go wild and have fun; that separating sex from emotions is sexually liberating; and that they're too young and career-focused for commitment. All of these ideas are widely circulated on campus—and all make reasonable sense—validating the choice to engage in casual sex while invalidating both monogamous relationships and the choice to have no sex at all.

For the students in my study who were enthusiastic about casual sex, this worked out well, but students who found casual sex unappealing often had difficulty explaining why, both to themselves or others. Many simply concluded that they were overly sensitive or insufficiently brave. "I honestly admire them," wrote one Latina student about her friends who enjoyed casual sex, "because I just cannot do that." A White middle-class student implored herself to not be so "uptight." "Sometimes I wish I could just loosen up," she wrote. A sexually sophisticated pansexual student wondered aloud if she was a "prude." "I'm so embarrassed by that," she confessed. "I feel as if by not voluntarily taking part in it, I am weird and abnormal."

If culture is a "toolkit" offering culturally competent actors a set of ideas and practices with which to explain their choices, to use Ann Swider's metaphor from her article "Culture in Action," then hookup culture offers students many tools useful for embracing casual sex, but few for articulating why they may prefer other kinds of sexual engagement, or none at all. Faced with these options, many students who are ambivalent decide to give it a try.

The New Culture of College

In the colonial era, colleges were downright stodgy. Student activities were rigidly controlled, curricula were dry, and harsh punishments were meted out for misbehavior. The fraternity boys of the early 1800s can be credited with introducing the idea that college should be fun. Their lifestyle was then glamorized by the media of the 1920s and democratized by the alcohol industry in the 1980s after *Animal House*. Today, the reputation of higher education as a place for an outlandish good time is second only to its reputation as a place of learning.

Not just any good time, though. A particular kind of party dominates the social scene: drunken, wild, and visually titillating, throbbing with sexual potential. Such parties are built into the rhythm and architecture of higher education. They occur at designated times, such that they don't interfere with (most) classes, and are usually held at large, off-campus houses (often but not always fraternities) or on nearby streets populated by bars and clubs. This gives the institutions plausible deniability, but keeps the partying close enough to be part of colleges' appeal.

Almost all of the students in *American Hookup* were living in residence halls. On weekend nights, dorms buzzed with pre-partying, primping, and planning. Students who stayed in were keenly aware of what they weren't doing. Eventually residence halls would empty out, leaving eerie quiet; revelers returned drunker, louder. Students were sometimes kicked out of their own rooms to facilitate a roommate's hookup. A few had exhibitionistic roommates who didn't bother to kick them out at all.

The morning after, there would be a ritual retelling of the night before. And the morning after that, anticipation for the next weekend of partying began. Being immersed in hookup culture meant being surrounded by anticipation, innuendo, and braggadocio. As one of the African-American men in my study wrote: "Hookup culture is all over the place."

For students who went to parties, hookups felt, as several put it, "inevitable." Sooner or later, a student had one too many drinks, met someone especially cute, or felt like doing something a little wild. For young people still learning how to manage sexual desire, college parties combining sex with sensory overload and mind-altering substances can be overwhelming. Accordingly, anyone who regularly participates in the routine partying built into the rhythm of higher education will likely find themselves opting in to hooking up.

Sex on college campuses is something people do, but it's also a cultural phenomenon: a conversation of a particular kind and a set of routines built into the institution of higher education. When students arrive on campus, they don't just encounter the opportunity to hook up, they are also immersed in a culture that endorses and facilitates hookups. Ceding to or resisting that culture then becomes part of their everyday lives.

"Even if you aren't hooking up," said an African-American woman about her first year on campus, "there is no escaping hookup culture." Residential colleges are what sociologist Erving Goffman called "total institutions," planned entities that collect large numbers of like individuals, cut them off from the wider society, and provide for all their needs. And because hookup culture is totally institutionalized, when students move into a dorm room on a college campus, they become a part of it—whether they like it or not.

Students wish they had more options. Some pine for the going-steady lifestyle of the 1950s. Many mourn the utopia that the sexual revolution promised but never fully delivered. Quite a few would like things to be a lot more queer and gender fluid. Some want a hookup culture that is kinder—warm as well as hot. And there are still a handful who would prefer stodgy to sexy. Satisfying these diverse desires will require a shift to a more complex and rich cultural life on campus, not just a different one.

9

Straight Girls Do Kiss on Campus, But What About Those Who Don't Go to College?

Jamie Budnick

"Straight girls kissing" has become something of a curious and controversial cultural phenomenon over the last 15 years.

Madonna and Britney Spears famously locked lips in front of millions during the 2003 Video Music Awards, with Scarlett Johansson and Sandra Bullock following suit seven years later at the MTV Movie Awards. In 2008, Katy Perry went platinum singing that she "kissed a girl" and "liked it." Meanwhile, we've seen portrayals of otherwise unlabeled women acting on same-gender desire in a number of popular primetime shows, from "Orphan Black" to "The Good Wife."

In one sense, this reflects real life. Many young women who identify as straight have had sexual or romantic experiences with other women. Research on sexual fluidity, hooking up and straight girls kissing has mainly focused on women living on college campuses: privileged, affluent, white women.

But studies have found that same-gender sexual experiences between straight women are common across all socioeconomic backgrounds. This means existing studies have been ignoring a lot of women.

As recent surveys have shown, women outside of the privileged spaces of college campuses actually report higher rates of same-gender sex. This happens even though they're more likely to start families at a younger age. They also have different types of same-gender sexual experiences and views of sexuality, all of which we know less about because they're often underrepresented in most academic studies of the issue.

As a sociologist who studies gender and sexuality, I wanted to know: How do straight women who don't match the privileged, affluent and white stereotype we see in the media make sense of their same-gender sexual experiences?

"STRAIGHT GIRLS KISSING" IN SOCIAL SCIENCE

Some social scientists have followed the media's fixation on straight girls kissing to further explore theories of female bisexuality.

Budnick, Jamie "Straight Girls Do Kiss on Campus, But What about Those Who Don't Go to College?" October 13, 2016.

In her 2008 book, psychologist Lisa Diamond developed the influential model of "sexual fluidity" to explain women's context-dependent or changing sexual desire. Meanwhile, sociologist Laura Hamilton argued that making out at college parties served as an effective, albeit homophobic, "gender strategy" to simultaneously attract men and shirk lesbians. And historian Leila Rupp, with a group of sociologists, theorized that the college hookup scene operates as an "opportunity structure" for queer women to explore their attractions and affirm their identities.

All of these scholars are quick to recognize that these ideas – and the studies on which they are based – focus mostly on a certain type of person: privileged women living on the progressive campuses of selective universities. In part, it is easier to recruit study participants from classes and student groups, but it leaves us with a picture that reinforces stereotypes.

Around the same time I conducted my study, the National Survey of Family Growth (NSFG) found that women with the lowest levels of educational attainment reported the highest lifetime prevalence of same-gender sex. The New York Times correctly observed that these findings challenged "the popular stereotype of college as a hive of same-sex experimentation." A 2016 update of the survey did not find a statistically significant pattern that varied by education level, but reiterated the high prevalence among women who didn't go to college.

Rich Insights Just below the Surface

In 2008, I started work as a research assistant on the Relationship Dynamics and Social Life (RDSL) study, which surveyed young women weekly for two-and-a-half years to learn about the prevalence, causes and consequences of unintended pregnancy. It was my job to handle participants' questions, comments and complaints. Most of the inquiries from the participants were about how to complete the surveys or receive the incentive payment.

But a few came from women unsure about how to answer questions on sex and relationships. They wondered: Were they supposed to include their girlfriends?

Many demographic surveys focused on health or risk do not explicitly collect data on sexual orientation or same-gender relationships. But valuable information on these topics often exists just below the surface.

In 2010, I decided to write new RDSL survey questions about sexual identity, behavior and attraction. Nearly one-third of participants gave some type of nonheterosexual response (including women who said they "rejected" labels or that gender was not a determining factor in their attractions). In 2013, I recruited 35 of these women to interview. Because RDSL had a racially and socioeconomically diverse population-based sample, I was able to interview women that many sexualities scholars struggle to access.

After Becoming a Mother, Goodbye to all That?

Many women I interviewed had become mothers in their teens or early 20s. All of these moms had hooked up with a woman, had a girlfriend in the past or said they were still attracted to women. Nonetheless, most identified as straight.

They explained that it was more important to be a "good mother" than anything else, and claiming a nonheterosexual identity just wasn't a priority once kids were in the picture.

For example, Jayla (a black mom with a four-year degree from a state school) broke ties with her group of LGBTQ friends after her daughter was born. As she explained, "I think what our relationship didn't survive was me becoming a mom... I kind of shifted away from them, because I know how I want to raise my daughter."

Women who married men or settled down in their early 20s also felt that their previous lesbian or bisexual identities were no longer relevant.

Noel, a white married mom with a General Educational Development certificate, dated girls in high school. Back then, being bisexual was a big part of her identity. Today, she doesn't use that term. Noel said monogamy made identity labels irrelevant: "I'm with my husband, and I don't intend on being with anybody else for my future."

SEXUAL FRIENDSHIPS EMERGE

Being a young mom can foreclose some possibilities to fully embrace an LGBTQ identity. But in other ways it created space to act on same-gender desire. I came to call these intimacies "sexual friendships."

Chantelle, a black mom with a high school diploma, was struggling to co-parent with her ex-boyfriend. In the midst of her frustrating situation, she had found intimacy and satisfaction in a sexual friendship with a woman. As she put it, "relationships have a different degree and different standards. But with a friendship it's kind of like everything is an open book."

Amy, a white woman working on her associate's degree, has had sex a few times with her best friend. They don't talk about that, but they have daydreamed together about getting married, contrasting their feelings with their experiences dating men: "I feel like a man will never understand me. I don't think they could. Or I don't think that most men would care to. That's just how I feel from the experiences I've had."

Some of the women I interviewed told me they strategically chose hookups with women because they thought it would be safer – safer for their reputation and a safeguard against sexual assault.

Tara, a white woman attending a regional public university, explained:

> I'm a very physical person and it's not all emotional, but that doesn't go over well with people, and you get 'the player,' 'whore,' whatever. But when you do it more with girls, there's no negative side effects to it.

Tara also said that men often misinterpret interest for more than it was: "Like if I want to make out with you, it doesn't mean I want to have sex with you. But in a lot of guys in party scenes, that's their mentality." I asked her if this happened to anyone she knew, and she uncomfortably said yes – "Not that they ever called it rape or anything like that."

LESS EXCITING, MORE REAL

Intersectional studies like the one I conducted can upend the way we frame the world and categorize people. It's not binary: Women don't kiss each other only for either the attention of men or on their way to a proud bisexual or lesbian identity. There is a lot of rich meaning in the middle, not to mention structural constraints.

And what about that popular image equating "straight girls kissing" with "girls gone wild"? It's more provocative cliché than reality. Many are at home with their kids – the father gone – looking for companionship and connection.

By using large-scale surveys as both a source of puzzles and a tool for recruiting a more diverse group of participants, the picture of "straight girls kissing" gets a little less exciting – but a lot more real.

10

'If I Could Really Say That and Get Away with It!' Accountability and Ambivalence in American Parents' Sexuality Lessons in the Age of Abstinence

Sinikka Elliott

INTRODUCTION

When Rose (43 years old, White) describes her 14-year-old son – who is just going through the physical changes of puberty – her face lights up: he is 'very intelligent', 'very responsible', and 'loves outdoor activities'. She thinks her son revels in the changes of puberty: he proudly shows off his armpit hair and is anxiously awaiting his 'happy trail' (a slender path of pubic hair running from the belly button to the pubic area), uses his deeper voice to be heard over his younger siblings, and, when he began to shave a year ago, displayed his shaving kit like 'a status symbol or something'. But Rose is also worried. Two years ago, she and her husband sat their son down for 'the talk': 'We told him the basics of what happens. You know, what sex is'. Since then, Rose said they have taken him aside regularly to talk about sex and dating: 'He got to the point where he was like, "Uh oh, oh no!" and he would like get scared every time we said we need to talk'. Rose has persisted, however, because 'I want to make sure he knows all the risks that are out there'.

Rose does not think her son is interested in sex yet, but she is concerned that girls might make advances toward him. The first time she and her husband talked with him about sex, 'We just sat him down and said, "You need to watch out for girls"'. As far as Rose is concerned, 'girls are more aggressive than boys … both in pursuing the boy and in having sex'. Rose has heard that some middle school girls now wear different colored hair bands as bracelets; each color represents what a girl will do sexually: kiss, let a boy feel her up, oral sex, and so on. Rose also relayed experiences that have solidified her belief that girls really are more forward than boys. A few months ago, Rose's husband stumbled across a topless picture of one of their son's female classmates in their son's email inbox. Rose immediately 'forwarded the picture to her mom, so her mom would know what her daughter was up to', and talked extensively with her son about the type of girl who would send such a picture: 'I told him she was probably trying to get him to be her boyfriend, but boys really lose respect for girls who act like that. Boys don't respect girls who are showy'.

Elliott, Sinikka. "'If I Could Really Say That and Get Away with It!' Accountability and Ambivalence in American Parents' Sexuality Lessons in the Age of Abstinence." *Sex Education* 10, no. 3 (2010): 239–250.

Rose has many concerns about teenagers having sex. She worries about sexually transmitted infections and teen pregnancy, but also thinks that young people approach sex too cavalierly. She says that popular teen movies and television shows contribute to this by portraying teen sex 'as if it's perfectly normal. It's like brushing your teeth. It *shouldn't* be that way. They just *should not* be that intense at that age'. For Rose, teenagers are not yet mature enough to understand the significance of sex. She passionately described her 16-year-old niece and her boyfriend: 'They're just *babies*. They're just too young, too immature. It would be a huge mistake for them [to have sex]. I've told my niece that too'. Rose hopes to instill these beliefs in her son as well, so that if the opportunity arises, he will think twice before having sex. She tells her son that sex is 'something special between a husband and a wife – that's how you have children', and would prefer that he remain a virgin until his wedding day.

Yet, even though she is committed to the idea that sex is for marriage, she doubts that her son will wait until he is married: 'We tell him to wait till he's married. I don't think he will. I mean, it's just a fact of life [laughing] … But I hope it won't be until he's in his twenties.' Although Rose expressed very strong opinions on a number of topics, on the issue of abstinence she is torn between what she would ideally prefer and what she thinks is realistic. She worries that if she pushes her belief that sex should only happen within marriage too forcefully, her son will feel guilt-ridden if he ever does have sex outside of marriage. As she put it, 'I don't want him to have a big guilty complex about it. But I don't want him to have sex when he's 14 either!' Thus, in talking with her son, she emphasizes his youth and vulnerability in a highly sexualized culture surrounded by sexually driven girls. She hopes that this will sufficiently scare him into waiting without producing too much guilt if and when he does have sex.

Rose's fears for her son, the scrutiny she and her husband employ to keep him safe, and their sense of accountability for his well-being, along with the ambivalence she expressed, were echoed by countless other parents I interviewed. In this paper, based on in-depth interviews with 64 American parents of teenagers, I examine how parents of teenagers navigate the complex landscape of abstinence, personal responsibility, and sexual well-being in their sexuality lessons to their children. Reflecting the dominance of the abstinence-only discourse, many parents promote abstinence in their sexuality lessons to their children, but doubt its practicality (and some, like Rose, worry about their children experiencing guilt if they have sex outside of marriage). My analysis suggests that abstinence is appealing to parents less for its moral message than its promise of psychological, physical, and financial well-being. That is, despite their ambivalence, many parents promote abstinence because they hope it will keep their children safe and safeguard their futures.

Background

Research on sex education suggests that Americans hold polarized views on sex education and teen sexuality. Luker's (2006) study of the battles over sex education finds that, when it comes to teen sexuality, Americans are divided into two groups: sexual liberals and sexual conservatives. According to Luker, sexual liberals and sexual conservatives disagree on a fundamental level about tradition versus modernity, values, and the role of information in people's lives. When it comes to information about sexuality, sexual liberals, for example, think that young people need plenty of information about sexuality in order to make good sexual choices, and thus promote comprehensive sex education (i.e. sex education that teaches about contraception). Sexual conservatives, in contrast, believe that too much sexual information can be confusing, at best, and dangerous, at worst, to young people, and thereby promote abstinence-only sex education.

Parents are often symbolically at the center of these debates. Although school-based sex education was historically predicated on the belief that knowledge about the dangers of sex would prevent youthful sexual activity and that parents, especially mothers, were ill-equipped to impart this information to their children, shifts in sex education over the past couple of decades have increasingly designated parents the 'guardians of their children's sexual lives' (Levine 2002, 105). The 'Chastity Act' passed early in Reagan's administration, for example, identified parents as the rightful dispatchers of sex education. As President Reagan put it in a speech expressing the prevailing view: 'The rights of parents and the rights of family take precedence over those of Washington-based bureaucrats and social engineers' (*New York Times* 1983). Since Reagan's speech, a number of states have implemented policies to increase parents' rights over their children's sexuality, such as parental notification and consent laws for teen abortions and parental consent for school-based sex education. Abstinence-only sex education is also described as a form of sex education that increases parents' rights over the type of information teenagers receive about sex. Calls for comprehensive sex education, by contrast, tend to be based on the notion that parents are largely out of touch and/or misinformed about issues related to sexuality and reluctant to talk to their children about sex. Yet, by focusing predominantly on activists and communities involved in fights over sex education, research on the sex education debates largely depicts reality as 'divided into people who are for or against someone or something' (Smelser 1998, 11). In this chapter, I argue that polarization does not accurately reflect the complexities of parents' understandings and management of their children's sexuality. Instead, I find that ambivalence and ambiguity characterize parents' discussions around and understandings of their teenagers' sexuality. I use the term 'ambivalence' less in the psychological than the sociological sense of the word. Psychologically, ambivalence broadly refers to 'the simultaneous existence of attraction and repulsion, of love and hate' (Smelser 1998, 5). Hence, psychologists tend to focus on individuals' contradictory states toward people, objects, or symbols. A more sociological understanding of ambivalence emphasizes that contradictory feelings or attitudes are often rooted in structured social relations. Ambivalence, sociologically defined, is 'the result of pressures imposed by contradictory demands or norms placed on an individual in a particular social location, role, or relationship' (Willson et al. 2006, 236). Sociologists thus examine how social conditions give rise to and encourage ambivalence. Ambivalence tends to arise from interdependence, for example, and often entails a sense of obligation. Given the extent to which parents' and children's lives are intertwined and interdependent, the parent-child relationship is rife with ambivalence. Ambivalence may also be rooted in contradictory cultural messages or images, such as those surrounding teen sexuality. Teen sexual activity is routinely linked to a whole host of negative outcomes, even as notions and images of teenagers as highly sexual and sexualized abound.

In this chapter, I examine parents' ambivalence about teen sexuality, in general, and sexual abstinence, in particular. I ask, in an era in which abstinence only until marriage has emerged as the dominant discourse around teen sexuality, promoted as the only surefire way to prevent the disease, heartache, procreative possibilities, and financial ruin regularly associated with teen sexual activity, how do parents make sense of teen sexuality and what do they teach their teenagers about sexuality? As I demonstrate, most parents feel accountable to promote abstinence in their lessons to their children about sexuality, and many view abstinence as a way for their children to safely and successfully get through adolescence and attain hopeful futures, even as they are skeptical that their children will in fact abstain from sexual activity until marriage. I argue that parents' ambivalence stems in part from their own life experiences and their social structural position as parents who are invested in, and feel accountable for, their children's safety and well-being, but it is also informed by the cultural contradictions around teen sexuality. In line with larger discourses around teen sexuality, parents view teen sexual activity as fraught with danger, heartache, and ruin while simultaneously depicting teenagers, in general, as highly sexually motivated but not yet mature enough to responsibly navigate the perilous terrain of teen sexuality.

METHODS

The data and analyses offered here are based on in-depth interviews with 64 parents (40 mothers and 24 fathers) of at least one teenage child between the ages of 13 and 19.

The sample comprises six fathers and 40 mothers who reside in Texas and 18 fathers in North Carolina. Both of these states received federal funding for abstinence sex education at the time of the interviews, although the actual content of school-based sex education varied across school districts. Over one-half of the parents identified as White (n = 38; 19 mothers, 19 fathers), one-quarter identified as Latino/Latina (n = 16; 15 mothers, one father), and about one-eighth identified as Black (n = 10; six mothers, four fathers). In terms of social class, just under one-quarter of the sample of parents are upper middle class, one-half are lower middle class, and slightly over a quarter are working class or poor. To take into account the social and cultural aspects of class, I determined parents' social class location using their reported annual income, as well as the types of jobs they hold and their education levels.

FINDINGS

My analysis suggests that abstinence is appealing to parents less for its moral message than its promise of psychological, physical, and financial well-being. That is, despite their ambivalence, many parents promote abstinence because they hope it will keep their children safe and safeguard their futures. This understanding is largely based on two dominant American discourses around teenagers and teen sexuality. First, parents think sex (by which they mean heterosexual intercourse) is enormously risky – resulting in innumerable negative physical, emotional, and financial consequences. As Melissa (43 years old, White) put it: 'You're dealing with life and death issues from seventh grade on'. In particular, most parents mentioned being concerned about HIV/AIDS and other sexually transmitted infections. Yolanda's (30 years old, Latina) description of her discussion with her 13-year-old daughter and 11-year-old son captures this concern:

> I've told them [my kids] the story of a friend of a friend. The girl was 17- years - old and she was dating an older guy and the first time she ever had sex with him, the guy gave her herpes. And, you know, that stuff lives with you forever. And I told them, 'You just never know. You know, it's just so scary.' And they're like, 'Oh no!'

Many parents described a sense of escalating sexual dangers since the 1960s and 1970s. Kirk (45 years old, White) expressed this when he said:

> There's more sexually transmitted diseases than when I was [young]. You know, I'm 45 that we didn't have – I mean maybe AIDS was out there but it wasn't something that people were too worried about. I never thought about it myself. You know, we had other types of sexually transmitted diseases but none of them killed you, so that's the thing that I warn [my 15-year-old son] about.

In addition to disease, parents described fears about teen pregnancy, emotional and psychological distress, as well as social and economic ruin. In line with the discourse of personal responsibility and school-based sex education, parents routinely used the word 'consequences', both in discussing their rationale for talking with their children about sex and in describing the content of these talks. Kim's (45 years old, Black) response was typical. Kim explained that she emphasizes consequences when she talks to her 17-year-old son, 12-year-old niece, and 10-year-old daughter: '[I tell them] "Procreation is real. I don't care what anybody says, when you have sex, there's only the potential for a baby to pop up, no matter what precautions you take"'. In line with abstinence-only discourse, Kim stresses to her children that the only safe sex is no sex. She also tries to instill an internal voice in her children that will lead them to think – 'there's things I want to accomplish and I know the consequences of having [sex] … the consequences can be quite detrimental' – before they act. In general, parents' discussions about sex appear to revolve around a time, in the future, when their children may either engage in or consider engaging in heterosexual intercourse and the omnipresent risk of pregnancy, disease, and victimization.

Second, in addition to emphasizing the dangerous consequences of sex, the parents articulated a view of teenagers as vessels of raging hormones who lack the capacity to approach sex responsibly. Patrick (43 years old, White), for example, said he tells his 13-year-old son: 'We're still animals and you can break down biology and it's very plain: You hit puberty [and] the drive, the hardwire is to reproduce. Everything that goes on is human drive, and there's nothing you can do about it'. As Corina (39 years old, Black) put it: '[Teenagers] got their cute little bodies and their raging hormones. They're like raring to go'. This understanding reflects a dominant discourse of sex as an uncontrollable drive to which teenagers, in particular, because of their raging hormones and lack of impulse control are susceptible. This discourse often runs alongside a risk-based discourse of teen sexuality. Indeed, parents frequently intertwined these two discourses. During their interviews, parents would often first describe how dangerous sex is and then point out that these dangers are magnified for teenagers because of their immaturity and irresponsibility coupled with their out-of-control hormones. For example, Paul (62 years old, White) explained why he does not want his 17-year-old son to be sexually active: 'Your limbic system is the area that lights up the most; you're mostly controlled by your emotions [in your teens]. [Sex at this time] is just very very risky'. Josephina (31 years old, Latina) described how she talked with her 14-year-old son about sex:

I explained that it's very risky, in the sense that a lot of your behavior is driven by your hormones. It's not that you are good or bad or you do this because you consciously want to do it and *decide* to do it, there's a lot of instinctive behavior and it's driven by your hormones. And it can drive you to very dangerous situations in which you can end up having AIDS or an unwanted pregnancy.

Some parents asserted that teens lack the judgment or capacity to, for example, use contraception at all or effectively. For example, in response to a question about whether she thinks it is acceptable for teenagers to experiment sexually, Paula (43 years old, Latina) said after a long pause:

I think … um … that's a hard one for me because you know, there's just so much more issues going on. It's not just the experimentations. I mean, you worry about sexually transmitted diseases and other things. And I still think there's a level of maturity that goes along with that too. So I don't know, I have a hard time with that one, as teenagers.

Sylvia (44 years old, Latina) also strongly expressed a belief that teenagers should not have sex. When I probed to find out more about why she feels this way, she responded: 'I think they would be more responsible [about sex when they're older] rather than being a teen [laughing]'. I asked, 'So in your opinion teenagers aren't responsible?' Sylvia replied, 'Yes! What teenager is responsible?'

These two discourses – the dangerous consequences of sex and the raging hormones of teenagers – shape parents' ambivalence about promoting abstinence. Reflecting a combination of these two dominant discourses, most of the parents professed that sexual abstinence until marriage (or adulthood) is what they would prefer for their children, but also a belief that this is probably not realistic. Josephina (31 years old, Latina) encapsulates this stance when she said, 'I mean, abstinence is the only way where you're 100 percent not going to get pregnant. You're not going to get any sexually transmitted diseases. But it's not real'. Beth (39 years old, White) discussed her ambivalence about telling her 16-year-old son he should remain abstinent until marriage:

I will say things like half-kiddingly, but he knows I'm not kidding, like 'Now remember you *cannot* have sex until you're married'. I just know that that's not going to happen. I think the no-sex-until-marriage thing is a religious thing and we're not that religious, so I do not have that expectation of him.
[*But you tell him anyway?*]
Yeah because you don't know what else to say.

Although she is not very religious, Beth uses the language of abstinence until marriage in discussing sex with her son because, despite her belief that it is unrealistic and that her son will not abstain until he is married, she does not know what else to tell him. Beth's response reveals that she lacks a cultural repertoire to talk about sex outside of marriage in a positive, affirming way. Indeed, teen sexuality is routinely framed in negative terms. Mainstream media reports tend to focus on teen pregnancy, sexually transmitted infections, 'casual' sex, and victimization. In addition, although the debates over sex education are often premised on the notion that abstinence and comprehensive sex education curricula are vastly different, these programs typically rely on a fear-based model of teen sexuality and stress the risks and negative consequences of teen sexual activity. A positive discourse of teenage desire and sexual pleasure, especially female desire, is notably absent in both popular discourse *and* sex education.

Beth has not talked with her son about contraception, finding it difficult to reconcile that discussion with her stance on abstinence only, her general discomfort, and her sense that her son is too young for this information. However, many of the parents who stress abstinence also said that they provide contraceptive information. Lorena (32 years old, Latina), for example, prefers that her 16-year-old son wait to have sex until he is married or until he has found the right person: 'I always instill in him, "You have to have somebody special. It has to be somebody special. Hopefully it will be the person you marry." But these days I can't expect that, but that's what I prefer'. Because she feels she cannot expect her son to abstain until marriage, Lorena has discussed contraception with him. However, when I asked her whether she thought it was acceptable for teenagers to have sex, she responded: 'I don't know. I think it depends on the individual. But my son, no. I don't think so.'

Importantly, parents' own experiences critically shape their understandings of teen sexuality and their ambivalence about what is best for their children. Lorena wants her son to wait in part because she was a teenage mother. Although she attributed being a mom to many positive things in her life, including becoming more responsible and goal oriented, she said being a mother at 16 also made it harder for her to achieve her goals. She is currently working full time in a low-wage job and taking college classes in the evenings, with the plan of someday becoming a probation officer. She would like her son to have an easier life.

Corina's (39 years old, Black) story provides further insight into this dynamic. Corina has three daughters – two are in their 20s, are married, and have children of their own. Her youngest is 14 years old. When her two oldest daughters were in high school, Corina had them sign a contract promising to abstain from sex until marriage. If they graduated from high school without having had sex (measured by the absence of a teenage pregnancy), she pledged to give them each $500. To reinforce the abstinence message, she took them to witness a friend's childbirth, what she calls 'the childbirthing class', so they could see for themselves, 'Look it hurts! This is what happens'. In addition, Corina was extremely vigilant. She never left her daughters' sides:

> I would go with them to the movies; I would go with them to the mall; I went to the dances; I was the chaperone at the prom (laughs)! I can just go on and on about all the little stuff I did. If there was a track meet, I was there. Everything they did, I did with them.

Corina also had several male friends talk to her daughters about the 'male point of view'. One friend in particular, whom Corina described as 'a player', told her daughters 'the truth,' 'I just want women for their body. I'm using them and if any other man tells you that's not what they're doing then they're lying to you.' Corina hoped that these talks would help her daughters realize the pitfalls of having sex outside of marriage.

Yet, in spite of her vigilance, the contract, the childbirthing class, and the talks, Corina still provided her daughters with information about contraception, including taking them to Planned Parenthood. When I asked her why, she explained:

> Because things happen, you know? I was a teenage girl. I snuck out the window. And I figured my girls will slip up and they'll do something crazy too. So they need to know the right methods to take. [I tell them], 'Make sure you use protection. You protect yourself. You protect him. You don't want to get no disease. And if he's out messing around then you'll most likely catch something'. Plus, Planned Parenthood, they show videos. They talk to you. They teach you about contraceptives. They tell you about the venereal diseases, what they all do to your body, how to prevent you from having children and everything else.

Corina desperately wanted her two oldest daughters to abstain from sex – to get through high school without an unplanned pregnancy or unwanted sexually transmitted infection and to have 'something left to save for your husband on your wedding night' – yet, based on her own recollection and understanding of what it is like to be a teenager, especially a teenage girl, surrounded by 'lying boys, saying all the right stuff', she decided it would be foolhardy to deny them information about contraception. In particular, stemming from her own experiences – she said, for various reasons, she could not rely on the fathers of her two oldest daughters, both conceived when she was a teenager – Corina emphasized that boys are not to be trusted.

Like Corina, the parents often constructed teenage intimate heterosexual relationships in adversary terms, a practice also common in school-based sex education. Notions of vulnerability and victimization, often based on a battle of the sexes paradigm whereby girls trap boys and boys use girls, permeate discussions about teen sexuality. These understandings informed many parents' ambivalence about teen sexuality as well. For example, Sharon (51 years old, White), a mother of two teen daughters, conveyed a highly sex positive perspective in her interview. She wants her 14- and 16-year-old daughters to feel sexually empowered and agentic. Yet she worries that this might be especially difficult for her daughters to achieve in a society that routinely denigrates sexually active young women while encouraging young men to carve another notch in their bedpost. Thus, despite her sex-positive perspective, Sharon has made it clear to her daughters that she would prefer they wait to have sex: '[I tell them], "There's lots of time to do that, why do it now?"'. Sharon's ambivalence is shaped in part by sexist conditions and cultural logics that encourage a climate whereby girls and women risk being debased and disparaged for expressing sexual agency. Indeed, Sharon described her own sexual debut at the age of 19 as 'planned' and 'great', but also expressed some ambivalence about the extent to which she controlled the experience for fear of being used: 'I'm not even sure it's the healthiest thing. It would be nice to have a little bit more [sexual] abandon, I guess. But I kind of like to be in control. The thought of being taken advantage of, just argh!'

Thus, how parents experienced and remember their own adolescence and sexuality shape how they think about and manage their teenagers' sexuality. Some parents said they would prefer that their teenagers abstain from sex until marriage but do not feel they can tell them this because they themselves did not abstain. Nicole (32 years old, White), who was a teenage mother, said that given her circumstances she cannot tell her 16-year-old son and 14-year-old daughter to abstain until marriage even though 'I would like for my kids to be married'. As Nicole put it:

> I can't really speak on it because I wasn't married. So I can't say, 'Hey, this is the right way to do something'. I can't tell them to live their life that way because I didn't. You know. And I don't want to teach my kids something that I didn't practice myself.

Some parents even wonder whether sexual abstinence is indeed the route to happiness it is so often chalked up to be. Sheila (48 years old, White), who has two sons in their 20s and a 16-year-old daughter, articulated this uncertainty:

> I will always discourage a teenager from having sex before marriage. Period. But really what I would want is that they wait to have sex until they're about 25 and figure out what they want first (laughs). If I could really say that and get away with it! But instead, I define it as wrong before marriage. I don't necessarily – with my own experience and my experience with my husband, I don't think our life would have been any better or worse if we had waited. It developed along the way. And you can wait until you get married and then hate the sex with the person you're with, even though you love them dearly.

Sheila and her husband of 28 years both had active sex lives as teenagers and were sexually active before they married. She does not think this harmed her in any way, yet she would not feel comfortable saying this to her children. She expressed annoyance that her 16-year-old daughter's sex education class at school 'did the condom route'. Yet, Sheila expressed doubts that her daughter will actually abstain until marriage and told me that she has told her daughter that she will help her get on birth control if she decides she is going to have sex in high school:

> I did tell her, 'I don't want to put you on the pill because I don't want you to think, at 16, that I've given you permission. But, if you're going to do that anyway, I'd rather have you on the pill than –'. Because at that point, I'm not going to talk her out of it. If she's made up her mind, I'm not going to talk her out of it ... I would rather it be like that, but I also know the world we live in. Yeah, it's been a while since I was young, but I do remember.

Like many parents I interviewed, Sheila relies on her own life experiences in making sense of her daughter's sexuality. These experiences are often more nuanced than the sex education debates might suggest. Sheila does not feel she was permanently scarred by her teenage sexual activity and, in fact, remembers it fondly. Nor does she believe her teenage sexual experiences prevented her from having a fulfilling sex life as a married adult, as the abstinence-only position asserts.

But Sheila is conflicted and expressed a sense of accountability for safely ushering her daughter to adulthood. As she put it when she wistfully said she would like to tell her daughter to abstain until she is an adult rather than until she is married: 'If I could really say that and get away with it!' Similarly, Beth (39 years old, White) – who has told her son to abstain from sex until marriage – expressed ambivalence about not yet teaching her son about contraception:

> I try to do what I am supposed to do as an obligation as a parent and just for society in general; so I don't put this kid out there who doesn't know anything about the consequences of his actions. It's probably long overdue – I haven't talked to him about contraception. I have friends that have, I just haven't.

Nicole (32 years old, White) suspects that her 16-year-old son is sexually active but, expressing a sense that her knowledge in this regard would make her accountable, said: 'Even though I know my son has probably possibly had sexual activities, I have not known, I have not seen, I have not heard. You know?'

Overall, parents said they are responsible for guiding their children through the teenage years and into adulthood. As the above comments suggest, giving your teen child 'permission' to have sex, inadequately teaching your teenager about the 'consequences' of sex, as well as knowing, or acknowledging to an interviewer that you know, your teen is having sex may make parents feel complicit in, and perhaps even responsible for, anything negative that occurs. But as well, parents and children's lives are deeply interconnected. Parents articulated a sense that what happens to children affects parents' lives too. As Fern (55 years old, White) put it, referring to her hopes for her 14-year-old daughter's future, 'I want her to be happy, [Her father and I] We won't be happy if she's not happy'.

CONCLUSION

Children's and parents' lives are complexly intertwined. Parents look forward to their children someday achieving productive, independent, fulfilling lives, replete with positive intimate relationships with adult others (many, but not all, parents hope these relationships are in the context of marriage). Indeed, this outcome is often how parents judge themselves, and are judged by others, to have done a good job parenting. Thus myriad worries, hopes, desires, and fears, along with parents' own complex life experiences, collide when parents contemplate their children having sex as teenagers. It is not surprising that these conversations are fraught and that parents are ambivalent – what is surprising is that parents have long been painted as either conservatives or liberals – as one-dimensional figures in the battles over teen sexuality and sex education.

In summary, parents hold themselves and other parents accountable for their children's sexual safety and well-being; yet they are deeply ambivalent about how best to guide and safeguard their children's sexuality. Given the parent-child relationship, some degree of ambivalence is inevitable. I argue, however, that parents' ambivalence is also shaped by their belief, on the one hand, that sexual abstinence, ideally until marriage, is the best and safest route for their children to follow – one that will ensure their sexual safety and well-being and future success and happiness – accompanied by the belief, on the other hand, that abstinence until marriage is not terribly realistic. Parents want abstinence to keep their children safe and to give them the opportunity to pursue successful and productive futures; yet they simultaneously expressed confusion, doubt, and ambivalence about teaching abstinence and about the practicality of abstinence. Parents' ambivalence, far from being anomalous, makes a great deal of sense given the context in which these meanings are constructed – a context in which parents hear a great deal about the negative consequences and bad outcomes of sex, are fearful for, and feel accountable for, their children's well-being, and believe that, as adults, their children will face an intensely competitive environment and that abstinence will give them an edge. Instead of suggesting ways to 'fix' parents' ambivalence, I suggest that public policy should address the culture of sexual fear and dominant constructions of masculinity, femininity, and adolescence, as well as social inequality, that structure parents' and their children's lives. Sex is risky in the US, but it is not inherently so. Gender, race, class, age, and sexual hierarchies and inequalities shape Americans' sexual experiences. Policy efforts should focus on promoting societal conditions that empower all youth to experience life, make mistakes, and pursue their dreams without fear of losing their rights to respect, care, and a good life. Safe neighborhoods, good schools, quality health care, including affordable and accessible contraception, and optimistic economic futures, along with social policy and school-based lessons that challenge gender and sexual inequalities, might help create an environment in which all parents are better able to embrace their children as sexual beings.

REFERENCES

Levine, J. 2002. *Harmful to minors: The perils of protecting children from sex*, Minneapolis and London: University of Minnesota Press.

Luker, K. 2006. *When sex goes to school: Warring views on sex – and sex education – since the sixties*, New York: Norton.

New York Times. 1983. Excerpts from President's speech to National Association of Evangelicals, March 9. http://www.nytimes.com/1983/03/09/us/excerpts-from-president-s-speech-to-national-association-of-evangelicals.html (accessed June 11, 2009).

Smelser, N.J. 1998. The rational and the ambivalent in the social sciences: 1997 presidential address. *American Sociological Review*, 63: 1–16.

Willson, A.E., Shuey, K.M., Elder, G.H. Jr and Wickrama, K.A.S. 2006. Ambivalence in mother–adult child relations: A dyadic analysis. *Social Psychology Quarterly*, 69(3): 235–252.

11

Think Teens Need the Sex Talk? Older Adults May Need It Even More

Heather Honoré Goltz and Matthew Lee Smith

Humans are sexual beings. This urge does not stop when the clock strikes 60. Or even 90.

Young adults may deny older relatives are having sex, but sexual activity is a strong indicator of healthy aging and vitality. In fact, sexual activity is roughly equal to climbing two flights of stairs.

Sex education and research use a medical model of sexual health focusing mainly on pregnancy, sexually transmitted infections (STIs), and sexual dysfunctions. However, sexuality is complex. Beyond genitals and Kama Sutra-like positions, it considers sexual and gender identity, sensuality, sexual response, intimacy, and positive and negative ways we use our sexuality.

Our research has explored sexuality among older adults experiencing healthy aging and also aging with health challenges. We found that older adults who routinely talk with health care providers about sexual matters are more likely to be sexually active, despite sexual dysfunctions or other health issues. These conversations become more important considering high HIV/AIDS and STI rates, even among older adults in the US.

SEXUALITY IS COMPLEX

As we age, the complex interplay among biological, psychological, cognitive, socioeconomic, religious, and even societal factors contributes to changes in our roles and responsibilities. For example, changes in physical or cognitive health over time can create differences in analytical thinking, mobility, and health care needs. We also experience changes in work, social and family roles, and responsibilities over time. Examples include transitions from working to retirement, parenting to empty-nesting, and child-rearing to caring for aging parents or partners.

These changes may alter our sexual desires, expression, and the frequency in which we engage in sexual activities with partners. For example, sexual functioning and activity may decrease over time, but having open communication with a partner who is responsive to our needs can increase our feelings of intimacy and desire, and in turn stimulate sexual activity.

Goltz, Heather Honoré and Matthew Lee Smith "Think Teens Need the Sex Talk? Older Adults May Need It Even More." *The Conversation*, December 13, 2018.

Evolving social support and activities may change opportunities for sex and intimacy. Partners may disappear through death or moving away, or appear, such as when meeting new people after moving to an aging community. Over one-third of adults over age 65 use social media or internet technologies. These tools may expand sexual interest or activities by increasing access to sexual aids and partners.

SEX AFTER 60

There are myths, misconceptions, and stigma associated with aging and sexuality that hinder older adults' ability to openly communicate with family, friends, and health care professionals. This misinformation limits their access to sexual education, health care, and, ultimately, their sexual rights.

The first myth is that older adults are not as sexually attractive or desirable as their younger counterparts. While an 80-year-old may not be as appealing to an 18-year-old, he or she may be very desirable to peers. More importantly, he or she may feel more sexually desirable and confident than their younger self.

A second myth is that older adults lack interest in and desire for sexual activity – and that they are somehow asexual. Research from ongoing national surveys supports the ideas that sexual interest, desires, and behaviors can decrease over the life course. For example, among women ages 57 years and older, over 80 percent of participants expressed interest in having sex, but less than two-thirds of women surveyed perceived sex as "important," and fewer than half reported having sex in the previous year. However, the reality is that these trends are not universal among older adults. Results from another recent survey found that 39 percent of men and 17 percent of women ages 75–85 years are sexually active.

Another myth is that older adults are so medically fragile that sexual activity is dangerous. This is simply not true in many cases. Recent studies have shown that healthy older adults are more likely to have sex. Even when chronic illnesses are present, sexual abstinence is not a foregone conclusion. For example, a 2012 American Heart Association statement contains evidence-based recommendations about sexual activity among patients with specific cardiovascular conditions. The recommendations generally advise assessing risks with a doctor and disease management, rather than abstention.

There are well-documented relationships between common medical conditions such as heart disease or diabetes and treatment-related effects on sexual functioning. Yet, older adults and their health care providers are not discussing sexual concerns during routine care. Missed opportunities during visits deprive older adults of access to newer treatments and other best practices in sexual medicine, which can impact their mental and physical health.

A bigger problem may be ageist attitudes among providers and internalized ageism in their patients that may interfere with sex education and application of newer standards. The result is that many believe older adults are uninterested in, or lack desire for, sexual activity and cannot engage in these activities.

LOVE HAS A LOT TO DO WITH IT

There is more to sexuality than physical acts. While much of the existing research focuses on sexual activity and intercourse as predictors or outcomes, most older adults also desire companionship, intimacy, and closeness. Non-intercourse-focused activities, such as hand-holding, cuddling, and massage, have not been studied as much as intercourse. Yet, there is reason to believe that they can enhance intimacy. Research about physical and mental health outcomes resulting from older adult sexual activity reveals additional benefits, including reduced cognitive decline, loneliness, and depression, and improved reported health status, physical functioning, and other aspects of quality of life.

Recent studies also reveal that sexually active older adults are more likely to communicate needs and concerns with health care providers and have them addressed. Providing high-quality sexual health care requires providers to take comprehensive sexual health histories from older patients and engage in direct, positive communication concerning gender and sexual identity, and sexual knowledge, beliefs, and practices.

Discussions should promote understanding about sexual risk behaviors for STIs and effects of physical and cognitive or psychological aging on sexual health and sexuality. To maintain or improve older adults' sexual health and well-being, health care providers should provide safe and welcoming environments for patient-provider collaboration, resources and interdisciplinary referrals to clinical social workers, sex therapists, physical therapists, and other allied health specialties.

SECTION III
Regulating Relationships: Marriage and Partnerships

INTRODUCTION

Marriage provides at least 1,138 legal and financial benefits that are written into federal law and is one of the ways individuals can gain formal recognition as a family. As discussed in Section I, formal recognition comes with benefits and obligations. In calculating the benefits that flow from legal marriage, the General Accounting Office, the federal agency charged with conducting research for Congress, calculated that in 2004, there were 1,138 provisions written into federal law that provide benefits, rights, and privileges based on marital status or in which marital status is a factor (Shah 2004). These include the ability to file joint income taxes, form family businesses from which income can be divided without tax penalties, give property or money to family members, or avoid inheritance tax. Beyond federal benefits, married people gain countless other social and legal benefits that unmarried people do not. For example, they can inherit without a will, assume medical or legal decision-making powers for one's spouse, have a court divide assets in divorce, jointly adopt or become foster parents, or apply for residency in immigration proceedings. Marriage extends spouses' government benefits including military or veteran benefits (like education, medical care, or special loans), Social Security, Medicare, retirement benefits, or disability benefits for spouses. Married people qualify for family leave to care for a spouse during an illness or bereavement leave after death. Legal marriage entitles a person to visit in hospitals or jails, request an autopsy after death, plan funerals, or sue for wrongful death. Marriage provides automatic renewal of leases or access to family housing. Spouses can claim tuition discounts for education, take advantage of corporate incentives for families, obtain insurance through a spouse's employer, maintain joint car or home insurance policies, or waive rental car fees for multiple drivers. They cannot be compelled to testify against a spouse in court. Marriage is a powerful institution that bestows a huge number of privileges as well as social recognition, including relief from pressure to be married. It is no wonder that marriage has always been regulated, with battles over who can access it.

LEGAL REGULATION OF MARRIAGE

The roots of American family law have grown out of English common law, a system based more on tradition than written legislation. Throughout the past 100 years, states have gradually written laws and courts have found many parts of common law to be incompatible with the US Constitution. Thus, few common laws remain today. Nonetheless, considering common law is useful for understanding the roots of family law.

Most common law was written down by Sir William Blackstone in the mid-1700s, in volumes known as the Blackstone Commentaries. These commentaries define women in marriage as little more than property. Once a woman married, her legal status as a person was suspended. She could rarely enter contracts on her own, make wills, or even control property she owned prior to marriage. Upon entering marriage, a woman entered coverture, a condition in which her legal status was covered by that of her husband. Because a man and a woman became one person in law, they could not enter a contract with each other. Women were incapable of testifying against their husbands because that would have been the equivalent of self-incrimination since they were one person in law. A woman could not be sued without making her husband the defendant. A husband could physically restrain his wife if he felt it necessary.

Marriage entitled husbands to sex on demand and thus made it legally impossible for husbands to be prosecuted for rape. One of the earliest legal challenges to this was in 1905 in the case of *Frazier v State*. In this case, the Fraziers were a couple who married in 1889 and lived together with their four children until 1902 at which time the wife, Emma Frazier, notified her husband she no longer wished to be married and saw them as separated (they did apply later for divorce, but their request was denied). They slept in separate bedrooms but lived in the same house, ate meals at the same table, and shared family resources. As the court decision described, "On the occasion of the alleged assault, appellant entered her room, and rather vigorously insisted upon what he believed to be his rights as a husband" (*Frazier v. State*, 86 S.W. 754 (Tex. Crim. App. 1905)). Mrs. Frazier wanted her husband to be prosecuted for trying to force her to have sex with him but was told that was impossible for two reasons. First, the court ruled that such a prosecution would require a wife to testify as a witness against her husband, which was not possible. Second, the court decision explained that a man cannot be guilty of rape of his wife, noting that it is impossible: "The matrimonial consent which she gives when she assumes the marriage relation, and which the law will not permit her to retract in order to charge her husband with the offense of rape."

It was not until 1993 that all US states passed laws criminalizing marital rape. Even as states addressed this issue in their state statutes, they did so in ways that communicated that marital rape was a less serious crime than other sexual assaults. For example, many states created different laws about and punishments for rapes within marriage and sexual assaults outside of marriage. States sometimes require that spouses live in separate residences or that the victim provides evidence of violence or threat. Some states require victims raped by a spouse to report it in a shorter time period than are required for unmarried victims, or have loopholes that forbid prosecution if the married victim was unconscious, even when drugged by her or his spouse. Legal response to spousal rape—and willingness to see it as different from sexual assaults between non-married people—illustrates the persistence of the view that women lose legal autonomy in marriage.

LEGAL ACCESS TO MARRIAGE

Americans have seen changes in the past 50 years in terms of regulation of who can marry whom. In particular, there have been dramatic shifts that have eliminated state bans on interracial marriage and have extended marriage rights to gay and lesbian couples. These changes occurred even when popular opinion was against them, based on arguments about what constituted individual rights and equal access to benefits. Legal challenges to discriminatory laws changed the law but also helped to define marriage—and the ability to freely choose it—as a core aspect of the individual right to pursue happiness.

Interracial Marriage Bans

Up until the 1950s, the majority of states had laws forbidding a white person from marrying a person from a different racial group or specifying that an African American could not marry anyone not of the same racial background (ACLU 2020). Rather than viewing these laws as a violation of the US Constitution, courts for a long time upheld these laws as a reasonable use of state power to "suppress what it is free to regard as a public evil" in order to "prevent the obliteration of racial pride" and "the corruption of blood," which would "weaken or destroy the quality of its citizenship" (*Naim v. Naim*, 197 Va. 80, 88–89 (Va. 1955)).

California was the first state in 1948 to eliminate such a law through a challenge in the courts (*Perez v. Lippold*, also known as *Perez v. Sharp* (32 Cal.2d 711 (1948)). Through the 1950s and 1960s, 14 states repealed their laws. Laws still on the books in 16 other states became unenforceable in 1967 when the US Supreme Court ruled in the case of *Loving v Virginia* that all such laws were unconstitutional.

That case originated in 1958, when police came into the bedroom of Richard and Mildred Loving, a white man and woman of color who had grown up together and married five weeks prior. At about 2:00 am, the police entered their bedroom while they slept and arrested them for violating Virginia's ban on interracial marriage. Facing a felony conviction and the possibility of up to five years in prison, the Lovings initially pleaded guilty and received a one-year jail sentence, which would be suspended if they left the state and did not return together for 25 years. The Lovings moved to Washington DC, and, five years later, contacted the American Civil Liberties Union (ACLU) to request help with their case. The ACLU requested that the original conviction be vacated, and the judge who heard that appeal—the same one who initially sentenced them—refused. In his 1965 decision, that judge wrote,

> Almighty God created the races white, black, yellow, malay and red, and he placed them on separate continents ... And but for the interference with his arrangement there would be no cause for such marriages. The fact that he separated the races shows that he did not intend for the races to mix.

Eventually, the US Supreme Court heard the Lovings' case and decided unanimously that the law was unconstitutional. The decision explained that

> marriage is one of the basic civil rights of man, fundamental to our very existence and survival ... Under our Constitution, the freedom to marry, or not marry, a person of another race resides with the individual, and cannot be infringed by the State.

(388 US 1 1967)

Marriage as a Fundamental Right

The centrality of individual freedom to choose to marry and privacy within marriage has been clarified in other US Supreme Court cases. The case of *Griswold v Connecticut* in 1965 struck down laws that banned married couples from using birth control by describing the sanctity of marriage:

> Marriage is a coming together for better or worse, hopefully enduring, and intimate to the degree of being sacred. It is an association that promotes a way of life, not causes; a harmony of living, not political faiths ... Yet it is an association for as noble a purpose as any involved in our prior decisions.

(381 US 479 1965)

In 1978, the US Supreme Court struck down a Wisconsin law that required non-custodial parents to demonstrate that their child support payments were current before they could marry. In that decision, the US Supreme Court also defined marriage as "of fundamental importance to all individuals" (*Zablocki v Redhail*, 434 US 374 (1978)). Arguably well intentioned, the law was unconstitutional based on this view of marriage. Other cases, including one in 1987 that guaranteed the right of prisoners to marry (*Turner v. Safley*, 482 US 78), continued to define marriage as a fundamental constitutional right.

Same-Sex Marriage

The articulation of marriage as an important freedom through the 1960s and 1970s seemed to logically apply to other groups, especially those who were gay and lesbian who sought marriage rights. These claims were unsuccessful for more than 40 years. Among the first was a 1971 challenge in Minnesota in which the state Supreme Court ruled that a gay couple was not discriminated against by being denied a marriage license because the term marriage in Minnesota state law had gender-specific language. This restriction, the judge writing the majority decision reasoned, was acceptable because procreation and child-rearing were central to marriage. The fact that many married opposite sex couples are childless, the decision explained, did not change this. The decision also clarified that this case was different than *Loving v Virginia* since "in commonsense and in a constitutional sense, there is a clear distinction between a marital restriction based merely upon race and one based upon the fundamental difference in sex" (Baker, 191 N.W.2d at 187). The US Supreme Court refused to hear an appeal of this case.

In the subsequent decades, same-sex couples around the country filed cases claiming that denial of the right to marry was a violation of religious freedom and sex discrimination, disadvantage in immigration processes, loss of the right to inherit an apartment lease as the surviving spouse, and even the right to legal divorce based on common law marriage law. Most argued that marriage was a fundamental right and the sexes of the participants did not justify limiting access to that right. All were unsuccessful until 1993 when a Hawaii court decision changed the terms of the same-sex marriage fight.

Federal Law and States' Rights to Regulate Marriage

Three same-sex couples in Hawaii applied for and were denied marriage licenses. They sued, pointing out that the Hawaii state constitution prohibits sex discrimination so sex could not reasonably be the reason their applications were denied. In 1993, the Hawaii Supreme Court ruled that their challenge could continue through the courts. Although this decision did not grant marriage rights to same-sex couples, it created the possibility that Hawaii eventually might. In general, states are expected to recognize each other's family laws. So for example, if one state allows someone to marry a cousin and another does not, the marriage of the couple who are cousins would be valid even as they travel to a different state with different laws. Adoption rules vary by state, but one is still an adopted parent even when crossing state lines. Had Hawaii legalized gay marriage, other states would have to recognize those marriages.

Fearing that Hawaii could legalize same-sex marriage, the US Congress in 1996 passed the Defense of Marriage Act (DOMA), which then-President Bill Clinton signed into law. DOMA stated that

> No State, territory, or possession of the United States, or Indian tribe, shall be required to give effect to any public act, record, or judicial proceeding of any other State, territory, possession, or tribe respecting a relationship between persons of the same sex that is treated as a marriage under the laws of such other State, territory, possession, or tribe, or a right or claim arising from such relationship.

It also clarified that in determining the meaning of marriage for federal rules, regulations, and agencies, "the word 'marriage' means only a legal union between one man and one woman as husband and wife, and the word 'spouse' refers only to a person of the opposite sex who is a husband or a wife."

By 1999, Hawaii's legislature along with dozens of other states passed their own version of DOMA, which meant that Hawaii would not be the first state to legalize gay marriage. Yet legal challenges continued and that same year, the Vermont Supreme Court agreed in the case of *Baker v State of Vermont* that denial of marriage licenses to same-sex couples was discriminatory. The decision acknowledged that marriage comes with many benefits and that couples denied licenses were disadvantaged. Rather than ruling that same-sex couples were entitled to marriage licenses, the Court ordered the state to extend similar benefits to same-sex couples. In response, the Vermont state legislature in 2000 passed "An Act Relating to Civil Unions," which created legal partnerships that would include the same recognition and benefits of marriage. Other states also experimented in the subsequent years with legal definitions of domestic partnerships, civil unions, or legal processes to claim "reciprocal benefits."

In 2003, the Supreme Court of Massachusetts heard a similar case and ruled that the state law barring same-sex marriage was unconstitutional under the Massachusetts constitution and ordered the legislature to remedy the discrimination within six months (*Goodridge v. Department of Public Health*). Although the state tried to enact civil unions in 2004, the Court ruled that offering civil unions instead of civil marriage was not adequate, effectively legalizing gay marriage. Connecticut's legislature voluntarily passed a bill to permit civil unions in 2005; when the courts deemed that inadequate, the state legalized same-sex marriage in 2008. In 2009, the Iowa Supreme Court also upheld the rights of same-sex couples to seek marriage licenses. Some states followed; others instead passed ballot initiatives to amend state constitutions to block courts from granting gay marriage rights.

Same-sex couples found themselves able to be legally married in some states but under DOMA, excluded from federal recognition and benefits. For example, spouses of federal employees could not get spousal health benefits. Couples could not file federal taxes as a married couple, even though they could in their states. Since, as we saw in Section I, virtually all state law, including the regulation of marriage, resides with the states, questions remained about whether Congress even had the power to pass DOMA.

In 2010, the ACLU successfully sued the federal government on behalf of a same-sex surviving spouse whose inheritance from her deceased spouse was taxed as if they were unmarried. The US Supreme Court decided in the *United States v. Windsor* (570 US 744 (2013)) that parts of DOMA were unconstitutional. In 2015, the US Supreme Court went further and struck down the remaining bans on same-sex marriage, thereby requiring all states to issue marriage licenses to same-sex couples and to recognize same-sex marriages validly performed in other places (*Obergefell v. Hodges*). This was indisputably an important moment in decades-long campaigns for equal rights for gays and lesbians. Yet, given the patriarchal history of marriage, access to the institution also raises important questions, many of which are explored in the chapter by Suzanna Danuta Walters.

Ongoing Limits to the Right to Marry

Based on the success of efforts to legalize same-sex marriage, there have episodically been efforts to expand marriage rights to include plural marriage. Plural marriage, or polygamy, is the practice of having more than one legal spouse and is illegal in all 50 states. Polygamy in the United States is practiced most often within sects of the Mormon Church and remains highly stigmatized as the chapter by Michael K. Ault and Bobbi Van Gilder shows. Many immigrants come from countries that practice some form of polygamy and bring their definitions of family with them. The United Nations estimates that polygamy is legal or generally accepted in 33 countries and is accepted for some groups of people in an additional 41 countries (United Nations 2011). As of 2017, as many of 17 percent of Americans said polygamy was morally acceptable, the highest level of approval ever recorded (Dugan 2017).

There have been a few challenges to laws banning polygamy. In 1878, the US Supreme Court heard a challenge brought by George Reynolds, a member of the Church of Jesus Christ of Latter-day Saints who was prosecuted for violating the law against polygamy in the Utah territory. He argued that his religion required him to marry multiple women and so the law violated his First Amendment right to freely exercise his religion; his challenge was unsuccessful.

More recently, Kody Brown and his four wives attempted and failed to have their challenge to anti-polygamy laws heard by the US Supreme Court. Brown and his wives made their polygamist family visible by starring in the television reality show, *Sister Wives*. Technically, Kody is only legally married to his first wife, but as Mormons, they and their 17 children see themselves as family. Utah's law at the time included cohabitation in the definition of criminal polygamy, which meant that they could be prosecuted. When the television show aired, the Browns were investigated, but were not prosecuted. Nonetheless, they filed a lawsuit and argued in court that the law negatively affected them and violated their right to privacy and religious freedom. The judge who heard their case ruled that the law's section prohibiting cohabitation violated constitutional guarantees of due process and religious freedom and could not be enforced, but did clarify that polygamy in the literal sense—of seeking marriage licenses with multiple people—could remain illegal. In the United States, only one spouse can receive legal benefits that come with marriage, a position courts have been willing to uphold. However, lack of legal recognition does not mean that many families with more than two spouses who lack formal recognition do not function as a family anyway.

DECLINE OF MARRIAGE

Although access to marriage has been broadened thanks for many legal challenges, the percentage of people who actually choose to marry is declining. Instead, people make a range of choices about their lives and relationships. An increasing number of couples choose to live together and cohabit rather than legally marry. In 1968, only 0.1 percent of adults between the ages of 18–24 years old cohabited, whereas 39 percent were married. Today, according to the US Census Bureau, 9 percent of those 18–24 cohabit (compared with 7 percent who are married). For those between the ages of 18–34, about 30 percent are married, compared to 40 years ago when 59 percent were (Gurrentz 2018). About half of people who cohabit are under the age of 35 years, but notably the number of cohabiting adults over 50 years of age is growing and now comprises almost a quarter of all cohabiting adults (Stepler 2017).

One in four parents living with a child today is unmarried. This marks a dramatic change from a half-century ago, when fewer than one in ten parents living with their children were unmarried (7 percent). However, being unmarried does not mean a parent is single. In fact, about 35 percent of unmarried parents live with a partner (Livingston 2018). Estimates are that by age 12, 40 percent of American children will have spent at least part of their lives in a cohabiting household (Kennedy and Bumpass 2008).

Patterns in marriage vary by education level and social class. In the 1960s, marriage and divorce rates were nearly identical for those who went to college and those who did not (Reeves and Pulliam 2020). Today, married couples are more than four times as likely to hold a bachelor's or advanced degree than are cohabiting biological parents (Reeves and Krause 2017). Income also looks different between married and unmarried couples; among adults ages 25–34—the age range during which first marriage is most common—43 percent of married individuals earn at least $40,000 per year, compared to 34 percent of unmarried individuals (Gurrentz 2018). Finances appear to be a factor in shaping couples' choices. One recent survey shows that 29 percent of cohabiting adults cite their partner's lack of financial readiness, while 27 percent cite their own as the reason why they are not engaged or married to their current partner (Graf 2019).

Singlism as Inequality

Since many rights and benefits come through marriage, it is worth considering whether and how those who are not married may be disadvantaged. The penalties, lost opportunities, costs to identify and legally empower someone to make decisions in an emergency or make other legal arrangements that come automatically with marriage, and other disadvantages are worth considering. Some advocacy groups, like Unmarried America and Unmarried Equality, have argued that programs like those created for domestic partnerships before legalization of same-sex marriage should be available to unmarried individuals to identify extended family members, close friends, or another person who functions like family for the purposes of accessing workplace or military benefits. Others highlight the discrimination unmarried people face and the material losses they suffer. There are also social hierarchies between those whose are married and those who are not, including stigma toward unmarried women (Sharp and Ganong 2011).

There appears to be increasing support for unmarried couples. A majority of Americans support extending legal rights to cohabiting couples. A 2019 survey showed that 65 percent say they support allowing unmarried couples to enter into legal agreements that would give them the same rights as married couples when it comes to things like health insurance, inheritance, or tax benefits, while 34 percent oppose this (Graf 2019).

In addition to the aforementioned chapters on polygamy and questions about the goal of marriage for gays and lesbians, the following chapters take on different aspects of life in partnerships. Katie Acosta's chapter explores experiences of sexually non-conforming Latinas to show how they make strategic decisions about disclosing their intimate relationships to their families. Carla Pfeffer's chapter looks at household responsibility, which is highly gendered in heterosexual cohabiting relationships, and examines how women partners of transgender men describe their household and emotional work. Gina Marie Longo looks at advice offered to couples where one partner is seeking to immigrate to the United States to show how views of these couples are gendered and make assumptions about abuse of the immigration process. Throughout, each chapter provides an opportunity to understand how individuals and couples make decisions about their relationships in dialog institutional rules and within existing systems of inequality.

REFERENCES

ACLU. 2020, "The Leadup to Loving." American Civil Liberties Union. (https://www.aclu.org/other/map-leadup-loving).

Defense of Marriage Act: Update on a Prior Report, 2004, General Accounting Office.

Dugan, Andrew. 2017, "Moral Acceptance of Polygamy at Record High – but Why?" Gallup. (https://news.gallup.com/opinion/polling-matters/214601/moral-acceptance-polygamy-record-high-why.aspx).

Graf, Nikki. 2019, "Key Findings on Marriage and Cohabitation in the U.S." Pew Research Center. (https://www.pewresearch.org/fact-tank/2019/11/06/key-findings-on-marriage-and-cohabitation-in-the-u-s/).

Gurrentz, Benjamin. 2018, "Living with an Unmarried Partner Now Common for Young Adults." (https://www.census.gov/library/stories/2018/11/cohabitaiton-is-up-marriage-is-down-for-young-adults.html).

Kennedy, Sheela and Larry Bumpass. 2008, "Cohabitation and Children's Living Arrangements: New Estimates from the United States." *Demographic Research* 19: 1663.

Livingston, Gretchen. 2018, "The Changing Profile of Unmarried Parents." Pew Research Center. (https://www.pewsocialtrends.org/2018/04/25/the-changing-profile-of-unmarried-parents/).

Reeves, R. V. and E. Krause (2017, April 5). "Cohabiting parents differ from married ones in three big ways." from https://www.brookings.edu/research/cohabiting-parents-differ-from-married-ones-in-three-big-ways/.

Reeves, Richard V. and Christopher Pulliam. 2020, "Middle Class Marriage Is Declining, and Likely Deepening Inequality." (https://www.brookings.edu/research/middle-class-marriage-is-declining-and-likely-deepening-inequality/).

Sharp, Elizabeth A. and Lawrence Ganong. 2011, ""I'ma Loser, I'm Not Married, Let's Just All Look at Me": Ever-Single Women's Perceptions of Their Social Environment." *Journal of Family Issues* 32(7): 956–980.

Shah, Dayna. 2004. Defense of Marriage Act: Update on a Prior Report, General Accounting Office. January 23.

Stepler, Renee. 2017, "Number of U.S. Adults Cohabiting with a Partner Continues to Rise, Especially among Those 50 and Older." Washington, DC: Pew Research Center.

United Nations. 2011, "Population Facts." Department of Economic and Social Affairs, Population Division. (https://www.un.org/en/development/desa/population/publications/pdf/popfacts/PopFacts_2011-1.pdf).

12

The Language of (In)Visibility

Using In-Between Spaces as a Vehicle for Empowerment in the Family

Katie L. Acosta

This chapter explores the ways in which sexually nonconforming Latinas negotiate both visibility and invisibility with their families of origin. Visibility is an ongoing process, not a state of being. Visibility itself implies movement and a pursuit to be seen, heard, and validated. For sexually nonconforming Latinas, the journey to gain such visibility from the family does not manifest itself in any given or predetermined form. For some sexually nonconforming Latinas, the process of achieving visibility and empowerment begins with verbal articulation of their sexual identity to family members. For others it does not. For some Latinas, tacit relationships can be empowering and can lead to visibility within the family. Their experiences highlight that verbal articulation of sexual identity is neither a prerequisite for nor a determinant of visibility. In this chapter, I explore how sexually nonconforming Latinas achieve empowerment and visibility with and without verbal articulation of their same-sex relationships. This work is driven by two main research questions. (a) What constitutes visibility for sexually nonconforming Latinas and how does this vary along lines of race, class, gender, and sexuality? (b) Are there manners through which to achieve empowerment through invisibility? The second question explores the notion that, at times, empowerment can arise even in a context in which visibility and validation are denied.

In this chapter, I advance the notion that invisibility is also a possible means to realize empowerment. I point to the flexibility that can stem from invisibility and to the creative ways in which sexually nonconforming Latinas can manipulate this status in order to serve their own needs. I offer an alternative approach to understanding empowerment for sexually nonconforming Latinas by exploring the spaces in which sexually nonconforming Latinas negotiate family. I call these spaces "in-between spaces" because they exist at the juncture of "in" versus "out" of the closet. I recognize that the metaphor of "the closet" is limiting as an analytical tool. The notion of the closet implies that it is possible for individuals to neatly fit into being either "in the closet" or "out and proud." This simple dichotomization does an injustice to the experiences of the sexually nonconforming Latinas described in this chapter. Their experiences are more adequately expressed by a concept that is flexible and malleable. I use in-between spaces to describe a space that sexually nonconforming Latinas inhabit with their families, a space that affords these women power and agency as they negotiate visibility and invisibility, silence and validation.

Acosta, Katie L. "The Language of (In) Visibility: Using In-between Spaces as a Vehicle for Empowerment in the Family." *Journal of Homosexuality* 58, no. 6–7 (2011): 883–900.

COMING OUT, TACIT RELATIONSHIPS, AND VISIBILITY

A modest but growing body of scholarship has begun problematizing the notion that outness is the correct way to be a "good" lesbian, gay, bisexual, transgender, or queer (LGBTQ) individual. Not coming out promotes feelings of political irresponsibility, inauthenticity, and negative judgments from the larger LGBTQ community as well as the academic community (Adams 2010). This fact, Adams argues, holds gay individuals to contradictory standards where coming out is the ideal, but doing so in everyday interactions can potentially put these individuals at risk as they must continuously engage in disclosure at every new encounter. For the individuals who inhabit these spaces, coming out can become unnecessary in so much as they are making a verbal declaration of information that is understood but has remained tacit. There is, therefore, agency to be found in having the autonomy to move in and out of visible spaces and to use the closet as a space to escape surveillance. I offer, then, that we look at verbal disclosures and tacit relationships as steps in an ongoing, dynamic process negotiated by individuals in their efforts to become empowered and visible.

Recognizing the limitations of the closet metaphor, more and more scholars are moving away from centering their analysis on coming out and, instead, are looking to a much broader concept: visibility. It manifests in different forms along race, class, gender, and sexuality lines, and our attempts to obtain visibility can produce both empowerment and disempowerment simultaneously. It is both empowering and disempowering because there are risks that come with being visible. Being visible leaves one susceptible to negativity, rejection, and potential violence. In light of these risks, it becomes important to understand the choices made about when and where to be visible and the relationship between these choices and silence. It is important then to look at the array of external factors that influence the choices individuals' made regarding when to be visible using an intersectional lens in order to better understand the complex rationale for these choices.

A great deal of the existing research has looked at visibility and coming out by analyzing people's public behaviors. Here, I explore visibility and outness in a semi-private space: the family. What follows is an analysis of how sexually nonconforming Latinas move in and out of visible spaces when negotiating family. I provide examples of how these women engage in both strategies of disclosure and tacit relationships based on specific social conditions. I argue that the participants found the most empowerment when using tacit and disclosure strategies in transient ways: deciding when and with whom to disclose their relationships versus when silence seemed a more appropriate or safe option. Despite its limitations, the in-between spaces that are sometimes created by these strategies are a powerful tool for those individuals who have found ways to manipulate and mobilize it in their individual lives. These spaces are powerful because, regardless of their level of achieved visibility, study participants are able to merge families of choice and origin within these spaces.

METHODS

This chapter is informed by 40 in-depth interviews with sexually nonconforming Latinas that were conducted between 2007 and 2008. All of the participants identified as lesbian, bisexual, or queer and were between the ages of 19 and 60. The overwhelming majority of the participants identified as lesbians, but there were also five bisexual women and three queer-identified women in the study. All of the participants were either immigrants from Latin America or second-generation immigrants living in the United States. They represented nine countries and included 12 women from Puerto Rico, six from the Dominican Republic, six from Peru, six from Mexico, three from Cuba, three from Colombia, two from Nicaragua, one from Ecuador, and one participant from Guatemala. All of the study participants had at least a high school education. Twenty-one had college degrees, and eight had graduate degrees that they received in the United States or in their countries of origin.

Interviews were conducted throughout the northeastern United States and lasted approximately 90 minutes. The interviewees had the choice of conducting the interview in English or Spanish, given their preference and comfort with the language. The transcriptions were recorded in the language in which the interview was conducted. In the instances in which I have included excerpts from the interviews conducted in Spanish, I have included the original Spanish as well as the English translation in this chapter. Retaining the original Spanish is important not only because of the specificity of language and the inherent loss of certain sentiments and connotations in translation, but also because, in this analysis, I pay particular attention to participants' and their families' specific words and the meanings behind them. Working with only the English, therefore, would unnecessarily flatten the richness of the data.

VERBAL ARTICULATIONS AND THE JOURNEY TOWARD VISIBILITY

The 23 participants who reported having engaged in verbal disclosure with their families had diverse experiences. Five of these women were forced into a verbal disclosure after their family members discovered information that compromised their privacy. Given these less than ideal circumstances, four of these five women described the verbal disclosure as a very negative experience resulting in their feelings and thoughts not being heard and their declarations being erased. The remaining 18 participants engaged in a voluntary disclosure to their families. Even among these 18 participants, the reactions from family members were very mixed. Three of the women who voluntarily disclosed their partnerships shared the experience of those who were forced to disclose and reported acrimonious fights with their families, which, ultimately, lead to their disclosure not being heard. The remaining 15 women who voluntarily disclosed reported more positive experiences or, at least, a moderate level of success with gaining acceptance from their families.

The participants who experienced the highest levels of success with disclosure overwhelmingly reported starting first by talking with their mothers. While many participants reported their mothers' struggle with the disclosure, they also reported bonding with their mothers who were often faced with disclosing their daughters' sexuality to the rest of the family. The study participants reported the bond stemming from their mothers' realization that they both shared the possibility of rejection. Yanet is a Chicana in her late 20s. During our interview, she described finding a new respect and admiration for her mother after disclosure.

> My mom outted me to the family, and I think that was very brave of her. I don't think that I would be able to do that: to come out to these people who could potentially be dangerous emotionally. It created a rift between my mother and her family whom she tries to be close to. But she definitely takes the risk every time and somehow manages to make it okay. I think it's definitely put space between her and her closest younger sister. They were very close until my mom said I was gay and then it was like oh … that's sinful.

Yanet's experience with coming out and finding in her mother an ally willing to stand beside her and face rejection did not come without struggle. Yanet's mother's initial reaction to her daughter's disclosure was neither positive nor supportive. However, it was the realization that they shared this potential rejection in common that helped the two overcome their reservations and move toward acceptance. Consistent with previous findings, in this study, mothers were instrumental in helping study participants move beyond verbal disclosures toward visibility in the context of family. Mothers played the mediator role with the extended family defending their daughters against the rejections of others and doing so even in instances in which they themselves struggled to accept the nonconformity. In another example, Inocencia's mother was instrumental in helping her grandparents come to acceptance. However, the passage below illustrates how she does so even while still reconciling her own reservations about her daughter's sexuality. Inocencia described the experience in the following way:

> I sent my coming out letter and I included a booklet published by PFLAG "Por qué Mi Hijo Es Gay?: Preguntas y Repuestas para los Padres de Hijos Gay" [Why is my Son or Daughter Gay? Questions and Answers for Parents of Gay Children]. My grandma spent a month crying because I was going to hell and she wanted me in heaven. My grandpa was infuriated … "How could I do that to the family?" And my mother was the angel that would always come and say something to make them shut up.

> Once my grandpa was saying "Oh I don't know, Inocencia with that girl, that is sinful" . . . and my mother said "Well Bladimar is using drugs and stealing things from you to buy them. Isn't that a greater sin? How is Inocencia affecting you? Is it in the 10 commandments that one can't be gay, because stealing is?" My grandpa didn't talk to her for two weeks after that. But mami would always come with something to make them think about what they were saying.

Here, Inocencia introduces us to her mother, boldly challenging her parents in an effort to defend her daughter. But there also exists a glimpse of Inocencia's mother's reservation. As she challenges her father, she does not imply that homosexuality is not sinful, but rather that stealing is a "greater sin." It is clear, then, that even as she defends her daughter, Inocencia's mother continues to struggle with the issue of homosexuality as a sin. Nonetheless, in this example, the way she assists her daughter in gaining visibility from the rest of the family is clear. Inocencia's parents and grandparents, ultimately, grow to accept her and her partner. Eventually, they come to welcome the couple in their home and to enjoy making special accommodations to make Inocenia's partner feel comfortable as a guest in their home in Puerto Rico. While it is Inocencia who takes the initial risk of engaging in verbal disclosure, it is her mother who later plays the instrumental role of making sure that this disclosure becomes visible and is not silenced.

Not all of the participants had as much success as Yanet and Inocencia in using their mothers to gain more visibility after verbal articulation. Seven of the participants who had disclosed to their parents had their verbal articulations rendered unheard. For these seven women, verbal articulations did not create greater visibility but rather silenced them. In these instances, study participants engaged in a larger performance of invisibility in an effort to appease the nonaccepting family members. Diana, a 22-year-old study participant of Dominican descent, describes this process:

> In 2000, things really blew up in my house, and my mom found out about me and like, what I was doing and that I was seeing other women and she was not okay with it ... I kind of reassured her that I had figured it out, that I was fine and that it was resolved and that it was over because all hell would have broken loose if she would have known otherwise.

It was never Diana's choice to come out to her mother. Her mother found out that she was dating women through an outside source. Given that the outcome of this disclosure was not ideal, Diana chose to perform invisibility by reassuring her mother that she was not, in fact, dating women. In these instances, the verbal articulation made the study participants' nonconformity more invisible to their families. The circumstances through which she was exposed to her mother made the experience less than empowering. On the contrary, in instances like Diana's, power comes from the performance and success in making oneself invisible once again.

For some participants the heightened invisibility stemming from coming out and being rendered unheard left them with the additional burden of trying to piece the family back together again. Participants in this situation are twice impacted by the negative outcomes of verbal disclosure. Verbal disclosure does not help them move toward gaining visibility or legitimacy, and they are burdened with the task of comforting upset family members. Milagros is one such participant. A Peruvian woman in her 40s, Milagros describes her mother's reaction to her coming out as very unsupportive. Her mother was unwillingly to talk about the issue or meet Milagros' partner for a number of years.

> Durante ese tiempo, mi mamá nunca me llamaba, nunca me visitaba, nunca quiso saber de esta persona, nunca fue capaz de ver como yo vivía. Solamente, la única comunicación que teníamos, si ella quería comunicarse conmigo, ella llamaba a mi papá para yo llamar. Y todos los jueves yo iba a cenar con ella. Sola. Y ya después de cinco años eventualmente la segunda pareja que yo tuve, ella como que fue reaccionando un pocito más. La veía como una amiga.

> During that time, my mother never called me, never visited me, never wanted to know about this person, was never capable of seeing how I lived. The only communication that we had, if she wanted to communicate with me, she would call my father so that I could call. And every Thursday, I went and had dinner with her. Alone. And after five years, eventually the second partner I had, she reacted a little better. She saw her like a friend.

It took Milagros' mother five years to begin acknowledging her daughter's relationships with other women. During those five years, the burden rested on Milagros to maintain the familial bond. Since her mother refused to call or visit her, Milagros was tasked with making her lesbian self invisible by always going to dinner with her mother alone and only communicating with her when her mother took a roundabout path of calling a third party to help facilitate the communication.

The experiences of all four women mentioned above highlight the process involved in verbal articulation for sexually nonconforming Latinas. Disclosure does not always result in visibility. Often we look at coming out as a final stage in accepting oneself, but in other ways, verbal articulation is the beginning of an entirely new process: pursuing visibility. This process is a pursuit because it involves pushing against heteronormative family structures in order to be seen and legitimized as a same gender loving individual. In this way, verbal articulation became the first of many steps in sexually nonconforming Latinas' quest for visibility. Those women who did not have the support of their mothers or others in moving beyond disclosure and toward visibility entered an in-between space with their families. These participants learned to utilize their invisibility as a tool to merge their romantic and familial relationships.

DEVELOPING IN-BETWEEN SPACES THROUGH INVISIBILITY

Power can manifest itself through invisibility because that which is not seen can, therefore, not be controlled, regulated, or demonized. Consider, for example, two couples walking in a public space. One is a same-sex, interracial couple; the other is an opposite-sex, interracial couple. In a country where most Americans read their surroundings through a heteronormative lens, the opposite-sex couple would be vulnerable to rejection for crossing racial boundaries. The same-sex couple could potentially remain invisible, and, by doing so, may not face rejection, threat, or violence. Frustrating as this may be, it also provides safety for same-sex couples in unfriendly circles.

The power in invisibility comes from learning how to manipulate this invisibility. By strategically remaining so unseen to the larger nonaccepting society, one cannot be chastised for nonconformity. Visibility carries assumptions of Whiteness, privilege, and the relinquishment of other identities. The quest for visibility is complicated by race, class, and gender, and it can lose potency when those seeking it are already marginalized on account of their gender, race, and class. Regardless of the strategies sexually nonconforming Latinas used to negotiate family and sexual nonconformity, they understood the complexities inherent in visibility and the possibilities inherent in not being seen. In this section, I will explore the in-between spaces inhabited by a particular subset of the study participants: those whose disclosures were completely unheard and those whose disclosures were avoided by family members. Eleven of the total 23 participants who disclosed their sexual nonconformity to their parents fell into this category. They include the seven participants mentioned above whose disclosures were unheard as well as four additional participants whose families initially heard their disclosures but later choose to avoid recognition of this fact. These additional four participants did not experience the acrimonious and hostile rejection reported by the other seven participants. Instead, these additional four participants experienced avoidance and denial from their families. In both instances, nonetheless, the participants were rendered invisible. I will show how these 11 study participants used invisibility as a tool to strategically manipulate their encounters with family. Their experiences with these negotiations will better explain how they were able to exercise freedom and agency from within invisibility.

In their efforts to maintain their familial relationships, these study participants allowed their sexuality to become invisible after disclosure. As a result, they came to inhabit a space that is in between in and out. Their families are aware of the fact that they are lesbian, bisexual, or queer, but they pretend the disclosure never occurred. These relationships complicate how we understand visibilities and invisibilities, for even after verbal articulation one cannot force another to recognize something they prefer to avoid. Such circumstances created an in-between space where these individuals often went along with their family's denial, allowing their disclosures to be unheard, and compromising certain aspects of their visibility.

Interestingly, the participants who inhabited this space found advantages to this arrangement that would have otherwise been lost to them. For example, one Cuban participant, Luz, verbally articulated her queer identity to her family. Her parents tried very hard to be nonjudgmental and, ultimately, came to some level of acceptance of their daughter's disclosure. However, the parents' method for dealing with Luz's nonconformity was to avoid it all together. The invisibility created by this avoidance is something that Luz has been able to manipulate to her advantage in her relationships with women. As long as her parents avoid her disclosure they must also ignore her relationships with other women. This, she finds, is not always a bad thing. Take for example, her description of bringing a woman home with her for a family wedding:

> Later, when I had that girlfriend, she came with me to the house. I never said to my parents, "This is my girlfriend" but they could tell. They knew, but they didn't want to talk about it. And I know they were really in denial because when she came to the house, the room that had been my bedroom in high school had two twin beds and they let us stay in there. Whereas when I had a boyfriend he would always have to stay in a different room. They were nice. They weren't mean to her. She came with me to my sister's wedding.

This example helps to clarify the in-between space Luz inhabits with her family. Her parents understood that the woman she brought home was her lover, but they did not want to address the issue, and Luz did not want to push the topic on them. Nonetheless, by not objecting to Luz bringing her partner to the wedding, they are, in a sense, tacitly acknowledging their partnership. However, by allowing them to share a room, they are avoiding the realities of this relationship. If Luz's parents had asked her and her partner to sleep in separate rooms they would have been validating the non-platonic aspects of their relationship. By engaging in an avoidance strategy, Luz's parents render her relationship invisible. In doing so, this same-sex couple is granted privileges that would be considered inappropriate in her family's home in a heterosexual context. The flexibility of this in-between space helps Luz move forward in merging her family of choice with her family of origin.

This in-between space comes with its own set of potential consequences. Luz was able to manipulate her parent's avoidance and use it to her benefit. Other participants were not as lucky. At first disclosure, Luisa's parents were tolerant of her coming out; however, like Luz' parents, Luisa's parents tried to avoid the issue. During this time, Luisa's experiences mirrored those of Luz. She often brought her partner with her to family functions although no one ever acknowledged them as a couple. Things changed, however, when Luisa announced that she was engaged to her partner and wanted to plan a wedding. This development sparked serious rejection from Luisa's family. She describes the experience below:

> And then we got engaged. I was elated. My friends were really supportive and with all of that elation I started to tell people in my family. And what I found out is that even the people who were pretending to be polite, when they realized I wasn't kidding, that I was engaged, that was like drawing the line in the sand. Very quickly my elation turned to the realization that, "Oh my God, these people who are my blood relatives who would otherwise lie in the street for me, not only will they not come, I'm not welcome in their house. She's not welcome in their house. They're not going to tell their kids. Because they think this is immoral and unnatural."

Luisa's parents had come to accept, through avoidance, that their daughter was in a serious relationship with another woman. However, by wanting to have a public wedding where friends and family are invited, Luisa was pushing her relationship too far outside of the in-between space with which her parents had grown comfortable. By pushing to move out of this in-between space and to create more visibility for herself and her partner, Luisa now faces further rejection. Upon experiencing this rejection from her family, Luisa postponed her wedding and did not bring up the topic again for four years. Luisa's excitement about making a public commitment to her partner in front of her family and friends is hindered by her parent's desire to not see their partnership. Although her parents had known of this relationship for years and had not outright rejected their daughter's same-sex partner, they drew the line at the point where Luisa wanted to make her commitment public. Luisa's quest for visibility among her extended family gave them the power to reject and injure her in a way that she had, up until that point, been shielded from.

The 11 participants who fell into this category built in-between spaces stemming from the invisibility they experienced in the familial realm. They found ways to manipulate invisibility to work to their advantage. They merged their familial and romantic relationships in in-between spaces, thus creating a space where their families could not avoid their disclosures, but also where they did not have to verbally acknowledge them. The transient nature of this space gave these women the flexibility to move in and out of visibilities. In in-between spaces, the participants could be seen even if not validated. They were invisible in the sense that their disclosures were not heard, but they were physically seen. In in-between spaces, study participants are able to merge families of choice and origin. It is important to note that an in-between space is very different from the closet. Despite their shared roots in invisibility, in-between spaces offer individuals the opportunity to be seen even if not heard. In this way, in-between spaces become fertile grounds for sexually nonconforming Latinas to create unique arrangements which fit their needs and those of their families.

NONDISCLOSURE/EXPLORING THAT WHICH REMAINS TACIT

In contrast to the 23 participants who had disclosed their sexuality to their families, 17 of the women who participated in this study had not. Nonetheless, most of these women did not live closeted lives around their families. The sexually nonconforming Latinas in tacit relationships would partake in familial events with their partners and accept visitors in their homes where they lived with their partners, but never verbally articulated the romantic nature of their relationships. Those study participants who maintained their relationships tacit inhabited an in-between space with their families similar to the one inhabited by those participants whose disclosures left them invisible. Thus, even by leaving unspoken that which is evident, the study participants were successful in linking their same-sex relationships with their extended familial relationships. Take for example Minerva, a woman in her 50s of Mexican and Nicaraguan descent. She enjoyed a life partnership with Daniela who recently died of cancer. When I asked Minerva about their relationship with her mother, she responded in the following way:

> With my mother, I never came out to her. And there was always this she-knew-and-she-didn't-know kind of situation. But what I used to tell myself was that I didn't want to lose my mom. How realistic that fear was, I don't really know, but that's what I told myself. And so I never came out to my mom. But, my mom adored Daniela and would cook for her. When she found out that Daniela liked lamb, she started making lamb; when she found out that Daniela didn't eat pork, she switched and started making all of her traditional dishes with turkey and chicken. They had a very, very warm connection to one another even though they didn't speak the same language. My mom loved Daniela, and Daniela enjoyed her. She appreciated her for who she was, and that came through despite the language barrier.

While Minerva never verbally articulates her sexual nonconformity to her mother, it is clear that she believes her relationship with Daniela was visible. Minerva's mother has passed away and, thus, she will never know if her mother really saw them as a couple; however, that is less important than the fact that Daniela was loved and accepted as a member of the family. How, then, can one make sense of this mother's appreciation for Daniela if, theoretically, she does not see Daniela as her daughter's lover? I argue that the answer to this question lies in the in-between space Minerva inhabited with her lover and her mother—the space that allowed Minerva's same-gender loving relationship to remain tacit but not unseen. Minerva's existence in this in-between space prompted her to use the language "she knew and she didn't know..." when describing her mother's awareness of the arrangement. Those are perhaps the only words which could capture the in-between nature of their relationship: a relationship without words but with deep understanding.

Tacit relationships do not only raise questions about one's visibility. They hold implications for what one says, what does not get said, and the behaviors that accompany this language. Study participants who allowed their sexual nonconformity to remain tacit had the ability to determine if and when they spoke to their family members about their partnerships. These women sometimes found power in the control that comes with being the withholder. At times, they played with this power, recognizing that a verbal articulation could confirm suspicions and silence rumors, but remaining unwilling to give up the power they gained from leaving certain things unsaid. Consider the following description, where a study participant, Josefina, describes a conversation with her aunt:

> Mi tía me ha puesto el tema varias veces. Lo último que me dijo fue que mi papá estaba muy triste porque él entendía que al fin de mi días, yo me iba a quedar sola. Entonces yo le dije a mi tía:

> JOSEFINA: ¿Pero cuando él se va a cansar del mismo tema? Yo desde que tengo 11 años a mí los varones no me gustan porque me prohíben en todo lo que yo quiero hacer. Entonces yo sé que eso es una decisión que yo tomé y yo sé que voy a tomar las consecuencias más adelante.
> TÍA: No, porque, yo le he dicho que yo nunca te he visto con nadie pero tú eres así tan tranquila. Yo le dije que él tiene que aceptarte como tú eres.

> Y ahí yo misma le cambié el tema. Yo no me voy a meter en ese gancho. Esta conversación está dentro de mí. No es con ella que tengo que tener la conversación. Y no le di más información.

> My aunt has brought up the topic with me several times. The last thing she said was that my father was very sad because he understood that at the end of my days, I was going to end up alone. And so I said to my aunt:

> JOSEFINA: But when is he going to get tired of the same topic? Since I was 11, I do not like boys because they inhibit me in everything I want to do. So, I know that this is a decision I made, and I know that I will have to deal with the consequences later.
> AUNT: *Well, I've told him that I have never seen you with anyone, but you are so calm. I told him that he needs to accept you the way you are.*

> And then I changed the subject. I'm not going to fall into that trap. This conversation is inside of me. She's not the one that I need to have this conversation with. And I didn't give her anymore information.

Josefina's agency is clear in this description. She decides how long she will allow the conversation with her aunt to continue. These carefully measured words send a clear and direct message, but they also fall short of a full disclosure. Josefina's greatest act of power in this encounter is in what remains unsaid. By changing the topic, Josefina leaves her aunt to read between the lines of her statement, "I don't like boys because." Josefina clings to a part of herself which she wants to remain tacit. In so doing, she owns the ambiguity surrounding her sexuality and denies her aunt the satisfaction of a confirmation which remains tacit.

The largest discrepancy in this study between those who chose to disclose and those who chose to allow their sexual nonconformity to remain tacit is that, for the latter, there was not a drawn out period of struggle, rejection, or resistance. The findings show that both those who disclosed and those who did not, ultimately, found ways to merge their families of origin with their chosen ones. It is unclear from the findings what will happen with those study participants who had recently verbally articulated sexual nonconformity to their families at the time of the interview. However, if the experiences of the other participants who did disclose several years ago are any indication of what will occur with those who recently disclosed, one can expect the experiences to have similar outcomes. The major difference observed was in the process taken by the various women who merged families of choice and families of origin and the level of visibility these women were able to obtain regarding their same-sex relationships.

In analyzing the alternative arrangements which sexually nonconforming Latinas created with their families, their movement in and out of visibility becomes evident. Some of the participants are empowered by the freedom they acquired to live a visible and verbally validated lesbian, bisexual, or queer life around their families. This was the case for Inocencia and Yanet. For these women, verbal disclosure resulted in more visibility among family. However, the data show another very strong trend of study participants who are, in fact, empowered through invisibility. Those participants whose disclosures were avoided or unheard found ways to use such invisibility to their advantage. Others still found empowerment through tacit relationships which they believed to still be visible. Many of these women, then, do not fit simply into a traditional I-am-out-and-proud paradigm; rather, they find power through moving in and out of visibility and by building in-between spaces. The flexibility that they gain from these more fluid arrangements grants them both the possibilities and the space to maneuver when, where, and if to be visible. Such maneuvers are pregnant with agency and power.

CONCLUSION

The participants included in this study made interesting use of space, visibility, and silence as tools to help them navigate familial relationships. They found agency in in-between spaces and in the flexibility to choose if and when to perform more or less overt expressions of outness. Sexually nonconforming Latinas' experiences highlight that visibility is not merely something present or dissociated from their same-sex relationships. Rather, there are levels of visibility in terms of their relationships that are constantly shifting within the family. By learning how to capitalize on the visibility they obtained from the family and to manipulate invisibility, the participants in this study appear to strategically utilize in-between spaces to their fullest potentials.

As Latina immigrants, the study participants relied on the support they received from their familial and immigrant communities in order to navigate the racial landscape in the United States and to combat anti-immigrant sentiment. Furthermore, their familial and immigrant communities relied heavily on them for this same kind of support. This co-reliance is something sexually nonconforming White women may not experience and, thus, may result in differences in how White and Latina sexually nonconforming women negotiate visibility in the family. Sexually nonconforming Latinas' unique needs have led them to create alternatives to the standard coming out process and the linear phases inherent in this process. Instead, these women have created new options for themselves that, at times, involve a verbal articulation of their sexual identity while under different circumstances they do not. Regardless of their choices, the study participants are finding ways to create empowerment for themselves as sexually nonconforming women through visibility and invisibility. In doing so, they are forcing a reconsideration of our understanding of invisibility and the uncritical ways in which society can and has associated it with repression.

In this chapter, I have drawn out the complex relationship between silence, repression, and invisibility. Clearly, given the information provided by those interviewed for this study, silence does not merely equate repression. I have argued that verbal articulations of sexual identity do not always help individuals in their quest for visibility. Even when there is language and verbal communication, invisibility happens.

This study pays particular attention to what is said and left unsaid in sexually nonconforming Latinas' familial relationships. In particular, I have explored the unspoken meanings behind the tacit relationships participants developed with their families and the in-between spaces they inhabited together. Here, I look at what both the participants and their families leave unsaid. An exploration of this nature requires us to consider the language of silence and the meanings present in spaces where there are no words. Silence is often associated with repression, but in this chapter, I have sought to complicate this understanding by pointing to the power inherent in leaving certain information unspoken. I encourage us to consider the existent silences not as closeted behaviors that prohibit individuals from being true to themselves, but rather as a strategy to allow for maneuverability in and out of visibility. The in-between spaces these individuals create should also not be seen as repressive but, instead, as a flexible environment where one can use the language of silence to maintain familial relationships.

REFERENCE

Adams, T. (2010). Paradoxes of sexuality, gay, identity and the closet. *Symbolic Interaction*, 33, 234–256.

13

Mothers and Moneymakers

How Gender Norms Shape US Marriage Migration Politics

Gina Marie Longo

Sarasusan, a white divorcee and single mother of two from Virginia, and Hicham, an Arab factory worker living in the desert town of Tan-Tan, Morocco, met on MySpace in December 2009, and immediately hit it off. In June of 2010, Sarasusan traveled to Morocco to meet Hicham for the first time. Over the course of three years, Hicham traveled to internet cafés daily to talk to his future wife and stepdaughters. In January 2013, she finally could afford to bring her daughters to Morocco to meet Hicham in person. Upon her return to the United States, she filed for a K-1 (fiancé) visa petition with the U.S. Citizenship and Immigration Services.

While they began dreaming of the day they could marry, they didn't realize their nightmare had already begun. After a year and a half, the first petition and subsequent appeal were denied. At his interview, the U.S. consulate officer in Morocco told Hicham that their relationship appeared fraudulent or strictly for immigration papers. He was given no further explanation. In July 2015, Sarasusan married Hicham in Morocco, but her daughters, due to high airfare costs, were unable to come. Upon returning home, Sarasusan saved money to start a new immigration petition for her husband. Sarasusan began seeking advice from other petitioners online, and crafted her evidence package based on much of this advice. It was not until September 2016 that Sarasusan and her daughters were able to embrace Hicham on U.S. soil.

Foreign nationals who marry U.S. citizens have an expedited track to naturalization, so immigration officials worry that some will use fake marriages to obtain a green card. Early U.S. immigration and citizenship policies addressed these concerns by blocking white women in racially mixed relationships. Native-born women citizens lost their citizenship status if they married foreign nationals, and could not initiate immigration petitions for foreign-born husbands. Consequently, this enabled a gendered and racialized citizenship model that defined white, native-born men as full citizens and women as second-class citizens.

Today, these policies have been replaced with preferential processing for immigrants with U.S. family ties. So, U.S. immigration officials require that "green card" petitioning couples demonstrate that their relationships are "valid and subsisting" (i.e., for love) and not fraudulent (i.e., for immigration papers). Immigration officials warn U.S. citizens in such relationships to beware of *red flags*, or details about a couple's relationship that raise suspicions of marriage fraud, such as large age differences, short courtships, or requests for money. These requirements and *red-flag* warnings are supposedly gender and racially neutral, but migration itself is

Longo, Gina Marie "Mothers and Moneymakers: How Gender Norms Shape US Marriage Migration Politics" *Gender & Society Blog*, August 3, 2018.

not. Thus, like Sarasusan, men and women petitioners with foreign partners from different world regions often seek advice from experts and other petitioners about how to overcome potential obstacles to their petitions' success.

I used an online ethnography and a text analysis of conversation threads on a large online immigration forum where U.S. petitioners exchange such advice. I compared two of the sites' sub-forums – the Middle East/North African (MENA) forum, where members are predominately white U.S. women coupled with MENA-region men, and the Belarus/Russia/Ukraine (BRU) forum, where white U.S. men pair with BRU-region women – and analyzed how forum members define *red-flag* warnings and the requirements for a "valid and subsisting relationship" to label a relationship "real" or "fraudulent." These conversations reveal members' own experiences with immigration officials and their understanding of genuine marriages for immigration purposes.

I found that petitioners connect generic relationship criteria and warnings in U.S. immigration policy with racialized and classed gender ideologies and expectations surrounding an idealized image of the white, Middle-class, "American family." Women should be mothers and caretakers, and men should be breadwinners. Both men and women petitioners use sexual and gendered double standards surrounding women's sexual agency, fertility, and desirability to determine which red flags will concern immigration officials and for whom. Women's sexuality and gender differentially structure the process of negotiating *red flags* for men and women petitioners, and the right to confer citizenship onto a foreign partner. This provides privileges to men citizens, allowing them to pursue of foreign women abroad and to bestow their citizenship status more freely upon their chosen mates. However, women citizens with the same intentions are considered desperate fools, incapable of controlling their emotions or the border. Consequently, citizen-women's relationships appear more suspect and in need of policing.

Why is this important? Although media coverage on U.S. immigration often centers on issues surrounding DREAMRs, refugees, and undocumented people, approximately 50 percent of the one million-plus immigrant visas issued in 2015 (i.e., "green cards") were for U.S. citizens' immigrant spouses/fiancés. These rates have remained consistent since 1908, making these beneficiaries the largest groups of visa holders with a pathway to citizenship. These immigration cases largely shape the nation and conceptions of citizenship. Through this online forum, members become unofficial border police before cases ever reach an immigration officer. Although discriminatory U.S. immigration and citizenship laws of old have been abolished, I find that when citizens use ideological understandings about gender and family themselves to give each other petitioning advice, explicitly discriminatory policies are not necessary to uphold and legitimize racialized and gendered citizenship hierarchies. My findings highlight how conversational negotiations in virtual spaces are consequential for re-imagining intersectionally gendered citizenship and the policing of national identities and borders.

14

Polygamy in the United States

How Marginalized Religious Communities Cope with Stigmatizing Discourses Surrounding Plural Marriage

Michael K. Ault and Bobbi Van Gilder

Centennial Park is a community of approximately 2,000 residents who perpetuate a lifestyle centered on religious beliefs, including plural marriage (or polygamy). Due to social and legal dangers associated with practicing an outlawed lifestyle, many polygamous communities, including Centennial Park, adopted policies of strict geographical and social isolation. Because of this isolation, group members have not, until recently, overtly attempted to negotiate their position or gain acceptance within the larger culture, so little was known in the outside world about the beliefs, practices, or lifestyles of these communities. However, recent public attention focused on polygamy has given voice to members of this community, thus providing them an opportunity to share their perspectives regarding their religion and lifestyle with members of dominant US culture. For many Centennial Park residents, their hope is to correct what they believe to be an "inaccurate definition produced at a distance with almost no input from those ... being defined" (Dockstader 2011, p. 2), and establish positive relationships with outsiders. The Centennial Park community is a site of theoretical interest because its current attempts to emerge from isolation have made salient its goals and expectations in maintaining its current culture while attempting to associate with the outside world.

Importantly, the stigmatization of plural marriage remains strong, so strategies must be employed by community members to cope with and negotiate their stigmatized cultural identities with outsiders. This is a critical period of change both within the community as it becomes more open to the outside world, and within the larger American culture as the idea of family and marriage is reinterpreted to include non-traditional lifestyles. In fact, the past two decades have brought about the emergence of the "postmodern" family, which is characterized by a variety of different family types including the following: working mothers, divorced families, single-parent families, adoptive parenting, domestic partnerships, lesbian, gay, bisexual, transgender, and queer (LGBTQ) families, and others. As such, the purpose of this study was to expand upon the existing literature and to investigate the identity negotiation processes of Centennial Park community members in their interactions with members of mainstream culture.

Ault, Michael K., and Bobbi Van Gilder. "Polygamy in the United States: How Marginalized Religious Communities Cope with Stigmatizing Discourses Surrounding Plural Marriage." *Journal of Intercultural Communication Research* 44, no. 4 (2015): 307–328.

CENTENNIAL PARK

Despite modern condemnation of the practice of polygamy, historical records indicate that in human history, 93 percent of societies allowed for some form of polygamy with 70 percent of them embracing polygamy as the preferred marital relationship. Historically, there are many reasons for the practice of polygamy such as forging kinship ties, demonstrating group or social dominance, and/or creating a labor force for family farms. Today, polygamy is predominantly limited to Northern African, Middle Eastern, and Southern Asian countries and is largely based on religion. Although polygamy exists in the United States outside of Mormon fundamentalism, those who practice it are very few and typically do not organize into larger communities.

The history of this faction of polygamy begins with the history of The Church of Jesus Christ of Latter-day Saints (LDS) of which it was a part until the 1890s. The history of the creation and development of the LDS Church and the origins of its practice of polygamy are well documented and therefore are not explained here. When the LDS Church abandoned polygamy in 1890, due to government pressure, the progenitors of the Centennial Park group continued to practice polygamy believing that it is an essential requirement for eternal salvation. Attempts to coexist with mainstream LDS members proved difficult for those who defied the Church and continued to enter into plural marriages. In 1926, many of the "fundamentalists," who renamed themselves "The Work of Jesus Christ" or "The Work" for short, established Short Creek, later called Colorado City, a community in an isolated and desolate stretch of land along the Utah/Arizona border, to avoid social persecution and legal prosecution.

Despite their efforts to isolate themselves physically and socially from the outside world, Utah and Arizona government leaders made several attempts to disband the community and eradicate their marital practices. Government officers performed raids of the community in 1935 and 1944 arresting community leaders. When these raids proved unsuccessful at persuading community members to discontinue living plural marriage, Arizona Governor Howard Pyle ordered a massive raid in 1953, during which nearly 100 police officers, inspectors, government officials, and members of the media descended on Short Creek. All of the men were arrested, and the women and children were forcibly relocated to shelters and foster homes throughout Arizona. Although the raid would be found unconstitutional by a federal judge, many families were separated for more than ten years before reassembling in Short Creek. In the years that followed the establishment of Short Creek, the fundamentalist movement experienced many schisms leading to the establishment of several organized groups and independent polygamous families. The Centennial Park faction of Mormon fundamentalism was founded in 1986 after political turmoil surrounding leadership succession led approximately one third of the community to split from the group and form a new settlement less than three miles from Colorado City, AZ, the traditional headquarters of the fundamentalist movement. Since the split, unlike with the fundamentalist church of Jesus Christ of Latter-Day Saints (FLDS) group, local and state governments have taken a "hands off" approach when dealing with the Centennial Park community. Although Centennial Park has not experienced much political or legal turmoil, social changes have strongly impacted the way its members live.

Rapid changes in social attitudes toward marriage and family have created a safer space for alternative families to interact with dominant culture. These changing views toward marriage and family are made evident by the recent repeal of the Defense of Marriage Act and by the legalization of same-sex marriages in states across the nation. In regard to polygamy, in a 2011 court ruling in Utah, instigated by the Brown family known for their television show "Sister Wives," Judge Clark Waddoups threw out an important aspect of Utah's anti-polygamy law prohibiting cohabitation. Although the ban on bigamy remains in place, polygamists cannot be prosecuted unless more than one official marriage license is issued (Brown v. Buhman 2013). These shifts in cultural discourses about marriage and family have enabled members of Centennial Park to speak openly about their cultural practices for the first time. With that, communication scholars have been afforded the opportunity to explore a theoretically interesting co-cultural community and their attempts to overcome public stigma and establish a new, more open relationship with the mainstream US culture.

Stigmatization and Cultural Exclusion

To better understand the stigmatization of polygamy, one must first understand the identity processes that shape intergroup encounters. *Social identity* refers to a person's sense of who he or she is based on his or her group membership(s). According to Turner (1982), individuals typically view themselves in terms of their group membership categories, such that one's group membership(s) becomes a key component of his or her individual identity. The groups to which individuals belong (e.g. social class, religion, family, ethnic group, and university affiliation) thus become a significant source of pride and self-esteem for group members. While social identity is crucial to individuals' self-concepts, social identities vary in their desirability. Consequently, individuals whose identities are perceived as undesirable by out-groups may encounter discrimination. These undesirable identities become stigmatized.

As noted by Goffman (1963), "differentness" is the primary means by which individuals become aware of identity assumptions. Stigma occurs when labeled differences are linked to stereotypes and perceived collectively as negative. Because identities exist within a system of social hierarchy, stigmatized individuals face inequalities, which are maintained and enacted through social interaction. In fact, once a person is assigned a stigmatizing social label, this labeling process connotes a separation of "us" from "them," which often leads to discrimination. Further, *deviance* refers to behaviors that do not fit the accepted standards or social expectations for appropriate behavior. So, by categorizing polygamy as a deviant practice, those who engage in plural marriage are deemed abnormal and are viewed as a threat to society. Consequently, fundamentalist Mormons who practice plural marriage remain marginalized as the dominant social structure works to maintain monogamy as the standard for marriage and to preserve the nuclear family.

This trend has been made evident by the persistent controversies concerning same-sex marriage and polygamy. In fact, labels such as "polygamist" have worked to mark the exclusion of fundamentalist Mormons from some of the rights afforded by citizenship (i.e. marriage). Polygamist marriages are not recognized by the state. As a result of stigmatization, individuals who are marked as deviant must adopt strategies for coping with stigma.

Communication Strategies for Coping with Stigma

In coping with a stigmatized identity, individuals must engage in identity management. Identity management is a communicative process through which identities are formed, maintained, and modified through symbolic interaction. Therefore, those who are stigmatized will typically respond to manifestations of stigma in ways that preserve their self-esteem and protect their individual identity. Stigmatized individuals, therefore, are "not passive, powerless individuals; rather, they are strategists, expert managers, and negotiators who play active (although not always successful) roles" in shaping their social environment (Herman 1993, p. 324).

Identity management processes are especially salient for individuals possessing unmarked stigmatized identities, or identities that are not easily identifiable by others. Put simply, while some stigmatized identities are easily identifiable (e.g. skin color, physical disabilities, developmental delays), others are invisible stigmas (e.g. mental illness, homosexuality, religion). Much like homosexuality, religious orientation and marital status typically become known only through a process of disclosure through which an individual either denies or allows others to access this personal information. Disclosure of membership in a stigmatized culture or group can take different forms. Often, disclosure occurs nonverbally as stigmatized people present symbols that demonstrate their membership in a stigmatized culture (e.g. wearing a yamaka or cross necklace). These choices regarding how much information to reveal or conceal are related to the social networks that stigmatized people maintain. While a consensus exists in the United States that individuals should not be penalized for being different, cultural demands insist that certain differences be muted. As such, stigmatized individuals are forced to manage and cope with stigmatized identities. Through the utilization of in-depth interviews, the objective of this study was to give voice to members of the Centennial Park community and to better understand a historically unobserved population.

Methods

Participants included 20 members of "The Work," and all currently reside in Centennial Park, Arizona. Of these participants, 13 were women. All participants in this study are Caucasian, which is representative of the population of interest (nearly 100 percent of the Centennial Park population is Caucasian). Participants' ages ranged from 20 to 64 years old. Participants varied in educational background, with education ranging from high school diploma to graduate degree, and in their occupations (e.g. nurse, teacher, home-maker, religious leader). Although all interviewees were married at the time of their interviews, several participants were not living plural marriage at the time of their interview. However, those not living plural marriage at the time of the interview all expressed a desire to live the principle in the future.

Key members of the community were contacted via email and community leaders solicited volunteers to participate. This study utilized face-to-face, in-depth interviews. The first author is a member of the LDS Church, which shares its history with this polygamous group from the Church's organization in 1830 until 1890 when the LDS Church officially discontinued the practice of polygamy. This affiliation with the LDS Church was helpful in interpreting these data.

Results

Findings revealed that *discursive cultural de-legitimation* of plural marriage motivates co-cultural members to engage in *network management*. In the following paragraphs, we explain how this theory emerged by describing the ways in which dominant cultural discourse de-legitimizes plural marriage culture and by highlighting the ways in which co-cultural members engage in behaviors aimed at controlling and managing social networks as a way to cope with stigmatization.

Discursive Delegitimation

Findings revealed that by denying the legitimacy of their cultural identity, dominant cultural discourse works to isolate plural marriage as a problem to be dealt with or resolved. Plural marriage culture is de-legitimized in five distinct ways: (1) *dehumanization*, (2) *cultural homogenization*, (3) *media misrepresentation*, (4) *stereotype propagation*, and (5) *legal persecution*.

Dehumanization

The first category of *discursive cultural de-legitimation* is *dehumanization*. Several participants in this study described a discourse from mainstream society that treated those practicing plural marriage as not "real people" (Pamela), thus taking away from their personhood. Participants described dehumanization commonly as the use of derogatory slurs used to label and degrade members of the community. Lena states, "I'd be walking down the street and people would holler out, there goes a plyg. Get out of here! We don't want you here." The linguistic slur "plyg" is used here to degrade members of the community. In addition to language, dehumanization was evident in actions that were meant to humiliate and frighten members of the community. As Leslie relates, not only was she the victim of hateful speech, but also fell victim to an act of discrimination and hate.

> One day I was in Wal-Mart shopping and I was in an aisle all by myself, walking down the aisle, almost to the end and all the sudden out of nowhere these two kids jumped out the aisle on each side of me one with a video camera and one with a can of the spray of party confetti stuff... String spray, yeah. Sprayed it all over me while the other one was recording it. And I was so freaked out because it just happened all the sudden that it didn't register to me until afterwards the comments they made as they were recording about how they "accosted this polygamist." And I was so frustrated that this would happen right there. I mean, if I hadn't been so caught off guard and so hurt and so emotional after the exchange, I would have gone to Wal-Mart and said "That this could happen in your store is appalling" [...] But I was really shook up after that, and I mean there's hundreds and hundreds of stories I could tell. I mean, from being a teenager and called a plyg and all that.

Despite Centennial Park's isolation, this experience demonstrates the everyday issues that these participants deal with because of their chosen lifestyle. As evidenced by the excerpts above, members of the Centennial Park community, and others practicing plural marriage, often fall victim to acts of dehumanization by cultural outsiders thus denying legitimacy to their cultural practices.

Cultural Homogenization

Cultural homogenization refers to the ways in which dominant cultural discourse has homogenized out-group members (i.e. polygamists). This is done in a variety of ways. One of the most commonly noted examples of this was the lumping of *all* polygamist communities together. In fact, almost all of the participants in this study highlighted this as a significant problem facing the community. For example, Andrea states, "they group us as polygamists and they group them as polygamists so in their mind we're not different than they are." This cultural homogenization becomes especially problematic when Centennial Park residents are associated with Warren Jeffs and the FLDS church, which many participants reported as a frequent association. The FLDS church is most known because of their child abuse scandal in 2011, when president, Warren Jeffs, was charged for felony child sexual assault after taking a child bride. Despite Centennial Park residents publically attacking the actions of the FLDS church and their openly expressed disgust toward child abuse, forced marriage, and domestic violence, they continue to be lumped in with the FLDS. Pamela indicated in her interview that this is a frequent misconception,

> I think in the eyes of the majority of the general populous today, Warren Jeffs equals polygamy. That is truly sad to me. Because he's a sick man and that's really sad. He's such a little small portion of the whole society of polygamists, you know, the FLDS are just a portion of that and we sit and watch him pretty much do everything that we've strived to stand up as in our culture and say, "This is not us, this is not what we represent," and watch him do everything that we said we don't believe in.

Adam expresses further frustration with this cultural homogenization. He states,

> Well it has been in the public eye because we've been lumped with the FLDS and that's why I have an issue with that because it was the Work, it was the Work and the Work was split then Brother Jeffs organized the FLDS and made himself the sole corporate... [Warren Jeffs] has done those things that a cult leader will do to capture the people, that's what's happened over there. You talk about a cult, he's perpetuated a cult. And the characteristics of a cult leader are the things he has exuded to be able to do that. So, there's no resemblance between the Work of God and the Fundamentalist, whatever you want to call it, movement.

The excerpts above illustrate the ways in which public discourse has homogenized plural marriage culture such that all polygamists are seen as the same.

Media Misrepresentation

Media misrepresentation refers to media representations in which faulty information is expressed, or when footage is edited in a way to misrepresent and sensationalize plural marriage culture. Several families took advantage of requests from television shows and networks such as The Oprah Winfrey Network, Dr Phil, and PBS to publicize their lifestyle, thinking that greater transparency might help outsiders to understand and eventually tolerate the plural lifestyle. These attempts to utilize the media as an outlet for engaging with the outside world often left the community frustrated and hurt as Jessica asserts,

> The media will go and interview people like that who have an agenda. Some of the things they say are outright lies or they will twist them, saying them in a way with different connotations. I resent that kind of coverage because it's just not true.

Jessica further expanded upon her point noting,

> My experience has been that people want the sensational story, not the truth. Our family did an interview with PBS when they did it on the Mormons and they just had a piece in there about polygamy and we were part of that. they made a couple promises, which they broke. We were very upset about that. One of which was that we do not want to be associated in any way with Warren Jeffs. We have never been a part of his church or associated with him. We are not in any way connected and we don't want to be. Well they did, they took some old footage and put it right in the middle of our piece. It upset us a lot because it connected us to him. So we felt like there was an agenda there.

Similarly, Thomas notes,

> People like to sell newspapers. And, when they find out that we're just a bunch of boring people, that doesn't necessarily sell newspapers [...] They look at it in a salacious way kind of, even though they try to give us a fair shake. I don't really think that most people that come out here to check us out, I don't really think that they're trying to understand us, so to speak. They're just trying to get a story and sell it.

Despite attempts from Centennial Park residents to correct the misinformation formerly propagated by media sources, misrepresentations of the co-culture continue to delegitimize their cultural practices.

Stereotype Propagation

Stereotype propagation refers to the perpetuation of negative stereotypes ascribed to polygamists in the United States. Pamela highlights a few of the most common stereotypes which are advanced in dominant discourses about polygamy: "child abuse, white slavery, neglect, fraud, lack of education, living in squalor, bleeding the beast, living on government funds" among others. Henry also reports a few of the stereotypes he had seen propagated via media outlets. He says, "Well, what I see mostly on the blog is that we are in it for lust or for deviant sexual behavior."

Another common stereotype is that of sexual abuse. Andrea expresses her frustrations regarding stereotypes about abuse,

> Yeah. I think it comes up in every interview and it sort of irritates me, mostly because it's a stereotype. And I don't know of any cases here, but I'm sure there are some because it happens across the spectrum of human nature. But no, I haven't had any personal experience with it.

Andrea also shared a story about how an ordinary errand for most people becomes a demonstration of how these stereotypes have shaped perceptions of polygamist women in general,

> I was getting my car serviced in Hurricane and the guy's like, "Okay, I need your card and your license to verify the signature." And he's like, "You're from Colorado City? When did you escape?" "I didn't escape! I still live in Centennial Park, thanks." But he had assumed I escaped because normally they wear the prairie dress and their hair is different.

Polygamists have long been associated with negative stereotypes, but public discourses continue to perpetuate old stereotypes thus reinforcing negative attitudes and beliefs about plural marriage families.

Legal Persecution

Finally, *legal persecution* refers to the legal policies and ramifications of plural marriage. Specifically, this refers to laws that criminalize polygamists along with lack of legal recognition for polygamist marriages. State and federal laws do not recognize plural marriages. Further, the criminalization of plural marriage functions as an explicit source of de-legitimization of cultural identities. In this study, many participants mention the raids that separated families and produced fear within the community. For instance, recalling her family situation living away from Short Creek following the 1953 raid, Lena stated,

> If my father ever came around, which was only a couple times a year, we had to call him Uncle George because the state would have put him back in jail again. They only allowed the first wives to come back two years after the raid was over and the other wives-my father's family at least-were scattered.

As Thomas explains further, "From the government intervention, as far as plural marriage is concerned... We've had a long history of the government taking our best and brightest and putting them in jail. So that's always a reality." He goes on to say, "because of the changes that have occurred in society where we're a lot more open about people's relationships, but in the back of your mind it's kind of always there." Here, Thomas described the ways in which the community has been more open about their practices in recent years, but the fear of legal prosecution is always ruminating beneath the surface.

Network Management

The *discursive cultural de-legitimation* of plural marriage functions as a force of stigmatization. Members of the Centennial Park community, their cultural and religious identities, and their religious practices become stigmatized. As such, the community members are rejected as deviant by dominant US culture. In response to this stigmatization, co-cultural members engage in communicative strategies of *network management*. Network management is described here as the management of social networks such that individuals control access to information through network ties, informational control, and strategic disclosure while also strengthening in-group bonds through shared values and practices. This entails the organizing, securing, and maintaining of information through social interaction, or the limiting of social interaction with out-group members. We found that co-cultural members engage in *network management* by making strategic decisions about how they interact with cultural outsiders and what information they will disclose to outsiders about plural marriage culture. *Network management* comprises four main strategies: *withdrawing from mainstream society*, *establishing in-group solidarity*, *concealing cultural identification*, and *educating cultural outsiders*.

Withdrawing from Mainstream Society

One coping strategy that was referenced frequently by participants was *social withdrawal*. Social withdrawal refers to the withdrawal from the broader community to create a separate community in isolation. This includes the development of a separate entity that remains united through shared values, the advancement of separatist ideologies, and the development of a self-sufficient community existing independently from mainstream society (e.g. separate schools, separate community center). Of course, complete separation/independence is not possible, as community members utilize modern technology such as the Internet and television, and this community still exists within the state of Arizona and is under the jurisdiction of the US and state governments. Everyday struggles that other stigmatized groups experience were viewed as less obvious in Centennial Park because they had created an isolated community away from day-to-day discrimination. Leslie describes the isolation of the community as a way to deal with the dangers of discrimination. She states,

> Arizona is more of a safe haven as far as a state goes and for us to be able to live according to the laws of the state with less threat of incarceration than it is in Utah, we are here in this remote area of the Arizona strip by choice just so that we can live freely because it's remote enough that we can live freely, so that we can live without threat of ignorant persecution if you will. So, it's a safe place to raise families, not in secrecy, but in safety.

Similarly, Rachel states,

> We are very guarded. We try to protect our children. Not only in a moral sense, but from harm also. So you know, there are walls there, there are barriers, but it is more of an umbrella protection that we

try to create and allow our children to grow in an environment where they can thrive in a healthy way without the bombardment of the evils of society.

Jessica further describes the importance of isolation for the community noting, "It [Centennial Park] was established so that the polygamists could live openly and freely with freedom and without scrutiny." As evidenced by some of the excerpts above, participants in this study recognized the stigmatization of plural marriage culture in the outside world, and accept the isolation as a way to be free of stigmatizing forces.

Establishing in-group Solidarity

Another coping strategy reported by participants was the *establishment of in-group solidarity*. As social identity theorists postulate, maintaining psychological distinctiveness between the in-group and the out-group is functional for individuals. As such, members of the Centennial Park community unite around shared values to enhance in-group status. They challenge stigmatizing discourses by defining their position/practices in religious terms. For instance, Lena states,

> I believe that this is the way God wanted us to live. You can't populate the earth with a man and one wife. If you ever did qualify to become a god, there is not a way to populate the earth with just two people.

As social identity theory explains, two key motivations in intergroup communication are self-enhancement and positive distinctiveness. Of course, self-enhancement is often accompanied by out-group derogation. By diminishing the status of out-group members, individuals within the Centennial Park community are able to combat the forces of stigma by seeing themselves in a positive light that transcends negative discourse. For instance, Adam states, "If we have it, and we are the correct order of authority and priesthood, then they don't because they're not under the authority that we have." By establishing themselves as the chosen people, and by uniting through a shared belief system, individuals are able to cope with the stigma that comes from mainstream culture. As such, network ties become tightened, and cultural beliefs, practices, and activities are shared among in-group members where trust and understanding are mutual.

Concealing Cultural Identification

Concealing cultural identification refers to the concealment of identification with the co-culture and the limiting of information disclosure to cultural outsiders. This may also include practices such as covering or passing, Henry expresses his desire for concealment:

> I was very private, protective of my family and the sacredness of our beliefs because they're so slandered by the world. They don't understand any of it. There was a Cherokee Indian that I worked with, very well-educated, and anthropology was his degree, and I could just about share anything with him because he was just so open and understanding of other cultures and so I did. I shared some things, quite a bit actually, but most of them, I hid my life from and in the end, I was there for 25 years, in the end, I made the right choice because I was able to make a living, provide income and benefits, all kinds of insurance coverage for my plural children even, that I received and I didn't want to threaten that in any way.

Because Henry feared that the stigma associated with plural marriage could threaten his employment, he felt that maintaining secrecy about his religious beliefs and practices was an ideal way to cope with stigma.

While Sarah did not express fear in losing a job, when she was asked how she would describe her family to outsiders she stated, "We lie. We absolutely lie. I have five kids, that's all I ever say. Just to make it more comfortable for everybody, we just don't say a whole lot." In the excerpts above, participants expressed a fear of discrimination. As such, many Centennial Park residents make the decision to conceal their identification with plural marriage culture. In these instances, secrecy was a method for protecting their social identities.

Educating Cultural Outsiders

Finally, *educating cultural outsiders* refers to taking initiative in correcting misinformation and educating the public about the community. While the previous network management strategies are defensive, this network management strategy is unique in that it is the only one that allows for openness and vulnerability with outsiders. Today, Centennial Park residents are publicizing competing discourses aimed at challenging dominant views about their religious practices. In fact, in response to several solicitations to participate in television programs, in 2006, the community founded the Centennial Park Action Committee (CPAC) as an organization "to get information out that responds against the stereotypes and misinformation about us when they lump us together with the other polygamous communities or other fundamentalist Mormon communities" (Adam). CPAC met with advocates for LGBTQ rights and formulated strategies to take advantage of the advancements made by those promoting gay rights and expand gay rights to polygamists as well. In this way, members of the community sought out media sources in an effort to educate Americans about the community in their own way. In employing this network management strategy, Centennial Park residents are also engaging in *social creativity* in that they are attempting to change the negative values assigned to their group into more positive ones. By interacting with, and working with the media, Centennial Park residents use creativity to change negative values placed on their cultural identities, by instead celebrating their community.

By appearing on television shows such as Oprah, Our America with Lisa Ling, National Geographic, and Frontline, people in this community attempted to differentiate themselves from the scandals of other polygamous groups and show the public that they are "more open than the general population's perception of us. We are more open to be talked to" (Jessica). Jessica further explained,

> Our family did an interview with PBS when they did it on the Mormons and they just had a piece in there about polygamy and we were part of that. PBS was the first thing our family did. We've since done several different kinds of interviews. That to us was huge because we are putting our lives out there to the public and for the PBS interview, everyone.

Nicholas explains the importance of engaging in this coping strategy, "Essentially, we came to the point where we realized in this community we needed to tell our own story." Brittany adds, "Stereotypes are broken down through those communications." As explained by the interviewees, by actively engaging in this process the community is better able to gain control over information, to challenge public discourses, and to educate the public.

DISCUSSION

Polygamists' cultural beliefs and practices are de-legitimized in five distinct ways: (1) *dehumanization*, (2) *cultural homogenization*, (3) *media misrepresentation*, (4) *stereotype propagation*, and (5) *legal persecution*. Not only did participants describe the legality of their practices and their fear of prosecution, but they also reported the discursive devaluation of their cultural identities through media representation and discrimination from cultural outsiders.

These manifestations of stigma are not new; however, because of changes in social perceptions, these polygamists believe they now have an opportunity to enact change. During the decades of isolation, these participants did not feel safe in combating the stigma that surrounded polygamy. The message was tacitly yet clearly communicated by government officials that as long as they were "good," the government would leave them alone to practice their beliefs in peace. This pressure to remain silent has gradually decreased as social acceptance of alternative lifestyles has gained momentum. In recent years, many members of this community have begun tentatively the process of combating these manifestations of stigma. In response to stigmatizing discourses, participants adopt a variety of coping strategies, which fall under the unifying term "network management." *Network management* refers the management of social networks such that individuals control access to information through network ties, informational control, and strategic disclosure, while also strengthening in-group bonds. *Network management* comprises four main strategies: (1) *withdrawing from mainstream society*, (2) *establishing in-group solidarity*, (3) *concealing cultural identification*, and (4) *educating cultural outsiders*.

Initially, many members of the Centennial Park community were excited to open their community to the outside world through various channels so as to combat negative stereotypes and differentiate themselves from other polygamous groups. However, they quickly came to realize that in doing so, they became vulnerable to further misunderstanding as their messages were often manipulated to fit the needs of the media rather than the needs of the participant or community. The strategies of network management identified above depict this struggle to balance the dangers and benefits of becoming open with the outside world. Most important to the community is protecting and maintaining their religious culture and lifestyle. Thus, it is not surprising that defensive strategies for coping with stigma are more abundant, illustrating the importance of caution when engaging with the outside world. Indeed, these defensive strategies of network management probably became more salient as the community opened itself up to the outside world's threats and dangers (real or perceived). However, the presence of *educating cultural outsiders* in the repertoire of coping with stigma is a large and important step for this community after experiencing nearly a century of social isolation.

References

Brown v. Buhman, 947 F. Supp. 2d 1170 (D. Utah 2013).

Dockstader, P. (2011, March). *Patriarchal living*. Speech presented at a 'Meet and Greet' at the Centennial Park Community Center between members of the Centennial Park Community and various political and government agency officials and service organizations, Colorado City, AZ.

Goffman, E. (1963). *Stigma: Notes on the management of the identity*. New York, NY: Simon and Schuster.

Herman, N. J. (1993). Return to sender: Reintegrative stigma-management strategies of ex-psychiatric patients. *Journal of Contemporary Ethnography, 22*, 295–330. doi:10.1177/ 089124193022003002.

Turner, J. C. (1982). Toward a cognitive redefinition of the social group. In H. Tajfel (Ed.), *Social identity and intergroup relations* (pp. 15–40). Cambridge: Cambridge University Press.

15

The Trouble with Tolerance

Suzanna Danuta Walters

I've been thinking about marriage a lot lately. Mostly, how to avoid it. Sometimes how to convince others to do a dramatic about face and, like Julia Roberts in Runaway Bride, run screaming from the altar. Or maybe Katherine Ross in The Graduate is a better role model; although she runs into the arms of another man (boring) she doesn't run into a different marriage, or at least not in the life span of the film.

But, post-Supreme Court gay-marriage bonanza, it's getting harder and harder to live the "alternative" in alternative lifestyle. One by one, non-marrying friends are dropping like flies. Queer Nation types who once marched down the streets proclaiming, "we're here, we're queer, get used to it" are now saying "I do" at alarming rates. And we're talking here about card-carrying feminists; die-hard dykes with dutifully unshaven legs and righteous rage against the patriarchy. When those sisters tie the knot you begin to realize that resistance is futile. Even Lily Tomlin is thinking of getting married to her partner of 40+ years, Jane Wagner, although she assures us—in an interview with E!—that there will be "no rings, no bridal dresses," and instead that, "maybe we'll be dressed like chickens."

First there were the friends who weren't much of a surprise, kinda traditional gals and guys whose commitments to anything alternative were more akin to liking alt-rock radio than embracing queer family values. I may have cringed when they talked of "proposals" and "engagement parties" but their desire to wear the white and join the married masses was no real surprise to me, although I was a bit perturbed that some have given up their own names, a fine patriarchal tradition if ever there was one! Then there were those whose weddings I only found out about on Facebook. These friends knew my political persuasions (which I thought they shared!) and wanted to avoid my snide remarks and vitriolic mockery. How rude of them!

To add insult to injury, I now see a bumper crop of marriage lemmings emerging. These new converts were—not so long ago—part of the small but hardy band of queers critical of the overweening focus on marriage, for reasons ranging from resource allocation (what happens to those queer youth centers if all our money goes to marriage initiatives?) to the more philosophical (why should social benefits come only through commitments to one particular form of intimacy? And what about the sexist and racist history of the institution of marriage?). Many of those critics have jumped ship too, like one high-profile lesbian couple I know who simply felt, after decades of devotion to each other, that it was "time," or the gay dudes—longtime radical activists—who apologetically invited me to their wedding, with a mumbled claim

Walters, Susanna Danuta "The Trouble with Tolerance." *Contexts* 13, no. 2 (2014): 87–90.

that "our parents just wanted this sooo much." But when my best friend Annie—valiant midwife, she of the unshaven bravado and unshakeable feminist faith—murmured that she too might be marrying her partner of 25 years, I was stunned. "You have," I declared, "put a knife through my feminist heart." To which she responded (after the obligatory eye roll), "Please. I am disgusted with myself. I so don't want to do this!" So why do it?

BENEFITS FOR ALL

Annie has one word for me: money. The lure of pension benefits and Social Security and joint tax returns has flipped even the most resolutely nonmarital and made it hard to just say no. For years, Annie's partner has been on her health plan and she's been taxed on it, an amount in the thousands. Add to that all the other aforementioned monetary perks and the reality of marriage as a financial and governmental institution is quickly revealed. One couple, about ten years older than me and seemingly just as unlikely to jump on the marriage bandwagon, shook their heads and said, "We did the math. Fifty grand more just in retirement benefits and much more down the pike." Surely many embrace the romantic storyline of love and marriage that permeates our media culture, but one of the things same-sex marriage reveals is the monetized core hiding in plain sight. As we sociologists are wont to repeat (endlessly and pedantically), a phenomenon is no less experienced or lived or felt if it is socially constructed. The heart wants what it wants, even as we recognize that wanting marriage per se is less a product of the heart than of a culture that has consistently sold and marketed it as sign of maturity, a marker of commitment, and a testament to the values of family, faith, and country.

The time is past to laboriously review the objections to the marriage mania, at least to a smart academic audience who should support the civil right, but be critical of both the normative familialism (see, we look just like those regular families!) and the hierarchical framing (marriage as the route to acceptance and as that form of socially and legally benefited public intimacy) that underlie the seemingly benign equality impetus. Feminists and queer scholars and activists have been writing about this—eloquently— for years. If you still think that marriage rights are an unalloyed mitzvah you need to wake up and smell the acrid stink of heteronormativity.

But as a topic for mass popular consumption, same-sex marriage couldn't be sexier and safer at the same time; it mixes up religion, the state, kids, and romance in a way that links love and legitimacy. More to the point, same-sex marriage is easy for liberal straight allies (who yearn to be "accepting") to glom on to; supporting gay marriage proves how über-tolerant one is but cannily avoids getting caught up in the messiness of queer difference, queer sex, and queer liberation. The gauzily iconic image of the wedding can replace the debased image of the (take your pick) gay bar/drag ball/dykes on bikes and is a win-win: gays get their marriage, and straights get their feel-good pat on the back. Same-sex marriage can be easily analogized to the repeal of miscegenation laws and can be framed in the language of love. It is, therefore, a media-friendly issue tailor-made for straight support. Let's face it: liberals love same-sex marriage. As blogger George Berkin puts it, "supporting gay marriage is fashionable."

THE TOLERANCE TRAP

But marriage rights are the bait that lures us into the tolerance trap. Support for same-sex marriage is a popular and safe demonstration of heterosexual goodwill and alliance; in this formula, rights are equated with access to marriage and the tolerant society grants it in exchange for quiescence on more troublesome exclusions.

And what, you may ask, is wrong with tolerance as our goal? Really, who doesn't applaud tolerance? What individual doesn't want to be seen as tolerant? It seems to herald openness to difference and a generally broad-minded disposition. Indeed, one of the primary definitions of "tolerance" concerns sympathy or indulgence for beliefs or practices differing from or conflicting with one's own. But it is a word and a practice with a more complicated history and with real limitations. The late Middle English origins of the word indicate the ability to bear pain and hardship. In fact, some of the first uses of the word can be found in medieval pharmacology and toxicology, dealing with how much poison a body can "tolerate" before it succumbs to a foreign, poisonous substance.

In more contemporary times, we speak of a tolerance to something as the capacity to endure continued subjection to it (a plant, a drug, a minority group) without adverse reactions. We speak of people who have a high tolerance for pain or worry about a generation developing a tolerance for a certain type of antibiotic because of overuse. In more scientific usages, it refers to the allowable amount of variation of a specified quantity—the amount "let in" before the thing itself alters so fundamentally that it becomes something else and the experiment fails. So tolerance almost always implies or assumes something negative or undesired or even a variation contained and circumscribed.

To tolerate something indicates that we think that it's wrong in some way. To say you "tolerate" homosexuality is to imply that homosexuality is bad or immoral or even just benignly icky. You are willing to put up with (to tolerate) this nastiness, but the toleration proves the thing (the person, the sexuality, the food) to be irredeemably nasty to begin with. Alternatively, if there is nothing problematic about something (say, homosexuality), then there is really nothing to "tolerate." We don't speak of tolerating a good book or a sunshine-filled day. We do, however, take pains to let others know how brave we are when we tolerate the discomfort of a bad back or a nasty cold. We tolerate the agony of a frustratingly banal movie that our partner insisted on watching and get points for our endurance. We tolerate, in other words, that which we would rather avoid. Tolerance is not an embrace but a resigned shrug or, worse, that air kiss of faux familiarity that barely covers up the shiver of disgust.

One of the central arguments of straight supporters of gay marriage reveals this tolerance motif at work. "How," they ask with righteous moral authority, "does Jim marrying Bob in any way challenge or undermine my wedded bliss with my wife?" And here's the conundrum: if it doesn't challenge your life, it's not very radical, and if it does challenge your life, we won't get it. Politically, gay rights advocates argue that this is a cut-and-dried (albeit difficult to achieve) civil rights issue, analogous to ending miscegenation laws years earlier. But they typically amend the civil rights push with a more personal insistence that gay marriage won't hurt or change or alter "your" marriage a bit. Worse, gay-marriage advocates can't seem to avoid the language of "just like you."

Activist leaders claim that we are just as capable of making committed relationships as "you" are and that our marriages are no different. The upshot of all this tolerance and sameness?: we ask nothing of you. There's the catch. Marriage as a right is a trap, at the heart of the misguided tolerance project. As sociologist Joe Rollins remarks, "Proponents minimize the imagined differences between gay and straight couples, opponents are striving to render an image of same-sex marriage as a cultural and political monstrosity, and the critically inclined worry that we are making a Faustian bargain." As long as marriage rights are framed as the pinnacle of gay liberation and, simultaneously, pose no challenge to hetero business as usual, then the jaws of the tolerance trap will have snapped shut, keeping out the more transformative possibilities. The overweening emphasis on this—not just as an obvious civil right, but as the sign of gay inclusion—is a contraction of the expansive potential of sexual freedom imagined by earlier activists. The shift to a rhetoric of "marriage equality," rather than "same-sex" or "gay" marriage, indicates a desire to take the messiness of sex out of the picture, to remove the specter of homosex from the hominess of marriage. Just as the main pro-gay-marriage organization has the bland name "Human Rights Campaign," effectively nullifying the specificity of queerness in the very title, so too does "marriage equality" implicitly de-queer our inclusion in that institution, making heterosexual unions the default point of comparison.

We must dethrone the reigning image of gay marriage as the civil rights achievement that will signal the death knell of homophobia and discrimination. For no other minority group do we imagine this: do we think misogyny has been vanquished now that legal gender discrimination is a thing of the past? Do we think anti-Semitism is gone because Jews no longer must wear the yellow star? Has the integration of women into the labor force eradicated sexism? Has the election of a black president and the end of legal segregation slain the scourge of racism?

An expansive and robust future of sexual and gender freedom can't be imagined when tolerance is the objective, marriage is the pinnacle, and sameness is the road most traveled. And that future is most assuredly further out of reach when we foolishly buy into the progress narrative that claims a "postgay" homo friendliness that just isn't there. The dominant frameworks we are working with today—acceptance, tolerance, sameness—may get us some traction but inevitably fall short or even actively undermine the potential for deeper challenges. Advocating for a tolerant society is like marrying your best friend: comforting but just not sexy. Let's hold out for the sexy.

16

"Women's Work"? Women Partners of Transgender Men Doing Housework and Emotion Work

Carla A. Pfeffer

This study responds to an existing gap in the sociology of families literature, in the context of increasing trans visibility and media representation, with regard to women's experiences in transgender family life. In this study, I address the following primary research question: What do narratives from women partners of trans men, on the performance, structure, and division of household labor and emotion work within their relationships, reveal about "doing gender" and "women's work" within contemporary families? This research builds on existing sociological literature on families to consider how emotion work may be a useful conceptual framework for understanding the particular forms of labor in which some women partners of trans men engage in the context of their relationships. Learning more about the everyday experiences of women partners of trans men holds the potential to expand not only how sociologists of the family understand and theorize about the work members of this minority group perform within their relationships, families, and communities but also the myriad understudied ways the work of *women, in general,* constructs and contributes to family life in the twenty-first century.

BACKGROUND

Notes on Language, Concepts, and Terminology

For the purposes of this study, "sex" is constituted by a perceived or actual convergence of hormonal, chromosomal, and anatomical factors that lead to a person's classification, usually at birth, as "male," "female," or "intersex." "Gender" can be understood as the vast array of social and cultural constructions (involving bodily comportment, manner of dress, social roles) that adhere to individuals once they have been assigned to a particular sex category (thus marking an individual as a "girl," "boy," "woman," or "man"). "Gender identity" is a concept that refers to one's subjective sense of being a boy, girl, man, woman, or some combination thereof. "Gender expression" refers to one's social presentation of gender in everyday life (through dress, bodily comportment, vocal expressions, etc.). Gender expression may also shift across social contexts depending on perceived safety and risks. To "transition" is to bring one's gender expression into closer alignment with one's gender identity. Transition may involve changes in

Pfeffer, Carla A. "'Women's Work'? Women Partners of Transgender Men Doing Housework and Emotion Work." *Journal of Marriage and Family* 72, no. 1 (2010): 165–183.

one's style of dress, hair, body comportment, pronoun or name use, legal sex or gender status, social roles, hormones (taking testosterone; "t"), or physical anatomy (e.g. bilateral radical mastectomy with chest wall recontouring or reduction mammoplasty ["top surgeries"] and hysterectomy, oopherectomy, metaoidioplasty, or phalloplasty ["bottom surgeries"]).

"Transgender" and "genderqueer" are umbrella terms for those whose gender identity or expression, or both, does not normatively align with their assigned sex. "Transsexual" (a particular type of transgender identity or embodiment) describes individuals who make surgical or hormonal changes, or both, to their body in order to bring it into closer correspondence with their gender identity. "Trans" is an abbreviated term that refers to "transgender" or "transsexual" or both. Individuals designated "female" at birth who come to gender identify as a man or on the masculine spectrum are referred to as "female-to-male" ("FTM") or "trans men." It is critical to distinguish between "gender identity" and "sexual identity"—all people have *both*. For example, some trans men self-identify as heterosexual (and partner with trans or non-trans women, or both), whereas others self-identify as gay (and partner with trans or non-trans men, or both), bisexual, or "queer" (those whose sexual identity cannot be neatly classified as heterosexual, gay, or bisexual).

Household Labor in (Non-Trans) Heterosexual and Lesbian Relationships

For over 30 years, sociologists have made great strides in documenting and theorizing unpaid household labor performed by women within (non-trans) heterosexual families. Despite continuing rises in the numbers of women working outside the home for pay, concomitant with supportive social attitudes for women's equality (among men and women), women still report experiencing "the second shift" at home. Despite increasingly liberal gender-role attitudes, heterosexual women continue to perform the bulk of household labor across both cohabiting and marital contexts. Even more surprising, some research demonstrates that men actually perform *less* household labor once married than when cohabiting with their women partners or when earning less income than their women partners.

One of the most lasting lessons from Hochschild's (1989) study was that men and women who are ideologically committed to egalitarian relationships co-construct elaborate "gender strategies" and "family myths," describing the division of housework as equal although women actually perform the majority of this labor. Rather than assailing women with claims of "false consciousness" regarding incommensurability between one's feminist self-understanding and participation in traditional, inegalitarian, sex-typed divisions of household labor and emotion work, this work demonstrates the complexity and function of family myths and gender strategies. These family myths and gender strategies serve important personal and social functions, as they allow individuals and couples to retain and preserve deeply held commitments to egalitarianism and keep relationships and families intact.

Increasingly, sociologists are studying *sexual minority women's* patterns and processes of cohabitation, partnership, and family work. Survey research often reports that household division of labor among cohabiting lesbian couples is relatively egalitarian. Some ethnographic qualitative research, however, has suggested that the issue is actually more complex. It may also be possible that notions of what constitutes an "egalitarian relationship" are shifting and multiple. Just as research demonstrates that household labor among (non-trans) heterosexual couples is often divided along gendered dimensions, we might expect that, even among (non-trans) "same-sex" partners, tasks might still be differentially allocated based upon differences in gender identity or expression between partners.

Emotion Work in (Non-Trans) Heterosexual and Lesbian Relationships

The concept of emotion work was first introduced 30 years ago (Hochschild, 1979). The contribution of this concept to earlier sociological thought was that emotion functions not only in highly personal and psychological ways, but is also determined by and through social rules, negotiation, and regulation. Researchers have proposed that emotion work is a critical component of family work and marital satisfaction among (non-trans) heterosexual couples, mediating against feelings of marital burnout—particularly when such work is also performed by men. Research on emotion work enabled sociologists to better understand how social actors engage in active management of their own and others' emotions and how this work is gendered in particular, predictable ways.

For example, the knowledge of family members' tastes and preferences is a form of (primarily) women's work that treads a thin line between instrumental household labor (such as shopping and cooking) and emotion work (such as keeping family members happy, satisfied, and feeling cared for). Even among same-sex couples, one partner tends to know tastes and preferences of another to a greater extent; this knowledge is generally associated with the partner who most often cooks and shops for the family. Researchers also proposed that, contrary to most sociological work that posits *sex* as the primary determinant of who engages in emotion work within relationships, *gender constructions* and *gender ideologies* may actually be better predictors. Conceptualizing emotion work in this way allows us to predict that women partners of trans men may be expected to perform greater or lesser amounts of emotion work than their trans partners on the basis of the way each partner's *gender* is constructed individually and interpersonally, rather than assuming an egalitarian division based on *sex*. As such, we should not necessarily expect to find egalitarian divisions of household labor and emotion work among "same-sex" couples whose *gender identities* are quite dissimilar.

Method

Methodological Approach and Interview Protocol

To get a sense of women's perceptions of division of household labor within their relationships, I asked cohabiting interviewees to tell me who has primary responsibility for a list of specific tasks (e.g. cooking, writing grocery lists, knowing a partner's tastes and preferences, fixing things around the house, garbage and recycling, shopping for and sending birthday and holiday presents, decorating, scheduling and attending doctor appointments, child care, elder care, pet care, lawn care, auto care, and driving). I also asked each participant the following questions: Can you tell me your feelings about how the household labor is divided between you and your partner overall? Has the division of household labor ever been a source of conflict and/or resentment in your relationship? (If "yes"): Can you tell me what happened and how you handled it? (If "no"): Why do you think you and your partner have never had conflict or resentment over the division of household labor?

Recruitment

Eligible participants included both current and former women partners of trans men who had been in a relationship with a trans man for at least three months. Three months was chosen as a minimum cutoff point for participation because I wished to gather data on perceived relationship dynamics from individuals across as wide a swath of relationship durations as possible, from those in the early stages of relationship development to those in long-term relationships. I sought to interview both trans and non-trans women as participants and all recruitment materials contained the recruitment phrase, "self-identified women partners." I sought to interview women partnered with trans men at various stages of trans identification and transition, from those who self-identify as "genderqueer," with no intention of taking testosterone or obtaining sexual-reassignment surgeries, to those who identify and are legally recognized as "male," who are taking testosterone and have had sexual-reassignment surgeries.

Participant Sample

The 50 participants in this sample provided detailed information on 61 individual relationships with trans men. Most participants (n = 42) were currently in a relationship with a trans man, whereas a minority (n = 8) were reporting on a former relationship (or relationships) and were not currently in a relationship with a trans man. Of those not currently in a relationship with a trans man, the median time elapsed since termination of the relationship was just under four years. Across all reported relationships, relationship duration averaged 2.2 years with a range from 3 months to 11 years at the time of the interview.

Of the 61 reported relationships, more than half (n = 38) were cohabiting, with an average cohabiting duration of 1.5 years. Several participants (n = 4) were in legally recognized, opposite-sex marriages (all in the United States) with their partner, and several others (n = 4) were engaged to be legally married and one participant was in a legally recognized same-sex marriage (in Canada). A few (n = 2) participants were actively engaged in raising children in the home with their partner and several others (n = 4) reported formerly raising children or involvement with raising children who did not live with the couple. Interview length averaged 103 minutes and ranged from 47 to 150 minutes.

Participants include women from 13 states across the United States and three Canadian provinces. The women in this study self-identified as "queer" (50 percent), "lesbian" or "dyke" (22 percent), "bisexual" (14 percent), "bisexual/queer" (4 percent), "heterosexual" (4 percent), "undefined" or "unsure" (4 percent), and "pansexual/omnisexual" (2 percent). According to the women I interviewed, their trans partners identified as "queer" (48 percent), "heterosexual" (34 percent), "heterosexual but bicurious" (8 percent), "bisexual" (8 percent), and "gay" (2 percent). Approximately 30 percent of participants were in a lesbian-identified relationship with their partner prior to his transition. None of the participants I interviewed considered their relationship with a trans partner "lesbian" once their partner began the transition process. In terms of gender identity, 30 percent of the women I interviewed self-identified as "femme." Trans partners were said to gender identify as "a man" (59 percent) or as "a trans man or genderqueer" (41 percent). In terms of feminist identity, 93 percent of the women I interviewed self-identify as "feminist" and 77 percent responded that their partner also identifies as "feminist." Despite aiming for a racially diverse sample, this sample reflects greater variation on age of participants (29 years on average with a range from 18 to 51 years) than on race or ethnicity. Participants in this study are largely White (n = 45), with non-White participants self-identifying as multiracial (n = 3), Black (n = 1), and Latina (n = 1). The sample does reflect somewhat greater variation in race or ethnicity when considering race or ethnicity of trans partners of participants (e.g. 19 percent were identified as "multiracial").

Participants reported higher than average levels of education (59 percent have at least a Bachelor's degree and 26 percent have a postgraduate degree), but household incomes were well below the national average (nearly 80 percent made $50,000 or less in combined annual household income with nearly 40 percent reporting less than $25,000 in combined annual household income). The trans men partners of the women participants were slightly younger than participants (27 years of age, on average) and, like the participants, were highly educated (though less so than their women partners), with 49 percent holding a Bachelor's degree or higher and 13 percent holding postgraduate degrees. Trans men partners of the women I interviewed were at various stages of sex or gender transition or both, with most being just a bit over two years into the process. Most were taking testosterone (69 percent), a considerable minority had had top surgery (38 percent), and a very slim minority had had bottom surgery of any kind (7 percent). Likely because (in large part) of testosterone, the majority (63 percent) of trans men partners of participants reportedly are "always or almost always" "read" in social contexts as male. Approximately 80 percent of women were involved with their trans partner's hormonal or surgical transition process, or both, over the course of their relationship.

RESULTS

"It's Not Because of Gender Issues for Us": Women Doing and Explaining Household Labor

Most participants in my sample (93 percent) and their trans men partners (77 percent) were feminist. As documented in the previous literature review, one of the primary contributions of feminist social research, over the past 30 years, has been to document striking inequalities in division of household labor between men and women. The feminist women I interviewed were not immune to these same social trends, often reporting inegalitarian, gender-stereotyped divisions of household labor between themselves and their trans men partners. Despite strong feminist selfidentification, the family myths and gender strategies that participants generated to explain these inconsistencies most often focused on individual choice and preference rather than systemic and structural gender inequalities.

Women frequently spoke about inegalitarian division of household labor, but rationalized the reasons for this division. Ani stated: "I do the dishes; but I'm so neurotic about having a clean house and he is not.... I definitely do more than he does but, again, I'm the one that happens to be a neat freak." Linda offered a similar description, echoing the direct reference to personal preferences, rendering the pattern more idiosyncratic or personal rather than a reflection of traditional gender roles:

> I think I would play a little bit more of an active role in laundry because it's one of those things that I have to have my way. Like if he was doing it, for example, everything just gets tossed in, whereas I have to do it my special way.

Lilia discussed some of the ways she experiences gender in relation to her partner and to household work:

> I feel very female when I'm cleaning up his room. He doesn't ask me to clean up his room, he's just very messy. So I clean up on my own free will and try and take care of him, which, sometimes he'll *let* [my emphasis] me do... It makes me feel very female.

Several women went to some lengths to assure their partners (and me) that choices they made were based *not* on gender stereotyping or roles, but on autonomous personal decisions. Veronica told me:

> I've been working full-time for a couple years now. My musical career has gone by the wayside because of that. So, for me, my own personality, I think I would be happier being at home, making a home, being able to work on my own, being able to practice and have that sort of freedom. And we were discussing it a lot and I made it very clear that if I do adopt those traditional roles, it's not because of gender issues for us, it's just because the nature of our own sort of goals and just the nature our own selves.

Linda echoed some of this same sentiment:

> I would say he's definitely more of an outdoors person than I am. Like I don't know how to drive a car, I don't have my driver's license where he's driven cars from a young age. He fixes the car outside. He's the one who scoops up the dog poo. He putters around in the garden. I cook a little bit more than he would though I don't think we do things like that because we feel we have to but that's just what our personal interests are.

Kendra offered another individualist explanation for what some may see as gendered roles:

> I'm the one who's always cooking, and I'm definitely more of a nurturer.... I could see how someone from the outside could say we have very gendered roles in our relationship, but I don't know that they're really that gendered. He's definitely going to be the bread winner, but that's because he's going to get his doctorate and I really have no desire to.... But I don't feel bad about it because he likes to do it.

These statements reflected a general unwillingness—or, in some cases, outright refusal—to link women's personal preferences, at least in the area of household labor, to women's gender roles or socialization. In the quotes above, interviewees either never discussed gender or gender roles or expressly rejected any connection between inegalitarian division of labor within their homes and women's traditional gender-role socialization. These quotes revealed a conceptual disjuncture of the personal from political, as they suggested traditional division of household labor was a rather unremarkable matter of individual free will outside the realm of gender-role socialization and imperatives. Women's narratives on the division of household labor in their families also did gender as they reflected predominant cultural scripts for men and women dividing household labor in accordance with seemingly "natural" tastes and preferences.

"Boy Energy": The Emotion Work of Managing Gendered Roles and Communication

Emotion work often involves not only managing one's own emotions, but the emotions of others as well. The women I interviewed often detailed elaborate routines of attending to (and being accountable for) both the mundane and extraordinary organization of the details of their partners' personal and emotional lives in ways that revealed traditionally gendered roles. For women with deep commitments to feminism, enactment of traditionally gendered roles within a relationship can be conceptualized as yet another form of emotion work that can result in personal and interpersonal stress and strain.

Michele offered one of the clearest examples of a woman partner's investment of physical, psychological, and emotion work for a trans partner's primary benefit. When I asked Michele about how much of her life, would she say, is comprised of taking care of her partner and issues related to his transition, she replied:

> A lot. I would say, percentage wise—and this is something I've been trying to change because I see it being a problem—I would say about 70% of my life. That's scaled back from what it was—which was, like, 80%.

When I asked Michele to reflect on what this has meant for her in her own life, she stated:

> I provide an enormous amount of support around maintaining the household, doing domestic tasks. I have assimilated massive amounts of [my partner's] own work—school work—to assist him in completely his work. [This is in addition to] a huge amount of emotional time spent in processing transitioning, family, frustrations around the transition process, ... a huge amount of work. I'm supposed to be writing a dissertation.... My own work has been very neglected .... I put it off since [my partner] started transitioning.

In this example, Michele described an emotional process of neglecting and postponing her own personal and educational goals and work in order to assist her partner in completing his, serving almost as a proxy or personal assistant during her partner's transition. Nina discussed her own involvement with organizing and managing both the mundane details of her partner's everyday life and his emotional lability:

> I remind him to do a lot, and am the planner and really sort of controlling about a lot of things. He is the one who is super flaky and forgetful .... His mood changes every 30 minutes. So the dynamic is me trying to keep on the ball about things and him assuming that I'm going to take care of it. Then, him not being on the ball about a lot of things and me assuming he's not going to take care of it.

Nina described this process as an exhausting, dynamic cycle.

When describing taking primary responsibility for organizing tasks and responsibilities, many participants' accounts portrayed these behaviors as a matter of personal style or a reflection of roles that were intrinsic or natural. For example, Charlene told me:

> I sort of call myself the secretary because he has trouble keeping that sort of stuff straight. It's a personality-type thing—I'm very organized-sort-of-minded. One thing that he remarks is that I make lists all the time and he is more scattered that way. So I tend to keep track of that stuff.

Robyn discussed the discrepancy between her and her partner's involvement in one another's lives:

> I guess that's, like, one of the female roles I take as his partner—someone who will always support him. I'm helping him do his trans stuff and he doesn't really look at the stuff .... He doesn't participate with my stuff so much—which kind of falls into the .... me-being-the-one-to-come-to-him a lot of the time [pattern]. Not that he doesn't always express appreciation for that, but it's the way things happen.

Robyn's description revealed a relatively unidirectional investment of emotional resources that she clearly understood as a gendered aspect of her relationship with her partner and one in which she (as the one occupying the "female role") got the short end of the stick.

Managing differences in communication styles and facilitating emotional expression between partners emerged as other examples of women's emotion work and clear manifestations of how gender is done within their relationships. Veronica stated:

> I think that we're pretty much egalitarian. I think that … I'm probably more of the one who gets us to talk about things. So I kind of have to be the provoker…. I have to be the one who gets him to say things. I kind of have to egg him on a little. I think that I help him be more expressive and he helps me to calm down my brain.

Anna described a similar pattern:

> I think he compartmentalizes. So he just doesn't like to talk about things. And not because they're things related to gender, but just like, "I don't like to process," kind of issues. I think about a whole huge range of issues. You know—his surgery coming up. I asked him, "Are you nervous?" He doesn't wanna talk about whether he's nervous. And his reaction is not just, "Oh honey, darling, I don't feel like talking about that," but kind of snappish like, [in a very annoyed voice] "Uggh, I told you already I don't want to talk about that." So yeah it feels like there's a whole huge universe of things that are off limits.

Lilia discussed some of the ways she felt her trans partner manifested what many might describe as male privilege:

> He's very forgetful and he doesn't take care of himself and he's messy and all this other stuff…. I feel like he's very specifically like a boy in this way. Like, this boy energy—being messy, not neat, being clumsy with my feelings sometimes.

Charlene, Robyn, Veronica, Anna, and Lilia all explicitly linked behaviors such as messiness, carelessness with others' feelings, not being able to "process" or discuss important issues, and lack of self-care to male gender roles and to their trans partners. They each discussed the extra emotion work and household labor in which they engage in order to draw their partners out or to care for them. These narratives were strikingly similar to those offered by women partners of non-trans men, extending theoretical contributions that doing gender is a social rather than biological process.

"You Have Bleeding, Oozing Stuff!": Women Doing Medical or Health Care Emotion Work

Although the women I interviewed discussed engaging in a wide range of emotion work within their relationships, one of the most compelling, frequent, and sociologically relevant activities they discussed was the provision of both basic and complex medical or health advocacy and care. Although women whose partner transitioned over the course of their relationship reported providing the most transition-related support for their partners, women whose partner had largely completed his transition prior to the start of the relationship still reported providing a great deal of transition-related support (in the form of emotional support, advocacy, bimonthly testosterone injection administration, etc.). Indeed, transition should be considered an iterative, relational, and lifelong process. The women I interviewed revealed their multiple roles as personal advocate, mediator, and emotional supporter for their partners, especially in terms of dealing with a partner's medical and health needs. Samantha stated:

> I've always been very active in his medical care. I've always known when his doctor's appointments are, known what they're for, made sure he's gone to them, found doctors in the area. I think it's sometimes hard for him to deal with the actual bureaucracy of things. I think I'm a lot better dealing with it.

Samantha continued by describing an encounter her partner had with an inept medical practitioner:

> [His doctor] was a recommendation from his pediatrician…. She sort of blew off his gender, … didn't acknowledge it. As soon as he told her that he was trans, she wouldn't look him in the eye and he just

felt like she rushed through his exam and did everything she could to not be around him. So he came out of it crying. He was really upset.... I'm very proactive ... and so I was ready to call the office and speak to somebody about it and educate them on their trans issues .... But he was like, "No, no it's okay, it's okay." ... He was really depressed.... He was suicidal.

Samantha was not the only interviewee who described emotion work invested in trying to help a partner with depression or even suicidal ideation. These testimonies indicated the level of involvement some women had in providing emotional support to (and advocacy on behalf of) their trans partners, sometimes at times of great personal crisis. Women described serving as islands of support during times when trans men wished to have little outside contact because of privacy, job security, or personal safety considerations or a combination of these.

Women offered many stories about feelings connected to administering a trans partner's testosterone shots. Linda stated:

> The first time, I was terrified that I was going to hurt him more than anything. Really, really scared. I've never given anyone a needle in my entire life. Yeah, my main fear was that I was going to fuck it up really bad and hurt him or hit a nerve or something like that. But now it's fine.

Kendra also spoke about giving her partner testosterone injections:

> He kind of developed this fear of needles and so he couldn't inject it any more. So I've done it for quite some time now.... At first, I was really nervous about it. You know, if you do one thing wrong, you could kill him; but it's just routine for me now.

These comments revealed that (at least in the beginning) administering testosterone injections could be events imbued with anxiety about one's own adequacy as well as fears of hurting, potentially seriously, one's partner. These quotes also revealed how performing medical care for a trans partner became a routinized aspect of everyday life. Interviewees discussed that their involvement with their trans partner's medical care sometimes extended far beyond the administration of testosterone injections.

Some of the most evocative and compelling aspects of women's narratives focused on their partners' surgical transitions. Interestingly, many of these narratives highlighted trans *partner's* experiences, despite me specifically asking women to reflect on *their own* impressions of the transition process, providing detailed descriptions of their *personal* involvement throughout. Samantha replied:

> Right now, we're trying to find a doctor in the area and we're looking at pictures of their results. And we're also trying to figure out how on earth to pay for it. We're basically in the beginning stages of it.... It was a decision that I already decided a long time ago that I would definitely help him pay for it.

Samantha's use of the collective "we" and "we're" at numerous points in her narrative reflected the degree to which she felt involved with her partner's transition on multiple levels—including economic. Samantha's narrative was one of many illustrating how tentative and artificial divides between intimacy and economics can be within families. Although some women reported discussions and negotiations with partners regarding details connected to transition surgeries, this was not always true.

Teresa discussed her sadness and frustration in connection to being left out of most of her partner's surgical transition decisions:

> In trans community, it's the idea that I will support my partner and will do cartwheels whenever he decides to [physically alter] his body and that I'll be really happy about it. Whereas, really, when my partner had chest surgery ... [the] process for me [was] that a body I had always known changed. I think it's important to let partners have that grief. I don't feel like I was given space to really feel things that I was feeling because there was this expectation that I just was going to support it wholeheartedly. That was really hard.

Kendra described her feelings about her partner's impending surgery:

> I was really concerned ... that he would need someone to help him with a lot of things after
> surgery.... I was just like, "If you're expecting me to help you with this—which I'm more than
> willing to do—then you need to help me help you. I need to know these things so I can help you."
> And so that was frustrating.

These comments revealed that some women were concerned about their trans partner's surgical transitions
in terms of the support *they* would be *personally* expected to provide. Women also expressed fears or concerns
about their partner's risk of death during surgery, ways their partner's body might change and/or the
fact that they loved their partner's body as it was. Tiffany discussed emotions connected to her partner's
impending top surgery:

> It's kind of weird because you get so used to somebody's body being a certain way—especially
> somebody you're close to. You get to a point where you memorize every single part of their body.
> And so it's very difficult when something changes—especially that quickly.... It's something
> that's important for him to do; so by the time he gets it, I'll be ready for it and I'll be supportive.
> But I really wish he didn't have to.... Having that piece of him cut off and tossed away is very
> difficult.

Despite the numerous concerns women reported in being excluded from surgical decision-making
processes, considering possible negative surgical outcomes, and mourning the loss of a partner's
familiar and beloved body, women still described enormous personal involvement with partners'
surgeries and postoperative care. Willow told me: "Oh God. It was like being an advocate for him,
getting him food, helping him with the pain stuff, helping him get dressed, keeping him company, just
being there, helping him sit up, helping him walk to the bathroom." Gail offered a particularly visceral
recollection:

> I remember it [top surgery recovery] being totally intense. It's like blood—and the smell was
> so intense—and that was the first time I was like, "Whoa—you have bleeding, oozing stuff!"
> And just feeling kind of like you're just kids taking care of each other. You're twenty-four [years
> old] and it's weird because you have no nurse or anyone telling you what to do.... It's so major.
> Someone just cut their body, had it reconstructed.... I didn't feel confident in it [taking care of her
> partner] .... I get kind of queasy and stuff and I remember the smell being really intense.... We
> were basically locked up in this room for three days.... I felt really disconnected from the outside
> world.

In this not uncommon example, an interviewee described involvement in postsurgical caretaking for
what is generally considered major (yet outpatient) surgery. This caretaking may take mental, physical,
and emotional tolls. Further, the pain and helplessness some trans men experienced after surgery were
sometimes taken out, in frustration, on their weary partner. Veronica said: "The person who is going through
the medical transition is really wrapped up in their own issues. And the person who is giving the support
feels neglected."

The women partners of trans men that I interviewed played critical roles in their partners' continuing
journeys from female-to-male identity, embodiment, and social status. Interviewees discussed extensive
involvement in processes of sex and gender transition; they served informally (and sometimes at great
personal cost) as personal assistants, medical aides, and advocates on a partners' behalf. Women described
these ways of doing gender and relationships as simultaneously exhausting, rewarding, challenging,
unprecedented, and transformative. Feelings of nervousness or worry in connection with a partner's
transition were reported almost universally across participants whose partner underwent hormonal
or surgical transition, or both, over the course of their relationship. Axial coding revealed that, among
participants whose partners largely completed their transition prior to the beginning of their relationship,
60 percent reported ongoing transition-related anxiety.

DISCUSSION

Feminist Self-Identified Women Doing and Explaining Household Labor and Emotion Work

In accordance with previous sociological research, women partners' explanations for inegalitarian divisions of household labor and emotion work might best be understood as instances of family myths or gender strategies that allow them to continue functioning within particular roles and relationships with relatively little reported discord or threat to their identities as feminist or nontraditional or both (Hochschild, 1989). What was less expected, however, was that these feminist-identified interviewees employed a distinct type of family myth or gender strategy predicated on ideals of individualism, free will, and choice. Further, participants whose relationships with their partner initially began as lesbian and those who went through a hormonal or surgical transition process, or both, with their partner over the course of their relationship were more likely to offer these individualist, choice-based, and free will explanations than those whose partner's hormonal or surgical transition was largely completed prior to the start of their relationship.

According to Scott and Lyman (1968), individuals manufacture socially accepted verbal "accounts" to explain socially unacceptable behaviors to others. These accounts arise in two primary forms, either as "excuses" or "justifications," intended to neutralize social judgments of stigmatized or unexpected behaviors. In excuses, social actors admit that they have engaged in behavior that might be negative or unexpected, but they excuse this behavior by denying full culpability. One excuses such behavior by explaining the ways in which this behavior was not under his or her direct control. In justifications, one admits he or she has engaged in behavior that might be negative or unexpected, but justifies this behavior by verbally minimizing the seriousness of the perceived transgression. In the context of women's accounts for stereotypically gendered inegalitarian divisions of household labor and emotion work (when speaking with someone presumed to hold negative valuations of such behaviors—the interviewer), justifications were most frequently invoked by study participants. More specifically, the women in my study employed the use of "self-fulfillment justifications" (Scott & Lyman, 1968, p. 52), in which they simultaneously *acknowledged* inequities in the division of household labor and emotion work in their relationships and *neutralized* the negative social stigma associated with such inequities by focusing on assertions of their own free will, personal power, performativity, and choice to act in such ways. Of important sociological consideration, these verbal justifications function to absolve social actors and behaviors from potential social critique.

As demonstrated through these analyses, gender and gendered identities are relational, social accomplishments arising from iterative, interactive practices of doing gender. The women partners of trans men that I interviewed reported acting in critical ways to shape, support, reflect, and coproduce seemingly normative forms of masculinity and femininity in ways that deserve more focused sociological exploration and consideration. We must remain cautious, however, that we do not make overly simplistic or reductive assessments about these women participants and their relationships. Without readily available, socially sanctioned and supported models for how to do (trans)gender and trans partnerships in counter-normative ways, these couples are navigating relatively uncharted territories. Further, scholars and trans community members have noted that it is irresponsible to place a disproportionate burden on those who are trans-identified (and, by extension, their partners) for reforming the entire gendered social order. The women I interviewed are no more and no less responsible for (or necessarily desirous of) the maintenance or overthrow of the gendered social order within the family than those whose lives have been more fully studied and documented by sociologists of the family over the past 30 years.

Women Doing Medical or Health Care Emotion Work in the Context of Managed Care

A growing body of literature in the medical sociology subfield documents women's increasing involvement as unpaid, untrained, amateur nurses for aging or ailing nuclear or extended family members. In many instances, women are called on to provide care for family members' chronic and acute health conditions or crises. Results from the present study expand this scholarship by introducing a previously unexamined population: women serving as a trans partner's unpaid and untrained personal medical and health care advocate, therapist, assistant, and nurse.

Results from the present study are unique insofar as they focus on performance of medical and health-care-based emotion work within families whose members (both care providers and recipients) are relatively younger than those reported in the medical and health care "work transfer" literature. Furthermore, the medical and health care procedures (testosterone injections, top surgeries, and bottom surgeries) described herein are frequently considered elective and are not covered expenses under most medical insurance plans. This places enormous emotional and material burdens on trans families.

The experience of assisting a partner with transition-related medical and health care was one shared by 80 percent of study participants. The tasks to which women reported attending included researching trans-friendly health care providers; scheduling and attending a trans partner's medical appointments; advocating on behalf of one's trans partner in the instance of encountering inept health care practitioners; obtaining medical insurance and negotiating with medical insurance companies; saving, raising, and contributing funds for transition-related medical procedures not covered by insurance; juggling family disclosures about transition-related procedures; arranging for time off from work or school to provide medical and health care services; administering testosterone injections; and providing aftercare for major surgical procedures (e.g. changing dressings, administering pain medications, monitoring surgical sites for signs of infection and milking fluid drainage tubes from surgical sites, and measuring, tracking, and disposing of their outputs).

This study also documents the personal and emotional costs of "women's work" in providing unpaid, untrained medical and health care for a trans partner undergoing transition-related medical procedures. Women's reports of providing care are frequently tinged with feelings of anxiety, frustration, fear, and inadequacy. Study participants reported feeling alone, sad, disgusted, terrified, angry, exhausted, unsupported, neglected, confused, and unprepared. Furthermore, participants described how providing transition-related medical and health care and dealing with the attendant emotions (both one's own feelings and the feelings of a trans partner) can become a consuming process that draws time, energy, and focus away from other activities such as work, school, friends, family, and self-care. Given most of these participants were providing medical and health care for trans partners during developmental time periods critical to personal educational and career success (their 20s), implications of such emotional and material investments in another's medical and health care deserve greater sociological attention, consideration, and inquiry.

References

Hochschild, A. (1979). Emotion work, feeling rules, and social structure. *American Journal of Sociology, 85,* 551–575.
Hochschild, A. R. (1989). *The second shift: Working parents and the revolution at home.* New York: Viking.
Scott, M. B., & Lyman, S. M. (1968). Accounts. *American Sociological Review, 33,* 46–62.

SECTION IV
Separation and Divorce

INTRODUCTION

Divorce marks a legal process in which a couple recognized as family comes to be no longer related in law. Yet, as a social experience, divorce represents a great deal more. Divorce represents the end of a commitment, often embodies disappointment and anger, and frequently requires former spouses to continue to interact as co-parents. The reasons marriages end vary, but there are some patterns. For the past decades, researchers have identified infidelity, incompatibility, alcohol or drug use, growing apart, personality problems, lack of communication, and physical or mental abuse as the leading reasons cited for divorce (Amato and Previti 2003). Marriage is stressful and takes a toll on relationships, and in the ways to be discussed in the section on motherhood, parenting also takes a toll on couples. (The chapter by Matthew Johnson in this section examines this issue.) Divorce can also be stressful, even as couples aim for a "good divorce" or as celebrities Gwyneth Paltrow and Chris Martin touted, "conscious uncoupling."

We are all accustomed to hearing that half of all marriages will end in divorce. That statement is not entirely accurate. In reality, about 43 percent of all marriages that began from age 15–46 ended in divorce. However, the probability of divorce depends on a range of factors. The chance of a marriage ending in divorce goes down as education goes up. About half of all marriages between people who did not complete high school end in divorce, compared with about 30 percent of marriages among college graduates (Aughinbaugh, Robles and Sun 2013). Delaying marriage until one is older reduces the risk of divorce, which is also more common as people continue their education. These patterns do not vary much by race or ethnicity.

Much evidence suggests that younger cohorts are waiting longer to get married—and fewer are actually getting married. Thus, divorce rates are coming down and will likely continue to do so (Cohen 2019). The greatest increase in divorce has come from those over the age of 50 years, dubbed "gray divorce." By 2010, one in four people getting divorced were over 50, a huge increase from 1990, when that figure was closer to one in ten (Brown et al. 2019). Gray divorces are still relatively rare, about eight per 1,000 married persons, but that number doubles for those in a second marriage (16 per 1,000). Among all adults 50 and older who divorced in 2015, 48 percent were in their second or higher marriage at the time of divorce (Stepler 2017). The chapter by Tera Jordan explores some of these factors, including why there is a general decline in the number of divorces.

LEGAL PROCESSES

Laws dictating how divorce happens procedurally, to whom it is available, and under what conditions are set by state law and have changed over time. In 1970, California became the first state in the United States to allow people to divorce without having to show fault. Prior to the advent of no-fault divorce, individuals wanting to leave a marriage would have to prove that someone did something to cause the demise of the marriage. Typically, divorce proceedings included claims of cruelty, adultery, abandonment, lengthy incarceration, or inability to have sex (that was not disclosed before marriage). Some states allowed mental illness or drug abuse to also serve as grounds for divorce. Notably, not loving one's spouse, growing apart, or being unhappy were not acceptable reasons for divorce.

In these divorce proceedings, spouses would typically need to testify against each other to substantiate the claims of fault. Judges would then decide if the allegations were believable, who was to blame, and whether those faults were serious enough to grant divorce. There are voluminous historic accounts of couples who would stage infidelity to be discovered or documented by a private investigator or create stories to justify a mutually acceptable divorce. As one California judge described court hearings prior to passage of no-fault divorce:

> Every day, in every superior court in the state, the same melancholy charade was played: the "innocent" spouse, generally the wife, would take the stand and, to the accompanying cacophony of sobbing and nose-blowing, testify under the deft guidance of an attorney to the spousal conduct that she deemed "cruel."[1]

Recognizing the deceptions that were common in divorce proceedings, the California legislature passed a law creating no-fault divorce, which allowed couples to divorce for irreconcilable differences. Other states in subsequent years began adopting no-fault divorce laws. By 1977, nine states had such laws. By 1983, 48 states had some kind of law allowing for divorce without proving cause. Notably, different states have different requirements before a person can petition for divorce, including evidence of separate residences for a specified period of time or a ban on divorce if a woman is pregnant. New York was the last state to create a no-fault option, adding that to law in 2010.

Making divorce easier may reduce conflict. It may also allow individuals in violent or abusive relationships to more easily leave. However, no-fault divorce has its critics. Some worry that more people will get divorced if accessing a divorce is easy. In the first few years after the passage of no-fault laws, states did see an uptick in divorces. Those rates did come back down, suggesting there was pent-up demand to access a divorce.

Fearing that easy divorce would erode the value of marriage, three states in the late 1990s (Arizona, Arkansas, and Louisiana) created the option of covenant marriage. Individuals may select to enter a covenant marriage when they get married (though couples often can adopt it after they are married). Covenant marriages require a participant to prove fault in order to divorce, may mandate counseling before marriage and prior to separation, and make the process of divorcing more difficult. Covenant marriage is declining in popularity since its introduction in 1997; at its height, fewer than 1 percent of couples opted for it.

POST-DIVORCE SUPPORT

As a legal process, divorce provides separation of property and assets, agreements for child custody and visitation, and assignment of ongoing financial support through child support or alimony (spousal support). Identifying what is fair is challenging after divorce. Research for more than 40 years has demonstrated the women's income and standard of living drops more than men's after divorce (De Vaus et al. 2017). Yet

---

1 In re *Marriage of McKim*, 6 Cal. 3d 673, 493 P.2d 868, 100 Cal. Rptr. 140, 1972 Cal. LEXIS 277 (Cal. 1972).

popular culture is full of examples of claims that women unfairly collect money from men, courts treat men unfairly in custody disputes, or family support programs after divorce punish men.

Processes for determining child or spousal support are gender neutral and despite these popular representations of conflict and manipulation, most divorces are not legally contentious. In fact, more than half of divorces are uncontested, meaning that the terms of the divorce, including division of property, child custody and visitation, and financial support, are settled through parental agreement or during mediation and not by a judge (National Center for State Courts 2018). Although many families have two income earners, data show that mothers spend about twice as much time caring for children as do fathers (Livingston and Parker 2011). That means they may also be more likely to be seen as a consistent caregiver after divorce if that was their primary role before divorce.

Custody and Child Support

During divorce proceedings, court decisions usually specify custody and visitation arrangements between parents and their children. In some cases, one parent receives sole custody, an arrangement where children primarily or exclusively live with that parent and the other parent might in some cases have a schedule for seeing the children, which might include a limited number of overnight visits. In cases where parents share custody, children usually stay overnight a significant number of days with each parent. Shared custody may not be equal between the two parents, with one parent having more time with the children or more overnight stays with the children than the other parent.

There are few studies of national patterns in custody arrangements, but one survey suggests, based on where people say their children live, that almost 82 percent of custodial parents are mothers and just over 18 percent are fathers (cited in Cancian et al. 2014). Increasingly, states grant shared custody. One group of researchers found that while mothers were awarded sole custody in 80 percent of cases in 1986, by 2008, they received sole custody only in about 42 percent of cases (Cancian et al. 2014). Mirroring this change, rates of shared custody also increased, with higher shared custody more likely in higher income families (Cancian et al. 2014).

When awarding custody, courts may consider a range of factors including who has served as the primary caregiver, what kind of relationship each parent has with a child, what parenting skills each parent has, home environments, history of domestic violence, parents' work demands, and what is in the child's best interests. Monetary contributions to support children come in the form of child support. States calculate child support in a few different ways, but all states consider each parents' income and the percentage of time each will have custody of the children when setting support levels.

Spousal Support

Alimony—or spousal support—aims to address unfair outcomes of divorce between adults. In concept, alimony provides income to a spouse who may not have worked for wages during the marriage or who earned less than their spouse. Orders of alimony are often based on the assumption that one spouse may have sacrificed opportunities to build a career, complete education, or advance professionally while supporting the other spouse's professional opportunities.

As seen throughout this book, states pass their own family laws. It is worth noting that many recommendations that become adopted into law, including those for estimating spousal support, are put forth by the Uniform Law Commission. This national organization with representatives from all states drafts model legislation on a range of topics that states can adopt as legislators craft their own laws. Thus, there is often variation across states, but most of the law tends to be similar in core ways.

In general, courts will likely consider a variety of factors in calculating spousal support. These might include the age of the spouse who might need support, his or her emotional or physical health, the financial resources of the couple, the family's standard of living during the marriage, the length of the marriage, how long an ex-spouse might need support to complete education or training to become self-sufficient, and how much the higher earning spouse can reasonably afford.

Unmarried Spousal Support

Child support goes to supporting minor children, so the marital status of the parents is irrelevant to calculations of that support. However, in certain cases, one member of a cohabiting couple that is breaking up may claim to need financial support akin to spousal support. The first legal case to carve out this legal recognition was in 1976, when singer Marvin Gaye was sued by his longtime girlfriend Michelle Triola. In this case, Ms. Triola argued that in the seven years she lived with Mr. Gaye, she had given up her own career to support Gaye's career and serve as a homemaker. She also said that they had agreed to share resources and as such, argued that she was entitled to support and a portion of the property accrued while they were together. In essence, she insisted they had entered into a verbal contract that he should honor. Although contracts and agreements between unmarried couples in the past were often not enforceable because they involved the exchange of sex (Bowman 2004), the California Supreme Court in this case felt their agreement did entitle her to support.

This case has had two lasting results. First, the California Supreme Court recognized that individuals who live together may have a legal contract, even if not in writing, that should be respected under state laws about contracts. Second, this case led Triola's attorney to coin the term palimony (pal + alimony) to describe a legal settlement resulting from the break-up of an unmarried cohabiting couple. Although not a legal term, the term palimony continues to be used.

In 1979, a similar claim in Illinois was unsuccessful. In the case of *Hewitt v. Hewitt*, the Illinois Supreme Court rejected a palimony claim, arguing that granting it would have been the same as resurrecting common law marriage, which the Illinois legislature had outlawed in 1905 (Ryznar 2019). The result is that all states except Illinois, Georgia, and Louisiana allow for contracts to be recognized between unmarried persons, including agreements for monetary support and shared resources, as was decided in the Gaye case (Bowman 2004).

POST-DIVORCE RELATIONSHIPS

The legal definitions of divorce do not necessarily adequately characterize the complicated and continuing relationships that follow from divorce. Several of the readings in this section examine the tensions of transitioning from married family to divorced spouses. One challenge described by lawyer Pauline Tesler is the process of divorce itself. In her chapter, Tesler argues that how attorneys are trained to carry out divorces and the ways divorce is set up as an adversarial process might foster ongoing conflict and increase harm to families in the long run. As a longtime advocate for what she terms collaborative law, Tesler suggests that the process of divorcing can and should be better.

Even as marriages end, many relationships continue in a variety of forms, sometimes with unclear boundaries. In many cases, ex-spouses will continue to co-parent and thus will need to find ways to communicate, collaborate, and co-exist. The chapter by Kristin Natalier looks at this issue and suggests models for how co-parents can do so well. Ex-spouses might continue to have relationships, even without young children in their homes. Family researcher Teresa Cooney and her colleagues examine how women provide care for their ex-husbands, which often leads to a sense of role ambiguity. Each of these readings illustrates how formal definitions of family do not adequately account for the myriad feelings and interactions that continue long after marriages end.

WORKS CITED

Amato, Paul R. and Denise Previti. 2003. "People's Reasons for Divorcing: Gender, Social Class, the Life Course, and Adjustment." *Journal of Family Issues* 24(5): 602–626.

Aughinbaugh, Alison, Omar Robles and Hugette Sun. 2013. "Marriage and Divorce: Patterns by Gender, Race, and Educational Attainment." *Monthly Labor Review* 136(10): 1–19. U.S. Bureau of Labor Statistics.

Bowman, Cynthia Grant. 2004. "Legal Treatment of Cohabitation in the United States." *Law & Policy* 26(1): 119–151.

Brown, Susan L., I-Fen Lin, Anna M. Hammersmith and Matthew R. Wright. 2019. "Repartnering Following Gray Divorce: The Roles of Resources and Constraints for Women and Men." *Demography* 56(2): 503–523.

Cancian, Maria, Daniel R. Meyer, Patricia R. Brown and Steven T. Cook. 2014. "Who Gets Custody Now? Dramatic Changes in Children's Living Arrangements after Divorce." *Demography* 51(4): 1381–1396. doi: 10.1007/s13524-014-0307-8.

Cohen, Philip N. 2019. "The Coming Divorce Decline." *Socius* 5: 2378023119873497.

De Vaus, David, Matthew Gray, Lixia Qu and David Stanton. 2017. "The Economic Consequences of Divorce in Six OECD Countries." *Australian Journal of Social Issues* 52(2): 180–199.

National Center for State Courts. 2018. *Family Justice Initiative: The Landscape of Domestic Relations Cases in State Courts.* Williamsburg, VA: National Center for State Courts.

Ryznar, Margaret. 2019. "Unmarried Cohabitation." *Marriage and Divorce in America: Issues, Trends, and Controversies.* doi: 10.2139/ssrn.3446220.

Stepler, Renee. 2017. "Led by Baby Boomers, Divorce Rates Climb for America's 50+ Population." Pew Research Center. (https://www.pewresearch.org/fact-tank/2017/03/09/led-by-baby-boomers-divorce-rates-climb-for-americas-50-population/).

17

Have Children? Here's How Kids Ruin Your Romantic Relationship

Matthew D. Johnson

Lots of women look forward to motherhood—getting to know a tiny baby, raising a growing child, developing a relationship with a maturing son or daughter. All over the world, people believe that parenting is the most rewarding part of life. And it's good that so many mothers treasure that bond with their child, because the transition to parenthood causes profound changes in a woman's marriage and her overall happiness … and not for the better.

Families usually welcome a baby to the mix with great expectations. But as a mother's bond with a child grows, it's likely that her other relationships are deteriorating. I surveyed decades of studies on the psychological effects of having a child to write my book "Great Myths of Intimate Relationships: Dating, Sex, and Marriage," and here's what the research literature shows.

NOWHERE TO GO BUT DOWN?

When people marry, they're usually in love and happy to be tying the knot. But after that, things tend to change. On average, couples' satisfaction with their marriage declines during the first years of marriage and, if the decline is particularly steep, divorce may follow. The course of true love runs downhill. And that's before you factor in what happens when it's time to start buying a carseat and diapers.

For around 30 years, researchers have studied how having children affects a marriage, and the results are conclusive: the relationship between spouses suffers once kids come along. Comparing couples with and without children, researchers found that the rate of the decline in relationship satisfaction is nearly twice as steep for couples who have children than for childless couples. In the event that a pregnancy is unplanned, the parents experience even greater negative impacts on their relationship.

The irony is that even as the marital satisfaction of new parents declines, the likelihood of them divorcing also declines. So, having children may make you miserable, but you'll be miserable together.

Worse still, this decrease in marital satisfaction likely leads to a change in *general* happiness, because the biggest predictor of overall life satisfaction is one's satisfaction with their spouse.

Johnson, Matthew "Have Children? Here's How Kids Ruin Your Romantic Relationship." *The Conversation*, May 5, 2016.

While the negative marital impact of becoming parents is familiar to fathers and mothers, it is especially insidious because so many young couples think that having children will bring them closer together or at least will not lead to marital distress. Yet, this belief, that having children will improve one's marriage, is a tenacious and persistent myth among those who are young and in love.

LOVERS MORPH INTO PARENTS

It seems obvious that adding a baby to a household is going to change its dynamics. And indeed, the arrival of children changes how couples interact. Parents often become more distant and businesslike with each other as they attend to the details of parenting. Mundane basics like keeping kids fed, bathed, and clothed take energy, time, and resolve. In the effort to keep the family running smoothly, parents discuss carpool pickups and grocery runs, instead of sharing the latest gossip or their thoughts on presidential elections. Questions about one's day are replaced with questions about whether this diaper looks full.

These changes can be profound. Fundamental identities may shift – from wife to mother, or, at a more intimate level, from lovers to parents. Even in same-sex couples, the arrival of children predicts less relationship satisfaction and sex. Beyond sexual intimacy, new parents tend to stop saying and doing the little things that please their spouses. Flirty texts are replaced with messages that read like a grocery receipt.

With nearly half of all births being to unmarried couples, some parents may think they have gamed the system by skipping the wedding. Not so. The relationship burden of having children is present regardless of marital status, gender orientation, or level of income. In addition, the adverse impact of becoming a parent is found in other countries, including those with greater rates of nonmarital parenting and more generous family policies.

MOMS BEAR THE BRUNT

Not surprisingly, it is mothers, not fathers, who bear the heaviest cost of becoming parents. Even when both parents work outside the home and even in marriages in which both spouses describe themselves as sharing the burden of household chores, most parents slide toward gender-stereotypical ways of parenting. Women are more likely to become the "on call" parent, the one who gets up in the night to bring a child a tissue or who's called by the school nurse.

As part of this pattern, new mothers tend to cut their hours in outside work, which often leads fathers to feel more of the burden of financial responsibility. A common pattern emerges in which dads start spending more time and energy on outside work and moms start doing an increasing percentage of the childcare and housework. Cue the feelings of frustration, guilt, and distress for both parents.

New mothers often talk about their social isolation, becoming disconnected from friends and colleagues and how their world feels like it's shrinking. All of these changes lead to fundamental and long-lasting effects on new mothers' circle of support, including with their spouses.

The consequences of the relationship strain can be serious. Marital stress is associated with many serious physical health problems as well as symptoms of depression and other mental health problems. The link between psychological and marital problems is strong enough that researchers have found that couples therapy is one of the most effective ways of treating depression and some other mental illnesses.

A LIGHT AT THE END OF THE TUNNEL?

If the arrival of children is hard on marriages, is the departure of children good for marriages? Some marriages do improve once the children leave the nest. In other cases, the successful launch of the children leads spouses to discover they have few shared interests and there's nothing keeping them together.

These downsides to having children may partly explain why more and more women in the United States and around the world are choosing not to procreate. According to the U.S. Census, the percent of childless American women (ages 15–44) increased a staggering amount in just two generations: from 35 percent in 1976 to 47 percent in 2010.

Despite the dismal picture of motherhood painted by researchers like me (sorry Mom), most mothers (and fathers) rate parenting as their greatest joy. Much like childbirth, where nearly all mothers believe the pain and suffering was worth it, most mothers believe the rewards of watching their children grow up is worth the cost to their romantic relationships.

18

Can This Relationship Be Saved?
The Legal Profession and Families
in Transition

Pauline H. Tesler

INTRODUCTION

Few would deny that the American legal system's response to families experiencing breakup and restructuring must change. Where and how to focus change strategies is murkier. Much ink has been spent on the poor fit between the needs of families in transition and the capacities of our court system to provide help, and on the adversarial habits of lawyers that exacerbate rather than heal conflict, and on the failure of our law schools to prepare family lawyers with the competencies needed to be helpful rather than harmful when working in the realm of broken relationships. Plenty has been written about how family court processes might be changed to serve families better—or at least, to do less harm. But it is useful to remember that if we were to start fresh and design a system for delivering professional dispute resolution services in this country to families restructuring because of the breakdown of an intimate primary relationship, no one aware of this body of literature would come up with a system remotely resembling our current adversarial, fragmented, and underfunded hodgepodge of court-centric approaches that seem to differ only in the degree of unintended harm they inflict upon the people they are meant to help. The reasons for that are also good reasons for looking elsewhere to effectuate meaningful change in how family lawyers help clients through divorce.

Because our state courts are highly decentralized, with power to implement or resist change dispersed down to the level of semi-autonomous individual judges and courtrooms governed by more than fifty separate sets of laws and rules, it seems improbable that tinkering with courts and court-centric programming can accomplish sweeping change in our culture's institutional response to divorce anytime soon. Additional barriers to change include vast numbers of unrepresented parties swamping family court dockets at the same time that budgetary resources to run those courts have shrunk. Thus, with many state courts already facing too few judges, insufficient court staff, and not enough money to answer telephones, pay court reporters, or buy pencils, proposals for change that involve delivering a richer or better mix of professional services to families in transition via the court system, desirable as that surely would be, seem doomed.

This chapter begins with the proposition that before we can settle on the best policy recommendations for reengineering the legal profession's services to divorcing families, we need to step outside the social

Tesler, Pauline H. "Can This Relationship Be Saved? The Legal Profession and Families in Transition." *Family Court Review* 55, no. 1 (2017): 38–58.

constructs about lawyers and courts that invisibly constrain our thinking. We need to ask some really basic questions, starting with: is divorce, like a fender-bender or a breach of contract action, a zero-sum matter that can be resolved by an efficient choice between clashing bundles of individual rights and entitlements followed by a simple transfer of resources? We know it is not. Family restructuring involves a complex multiplicity of financial and relational issues, driven by powerful emotions of traumatic dimensions that often overwhelm parties' thinking and coping capacities as well as their physical and mental health. It often requires ongoing parenting of children after judgment, calling for nuanced recalibration of solutions as children grow up, parents relocate, and blended post-divorce families form and come apart again. Moreover, divorce and family restructuring implicate interests that go far beyond the individual spouses, affecting not only children, but also extended family and friendship networks as well as significant relationships in the community and workplace. Badly managed divorces generate consequences that affect public health, community engagement, the workplace and economy, and the raising of a healthy next generation in ways that extend far beyond what any divorce court's orders can address, making the broader community itself an invisible stakeholder in every divorce.

A sensible starting point for developing a change strategy is to consider what kinds of needs most divorcing couples and families generally experience, and what normative mix of professional services, delivered in what context, might best meet those needs, instead of working backwards by accepting existing service delivery systems, resource constraints, and the limitations and public resentment of the legal profession as givens and then seeking workarounds. With awareness of the human and legal needs implicated in divorce, we can then think about how to prepare lawyers—and other professionals—to do their part well, considering what they need to know, and how and where we can best teach the necessary content and skills to them. With that knowledge, we would have a basis for designing systems through which effective family-friendly professional services could best be delivered to families in need of help, regardless of wealth. At that point, we would be in a position to examine what laws, rules, and ethical standards that govern the practice of law would need to change in order for lawyers to participate effectively in such service delivery systems. Only then would it make sense to consider where and to what extent the court system should play a role.

What Couples and Families Need from Professionals during Family Transition

Though we have become accustomed to the construct of divorces as legal matters and lawyers as the professionals designated to handle them, couples experiencing family breakdown and transition tend not to think of their challenges in terms of abstract legal rights and remedies. Their problems present themselves in human and practical terms:

> how will I pay the mortgage or rent, find a new place to live, decide who keeps the house, keep food on the table, retire, find money to pay support, figure out how to divide assets fairly, tell the children why we are divorcing, separate my own feelings from those of the children about this marriage ending, figure out a fair way to co-parent that doesn't harm the children, recover from the humiliation of my spouse having an affair, find a job after years as a homemaker, learn how to be responsible for a toddler without my wife helping me, learn to live within a budget, have a conversation with my spouse about who gets the house that doesn't end in shouts and tears, figure out what I want to receive as my part of complex assets I don't understand and so forth.

These are intrinsic practical concerns associated with creating two households where previously there was one, colored by the inevitable emotional challenges and communication difficulties associated with unraveling the bonds of a primary intimate relationship. What these concerns are not, at least initially, are legal issues. While some of these problems involve potential legal considerations that do fall within the professional domain of lawyers, obviously many if not all of them involve interests and needs falling outside any specialized knowledge lawyers bring to the table.

For many years, I have included an exercise in my advanced collaborative divorce workshops that asks the participants to forget everything they think they know about legal rights and about how divorces are presently handled, and simply to brainstorm as complete a list as they can of needs that adults and children typically experience as they move through the divorce transition. The resulting lists are surprisingly long. We then classify these needs as core, meaning most couples and families would experience this as a need or concern, or else ancillary, meaning some but not most couples or families are likely to experience this need. Next, we decide which profession might be in the best position to help address each core need. What we invariably discover is that the core needs of most divorcing families fall into three categories: those that require lawyers, those that can best be addressed in the first instance by a properly trained financial services professional, and those that can best be addressed by a mental health professional with family systems training.

If we think about better ways of providing professional services to couples and families during divorce by starting from their perceived needs, rather than with what we as lawyers or judges are accustomed to doing, it seems apparent to me that an adequate service delivery system that considers children's needs as well as those of adults would necessarily be interdisciplinary and team-based. It is not obvious that lawyers would be more important than other professional service providers in such a system and for that reason not clear that courts would be the best structure within which to provide such services.

Courts Are Not the Right Place for Most Divorcing Couples and Families

Reform efforts that place the family court at the center of a triage, referral, and service delivery system in my view are doomed to fall far short of what is needed. The evidence is strong that the experience of taking a family restructuring problem into or near a court increases mistrust between the parties, reduces the likelihood of durable settlement, and fosters more, rather than less, litigation by exacerbating parental conflicts and prolonging discord. The demands and stresses inherent in litigation-matrix processes drain economic resources, strain parent–child relationships, and diminish the quantity and quality of attention parents can give their children at the very time when their need for attentive parenting escalates.

Courts by their nature are reasonably well suited to resolution of business or commercial disputes, many or most of which routinely reach resolution without need for a judgment incorporating settlement terms, without any involvement of a court or other governmental institution, and often even without lawyers. Yet, paradoxically, family law matters, which constitute a high volume of civil filings, and which require sensitive, well-informed professional expertise brought to bear over a broad range of matters affecting personal relationships fundamental to the health of a society, are consigned to a court system that operates on principles and methods antithetical to the health of children and families.

Our courts and lawyers reflect who we are as a culture. Americans seem driven by deeply rooted attitudes and values that treat conflict as warfare, with opposing sides battling to crush one another in business disputes, scholarly and political debate, and even ordinary conversations about matters large and small. If our argument culture were a pyramid, the very top of it would house lawyers, judges, and courts, a professional domain in which conflict is institutionalized in thought and word, procedure and practice, and even the furniture.

The idea of a legal dispute abstracted from the human context in which it arises, that will routinely be taken to a third-party authority figure empowered to decide which of two opposing arguments will prevail, is a social construct, not an intrinsic characteristic of the normal challenges that must be addressed during relationship breakup and family restructuring. Other social constructs, based on values of civility, cooperation, and restoration of harmony in family systems, could be the ground from which policies and solutions emerge that would better fit the needs of most families in transition. Such constructs would support cultural norms like these: that intimate partnerships do not always last till death do we part, that family breakdown and transitions are normal experiences many or most of us will have, and that adults are expected by their society to unravel their intimate partnerships in socially responsible ways by participating in processes imbued with constructive, problem-solving, non-zero-sum frames for negotiations. With social norms calling for cooperation and consensual problem solving in divorce, informal service delivery systems and methods would become the expected first stop for divorcing couples. Except in unusual circumstances of risk, couples might begin in a community conflict resolution center offering a combination of subsidized and market rate interdisciplinary professional services. Most couples would achieve resolution there, but if they did not, they might then be certified to move on into an administrative process that might resemble med/arb or small claims court. In most instances access to the courts might be permitted only after exhaustion of community and administrative remedies. Adversarial third-party decision making in this kind of peacemaking, problem-solving social construct would be an alternative reserved for those few who fail at the normal, expected, culturally appropriate way of resolving differences.

Because divorcing spouses who have children will forever be linked to them as extended family long after the parenting challenges during their minority are over, it seems to me fundamental that lawyers who work with families in transition must learn core skills and understandings based on a social construct of conflict as an opportunity rich with possibilities for consensual resolution and even transcendence. Lacking such core competencies, family lawyers are likely to stoke conflict whether working in or outside the courtroom, because that's the baked-in-the-cake war construct they learn in law school and on the job. With such new core competencies, family lawyers can become part of the solution wherever they may be working, instead of remaining at the heart of the problem. That is why I believe what, where, and how we teach family lawyers and what they understand to be their identity and purpose are the places where effective change must begin.

Changing the Social Constructs that Family Lawyers Learn

But, some object, is this kind of conflict resolution really the job of a lawyer? That depends on what social construct we lawyers are taught to bring to our work in the land of broken relationships. The legal dispute resolution construct lawyers are socialized into, starting with law school and continuing on the job, sees clients as dueling bundles of individual rights and entitlements colliding with each other until, with our zealous advocacy, the stronger bundle wins. If that is our construct, then we would agree with the American Bar Association (ABA) Litigation Section that divorce is war, our job is to be the front line commanders, and approaches like collaborative law represent a risky departure from the real work.[1]

Since the late 1970s, however, when California became the first jurisdiction in the country— perhaps in the world—to enact no-fault divorce legislation, family law professionals have been building a different, collaborative, interdisciplinary, problem-solving social construct for divorce and advocating for its place as the normative way our culture handles family restructuring. But we still fall far short of the goal of inculcating that new construct broadly in the hearts and minds of new lawyers. Law schools and law firms still produce for the most part traditionally prepared adversarial family lawyers. Thrown into the cauldron of court-centric war-model practice, many become disheartened, depressed, and unwell. While some eventually find their way into the new social construct—the new paradigm—of interdisciplinary collaborative team divorce or transformative mediation, that is a painful, inefficient pathway from old to new, reflecting the absence of consensus about the need for a client-centric, family-friendly, constructive professional identity for family lawyers.

Law school trains us to abstract from the pain-saturated stories clients bring to us those elements that constitute a justiciable issue. Those are the issues judges address after motions and trials, and they form a frame around what family lawyers generally talk about when they engage in traditional settlement negotiations. But for our clients, the divorce experience is not divided into law school disciplines or elements of causes of action. Justiciability as a frame for the conversation with a lawyer too often means a sequence of leading questions from the lawyer, frustration on the client's side at the lawyer's unwillingness to hear the full story, and impatience on the lawyer's side, waiting for the client to calm down and answer the question. This is a consequence of a cultural construct that says divorce conflict is not essentially different from other legal disputes.

When I left public interest law to join a family law firm, the founding partner—a tough-minded Hungarian woman in her eighties—gave me the first of many lessons in humanistic law practice by observing that when clients first seek professional help in a relationship breakup, they usually think of lawyers, and when clients come to a lawyer's office, what they get is a divorce. But, she asked, what if they are in the wrong office? Suppose their needs would be better served by a psychotherapist, or a minister, or a financial planner? Suppose they need not a divorce, but a postnuptial agreement? Or a vacation? Later, I gradually understood that when clients first consult a family lawyer they are often so distraught, fearful, angry, or guilt ridden that from a neurochemical perspective, they can barely think straight, that what lawyers are taught to do can sometimes be exactly the wrong way to serve the long-term welfare of the client and those she cares about, that interdisciplinary resources benefit almost all divorcing couples, and that while lawyers are impatient for results and courts want to clear their dockets, going slow and allowing the parties time to adjust to their new circumstances before commencing negotiations can be an excellent way to prevent a high-conflict divorce. These ideas are significant threads in the fabric of a conflict-resolution social construct for divorce.

A new dimension to my thinking about the pernicious impact of the divorce-is-war construct in family law was prompted by Justice Robert Benham, who as chief justice of the Georgia Supreme Court gave a keynote address to the International Academy of Collaborative Professionals (IACP) in 2005.[2] He explained that every known human culture has always had three core professions (whatever the name or methods): religion, law, and medicine. The true and essential purpose of religion is to heal the soul, of medicine is to heal the body, and of law is to heal breaches in the social fabric. Law as codified in the law books and in appellate decisions, Justice Benham explained, represents the floor below which you cannot go in a civilized society without getting into trouble of some kind—a tort or breach of contract action, a statutory discrimination suit or criminal proceedings. But the written law says only what you must or cannot do, and nothing about what you should aspire to do. Toward the end of the twentieth century, in his view, the legal profession lost its way, redefining its mission as seeing how low that floor could be pushed for each client. The collaborative family law movement, on the other hand, inspired admiration in him because it was breaking new ground, reclaiming law as a healing profession by occupying the space between the floor which is the law, and the highest shared values that a disputing couple could be invited to discover. Collaborative lawyers were changing the narrative, inviting divorcing couples despite their hurt and anger to aspire to a respectful, socially responsible divorce process that could take into account integrity, values, and the long-term welfare of their children.

The mismatch between what law schools teach and what families need from their professional advisors remains profound. Thinking like a lawyer (or more accurately, thinking like an appellate lawyer or a law professor), which the prevailing case method focuses on to the exclusion of all other values, and the subsequent socialization of new lawyers into the practicing bar result in placing disproportionate value on technical argumentation skills and "client control" (meaning control of, not by, the client), and discounting considerations in the emotional or relational realm as the job of some other profession to deal with, not lawyers.

The stakes could scarcely be higher. Whether in law school or afterward, a family lawyer must learn quite a lot more... if she is to be a constructive rather than a damaging presence. This need exists for any lawyer working with personal relationship disputes, but is particularly compelling in family law matters, where by definition we are dealing with a dysfunctional family system—one that, if young children are involved, will need to remain connected and make joint decisions for years into the future. When the dispute resolution system that serves these clients is itself dysfunctional, when insufficiently or badly trained family lawyers behave as they believe they were taught and adopt alter ego behaviors that mirror the irrational thinking of their clients, or conduct litigation and negotiations in power-based ways that polarize negotiations and cripple the possibilities for compromise and for acts of generosity that might have been supported by a more constructive system of professional helpers, the parties will leave the divorce process more rather than less conflicted, and less rather than more able to cooperate in effective co-parenting of their children, our next generation.

Preparing Family Lawyers to Meet Their Clients' Needs

The additional knowledge that would support settlement-focused client-centric family lawyering includes: specific techniques for negotiating and resolving issues (such as interest-based and narrative-based negotiations), apology and forgiveness in negotiations, preventive law, client counseling, problem-solving approaches, empathic awareness, cognitive biases, out of court consensual service delivery methods (such as facilitative and transformative mediation and interdisciplinary collaborative divorce team practice), deep communications skills, self-reflective practice, self-care and mindful awareness practices, systems theory and interdisciplinary teamwork, techniques for reducing stress and reinforcing client resilience and optimism, a basic introduction to psychodynamics of family breakdown and restructuring, basic concepts of child development and attachment, and some familiarity with the growing wave of immensely useful knowledge emanating from the fields of decision science, behavioral economics, neuro-morality, and positive and social psychology that can give depth and confidence to a lawyer's professional identity as peacemaking problem solver. "[The] traditional conception of lawyering as a detached and emotionless exercise does not suit legal practices that deal in the consequences of human suffering," concludes Donald Murray, QC and a respected criminal barrister. Rather, he counsels in a desk book written for the Canadian Bar Association, lawyers engaged in high stress practices like family law which require daily empathic engagement with clients' pain and trauma need tools and capacities that reinforce attunement in their daily work lives to personal needs, limits, emotions and resources, awareness of one's own inner state, the capacity for self-care, a balance between work and other priorities, and sustained connection to self and others.[3]

Conclusion

Tremendous intellectual and increasing financial resources are finally being devoted to addressing what we know to be wrong about the fraught relationship between families in transition, the court system, and the legal profession. While the slow pace of reform in law school education of family lawyers and the difficulties of implementing change in local family courts seem unlikely to change dramatically anytime soon, there is much cause for optimism about the family law bar as a focal point for normalizing a new construct: lawyers as peacemaking problem solvers. Although too many lawyers work with divorcing couples in ways that engender rather than resolve conflict, practicing lawyers also constitute an underutilized resource for broad scale implementation of solutions. Family law firms tend to be small, without the entrenched institutional culture characteristic of large firms that can be impervious to new ideas and deeply attached to the bottom line. This means that opening the mind and heart of even one family lawyer in a community can alter how the firm practices and what kind of new hires it seeks out.

Notes

1 The Litigation Section of the ABA vigorously opposed a 2010 resolution in the House of Delegates that would have lent ABA support to the Uniform Collaborative Law Act. Letter dated April 15, 2009, to Peter K. Munson, Chair of the Drafting Committee on Uniform Collaborative Law Act, from Robert Rothman, Chairman, ABA Section on Litigation.

2 Justice Robert Benham, SUP. CT. OF GEOR., http://www.gasupreme.us/court-information/biographies/-justice-robert-benham/ (last visited July 12, 2016). His 2005 keynote address, given in Atlanta in 2005, was not published.

3 The Board of Legal Specialization of the State Bar of California has for decades required ongoing continuing education in "psychological and counseling aspects of family law" in order to obtain and renew certification as a specialist in family law. Standards for Certification and Recertification in Family Law 2.1.12, available at http://rules.calbar.ca.gov/LinkClick.aspx?fileticket58X1vLyj1V1w (last visited July 15, 2016).

19

What It's Like to Get a Queer Divorce after Fighting for Marriage Equality

Shannon Weber

In a Few Words: It Sucks

Breakups are horrible things, even if, as in my case, they really need to happen. And getting a divorce, with the complications of being legally entangled with someone else and having to get government institutions involved in order to start rebuilding your life, is a unique brand of horrible. But getting a divorce after being denied the right to enter into a marriage, fighting for it in high-profile ways for years while being attacked by the Right and often mocked by the Left, and being seen by your community as a poster child for queer marriage? That is its own universe of awkward, devastating hell.

I found my way into a queer marriage by way of my college girlfriend, who was both my first relationship and who also, I would come to realize over the course of almost six years, was emotionally abusive. We fell very much in love in the spring of our sophomore year, when the trees were in full pink bloom and the air smelled like freshly cut grass warmed by the sun. I was so excited to finally be experiencing all of these relationship and sexuality "firsts" that I ignored the red flags. There never seemed to be enough time to slow down and have the space to think about my own needs in the relationship—my girlfriend was ever planning our relationship far into the distant future. For example, we got into a fight about whether I wanted to marry her two weeks into dating, spurred by seeing a wedding vendor at the first Pride festival we ever attended together.

The reasons why I ultimately agreed to marry her, and the nuances of what happened in our relationship over time, could fill a book. A major reason, though, was connected to the fact that we were planning to move to California together and that Proposition 8, the 2008 ballot initiative to take away same-sex marriage in California, was looming on the horizon. As the polling on Prop 8 grew bleaker and bleaker as the election approached, my girlfriend convinced me that we needed to get married in case Prop 8 passed. After arguing about this, a sense of *carpe diem* took over and, about a year and a half after we first met, I eloped with her to San Francisco. The next week, Prop 8 passed, and it would take years of multi-pronged social justice organizing and legal appeals before marriage equality would return to the state of California in 2013 and, on the same day in 2015, extend to the whole of the United States.

Weber, Shannon. "What It's Like to Get a Queer Divorce after Fighting for Marriage Equality." *The Body Is Not an Apology*, February 17, 2018.

FIGHTING FOR MY QUEER MARRIAGE

Let's back up, though. The summer before Prop 8 passed, I volunteered in the rather conservative state capitol of Sacramento—where my parents live, as well as the home base for the Proposition 8 campaign—to go door-to-door talking to residents about marriage equality. I didn't last long doing this. The worst memory that sticks out to me during this stint was knocking on the door of a family who had wooden decorations featuring Bible passages on their front door. As someone who grew up surrounded by conservative Evangelical Christians, this raised my spidey senses, and when a man came to the door, I realized he was in the middle of leading a prayer group in his living room. Once he understood what I was trying to talk to him about, he called me an "abomination" and closed the door in my face.

Similarly, at the Sacramento Pride festival that summer, pro-Prop 8 activists showed up to disrupt our celebration, bringing their kids dressed in heterosexually coupled wedding outfits and holding huge signs about how we were filthy, disgusting, AIDS-carrying monsters whom God despised.

Just as I had conservatives on the Christian Right telling me I was a sinner who would cause straight people to try to marry their cats and salad bowls, I also would go on to have self-righteous acquaintances and colleagues on the Left tell me how conformist, neoliberal, and heteronormative it was for queers to get married. After I'd gotten married and started my PhD program in gender studies, I was subjected to constant comments from other grad students and gender studies scholars about how pathetic and stifling the institution of marriage was, how queers who got married were non-radical sell-outs, and so on. My daily life continued to be a hot-button political issue, and not just on the part of Fox News anchors.

While marching for years in protests and rallies and fundraising and signature gathering and watching my daily life be treated as a political football by reactionary and hateful forces, my relationship was also a hot mess. My wife felt isolated moving to California with me, where she had no friends or family, and felt alienated by the elitist, exclusive circles of academia, in which anyone outside academia's orbit was seen as a nobody. She was perennially depressed, anxious, and moody, and we fought constantly on a range of topics, from our sex life to whether we wanted kids and so on. **She deepened her habit of flirting with people both in front of me and behind my back despite our ostensibly monogamous relationship. She would berate me with cutting, below-the-belt insults during our screaming cry-a-thons and then apologize after the damage had already been done, making it about how she hated herself.**

When we moved to the East Coast for my wife to start grad school in 2012—about four years after marrying and as more and more states were passing marriage equality legislation and voting for it at the ballot for the first time, all as the federal court cases snaked their way through layers of appeals—the cycles of emotional abuse only intensified. My wife became increasingly angry, callous, and emotionally removed, to the point where I would frequently be in tears over her behavior and she would barely take notice. She would tell me over and over again that I was "just so infuriating" while continuing her pattern of flirting with other people and spending more and more of her time with others. **We decided to try an open relationship, and by the time I acted on this, I realized what I was missing out on and how I deserved to be treated.** Following this realization, not long into 2013, our relationship spiraled irreparably into divorce territory.

WHAT I LEARNED FROM THE QUEER DIVORCE

One of the hardest parts of telling my social networks that I was getting a divorce is the extent to which my wife and I had been built up as the poster couple for queer wedded bliss. I wondered if I was being paranoid and narcissistic for thinking that I'd be shocking and disappointing so many people, but my concerns were verified by multiple friends telling me how depressing and jarring it had been to hear, including one person who confessed that the news actually made her cry and wonder whether true queer love can really exist. We were the (dysfunctional, working-class, 20-something, married-way-too-young) Ellen and Portia of our social world, and now it was over.

It was a strange and somewhat cruel twist of fate that on June 26, 2013, the day Prop 8 was officially struck down by the Supreme Court as part of the court's ruling against the Defense of Marriage Act, I was sending in my divorce papers as joyous couples embraced in front of the Supreme Court and on the steps of city halls across the country.

Queer people's lives are constantly under a microscope in ways that heterosexual people's lives aren't. The long fight for same-sex marriage in the United States illustrates how simply living our lives and making important decisions about our relationships was turned into something else: a literal referendum on the legitimacy of our relationships, the worthiness of the families we made, the right for us to take up space in this society so premised on heterosexual male control of women. In the midst of all that, a lot of queer people, myself included, operated from a place of scarcity, where we decided to take what we could get when we could get it, marrying because it might not be there the next day. That's a tragically absurd place from which to approach a huge life decision like marriage, and when someone is in a toxic or abusive relationship, it makes for a particularly distressing combination.

But it wasn't all bad. My divorce taught me the indescribable importance and power of listening to my intuition and fighting my way out of a situation so toxic it had become my listless normal. It taught me to wake up and realize that I deserved so much better. **It was the beginning of my journey in realizing that it's not up to me to save other people, that it's unspeakably cruel to destroy myself for the comfort of anyone else.** It showed me that even though straight people's relationships are hella dysfunctional, two women in a relationship aren't inherently feminist or empowering. And it taught me that I didn't have to be ashamed of my own marriage dissolving despite my marriage equality activism. Indeed, my persistent belief in the power of love and dignity, enriched by my activism, is what saved me from my marriage, and this belief continues to buoy me in my current relationship.

Far from being hardened against love or even marriage, my heart has been softened, opened, grateful for my past experiences and what they've taught me about what love should be. My divorce brought me back to myself, to begin again, again and again and again.

20

What Type of Relationship Should I Have with My Co-Parent Now We're Divorced?

Kristin Natalier

When talking about separation and divorce, media and personal stories often focus on relationships characterised by ongoing conflict or violence. In contrast, Australian research suggests low conflict or cooperative post-separation relationships are common.

These are negotiated in contexts that require what British sociologist Carol Smart described as an "indelible" joint-parenting contract. This means people can end an intimate relationship but it's very difficult to disengage from each other as parents.

We know very little about how people define and experience "good" relationships after separation. So a recently conducted and soon to be published study sought to explore what this might look like.

GOOD RELATIONSHIPS AREN'T ALL THE SAME

The study found three types of good post-separation parental relationships: allied, arm's length and autonomous. These differed in their communication and family practices shared by parents.

ALLIED RELATIONSHIPS

Allied relationships were the most common type of relationship. Parents described emotionally close connections with their former partner. They often used terms such as "family" or "friends". People liked their former partner but recognised their children were the reason they remained close.

Parents in allied relationships described a lot of practical support and responsiveness to their former partner's needs. They were typically flexible in their care arrangements to meet changes in the other parents' work, personal and health situations. Parents also reported more mundane supports such as feeding pets or sharing laundry duties.

Natalier, Kristin. "What Type of Relationship Should I Have with My Co-Parent Now We're Divorced?" *The Conversation*, August 29, 2018.

They emphasised the importance of shared events such as regular family dinners and birthday celebrations. They saw their approach as an important way to signal to their children they were "still a family". This helped balance children's and parents' needs so no one missed out on important events and relationships.

ARM'S LENGTH RELATIONSHIPS

Parents in arm's length relationships were present in their children's lives and absent from their former partner's life. Their dealings were civil and cooperative, but they did not look for emotional closeness or shared activities. Any connection was built on and limited to their shared focus on their children's well-being.

For example, one father in the study had almost no contact with his former wife outside of their children. He said:

She rings me with issues, if the kids have got, if she thinks the kids need anything she rings me and asks me about it or whatever you know, so we've got a kind of contact. It's probably, functional is the best thing I can say.

People imposed clear boundaries to limit interactions to child-specific issues. There were none of the family rituals that were such an important part of allied relationships. Parents were not particularly responsive to the needs of their ex-partner and their care arrangements were fixed in place. Parents described their relationship as good, because both parents cared about their children and worked together to meet their children's needs. As a result, their children were happy and thriving.

AUTONOMOUS RELATIONSHIPS

Parents in autonomous relationships did not communicate with their former partner beyond basic logistical information about children's routines. However, each parent loved and responded to their children's needs in their individual ways.

This separate approach also created economic, emotional and logistical freedoms for each parent. One mother in the study put it this way:

I don't have to go into any negotiations, the playing field is clear, I have clarity and my kids are unbelievably healthy, they're really, really happy.

Parents did not interpret limited communication as an indication of their former partner's lack of care or ability to parent. They recognised that after separation, what counted were parents' emotional and practical contributions to their children's lives – not to each other's lives.

WHY DO GOOD POST-SEPARATION RELATIONSHIPS MATTER?

Interview studies such as the one we conducted can't show statistical links between good post-separation relationships and children's outcomes. But regardless of the type of relationship they had, parents believed their child-centred focus was central to their children's happiness and development. This focus was the basis for parents defining their relationship as good.

Existing literature suggests it's the tenor and practice of relationships rather than how much time children spend with each parent that makes the most difference in children's post-separation lives. Yet debates continue to centre on the importance of how much time children spend with each parent.

Good post-separation relationships are hard work. They require constant emotional thoughtfulness, careful negotiation and letting go of past wrongs. But when the payoff is a happy and healthy child the hard work is well worth the effort.

21

Role Ambiguity among Women Providing Care for Ex-Husbands

Teresa M. Cooney, Christine M. Proulx, Linley A. Snyder-Rivas, and Jacquelyn J. Benson

INTRODUCTION

The marital and relationship histories of aging baby boomers are vastly different from those of past cohorts of older Americans. Due largely to the divorce revolution of the 1970s–1980s, a greater share of baby boomers are arriving at midlife and young old age either currently divorced or with a history of marital disruption. Divorce adds complexity not only to family structures but also to family functioning. Spouses become ex-partners with divorce, a designation that is not accompanied by clear and widely accepted normative guidelines. In addition, relationships with and roles vis-à-vis ex-partners change over time; frequency of contact, for example, is inversely related to time since the divorce. Yet little is known about the longer-term interpersonal dynamics of divorced spouses as they age.

The aging of the U.S. population, and the large baby boom cohort especially, creates serious care challenges due to the association between age and poor health. The likelihood of chronic conditions is substantially greater among those aged 75 and older than for those 45–54 years old. In addition, the proportion of the population having functional impairments increases from 20 percent for 55- to 64-year-olds to 60 percent for persons over age 80. Moreover, analysis of health and morbidity among aging baby boomers suggests that this cohort may actually have a greater need for health and personal care than recent cohorts of elderly. Added to this potential for an increased need for care and a longer life span, baby boomers are the cohort most likely to have ever experienced divorce, and they also are the generation most likely to be currently divorced. This raises the question of who divorced aging individuals turn to when care needs arise.

Typically, care demands are met by family members. Married individuals usually rely on spousal care, with adult children assisting next if a spouse is unable or unavailable. Among the unmarried, however, men are less likely than women to rely on their offspring for assistance. Men with a history of divorce are especially unlikely to view family members as potential caregivers. Thus, how the growing number of divorced men will meet their care needs as they age is of serious concern.

This chapter emerges from qualitative interviews with 21 women providing care for former husbands diagnosed with a serious illness. Thematic analyses revealed that giving care to an ex-spouse elicits mixed

Cooney, Teresa M., Christine M. Proulx, Linley A. Snyder-Rivas, and Jacquelyn J. Benson. "Role Ambiguity among Women Providing Care for Ex-Husbands." Journal of Women & Aging 26, no. 1 (2014): 84–104.

reactions. Unlike providing care for a sick or dying spouse or parent, social norms are unclear as to the appropriateness of assisting and caring for a former spouse. Ex-wives in this research experienced role ambiguity on three distinct levels: interpersonally in their informal social networks; institutionally, as they interacted with formal settings such as the health-care system and their workplace; and intrapersonally, as they faced their own reactions to being an ex-wife and providing care. The goal of this chapter is to describe women's experiences with these distinct forms of role ambiguity and identify some of the consequences of role ambiguity for middle-aged and older women's role performance and well-being. Given the aging of the high-divorcing baby boom cohort, such roles may become more common, especially for women. Thus, we conclude by using our findings to offer recommendations for interventions and policies that may benefit these caregivers' role performance and well-being.

METHODS

Procedure

Seventeen of the 21 women providing care for their ex-husbands in our sample were recruited with help from The Population-Based Palliative Care Research Network at the University of Colorado Denver. Through this national network, approximately 25 hospice agencies agreed to assist with recruitment for the project. Another three women in our sample were recruited through word of mouth. One respondent was recruited via a LISTSERV of university announcements. Two forms were subsequently mailed to those caregivers who agreed to participate: a short questionnaire with demographic questions about the caregiver and her ex-husband, and a relationship history timeline. Completed forms were returned to the research staff, and upon receipt a telephone interview was scheduled with the caregiver. These semistructured interviews lasted from 1 to 2.5 hours.

Sample

The 21 female caregivers were from ten different states across the United States and varied in racial-ethnic background. Most of the women (n = 17) were non-Hispanic White, though the sample included two Black, one Latino, and one Middle Eastern woman. They ranged in age from 45 to 77, with an average age of 59. Their ex-husbands were between ages 40 and 80, with an average age of 63 at the time of the interview (or death, if deceased at time of interview). The average length of marriage was 19 years, although the range varied from 3 to 53 years. All but two women had had children with this ex-husband, and most offspring were now adults. The average interval to caregiving, defined as the length of time between the separation/divorce and commencing of care for the ex-husband, was 14 years, though again there was a wide range of elapsed time reported (0–41 years). About half of the respondents were caregiving at the time of their interviews; the others had provided care within the last year, typically within a few months of their interview. Of the former caregivers, all but one were no longer in the role due to the ex-husband's death. All ex-husband care recipients were seriously ill, many with multiple diagnoses. Cancer was the most common, with 13 of the care recipients being diagnosed. Other diagnoses included congestive heart failure, alcoholism/cirrhosis of the liver, kidney failure, and various forms of advanced dementia.

FINDINGS AND DISCUSSION

Interpersonal Experiences of Role Ambiguity

For ex-wife caregivers, role ambiguity was most commonly experienced at the interpersonal level. Fifteen of the 21 respondents reported encounters in which they were confronted by informal network members about the appropriateness of their role as ex-wife caregivers for their ex-husbands. These experiences involved their own relatives, those of their ex-husband, friends, coworkers, and casual acquaintances.

The comments offered by others about the ex-wife's current role focused on whether it was appropriate for an ex-wife to devote herself, even temporarily, to the care of a former spouse because caregiving typically reflects concern and involves fairly intimate, private behaviors (e.g. bathing, toileting, dressing). Such remarks seemed judgmental and disrespectful to the caregivers who experienced them. Moreover, comments from others that they "were crazy" to take care of an ex-husband were perceived as hurtful, as Anne conveys when sharing the negative reactions of coworkers at the store where she had worked for over two decades:

> They just thought I was stupid... They came out and said ... Some people laughed and made jokes about it ... The people that knew me and cared about me, they understood, but... I had a supervisor say, "Are you stupid or what? Why would you do that?"

Occasionally, the disapproval expressed by network members was offered in a protective, nonjudgmental way. Grace's friends caringly told her that she should not *have* to be the one to assume care for her ex-husband. Her situation was particularly unusual because her ex-husband was remarried to another woman (who refused to care for him) when Grace took him in 23 years after their divorce.

That caring for an ex-spouse might be viewed publicly as unacceptable did not surprise some caregivers. Tess recalled how her son anticipated social disapproval when he asked for her help in providing care for her ex-husband: "'I hate to ask you,' he said. 'I know people's gonna say something.'" The highly critical reactions of Tess's ex-husband's family focused on the intimacy of particular care tasks and whether it was right for an ex-spouse to do them. A former in-law badgered her: "What ex-wife goes in and takes care of an ex-husband and even has to bathe him?"

Close family members, such as children, parents, and siblings, were less likely to question the care these women provided for their ex-husbands than were more casual acquaintances, friends, and more distant kin, unless the former marriage had involved serious transgressions like affairs or abuse. In such cases, close network members also had a difficult time understanding and accepting the care and devotion given by these women to their ex-husbands. For example, Maxine's best friends questioned her decision to care for her ex-husband because of his extraordinary meanness. Anne, whose marriage was fraught with abuse, said those who really knew the couple were "shocked and amazed" that she provided care "after everything that happened" between them. Meg joked about her decision to care for an ex-husband who not only mistreated her, but their children as well. She laughed as she told the interviewer, tongue in cheek, that she "worried that people would think I just brought him home to kill him," because those close to the couple were aware of her ex-husband's abusive behavior during the marriage, which had ended 25 years prior. A few of the caregivers' own children acknowledged what they perceived as their mother's misplaced devotion for a former spouse. Mary's daughter forcefully reminded her, "Mom, you're divorced from this guy. He's done nothing nice for you for a long time." Ellen's ex-husband was viewed by others as completely undeserving of her assistance because he was selfish; at one point in their marriage he had refused to care for her when she was sick and needed surgery.

Finally, a few women shared incidences illustrative of role ambiguity in which former in-laws accepted their caregiving or even *expected* it of them but did not fully trust them with the job. In Mary's case, her in-laws expected her to be the primary caregiver and entrusted to her difficult care duties; yet they did not trust her enough to discuss her ex-husband's financial matters in her presence because of lies he had told them about her stealing his money. Mary finally confronted her ex-husband's family, threatening to abandon the caregiver role unless their treatment of her improved.

Clearly, society does not expect favorable and caring interactions between former spouses. Rather, we assume episodes of conflict and tension will exist between ex-spouses after divorce. Thus, it is not surprising that most of the experiences of role ambiguity that ex-wife caregivers in this study reported involved interpersonal encounters with members of their informal social networks who voiced disapproval or incredulity regarding their caregiving role.

Consequences of Interpersonally Experienced Role Ambiguity

As a result of unsolicited, sometimes judgmental and hurtful comments about their roles as ex-wife caregivers, participants noted both behavioral and psychological consequences. One behavioral consequence of role ambiguity is that most of these women did not receive much assistance in their caregiving role. In some cases, ex-husbands refused help other than that from the ex-wife, or the ex-wife caregivers believed they could provide the best care, and essentially took over the role. According to Anne, her ex-husband strongly rejected help from any friends or family members: "I don't want 'em. You [Anne] can do it. ... I just want you to do it." Melanie, a trained nurse, believed she was the best person for the job: "I honestly ... didn't want anybody else to take care of him." For other caregivers, though, the lack of help they received resulted from others' disapproval of their care role. For example, neither Mary's children nor her friends wanted her to be the caregiver, and thus they kept their distance from the care situation. She noted, "Mark [her ex-husband] is gonna get worse, and there's nobody for me to say, 'This sucks, this is really hard.'"

Another consequence of interpersonal experiences with role ambiguity is that some caregivers avoided talking about caregiving challenges and experiences in an attempt to prevent further disapproval from others. Mary said she kept her life "compartmentalized": "It feels like I'm, I'm a pie, you know, there's pieces of me." She wished "that it didn't have to be secretive." Donna, who was preparing to remarry her ex-husband at her children's prompting, kept her caregiving situation private, too. Expecting severe social disapproval of her caregiver role in her current divorced status, she reported, "I don't talk to anyone....I don't want to discuss [the experience] with anyone ... until I get [re]married to him."

Maintaining such closed boundaries around the caregiving situation was challenging. Mary acknowledged that, "I miss not being able to like say to somebody at work, 'Oh shit, do you have any idea what he did yesterday?'" Most important, being secretive about the role interfered with caregivers' ability to seek and receive social support. This was evident from Mary's comment that, "You just feel isolated. You know, isolated and very much alone." Thus, ex-wife caregivers experienced emotional consequences due to the role's ambiguous nature.

Intrapersonal Experiences with Role Ambiguity

Over half (12 of 21) of these ex-wives struggled personally with the appropriateness of adopting the care role for their ex-husbands or confusion regarding their feelings as an ex-wife caregiver. The origins of this internal type of role ambiguity varied across women. For some respondents, self-doubt about their role was prompted by others' negative reactions to their caregiving. (Of the 15 women noting interpersonal experiences with role ambiguity, nine also reported intrapersonal struggles over the role.) Tess was so bothered by the vehement opposition to her role that came from her ex-husband's family [focused largely on the intimacy of the care tasks that she performed] that she finally sought advice from clergy at a local church: "They said, 'you know what's right and what's wrong.... What's wrong with a female nurse giving a male patient a bath?' They said, 'That's your capacity at this moment. You are a caregiver.'" The acceptance and understanding of her caregiving conveyed by these church leaders seemed to calm Tess's internal struggle and distress over role ambiguity.

Most of the caregivers who reported intrapersonal experiences with role ambiguity seemed torn because of a lack of clear internalized norms about the appropriate roles of ex-spouses. Anne's repeated self-questioning of "Why is this my responsibility?" reflects a view of expected disengagement with an ex-spouse that we noted earlier is common among the public. Still, some caregivers believed that, despite being divorced, they owed something to their ex-husbands and that helping them was necessary. Mary explained that "I married this guy, and I only got married once." Mary reported feeling guilty when she set limits on how much she did for her dependent ex-husband. Similarly, Sara, who also was actively providing care for a chronically ill ex-husband at the time of the interview, noted that, "I know I can't, you know, have him in my home so I have to distance myself, but it, I, I sometimes feel like I'm sentencing him to death or something." Aside from these few cases, guilt was not widely expressed by these caregivers.

It was noted earlier that network members often questioned the caregivers about their choice to provide care if the ex-husband was perceived as undeserving. Conflicted emotions were common in these cases (eight of the nine women reporting abuse conveyed intrapersonal experiences with role ambiguity), making caregiving especially challenging. Ruth, whose two-decade-long marriage was wrought with emotional abuse and mutual partner violence, spoke of her efforts to "put all my feelings, my ill feelings [about ex] aside and just focus on his—focus on him because I knew that he didn't have long to live." Kathy struggled daily with caring for a man for whom she had very mixed feelings and who had refused to assist her as she battled cancer earlier in their marriage. She noted, "I had days I really wanted to [help him] and then days that I didn't really want to be involved."

Finally, several caregivers shared powerful, often confusing, emotional reactions to their ex-husbands' illness, and, in some cases, death. The intensity of emotion felt at the loss of the ex-husband shocked several of the bereaved caregivers, especially when some of these men had provoked such strong unfavorable emotions at earlier points in their lives. As Melanie noted:

> I was surprised at my feeling for him and my reaction...I was devastated when he died. Five years ago I could have cheerfully backed over him in the van. I mean, I would have, I'm not kidding you. I was so angry with him. I could have killed him with my bare hands, you know. I did not expect this. I'm still grieving.

Melanie shared this response three months after losing her ex-husband; they had been married for 14 years and were divorced for 5 years prior to her providing care for him. Even for women who had been divorced much longer, like Anne, who lived apart from her husband 17 years before providing care, the grief was sometimes overwhelming:

> I'm surprised because it has taken me time, and it's been almost a year, and there's not a day goes by that I don't think about him or think about us... It's just a whole other realm of reality that it hit me like a ton of bricks.

In addition to being caught off guard by the emotions that their ex-husbands' illness or death elicited in them, some of these women reported spending considerable time trying to understand why they reacted the way they did. Meg puzzled over her feelings of shock when her ex-husband of 26 years died.

> I didn't understand why it bothered me. I hadn't lived with him for over 25 years.... I was just mourning this whole idea maybe, [a] fantasy I had of marriage and family and it, it was a huge piece of me that I have a family and take care of it and that it be happy and successful. And, of course, that never happened. So, when he died, it was the absolute realization of the loss of a dream.

Sheila struggled to handle the mismatch she experienced between her social status as a bereaved ex-wife and her severe and lingering emotional response:

> [There is] a real disconnect there with how I emotionally felt and what [I] was.... People don't understand I'm still mourning [be]cause I never thought of myself as anything but his wife, even though we were divorced. There was always a connection.

Consequences of Intrapersonal Role Ambiguity

The emotional struggle these women experienced over an ex-husband's illness or death was exacerbated by the lack of validation they received from others for their grief. Audrey, who was happily remarried at the time of the interview, told her son about her unexpected feelings following her ex-husband's death (they had been divorced 26 years): "I don't know what's wrong with me.... I didn't even know your dad for the last, I mean 10 years. I haven't talked to him or anything, and all of a sudden..." Though her son understood her response ("It's okay you know. It's really okay, Mom."), others, including friends, did not. Audrey referred to a recognized counseling term in explaining the situation she encountered with friends: "It's kind of a *disenfranchised kind of grief* where people are like, 'Well, why don't you just get over it [her ex-husband's death], you know? You're remarried.'"

Disenfranchised grief is a term Doka (1986) introduced to capture situations where individuals' mourning and grief are not recognized or validated by others because their status vis-à-vis the deceased is not socially recognized, or may even be socially sanctioned (e.g. gay partners, persons involved in extramarital affairs, and ex-spouses). This clearly was the case for Mary, whose ex-husband was suffering from early onset Alzheimer's disease at the time of the interview. She expressed the loss of the ex-husband that she knew, as well as the hurt she feels having no one who understands her situation and with whom she can talk. "People don't want to hear that" [about her emotional distress]. "He's nothing to you. What are you upset about? He's nothing to you," is what she hears from others, rather than receiving empathy and support. Such responses compound the emotional struggle of those who are grieving the loss of an ex-husband for whom they provided care.

Institutional Instances of Role Ambiguity

Ex-wife caregivers also experienced role ambiguity in their interactions with formal institutions, though role ambiguity of this type was least common (six of 21 cases). It was generally the representatives of formal institutions, such as doctors, nurses, funeral directors, and bosses who questioned or challenged the role of ex-wife caregivers. Often, role ambiguity surfaced in interactions with institutions because formal policies did not recognize the relationship between ex-wife caregiver and ex-husband care recipient as legitimate, legal, or "authorized" for medical purposes or various benefits and services.

A few caregivers shared the difficulties and frustration they experienced trying to meet their caregiving responsibilities as they encountered institutional roadblocks from hospitals and doctors. Ruth explained the trouble she initially had getting a clear diagnosis and prognosis of her ex-husband's condition when she took him in for the last five months of his life:

RUTH: I got a hold of the nursing report because, see, they [the medical professionals] kept a lot of things from me because I was no longer his wife.
INTERVIEWER: Oh, okay. So you weren't getting that information?
RUTH: At the nursing home he put me down as the only contact person, so they shared a lot of it with me at the nursing home. And then one day I went to his doctor's appointment, and the cancer doctor brung [sic] it up on his screen, telling me that he had a Stage 4 Cancer.
 Anne reported that not only were workers at the Veteran's Administration (VA) Hospital surprised when she accompanied her ex-husband to appointments, but, because of her unrecognized status, she often got the runaround when trying to meet his care needs.
ANNE: It's so hard. Like say someone would call and the doctor would call or, you know, like the pharmacy would call. "You gotta put Steve [her ex-husband] on the phone." You try to talk to the VA people—they won't talk to me [she told her ex-husband].
INTERVIEWER: Oh, really?
ANNE: I gotta put Steve on the phone because they don't have on record that I'm, that I have power of attorney and I'm his ex-wife so I'm not legally related to him. So they gotta speak to Steve. So, it was hard … that was all challenging to still care for him but not have the legal rights that I needed to have to do the things I needed to do.
 Sheila discussed challenges that she faced when trying to conduct official business related to her ex-husband's illness and death:
SHEILA: Probably one of the hardest things for me was I kept acting like a wife, and I wasn't the wife.
INTERVIEWER: In what WAY do you think you acted like that?
SHEILA: Every way. I wasn't in the position to make any decision for him. Wanted to, but didn't.…He had said that week before he died, he said "Well, I suppose we can have a service at St. Paul's Methodist Church," and that's where we were married and that's where he was baptized. But I totally let the kids, his son and daughter, make the plans, but I wanted to make the arrangements. I totally let them handle his cremation. I wanted to. I let them do it. So, and I guess it was okay. I wasn't the wife.

Clearly, a major barrier to effective and efficient caregiving for many of these ex-wives was the lack of recognition (legal and informal) of the role they had assumed. In some cases, though care roles had been legally authorized through medical power of attorney, professionals were not always aware of this or perhaps were surprised by and did not fully accept the decision.

Finding appropriate support services, either while caregiving or after care ended, also was a problem noted by a few of the participants due to their unrecognized status and ambiguous role. Mary claimed that ex-wife caregivers would have trouble getting any formal assistance or financial support for providing care to ex-husbands: "I don't know that any of the senior organizations or anybody would offer to help because, well, you know ... find a title for us."

Much of our discussion to this point has considered the absence of clear agreement regarding the accepted and expected behaviors, emotions, and attitudes that former spouses *should* convey toward one another. Mary's comment reminds us that it is often the label applied to a status that conveys the normative expectations associated with it. For ex-wife caregivers, it appears to be the "ex" part of their label that confuses others, even professionals. Mary reported that physicians and other medical professionals "don't know *who* the hell I am." Mark, her ex-husband, had asked her to wear her wedding ring again to simplify their situation in dealing with others. She says, "For me, it [wearing a ring] would shorten answers by about 50 words. If you have a ring, it says 'I'm attached to this guy.' If you don't have a ring, then *who are you?*" Mary was not the only ex-wife caregiver who reported that in dealing with professionals their ex-husbands would just refer to them as their "wives" to avoid role ambiguity problems. Sheila also told how she personally struggled to find an appropriate term for her social status. The connotations associated with the terms "ex-wife" or "ex-husband" tend to be negative, and, as Sheila conveyed in referring to her former husband, she "didn't want to say he's my ex-husband because he was more dear to me than that." In the end, Sheila coined the term "wasband" to refer to her former spouse as it seemed to capture her lingering love for and connection to this man.

A few women noted the unavailability of appropriate support and professional counseling services for persons in their role. Sheila did not specify why she found the hospice grief groups were not for her but commented to that effect. Perhaps women like Sheila felt as if their relationships are not fully validated in traditional bereavement support groups. Mary's explanation for the discomfort she experienced as an ex-wife attending a caregiver support group confirms this:

> But I'm not a wife. You know, the caregiver groups and all that stuff are for wives and children. The girls [her daughters] would go, but I don't know that I would be accepted there ... People just don't believe that you could care for somebody after you're divorced.

Institutional responses reflective of role ambiguity for ex-wife caregivers were also documented in the workplace. Of the women in our sample, nearly half (n = 9) held jobs or were on leave from work while providing care for their ex-husbands. A few employed women conveyed the hassles they confronted at work trying to secure time off to provide care for an ex-husband when the Family and Medical Leave Act (FMLA) did not apply. Anne told of how her job was jeopardized because of "penalty points" she acquired when she took time off for caregiving. When the interviewer asked what that meant, she explained, "You're only allowed so many points and you get fired." Anne tried other approaches to her situation, like using vacation time to care for her ex-husband. She also explained her situation to human resources staff, but that did not help: "I called the HR lady up and I told her what was going on. . . She goes, 'That's [caregiving for her ex-husband] not your responsibility.'" Anne's daughter was allowed to use FMLA for a while to help out, but "she [the HR person] wouldn't give me FMLA cause she said he's not related to me ... but then he passed away that week."

Mary recounted a similar unsupportive work setting in dealing with her ex-husband's illness and care needs. Her boss outright told her, "You're making choices. We think they're bad choices." Mary suspected that this disapproving boss would look unfavorably on her rearranging scheduled work appointments so that she could take her ex-husband to doctor's appointments on her lunch hour. She reflected:

> They're okay with me going to lunch with a colleague, but they don't want to hear that about Mark [her ex-husband]. They would have more respect if I had an issue with a dog and had to take a dog to the vet.

Mary hears repeatedly from her supervisor, "He's not related to you, we have no obligation to honor any request [for time off] from you." Fortunately for Mary, her ex-husband has been institutionalized and receives full-time professional care, which has reduced the care demands that she has to meet.

The narrow definition of family used in the FMLA legislation is especially problematic, given reductions in public resources for persons needing medical care. In fact, a few ex-wife caregivers had the impression, based on their experiences with their ex-husbands, that the health-care system and its representatives are more than willing to turn to "nonfamily" to provide care as a means of reducing the demand on the health-care system and its workers. Consider the comment of Sara, a social worker who formerly worked as a nurse:

> People that are involved in any way with his [ex-husband's] care, they want, they want me to do everything because that's kind of the nature of the system right now. You look for whoever is a support to the person and you bleed them dry, basically. I mean, that's just how it's set up because people are let out of the hospital too soon. They're forced out of the nursing home too soon because their payments run out. I mean, it just, if you don't have the financial resources and the, or the personal resources or whatever, you, it just falls back on whoever is, is stupid enough or whatever to do it.

Similarly, another nurse in the study, Mary, reported that social workers are "glad you're there 'cause that means [they] don't have to provide this dying guy with support." Yet, she sensed that the attitudes social workers often conveyed to ex-wife caregivers were critical and judgmental. Such mixed messages from formal providers were also evident to Ruth. Like Sara and Mary, she interpreted relief from professionals that *someone (anyone?)* would accept responsibility for these dying men:

RUTH: The VA and the social workers, they loved it that I took over.
INTERVIEWER: Why is that? What, what do you mean?
RUTH: Because they could tell that he wasn't getting the proper care from his own daughter …
INTERVIEWER: So, you think they were, again, just kind of relieved that someone [was handling it] appropriately?
RUTH: Oh, they were relieved. Totally relieved. Yeah, totally relieved.

Despite this acceptance and satisfaction that a nonfamily member—an ex-wife—would agree to provide the proper care, recall that earlier we shared Ruth's extreme frustration over being denied health information about her ex-husband and being unable to order prescriptions for him because of her unauthorized relationship to him. Inconsistent institutional responses of this nature interfere with the conduct of efficient caregiving. They also could jeopardize the willingness of nonfamily caregivers, like ex-wives, to continue performing care duties, which appear to be highly valued by the medical care system.

IMPLICATIONS AND RECOMMENDATIONS

This study provided rich description of the ways in which 21 middle-aged and older women encountered role ambiguity in providing primary care for their ill or dying ex-husbands. Most common among the three forms of role ambiguity that were identified were interpersonal experiences with role ambiguity, which involved network members questioning and challenging the assumed caregiver role. In response to such challenges and unclear internalized norms about appropriate behavior toward ex-husbands, several caregivers struggled intrapersonally with their assumed care role. Finally, several ex-wife caregivers noted role ambiguity at the institutional level, as they interacted with the medical establishment in providing care or with their workplace as they juggled the dual roles of employee and caregiver. Only three of the 21 interviewed women conveyed no experiences of role ambiguity.

As noted in the caregivers' responses, situations characterized by role ambiguity—whether interpersonally, intrapersonally, or institutionally experienced, may trigger a variety of negative emotional reactions (e.g. stress, self-doubt). Role ambiguity may also interfere with the ability of ex-wife caregivers to offer their best possible care. In response to these women's experiences and the apparent consequences of role ambiguity, we offer several suggestions.

At the interpersonal level, encouraging greater communication within families (especially extended families) regarding the care preferences of the patient could help to reduce role ambiguity for the caregiver. When patients' families are aware of their caregiver preferences, they may be more supportive of the caregiver and create less conflict, resulting in better adjustment for the caregiver and enhanced care for the patient.

Alternatively, in some cases it may be best for ex-wife caregivers to find ways to limit negative interactions with both family members and others.

Ex-wife caregivers also need more options for accessing social support through formal means. Offering support groups that are specifically targeted to less-traditional family forms and relationships may help to create alternative safe spaces/settings for people in a variety of relationships to express and explore their grief and to have it affirmed. As the baby boomer generation ages and the diversity of later life family forms increases, this need becomes especially critical.

Institutionally, professionals must be better prepared to serve diverse populations and family forms, and policies should be more inclusive and responsive to contemporary family life. Training professionals in the health-care and human-services fields to be more attentive to the unique needs of different populations and patients ... would be highly beneficial. Ideally, diversity training would extend beyond sexual orientation and culture differences to emphasize that families and caring relationships come in many forms, all deserving recognition and respect.

Regarding policy changes, our findings suggest that FMLA is too narrowly targeted to traditional family relationships. If the medical system is increasingly depending on a variety of relational partners to assume care roles, as alluded to by caregivers in this study, then expansion of FMLA is necessary to meet the care demands of a growing number of Americans. Because of the severe economic consequences divorce presents for many women, and their pattern of extended employment into later life it is especially critical that workplace policies support ex-wife caregivers. Finally, in terms of medical policies, it would be beneficial to make information about advanced directives and durable power of attorney for health care more widely available to patients so they can ensure that health-care rights and legal protections are appropriately offered to themselves and their intended caregivers.

REFERENCE

Doka, K. J. (1986). Loss upon loss: The impact of death after divorce. *Death Studies, 10*, 441–449.

22

Why Fewer and Fewer Americans Are Getting Divorced

Tera R. Jordan

Fewer and fewer Americans are getting divorced, with the rates falling 18 percent between 2008 and 2016.

Among American adults, there is support for divorce when couples do not get along. Women, people from underrepresented racial and ethnic groups, and adults who have experienced divorce personally or among friends and family are especially likely to be accepting.

Despite this growing acceptance, the divorce rate dipped again in 2018. The decline began in 1980 or 1990, depending on the data source and experts. According to the Centers for Disease Control, the number of divorced persons per 1,000 Americans fell from 4.7 in 1990 to 2.9 in 2016.

Who is driving this downward trend? Adults age 45 and younger.

YOUNGER ADULTS

Young adults are being more decisive – in not only the timing of their nuptials, but also their choice to marry.

Many of these younger adults choose to marry after they have achieved their desired levels of education, established careers and stabilized their finances. They also want to be "bonded" with a mate based on love, friendship and common interests, not social obligation.

In the United States, the median age at marriage has risen, from 26.1 for men and 22 for women in 1890, to 29.8 for men and 27.8 for women in 2018.

I am a human development and family studies scholar who has spent 20 years studying intimate relationships. In one study, I examined the perspectives of 52 married black men. Achieving their goals relative to education, work and finances was a significant factor in deciding when to marry their wives.

Men praised how the unions with their wives afforded them secure attachment and emotional support, as well as enhanced life success. Nearly one-quarter emphasized the role of individual development and being ready for the type of commitment that a successful marriage requires.

Jordan, Tara. "Why Fewer and Fewer Americans Are Getting Divorced." *The Conversation*, May 30, 2019.

These considerations promote the likelihood of long-term, happy marriages in a culture that values fulfilling one's goals and happiness.

GRAY DIVORCE

Meanwhile, older adults are actually becoming more likely to get divorced.

Among those 50 years of age or older, scholars have reported a rise in divorce from 1 in 10 in 1990 to nearly 1 in 4 in 2010. This trend is called "gray divorce."

A report commissioned by the AARP offers insight into the nature and consequences of gray divorce. Women's economic independence may help them opt out of these unhappy marriages.

Some older adults end their unhappy unions because they have grown apart. In her dissertation and forthcoming book, marriage and family therapist Crystal Hemesath defines falling out of romantic love as a lack of sexual attraction, emotional connectedness or sense of relationship togetherness.

After older adults have perhaps cared for dependent children, parents or other relatives, spouses may reassess their marriages and ask, "What's next?," "Who are you?" or, better yet, "Who am I?"

Hemesath interviewed 15 adults. Laura, a 59-year-old woman who was married for 18 years, said this:

> It wasn't until my dad became gravely ill. I would say to my husband, 'Will you go in and see if dad's okay?' He'd say, 'He's fine.' It causes you to look at your own mortality. This person is still emotionally unavailable and distant and if I don't get out now, I'm doomed. I was unhappy in year one and I stayed 17 more. I hoped that it would change. I didn't really have the courage to get out. I think a lot of people stay in … for fear of the unknown. It sort of takes your soul away.

Among those 50 and over, there may simply be irreconcilable differences with how one chooses to live the rest of his or her life and the type of love and companionship one desires.

CHOOSING MARRIAGE

The pattern in marriage and divorce across both age groups highlights the rise in individualism in our culture. Today, adults have more agency to chart their own life paths based on options they perceive as being available to them.

And because society is more supportive of other ways of forming families, adults are more apt to take their time to marry, if they want to, and exit, if they need to, in order to be happy.

Sociologist Philip Cohen summed up this issue in a September 2018 Bloomberg article. "Marriage is more and more an achievement of status, rather than something that people do regardless of how they're doing," he said.

This is an important change in the way in which adults approach marriage.

SECTION V
Reproducing Families

INTRODUCTION

Reproduction is not only a biological process, but is socially, politically, symbolically, and legally meaningful. As such, who reproduces, how people reproduce, and what rights and responsibilities they should have as a result have been a subject of regulation. This regulation matters in determining how formal familial relationships—and new additions to families—are to be recognized. In these ways, reproduction is simultaneously personal and political. Policies may aim to encourage more births, control population growth, or limit access to birth control, beliefs about who should reproduce and which people are seen as undesirable reproducers—usually defined by race, ethnicity, class, immigration, or disability—have informed law and policy around reproduction. This section examines how law has regulated reproduction by examining policies ranging from access to birth control and abortion to the costs of childbirth to arguments about the use of reproductive technologies to demonstrate how inequality infuses regulation of reproduction, which, in turn, configures families.

EUGENICS AND STRATIFIED REPRODUCTION

Many legal efforts to regulate reproduction in the United States and elsewhere have been built on eugenic ideas, which hold that the genetic quality of society can be manipulated by controlling who reproduces. From the Holocaust in Europe to mass sterilization campaigns in the United States, these state-sponsored efforts build on the myth that socially desirable traits are genetic and inheritable. This has meant, on the one hand, that people who are deemed to have undesirable traits—which has historically targeted people of color, immigrants, people with disabilities, those with mental illness, and poor people—are discouraged or prevented from having children. On the other hand, those with purported desirable traits are encouraged to reproduce—which has included those who are white, wealthy, native-born, and Protestant. This kind of stratified reproduction, in which the ability to control one's own reproduction is based on individual and social group characteristics, informs laws and policies around reproduction (Ginsburg and Rapp 1995).

Sterilization Abuse

Legal efforts to prevent people seen as undesirable from reproducing, known as negative eugenics, were commonplace through the twentieth century, with federally funded sterilization programs operating in 32 states. In one landmark case in 1927, the US Supreme Court upheld the constitutionality of a Virginia law that allowed the state to sterilize people without consent for the good of society. In that case, *Buck v Bell*, a young woman who had been institutionalized for "feeblemindedness" and "promiscuity" was sterilized after giving birth to a baby that resulted from being assaulted by the son of her foster family (Aultman 2006). Supreme Court Justice Oliver Wendell Holmes famously wrote in his decision, "It is better for the world, if instead of waiting to execute degenerate offspring for crime, or to let them starve for their imbecility, society can prevent those who are manifestly unfit from continuing their kind." Pointing to her, her newborn baby, and her mother, he wrote, "Three generations of imbeciles are enough."

In the subsequent decades, the use of sterilization grew, often targeting girls as young as nine years of age. The 1974 US Supreme Court case of *Relf v Weinberger* brought to light the widespread use of sterilization without consent. In this case, Mary Alice and Minnie Relf, girls who were 14 and 12 years old, were sterilized after a public health nurse told their mother she was giving them a birth control shot. Their mother, who could not read or write, signed the consent form with an X. The Southern Poverty Law Center sued on their behalf, which led to the discovery that an estimated 100,000 to 150,000 poor people were sterilized annually under federally funded programs, and many others were forced to consent to sterilization when threatened with the loss of their welfare benefits. The case resulted in a ban on federal funds being used in such situations, but did not outlaw sterilization abuse (Southern Poverty Law Center 1974).

A year later, ten women in California sued a hospital for sterilization abuse after a whistle-blower exposed common practices that coerced or deceived women in efforts to sterilize them. In *Madrigal vs Quilligan* (1975), the women showed that doctors taunted Mexican American women while they were in labor with promises of pain medications if they signed a consent form to be sterilized. Many testified they were told the procedure was reversible or were not told what the procedure was. The judge in that case ruled that the sterilizations resulted from "a breakdown in communications between the patients and the doctors," and not the result of malice, and ruled in favor of the hospital. Nonetheless, the case led to policy changes, including a waiting period between consent and performance of sterilization and requirements to translate materials from English into Spanish.

The eugenics beliefs that led to sterilization abuse also led to heavy-handed ways to encourage women with traits deemed desirable to have more children. This practice of positive eugenics led President Theodore Roosevelt to chastise white Protestant women who had begun having fewer babies—with two children becoming the norm. Delivering his speech in 1905 and drawing on fears of immigration and population growth among people of color, Roosevelt referenced white women's decisions to have fewer children as "race suicide." In his national address, he cautioned that

> if the average family in which there are children contained but two children the nation as a whole would decrease in population so rapidly that in two or three generations it would very deservedly be on the point of extinction.

Blaming women for acting on what he called "this base and selfish doctrine," Roosevelt argued they would deserve this collapse, explaining that "a race that practised race suicide would thereby conclusively show that it was unfit to exist, and that it had better give place to people who had not forgotten the primary laws of their being" (Roosevelt 1905).

Recognizing the history of sterilization abuse, some southern states have begun offering financial compensation to the surviving victims of forced sterilization. Nonetheless, efforts to coerce sterilization continue. Judges across the country have offered women and occasionally men shorter criminal sentences, preservation of welfare benefits, or to reduce punishment for non-payment of child support, contingent on their consent to use long-acting birth control or become sterilized.

Stratified Access to Preventative Care

Inequality shapes experiences of reproduction in ways that are significant but might not always be visible. Low-income women in the United States are more likely to suffer from infertility than their wealthier counterparts. They may live in communities with greater environmental hazards that can affect their fertility and pregnancy outcomes. Nationally, about 7.4 percent of married women in the United States suffer from infertility. Among African Americans, that number is 11.5 percent (Armstrong and Plowden 2012).

Inequality also shapes birth outcomes. Women who are poor and women of color are more likely to give birth to babies with low birth weight and have babies who have health problems. As the chapter by Maria Rodriguez and Jens Hainmuelle shows, immigration status and access to preventative care can affect long-term health outcomes for babies. Even in the best of circumstances, prenatal and birth care can be costly, as the chapter by Simon Haeder shows. Black, American Indian, and Alaska Native women are two to three times more likely to die from pregnancy-related causes than are white women. According to the Centers for Disease Control and Prevention, these disparities increase with age, with Black, American Indian, and Alaska Native women over 30 years of age dying of pregnancy-related causes at four to five times the rate of white women. These patterns persist, irrespective of educational levels.

REPRODUCTIVE SELF-DETERMINATION

Because reproduction is politically contentious and stratifies along lines of inequality, women have faced challenges both in having children they want—as illustrated in the stories of sterilization abuse—but also in avoiding pregnancies they do not want. The ability to control one's own reproduction and determine how many offspring one has is a fundamental desire that spans geography, history, legal context, and cultures. As just one example, estimates are that 99 percent of sexually experienced women in the United States have ever used contraception (CDC 2012). Nonetheless, laws and policies affect an individual's ability to do so.

Birth Control

Women in the United States have used contraception widely since the nineteenth century. The invention of vulcanized rubber in the mid-1800s allowed for better access to methods like condoms and syringes (a device that aimed to wash sperm away), but many people relied on a variety of folk methods that worked with varying degrees of success. During this time, there were few attempts to regulate birth control. That changed in the late 1800s.

In 1873, Anthony Comstock founded the New York Society for the Suppression of Vice, an organization that aimed to stop pornography and other material he saw as "obscene, lewd, or lascivious." Comstock became a US postal inspector and successfully lobbied for the passage of the Comstock Act, which made it illegal to publish, possess, sell, lend, exhibit, or give away a wide range of materials, including

> an obscene book, pamphlet, paper, writing, advertisement, circular, print, picture, drawing or other representation, figure, or image on or of paper or other material, or any cast instrument, or other article of an immoral nature, or any drug or medicine, or any article whatever, for the prevention of conception.

Among the materials he classified as obscene were educational books and pamphlets that provided information about birth control as well as devices to prevent pregnancy. The penalty for violation was six months to five years in prison or fines between $100 and $2,000 for each offense. The federal Comstock Act and state versions remained in place for more than 70 years.

At the same time Comstock was crusading against family planning, Margaret Sanger, a public health nurse and family planning activist, worked to distribute birth control information and devices, including an early version of a diaphragm. She opened a birth control clinic in Brooklyn in 1916 that was immediately shut down by police, and she was prosecuted for violating the Comstock law. In 1921, she founded the American Birth Control League, which eventually became the Planned Parenthood Federation of America. Sanger's legacy is complicated. She was a powerful advocate for women's rights to self-determination but also worked closely with, and accepted funding from, eugenicists who wanted to promote birth control among poor and immigrant communities. One of Sanger's legacies is that she was instrumental in bringing together researchers and investors to create the birth control pill.

The oral birth control pill has dramatically changed the world of family planning. It was first licensed in the United States in 1957 after a year of clinical trials in Puerto Rico on women who did not knowingly consent to participate in research. The pill was initially approved to treat "menstrual disorders," a condition that skyrocketed after the pill was made available. In 1960, the pill became officially available for contraceptive use. Within five years, 6.5 million women were using it.

The widespread use of birth control led to cultural changes in the subsequent decades. Individuals could be sexually active with a much lower risk of pregnancy. This facilitated women's ability to complete education, earn graduate degrees, and enter the workforce in greater numbers. Birth control also allows women to escape many of the health risks associated with pregnancy. Newer hormonal methods, such as long-acting reversible contraception (IUDs, implants, and injections), provide some of these same benefits. For this reason, the Institutes of Medicine, a body of medical experts charged by Congress to review medical evidence and make recommendations improve the nation's health, issued a report in 2011 defining contraception as a key part of women's preventative health. As a result, the Patient Protection and Affordable Care Act (ACA) included contraception for women as a part of preventative healthcare that should be provided without cost to the user. This federal policy aims to make access to birth control affordable. The chapter by Krystale Littlejohn explains why this coverage for prescription contraception matters to men and women.

Abortion

About half of all pregnancies in the United States are unintended, and about 18 percent of pregnancies (excluding miscarriages) in 2017 ended in abortion (Guttmacher Institute 2019). Abortion is defined as a medical procedure that leads to the deliberate termination of a pregnancy after a fertilized egg (a pre-embryo) has implanted in the uterine wall (implantation usually takes several days to more than a week after conception). Ninety percent of abortions occur in the first 12 weeks and only about 1 percent takes place after 20 weeks. In the United States, there were 862,320 abortions performed in 2017, down 7 percent from 926,190 in 2014. Despite stigma associated with abortion, about one in four women will have an abortion by the age of 45 years, based on 2014 estimates (Guttmacher Institute 2019).

The reasons women give for seeking abortion services suggest that inequality plays a role. About 59 percent of women who have abortions are already mothers. Of women who received abortions in 2014, about 75 percent were poor (having an income below the federal poverty level of $15,730 for a family of two in 2014) or low-income (having an income of 100–199 percent of the federal poverty level) (Guttmacher Institute 2019). Women consistently rank concerns about money as the leading reason they choose to terminate their pregnancy (Chae et al. 2017).

The small percentage of women who seek abortions after 20 weeks do so for a few different reasons. Some learn late in their pregnancies that their fetuses have serious genetic disorders or are not developing in a way in which they will survive. Some face threats to their own health because of the pregnancy. Some are unable to raise funds to pay for an abortion, which can delay access. Some women, often younger teens, may not realize they are pregnant until later in their pregnancies. The chapter by Diana Greene Foster, Rana E. Barar, and Heather Gould shows the different outcomes between women who were able to obtain an abortion and those who were not.

Reproductive Technologies and New Family Configurations

Assisted reproduction refers to pregnancies conceived in ways other than through sex, and often with a medical intermediary and/or the use of technology. This section provides an overview of the technologies and highlights how they have challenged legal definitions of family.

Insemination involves inserting sperm into a woman's body to increase chances of conception. This technology is relatively "low-tech" and has been in use for more than a century. Medical providers are often involved but are not required. The sperm may come from a man who intends to be the father or from a donor, depending on the circumstances surrounding the intended conception. So in one case, a man who intends to parent the child may use his own sperm to increase chances of conception, while in another scenario, a man who wants to be a parent but is infertile may see his female partner inseminated with sperm from another man. In yet another configuration, a lesbian couple may use sperm from a donor to conceive their child. In some cases, donors are known to the parents, such as when they ask a friend to provide sperm. In other cases, sperm is purchased from sperm banks, where donors are paid and are generally anonymous, although they may agree to be contacted in the future by their offspring. The chapter by Maura Ryan and Amanda Moras examines some of the ways lesbian couples select donors. The question of whether men who donate sperm can claim parental rights has been the subject of a many lawsuits. (There is some discussion of paternity and law in Section X).

In vitro fertilization (IVF) is a newer technology in which sperm and egg are fertilized outside of the human body before being implanted in a uterus where it can grow into a baby. This technique typically requires a woman to inject drugs that suppress her natural menstrual cycle and then induce the ovaries to release many more eggs than would be normal. A medical provider then retrieves the eggs by inserting a needle connected to a suction device into the vagina. Placed in petri dishes with sperm, these eggs ideally will be fertilized and allowed to grow for a few days in the lab before being transferred to a woman's body. Newer technologies involve injecting a single sperm into a single egg or genetically testing the fertilized eggs, known as pre-embryos, to screen for genetic disorders.

Gestation is an essential part of reproduction. Embryos must be gestated inside a uterus to develop into a baby. The person whose uterus it is could intend to be a parent, or it could be someone who has agreed to carry the pregnancy for someone else as a surrogate—either for pay or for other reasons. There can be a lot of variation in the social and genetic relationships between a child and the providers of sperm and eggs, the person who will gestate the pregnancy, and the intended parents. For example, egg and sperm can come from one or more intended parents but be gestated by a third person as a solution for infertility or if a woman wants or needs to avoid pregnancy. In another example, eggs and/or sperm can come from donors and be implanted into an intended parent or a surrogate. There are myriad combinations. While the technology may be the same, the social and legal definitions can vary dramatically.

Louise Brown was the first baby born from IVF in 1978—dubbed the first "test tube baby." Estimates from the Centers from Disease Control and Prevention are that 1.7 percent of babies born each year in the United States are the result of reproductive technologies like IVF. In 2016, about 26 percent of IVF procedures led to a live birth (Eskew and Jungheim 2017). Although infants resulting from reproductive technologies accounted for a small proportion of all infants born, these technologies contributed to 16.4 percent of all multiple infants (such as twins, triplets) born in the United States (CDC 2019). As the chapter by Danielle Czarnecki shows, how women perceive these technologies are highly personal and often depend on their own faith beliefs.

Technology and Legal Parentage

Since their earliest uses, significant questions have arisen about who should be recognized as a legal parent when a child is born through use of reproductive technologies. In theory, a child could be born with at least five people who all feel a claim to them, either biologically, genetically, or socially. A child could have a person who provided the ovum, a person who provided sperm, another person who gestated them, and any number of intended parents. Since the law only recognizes a maximum of two legal parents, courts have frequently been asked to sort through competing claims. As the chapter by Barbara Katz Rothman shows, courts have most often chosen to recognize "seed," or genetics, when granting parental rights. This means that surrogates, who are not genetically related to the child because someone else's ovum was used, are virtually never granted parental rights. Sperm and egg donors who provide their genetic material through a medical provider also rarely have claims. However, in some instances, the lines between these roles are not entirely clear. Two cases illustrate how these technologies complicate parental determinations.

In the case of *Johnson v Calvert*, a Superior Court considered whether a surrogate could be recognized as a legal parent. Crispina Calvert, a Filipina woman, and her husband Mark, a white man, wanted children. Crispina's uterus had been surgically removed, but since she still had ovaries, she and her husband opted to hire a surrogate to gestate a pregnancy using their eggs and sperm. They entered a contract with Anna Johnson, an African American single mother, who agreed to gestate the pregnancy and would receive payment after giving the Calverts the baby. Shortly after the baby's birth, Anna filed suit to be declared the legal mother while the Calverts also requested to be legally recognized as the parents. The court accepted that Crispina Calvert was the child's genetic mother (confirmed with testing) and that Anna Johnson was, as defined in law, the child's "natural mother" because she gave birth. Yet, as the court summarized, "for any child California law recognizes only one natural mother, despite advances in reproductive technology rendering a different outcome biologically possible."

In deciding which mother should have legal rights, the court sided with Crispina Calvert. The decision noted that when "the two ways do not coincide in one woman, under state law, the natural mother is the one who intended to bring about the birth of the child whom she intended to raise as her own." The surrogacy agreement makes clear the intention of the relationship. The majority decision argued that

> a woman who enters into a gestational surrogacy arrangement is not exercising her own right to make procreative choices; she is agreeing to provide a necessary and profoundly important service without (by definition) any expectation that she will raise the resulting child as her own.

Although many advocates and scholars have pointed to the coercive nature of surrogacy contracts that include payment, the court also rejected the notion that women "cannot knowingly and intelligently agree to gestate and deliver a baby for intending parents." Instead, they accepted that Anna Johnson, a vocational nurse who already had a child of her own, was capable of making an informed choice to enter into the surrogacy agreement and rejected her claims to motherhood. (*Johnson v. Calvert*, 1993). It is worth noting that not all states allow surrogates to enter contracts or receive payment, and not all states allow intended parents to immediately claim parentage. In addition, a growing number of countries allow intended parents from other countries to hire surrogates, which changes processes and rules of consent considerably.

A different case illustrates the complications in defining family in novel ways, which technologies can facilitate. KM and EG became a couple in 1993 and registered as domestic partners in 1994. After failing to become pregnant after 12 attempts with donor sperm and another with in vitro fertilization, EG agreed to use KM's ova and donor sperm. This worked and EG gave birth to twin girls in 1995. About two weeks later, EG and KM were married in a secular ceremony that was not a legal one (since same sex marriage was not yet legal).

Whether or not KM was a legal parent became a question when the couple separated in 2001. At the time of the twins' birth, EG had asked KM not to tell anyone she was genetically related to the twins and was hesitant to allow KM to legally adopt them. EG listed only herself on the children's birth certificate, but medical records indicate both women were present. Only EG's name was on baptism records, but KM appeared as a second parent on preschool registration forms. Friends hosted a joint baby shower for them as a couple and they received joint gifts. At the time of the ovum transfer, KM signed a consent form that read,

> I waive any right and relinquish any claim to the donated eggs or any pregnancy or offspring that might result from them. I agree that the recipient may regard the donated eggs and any offspring resulting therefrom as her own children.

The children called KM's parents "Granny and Papa" but no one told those grandparents of KM's genetic relationship to the children. When EG wanted to move out of state with the children after the couple separated, KM requested formal recognition as a co-parent and the right to visitation.

A lower court initially ruled that KM was not legally a parent and had surrendered those rights when she consented to egg donation. However, the California Supreme Court overruled that decision and noted that when looking at intent, they recognize that KM and EG had a committed relationship before the conception of the twins and that they "planned to provide together a stable and nurturing home for the children." Drawing on the Uniform Parentage Act (discussed in length in Section X), a law aimed to define fatherhood for unmarried genetic fathers, the decision explained that "K.M.'s genetic relationship to the children in the present case constitutes evidence of a mother and child relationship as contemplated by the Act" (*K.M. v. E.G*, 118 Cal.App.4th 477, 482-0 (Cal. Ct. App. 2004)).

These cases, and many others, demonstrate the challenges courts have faced in determining parental rights, and sorting through the new family configurations that can result from technology. Most states do not have laws specifically about reproductive technologies, so courts have relied heavily on laws intended to recognize paternity of unmarried fathers, adoption, or surrender of parental rights. The result is that courts have overwhelmingly favored genetics. In surrogacy cases where the surrogate also uses her own ovum, she often is able to assert parental rights in a way Anna Johnson was not. It is not insignificant that most surrogacy agreements (excluding those between close friends and family members) cross lines of race, class, and education, in which surrogates usually having fewer monetary and cultural resources and status than the intended parents do.

The social meanings of reproduction do not always align with the legal definitions. The ongoing insistence, with a few notable exceptions, that children may only have two legal parents complicates new lived realities of family.[1] The increasing number of transgender men who have uteruses and trans women who produce sperm that lead to pregnancies also challenge legal and medical systems in new ways. Race, class, gender, ethnicity, disability, and immigration continue to be significant social and structural forces that shape lived experiences of reproduction, but also the regulation of reproduction and families.

REFERENCES

Armstrong, Alicia and Torie C. Plowden. 2012. "Ethnicity and Assisted Reproductive Technologies." *Clinical Practice* 9(6): 651–658. doi: 10.2217/cpr.12.65.

Aultman, Julie M. 2006. "Eugenomics: Eugenics and Ethics in the 21st Century." *Genomics, Society and Policy* 2(2): 28.

CDC. 2012. "Current Contraceptive Use in the United States, 2006–2010, and Changes in Patterns of Use since 1995." *National Health Statistics Report*, Atlanta, GA: Centers for Disease Control and Prevention. (https://www.cdc.gov/nchs/data/nhsr/nhsr060.pdf).

CDC. 2019. *State-Specific Assisted Reproductive Technology Surveillance*, Atlanta, GA: Centers for Disease Control and Prevention. (https://www.cdc.gov/art/state-specific-surveillance/index.html).

Chae, Sophia, Sheila Desai, Marjorie Crowell and Gilda Sedgh. 2017. "Reasons Why Women Have Induced Abortions: A Synthesis of Findings from 14 Countries." *Contraception* 96(4): 233–241.

Eskew, Ashley M. and Emily S. Jungheim. 2017. "A History of Developments to Improve in Vitro Fertilization." *Missouri medicine* 114(3): 156–159.

Ginsburg, Faye D. and Rayna Rapp. 1995. *Conceiving the New World Order: The Global Politics of Reproduction*. Berkeley, CA: University of California Press.

Guttmacher Institute. 2019. "Induced Abortion in the United States." (https://www.guttmacher.org/fact-sheet/induced-abortion-united-states).

Roosevelt, Theodore. 1905. "Address by President Roosevelt before the National Congress of Mothers." Theodore Roosevelt Collection. Houghton Library, Harvard University.

Southern Poverty Law Center. 1974. "Relf V. Weinberger Case Number Civ. A. Nos. 73-1557 (Consolidated with 74-243)." Southern Poverty Law Center. (https://www.splcenter.org/seeking-justice/case-docket/relf-v-weinberger).

NOTE

1 Notably, about a dozen states allow for a three-parent (or tri-parent) family, but there are no statistics to know whether this is yet routine. In some cases, courts will decide an adult is "a psychological parent" and will recognize them as a third parent. In other cases, a gay or lesbian couple with a genetic co-parent have also all gained legal recognition.

23

Beyond Mothers and Fathers

Ideology in a Patriarchal Society

Barbara Katz Rothman

Something has gone seriously awry in our cultural understanding of motherhood in America. We find ourselves surrounded by contradictions that would give George Orwell pause: the return of the midwife, and the rise of the cesarean section; cigarette ads, clearly aimed at young women, carrying a warning that smoking harms fetuses; the infant formula companies distributing sample packages of formula for new mothers, labeled "In support of your decision to breast feed." An angry Black social worker says of a grieving white woman whose Black foster child was taken away after three years: "She had no right to love that child. It was just a *job*." Much the same is said of a pregnant woman who is not the "mother" of the fetus in her belly, because it was contracted to be there. Childbearing at 40 is chic, at 50 is the new frontier, at 18 is pathetic.

To understand it, to explain it, we need to step back and try to disentangle the contradictions. When we do, we find ourselves unweaving the strands of a fabric, understanding the pattern as we work it backwards to the underlying threads. American motherhood now rests on three deeply rooted ideologies that shape what we see and what we experience, three central threads of motherhood: an ideology of patriarchy, an ideology of technology, and an ideology of capitalism. As these three come together, with all of their multiplicity of meaning, they give us the shape, and the discordance, of our experience—the fabric of motherhood.

As used in this chapter, ideology is the way a group looks at the world, the way it organizes its thinking about the world. An ideology can let us see things, but it can also blind us, close our eyes to our own lived reality, our own experiences, our own bodies. The ideologies of patriarchy, technology, and capitalism give us our vision of motherhood while they block our view, give us a language for some things while they silence us for others.

The ideology of patriarchy is perhaps the easiest to understand of the three ideologies that shape motherhood. More than half the world has another reality called women's reality to contradict it. But women's reality is not the dominant ideology, and women's view of the world is overruled by men's view. Motherhood in a patriarchal society is what mothers and babies signify to men. For women this can mean too many pregnancies or too few; "trying again" for a son; covering up male infertility with donor insemination treated as the deepest darkest secret; having some of our children called "illegitimate"; not having access to abortions we do want; being pressured into abortions we may not want. The ideology of

Rothman, Barbara Katz. "Beyond Mothers and Fathers: Ideology in a Patriarchal Society." In *Mothering*, pp. 139–157. New York and London: Routledge, 2016.

capitalism, that goods are produced for profit, is also something clear to us; we know that some societies avoid the profit motive, and that most societies feel there should be *some* limits to how much of life should be viewed as a commodity. It may seem farfetched to apply this ideology to motherhood and to children. But the family has always been an economic unit as well as a social and psychological unit. What is new, perhaps, is the shift from children as workers to children as commodities, accompanying the change in the family from its role as a unit of production to its new role as a unit of consumption. Finally, the ideology of technology shapes motherhood. No longer an event shaped by religion and family, having a baby has become part of the high-tech medical world. But as an ideology, a way of thinking, technology is harder to pin down, so pervasive has it become in Western society. The ideology of technology encourages us to see ourselves as objects, to see people as made up of machines and part of larger machines. It is this mechanization that connects the ideology of patriarchy with capitalism, to create a worldview. This chapter addresses each of these ideologies as separate ways of thinking; then, most importantly, it turns to the ways they weave together to create a pattern, a fabric, both a curtain and a cage.

THE IDEOLOGY OF PATRIARCHY

The term "patriarchy" is often used loosely as a synonym for "sexism," or to refer to any social system where men rule. The term technically means "rule of fathers," but in its current practical usage it more often refers to any system of male superiority and female inferiority. But male dominance and patriarchal rule are not quite the same thing, and when the subject is motherhood, the difference is important.

Patriarchal kinship is the core of what is meant by patriarchy: the idea that paternity is the central social relationship. A very clear statement of patriarchal kinship is found in the Book of Genesis, in the "begats." Each man, from Adam onward, is described as having "begat a son in his likeness, after his image." In a patriarchal kinship system, children are born to men, out of women. That is, women, in this system, bear the children of men.

While all societies appear to be male dominated to some degree, not all societies are patriarchal. In some, the line of descent is not from father to son, but along the lines of the women. These are called "matrilineal" societies: it is a shared mother that makes for a shared lineage or family group. Men still rule in these groups, but they do not rule as fathers. They rule the women and children who are related to them through their mother's line. Women in such a system are not a vulnerability, but a source of connection. As anthropologist Glenn Petersen says, in a matrilineal system "women, rather than infiltrating and subverting patrilinies, are acknowledged to produce and reproduce the body of society itself."[1] People are not men's children coming through the bodies of women, but the children of women.

In a patriarchal system, in contrast, the essential concept is the "seed," the part of men that grows into the children of their likeness within the bodies of women. Such a system is inevitably male dominated, but it is a particular kind of male domination. Men control women as daughters, much as they control their sons, but they also control women as the mothers of men's children. It is women's motherhood that men must control to maintain patriarchy. In a patriarchy, because what is valued is the relationship of a man to his sons, women are a vulnerability that men have: to beget these sons, men must pass their seed through the body of a woman.

In a patriarchal system, when people talk about blood ties, they are talking about a genetic tie, a connection by seed. In a mother-based system, the blood tie is the mingled blood of mothers and their children: children grow out of the blood of their mothers, of their bodies and being. The shared bond of kinship comes through mothers. The maternal tie is based on the growing of children. The patriarchal tie is based on genetics, the act of impregnating.

Each of these ways of thinking leads to different ideas about what a person is. In a mother-based system, a person is what mothers grow—people are made of the care and nurturance that bring a baby forth into the world, and turn the baby into a member of the society. In a patriarchal system, a person is what grows out of men's seed. The essence of the person, what the person really is, is there in the seed when it is planted in the mother.

Modern procreative technology has been forced to go beyond the sperm as seed, however. "Daddy plants a seed in Mommy" won't work any more; modern science has had to confront the *egg* as seed also. Scientific thinking cannot possibly hold on to old notions of women as nurturers of men's seeds. The doctor who has spent time "harvesting" eggs from women's bodies for *in vitro* fertilization fully understands the significance of women's seed. But that does not mean we no longer continue to think of the seed as the essence of being. It is not the end of the belief that the seeds, the genes, are everything, that they are all that really matters in the making of a baby, that they are what *real* kinship is based on.

The old patriarchal kinship system had a clear place for women: they were the nurturers of men's seeds, the soil in which seeds grew, the daughters who bore men offspring. When forced to acknowledge that a woman's genetic contribution is equal to a man's, Western patriarchy was in trouble. But *the central concept of patriarchy, the importance of the seed, was retained by extending the concept to women.* Valuing the seed of women extends to them some of the privileges of patriarchy. That is, when the significance of women's seed is acknowledged in their relationship with their children, women, too, have paternity rights in their children. Unlike what happens in a mother-based system, however, this relationship between women and their children is not based on motherhood per se, not on the unique nurturance, the long months of pregnancy, the intimate connections with the baby as it grows and moves inside her body, passes through her genitals, and sucks at her breasts. Instead, women are said to own their babies, have "rights" to them, just as men do: based on their seed. This does not end patriarchy, and it does not end the domination of the children of women by men. Instead, by maintaining the centrality of the seed, the ideology maintains the rights of men in their children, even as it recognizes something approaching equal rights of women in their children. Since men's control over women and the children of women is no longer based simply on men's (no longer) unique seed, men's economic superiority and other privileges of a male-dominated social system become increasingly important. Children are, based on the seed, presumptively "half his, half hers"—and might as well have grown in the backyard. Women do not gain their rights to their children in this society as *mothers*, but as father equivalents, equivalent sources of seed.

The ideology of patriarchal society thus goes much deeper than male dominance. It means far more than just having men in charge, or men making more decisions than women do. The ideology of patriarchy is a basic worldview, and in a patriarchal system that view permeates all of our thinking. In our society, the ideology of patriarchy provides us with an understanding not only of the relations between women and men but also of the relations between mothers and their children.

In a patriarchal society, men use women to have their children. A man can use this woman or that woman to have *his* children. He can hire this woman or that woman to substitute for one or another aspect (biological, social, or psychological) of the mothering his child needs. From the view of the man, his seed is irreplacable; the mothering, the nurturance, is substitutable.

And from the woman's point of view? We can use this man's sperm or that one's to have our children. With this or that man as father, our bellies will swell, life will stir, milk will flow. We may prefer one man's seed to another, just as a man may prefer one woman's nurturance to another for his child, but they are substitutable, they are interchangeable. For a man, what makes the child *his* is his seed. For women, what makes the child ours is the nurturance, the work of our bodies. Wherever the sperm came from, it is in our bodies that our babies grow, and it is our physical presence and nurturance that make our babies ours. But is that inevitable? Did not some women substitute other women's bodies when they hired wet nurses? Don't some women substitute other women's arms, other women's touch, when they hire housekeepers and baby-sitters and day-care workers? And now the new procreative technology lets us cut our seeds loose from our bodies, and plant them in other women's bodies. The seed, the egg, of one woman can be brought to term in the body of another.

We have a technology that takes Susan's egg and puts it in Mary's body. And so we ask, *who* is the mother? Who is the surrogate? Is Mary substituting for Susan's body, growing Susan's baby for Susan? Or is Susan's egg substituting for Mary's, growing into Mary's baby in Mary's body? Our answer depends on where we stand when we ask the question.

When we accept the patriarchal valuing of the seed, there is no doubt—the real mother, like the real father, is the genetic parent. When we can contract for pregnancy at the present rate of 10,000 dollars, we can choose which women to substitute for us in the pregnancy. The brokers have books of pictures of women for potential parents to choose from, to take this woman or that woman to carry the pregnancy, to nurture the seed.

But for which women are these substitutes available? Who can afford to hire substitutes for the various parts of mothering? The situation today is exactly what it has been historically: women of privilege, wealthy or fairly wealthy women, hiring the services of poor, or fairly poor, women. Upper-class women can have some of the privileges of patriarchy. Upper-class women can buy some of the privileges of their paternity, using the bodies of poorer women to "bear them offspring." And upper-class women can, as they so often have, be bought off with these privileges, and accept men's worldview as their own. And so we have women, right along with men, saying that what makes a child one's own is the seed, the genetic tie, the "blood." And the blood they mean is not the real blood of pregnancy and birth, not the blood of the pulsing cord, the bloody show, the blood of birth, but the metaphorical blood of the genetic tie.

This is the ultimate meaning of patriarchy for mothers: seeds are precious; mothers are fungible.

The Ideology of Technology

In technological society we apply ideas about machines to people, asking them to be more efficient, productive, rational, and controlled. We treat our bodies as machines, hooking them up to other machines, monitoring and managing bodily functions. When a doctor manages a woman's labor, controlling her body with drugs and even surgery, it is to make her labor more efficient, predictable, rational. And so it is when mothers and fathers push their babies into a schedule, so that feeding the baby meshes into the nine-to-five day. When we think of our *relationships* with our children as a job to be done well, we are invoking the ideology of technology.

To do these parenting tasks efficiently, we divide them up into their component parts, organize them, systematize them, rationalize, *budget* our time, *order* our day, *program* our lives. All of this rationalizing, reducing, dividing, systematizing, organizing, in the name of efficiency, however, does harm to the human spirit. Clearly, not everything is best viewed as a resource.

The most obvious application of the technological ideology to motherhood has occurred in the medicalization of pregnancy and of childbirth. From the medical management of pregnancy, with its new, quality-control technology of prenatal diagnosis, through the rigidly monitored control of women's labor, the focus is on the "mechanics" of production, and not the social transformation of motherhood. It is as if biology were beyond culture, beyond ideology. The "mechanism" of contraception, the "mechanics" of labor, the "programming" of genetic development—these things are often seen as simple biological givens with which we must cope. But remember, that is the nature of ideology: the constructs look like common sense, the ideas are obvious, the descriptions are simply how things are, "naturally."

In our society, when we look at what we know, what our taken-for-granted reality about physical motherhood is, we are looking at medical ideology, a particular type of mechanical thinking, of technological ideology. Medical ideology is deeply rooted in the mind-body dualism expressed by Descartes: the body is a machine, the structure and operation of which falls within the province of human knowledge, as distinguished from the mind.

In the management of childbirth we see the ideology of technology played out, in all its inhumane absurdity. Pregnant women become workers in an unskilled assembly line, conceptualized as machines, containers holding precious, genetic material.

It is not only the body that we treat as mechanical, but the social order as well. Rather than seeing society as an organic, deeply interconnected whole, technological ideology encourages us to see society as a collection of parts. Liberal philosophy, the intellectual underpinning of the American Revolution and American government, is the articulation of the technological ideology in the social order.

The difficulty in reconciling the image of people as "atomized parts" with our very real desire for community, for interconnectedness between people, remains one of the ongoing problems of liberal society. And against this, we have motherhood, the physical embodiment of connectedness. We have in every pregnant woman the living proof that individuals do not enter the world as autonomous, atomistic, isolated beings, but begin socially, begin connected. And we have in every pregnant woman a walking contradiction to the segmentation of our lives: pregnancy does not permit it. In pregnancy the private self, the sexual, familial self, announces itself wherever we go. Motherhood is the embodied challenge to liberal philosophy, and that, I fear, is why a society founded on and committed to liberal philosophical principles cannot deal well with motherhood.

When the authors of the American Constitution declared "All men are created equal," they were drawing on this philosophical tradition of the Enlightenment. What made that statement reasonable was that the equality they spoke of was of the mind, of the rational being. Certainly some men were weak and some strong, some rich and some poor—but all shared the human essence, the rational mind. The extension of such "equality" to Blacks and to women is based on the claim that these groups, too, share the essence of humanity, the rational mind—housed, in the "accident of birth," in the body of the Black, the body of the woman.

If we believe, then, as this liberal philosophic tradition holds, that what is especially valuable about human beings is the capacity for rationality, then the ordering, rationalizing, and purposeful efficiency of technology will be seen as good. But hand in hand with the valuing of rationality is a "theoretical disdain for the significance of the body," and a disdain for physical work in preference for "mental" work. The latter, dividing the physical from the mental work, and then using machines and people interchangeably to do the menial physical work, is the essence of technological organization. Physical labor, the work of the hands and the bodies, is of low status.

This division of labor is a particular problem for women as mothers: mothers do the physical work of the body, we do the "menial" work of body maintenance. Thus women become identified with the physical, the body, and men with the higher, the rational. The distinction between menial physical labor and highly valued rationality goes a long way toward explaining the utter disdain with which a laboring woman may be strapped down and ignored or even insulted, while the doctor who "manages" her labor—reading her chart and ordering others to carry out his decisions—is held in such high esteem. Or similarly, why the woman who produces perfect nourishment from her body is seen as cowlike, animalistic in a negative way, while the pediatrician who "prescribes" a "formula" deserves such respect—and high pay.

The mind-body dualism has consequences at the macro level as well: viewing the body as a machine encourages us to see it as a resource to be used. If the mind and rationality are held as "above" the body, it becomes relatively easy to see the body as a resource for the use of the mind, and specifically, women's reproductive bodies as "societal" resources. So if the factories or the armies need fodder, women's bodies are the resources from which the young are produced.

In sum liberal philosophy is an articulation of the values of technological society, with its basic themes of order, predictability, rationality, control, rationalization of life, the systematizing and control of things and people as things, the reduction of all to component parts, and ultimately the vision of everything including our very selves, as resources.

THE IDEOLOGY OF CAPITALISM

From the standpoint of the ideology of technology, we have seen that motherhood is perceived as work, and children as a product produced by the labor of mothering. Mother's work and mother's bodies are resources out of which babies are made. From the standpoint of the market, however, not all work is equally valuable, and not all products are equally valued. In other words there is not a direct relationship between the value of the worker and the value of the product.

What is essential to capitalism is the accumulation and investment of capital, of wealth, by people who are in a position to control others. Under capitalism, workers do not own or control the products of their own labor. This means we are no longer talking about mothers and babies at all—we are talking about laborers and their products. Babies, at least healthy white babies, are very precious products these days. Mothers, rather like South African diamond miners, are the cheap, expendable, not-too-trust-worthy labor necessary to product the precious products. This is where it is all heading; the commodification of children and the proletarianization of motherhood. This is the end result of the evolution of these three ideological perspectives. This is what ties together the patriarchal and technological ideologies with the recreation of motherhood.

Because capitalism is complex, both as system and as ideology, here I will focus on only one essential aspect—the extension of ownership or property relations. There is a great deal of modem social criticism that claims the ways in which ownership has been extended are at best inappropriate, and too often morally wrong. For example, ecologists argue that it is inappropriate to think we can own the land, the waters: the earth, they claim—significantly—is our *mother*, not our property. The actual word *property* gets used relatively infrequently in discussions of human relations. More often the term is *rights*. Janet Farrell Smith says:

"A right can be interpreted as an entitlement to do or have something, to exclude others from doing or having something or as an enforceable claim."[2] What happens, then, when we start thinking of motherhood itself in terms of property? There are two directions in which property rights have extended that are directly relevant to motherhood: rights of ownership of one's own body, and rights to one's own child.

The way an ideology works is to focus our attention in certain ways, to give us a point of view, a perspective—often expressed in language as metaphor. People do not necessarily talk of or even actively think of their bodies or their children as *property* in the sense of real estate. As Smith points out,

> In applying a property model to parenting, it is important to remember that a parent may not literally assert that a child is a piece of property, but may work on assumptions analogous to those which one makes in connection with property.[3]

Within the American system, intelligent feminist use of the individualist ethos has been invaluable in assuring women's rights in procreation. Once women themselves are recognized as full citizens, then individual women must be accorded the same rights of bodily autonomy and integrity that men have. For women, that means sexual and procreative autonomy. Because it is her body, she cannot be raped. Because it is her body, she cannot be forced to bear pregnancies she does not want. Because it is her body, she cannot be forced to abort pregnancies she does not want.

This does not mean that women are not forced by circumstance into these very situations and eventualities. It only means that the society will not use the official power of the state to force her. Women are in fact prevented from having abortions they might want by family pressure, by economic circumstances, by religious and social pressures. And women are forced into having abortions they might not want to have because of poverty, because of lack of services for children and mothers, because of lack of services for disabled children and adults. By offering amniocentesis to identify fetuses who would have disabilities, and by cutting back on services for disabled children and their families, we effectively force women to have selective abortions.

Because of our current battles over the right to abortion, Americans tend to think of the state as "permitting" women to have abortions, as if the drive for continuing pregnancies came from the state, and the drive for abortions from women. In fact, the legal protection works also to permit women not to have abortions. When women's ownership rights over their bodies are lost, the rights to have and the rights *not* to have abortions are likewise lost. In American society, when we bring it back to the simple legal questions—who can force an abortion or forcibly prevent one—we wisely retreat to safety, calling forth our most sacred value. It's *her* body. We invoke a higher power, the power of ownership.

This then is the way that women have been able to combine dominant American liberal philosophy with capitalist ideology to our benefit. We've made use of the mind-body dualism, to allow a view of the body as owned, like a shelter which houses the more important mind. If one claims rationality for women—the essential liberal claim for all people—then simple fairness gives women the same rights of bodily ownership that men have, and the very high value of ownership, of property rights, is then turned to the advantage of women, who can claim exclusive rights to our own bodies. In the name of ownership, women have demanded access to contraception, sterilization, and abortion. And given the prevailing liberal philosophy, we've gotten those rights to control our fertility—although given the capitalist class system, we have fared less well with access to the necessary means.

While the "owned-body" principle has worked for women in avoiding motherhood, it is less clear how it can be made to work to empower women as mothers. Our bodies may be ours, but given the ideology of patriarchy, the bodies of mothers are not highly valued. The bodies are just the space in which genetic material matures into babies. In a patriarchal system, even if women own their bodies, it may not give them any real control in pregnancy. Women may simply be seen to own the space in which the fetuses are housed. This is the argument on which attempts to control women's behavior during pregnancy are based: owning her own body is not enough to assure her civil liberties if her body is believed to contain the property of someone else, somebody else's baby.

Of course, if women's bodies are understood to be the space in which sperm and egg grow to be a baby, and women are understood to be the owners of that space, then the acceptance of "surrogacy" follows logically, almost inevitably. The woman can rent out space in her body just as she can rent out the spare back bedroom. And she will have no more ownership rights over the inhabitants of that space in her body than over the boarder in her home. Whether she chooses to "rent" or not, the state can claim rights of passage through her body in the interests of the "citizens" within.

REWEAVING THE FABRIC

From these ideologies of patriarchy, technology, and capitalism we get the supportive fabric for the strange patterns we see emerging. In varying combinations, with sometimes one thread dominating, and sometimes another, these patterns explain things as disparate as genetic testing, including prenatal diagnosis for selective abortion; micro and macro level eugenics programs; reproductive technologies that commodify and commercialize babies and pregnancy, including breast milk substitutes, "gestational surrogacy," electronic fetal monitoring, and 8,000-dollars-a-cycle in vitro fertilization; minimum wage for child care; the "mommy track"; the simultaneous commercialization and politicization of abortion; and—well, you get the picture.

Over the years many of us have railed against each of these emerging patterns... But our real concerns must go deeper. Our question must be: How best to create a supportive fabric for intimate human relations, including that most intimate of human relations that is motherhood, that is not blinded by the limitations of the ideologies of patriarchy, technology, and capitalism, and that is truly feminist in all its complexity.

The simplest and least threatening version of feminism is to ask for what is seen in North America as simple fairness. Even lots of Americans who would never ever think of themselves as actually being feminists nonetheless expect fairness for women. Demands for fairness are generally based on insistence that prevailing liberal ideals be applied to women: ideals like equal pay for equal work. Since we are living in a society founded on liberal principles, it is liberal feminism that comes closest to mainstream values, and consequently often sounds like the very voice of reason, especially when juxtaposed with the more "strident" feminist positions.

Liberal feminism works best to defend women's rights to be like men, to enter into men's worlds, to work at men's jobs for men's pay, to have the rights and privileges of men. But what of our rights to be women? The liberal argument, the fairness argument, the equal rights argument, these all begin to break down when we look at women who are, or are becoming, mothers. A woman lawyer is exactly the same as a man lawyer. A woman cop is just the same as a man cop. And a pregnant woman is just the same as ... well, as, uh, ... It's like disability, right? Or like serving in the army? Pregnancy is just exactly like pregnancy. There is nothing else quite like it. That statement is not glorification or mystification. It is a statement of fact. Having a baby grow in your belly is not like anything else one can do. It is unique.

The question is: how can uniqueness be made to fit into an equality model? Strangely enough, albeit for different reasons, both patriarchal ideology and liberal feminist thinking have come to the same conclusion about what to do with the problem of the uniqueness of pregnancy—devalue it; discount it so deeply that its uniqueness just doesn't matter. In strongly patriarchal systems, as described earlier, the genetic tie for men is the most important parental tie: women grow men's children, what Caroline Whitbeck calls "flower pot theory of pregnancy."[4] Men have the seeds and women are the flower pots. Liberal feminists, seeking equality and recognition of women's rationality and rights, claim equality of parenthood between men and women. Women too have seed, they argue, and men too can nurture children. Men cannot nurture with their bodies, not with their blood or their milk as women do—but that is just menial, body work. What matters is that both parents have seeds. Children are "half hers, half his." Instead of a flower pot, the woman is seen as an equal contributor of seed—and the baby might just as well have grown in the backyard. It is, after all, only women's bodily experience that is different from men's.

Equal rights sounds good, and in many ways it is a fine goal, and one that has yet to be achieved for any of these groups: radical minorities, old people, women, disabled people. But a focus on "rights" ignores *needs*. Special attempts to get help based on need is called "reverse discrimination." Women as mothers are especially hard hit by this narrow equal rights approach. For one thing, those individuals who are not yet rational—our babies and children—need an awful lot of care and attention, and that falls to our lot. Liberal thinking, including liberal feminism, is a bit shy on what to do with the children—and the other deeply needy people. Even achieving a liberal goal of including men as child-tenders does not solve the problem: it remains individualized, privatized.

It is the nature of this complex worldview, constructed of interlocking ideologies, that we cannot see through it clearly. And so we fear to pick at the fabric, fear to pull at the individual loose threads for fear of falling into some abyss. If we challenge any piece of the system, other pieces block our way. When we challenge technological ideology, people hear the sound of the baby being chucked out with the bathwater, fear and return of the angel of death hovering at every birth, fear unchecked fertility and untreatable infertility, women captured and held hostage to some mad biology. When we challenge ownership models of bodily integrity, we hear the enormous fear of someone else claiming ownership. So deep the ownership model lies that the only askable question seems to be: *whose* property? When we challenge patriarchal models of genetic-based parenthood, we hear the fears of women of privilege who have gained for themselves some of the privileges of patriarchy—often at the expense of other women, particularly women of color.

What if we genuinely valued that work that is motherhood? What if we valued intimacy and nurturance, and human relationships, not just as means toward some end, but in themselves? Would such a valuing privilege women as mothers—but simultaneously lock out nonmothering women and all men? I genuinely do not think so. Such a valuing would open up, and not close down, acts of nurturance and caring, free up, and not constrain, the gender boundaries of intimacy we now face. It would expand, and not restrict, the very definition of mothering.

Looking at motherhood as a discipline, a way of thinking, a response to the needs and demands that exist outside of the mother, shifts our focus from who the mother is to what she is doing. Who she *is*, who she feels herself to be, is deeply gender-based: she is a woman, a mother. What she is *doing* is not gender-based: the similarities in behavior of mothers have more to do with the similarities in their situations, in the demands they face from their children and from their societies, than it has to do with the similarities in the women. And so the person engaged in this discipline of motherhood need not be a mother, need not be a woman, to engage in these activities, this way of thought and practice that is mothering.

The social relationship of parenting, of nurturing, and of caring needs a social base, not a genetic one. Through their pregnancies, women begin to establish that base. Through their relationships with women, and then with children, men too can establish that base. Pregnancy is one of the ways that we begin a social relationship with a child, but obviously not the only one.

If women are not to drop from exhaustion and lose all pleasure in life, someone is going to have to help with the kids. If women are sharing their lives, and sharing their children, with someone, then that is the obvious person to share the work of child care. For some it is a lesbian partner, for some it is one's own mother, and for many of us it is our husband. It is not by virtue of their paternity, their genetic ties to children, that men have an obligation to rear and to nurture them, but by virtue of their social relationship.

If someone, man or woman, is going to be the life partner, the mate, of a woman who mothers, then that person must share the child care. And, in turn, it is by sharing the care and rearing of the children that the partner comes to have a place in the life of the child. We have to move beyond a paternity standard to a standard of nurturance.

Mothers also need men who can mother because we *ourselves* need that mothering—women are tired of mothering the whole world. Mothering, like everything else in life, is best learned by doing. Mothering women have taught many of us the skills of listening to what is said and to what is not said. In mothering we hone our empathic abilities, learn to understand the vulnerability in others without profiting from it. The experience of mothering teaches people how to be more emotionally and intellectually nurturant, how to take care of each other. It is not the only way we learn that lesson, but it is hard to mother and not learn it.

And finally, men should join women in mothering because it is the only way to avoid recreating the gender and class system and still live together. We can pool our resources, join together in infinite varieties of social arrangements to rear our children, but we must not recreate endlessly the separate worlds of power and of care. We must not do this in any of its guises: not as separate public and private worlds, not as separate worlds of men and of women. It is morally wrong to have children raised by one group for another group, whether it is Mrs. John Smith raising John Smith Jr. in her husband's image, slave nurses raising their masters, or hired caregivers raising the children of dual-career couples.

Caring people can and do raise whole and healthy children, and they do it across lines of gender, class, and race. It is not that the children are "subhuman," but that we ask them to turn away from humanity, away from care, and toward power. We do that whenever we separate the world into the kinds of people who take care of children and the kinds of people who rule the world.

Notes

1 Glenn Petersen, "Ponepean Matriliny: Production, Exchange and the Ties that Bind," *American Ethnologist* vol. 9 No.1, 1982, p. 141.
2 Janet Farrell Smith, "Parenting and Property," in Joyce Treblicot, ed., *Mothering: Essays in Feminist Theory* (Totowa, NJ: Rowman and Allenheld, 1984), p. 202
3 Farrell Smith 1984, p. 201.
4 Caroline Whitbeck, "Theories of Sex Difference," *The Philosophical Forum* 5 (1973), 1–2.

24

Why Coverage of Prescription Contraception Matters for Men as Well as Women

Krystale Littlejohn

Contraception – who should be able to use it, and the role of government in its provision – has become a contentious issue, in part due to disagreements over the Affordable Care Act mandate positing that all private insurance plans must cover prescription contraception for women. The issue is not trivial, because nationally representative surveys show that more than 10 million women in the United States use the pill as their current method to prevent pregnancy. The pill is the most popular form of reversible birth control.

Across the political spectrum, both citizens and public officials tend to understand birth control as a "women's issue" rather than as a healthcare or social policy issue. Usually, birth control is discussed as a matter of reproductive health and rights or treated as an aspect of women's personal responsibility for managing their own sexuality. But where do men fit? How do they benefit from the availability and use of prescription birth control coverage? Could a better understanding of the ways prescription birth control coverage benefits heterosexual couples improve bipartisan discussions about coverage for contraception? My research provides insight into both of these questions.

WOMEN'S CONTRACEPTIVE USE AND COUPLES' PROTECTION FROM PREGNANCY

Contraception presumes the sexual involvement of couples, but surveys typically ask *individual* people about what method(s) *they as individuals* use to prevent pregnancy. By default, a woman who uses the pill for contraception also provides her partner with protection from pregnancy; and if her partner wears a condom, then both participants benefit. Contraception and condoms can be used together, but research shows that, in practice, couples in long-term relationships often move from using condoms to relying solely on prescription contraception.

Notably, interviews I conducted revealed that women who use prescription contraception for long periods of time rarely receive financial help from partners in purchasing it. Thus, although women's birth control covers men, too, the men do not have to pay for this coverage and its benefits.

Littlejohn, Krystale. "Why Coverage of Prescription Contraception Matters for Men as Well as Women." *Scholars Strategy Network*, August 21, 2017.

Men reap the positive effects of women's use of prescription contraception in at least three ways: they gain protection from pregnancy without much effort; they avoid using condoms when couples transition to solely using prescription contraception; and they can spend money they might have spent on contraception on other items and pursuits. There is also another way that men benefit from female contraceptive use that is not often mentioned. Women must deal with the downsides of whatever type of prescription birth control they use – including downsides such as physical side effects like nausea or depression and hassles like having to repeatedly refill prescriptions at the pharmacy. Their male partners are freed from such issues.

Contraceptive Use and the Unequal Burdens of Dissatisfaction

Preventing pregnancy is generally not something that couples enjoy, because it can be stressful, costly, and bothersome. Although public attention focuses on men's dissatisfaction with condoms, much less attention is paid to women's dissatisfaction with prescription birth control methods. My research using survey data finds that nearly 40 percent of women aged 23 to 44 who had ever used hormonal contraception had stopped using it at some point because they were dissatisfied. Yet even though many women stop using a particular type of prescription contraception, they rarely stop contraception use altogether. They try various methods – different pills, or long-acting reversible contraception devices like implants and intrauterine devices – until they find something that feels right for them. As my in-depth interviews show, although many women experience dissatisfaction with side effects of particular birth control methods, they still believe that they should continue using some kind of prescription method.

Discussions that focus only on the benefits that prescription contraceptive coverage provides to women hide the ways that prescription birth control is very much like other medications – it can cause unpleasant and consequential side effects. By persisting despite dissatisfactions in their search for effective ways to prevent pregnancy, women provide tangible benefits for their partners, who get to avoid pregnancy without sharing such costs. Even when women find it difficult or unpleasant to use certain methods, they cannot always count on getting male partners to wear condoms – or otherwise take responsibility for the couple's contraception. This may explain why data from nationally representative surveys show that women who experience dissatisfaction with contraception are at higher risk of unintended pregnancy. When the burden of responsibility for birth control is too great, some male partners cannot be counted on to pick up the slack.

What Does the Full Picture Mean for Debates about Contraception Coverage?

Recognizing that men as well as women benefit from prescription birth control coverage is crucial for appropriately evaluating the costs of rolling back the Affordable Care Act mandate for prescription contraception coverage. A nationally representative survey shows that only a very small percentage of people recognize that married women are the most likely to use prescription birth control. This may be because many of us are conditioned to see birth control as something affecting women rather than couples. Public debates might very well change if more Americans understood all the ways that women, men, and society at large benefit from women's access to prescription birth control – and their willingness to use it despite dissatisfaction. Too often, pundits and partisan debates treat contractive coverage as simply a women's issue or benefit. But if women, especially married women or women in long-term relationships, lose access to the most popular form of reversible contraception, so will men. Both men and women will experience new frustrations and costs.

25

New Evidence about Women's Experience with Abortion– Compared to Carrying Unwanted Pregnancies to Term

Diana Greene Foster, Rana E. Barar, and Heather Gould

Myths about the potential harm that abortion poses to women's physical and mental health are widespread. Proponents of laws restricting access to abortion often claim, for instance, that abortions put women at increased risk for breast cancer or other serious health problems. Amid heated public debates, such claims can be accepted as fact, despite a paucity of data to support them. Warnings about harms from abortion also fail to consider the real-life alternative: what happens when women who experience unwanted pregnancies have to carry them to term? Drawing from many research papers, we report on an important new study investigating a range of effects on women's well-being, comparing women who get abortions to those turned away.

THE TURNAWAY STUDY

A team of researchers under the direction of Diana Green Foster, based at the Advancing New Standards in Reproductive Health (ANSIRH) program at the University of California, San Francisco, has conducted a unique longitudinal study of women seeking abortion care. The Turnaway Study, as it is called, employs an innovative design to rigorously examine the health and socioeconomic effects of receiving an abortion compared to carrying an unwanted pregnancy to term. From January 2008 to December 2010, we recruited approximately 1,000 women seeking abortions from 30 facilities located in 21 U.S. states from Maine to Washington, Texas to Minnesota. Some of the women we studied received an abortion and others were "turned away" – that is, denied an abortion – because they presented for care past the gestational limit set by the clinic. We followed these women who had sought abortions through telephone interviews every six months over five years. This long-term approach allowed us to gather quantitative data on these women's mental health, physical health, relationships, and employment, as well as on their children's development and well-being. In addition, Project Director Heather Gould conducted personal interviews with a subset of the women, allowing them to share their stories in their own words and describe the effects of abortion and childbearing on their lives.

Foster, Diana Greene, Rana E. Barar, and Heather Gould. "New Evidence about Women's Experience with Abortion." *Scholars Strategy Network*, May 25, 2016.

FINDINGS ABOUT MENTAL AND PHYSICAL WELL-BEING

Final phases of data collection for the Turnaway Study were completed in January 2016 – but, for several years, – researchers have been analyzing early results. New evidence speaks to the ongoing public policy debates about the health consequences of abortion and unwanted childbearing:

- **Mental health effects.** Several analyses have examined the potential link between abortion and subsequent mental health, including depression and PTSD, and have found no evidence that abortion causes mental health problems. Our colleague Antonia Biggs and others have looked at self-esteem, social support, stress, and life satisfaction and found that women who have abortions fare no worse or better than women who carry unwanted pregnancies to term. Corinne Rocca and colleagues find that women feel a range of emotions when they experience unwanted pregnancies and seek abortion. Relief is the most common emotion that women report after having an abortion, but some experience other emotions, both positive and negative. Over three years, the vast majority of women – 95 percent – say that abortion was the right decision for them. And for most women, both positive and negative emotions become less intense as time passes.

- **Changes in substance abuse.** Abortion does not cause women to abuse alcohol, drugs, or other harmful substances, according to research by Sarah Roberts. However, women who are denied abortions are sometimes unable to reduce drug and tobacco use during their pregnancies.

- **Effects on relationships.** Data from the Turnaway Study reveal that women who are unable to obtain a requested abortion are more likely to remain in contact with the men involved in their pregnancies – and are, in some instances, unable to extricate themselves from violent relationships. Sarah Roberts and colleagues find that women who obtain abortion care experience a reduction in physical violence from male partners, probably because they dissolve their relationships with them more quickly, while women who carry their pregnancies to term remain exposed to violence. Jane Mauldon and her colleagues find a similar pattern in that carrying a pregnancy to term slows the dissolution of romantic relationships, but the effect is short-lived. By two years post-pregnancy, women who carry to term have the same likelihood of being in a romantic relationship with the man involved in the pregnancy as women who obtain abortions.

- **Physical health consequences.** Here Turnaway findings are in line with the larger medical literature showing that childbirth poses a far greater risk to women's physical health than abortion. Caitlin Gerdts finds that compared to women who obtained abortions, women who carried their pregnancies to term had longer periods of disability and reported more serious, potentially life-threatening complications. One such woman died of an infection that was complicated by childbirth.

BROADER LIFE IMPACTS

Beyond good physical and mental health, women's well-being includes being able to set and achieve life goals. Using data from the Turnaway Study, Ushma Upadhyay finds that women who are able to access abortion care are six times more likely to have aspirational life plans – such as becoming financially stable or finishing school – and are about twice as likely to achieve such goals as women who are engaged in parenting after an unwanted pregnancy. We are currently looking at socioeconomic effects, and preliminary results indicate that women who carry pregnancies to term and parent the child are more likely to live in poverty, less likely to work full-time, and more likely to receive public assistance. Such hardships have repercussions for the children women already have at the time they are denied abortions.

The most important lesson from our study is that women are thoughtful, even prescient, in the reasons they give for wanting to end their pregnancies. They most often cite financial worries and concerns about existing children and their partner. As researchers, these are exactly the risks we see playing out in the experiences of women denied wanted abortions. Policymakers should consider women's thoughtful reasons for wanting to end their pregnancies and understand that restricting access to abortion can have serious negative effects on women and their families.

26

Moral Women, Immoral Technologies

How Devout Women Negotiate Gender, Religion, and Assisted Reproductive Technologies

Danielle Czarnecki

Sexuality, gender, and reproduction are sites in which what is "natural" and "morally acceptable" are perpetually contested. Advances in assisted reproductive technologies (ARTs) such as in vitro fertilization (IVF) pose a challenge to the idea of "natural" procreation… While ARTs were not widely accepted 30 years ago, they have become part of the normal means by which life can be created. Their use has doubled in the last decade, underscoring the importance of biological[1] motherhood. Studies on the experience of infertility show that one's identity as a woman is often defined by the ability to have a biological child, which is "reified as the gold standard of motherhood" (Martin 2010, 540). This results in a "cataclysmic role failure" for women who desire but are unable to have children (Greil, Leitko, and Porter 1988, 191). Women with access to ARTs thus often feel compelled to use them. But some are still unable to bear a child, because they may not have access to ARTs, the treatments may fail, or they may not pursue ARTs at all. These women must then work to "redefine normalcy" via other forms of parenthood or by expressing other forms of "normative femininity" when childless.

For many, religion matters and plays a potentially critical, unexplored role in how women navigate messages about infertility and gender. Importantly, religious women negotiate not only wider cultural messages about gender, infertility, and ARTs but also their religion's positions on these issues. The Catholic Church provides an especially critical case for examination because it venerates motherhood and family but is the most restrictive world religion in its position on ARTs, creating potential moral dilemmas for those who adhere to Church doctrine. Devout women are members of a pronatalist society that supports the use of ARTs, but they are also members of a religion that emphasizes motherhood while restricting the technological means for achieving it. How do these women reconcile being outsiders who do not meet the expectations of their religious and secular communities?

The study highlights devout women's distinctive understandings of ARTs and experiences of infertility. Drawing on both religious and secular schemas, devout women's experiences of infertility are both medicalized as a biomedical problem *and* infused with religious meaning. Religion allows devout women to refuse technologies, but it also allows them to rework their sense of what it means to be a Catholic woman who is unable to have a biological child—a process I describe as achieving a *moral femininity*. Devout women attain this by embracing suffering as meaningful and constructing alternative maternal identities. Their

Czarnecki, Danielle. "Moral Women, Immoral Technologies: How Devout Women Negotiate Gender, Religion, and Assisted Reproductive Technologies." *Gender & Society* 29, no. 5 (2015): 716–742.

rejection of ARTs becomes a testament of their devotion to God that results in a deepened piety. They become "moral guardians" working to protect the natural social order as ordained by God. Thus, while religion increases the burden of reproduction for devout women, it also provides the cultural resources to resist the financial, emotional, and physical difficulties experienced by women who use ARTs.

THE CATHOLIC CHURCH AND ASSISTED REPRODUCTIVE TECHNOLOGIES

The Catholic Church's opposition to ARTs is articulated in the instruction *Donum Vitae* (Respect for Human Life in Its Origin and on the Dignity of Procreation). First, marriage is a sacrament—a ritual signifying God's presence—and procreation within marriage is a sacred act in which couples co-create with God. Children are considered a gift from God created when the corporeal and spiritual unite during intercourse. In the laboratory, the divine nature of procreation is ruptured, as scientists supplant God as the creators of life. In contrast to embryo formation within the womb, the laboratory environment is not considered respectful to human dignity or divine intention.

The Church is not entirely opposed to science and technology. Artificial insemination is not prohibited as long as it does not replace the conjugal act. The Church permits the use of a perforated condom to collect semen during intercourse that can later be used for insemination. In addition, Natural Procreative Technology (NaPro), developed by a Catholic doctor, is a Church-sanctioned infertility treatment that teaches women to monitor their cervical mucus and track fertility. Surgical procedures such as laparoscopic diagnostic techniques, hormonal therapies, and medications are also permitted to address imbalances. Unlike Judaism and Islam, Catholicism does not privilege biogenetic kinship, and thus infertility is not a legitimate reason for divorce. Biological reproduction remains the cultural ideal, but it is not mandated and alternatives such as adoption are valued.

METHODS

To understand how Catholic women experience infertility and ARTs, I conducted in-depth, semistructured interviews with 33 Catholic women[2] who experienced infertility. I recruited participants who responded to flyers posted at fertility clinics, cafes, Catholic Social Services, and grocery stores; and online via Craigslist, infertility blogs, and forums. I limited recruitment to Catholic, infertile women ages 18–50 who had considered infertility treatments. One non-Catholic woman who was married to a Catholic man asked to participate and was included.

Thirty-two of the respondents were U.S. citizens from across the country. One interviewee was from Latin America. The median age of interviewees was 33. Thirty of the respondents identified as Caucasian, one as African American, and two as Hispanic. Twenty-eight women were employed and five were stay-at-home mothers. I focus on the majority of the sample that is devout (n = 20). Any comparison between devout and nondevout women is limited because nondevout women experienced infertility for a significantly shorter time (median = 2 years) than devout women (median = 5 years). When appropriate, however, I include experiences of the nondevout women as a point of comparison. Women were classified as devout if they attended Church at least once a week, confessed at least once a year, and used words such as "very" or "extremely" to describe the importance of religion in their lives. Nondevout women typically described themselves as "not very religious," "casual," "moderate," or "nonpracticing" Catholics.

DEVOUT WOMEN'S NARRATIVES OF INFERTILITY

Both groups of women typically begin their infertility journeys by seeking medical solutions. But when the next line of treatment involves technologies that the Church forbids, devout women's treatment trajectories become distinct. I show how devout women draw on religious schemas in order to avoid the use of ARTs, while also achieving a *moral femininity* not rooted in biological motherhood. First, I show that the Church's veneration of motherhood and its silence regarding infertility amplifies the suffering of those who are without children. Those who refuse ARTs feel isolated from the broader society in which their use has become normalized, even expected. Second, I show how devout women draw on religious teachings about procreation to construct some reproductive technologies as artificial and others as natural. Third, religious schemas provide a means to critique the commodification of reproduction by understanding children as a gift from God, as opposed to a right. Fourth, by attributing their infertility to a "greater plan," devout women are able to move beyond a strictly biological understanding of infertility and find meaning in their suffering. Finally, they draw on religion to construct alternative maternal identities not defined by biological motherhood.

"All Mothers Must Be Important"

The Church plays an important role in how Catholic women think about motherhood. One devout woman explained, "[Motherhood] is a very important part of life, of femininity, of a marriage. Of actually being a co-creator with God … I see it as a very natural part of Catholicism." Another woman described the Virgin Mary as an exalted model of motherhood: "If the Blessed Mother is important, then all mothers must be important." Because the Church is family-centered and infertility is rarely acknowledged by their local priests, most women felt like outsiders at Mass. Some felt judged for not having children, as one devout woman described: "People wonder, 'Are they not really good Catholics? Are they on contraception?'" Women opposed to ARTs must also contend with broader society's embrace of these technologies, as one woman explained:

> You're living in a society that not only does what you can't do, but thinks it's a huge blessing and medical advance and a procedure given to us by God. … So you have to deal with that on top of everything. … You can't just go to generic support groups; you can't go to a generic blog online. … You realize, "I'm totally alone … everybody else I know can do IVF."

Devout women are thus in a double bind. They face pressures from society and their religious community to have children, but they feel judged by their Church community and isolated from secular society for refusing ARTs.

"Playing God": Differentiating the Natural and Artificial

Prior studies on infertility show that women pursuing ARTs struggle with their inability to conceive "naturally." I show how devout women construct ARTs as artificial and "strategically naturalize" medical treatments that are compatible with Catholic doctrine. Marilyn, a devout, 34-year-old writer living in a Boston suburb who suffered from primary infertility for four years, described IVF by contrasting it with "natural" procreation:

> I just feel like IVF demeans a person so much, because the conception happens not in the throes of love, but rather in a scientific laboratory and it just sounds so disgusting to me … they're not embracing each other, and they're not participating in this great procreative act.

For Marilyn, IVF eliminates the sanctity of intercourse within the marital union. According to the Church's instruction of *Donum Vitae*, this threatens not only "natural" reproduction but also the moral foundation of society.

Though opposed to ARTs, devout women do pursue medical treatments that they "strategically naturalize" as facilitating procreation within marital intercourse. NaPro, a technology that purports to monitor and maintain a woman's reproductive and gynecological health, for example, provides a morally acceptable alternative because procreation remains within the bounds of marital intercourse. Margaret, a 30-year-old manager suffering from primary infertility for a year, explained why she prefers NaPro:

I left the reproductive endocrinologist, and that's one thing I liked about the NaPro doctor. He would never perform any artificial reproductive procedures. He focused on diagnostics and helping me fix the problem from a hormonal and medical kind of way.

Margaret naturalized NaPro by contrasting its "medical" treatment with the reproductive endocrinologist's "artificial" procedures. Devout women view NaPro as preparing the spousal bodies for procreation through intercourse. One woman explained, "They must make your body so healthy that the result of sex is a baby."

The boundaries between the natural and the artificial are complicated by the fact that while the Church explicitly opposes most ARTs, its position on intrauterine inseminations (IUIs) is undefined. Nonetheless, all but two devout women chose not to use IUIs. Kayla, a 35-year-old banker from New England, suffered from primary infertility for one year. She described an IUI as almost "natural" if using a Church-approved perforated condom to collect semen during intercourse, but even she ultimately decided against the method:

> I think the Church is undecided. So I was telling myself that [IUI] would probably be as far as we'd go because we weren't harming any life. It was not quite natural, but if he used a condom with a hole in it for collection and we had sex, it would still be the act, and you would never really know. So I kind of worked my way around that, but in the end we canceled the appointment. We just weren't comfortable with it.

But Kayla also expressed doubts about her decision: "After I've seen ten women that go on to have IVF and now they have babies, I think, am I making a huge mistake?" Her desire for a child and the cultural acceptance of ARTs by other women contributed to her moral uncertainty.

Audrey, a 40-year-old manager suffering from primary infertility for 12 years, described engaging in "private negotiations" with God. She knelt down to pray before her insemination and held a concealed rosary during the procedure. She explains that an IUI is not "playing God" because it is just moving the sperm "closer." By having sex postprocedure, it is unclear if the artificially inseminated semen or the semen from intercourse will reach the egg. Conception is still in God's hands, as Audrey explained: "[IUI is] not really anti-Church. It's taking his sperm and putting it closer to my egg. You were told to go home and have sex. So was it the sex? Which sperm cell is it?"

Nondevout women in this study naturalize IVF. Christine, who described herself as "not religious," suffered from premature ovarian failure for one year. She understood IVF as assisting nature: "Basically, [IVF is] just like additional help, right? I would do it. I think we're very fortunate to have that ability to do that. I wouldn't even think twice about that."

Both nondevout and devout women expressed uncertainty about or objected to the use of donor semen and eggs. While devout women framed their objections as "playing God," some nondevout women described the use of donor egg or sperm as "weird" or "strange." Adopting an embryo or traditional adoption were considered better alternatives. Christine, who had no misgivings about IVF, was opposed to using an egg donor. But it was her only option, as she described:

> I don't want someone else's egg. I feel really weird about it and uncomfortable. I don't like the idea at all. … People do what they have to do. I'm one of them. I'm considering something that I would have never ever considered. We do these crazy things so that we can be mothers.

Both devout and nondevout women described feeling it would be unfair—even akin to adultery—to use donor eggs or sperm. They wanted the embryo to be completely genetically related to the couple or not at all. One nondevout couple decided to use their respective siblings as donors so that their child would be genetically related to each spouse. They "strategically naturalized" their siblings' donor gametes so that each spouse could establish an "equitable" genetic affinity to the child.

Nondevout women were less concerned with the Church's teaching that procreation must occur within marital intercourse, though they did express concerns about the moral status of the embryo. In response to critiques of "playing God," nondevout women often cited their good intentions when using IVF. Celeste, an editor from a Midwestern city who was undergoing IVF for male-factor infertility, reflected:

> I truly don't want to be "playing God." … I feel that we're trying to do things out of love. … I really don't want to destroy life, and I do believe that clearly is life. … Not to boil this down to something odd. But it's like endangered species. … Sometimes people have to do things to procreate that maybe weren't the way it was supposed to happen.

Like many nondevout women, Celeste characterized undergoing IVF as an expression of love for her husband. Nondevout women undergoing IVF also naturalized embryo disposition, as one woman described: "These embryos weren't killed; they just happened to die, and a lot of embryos die in nature too." Others limited the number of eggs they would fertilize in order to prevent dilemmas over embryo disposition. Leah, a nondevout scientist who grew up in a devout family, drew on science to reason through embryo disposition: "I think the biologist side of me that thinks they're just cells—I'm not completely convinced they're just cells—but they're not that different from my skin cells." She uses a scientific framework that is salient in her everyday life to reason through a moral gray area.

Devout women critique IVF by defining a child as a gift from God rather than a right. They describe the ART industry as a business that commodifies (future) babies, to which people then feel entitled. Carmela, a devout 34-year-old lawyer from Houston who has primary infertility and has pursued adoption, reflected:

> A child is a gift. It is not a given. Because you want a child doesn't mean that you have to have it, and that you have to do everything to get it and break all of the laws of God and society to do it.

Some secular parents also describe their children as "gifts," to be sure, but devout women draw a distinction between a divine gift and the right to a child. The concern is that when procreation is delinked from marital intercourse, people are dehumanized in the process and become products in an economic market that focuses on profit and self-interest.

Like women in treatment-based studies, nondevout women described IVF as an undesirable but necessary way to have children. They did not voice strong objections to the industry. Ashley, an executive from Nashville who had an unsuccessful IUI after suffering from primary infertility for a year, explained: "Because we have the technology, the outcome is not something that's wrong. I honestly don't think God cares how we get our child. We have the technology and he gave someone the gift to come up with this technology." For many nondevout women, the technology is described as "God-given" and assisting nature. Another nondevout woman described having a right to a child: "I just feel like everyone should have their right to have a child or children."

God's Plan: Suffering for a Greater Purpose

Early in their infertility narratives, devout women have confidence in medical treatments and draw on secular schemas regarding biomedical technologies as successful. Like women in prior studies, devout women described wanting to control every aspect of their infertility. They traveled to consult with doctors, read medical journals, and timed, measured, and tested their own bodies. But when IVF was the only option left, they surrendered their control to God. This transition illustrates how biomedical and religious schemas become salient at different moments. It also shows that religious women can value Western, liberal ideals of autonomy while also accepting limitations on their choices and actions. Anna described her transition:

> I've always achieved anything I wanted to. … And that can give you an ego and make you think that you're doing all this, and that God really isn't part of the equation. … Now, with this cross, I've been humbled to the point where I step back and say, "I understand that I'm not in control of this."

This shift was also poignantly captured by Audrey:

> Earlier it was, "I wish God would let me know what his plan is for me." Then it was my life is like a tapestry, how one side has the pretty picture and the other side is all ugly with the threads showing. All I can see are the threads. He can see the beautiful parts.

These were common narratives in devout women's accounts. By eventually locating their infertility within a cosmological order, devout women challenged a strictly biomedical understanding of infertility.

This conceptualization of God's plan also allowed women to expand their maternal desires beyond biological motherhood. Framed as part of a divine plan, devout women could naturalize their adopted child as meant to be. Rina, a 30-year-old stay-at-home mom who struggled with primary infertility for 12 years, reflected:

> We looked at it as there's a reason, there's a purpose ... now that we have our daughter, a friend said, "Thank God you never were able to get pregnant." She, for me, is ... that's the reason that I was waiting for, because I can't imagine not having her. I wouldn't trade ten pregnancies for her.

Leah, a nondevout woman and scientist who underwent several cycles of IVF, also questioned the reasons for enduring treatments and why she hasn't been able to adopt. She explained that a biological child is symbolic of her love for her husband:

> We'll either have a baby or we won't and then we'll adopt—it's simple, right? [laughs] ... But you've spent all of this effort. ... There must be a reason they're doing that, right? ... It's because I love my husband very much. He has these wonderful qualities, and I want to be able to give him a child.

Leah also struggled to make sense of her infertility, but its meaning does not extend beyond the material world. While devout women's refusal of ARTs is a testament to their religious devotion, nondevout women's use of ARTs is often described as a testament of love for their spouse.

Devout women draw on religious texts that provide a language of morality and redemptive suffering to make sense of their infertility. They find solace in biblical stories of infertility. Georgia, a devout woman, suffered from primary infertility for six years and eventually adopted a child, whom she now views as a miracle. She reflected:

> I'm not just blindly following these rules. I do believe in them. ... Our faith teaches us that Jesus died on the cross, and we are called to carry our crosses. I read a lot about suffering. Almost all of the greatest saints have had the worst things happen in their lives in these very dark times. It taught me that suffering has value in our lives.

Georgia has used religious writings about suffering to realize the value of her own difficult experience. Another devout woman described how infertility was the perfect cross for God to have chosen for her:

> What greater suffering can a woman who has always wanted to be a mother have than not being able to have children? So it was the perfect thing for God to have chosen because it allows us to suffer so greatly that we can redeem ourselves. If I had been paralyzed in a car accident, I would suffer greatly. But to me, that wouldn't to me be as great a suffering as not being able to have children.

Devout women come to understand their infertility as not just a disruption, but as a coherent part of God's plan for them... Devout women in this study not only found their suffering meaningful but also critiqued the notion that all suffering should be avoided. One devout woman argued:

> In the modern world everybody is always trying to relieve suffering. Like, you're suffering from being fat? Try the stomach pill. You can't see? Do LASIK surgery. I'm not denying that I'm very grateful for modern science, but at the same time, some suffering is meant to be, and it helps you grow as a person.

For some nondevout women, however, religion actually contributed to their suffering. Celeste was undergoing IVF due to male-factor infertility. She described feeling judged by Catholics for undergoing IVF:

> Rather than comfort there is judgment and isolation. There is not enough support within the Church for people, and waiting for an unpredictable adoption after we'd been through so much heartache simply seemed cruel. ... IVF was the shortest way to achieving the family we always dreamed of having.

Religious schemas were thus most meaningful for those who described themselves as more religious. Trusting God's plan and drawing on women's vocation to suffering helped devout women transition from desiring only biological motherhood to realizing other forms of maternal identity.

MORAL FEMININITY

When IVF fails, women must redefine normalcy and rework their gender identities. Devout women refuse ARTs and redefine normalcy by drawing on religious schemas such as Catholicism's openness to adoption, marriage without children as still meaningful, and a lack of emphasis on biogenetic lineage. These schemas allow them to expand their expressions of maternal identities beyond biological motherhood.

Devout women describe achieving a strengthened Catholic identity and an expanded understanding of their gendered identities. I call this co-construction of their religious and gendered identity a *moral femininity*, in which infertility and the refusal of ARTs become a combined source of value and self-worth—an expression of Catholic womanhood that brings them closer to God. In using the term *moral*, I am neither imposing an assessment of one's morality nor essentializing femininity as "moral." Rather, I use the term to point to the women's sense of their own morality. They reflect on their infertility as a journey toward salvation, through which Church teachings enable them to save their marriages, financial security, and bodies from the effects of fertility treatment. One woman explained, "One couple I knew broke up because of infertility ... we had boundaries that allowed us to focus on each other as opposed to throwing our lives into [ARTs]."

While the nondevout women in this study were earlier in their infertility journeys, none adopted or were in the adoption process; 12 of 13 had used ARTs. Some wanted to try for a biological child first; one woman explained, "We're open to adoption, but we wanted our own child. We wanted to try to get a biological child." For some, the experience of pregnancy was most important, while others described the biological connection as being particularly important to their husbands. Devout women were able to construct maternal identities around other forms of parenting, nurturing, and caring. Women drew on Biblical stories of infertility that emphasized women's value aside from biological motherhood, as one woman explained:

> There are women who suffered through infertility in the Bible, and that is a source of comfort: Hannah, Elizabeth, saints, or even nuns that give up their fertility because they have been called for something greater. It makes you feel like your life is still worthwhile even if you are not able to have a biological baby.

Carmela, who had a miscarriage and eventually adopted, challenged a strictly medical understanding of her infertility:

> I don't consider myself infertile in either sense. Neither in the physical sense because I have a baby in heaven that I'm not able to hold, but I was a mother ... because infertile means you don't give fruits, and I think I give fruits in many other ways.

These expanded expressions of fertility and motherhood helped devout women repair their gender identities, untethering their femininity and their status as mothers from biology.

Devout women also constructed alternative maternal identities as protectors of life. Elaina, who adopted, explained, "It's not that the Church is against everything. Actually, we're promoting life by helping women have their babies, by saving babies of abortion, by saving babies from IVF. It's very coherent." Kristine, a 30-year-old scientist from Houston, suffered from primary infertility for six years and eventually adopted a foster child. She described reconceptualizing her own maternal identity: "The key word there is I can be a mother without being pregnant. ... There are all kinds of kids who need help. I'm always a big advocate. I will always say I'm pro-life. Foster care, NaPro—I'm going to promote it."

Devout women are also able to achieve a sense of self-worth and value by focusing on what they see as a righteous path. Elaina explains:

> Being Catholic has made my life more difficult. On the other hand, it is an amazing source of value. ... I'm valued because I value life. Very Catholic people know that we're choosing life by not doing IVF. ... In that sense, the Church has given me a tremendous source of support.

As "moral guardians of life," devout women seek to preserve their souls and a divinely informed social order. While infertility marks them as potential outsiders in the Church community, their opposition to ARTs and their "bearing of the heavy cross" of infertility transforms them into exemplars of Catholic femininity instead. Women noted, in particular, the recognition of this status within the online community of Catholic infertile women—a place where their suffering, beliefs, and faith were understood.

CONCLUSION

In both their religious communities and in their social relationships outside of them, devout women contend with cultural interpretations of gender that conflate fertility and femininity. Devout women also experience a disjuncture between cultural expectations for them to use ARTs and a Church doctrine that forbids them to do so. Yet, despite religious traditions often compounding the larger societal pressure for women to be mothers, devout women *value* the limitations placed by the Church on the use of ARTs. In many ways, the religious restrictions provide a sense of meaning and stability as women grapple with profound uncertainty. This is not to say that devout women do not still struggle with aspects of their experiences. But they draw on religious schemas to construct moral boundaries around licit and illicit reproductive practices, to come to terms with the failure of medical treatments, and to reconceptualize themselves as feminine women and mothers in ways that transcend biological fertility. In doing so, they are able to recover a sense of womanhood that others experiencing infertility often feel they have lost. By "bearing the heavy cross of infertility," devout women achieve a *moral femininity* as virtuous women who endure suffering for God's larger plan.

Ultimately, religion is a multilayered and dynamic part of these women's lives. It contributes to the pain of infertility in various ways, but also offers cultural resources that help devout women construct meaningful, alternative maternal identities. Like their secular counterparts, devout women display admirable strength in facing the pain of infertility, but their religious beliefs enable them to locate their experiences within a larger cosmological order where God—not the individual—determines one's destiny. This relinquishing of control is, itself, a meaningful form of agency.

NOTES

1 By "biological" I mean biogenetic and gestational.
2 All names and places have been changed to protect confidentiality.

REFERENCES

Greil, Arthur L., Thomas A. Leitko, and Karen L. Porter. 1988. Infertility: His and hers. *Gender & Society* 2: 172–199.

Martin, Jade L. 2010. Anticipating infertility: Egg freezing, genetic preservation, and risk. *Gender & Society* 24: 526–545.

27

Race Matters in Lesbian Donor Insemination

Whiteness and Heteronormativity as Co-Constituted Narratives

Maura Ryan and Amanda Moras

In 2014, a white lesbian couple from Ohio filed a lawsuit against Midwest sperm bank when the birth of their biracial daughter revealed that they did not receive their requested donation from a white donor. The couple argues that they will experience unanticipated 'costs' now that they are raising a child of colour, including having to move from their current home in Uniontown, Ohio that they describe as white, conservative, and racially intolerant. Other 'challenges' they note are raising their daughter, Payton, with racially insensitive extended family, lack of their own cultural competency, and having to drive far from where they live to an 'all-black' neighbourhood to have their daughter's haircut. If there are costs involved in white lesbians raising children of colour, what are the unnamed benefits of raising white children? How does the naturalized assumption of whiteness function in white lesbian donor choices?

Moreover, this was not the first time there had been such a case; in 2004 Laura Howard, an African American woman, was inseminated with the 'wrong' sperm, her doctor mistakenly inseminated her with white sperm (she had intended to use a black donor) and 14 years earlier another such case in which a white woman was inseminated using sperm from a black donor (she has intended to use a white donor). Media coverage of each of these referred to such events using words such as: a nightmare, tragedy, and fiasco.

As sociologists have long argued, the state is instrumental in defining and legitimizing some family structures and not others, in defence of the hegemonic hetero-patriarchal family. Hierarchies of race, class, gender, and sexual orientation are of central importance in these legitimating projects, as evidenced by public policy and legal precedent. While American families are incredibly diverse in structure and definition, the mythical ideal type of family continues to hold mammoth ideological weight. In this arrangement, the husband works as the primary breadwinner, while the wife is charged with the primary responsibility of taking care of the home. All members of the family are also of the same religion and race, and perhaps even of the same ethnicity. The assumption that functioning families are built on a foundation of married, heterosexual parents who perform dichotomous gendered tasks in the home is precisely what rationalizes stigma against gay-headed families.

Many believe that one possible threat to the stability of hetero-patriarchal families is the new (relative) ease offered to single women and lesbians through reproductive technologies. Certainly,

Ryan, Maura, and Amanda Moras. "Race Matters in Lesbian Donor Insemination: Whiteness and Heteronormativity as Co-Constituted Narratives." *Ethnic and Racial Studies* 40, no. 4 (2017): 579–596.

lesbians have been raising children for several decades; however, new reproductive technologies and the relaxation of heteronormative policies for accessing these technologies have enhanced opportunities for women to conceive children through assisted reproductive technology in the last 15 years. Donor insemination is a key reproductive technology that many lesbian couples use to achieve pregnancy. The intentional selection of a particular donor opens up new questions for sociological analysis, specifically regarding how couples choose donor characteristics, in both known and unknown donor insemination attempts.

In this chapter, we analyse how our lesbian participants made decisions regarding their donor's race when they were choosing to conceive. Our data are composed of 18 in-depth qualitative interviews with white lesbian women who used both known and unknown donors to become pregnant. We specifically explore their raced narratives of pregnancy, discourses around race choices for donors, and conceptions of racial homogony in family imagining. Like in other areas of social life where the privileging of whiteness is rendered invisible, while many white women did not *overtly* articulate this decision-making process, the assumption of whiteness provides rich data for analysis.

DONOR INSEMINATION AND LESBIAN-HEADED FAMILIES

Donor insemination is the process of inserting sperm into the vagina or uterus of a female gestator. This can include couples who self-inseminate or inseminate through medical channels. Both heterosexual and lesbian women have used donor insemination as a means of getting pregnant; however, there are substantive differences in these two experiences due to sexual orientation. As Chabot and Ames (2004) point out, lesbian couples 'eliminate the gendered identities of man as father and woman as mother that united to produce children in the "natural" sense' (348). Furthermore, lesbian women have to make unique decisions including which parent is the biological mother, how to negotiate medical processes within hetero-normative medical institutions, and find known donors or sperm banks amenable to facilitating a lesbian family, in addition to longer-range choices such as choosing a surname for the child. While there is clearly some overlap between these experiences with heterosexual couples, lesbian couples face legal restrictions (for instance, inconsistent state laws regarding who can be on the birth certificate and second parent adoption) in addition to having to negotiate these issues in a heterosexist system that often withholds support such as not recognizing both mothers as 'real' parents.

DATA COLLECTION

Our analysis draws on audiotaped, in-depth interviews conducted with a sample of 18 lesbian birth mothers. All of the lesbian birth mothers in this study identified themselves as white. They were also overwhelmingly middle-class and upper-middle-class, based on self-reporting of their occupations and perceived social classes. Of the 18 birth mothers, three were in interracial relationships during their pregnancies (two with African American women and one with a Latina woman). The white woman with a Latina partner and one of the women with an African American partner chose a sperm donor who was Latino and African American, respectively, in order to create biracial children; one white woman with an African American partner chose a white donor in order to produce a white child.

All of the participants in this project were biological mothers and/or carried their children to term through pregnancy (one interviewed mother experienced pregnancy, but she and her partner employed the use of a purchased embryo). Although the lesbian participants' intentions toward and experiences with pregnancy varied slightly, the majority of them – 14 of 18 – acquired sperm (or in one case, an embryo) from sperm or embryo banks. Two of the birth mothers became pregnant using a known donor's sperm, with whom they do not currently share a parenting relationship, and one of the birth mothers became pregnant during an ongoing sexual relationship with a male partner (although she identified as a lesbian). Among the 18 mothers interviewed, two women were raising their children as single mothers and the other 16 were partnered.

'I Wanted My Child to Look Like Me':
Biological Relatedness and Race

Many lesbian women who plan families utilize donor insemination (DI) rather than adoption because of institutional discrimination in granting children to lesbians and because of a deeply rooted preference for biological connectedness. Here, we offer findings that emphasize the unspoken racialized process imbued in this kind of family building project.

Looking Alike

All participants who chose a donor (16 out of 18) expressed a desire for donors to have similar traits to either them or their partners. This desire reflects dominant family ideologies that claim members of families should – and will naturally – look alike, not only in terms of facial features but also hair colour, eye colour, and skin tone. This ideology reflects the emphasis placed on biological connectedness among all 'real' family members. However, same-sex couples do not have the option of having children who are biologically connected to both parents and instead may attempt to manipulate technology in a manner that makes families appear biologically connected. For example, in interviews there was a large emphasis placed upon matching the physical characteristics of donors in a manner that would mimic biological connectedness. Illustrating this, Lydia stated, 'Obviously there's no biology of my kid that's connected to my partner [but] we're a family and if we have the chance to increase our chances of our kid looking like both partners *of course we would do that*' [emphasis added]. This matching is inextricably connected to social expectations of families, and the negotiation of institutional structures in relation to family life. 'Of course' Lydia and her partner would try to have a child that looks like both of them because she knows that a lack of family homogeneity is used to deny the legitimacy of same-sex families, non-biologically related families, and single-parent families. Even if she was only referring to how 'looking alike' would make her and her partner feel about their own family, 'of course' they would still strive for this ideal because homogeneity is a leading social script of bonded families. It is both how they can *look* like a family to others, and how they can *feel* like a family amongst themselves.

An emphasis on looking like each other needs to be contextualized as both an interactional process in terms of how one negotiates family scripts and an institutional process. Illustrating this, Carol explained, 'I just wanted him to look like me, [for other people] to say "oh yeah, he looks like you", you know? ... Like I wanted someone to know that he is mine.' Immediately she followed her explanation by reflecting, 'That's kind of selfish I guess.' Her speculation that this may have been a 'selfish' decision is likely only because she chose a donor who would resemble only her and not both her *and* her African American partner. In other words, Carol only felt selfish because she defied the logic of how lesbians build families – making sure their child looks like both mothers. None of the biological mothers who chose donors that resembled their partners described this decision negatively, although they did note a shared interest in the child looking like them. For instance, Blanche said she wanted 'a reproduction of me' so she could 'see the traits, you know, from myself.' She goes on to say, 'especially because we knew we were using the same donor – to have two children, and see them, the similarities between the two of them.' While Blanche is interested in her own genetic traits being passed on to children, she is also excited about watching the genetic traits of a stranger develop in her sons. She made sure to use the same donor for both of her children so that they can *feel* biologically connected. If they share a smile that is not Blanche's they will presumably 'know' it came from their biological father, and Blanche believes this will make them closer siblings. This common emotion – the closeness generated by physical similarity – goes beyond interactional and institutional reasons for choosing physical likeness; it is a symbolic doing of family.

Both Carol's and Blanche's comments speak to the desire to have children look like themselves in a way that would make the child identifiable as theirs. Given the legal and social exclusions that same-sex-headed families confront, which challenge their rights and legitimacy as families, it is clear that many same-sex couples have a vested interest in making their families appear as connected as possible. It is not unrelated that Carol's 'selfish' desire to have 'someone know that he is mine' was also connected to the statement, 'you know, when he's going through school.' The only specific context Carol mentions where looking alike would be useful is in the institutional setting of the education system, where parents and children who do not meet a conventional family model may be marginalized. Perhaps she would like to avoid, for instance, being questioned by his teachers about her biological – or even legal – connection to her son. Discussed later is how Carol's African American partner navigates life with a son who does not resemble her. These concerns about family legibility speak to both the struggle for visibility within heterosexist family systems and internalized ideas about what families are 'supposed' to look like. The negotiation of biological ties that women we interviewed describe both subverts conventional meanings of biological kinship and reinforces preferences for biological connectedness.

Matching Racialized Characteristics

While participants were also concerned with personality characteristics and medical histories when selecting a donor, the physical features of the donor were of utmost importance. For most interviewees, the idea that families should look alike extends beyond 'looking like me' and manifests in the desire for similarly racialized features. These desires were present in all the interviews, although the racialized features discussed in these white families were not discussed as such. For example, Cassandra explained:

> So the first thing we looked at was physical characteristics like hair color, eye color, complexion, things like that. If possible, even the ethnic background – [my partner] has some English and Italian, we tried to find that kind of a thing. Then as we narrowed it down to physical characteristics that looked good, we would then go through the profiles or answers that donors would give on their questionnaires to see how they think.

Characteristics were framed as ethnic similarities or presented as a random set of isolated features such as eye colour and skin tone. Lydia also described a decision process wherein race was foundationally important to their choice, yet unnoticed:

> We chose a donor that had the same coloring as my partner so light brown hair, blue eyes, medium skin tone – my partner is really fair and I'm really fair and we thought, you know, if we have the choice we want to give the kid some pigmentation just to give him a chance in the sun so we went with medium skin tone. Otherwise, just somebody that seemed healthy.

While participants placed substantial emphasis on matching certain physical/ethnic characteristics, none specifically mentioned race. Yet the assumption of whiteness was implicit in many statements. Notice how, in terms of complexion, Lydia and her partner decided on a donor who matched neither of their fairness; they wanted someone with 'some pigmentation' to 'give him a chance in the sun.' Although they did not require their child to be as pale as they are, they did require their child to be white – and they did so without saying so. Again, we do not mean to imply that white lesbian mothers *should* be raising children of colour; we only mean to illuminate how decisions around whiteness can be achieved without talking about race.

Comments regarding eye colour, hair colour, and ethnicity are clearly marked with racial preferences. Rhonda, however, was the only participant who drew some connection between this matching and race preferences, albeit in a non-critical manner. She stated:

> We picked someone to match my partner… Both her interests and her physical attributes… We just thought that it might make a little bit more of a close family … we wanted her to resemble us somewhat. We were looking as far as features and coloring and things like that so I don't think it was too hard. Had [my partner] been African American or Hispanic or something we probably would have picked a donor to match that as well.

While her description of donor characteristics is typical of white participants with white partners, Rhonda was the only participant in this kind of relationship who mentioned race. However, she implies that race would only become an important aspect of family planning if 'race' – or being a person of colour – occurred in her family. While she states that 'had [my partner] been Hispanic or African American we probably would have picked a donor to match that as well,' she does not mention that they did in fact pick a donor based on being white. This raced silence in Rhonda's discussion, as well as in the other interviews, suggests that the option for a white donor was treated as an inevitable outcome, and not as a manifestation of racial preference.

Even a desire for a donor to belong to a certain ethnicity was couched in seemingly non-racial terms. What manifested in these interviews was the explicit mobilization of 'optional ethnicities' and a simultaneous silence around race. In our interviews, white mothers who never mentioned their own whiteness or the desire for a white donor did describe an attachment to a donor's racially specific ethnic identity. For example, Dot told Maura:

> We looked for an ethnic background that was like my partner's. Again, we started this when we were first looking for donors thinking that it would have half of my characteristics so we were specifically looking for her background as far as German, Scottish kind of – ethnic kind of stuff. And then, again, we did this process for about 2 years and at first we were very specific – we picked height, we picked build, we picked skin type.

It is somewhat puzzling what Dot means by 'skin type.' Although she is choosing whiteness, it is likely that – like Lydia – choosing 'skin type' means only what kind of complexion her white child will have. After all, being German or Scottish is presented as only 'ethnic kind of stuff,' not characteristics associated with a particular racial group. Instead of talking about whiteness, Josie also framed her choices as selection for a range of Eastern-European ethnicities: '[My partner] is Czech and Polish and Hungarian so we searched based on her ethnicity. We tried to make her as much a part of these babies as possible.' While Josie 'always knew [the donor] was going to be Czech, Hungarian, and Polish,' she and her partner miscommunicated the donor's profile number to their physician and accidentally chose a donor of an unintended ethnic composition. When they found out that the donor was, in part, Italian, they worried about the child's impending characteristics:

> We had actually gone to the doctor's for the last two inseminations and um, I read his profile and he's only half Czech and I remember I'm sitting in the office and I scream, 'Hey, honey?' – This is a classic line in our house – 'Did you know the kid's Italian?' She had picked somebody with an Italian mom! And we spent the next nine months going places and we'd always see this redhead next to this dark-haired kid and I always made fun because he was Italian that there was 'Coulda Be' and 'Would Be' and 'Would Be' didn't look like anybody, but 'Coulda Be' looked like me.

Similarly, for Roslyn, presumed cultural and ethnic heritage provided a framework to make sense of her racialized choices about a donor:

> [We wanted to choose] someone who was like my partner… She is half Jewish and the donor was all Jewish which means that our daughter will be half Jewish just like my partner… Curly brown hair, they were born the same year, they both have a science background, Russian, Polish, I don't know what you call that – their heritage.

The importance of 'heritage' can be understood as largely symbolic. After all, Dot, Josie, and Roslyn are describing an anonymous donor, not someone who will be present to transmit culture to their children – there will be no sharing of German children's tales, Hungarian goulash recipes, or Polish pet names. We can understand these descriptions as a deployment of 'optional ethnicity' because these families are placing an importance on an ethnic origin that has no practical value. Actually, the only practical measure of choosing a donor based on their ethnicity is that it is a way of approximating racial features. Interviewees never had to explicitly state that they wanted a white child because social expectations about family racial homogeneity and the privileging of whiteness rendered these choices benign. Comments such as wanting Scottish and German heritage, for example, erase choices about whiteness while simultaneously reinforcing the US ideology of colourblindness. What our interviews reveal is that ethnicity is expounded upon, deployed, and managed in order to discuss the complexities of skin colour, hair colour, and eye colour without engaging the language or realities of race and racial hierarchy.

The significance of these racial assumptions and individuals' efforts to elide race is evident when compared to how white participants who were partnered with women of colour explicitly addressed questions of race. White women in interracial relationships explicitly addressed questions about race in their decision-making process, without exception, regardless of whether they eventually chose a white donor or a donor of colour. For example, Susan chose an African American donor for her first child because she was partnered with an African American woman. After their breakup she began planning a second pregnancy and shared that 'it was definitely a consideration' to choose a white donor as a single white woman. In the end, she decided to use the same donor that produced her first child, 'I don't necessarily want to go with a completely white child because maybe [my first son] would feel left out.' This explicit negotiation highlights how whiteness was able to remain invisible in other white lesbian narratives only because they relied on hegemonic assumptions about race and family structure; race-based donor decisions made by interracial couples were more complex and more consciously negotiated.

Women choosing white donors were given much more freedom to make choices based upon education, hobbies, medical history, etc., whereas women looking for donors of colour were forced to select almost exclusively based upon race. Susan, a white woman who was planning a family with an African American partner, decided that her child should resemble both her and her partner, 'I was like, you know, we're together, we're a biracial couple, doesn't it make sense for the child to be more a representation of us than just of me? So, [my son] is biracial.' Because of this, as she says, 'race was the number one,' in their decision-making process, as their local cryobank only had three African American donors. She continued, 'Really nothing else. I mean, I wasn't really looking for any height or occupation or anything … Other than [his race], really nothing specific.' Carol, a white woman with an African American partner who chose a white donor, had the option of choosing a donor whose childhood photographs mirrored her physical appearance, had interesting hobbies, and offered a clear medical history for generations.

Carol explained that she had chosen a white donor before entering into a relationship with her African American partner, Regina. During Carol's family planning stages they entered into a serious relationship and decided that they would be raising the child together. During this shift in what her family would look like – from a single mother household to a dual mother household – Carol did not reevaluate her donor choice because even though she 'would have totally [changed donors]' her partner 'could [have] care[d] less.' Still, when reflecting on her choice she said, 'In fact, I felt really really really guilty that it wasn't a mixed baby, and I felt really selfish.' One would imagine that Carol felt selfish because Regina is not able to experience what she does – an easy assumption that she and the child are mother and baby. However, when offering how her partner felt about the situation, she reassured herself, 'but she could care less, this is her baby, you know.' One wonders why *Carol* would not have felt that her son was 'her baby,' no matter his racial composition.

Because of assumptions about the racial homogeneity of families that we have expounded upon, and because of heterosexist assumptions about parenting dyads, most people do not assume that both Regina and Carol are their child's mother. Carol mused about strangers' confusion:

> We got a lot of looks … people look at her, then they look at the baby, then they look at me, then they look at the baby, then they look at her… and they're like okay we know it's not [Regina's] baby. You know, they're like, we know it's her baby, but they seem awfully close, you know, like what's up here?

Notice how their lesbianism *and* the interracial nature of their relationship made them illegible as a family in public settings. Surely Carol's fears that raising a child of colour would detract from the assumption that she is his mother are not unfounded. Still, it is not only racial difference between parent and child that matters but also the racial status of the mother in question. That is to say, Regina's experiences as a black woman raising a white child are significantly different than Carol's would have been as a white woman raising a biracial child. For example, Carol explained further, 'when Regina is with the baby shopping she gets a lot of looks … everyone thinks she's just the nanny.' Regina is not just marked as not-mother, but as someone who is employed in service to the infant, which considering the racialized field of domestic labour is less likely for white women with biracial children.

Yet, there are further complexities to Carol's conscious decision-making process. She also told Maura,

> [Life's] going to be less [hard] on him than if he were a minority too… think of it that way. You know, so the poor kid's going to have a lot of stress anyway, much less being a minority himself.

At least part of her decision was not based on the 'selfish' dedication that her child look like her, but instead in trying to limit the discrimination her child would face. She also explained:

> I thought to myself, well, this boy, he's going to be going through so much in his life anyway, you know? Because right now he's a white baby you know, he's a white Anglo-Saxon baby. You would never know he had two lesbian moms in an interracial, you know, relationship. So, in a way he's not going to have any prejudice on himself because he just looks like this white, Anglo-Saxon kid.

Racial difference complicates issues of passing as a member of a nuclear, heterosexual, and racially homogenous family. Notice that when she says one would never know that her son had 'two lesbian moms in an inter-racial, you know, relationship' she is also talking about the benefits of whiteness. How does his race mark him as a coming from or not coming from lesbian parents? One can imagine many social interactions in which a visibly biracial child is asked to answer who is white and who is black – his mother or his father? When his answer is that he has lesbian mothers, he will become marginalized because of his family background, when he is already marginalized for his status as a person of colour. Notably, there are many circumstances where white children with white, lesbian mothers will be forced to out themselves about their families, but explaining their racial composition is not one of them.

Unlike lesbian couples, fertile heterosexual couples produce children in a context where they do not have to investigate the genetic characteristics they desire for reproduction; the decisions they made in partner selection make this invisible. While white lesbians in intra-racial relationships do have to consciously negotiate desired donor characteristics, they similarly naturalize the racial homogeneity of families, and they similarly make invisible the subconscious value they assign to whiteness.

DISCUSSION: WHITENESS AND HETERONORMATIVITY

All families who fall outside of hetero-patriarchal ideals are to some degree challenging heterosexuality, and, as such, are disciplined by a heteronormative system. It is perhaps especially intriguing that families who explicitly break with heterosexist ideologies about families – (white) lesbian mothers – are able to divest from the silencing structures of heteronormativity while furthering the powerful silence around their own whiteness and the whiteness in their families. However, it is not all that surprising. Because of how whiteness is constructed as an empty category devoid of meaning on its own, race, like gender, is only thought to be important when it functions as a disadvantage. Allowing privilege to remain invisible enables whites to deny their connection to, maintenance of, and profit from racism. In the US context, white people have the privilege of being un-raced, the proxy for normalcy. It is only through contact with people of colour that white identity is given meaning, is fleshed out, and personified.

This same privileging has been endemic to sociological studies of families. White, middle-class families have been used as a cultural measuring stick by which all other families are judged. Families who do not meet this hegemonic ideal of a white middle-class family have been labelled both by social scientists and policy makers as somehow deficient. As part of this privileging of white, heterosexual families, individual choices about the race of potential children are de-racialized and de-politicized. The individuals we interviewed rarely (if ever) questioned their decision to use white donors, or even verbally acknowledged their decision. For instance, while no participants explicitly stated, 'I wanted a white child,' they did display preferences in terms of skin colour, hair colour, eye colour, and ethnicity. That is, individuals assumed whiteness, and assumed this decision did not have to be explained.

Identifying the discourse and decisions surrounding a donor's race, as we have done in this study, illuminates an integral nexus between gender, race, and sexualities, and how these various social locations intersect in our conceptions of family. Many scholars have pointed out the multiple ways that Lesbian, Gay, Bi-sexual, Transgender, Queer (LGBTQ) families are transforming traditional notions of kinship and family, and transforming the gendered institutions of labour within the home. The narratives presented here did not suggest freely chosen familial practices or 'oppositional to heterosexual assumption' but instead reflected largely traditional family discourses. Our research suggests that we must keep other power structures in mind as well. Specifically, scholars who are engaging the topic of LGBTQ families have a responsibility to pay attention to the ways in which race – and in this case, whiteness – constitute specific family meanings. If we make race – and whiteness – more visible then we can begin to dismantle the white privilege that advantages some families, and we can have a more complicated discussion around the ways in which gay and lesbian families are differently and hierarchically located.

REFERENCE

Chabot, Jennifer M., and Barbara D. Ames. 2004. "'It Wasn't 'Let's Get Pregnant and Go Do It':" Decision Making in Lesbian Couples Planning Motherhood via Donor Insemination." *Family Relations* 53 (4): 348–356.

28

Immigration Policies Can Make the Difference between Life and Death for Newborn US Children

Maria Rodriguez and Jens Hainmueller

The health of children born to unauthorized immigrants – who are US citizens – is affected by local and federal immigration policies. There are as many as 4 million children who have at least one parent who is undocumented.

Along with colleagues at Stanford's Immigration Policy Lab and Oregon Health & Science University, we measure the impact of immigration policy on the health of individuals and communities. Our research reveals the public health benefits of laws that make it easier for unauthorized immigrants to integrate into society.

An Obama-era policy that temporarily shielded some Dreamers from deportation, Deferred Action for Childhood Arrivals (DACA), offers a dramatic example of how this has worked at the federal level.

POWER OF POLICY

We looked at Oregon's Emergency Medicaid program, which overwhelmingly covers the medical expenses of unauthorized immigrant mothers when they give birth.

We identified mothers who were born just before and just after the cutoff to be eligible for DACA. Their children, native-born US citizens, were all covered by Medicaid. This allowed us to follow their children's health over time and compare those whose mothers were either eligible or ineligible for DACA. We studied 8,610 children.

After the DACA policy was announced in 2012, the two groups of children suddenly diverged. Children whose mothers were eligible for DACA saw an immediate improvement in their mental health; they were diagnosed with anxiety and similar stress disorders at half the rate of the other children.

These findings suggest that in the absence of protections included in DACA, children inherit the stress and anxiety of their parents' lives without legal status. Mental illness in childhood is associated with a cascade of long-term challenges: struggles in school, limited job prospects, chronic health problems, and substance

Rodriguez, Maria and Jens Hainmuelle. "Immigration Policies Can Make the Difference between Life and Death for Newborn US Children." *The Conversation*, April 25, 2018.

abuse. Child and adolescent mental health is also a growing concern among medical professionals. Up to one in five children and adolescents experience mental disorder in a given year, according to a recent Centers for Disease Control and Prevention report. Our study's findings identify the critical role immigration policy may play in this growing problem.

GOOD HEALTH BEGINS BEFORE BIRTH

An inclusive approach to unauthorized immigrants can also benefit their children's health as early as birth, our research suggests. Health care during pregnancy has far-reaching implications for women and their children: It often involves diagnosing and treating chronic conditions, and it can help reduce preterm birth. However, Medicaid, the nation's largest payer for obstetric care, excludes otherwise eligible immigrant women from coverage based on their citizenship status.

Recognizing this problem, Oregon is one of 32 states that use a provision of the federal Children's Health Insurance Program (CHIP) to extend prenatal care coverage to unauthorized immigrant women. CHIP's unborn child option allows states to receive federal funds for prenatal care to immigrant women because the care benefits a future US citizen. However, maternal coverage only includes care that benefits the fetus, and coverage ends the day a woman gives birth.

Because Oregon expanded the program gradually, county by county, we were able to compare women and their babies who were covered with those who were not.

Women who got prenatal care coverage had an average of seven more doctor visits per pregnancy. They were 61 percent more likely to be screened for gestational diabetes and were 74 percent more likely to receive a fetal ultrasound.

Access to prenatal care significantly reduced infant mortality. That means, conversely, that failure to provide prenatal care may contribute to infant deaths. And the protective effect of increased prenatal care continued through the first year of life: Infants of mothers who received coverage were more likely to receive vaccinations and screenings.

The federal government has yet to take action to address undocumented immigration. So state and local governments across the country are experimenting with policies of their own. Evidence shows that states with inclusive policies can benefit both individual health and community in profound ways.

29

Born in the USA

Having a Baby Is Costly and Confusing, Even for a Health Policy Expert

Simon F. Haeder

It is hard to believe that it has been just over since five months since our second son, Lukas, was born on February 3. His mother, Hollyanne, is doing well, which is something to be thankful for, given the excessive maternal mortality rates in the United States. Lukas is also healthy and growing, albeit sleeping little at night. What is unbelievable is the fact that I am still receiving bills for his birth.

Of course, I "knew" what was going to happen when we found out that my wife was pregnant. I study health policy for a living, and I have written extensively about the American health care system. Yet for all the reading and writing, experiencing health care in America personally is a rather shocking experience. Keep in mind, our birthing experience was without any complications and we have health insurance.

I cannot imagine how overwhelming the experience must be for someone with fewer resources and less of an understanding about health care in America.

BEING PREGNANT AND GIVING BIRTH: NOT WHAT IT USED TO BE

From the first doctor's appointment, we were introduced to what to expect: lots of paperwork and lots of bills. There are of course all the monthly, then biweekly, and then weekly doctor's visits with the corresponding bills.

In West Virginia, due to the opioid epidemic, most doctors will also insist on a drug screen.

As it turned out, my wife's doctor ordered copious amounts of blood work and ultrasounds – "outpatient diagnostic services," totaling thousands of dollars. It is hard to question any of these when all you want is a healthy baby – and your doctor is the only one who knows which tests are necessary.

Like most parents, we also wanted to know whether our baby was going to be healthy. Here is the total amount of the bill for genetic testing sent to our insurance company: US$26,755.

Haeder, Simon. "Born in the USA: Having a Baby Is Costly and Confusing, Even for a Health Policy Expert." *The Conversation*, July 16, 2018.

Giving birth to our first son, Nico, had been quite an arduous experience for my wife. She labored for more than 30 hours. Determined not to spend hours in the hospital, my wife practically gave birth this time in the front seat of our car. Ultimately, I was able to throw my wife onto a bed in the maternity ward, and Lukas popped right out.

I joked to my wife: "At least they cannot charge us for delivery." At the very least, I should file a claim with our insurance company.

I am still not quite sure how wrong I was, because every time I ask for a detailed bill, new items appear while others miraculously disappear.

About $65 an Hour, for Lodging

The delivery room, which we used for all of one minute, cost about $7,000. Room and board for my wife for 48 hours cost just over $3,100. Two Tylenols for my wife: $25. Laboratory work: $1,200.

That does not account for Lukas. Room and board for him was just over $1,500. Various laboratory work charges added another $1,400 or so. The hearing test cost $260.

I tried to keep track of all the medical personnel coming and going, but after a while it all became a blur. The doctor, who was not present at birth, charged $4,200 for delivery and care. Pediatricians stopped by a few times to check on Lukas for $150 per look.

We were not able to take advantage of a tax-favored flexible spending account for most of these expenses, because "being pregnant" does not count as a "life event." While "giving birth" does count, the added contributions cannot be applied to previous costs associated with the birth.

Bringing the Baby Home

As demanding as giving birth is, in many ways, the real challenges of raising children start when one leaves the hospital.

Like many American women, my wife, a teacher, did not have access to paid maternity leave. Hence, we had to make do with one income for a few months. Of course, this could not have been a more inconvenient time to lose a paycheck, because literally every day we received medical bills. Many of the bills misspelled someone's name or got another fact wrong, which led to countless phone calls with providers and our insurer.

Diapers and other baby items, naturally, are also not cheap.

Once my semester ended in early May, my wife went back to work as I watched Lukas. This brought new challenges with it.

For one, as a professor, I am also not getting paid over the summer.

Moreover, while the Affordable Care Act provides added benefits and protections for breastfeeding, there are limitations. For one, not all breast pumps are covered, and insurance companies are getting stingier. This is of course ironic given that there is a whole other effort going on to encourage mothers to breastfeed more because it has been found so beneficial for mother and child.

Finding an appropriate place and time to pump breast milk at work, even with a decent pump and governmental protections, comes with a slew of challenges. Currently my wife is using every free minute she can find and locks her classroom. Finding the time and space when doing continuing education or field trips is, of course, a whole other story.

Going forward, we are rather lucky.

Thanks to the Affordable Care Act, well-child visits and preventive care like immunizations will be included in our insurance. Of course, should something serious happen, like a hospitalization, we will be on the hook again for potentially thousands of dollars.

My employer allows me to work from home during the fall semester so I can take care of Lukas at the same time. Of course, while I do not have to teach a class on campus, expectations about research and service will not diminish.

Yet soon, we will have to put Lukas into day care. We have been on several waiting lists since the moment we found out my wife was pregnant. Last time, I had to drive my son Nico 45 minutes one way to a day care we were comfortable with in Pennsylvania. Even if we are lucky to find a nice day care close by, fees will exceed in-state tuition at West Virginia University, my employer.

PUTTING OUR EXPERIENCE IN PERSPECTIVE

Our experience is, of course, not unique.

America's poorest members of society are somewhat shielded from medical costs. Medicaid generally does not require out-of-pocket contributions. For those on the Children's Health Insurance Program and those with cost-sharing subsidies on the Affordable Care Act insurance marketplaces, out-of-pocket contributions are limited. In both cases, the high costs of giving birth are passed on to public sources and those of us with private insurance.

The real struggles of the poor begin as they seek to raise their children with limited resources and diminishing governmental support.

Yet the middle class more and more often finds itself squeezed between a rock and a hard place when it comes to health care. Premiums, deductibles, and co-payments continue to increase while services and choices grow narrower every year.

With Republican efforts to undo much or all of the Affordable Care Act, even those of us with employer-sponsored insurance may lose many protections.

Many of us are simultaneously struggling to pay back our student loans, which already forces many to delay marriage, have kids, or buy a house.

For us, and many others, this also meant cutting back on virtually everything, including family vacations and replacing appliances. It also meant taking up every opportunity to add income for both of us by taking side jobs.

Any potential future pay raises are likely to be swallowed up by premium increases and co-payments as health care costs continue to grow unabated.

TOO RICH FOR GOVERNMENT PROGRAMS, YET TOO POOR TO AVOID FINANCIAL HARDSHIP

Given these struggles, it is perhaps not surprising that the frustrations of the middle class breed resentment toward publicly supported programs. Support for work requirements and more punitive and stigmatizing approaches to social programs are perhaps the understandable result.

Our current approaches to encourage and support parenthood are willfully inadequate. Health care, parental leave, day care, parental support, education. As a country, I think that we should strive to do better to support our families.

SECTION VI
Building Families through Adoption

INTRODUCTION

The beginnings of the practice of adoption are unknown. Many point to biblical stories of women caring for children they did not birth. Yet, adoption as a legal and bureaucratic process has changed a great deal over time, even as caring and loving a non-biological child may be ancient. Because there is no record of total adoptions in the United States, it is challenging to even know how many children are adopted each year. Data on the number of adoptions from the child welfare system (foster care) and intercountry adoptions are available from government agencies. However, no agency is charged with systematically collecting data from private agencies. Estimates are that in 2014, there were about 111,000 adoptions—a decrease from almost 134,000 adoptions in 2007 (Jones and Placek 2017). More than half of this decline can be attributed to the significant drop in the number of Americans adopting from other countries.

There are different paths through adoption, as the chart below shows. First, there are domestic adoptions: adoptions of children born in the United States. Then there are adoptions of children born in other

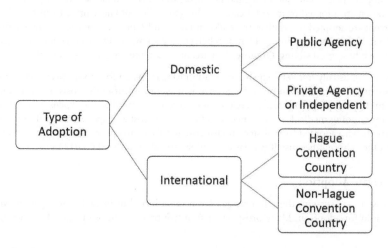

Pathways to adoption.

countries, known as intercountry or international adoptions (about 4,000 in 2018). There are different legal processes for both paths. For domestic adoptions, some come through public agencies in which prospective parents adopt children from the foster care system (about 61,000 adoptions in 2018) (DHHS 2018), and some through private arrangements where a child is relinquished by their birth parents. Virtually all adoptions require a home study, which will likely include information about prospective adoptive parents' health, finances, home, and background, and all require legal proceedings to finalize the adoption and bestow parental rights to the adoptive parents. Different processes have different costs, timing, and obligations, as the following sections explain.

DOMESTIC ADOPTION

Public Agency Adoption

A public agency adoption is one in which a child is adopted from the foster care system. In most cases, social workers charged with investigating child maltreatment have removed a child from his or her home due to abuse or neglect. If the parents are not able to successfully complete court-ordered services and regain custody of their children, a judge will terminate their parental rights, and the children become available for adoption.

The children who are available for adoption from foster care are more likely to be children of color and to have some disability than the general population of children. For example, 56 percent of children in the U.S. population are white, but only 37 percent of those adopted from foster care are white. Black children comprise 14 percent of the general population but are 35 percent of the children are adopted from foster care. About half of children adopted from foster care have special healthcare needs, compared to 19 percent of all children, though the signficance of those diagnoses is unclear. Notably, the Department of Health and Human Services finds that

> 76 percent of children adopted from foster care with special health care needs are considered by their parents to be in excellent or very good health. While this may appear contradictory, many children with special health care needs have conditions, such as asthma, that may be well controlled with medication or other treatment.

About 20 percent of children adopted from foster care are six years or older and 45 percent are under the age of one year (ASPE 2011).

Some public agency adoptions begin as foster care placements, known as fost-adopts. In foster placements, the biological parents still hold some legal rights to the child and if they are able to improve their lives, they can reunify with their child. Since 1997, federal law has stated a priority to identify foster placements that can become adoptive placements should a child be unable to return to their parents (ASFA 1997). About 55 percent of children are adopted from foster care by adults they did not know prior to entry to foster care. About 17 percent are adopted by relatives the children knew and 6 percent are adopted by relatives they did not know. About 22 percent are adopted by non-relatives they knew. About 82 percent of children in foster care have a known biological sibling. Of those, 41 percent are adopted together (ASPE 2011).

Public adoptions are usually not very expensive for adoptive parents. In fost-adopt placements, foster parents will usually receive payment from the government agency to offset the costs of caring for a child. Sometimes, children adopted from foster care continue to receive subsidies for expenses like health insurance or for ongoing medical or social needs. Differences in cost and speed are significant. About 60 percent of parents who adopted from foster care list cost as a factor in choosing that path, and about 28 percent report they chose it because it was faster than private adoption (ASPE 2011).

Domestic Private Adoption

Outside the foster care system, there is a range of ways to adopt, but in each, birth parents voluntarily relinquish a child for adoption. Many prospective adoptive parents choose licensed private agencies to increase their chances of adopting an infant. Agencies often allow prospective parents to submit letters, videos, photos, profiles, or other information from which birth parents can select an adoptive family for their child. In some cases, birth parents may get to meet prospective adoptive parents when deciding whether to place their child with them. Private agency adoptions are much more expensive than public adoption. Agency fees can range from $15,000 to $30,000. Prospective adoptive parents may also pay additional expenses, including legal representation for the adoptive and birth parent(s), medical costs, counseling, rent, phone and travel for the birth parent(s), and travel for adoptive parents, court costs, required home evaluations, and networking/advertising costs. Total costs are estimated to be between $25,000 and $50,000 (Adoption Network 2020). Many private agencies are religiously affiliated and may set additional requirements on adoptions beyond those required by the state Duncan 2016).

Independent adoptions are in many ways similar to private agency adoptions. However, most commonly, the adoptive parents identify the pregnant woman without the help of an agency. All states except four (Connecticut, Delaware, Massachusetts, and North Dakota) allow independent adoption. However, some additional states ban the use of advertisements to birth parents or limit financial compensation to be paid to birth parents. With independent adoptions, infants are likely to be placed with adoptive parents at birth.

In some cases, an unlicensed adoption facilitator may help connect birth parents and adoptive parents in exchange for a fee. These workers are usually unlicensed and have the least amount of government oversight. Families working with facilitators may also have the least amount of protection should the adoption not work out as promised. Some states regulate facilitators and others ban them completely.

Consent to Domestic Adoption

All voluntary adoptions (in contrast to court-ordered termination of parental rights in the public adoption system) require parents to give consent to the termination of their parental rights, although the timing of this varies by state. About 47 states and the District of Columbia specify in statute when a birth parent may legally consent to adoption. Sixteen states allow birth parents to consent at any time after the birth of the child. Approximately 14 states allow an alleged birth father to execute consent at any time before or after the child's birth. Only two states (Alabama and Hawaii) allow the birth mother to consent before the birth of her child; however, this decision must be reaffirmed after the child's birth.

Thirty states and the District of Columbia require a waiting period after the birth of a child before consent can be executed. The shortest waiting periods among states that require waiting periods are 12 hours (in Kansas) and 24 hours (in Utah), and the longest is 15 days (in Rhode Island). The most common waiting period, required in 16 states and the District of Columbia, is 72 hours (three days). The waiting period in Vermont is 36 hours, and it is 48 hours in Connecticut, Florida, Missouri, Nebraska, New Mexico, Texas, and Washington. In Massachusetts, consent can be provided on the fourth day after the child's birth. In Louisiana and South Dakota, parents can provide consent after five days. In California, a birth mother who is placing her child directly with adoptive parents must wait to consent until she has been discharged from the hospital following the child's birth. If the child being relinquished is an American Indian child, California and Washington impose a ten-day waiting period (Child Welfare Information Gateway 2017).

Once birth parents give consent, it can be very difficult to revoke it. Ten states and the District of Columbia specify a period of time in which birth parents can revoke consent. This can vary from seven days (in Virginia) to six months (in Mississippi). In addition, consent may be revoked in some states if it resulted from fraud or coercion, if doing so is in the best interest of the child, if consent was given under duress, or if it is by mutual agreement (Child Welfare Information Gateway 2017).

International/Intercountry Adoption

International adoption is an adoption where a child is born in one country and adopted by parents from a different country. The legal process of adoption varies based on the rules in the country where the child is from and the agencies with which adoptive parents are working. American parents adopt children from a wide range of countries. The countries that most commonly allow American parents to adopt change over time depending upon changes in political climate, economic conditions, and government regulation. In 2018, there were 4,059 intercountry adoptions to the United States, a decline of 655 from the prior year (and representative of a pattern discussed in the chapter by Montgomery and Powell). The majority of this decrease (430) occurred in China, which has been steadily decreasing over the past several years as a result of an improving economy, newer plans for adoption options within China, and legal changes relating to non-government organizations (NGOs). Ethiopia, which had recently become a more popular country for adoption imposed a ban in 2018 on intercountry adoption based on "concerns about the welfare of children in the United States whose adoptions had been disrupted, instances of adoptive parents returning children to Ethiopia, and concerns about corruption" (U.S. Department of State 2019a). Other countries have recently increased the availability of children for adoption, including Colombia, India, Afghanistan, South Sudan, Indonesia, and Croatia. Although seldom acknowledged, 81 children in 2018 were adopted from the United States to nine countries, including Canada (38 adoptions), the Netherlands (20 adoptions), Mexico (nine adoptions), and Ireland (six adoptions) (U.S. Department of State 2019).

Adoption from Hague Convention Countries

Countries may regulate the conditions of adoption of children from their country, but some international agreements do exist. The Hague Convention on the Protection of Children and Co-operation in Respect of Intercountry Adoption is an international agreement, written in 1993 and implemented in the United States in 2008, that aims to protect individuals from corruption, abuse, and exploitation relating to international adoption, including child trafficking. The Hague Convention requires that countries have a central authority to oversee adoption processes, including verifying whether a child is eligible for adoption, conducting or verifying home studies or background checks of adoptive parents, and working with certified agencies. It also limits adoptive parents' abilities to work directly with birth parents to prevent coercion and exploitation. The Hague Convention requires that agencies disclose fees in advance in writing and provide paperwork and certificates to adoptive parents to make it easier for them to bring their adopted child home. Hague countries also require prospective adoptive parents to complete ten hours of parent education.

Adoptions from Non-Hague Convention Countries

Americans adopting children from countries that have not signed on to the Hague Convention still face requirements imposed by U.S. states and federal agencies as well as those enacted by the country of origin. Those wishing to adopt must find an agency licensed in their state and accredited by federal agencies to do a home study. Prospective adoptive parents may not be required to complete training, which is required in Hague countries. Those wanting to adopt must apply to the U.S. Citizenship and Immigration Services and be recognized as eligible to adopt. This will depend on citizenship or immigration status and on evidence that the prospective adopting parents can provide "a suitable and stable home" with evidence from the home study and a background check. Once matched with a child, the prospective parents must provide evidence that the child is eligible for adoption as an orphan as defined under U.S. law. Non-Hague countries are not obligated to disclose fees. Usually, the country in which the child lives will then allow the prospective adoptive parents to adopt or assume guardianship in that country, which will allow the parents to return to the United States with the child. Assuming the child meets the U.S. definition of an orphan (which is easier in Hague countries), parents will submit more paperwork to embassies or consulates to eventually get an immigrant visa for their child. In contrast, those adopting from Hague countries can submit much of this before adoption processes in the child's country have started. The U.S. federal government generally does not recognize adoptions of children older than 16 years of age unless they have a biological sibling adopted by the same parents (U.S. Department of State 2019b). Hague countries must maintain adoption records for at least 75 days. Non-Hague countries have no such requirements.

Even with definitional and procedural differences, different countries—whether or not they signed on to the Hague Convention—can enact additional requirements. For example, China specifies that adoptive parents cannot smoke, have disabilities (including hearing loss), have had an organ transplant in the past ten years, or have a body mass index over 40. India, for example, suggests that married couples should not have a combined age over 90 years. Other countries do not allow gay and lesbian couples to adopt. In sum, some countries may be more or less restrictive. Countries will have varying levels of organization of the process. Typically, and varying by country, international adoptions cost between $20,000 and $50,000.

WHO ADOPTS?

Who adopts children varies dramatically, though there are some patterns. About 2 percent of Americans have adopted children. That number is twice as high for men (2.3 percent) than women (1.1 percent). On average, adoptive mothers are older than are non-adoptive mothers; only about 3 percent of adoptive mothers are between ages 18 and 29 years compared with 27 percent of biological mothers. Women who adopt are about ten times more likely to have used medical services for infertility and are more likely to have an income above 150 percent of the federal poverty line. Men who have biological children are more likely to also have adopted children than are men who do not (Jones 2009). Adoption is a significant pathway to parenting for gay and lesbians. National data show that more than 21 percent of gay and lesbian couples are raising an adopted or foster child, compared with only 3 percent of heterosexual couples (Goldberg and Conron 2018). The chapter in this section by Dana Berkowitz explores the challenges and choices involved in gay adoption.

OPENNESS AND CONTACT AFTER ADOPTION

Adoption does not always mean the end of contact between a child and her or his biological family. The kinds and quantity of contact between biological and adoptive families following a child's placement fall on a continuum. On one end is the closed or confidential adoption where no information-sharing takes place. Next, there are arrangements (semi-open) in which there is mediated contact between families through an adoption agency (Child Welfare Information Gateway 2013). On the other end, there are families who have open adoptions, in which they directly interact and share information. Openness can range from letters, photographs, and cards to in-person meetings (Frasch, Brooks and Barth 2000). Unlike earlier time periods discussed in Rickie Solinger's chapter in this section, adoption has become less stigmatized over time. Today, most adopted children and youth know that they are adopted, and many adoptive families have had some contact with birth families. One national study of adoptive families in the United States found that in approximately one-third of all adoptive families, the adoptive parents or the adopted child had some contact with the birth family after the adoption. Post-adoption contact is more common in private domestic adoption (68 percent) as compared with adoption from foster care (39 percent) and international adoption (6 percent). Another study among U.S. adoption agencies reported that almost all (95 percent) of their domestic infant adoptions were open (Child Welfare Information Gateway 2013).

Frequency of interaction can vary over time. Independent adoptions are more likely to have openness and contact than are public agency adoptions. However, openness and contact do occur in public adoptions as well. Among children not adopted by relatives, 39 percent have had some post-adoption contact with birth family (by definition, all children adopted by relatives do as well). One might logically assume that children adopted at an older age would be more likely to have contact or that fost-adopt placements would be more likely to have ongoing contact with birth families than children whose parents' rights were already terminated at the time of the placement. However, studies show that post-adoption contact does not vary significantly by whether the child was older or younger than age six at placement and does not vary by whether an adoptive parent was a foster parent first (ASPE 2011).

Although there are concerns about ongoing contact, most research suggests that these relationships are positive. One study found that adoptive families with contact reported having higher levels of satisfaction about their openness arrangements, experienced more positive feelings about the birth mother, and possessed more factual and personal knowledge about the birth mother than did families without contact (Grotevant et al. 2007). Longitudinal studies show that contact over time may ebb and flow, but that overall, "adoptive parents reported greater levels of comfort with contact over time and that this contact had generally positive repercussions for the child and adoptive family" (Crea and Barth 2009). Openness and contact have become normative in domestic adoptions. However, as Leslie Kim Wang, Iris Chin Ponte, and Elizabeth Weber Ollen show in their chapter, openness and contact are becoming an option in intercountry adoption too.

FORMAL FAMILIES THROUGH ADOPTION

Adoption is a highly regulated way to create a legally recognized family. After adoptions are finalized, adoptive parents have all the same rights and responsibilities to their children as do genetically related parents. Estimates are that about 5 million living Americans are adoptees, that 2 percent of all children in the United States are adopted, and that between 2 and 4 percent of families in the United States have adopted. Adoptive families are on average more racially diverse, have higher levels of education, and are wealthier than families in general (Herman 2012, Kreider and Lofquist 2014). The readings in this section provide historic background on adoption in the United States and show the significant role of race in adoption, explore intercountry adoption, and show the challenges gay men encounter in seeking to adopt as well as the ways that economic and social resources affect their experiences. In each, the intersections of regulation and experience are visible.

REFERENCES

Adoption Network. 2020, "How Much Does It Cost to Adopt a Child?" (https://adoptionnetwork. com/cost-of-adoption/how-much-does-it-cost-to-adopt-a-child).

ASFA. 1997. "Adoption and Safe Families Act of 1997." U.S. Congress. Public Law 105–89—NOV. 19, 1997 111 STAT. 2115.

ASPE. 2011. "Children Adopted from Foster Care: Child and Family Characteristics, Adoption Motivation, and Well-Being." Washington, DC: Office of the Assistant Secretary for Planning and Evaluation. U.S. Department of Health and Human Services.

Child Welfare Information Gateway. 2013. *Openness in Adoption: Building Relationships between Adoptive and Birth Families.* Washington, DC: U.S. Department of Health and Human Services, Children's Bureau.

Child Welfare Information Gateway. 2017. *Consent to Adoption.* Washington, DC: Department of Health and Human Services, Children's Bureau.

Crea, Thomas M. and Richard P. Barth. 2009. "Patterns and Predictors of Adoption Openness and Contact: 14 Years Postadoption." *Family Relations* 58(5):607–620.

DHHS. 2018. *The AFCARS Report.* Washington, DC: U.S. Department of Health and Human Services, Administration for Children and Families.

Duncan, Melanie L. 2016. "Adoption, Laws, in the United States." in *Encyclopedia of Family Studies* 1–7. C.L. Shehan (Ed.). Wiley. doi:10.1002/9781119085621.wbefs439.

Frasch, Karie M., Devon Brooks and Richard P. Barth. 2000. "Openness and Contact in Foster Care Adoptions: An Eight-Year Follow-Up." *Family Relations* 49(4):435–447.

Goldberg, Shoshana K and Kerith J Conron. 2018. *How Many Same-Sex Couples in the Us Are Raising Children?* Los Angeles, CA: Williams Institute, UCLA School of Law.

Grotevant, Harold D., Gretchen Miller Wrobel, Lynn Von Korff, Brooke Skinner, Jane Newell, Sarah Friese and Ruth G. McRoy. 2007. "Many Faces of Openness in Adoption: Perspectives of Adopted Adolescents and their Parents." *Adoption Quarterly* 10(3–4): 79–101.

Herman, Ellen. 2012, *The Adoption History Project*. Eugene, OR: University of Oregon (https://pages. uoregon.edu/adoption/topics/adoptionstatistics.htm).

Jones, Jo. 2009. "Who Adopts? Characteristics of Women and Men Who Have Adopted Children." NCHS *Data Brief No 12*. Hyattsville, MD: National Center for Health Statistics.

Jones, Jo and Paul Placek. 2017. *Adoption by the Numbers*. Alexandria, VA: National Council For Adoption.

Kreider, Rose M. and Daphne A. Lofquist. 2014. "Adopted Children and Stepchildren: 2010". U.S. Census Bureau (https://www.census.gov/prod/2014pubs/p20-572.pdf).

U.S. Department of State. 2019a. *Fiscal Year Annual Report on Intercountry Adoption*. Washington, DC: Department of State Bureau of Consular Affairs.

U.S. Department of State. 2019b. *Non-Hague Adoption Process*. Washington, DC: U.S. Department of State Bureau of Consular Affairs. April 11, 2020 (https://travel.state.gov/content/travel/en/Intercountry-Adoption/Adoption-Process/how-to-adopt/non-hague-adoption-process.html).

30
Race and "Value"
Black and White Illegitimate Babies, 1945–1965

Rickie Solinger

There are two histories of single pregnancy in the post-World War II era, one for Black women and one for white. But for girls and women of both races, being single and pregnant has revealed that, either publicly or privately, their fertility can become a weapon used by others to keep such females vulnerable, defenseless, dependent, and, without male protection, in danger. One aspect of single pregnancy that sharply and powerfully illustrates both the common vulnerability of unwed mothers and the racially distinct treatment they have received is the question of what an unmarried girl or woman can or will do with her illegitimate child.

Throughout my study of unwed pregnancy in the pre-*Roe v. Wade* era, racially distinct ideas about the "value" of the illegitimate baby surface again and again as central to an unmarried mother's fate. In short, after World War II, the white bastard child was no longer the child nobody wanted. The Black illegitimate baby became the child white politicians and taxpayers loved to hate. The central argument of this essay is that the "value" of illegitimate babies has been quite different in different historical eras, and that in the United States during the mid-twentieth century, the emergence of racially specific attitudes toward illegitimate babies, including ideas about what to do with them, fundamentally shaped the experiences of single mothers.

Social, cultural, and economic imperatives converged in the postwar era in such a way as to sanction very narrow and rigid, but different, options for Black and white unwed mothers, no matter what their personal preferences. Black single mothers were expected to keep their babies, as most unwed mothers, Black and white, had done throughout the history of the United States. Unmarried white mothers, for the first time in this country's history, were urged to put their babies up for adoption. These racially specific prescriptions exacerbated racism and racial antagonism in postwar America, and have influenced the politics of female fertility into our own time.

During the Progressive era of the late nineteenth and early twentieth centuries up through the 1930s, social commentators and social service professionals typically considered an illegitimate baby a "child of sin," the product of a mentally deficient mother. As such, this child was tainted and undesirable. The girl or woman, Black or white, who gave birth to it was expected by family, by the community, and by the state to bring it up. Commentators assumed that others rarely wanted a child who stood to inherit the sinful character—the mental and moral weaknesses—of its parent. Before World War II, state laws and institutional regulations supported this mandate, not so much because there were others vying for the babies, but so as to ensure that

Solinger, Rickie. *Wake up little Susie: Single pregnancy and race before Roe v. Wade*. New York and London: Routledge, 2013.

the mothers would not abandon the infants. State legislators in Minnesota and elsewhere required mothers seeking care in maternity homes to breast-feed their babies for three months and more, long enough to establish unseverable bonds between infant and mother.

Prewar experts stressed that the biology of illegitimacy stamped the baby permanently with marks of mental and moral deficiency, and affirmed that moral conditions were embedded in and revealed by these biological events. Likewise, the unwed mother's pregnancy both revealed her innate biological and moral shortcomings, and condemned her, through the illicit conception and birth, to carry the permanent stain of biological and moral ruin. These attitudes reflected, in part, the importance of bridal virginity and marital conception in mainstream American culture. They also reflected early twentieth-century ideas among moral and medical authorities regarding the strong link between physical, mental, and moral degeneracy and the degeneracy of sex.

WHITE UNWED MOTHERS AND THEIR BABIES: THE POSTWAR ADOPTION MANDATE

After the war, state-imposed breast-feeding regulations and institutional policies asserting the immutability of the white unwed mother's relationship to her illegitimate baby became harder to sustain in the face of a complex and changing set of social conditions. First, the demographic facts of single pregnancy were changing. White birth control and abortion remained illegal and hard to obtain. More girls and women were participating in nonmarital, heterosexual intercourse; thus more of them became pregnant and carried babies to term. As nonmarital sex and pregnancy became more common (and then very common during the later postwar period), it became increasingly difficult to sequester, punish, and insist on the permanent ruination of ever larger numbers of girls and women. This was particularly the case since many of these single pregnant females were members of the growing proportion of the population that considered itself middle class. As a result, it became increasingly difficult for parents and the new service professionals, themselves members of the middle class, to sanction treating "our daughters" as permanently ruined.

In addition, a strain of postwar optimism emerged that rejected the view that the individual, white, unwed mother was at the mercy of harmful environmental or other forces having the power to determine her fate. The modern expert offered the alternative claim that illegitimacy reflected an emotional and psychological, not environmental or biological disorder. It was, in general, a symptom of individual, treatable neuroses. Reliance on the psychological explanation redeemed both American society and the individual female.

Psychological explanations transformed the white unwed mother from a genetically tainted unfortunate into a maladjusted woman who could be cured. While there was no solvent that could remove the biological stain of illegitimacy, the neuroses that fostered illegitimacy could respond to treatment. The white out-of-wedlock child, therefore, was no longer a flawed by-product of innate immorality and low intelligence. The child's innocence was restored and its adoptability established. At the same time, psychologists argued that white unwed mothers, despite their deviant behavior, could be rehabilitated, and that a successful cure rested in large measure on the relinquishment of the child.

In postwar America, the social conditions of motherhood, along with notions about the psychological status of the unwed mother, became more important than biology in defining white motherhood. Specifically, for the first time, it took more than a baby to make a white girl or woman into a mother. Without a preceding marriage, a white female could not achieve true motherhood. Experts explained that the unwed mother who came to terms with the baby's existence, symbolically or concretely, and relinquished the child, enhanced her ability to "function [in the future] as a healthy wife and mother."[1]

Release from the biological imperative represented a major reform in the treatment of the many white unwed mothers who desperately desired a way out of trouble, a way to undo their life-changing mistake. The option of placing an illegitimate child for adoption became, in a sense, an unplanned but fortuitous safety valve for thousands of white girls and women who became unwed mothers but—thanks to the sanctioning of adoption—could go on to become properly married wives and mothers soon thereafter.

This arrangement could only work if there was a sizable population of white couples who wanted to adopt infants, and who didn't mind if the babies had been born to unwed mothers. In the postwar period, this condition was met in part because the postwar family imperative put new pressures on infertile couples who in the past would have remained childless. A social scientist in the mid-1950s referred to illegitimate babies as "the silver lining in a dark cloud":

> Over one in ten of all marriages are involuntarily childless. Since most of these couples desire to adopt a baby, illegitimacy is a blessing to [them]. Curiously, from their standpoint there are not enough illegitimate births because most of these couples must wait one or two or three years in order to adopt a baby, and some are never able to have one because there is not enough for all who want them.[2]

Through adoption, then, the unwed mother could put the mistake—both the baby *qua* baby and the proof of nonmarital sexual experience—behind her. Her parents were not stuck with a ruined daughter and a bastard grandchild for life. And the baby could be brought up in a normative family, by a couple prejudged to possess all the attributes and resources necessary for successful parenthood.

Some unmarried pregnant girls considered abortion the best way to efface their mistake, but the possibility in the mid-1950s of getting a safe, legal, hospital abortion was slim, in fact, slimmer than it had been in the prewar decades. If a girl or woman knew about hospital abortions, she might appeal to a hospital abortion committee, a (male) panel of the director of obstetrics/gynecology, and the chiefs of medicine, surgery, neuropsychiatry and pediatrics. In hospitals, including Mt. Sinai in New York, which set up an abortion committee in 1952, the panel of doctors met once a week and considered cases of women who could bring letters from two specialists diagnosing them as psychologically impaired and unfit to be mothers.

The doctors were apparently not concerned with questions about when life begins. They were very concerned with what they took to be their responsibility to protect and preserve the links between femininity, maternity, and marriage. One doctor spoke for many of his colleagues when he complained of the "clever, scheming women, simply trying to hoodwink the psychiatrist and obstetrician" in their appeals for permission for abortions.[3] The mere request, in fact, was taken, according to another doctor, "as proof [of the petitioner's] inability and failure to live through the destiny of being a woman."[4] If such permission were granted, one claimed, the woman "will become an unpleasant person to live with and possibly lose her glamour as a wife. She will gradually lose conviction in playing a female role."[5] An angry committee member, refusing to grant permission to one woman, asserted, "Now that she has had her fun, she wants us to launder her dirty underwear. From my standpoint, she can sweat this one out."[6]

The bottom line was that, if you were single and pregnant (and without rich or influential parents who might, for example, make a significant philanthropic gesture to the hospital), your chances with the abortion committee were pretty bleak. Thousands of unhappily pregnant women each year got illegal abortions, but for thousands of others, financially, morally, or otherwise unable to arrange for the operation, adoption seemed their only choice.

After World War II, social workers struggled to discard the two most basic assumptions that had previously guided their work with white unwed mothers. These girls and women were no longer considered the best mothers for their babies. And they would no longer be expected to pay for their illicit sexual experience and illegitimate pregnancy by living as ruined women and outcast mothers of bastard children. Social workers were now to offer them a plan which would protect them from lasting stigma and rehabilitate them for normative female roles.

To meet the demand and to justify their own existence, agencies and individual operators not infrequently resorted to questionable tactics, including selling babies for profit. While illegitimate pregnancy and babies had, in the past, been a private matter handled by family members, perhaps assisted by charity workers, by mid-century, these issues had become public concerns and public business. The State determined what types of agencies and individuals an unmarried mother could deal with in planning for her child, and either strongly suggested or legislated which ones were "morally wrong." These state prerogatives allowed some agencies and individuals to abuse and exploit childbearing, single, white women.

A very articulate, 18-year-old, unmarried mother from Minnesota wrote to her governor in August, 1950, illustrating how some public agencies took direct action to separate white babies from their mothers, even against the mother's will. She said that a welfare worker in her city told her she could not keep her baby, "that the baby should be brought up by both a mother and a father." Having gotten no satisfaction, she wrote in frustration and anger to President Truman:

> With tears in my eyes and sorrow in my heart I'm trying to defend the rights and privileges which every citizen in the United States is supposed to enjoy under our Constitution [but are] denied me and my baby.... The Welfare Department refuses to give me my baby without sufficient cause or explanation.... I have never done any wrong and just because I had a baby under such circumstances the welfare agency has no right to condemn me and to demand my child be placed [for adoption].[7]

Finally, this case illustrates that agency workers believed that a successful separation often depended on an early and very quick transaction. This was noticed by contemporaries, including the authors of a state-certified report on adoption in Cook County, Illinois that warned about the problems that arose when

> mothers come into court service division to sign a consent either on the day they are released from the hospital, or shortly thereafter [and] are physically and emotionally upset to the extent that they are not capable of making rational decisions.[8]

Courts also facilitated adoption abuse. A chief probation officer in the Richmond County, Alabama, Juvenile Court spent a great deal of her time finding and "freeing" white babies for adoption, using her position to legitimize these activities. One unwed mother told of her encounter with the officer, a Miss Hamilton. She said:

> Several hours after delivery [Miss Hamilton] informed me that my baby had been born dead. She told me that if I signed a paper she had, no one, my family or friends, would know about the situation, and that everything would be cleared up easily. She described the paper as being a consent authorizing the burial of the child.... I signed the paper without really looking at it, as I was in a very distressed and confused condition at the time.

This young woman went on to say that, "Two years later I was shocked to receive in the mail adoption papers from the Welfare Department in California since I was under the impression that the child was deceased."[9]

Illegalities and abuse existed in some mainstream institutions, but a great many of the worst abuses were committed by individual baby brokers—lawyers, doctors, and non-professionals cashing in on the misfortune of unwed mothers. In postwar, consumerist America, institutions promoted services and attitudes to protect the out-of-wedlock child from market-driven deals, and to see that it was well placed. On the other hand, these same institutions were themselves behaving in market-oriented ways as they promoted a specific, socially beneficial product: the two-parent/two-plus child family. This double message justified the baby brokers' commodity like treatment of unwed mothers and their babies. Charlton G. Blair, a lawyer who handled between 30 and 60 adoptions a year in the late 1950s, justified his operation by denying he ever "paid one red cent" to a prospective mother of an illegitimate child to persuade her to part with the baby. But in suggesting why the adopting parents were willing to pay up to 1,500 dollars for a child, which included the lawyer's 750-dollar fee, Blair defined his sense of the transaction very clearly: "If they're willing to pay three thousand dollars for an automobile these days, I don't see why they can't pay this much for a child."[10]

Again, there is no question that for many white unwed mothers, the opportunity to place their babies independently meant that they could get exactly what they needed when they needed it: money to live on, shelter, medical care, and assurances about the placement of the baby, all with no questions asked. These girls and women were often spared the delays, the layers of authority, the invasions of privacy, the permanent black mark engraved in the files of the welfare department, and they were spared the pressure to reveal the father's name, all of which characterized the bureaucratic agency approach. Their experience demonstrated how difficult it was for institutions to perform simultaneously as agents of social control and as sources of humanitarian assistance for the needy and vulnerable.

The stories of unwed mothers abused by the baby market reveal how class, gender, and (white) race together created the possibilities to use these girls and women for profit. Cultural constructions of female sexuality and maternity in the postwar decades, and the sanctions against sexual and maternal nonconformity, sent unwed mothers with few resources into the anonymous marketplace which offered, simultaneously, protection and danger.

THE BLACK UNWED MOTHER AND HER CHILD:
A TAXPAYERS' ISSUE

In postwar America, there was only one public intention for white, unwed mothers and their babies: separate them. Toward Black, single mothers and their babies, however, there were three broadly different public attitudes. One attitude, often held by middle-of-the-road politicians, social service administrators, and practitioners, maintained that Blacks had babies out of wedlock because they were Negro, because they were ex-Africans and ex-slaves, irresponsible and immoral, but baby-loving. According to this attitude, the state and its institutions and agencies could essentially ignore breeding patterns, since Blacks would take care of their children themselves. And if Blacks did not, they were responsible for their own mess. I call this public attitude toward Black illegitimacy *benign neglect*.

A second response to Black mothers and babies was *punitive*. The conservative, racist politicians who championed this position argued simply that the mothers were bad and should be punished. The babies were expendable because they were expensive and undesirable as citizens. Public policies could and should be used to punish Black unmarried mothers and their children in the form of legislation enabling states to cut them off from welfare benefits, and to sterilize or incarcerate "illegitimate mothers."

I label the third way of seeing this group *benevolent reformist*. Employees at the United States Children's Bureau and many in the social work community who took this position maintained that Black girls and women who had children out of wedlock were just like whites who did the same. Both groups of females were equally disturbed and equally in need of help, particularly in need of social casework. Regarding the baby, benevolent reformers held that Black, unwed mothers should be accorded every opportunity to place the infant for adoption, just like whites.

Despite these different attitudes toward Black women and their babies, proponents of all three shared a great deal. First, they shared the belief that the Black, illegitimate baby was the product of pathology. This was the case whether it was a pathology grounded in race, as it was for the benign neglecters and the punishers, or in gender, as it was for the benevolent reformers. Second, all commentators agreed that the baby's existence justified a negative moral judgment about the mother and the mother-and-baby dyad. The Black illegitimate infant was proof of its mother's moral incapacities; its illegitimacy suggested its own probable tendencies toward depravity. Because of the eager market for white babies, this group was cleared of the charge of inherited moral taint, while Black babies were not. Indeed, proponents of each of the three perspectives agreed that the unwed, Black mother must, in almost every case, keep her baby. Where they differed was in explaining why this was so. The different answers reflected different strains of racism and carried quite different implications for public policies and practices regarding the Black, unmarried mother and her child.

The benign neglecters began to articulate their position at about the same time that the psychologists provided new explanations for white, single pregnancy. According to these "experts," Black and white single mothers were different from each other in several ways. When Black, single girls and women had intercourse, it was a sexual, not a psychological act, and Black mothers had "natural affection" for their children, whatever their birth status. The white, unwed mother had only neurotic feelings for her out-of-wedlock child. The "unrestrained sexuality" of Black women and their capacity to love the resulting illegitimate children were perceived as inbred traits, and unchangeable parts of Black culture.

Thus, by becoming mothers, even unwed mothers, Black women were simply doing what came naturally. There was no reason for social service workers or policymakers to interfere. It was also important in this regard that the operative concept of "culture" excised considerations of environment. Environment was not a primary factor in shaping female sexual behavior or the mother's relationship to her illegitimate baby. These were determined by "culture," an essentially biological construct. Therefore, since professionals could only have an impact on the immediate situation—and could not penetrate or rearrange Black "culture," it was doubly futile to consider interfering. The absence of services for these women and their children was justified in this way. Issues regarding Blacks and adoption were quickly dismissed by those who counseled neglect. Agencies claimed that Blacks didn't want to part with their babies, and, just as important, Black couples didn't want to adopt children.

White policymakers and service providers often pointed to the Black grandmothers—willing, able, loving, and present—to justify their contentions that the Black family would take care of its own, and that no additional services were necessary. Yet when grandmothers rendered such service, policymakers labeled them "matriarchs" and blamed them for "faulty personality growth and for maladaptive functioning in children."[11] The mother was similarly placed in a double bind. She was denied services because she was black, an alleged cultural rather than a racial distinction, and then she was held responsible for the personal and social consequences. The social service system was, in this way, excused from responsibility or obligation to Black, unwed mothers.

The punishers, both Southern Dixiecrats and Northern racists, drew in part on the "cultural" argument to target both the unwed mother and her baby. They held that Black culture was inherited, and that the baby would likely be as great a social liability as its mother. Moreover, they claimed that for a poor, Black woman to have a baby was an act of selfishness, as well as of pathology, and deserved punishment. Once the public came to believe that Black illegitimacy was not an innocuous social fact, but carried a direct and heavy cost to white taxpayers, many whites sanctioned their political representatives to target Black, unwed mothers and their babies for attack.

The willingness to attack was expressed, in part, by a special set of tropes which drew on the language and concepts of the marketplace. The "value" assigned to the illegitimate child-as-commodity became useful in classifying the violation of the Black, unwed mother in a consumer society. Repeatedly, Black, unmarried mothers were construed as "women whose business is having illegitimate children."[12] This illicit "occupation" was portrayed as violating basic consumerist principles, including good value in exchange for a good price, for a product which, in general, benefits society. Black, unmarried mothers, in contrast, were said to offer bad value (Black babies) at a high price (taxpayer-supported welfare grants) to the detriment of society, demographically and economically. From this perspective, Black, unmarried mothers were portrayed as "economic women," making calculated decisions for personal, financial gain.

The precise economic principle most grossly violated by these women was, according to many, that they got something (ADC) for nothing (another Black baby); they were cheating the public with a bad sell. The fact that it was, overwhelmingly, a buyers' market for Black babies "proved" the valuelessness of these children, despite their expense to the taxpaying public. White babies entered a healthy sellers' market, with up to ten couples competing for every one adoptable infant.

The public's interest in casting Black, unwed mothers and their babies as consumer violators was reflected in opinion polls that suggested the American public wanted to withhold federal support, or food money, from illegitimate, Black babies. Among dissenters were people who believed it was wrong "to deny food to children because of the sins of the parents."[13] Both groups, however, fell into a trap set by conservative politicians who found it politically profitable to associate Black illegitimacy in their constituent's minds with the rising costs of public welfare grants. While white sentiment was being whipped up to support punitive measures against Black "subsidized immorality," only about 16 percent of nonwhite, unwed mothers were receiving ADC grants. Adoption, which was not an option for most Blacks, was the most important factor in removing white children from would-be ADC families. Of unwed, white mothers who kept their children, 30 percent, or nearly twice as large a percentage as Blacks, were receiving Aid to Dependent Children grants in 1959. Yet in the minds of large segments of the white public, Black, unwed mothers were being paid, in welfare coin, to have children.

Benevolent reformers typically took the position that it was unacceptable and potentially racist to assume that Blacks did not want every opportunity that whites had, including adoption. But it was extremely difficult for the reformers to suggest that some Black, single mothers wanted their children, and others did not. It was not simply unwed mothers and their babies at issue, it was the race. For the reformers, constructing an equivalency between Black and white unmarried mothers was the most promising and practical route to social services and social justice.

But even if a Black, single mother did consider placing her child for adoption, she knew that the likelihood that the agency would expeditiously approve a couple as adoptive parents was slim. While a white, unwed mother could expect a rapid placement, the Black one knew that her child would be forced, in part because of agency practices, to spend months in foster homes or institutions before placement, if that was ever achieved. For example, adoption agencies frequently rejected Blacks who applied for babies, claiming they did not meet the agency's standards for adoptive parents. They also neglected to work with schools and hospitals in contact with Black, unwed mothers to improve referral services between these institutions and the agencies, because they feared recruiting Black babies when there might not be homes for them. In these ways the organizations that reformers depended on to provide services for Black, unwed mothers equal to those for whites, and to make it more possible for society to perceive these Blacks in the same way as they saw whites, did not hold up their end.

In fact, the evidence from postwar Black communities suggests that the Black, unwed mother accepted responsibility for her baby as a matter of course, even when she was sorry to have gotten pregnant. A study in the mid-1960s cautioned the social work profession: "Social work wisdom is that Negroes keep because there is no place to give the baby up, but the study showed ... that Negroes did not favor adoption, opportunities or their absence notwithstanding." Findings showed that the issue of disposition of the child was the only one that consistently yielded a difference between Black and white respondents, no matter whether they were the unwed mother, her parents, or professional staff. In fact, the Blacks revealed their determination to keep mother and child together and the whites their determination to effect separation, "no matter how [the investigator] varied the content of the questions."[14]

For many Black, unwed mothers, the reasons to keep a baby were simply grounded in an immutable moral code of maternal responsibility. A young, Black woman said, "Giving a child away is not the sort of thing a good person would do"; and a teenager asserted, "My parents wouldn't let me give up the baby for adoption."[15] Two Black women in Philadelphia subscribed to this morality. One said:

> I sure don't think much of giving babies up for adoption. The mother mightn't be able to give it the finest and best in the world, but she could find a way like I did. My mother had thirteen heads and it was during the Depression.... *She* didn't give us away.

The other commented, "If you have a child, bring it up. Take the responsibility. Hard or easy, it's yours."[16]

The central question for all of these Black, single mothers was how good a mother you were, not whether you were legally married. The overriding stimulus in structuring the personal decisions of these girls and women was a "powerful drive toward family unity, even if the family is not the socially approved one of father, mother and children."[17]

CONCLUSION

A research team in North Carolina investigating illegitimacy concluded in the early 1960s that one major difference between white and Black unwed mothers was that the white girl generally felt that a "new maturity" had come with the experience of conceiving out of wedlock. The team claimed that this was not true for the Black subjects, and explained: "The white subculture demands learning from experience," so the white unwed mother must learn her lesson. The white girl "has probably been encouraged to look within herself for the reasons for her mistake because the white subculture stresses individual responsibility for error."[18]

These observations capture a great deal of the intentionality underlying the white culture's treatment of unwed mothers under the adoption mandate. For these girls and women, the "lesson" was twofold: no baby without a husband; and no one is to blame but yourself. Learning the lesson meant stepping on the road to maturity and womanhood. The illegitimate child was an encumbrance or an obstacle to following this route. The ability to relinquish was constructed as the first, most crucial step in the right direction.

Both Black and white women in the postwar era were subject to a definition of maturity that depended on motherhood. The most pervasive, public assumption about Black and white unwed mothers, however, was that their nonmarital childbearing did not constitute maternity in the culturally sanctioned sense. The treatment of these girls and women reinforced the notion that legitimation of sexuality and maternity were the province of the state and the community, and were not the rights of individual girls and women. In the case of white, unwed mothers, the community (including the mother herself, and her family) with government support was encouraged to efface episodes of illicit sex and maternity. Outside of marriage neither the sex nor the resulting child had "reality" in the community or in the mother's life. They became simply momentary mental aberrations. In the case of Black, unwed mothers, sexuality was brute biology and childbearing its hideous result. The state, with the support of public institutions, could deface the Black, single mother's dignity, diminish her resources, threaten her right to keep her child, and even threaten her reproductive capacity.

In both cases, the policies and practices which structured the meanings of race and gender, sexuality, and motherhood for unwed mothers were tied to social issues—such as the postwar adoption market for white babies, and the white, taxpaying public's hostile identification of ADC as a program to support Black, unwed mothers and their unwanted babies—which used single, pregnant women as resources and scapegoats.

In the immediate pre-Roe v. Wade era, the uses of race combined with the uses of gender, sexuality, and maternity in ways that dealt Black and white unwed mothers quite different hands. According to social and cultural intentions for the white, unwed mother and her baby, relinquishment of the baby was meant to place all scent of taint behind them and thus restore good value to both. The Black, unwed mother and her child, triply devalued, had all their troubles before them.

Notes

1 Janice P. Montague, "Acceptance or Denial—The Therapeutic Uses of the Mother/Baby Relationship," paper presented at the Florence Crittenton Association of America Northeast Conference, 1964.
2 Winston Ehrmann, "Illegitimacy in Florida II: Social and Psychological Aspects of Illegitimacy," Eugenics Quarterly 3 (December, 1956), p. 227.
3 Nicholson J. Eastman, "Obstetric Forward," in Rosen, Therapeutic Abortion, p. xx.
4 Theodore Lidz, "Reflections of a Psychiatrist," in Rosen, Therapeutic Abortion, p. 279.
5 Flanders Dunbar, "Abortion and the Abortion Habit," in Rosen, Therapeutic Abortion, p. 27.
6 Mandy, "Reflections," p. 289.
7 Duluth, Minnesota to Governor Luther Youngdahl, August 2, 1950, and to President Truman, August 14, 1950 Box 457, File 7–4–3–3–4, Record Group 102, National Archives.
8 U.S. Congress, Commercial Child Adoption Practices, May 16, 1956, p. 86.
9 Ibid., p. 120.
10 New York Times (July 10, 1958).
11 Patricia Garland, "Illegitimacy—A Special Minority-Group Problem in Urban Areas," Child Welfare 45 (February 1966), p. 84.
12 See, for example, the New York Times, August 28, 1960, which quotes Louisiana Governor Jimmie H. Davis justifying the recent state legislation targeting "those who make it their business to produce illegitimate children."
13 Milwaukee Journal, August 9, 1961.
14 Deborah Shapiro, "Attitudes, Values and Unmarried Motherhood," in Unmarried Parenthood: Clues to Agency and Community Action (New York: National Council on Illegitimacy 1967), p. 60.
15 Shapiro, "Attitudes, Values," p. 61.
16 Renee Berg, "Utilizing the Strengths of Unwed Mothers in the AFDC Program," Child Welfare 43 (July 1964), p. 337.
17 Berg, "A Study of a Group of Unwed Mothers Receiving ADC," pp. 95–96.
18 Charles Bowerman, Donald Irish, and Hallowell Pope, Unwed Motherhood: Personal and Social Consequences (Chapel Hill: University of North Carolina, 1966), p. 261.

31

International Adoptions Have Dropped 72 Percent Since 2005 – Here's Why

Mark Montgomery and Irene Powell

When Ethiopia stopped allowing its children to be adopted by foreign parents in January, it became the latest country to eliminate or sharply curtail the practice. In recent decades South Korea, Romania, Guatemala, China, Kazakhstan and Russia – all former leaders in foreign adoption – have also banned or cut back on international custody transfers.

In 2005, almost 46,000 children were adopted across borders, roughly half of them headed to a new life in the United States. By 2015 international adoptions had dropped 72 percent, to 12,000 in total. Just 5,500 of these children ended up in the United States, with the remainder landing in Italy and Spain.

Today, most children adopted internationally come from China, Democratic Republic of the Congo and Ukraine. But even China, which has been the top sending country since the late 1990s, has decreased its foreign adoptions by 86 percent.

Why are international adoptions imploding? Our recent book, "Saving International Adoption: An Argument from Economics and Personal Experience," explores the rationale – both real and invented – that countries use to explain curtailing foreign adoptions. Here's what we found.

It's in the Child's 'Best Interest'

When countries with high rates of international adoptions suddenly put an end to the practice, officials usually cite examples of abuse. The policy change, they say, is in "the best interest of the child."

In 2012, when the Russian parliament voted to ban adoptions by Americans, for example, lawmakers named the new law after two-year-old Dima Yakovlev, who died in 2008 after being locked in a hot car by his adoptive father.

Ethiopian lawmakers likewise recently invoked the 2012 case of a neglected Ethiopian 13-year-old girl who died of hypothermia and malnutrition in the United States to justify their new ban on international adoptions.

Montgomery, Mark and Irene Powell. "International Adoptions Have Dropped 72 Percent since 2005 – Here's Why."
The Conversation, February 28, 2018.

Such events, though high profile, are rare. Of 60,000 adoptees from Russia to the United States, only 19 have died from abuse or neglect in the last 20 years, according to The Christian Science Monitor. That's an abuse rate of about 0.03 percent. In Russia, the rate of child abuse is about 25 times higher.

Such statistics call into question whether "the best interest of the child" is really why countries cancel international adoptions.

POLITICS AND HUMILIATION

Our analysis suggests that politics may more strongly influence many countries' adoption policies.

Russia ended U.S. adoptions two weeks after the 2012 U.S. Magnitsky Act, which imposed sanctions on some allegedly corrupt Russian officials. Asked about the new ban, Putin essentially linked the two events, saying, "The country will not be humiliated."

Political pressures can also be external. As it sought to join the European Union in the early 2000s, Romania – which in 1990 and 1991 sent more than 10,000 adopted children abroad – halted all international adoptions. The EU's rapporteur for Romanian accession to the union, Baroness Emma Nicholson, was famously opposed to the practice.

We also found that embarrassment can spur countries to halt international adoptions. After bad publicity during the 1988 Seoul Olympics, South Korea – which had been allowing adoptions to the United States since the 1950s – temporarily banned overseas adoption. The remark of sports commentator Bryant Gumbel that the country's "greatest commodity" for export was its children likely helped trigger this policy change.

And after Guatemala imposed a moratorium on foreign adoptions – which dropped from 4,100 in 2008 to 58 in 2010 – a former member of the country's National Adoption Council expressed pride. "Our image as being the number one exporter of children has changed," he said. "Guatemala has dignity" again, he added.

Adoption scandals can also lead countries to rethink international adoptions. Every major sending country has seen accusations of "child trafficking" because some birth parents were paid to give up their children. There have been rare cases, too, where a child was kidnapped and put up for adoption.

Although infrequent, such incidents bring bad press, and with it pressure from international child welfare organizations like UNICEF and Save the Children to improve – or shut down – foreign adoptions.

WHO'S IN CHARGE HERE

The Hague Convention on International Adoption was supposed to resolve such problems by making adoption safer and more straightforward. This 1993 global agreement, which 103 countries signed by 2016, creates uniform regulations for adoptions worldwide.

But rather than encourage foreign adoptions, many experts argue that the convention has contributed to their decline.

Poor countries often struggle to meet The Hague's high international standards, which include creating a central adoption authority, accrediting local agencies and tightening approval procedures.

Even after Vietnam ratified the international adoption convention in 2008, the United States refused adoptions from the country because the State Department found it fell short of Hague rules. Vietnamese adoptions of special needs children to America reopened in 2016.

Rigorous international regulations have also made adoptions more expensive by imposing fees on agencies, adoptive parents, orphanages and countries. We believe that rising costs – which may have increased up to 18 percent in some countries – will lead to a decrease in the number of international adoptions.

The High Costs of No Adoptions

Critics will likely welcome the current decline in international adoptions, citing concerns that foreign adoptions remove children from their "birth culture," exploit poor birth mothers and enable illicit child trafficking.

But our book finds powerful – if uncomfortable – arguments in favor of foreign adoptions. When the child of a desperately poor family is taken in by parents from a wealthy country, the material benefits to that child are significant.

Children raised in rich countries are far more likely to receive a good education, for example. While the literacy rate in Ethiopia is 50 percent for males and 23 percent for females, 100 percent of people in most high-income countries, such as Canada and Norway, can read.

Our research shows that adoption can even save lives. We examined mortality figures for children under the age of five in Ethiopia and Guatemala and found that adoptions to the United States likely prevented the deaths of more than 600 children between 2005 and 2011.

Studies also show that the emotional costs borne by children of color being raised by white parents – which often occurs with international adoptions – are less dire than critics believe. Such adoptees do about as well on a wide range of indicators of self-esteem and ethnic identity formation as their non-adopted siblings.

Foreign adoptions can't solve global poverty. But ending them merely punishes thousands of vulnerable kids and their potential parents worldwide. And that's in nobody's best interest.

32

Letting Her Go

Western Adoptive Families' Search and Reunion with Chinese Birth Parents

Leslie Kim Wang, Iris Chin Ponte, and Elizabeth Weber Ollen

Over the past two decades more than 130,000 children from the People's Republic of China (PRC) have been adopted by foreign parents. Moreover, since 2000 the PRC has been the top "sending country" of adoptable children in the world. Chinese adoptees are growing up in first-world societies where open adoption, or "varying levels of ongoing connections between adoptive families and their children's families of origin" (Siegel & Smith, 2012, p. 5), has become the norm. This increased openness reflects a major cultural shift toward more transparency in Western adoption practices. In comparison, all adoptions from China are "closed" placements in which birth and adoptive families do not have contact or access to one another's information, a situation that has resulted from children having been illegally abandoned.

Within Western countries, this climate of openness has motivated many domestically adopted adults to search for and reunite with their birth parents. In the case of China, however, the obscurity of children's origins has long led to the assumption that locating birth parents was impossible.

Nevertheless, interest in learning about children's pre-adoption histories is on the rise. Over the past decade thousands of Chinese adoptees and their adoptive parents have initiated preliminary forms of searching by returning to the PRC on "homeland" trips, visiting orphanages and sites where children were abandoned in order to garner information about their early lives. Some of the families that have participated in homeland trips have furthered their searching efforts by attempting to locate children's birth parents. Although no official statistics exist, one online adoptive parent Listserv devoted solely to Chinese birth parent search has over 500 subscribed members.

At present, questions regarding children's origins and the politically sensitive nature of the PRC's foreign adoption program have created a lack of consensus. Holt International Children's Services—one of the world's most highly regarded and influential foreign adoption agencies—has even taken a firm stand against birth parent search in China, warning against a range of negative consequences that may result from searching:

> At this point Holt recommends that you do not search for your birth parents in China. It is illegal to relinquish children in China. As a result, there is also no legal means to search for birth parents.

Wang, Leslie Kim, Iris Chin Ponte, and Elizabeth Weber Ollen. "Letting Her Go: Western Adoptive Families' Search and Reunion with Chinese Birth Parents." *Adoption Quarterly* 18, no. 1 (2015): 45–66.

Searching at this time could put your birth parents, if found, at risk for legal penalties. Searching
might also jeopardize the possibility for other children to find adoptive families.

(Holt Adoption Agency, n.d.)

The controversy surrounding this topic has had a silencing effect, with few individuals being willing to
openly discuss their experiences. Therefore, this study, which is based on in-depth interviews with children
and adoptive parents from seven Western families who located and reunited with Chinese birth parents,
represents the first empirical analysis of its kind.

Birth Parent Search in the Context of Openness and Loss

In Western countries, an estimated 40 percent to 50 percent of domestic adoptees attempt to locate their
birth parents at some point. These numbers are remarkably high since merely decades ago an individual's
desire to search was seen as symbolic of larger problems with one's adoption. Until relatively recently,
searching was not even possible in the United States due to the closed, confidential nature of adoption
and sealed birth records; this secretive climate surrounding adoption reflected dominant cultural and
legal interpretations of kinship that were based solely on genealogy and blood ties. During the 1970s and
1980s, however, a vocal movement of domestic adoptee activists and birth mothers successfully advocated
for the unsealing of birth records, increased transparency, and more open adoptions. The changes have
been significant: Based on a recent survey of 100 American adoption agencies, 95 percent of domestic
adoptions now include some form of contact between birth parents and adoptive families (Siegel & Smith,
2012).

Despite increasingly liberal attitudes toward adoption and a major upsurge in transnational and transracial
placements in Western societies, bloodline continues to be the primary determinant of kinship and
family bonds. Privileging heredity has caused adoption to be equated with feelings of emotional loss that
are experienced by each part of the adoption triad, including the child's early loss of her "real" parents
and origins, the birth mother's loss of her child, and the adoptive parents' loss over their (presumed)
inability to bear biological offspring. Furthermore, internationally adopted children experience an even
wider range of painful losses, not only of their birth families but also of their "cultural 'authenticity,' of
psychic wholeness, of personal history and memory, and of legitimate citizenship" in their countries of
origin (Kim, 2003, p. 62). This atmosphere has motivated certain adopted individuals to search for birth
parents.

Taken together, the perception that adoption entails severe emotional loss that must be resolved is now so
prevalent that adoptees are often *expected* to try to find their birth parents. Adoptees who do lack information
about their personal backgrounds are considered to be missing a piece of themselves. Rather than feeling
a sense of shame or guilt over searching, many adoptees today are actually burdened with an "obligation
to find, know, and grasp material origins" (Homans, 2007, p. 59). As our interviews reveal, this larger
backdrop of openness and the desire to resolve loss has motivated certain Western adoptive families to search
for children's Chinese birth parents.

The Politics of Transnational Adoption and Search in China

As noted earlier, all international adoptions from the PRC are closed. This lack of transparency results from
Chinese government policies that not only regulate adoption but have also inadvertently contributed to the
illegal relinquishment of certain children. We suggest that the ambiguity of children's origins may exacerbate
feelings of loss and stimulate the desire to verify the exact circumstances by which they became available
for adoption. In brief, China's international adoption program is intertwined with a range of government

policies meant to regulate its economy and population. As the PRC began transitioning to a market economy in the late 1970s, central authorities also instituted the world's strictest family planning regulations, limiting couples to one, or sometimes two, children. In combination with long-standing cultural preferences for sons and a newly competitive economy, these changes led many rural parents to illegally abandon daughters and special needs offspring in order to ensure the birth of a healthy male heir. After sweeping family planning campaigns triggered the abandonment of overwhelming numbers of children to state orphanages, China began its international adoption program in 1992.

Because orphanages that participate in international adoption receive compulsory donations of US$5,000 per child, foreign adoption has provided immense financial resources to China's child welfare system as well as incentivized corruption, issues that further complicate birth parent search. Although the nation was once considered to have one of the world's cleanest, most efficient, and dependable programs, its reputation has since been tarnished by proven instances of baby trafficking and confirmed cases of forced removal of children from their birth families by government officials "with the specific motivation to sell them to orphanages participating in intercountry adoption" (Smolin, 2011, p. 60). In the most highly publicized case, officials from six child welfare institutes in Hunan Province were found guilty of having purchased up to 1,000 healthy baby girls who were subsequently sent abroad.

Widely publicized reports of baby trafficking have heightened the concerns of many adoptive parents, some of whom are choosing to conduct birth parent searches in China on behalf of their young children. Thus, adoptive parents are serving as instigators, facilitators, and funders of search and reunion—a unique dynamic that influences each stage of the process.

METHODS AND PARTICIPANTS

This study examines the experiences of seven families with adopted Chinese children who searched for and reunited with their birth parents. Four of the families were American, two were from the United Kingdom, and one was from the Netherlands. We interviewed a total of six children (five girls and one boy) and eight parents (six mothers and two fathers). In order to protect the privacy of those involved, all names are pseudonyms and no specific locations are given. Even though there was one male child participant, this chapter uses the feminine pronoun when referring to all adoptees to further prevent identification.

Except for one Chinese American father, all of the parent participants were White, middle-class college graduates. Children were between the ages of 5 and 19 at the time of interview. Two other than 19-year-old participants are included because they were both children at the time of reunion. We recognize that children's ages and levels of emotional and cognitive development affect their perception of events. Accordingly, this study relies primarily on the responses of the four teenage participants (their ages at the time of interview are listed next to their responses).

FINDINGS

Parent-initiated Searches: Wanting to Find Out the "Truth"

Two sets of adoptive parents decided to search immediately upon or even before adopting their children. These parents shared in common two major characteristics: extensive experience with China and a strong desire to discover the circumstances that led to their daughters' relinquishments. The Chans began their search during their initial trip to adopt their daughter Emma. Lauren described her sense of urgency:

> I'm familiar enough with China to know how quickly things are changing there ... I don't think that I thought her birth family would be findable at that point, but it was important to me to find as much information as we could get right away because I knew there was a good chance that it wouldn't be available later.

Husband Jeff also noted that he felt searching early was important due to the connection between one's history and the formation of personal identity. He stated:

> If a kid understands their story from a young age, it doesn't become some kind of "thing" they have to process later on. It just is integrated into their identity when their identity is forming. And I always thought that would be a preferable way to deal with those issues.

When Emma was four years old the couple hired a local Chinese searcher who was able to locate her birth parents. The couple was perplexed to have been contacted and immediately assumed that something was terribly wrong with the child. According to Lauren, "The only way they could fathom that [the reunion] would happen is if we wanted something from them. And they said, 'Is she sick? Does she need an organ? Does she need something? We'll give her whatever she needs.'"

In the second case, Katie Lewis also had significant experience with Chinese culture. She and her husband decided to begin searching soon after adopting their 15-month-old daughter Claire, wanting to act quickly before information disappeared. Katie was aware of child trafficking for adoption and had heard rumors of aggressive family planning campaigns in her daughter's region of origin. Because of this, the couple sought to verify the "real" reasons for her relinquishment. She explained:

> I guess the driving force… behind the search was not so much that we wanted to find the birth family [or] that we wanted our daughter to have a relationship with a birth family, it was really just to find out the truth. I wanted to make sure she hadn't been removed from her birth family.

Several years later they hired a local searcher to go back to Claire's village and put up posters with her photo and information. Within weeks the searcher received a text message from her birth father explaining that the child was the result of an extramarital affair. The man inquired about his daughter's life, confirmed her actual birthday, provided the birth mother's name, and apologized for his actions. In total, the Lewises exchanged messages with the man on four separate occasions. Although they have not yet experienced a face-to-face reunion, Katie noted that she felt "quite relieved and extremely pleased" to have confirmed that her child had not been trafficked.

Parent-initiated Due to Child's Sense of Loss

Children's expressed sense of emotional loss was the impetus for three sets of adoptive parents to initiate searches in China. According to Beth Thomas:

> We decided to search when [daughter Abby] started to really grieve for [her birth parents] and to be very upset at times wondering where they were and why they left her and thinking that they may not even be alive. She used to get so upset that I… wanted to be able to say when she grew up that we've done everything we could to try and find them.

The Thomases first returned to China on a homeland trip when Abby was six years old to visit her orphanage and finding location. When Abby was 10, Beth hired a local searcher and the adoptive family returned for another visit to her village. On their arrival day a family came forward claiming that Abby was their child.

Anne and Brian Peters' daughter Sarah also experienced intense grief and longing for her birth family from a young age. Sarah (age 14) articulated:

> I had many questions about whether [my birth parents] would still be alive, what they looked like, and whether I had brothers or sisters. Because of all these questions I often could not sleep and it made me really sad. My parents thought it was very important [to search] because they could see that it was difficult for me.

Unlike other parents, the Peters did not explicitly intend to search. However, a Chinese acquaintance from the same region as Sarah offered to help find her birth family, traveling to the girl's finding place and putting up posters. A local newspaper reporter published a story about the search and within one week, the child's birth parents were located.

Last, Patti Harris—a single mother who adopted her daughter Mei at age seven—began seeking information after the girl mentioned having parents. When Patti contacted the orphanage, the officials refused to provide any details. Instead they responded, "No need to worry about that now, she's going to America!" She reflected on her feelings at the time: "It was heartbreaking... I felt that we should have that information. I knew it wasn't right that she was talking about this family and nobody talked about it."

Unlike other participants who conducted lengthy, expensive searches, the Harrises underwent a relatively quick and inexpensive process. Because Mei had been with her family until age six, she remembered key details about her parents and different places. Patti provided this information to a Chinese student from Mei's city who was returning home. She described the simplicity of his search: "He just went and found them. I think he even looked them up in the phonebook or something. It was that easy."

Child-initiated Searches

While in the United States adoptees generally do not actively begin searching until they reach adulthood, the closed nature of Chinese adoptions eliminates those restrictions. Thus, with the financial and emotional support of their adoptive parents, two teenage participants made the decision to search prior to the age of 18.

Natalie Clark initiated her search to resolve emotional loss. Like Mei Harris, the girl had been adopted at an older age by a single mother and also remembered details about her former life. For years adoptive mother Marie kept detailed notes about her child's recollections but did not actively search, believing it was her child's choice. She explained, "I knew she had a history before the orphanage... I just wrote everything down with the intent that probably someday she would want to search." Natalie struggled emotionally throughout adolescence and asked her adoptive mother to make a serious effort to find her birth family upon turning 17. Marie e-mailed a Chinese volunteer organization that helps lost and missing children. Using her notes, the group was able to locate Natalie's birth family soon after.

THE LIVED EXPERIENCE OF REUNION

Regardless of where they take place, reunions are extremely emotional, unpredictable events. However, those that occur in China are even further complicated by cultural and language differences, the young age of many adoptees, and the presence of adoptive parents. The recurrent theme that emerged from all of the interviews was that of individuals not feeling emotionally prepared for the reality of reuniting with Chinese birth parents. Unlike most media representations that portray such occasions as exclusively joyful and happy, most participants claimed that their initial meetings produced a perplexing mixture of positive and negative feelings.

The Initial Meeting

All of the reunions occurred in public places—usually hotels—and typically involved other parties besides family members such as translators, guides, and even journalists. Sarah Peters met her Chinese parents in a hotel lobby. Although she couldn't understand what her birth parents were saying, Sarah (age 14) recalled her excitement: "I felt very happy when I saw them and it made me really nervous." Instead of experiencing delight, both sets of Sarah's parents reportedly had a more difficult time during the reunion. According to adoptive mother Anne, the girl's birth parents apologized repeatedly and were "very emotional. They felt so guilty because they had to give away their child... they were so afraid that Sarah would hate them and would not forgive them." For her part, at the reunion Anne also realized that she was now going to have to forfeit a certain amount of control over her daughter. She stated poignantly, "When [Sarah] was going to her parents, I thought, 'this is the moment I have to let my child go.'"

Natalie Clark's (age 19) initial meeting was also tremendously emotional. At the reunion, her father wept uncontrollably and asked for forgiveness. Unexpectedly for Natalie, seeing her Chinese family again unleashed a wave of anger and repressed memories. She recalled her reaction: "I walked in the room and [saw] my parents… and then they all ran up and started giving me a hug and started crying. And I… just stood there, and kind of didn't have any expression on my face."

In Abby Thomas' case, the reunion lasted merely half an hour and was primarily limited to a discussion of whether she was the right child—an issue that was later resolved by a DNA test. Ten-year-old Abby reportedly had difficulty reconciling the real couple in front of her with the romanticized mental image that she had developed over the years. Adoptive mother Beth recounted:

> [Abby] leaned into me at one point and she whispered, "these aren't my birth parents." Because I think she kind of liked the fantasy of a beautiful, tragic Chinese woman, and this was two quite careworn people—honest, hardworking, careworn people.

For her part, Beth admitted to grappling with unanticipated feelings of doubt and worry that arose in her immediately after the reunion—even though she was the one who had taken the lead in searching. Beth expressed feeling emotionally insecure:

> It seemed like… I'd lost her to them and that she wasn't mine anymore [and] at the very least I've got to share her. I fear that she'll want them more than me, you know, all those very natural feelings. Even though I know it's the right thing… I won't deny that there were feelings that I had just never expected to feel.

Jamie Ross (age 16) also stated that she was unprepared for the reunion because she had assumed the likelihood of finding her birth family was extremely low. She described her state of mind at that time: "I don't think I had gotten to the point emotionally to be worried about anything. I thought it was like a fun adventure and such. I didn't really realize the gravity of what was going on." At her initial meeting with her birth father and sister Jamie recalled going into a mild state of shock and feeling "pretty much numb," an experience that was influenced by the lack of certainty about their biological kinship. She recalled the moment she saw her birth father: "I was thinking, 'this is really great. This guy looks like he could be my dad!' But I was also thinking I need to kind of keep myself in check because he could possibly not be."

Children's ages and level of cognitive development also compounded the emotional nature of reunions as adoptive parents needed to serve as mediators for young children. Lauren Chan described facilitating an intimate discussion between four-year-old Emma and her birth mother. When the child inquired as to why the woman wanted to hold her, Lauren explained, "She is your Chinese mama. You were a baby in her tummy and she misses you." Emma then asked, "Does she miss me?" Her birth mother replied in Chinese, "I miss you every day… I love you so much!"

Perhaps due to the low awareness of international adoption in the PRC, birth parents were often shocked to learn that their child had been sent abroad. However, many of the Chinese birth parents in this study expressed gratitude to adoptive parents. Emma's birth mother told Lauren, "I'm so glad you adopted Emma… if it was anybody else, we would never know her, so thank you." It's important to note that despite widely held fears, none of the birth families sought to reclaim custody of their children, although all were eager to maintain contact in the future.

Questions Answered by Reunions

Reunions were an opportunity for individuals to gain an understanding of children's lives prior to adoption. As stated earlier, most individuals wanted to find out the real circumstances behind children's relinquishments. In all seven cases, participants learned that strict family planning regulations had played a key role in children being internationally adopted. For example, because Claire Lewis' parents had not been married to one another, her birth was rendered illegal. Two other children were the second offspring of urbanites in strictly enforced one-child policy areas.

Many participants gained information regarding heredity, including details about their medical history and real birthdays. Akin to other studies of reunion, both the children and adoptive parents scrutinized birth relatives for similar physical and personality characteristics. Jamie was gratified that she strongly resembled her birth parents and noticed obvious physical similarities between herself and her birth sisters, mother, and grandmother. She said: "They all share common facial characteristics and we *all* have the same smile. Thank you, DNA!"

Likewise, Sarah expressed pleasure in discovering "that I look a lot like my sisters." The obvious family resemblance also had a positive side effect for Sarah's adoptive parents. According to adoptive mother Anne, knowing the birth family limits her from thinking that all of her daughter's issues relate to adoption. She explained:

> If I didn't know them… if there were problems when she is growing up, maybe I would say "oh, she did something [because] she is adopted."… Now I don't think, "This has something to do with adoption, or problems with adoption, or she isn't accepting that she is adopted." No! She just is who she is, and she looks just like her [biological] mother and just like her sisters.

The Development of Relationships between Adoptive and Chinese Birth Families

The greatest challenge after the initial meeting "lies in establishing intimacy when neither daily interactions nor conventional generational distances control the expression of that intimacy." Previous research on birth parent search has tended to focus on short-term, rather than longer-term, outcomes of reunions. For China adoptive families, establishing familiarity and emotional closeness with birth parents was especially challenging because of cultural and language divides, geographic distance, and the need for some adoptive parents to maintain contact on behalf of their children.

The major theme that emerged from interviews was that of disconnection between participants' expectations of reunion and the reality of managing long-distance ties with birth families. Because of the intense focus on the search itself, no one felt adequately prepared for what might happen after the initial meeting. While some adoptive families struggled to communicate, others were able to develop comfortable, close relationships.

All of the participants reported that they had kept in touch with birth parents to varying degrees since the initial meeting, using both in-person visits and virtual methods such as e-mail, Skype, and QQ, a Chinese instant messaging system. Five out of seven families reported that they spoke with children's Chinese relatives on the phone every one to two months and used instant messaging somewhat more frequently. Moreover, six families had returned for at least one additional visit with birth relatives.

Two of the families found it especially challenging to develop a relationship with birth parents. In both cases, the adoptive mothers described having become the main intermediary between children and birth parents. For Natalie Clark (age 19), the reunion triggered difficult memories that caused her to discontinue contact with her birth family. A year after the initial meeting she expressed mixed emotions:

> I thought [the reunion] was just going to be a greet-and-meet and leave, instead of having a relationship with them now… I don't know if I am supposed to feel bad that I am not living with them now or I'm not going to see them every couple of years. I am not sure what to do with that, but I am figuring it out.

Adoptive mother Marie continued to speak regularly with her daughter's Chinese relatives in the hopes that she will eventually reestablish communication with them, a situation that she described as "emotionally hard." Marie elaborated, "Every time I call, they beg to speak to her. They want to just hear her voice… [but] I can't make her get on the phone, on the computer and talk to them if she is not ready to."

Lauren Chan also expressed reservations about maintaining a relationship with her young daughter's birth parents. Soon after their initial meeting, the two families experienced a serious cultural misunderstanding. Although it was ultimately resolved, the situation left Lauren feeling wary of making a decision that might adversely impact her five-year-old child. She wondered,

> What if… a cultural misstep means we never talk to them again? You know, to me it would be devastating if I screwed up this relationship that I've carried for her until she is old enough to carry it for herself.

In comparison, three families described having developed quite intimate relationships with birth relatives. Returning to China for extended periods—an effort that requires substantial time, planning, and financial resources—has been integral to creating closer bonds. For example, within the space of two years Jamie Ross (age 16) made three more trips to China to spend time with her birth family. She described maintaining regular online contact with one of her English-speaking sisters, chatting frequently about their shared life experiences.

During the four years since Sarah Peters' reunion, the two families have reunited again on several occasions. Although extremely happy to be reacquainted, Sarah (age 14) described the challenges of a transnational relationship: "It's difficult that I can't be with them that often and that, once I've been there, I have to say goodbye again." The two families have even incorporated one another into their kinship circles. As Brian explained, "We feel a little bit like we are also their parents, too. So we have this kind of strange family where there are two sets of parents and… six children." Adoptive mother Anne emphasized that their choice to locate Sarah's Chinese family obligated them to maintain contact:

> Given [that] I had decided to search for the birth parents, now that we found them it is also our responsibility to keep in touch with them.… We can't say, okay now we found them, now we know who you are, and go.

Similarly, Mei Harris (age 19) characterized her relationship to her Chinese family as "extremely close." She described herself as having two sets of parents and, in the decade since their initial meeting, has spent each summer in China with her birth relatives. Mei articulated, "I think the best thing families can say is something like, 'There is no competing. We all love you and want you to be happy.'"

POST-REUNION VIEWS OF SEARCHING

In addition to investigating search processes, the initial meeting, and post-reunion relationships, we sought to discover how participants now regard birth parent search. The central theme that emerged from interviews was that of encouragement tempered by caution; while all individuals agreed that searching could potentially bring about many positive outcomes, they also held serious reservations. Specifically, adoptive parents mentioned the following factors: the unpredictability of what might be discovered, the need to consider the birth family's perspectives, and the suggestion that adoptive parents search early but only reveal information to children if (and when) they are ready for it. For their part, adoptees were conflicted over who should have the power to decide whether or not to search.

Due to the closed nature of Chinese adoptions, each of the families in this study confronted troubling facts concerning children's origins. Nonetheless, all of the adoptive parents felt that knowing the truth outweighed any uneasiness. Lauren Chan explained:

> I always felt like knowing was better than not knowing. Because my theory on it was, we don't have a story, we have a big blank. And [Emma] could fill that in with every terrible story: "I was thrown out with the garbage, my parents hated me, they threw me away, I was kidnapped." I mean, she had a hundred stories, and each was worse than the next. And right now, we only deal with one story, and that story is the truth.

Even so, Katie Lewis advised adoptive parent searchers to be prepared for the possibility of discovering unethical practices:

> There was probably quite a bit of illicit activity going on in terms of orphanages procuring children… if you start to search there is a possibility that that is what you may find. And whether or not you want to, you and your child have got to [be capable] of handling that kind of information.

Second, all of the adoptive parents reinforced the notion that finding birth parents does not only mark the end of search but in fact constitutes the *beginning* of a new and complex process of communicating with a real family. Anne Peters encouraged adoptive parents to consider the emotional needs of their child's Chinese relatives:

> If you are starting the birth parent search, what will you do with the birth family? Because there are still three parties involved: You have the adoptive family, the child, and the birth family. So [searching should] not only be because… "I think my child needs this."

Marie Clark similarly cautioned, "Don't start searching unless you are prepared to follow through with it." Despite facing emotional challenges post-reunion, Marie was thankful that her daughter had obtained answers about her past that will eventually allow her to move forward. She reflected, "No matter how bad the story is, you can always heal in time from it. But without knowing what it is, you can't. You are still just in limbo."

A third theme involved the importance of timing due to China's rapidly changing political and social context. All of the adoptive parents and the four older children underscored the importance of searching before information disappears. Patti Harris stated: "I will always say to find out whatever you can, as soon as you can…. Once it's too late, it's too late." However, participants also advised adoptive parents to conduct DNA tests before revealing results to children and to take extreme care because not all children have the capacity—or the desire—to understand their past. Brian Peters conveyed, "Whatever information you get, whatever goes to your child, you have to control it. And make sure that the child can handle it and really, really wants it."

Last, the teenagers in this study each expressed mixed feelings regarding who should make the decision to search. Natalie Clark was thankful that her adoptive mother had left the choice to her. While the children generally felt that the choice should be left to adoptees, both Mei and Sarah also acknowledged how grateful they were that their adoptive parents had made the decision to search early on. Mei's comment underscored this sense of ambivalence:

> I don't think everyone should search because you should not have to if you don't want to—only if you want to. I did not search. My [Chinese] family and I found each other again because of my [adoptive] mom. It was not my decision. If she didn't though, I would have lost them forever.

DISCUSSION

This preliminary study has explored the complex experiences of adoptive families that have searched for and reunited with children's Chinese birth parents. We have argued that this growing trend has been influenced by larger cultural shifts in Western receiving countries—particularly increased openness and the view that adoption entails deep emotional loss that may be resolved through locating birth family.

Searching in China entails a wide range of logistical and ethical considerations due to the politically sensitive nature of the nation's international adoption program. The overlap between national family planning regulations, child abandonment, and confirmed instances of baby trafficking for foreign adoption has caused wide speculation regarding children's origins. Moreover, China's rapid modernization has shifted traditional decision-making processes of birth parent search with adoptive parents proactively taking the lead (often without first consulting their young children) to garner information before the window of opportunity closes.

We found that searchers were motivated by two primary factors: (a) the desire to verify children's origins and (b) the desire to help children resolve feelings of loss for birth parents. Most searches unfolded in stages spread over several years, involving many false starts and stops. Searching could also be quite expensive depending on the circumstances such as whether parents decided to hire local searchers or make repeated visits to China to gather information.

This study has also explored the implications of establishing contact with Chinese birth families, both during the initial meeting and longer-term. While media representations tend to highlight only their most positive aspects, initial meetings are emotionally charged, highly unpredictable events that challenge dominant perceptions of kinship. Interviews revealed that the first meeting brought myriad unforeseen emotional challenges as both children and adoptive parents tried to reconcile their expectations with reality. Due to their fixation on the search itself, most participants reported that they did not feel adequately emotionally prepared to meet actual birth families. Nevertheless, no one expressed regret over locating children's Chinese relatives.

Emotional challenges notwithstanding, the respondents in this study report largely positive outcomes of their reunions. Participants were gratified to observe physical similarities between adoptees and their birth relatives and to have clarified aspects of children's histories. By the same token, despite some feelings of displacement soon after the initial meeting, adoptive parents expressed that they were relieved to "know the truth" about their children's early lives. However, many questions still remain for participants, even years after establishing contact.

Interviews suggest that the adoptee's life stage at the time of reunion is an integral factor in the development of ties between adoptive and birth families. Unlike domestically adopted searchers who locate birth parents as adults, a number of adoptees in our study were young enough to create genuine parent-child relationships with their Chinese mothers and fathers. Thus, establishing contact with birth parents at a relatively young age appears to allow children to make an easier post-reunion transition, a situation that would be impossible without the assistance of adoptive parents.

In conclusion, search and reunion in China is an emotionally complex journey that does not end at the initial meeting with birth parents. As this trend continues to unfold, it remains to be seen how experiences of reunion impact children's relationships and personal identities. However, even for those adoptees who have reunited with birth families, resolving loss and making sense of one's history is clearly a continual process that involves both ups and downs. Natalie reflected on this reality, "It is good to search, but don't let that impact your whole life… and don't let that affect you being happy."

REFERENCES

Holt Adoption Agency. (n.d.). Retrieved from http://www.holtinternational. org/adoptees/chinesefaq. shtml

Homans, M. (2007). Origins, searches, and identity: Narratives of adoption from China. *Contemporary Women's Writing*, 1, 59–79.

Kim, E. (2003). Wedding citizenship and culture: Korean adoptees and the global family of Korea. *Social Text*, 21(1), 57–81.

Siegel, D., & Smith, S. (2012, March). *Openness in adoption: From secrecy and stigma to knowledge and connections.* New York, NY: Donaldson Adoption Institute.

Smolin, D. (2011). The missing girls of China: Population, policy, culture, gender, abortion, abandonment, and adoption in East Asian perspective. *Cumberland Law Review*, 41, 1–65.

33

"It Was the Cadillac of Adoption Agencies"

Intersections of Social Class, Race, and Sexuality in Gay Men's Adoption Narratives

Dana Berkowitz

INTRODUCTION

The heterogeneity of families constructed through adoption and fostering mirrors the kinds of diversity that characterizes contemporary American families. Gay adoptive families represent one segment of these diverse family constellations. Increasingly, adoption is becoming a major pathway for parenthood among gay men; yet they are still the minority of adopters when compared with lesbians or heterosexuals. Understanding how gay men construct and negotiate family bonds through adoptive fatherhood draws attention to how those marginalized from traditional family pathways navigate an institution embedded with heteronormative, racialized, and biolegal prescriptions. The purpose of this study is twofold: First, to generate knowledge on the ways by which gay men negotiate the potential challenges faced in the transition to adoption. Second, to unpack the social and symbolic meanings gay men attach to themselves and their children during this transition. My analysis draws upon in-depth interviews to generate theoretical and practical insights about how institutionalized structures and (hetero) norms shape the social psychological processes by which gay men imagine and experience adoptive fatherhood.

THE POLITICS OF ADOPTION

The politics of the adoption and foster care system in the United States provide a window into our nation's broader race and class inequalities. Recent data estimate that roughly 500,000 children live in foster care in the United States and more than 100,000 children currently await adoption. The most desired adoptees among children awaiting adoption are healthy white infants, and the least desirable, who are often referred to as hard to place, include African-American children, older children, and ill or disabled children. What this means then is that there is a short supply of healthy white babies, and the circumstances of African-American children and other hard-to-place children are dismal. Although it is a truism that white prospective adopters prefer to adopt white children, the limited pool of these babies means that many must settle for a child of color—and often adoptive parents are willing to accept an Asian, Latin American, or even biracial child. However, although many Americans might be willing to adopt a non-white child, most prefer

Berkowitz, Dana. "'It Was the Cadillac of Adoption Agencies': Intersections of Social Class, Race, and Sexuality in Gay Men's Adoption Narratives." *Journal of GLBT Family Studies* 7, no. 1–2 (2011): 109–131.

that these children are not black. In fact, white Americans who adopt transracially are five times more likely to adopt a non-African-American child than an African-American child (Maldonado, 2006).

The facts that African-American children in foster care wait significantly longer to be adopted and that many adoption agencies and facilitators charge lower fees for placing African-American children expose the racial hierarchy of adoption. Adoption in the United States (and globally) has become a business—one that is guided by the laws of supply and demand. Agencies charge lower fees for African-American children, higher fees for children who are half African-American or Latino, Asian, or Native American, and the highest fees for white children. The business is also based upon a ranking and matching system wherein available children are rated and paired with available parents in terms of their desirability. Historically, social workers and adoption agencies viewed sexual minorities as their least desirable applicants. Thus, in an attempt to match the least desirable applicants with the least desirable children, gay men (and lesbian women) were often matched with hard-to-place and special-needs children. Today, however, more affluent gay men can circumvent this ranking and matching process by spending relatively large amounts of money to work with private agencies or facilitators.

Gay Men and Adoption

Although no exact statistics of gay adopters exist, recent data from the United States Census reveal that of the 1.6 million adopted children in the United States at least 65,000 are currently residing with lesbian or gay parents. Of the quarter-million children living in US households headed by same-sex couples, 4.2 percent were either adopted or foster children, a figure that is almost double that of heterosexual couples. Although gay adoptive families are diverse, certain patterns differentiate them from both heterosexual and lesbian adoptive families. For example, statistics indicate that the adopted children of gay male couples are older than those of their female counterparts; more than 1 in 5 children of male couples are age 13 and older compared to only 1 in 10 among the children of female couples. In addition, some evidence shows that same-sex couples as a whole are more likely than their heterosexual counterparts to adopt transracially. Among adopted children of gay and lesbian couples, 14 percent are foreign born, a number twice the rate among adopted children by heterosexual couples. Finally, among same-sex couples, gay men are more than three times more likely than their lesbian counterparts to be raising an adopted child with a disability.

Despite the fact that multiple organizational bodies have endorsed adoption by gays and lesbians and advocate for second-parent adoption, some states continue to prohibit the recognition of adoption by same-sex parents. Because adoption is primarily a matter of state law and is usually left to the discretion of county family court judges, there is much diversity among how individual states and jurisdictions regulate same-gender adoption. The absence of explicit policies can mean that a potential adopter's sexuality is taken into account by adoption agencies and individual adoption personnel in nuanced ways. Many adoption agencies and practitioners follow a "don't ask, don't tell" policy when it comes to adoption by non-heterosexuals by presuming the heterosexuality of their potential adoptive parents unless told otherwise. As such, particularly in the initial stages of the adoption process, one partner alone is most often the primary adoptive parent. Hence, the nonlegal parent can become peripheral to the adoption process itself. Even in the midst of a growing openness on the part of lesbian and gay potential parents and in states where it is legal for non-heterosexuals to adopt, some couples still opt for silence—afraid that their openness will hinder their chance of success.

The legal and interpersonal barriers that gay men and lesbians face in adopting have been well-documented… Arguably, the most empirical and systematic analysis to date is the Evan B. Donaldson Adoption Institute's national study of adoption agencies' attitudes, practices, and policies with gay and lesbian adoptive parents (Brodzinsky et al., 2003). Findings of their nationwide analysis revealed that while 65 percent of agencies had accepted applications from non-heterosexuals, only 39 percent had actually placed a child in the care of a gay or lesbian adopter. Moreover, close to 20 percent reported rejecting applications from lesbian or gay individuals or couples on at least one occasion either because of the agency's religious beliefs, prohibitive state laws, or a policy of placing children only with married couples.

Beyond becoming experts on adoption and child welfare bureaucracies, gay and lesbian prospective adopters also must become proficient in consorting with birth mothers, policymakers, judges, and social workers who may perceive them to be unfit parents, despite an abundance of research that shows sexual orientation is irrelevant to one's parental ability. Gay and lesbian adoptive family formation is dependent on others, on birth mothers who may have homophobic beliefs, or on adoption agents whose chief job is governed by the economics of placing and matching children in a hierarchal system that positions both lesbian and gay parents and hard-to-place children at the very bottom.

Method

This chapter is part of my dissertation research that uses in-depth interviews with 19 childless men and 22 fathers to explore the procreative consciousness and fathering experiences of gay men. One of the major themes that emerged in my findings concerned gay men's challenges in their transition to fatherhood. In this chapter, I explore this theme further, specifically attending to how gay men imagined and traversed challenges in the transition to adoptive fatherhood. As such, my analysis in this chapter predominantly draws from my conversations with the 12 adoptive fathers in my sample. However, at times I interweave the narrative fragments of some of the 19 childless men I interviewed through my analysis to illustrate how childless gay men perceive, imagine, and plan for adoption.

Recruitment and Participants

The fathers participating in my research were white, and most were financially well off. In the analysis that follows, I show how participants' negotiations with the adoption system are not only products of their gay identities, but also their social location as white, economically privileged men. Although all fathers were white, 6 (two couples and two single men) out of the 12 men were raising children of color. All except two fathers had completed college, with five holding an advanced graduate degree. All except for two of these men earned more than $75,000 annually, and the remaining two earned between $30,000 and $60,000. Fathers' ages ranged from 36 to 55.

Findings

Becoming and Being a Gay Adoptive Father

I separate my analysis and findings into two main sections. First, I detail how adoptive fathers navigated legal, structural, and institutional barriers that oftentimes plagued their pathway to adoptive fatherhood, paying specific attention to how class privilege shaped their transition to adoption. I then explore the question of what it means to be a gay adoptive father. I consider the meanings gay fathers attach to themselves and to their prospective children and unpack how these meanings are created within a multilayered system wherein genetic privilege, heteronormativity, socioeconomic power, and racial hierarchies coexist.

Negotiating Obstacles/Overcoming Challenge

The fathers I spoke with all assumed that they would never have children unless they chose to reproduce within a heterosexual relationship. Usually some particular event, identity transition, or turning point transformed how they were able to envision their future as one that could integrate gayness with fatherhood. Randy, a single gay father who adopted two boys in the mid-1980s, told me about the day that changed his life. One afternoon a woman came into his natural foods shop inquiring about baby formulas. Randy replied that the healthiest and most natural option was to breastfeed. She retorted that this was not an option because she was adopting. When he replied, "But I thought you were single," she explained that she was a single woman adopting. Randy immediately followed with, "Do they let single gay men adopt?" She lowered her voice and said, "Well, there are two guys in our group, New York Singles Adopting Children (NYSAC), and I don't know for sure, but they both appear to be gay." Randy was at the very next meeting for NYSAC. He introduced himself to these men, who ultimately guided him through the adoption process. It was this chance encounter with a single woman at his natural foods shop that Randy reflects on as the instrumental moment at which he came to embrace a significantly different perspective on his life. This new perspective enabled him to become exposed to his possible self as a gay adoptive father—an identity that until that day was incomprehensible for him to imagine. This turning point marked the beginning of a complex journey through a labyrinth of social workers, attorneys, and other gatekeepers before he would be able to fulfill his fantasy of becoming an adoptive father.

When men like Randy decide that they want to pursue adoption, they are unsure how to begin, where to turn, and what to do. Because very few agencies actively recruit gay adopters, many men were forced to rely on an informal and unorganized network of referrals. Some men turned to friends who had already adopted for advice, while others looked to more formal sources of information such as studying adoption pamphlets and actively attending meetings. Regardless of where they turned, men reported being overwhelmed by feelings of powerlessness and confusion. Lawrence, one of the pioneering fathers I spoke with, remembered his experience in New York in the mid-1980s:

> So there were all these people at this adoption conference, you know, talking about all the different ways of adopting; you could do domestic adoption, but domestic had two ways, you could do public or private. You could do your own private adoption with a lawyer, you can go to these, also these places like Friend of Adoption or just facilitators; you could do international adoption. There were just all these options, and we came home and we were like exhausted because we had all these things to think about. And it just seemed overwhelming.

Parker, a father who adopted his children nearly a decade after Lawrence did, recalled a similar experience:

> There are so many options ... we took like a good like two years doing just research ... not every day, like on the weekends we would sit down and talk about it and you know, just try to figure it out.

After the men decided on an adoption route, their days became consumed with interacting with social workers, attending classes and workshops, and preparing for home studies. While this phase of the adoption process is experienced by most, if not all, prospective adopters, gay men pursuing adoption face added layers of complexity because of the heteronormative assumptions governing family and gendered norms that view parenting as the alleged natural domain of women. Participants experienced this phase of the adoption process differently, with some reporting overwhelmingly positive memories and others reflecting on this time with disdain. Randy, a single father who adopted in New York in the 1980s, recalled how he was able to convince a social worker to work with him:

> The social worker who did the home study—I was open with her. She was from Long Island, and she had a brother that was gay, and she was friendly. But when I first called, then you know I'm applying, she said, "oh I'm not doing any more home studies with gay men. I don't want to get in trouble. You're going to have to wait," because you see, she thought she was going to end up on the cover of *New York Times* like too many gay adoptions.... I didn't take no for an answer, so I just went full speed ahead so she had to do the home study.

Other men found it more difficult to secure these necessary allies. Lawrence, who also adopted in New York in the 1980s, remembered how he was constantly dealing with adoption agencies giving him the cold shoulder:

> This is what you get, you know when you're gay, it was like the last bastion of a place where people could be prejudiced and biased and not be reprimanded, not be punished for it ... they were allowed to kind of push you aside ... if you wanted a child you had to put up with this.

Lawrence did eventually find an agency to work with him—one that was publicly discounting of gay adoption but willing to facilitate the adoption discretely as long as either he or his partner agreed to remain completely invisible. It was Lawrence who agreed to be the invisible one, and he remembered with dismay hiding in the upstairs apartment the day the agency brought his first son home, pressing his ear to the floor so that he could hear the sound of his new baby. On a positive note, the adoption experience for gay men in states with more favorable policies, such as New York, Massachusetts, and California, has improved since Lawrence's experience two decades ago, illuminating how the sociohistorical context and changing legalities in adoption shape how gay men experience this transition. Simon and Theo, the couple living in Los Angeles, told me about their open-adoption experience using a private agency in the late 1990s with nothing other than praise for their social worker, the birth mother, and the agency personnel. Spencer, too, recalled his adoption process as positive, though more labor intensive than Simon and Theo's because of his choice to foster a boy with mental trauma. He elaborated on the months preceding the adoption of his 10-year-old son in Massachusetts:

> Well the first thing I had to do was to take an eight-week parenting course, and it was specifically for people adopting from DSS (Department of Social Services), and the parenting taught is essentially parenting traumatized kids who have attachment issues and behavior problems and so forth.... I do think they design it for people who would just not be able to handle it. But for me ... it convinced me to go ahead and do it.... Then you're committed to the adopting process and you go through a home study. The social worker came to my house I think four times, they look for cleanliness, safety hazards.... I had identified a bedroom for him and there was ample play and closet space and a decent bathroom. Then the time came for him to transition into my house. Needless to say, it was a long process.

The transition to fatherhood was remembered as one prolonged by bureaucratic red tape even for those men who did not adopt children with disabilities or trauma. However, gay men who lived in Florida faced the additional stress of having to circumvent explicit legal statues prohibiting them from adopting. The men in Florida who I spoke with shared how they fulfilled their fantasies of becoming adoptive fathers in a state that categorically prohibits them from doing so. Parker explained that he adopted through a private agency—a process that can cost up to $20,000. At the time of the adoption, Parker's partner was earning over a six-figure salary while Parker was able to stay home and manage the adoption process. Although their financial resources afforded them the luxury of bypassing the discriminatory policies of the state, their adoption experience was not without its sacrifices. Stated Parker:

> My partner is the legal father, and they hold his last name.... It's one of those things that if you live in Florida, you, there are sacrifices that you make and there are things that you know, you do to get to where you want to be.

Despite the fact that Parker and his partner possessed supplemental documents identifying both men as fathers, their family remains legally unrecognized by the state, as only one father is listed on the birth certificate. Brian, another adoptive father in Florida, explained that he and his partner managed to dodge state prohibitions on gay adoption by traveling to Vermont where they eventually established residency and adopted a daughter. This way, stated Brian, "We are both on the birth certificate, and Florida is forced to recognize it." Brian continued to detail how he and his partner rented an apartment in Vermont for two years in order to establish residency and were required to make monthly visits to meet face-to-face with the social worker and the adoption agency. However, many prospective adopters do not have the financial wherewithal to finance out-of-state monthly flights and an additional apartment. When I mentioned to Brian that the adoption for him seemed to be rather costly of both his time and money, he replied, "No, it didn't cost too much. We flew JetBlue and rent in Vermont is more reasonable than in South Florida." While Brian's class privilege may have been less salient to his identity than the societal marginalization he experiences as a gay man, his story further highlights the extent to which financial factors shape how potential gay adopters navigate their way through a complex system beset with subtle and explicit discriminatory practices.

The most financially accessible way to become an adoptive parent is through the foster care system. Many children in foster care are considered undesirable as a result of their age and the trauma that oftentimes accompanies time spent in the child welfare system. Spencer was the only father I interviewed who adopted a special-needs child and receives an un-taxable $606.00 stipend every two weeks from the state for providing his son with a safe, secure, and sanitary environment. However, his son, Joseph, who is a victim of childhood trauma, consumes a great deal of his time and energy because of his behavioral challenges. Spencer, a single father, recently decided to quit his high-paying job and is now employed as a part-time consultant who works from home. Ironically, even though Spencer receives money from the state, his decision to father a special-needs child has resulted in a substantial decrease in his annual income. Fortunately, Spencer is able to dip into his savings—a luxury that not all adoptive parents possess. Thus, even adoption routes considered to be economically accessible are only possible for those men who either have the financial resources to cut their work hours and dip into their savings, or have the ability to rely on social support from partners, close friends, and family.

The earlier narratives underscore how sociohistorical context, state legalities, and social location intersect to construct how gay men experience the transition to adoption. Where for many of these men the adoption process was rife with complications and hurdles, the majority looked back on this process as a blessing in disguise. Simon's comment sums up how participants felt following the adoption process: "Unfortunately in the real world any bonehead can make a baby and not be responsible for it, but in the adoption world they make you very responsible, which is a good thing." Simon's concluding statement underscores that although these men's stories are representative of a particular family category constructed through class privilege, gay fathers can reflect on and appreciate the challenges in the adoptive realm as equipping them with a cultural and interpersonal tool kit necessary to handle the unpredictability of parenthood.

I now ask what it really means for these men to be adoptive gay fathers in contemporary US society. How are these meanings constructed within socioeconomic and race hierarchies? How do these men position themselves and their families in a broader societal context after going through what for many was such a tumultuous process? How do these men plan for and control the kinds of families they are prepared to raise?

Father's Identity/Children's Identity

Hereafter, I explore and unpack the social and symbolic meanings of adoptive gay fatherhood. My conversations with the 12 men in my sample who became fathers through adoption highlight the extent to which their children are perceived as having been destined to complete their families regardless of (or perhaps because of) the absence of a genetic relationship. Ethan is the adoptive father of a 13-year-old girl. He eloquently summed up how many of my participants spoke about their bonds to their adoptive children:

> I feel that before you adopt, you ask a question that you never ask after you adopt. The question was, am I going to feel the same about an adopted child as I would about a biological child? … Once you hold your child, I mean, I couldn't feel more attached to my daughter if I carried her in my own belly for nine months and there's no, it's like a strange feeling of that there was no question that I am her father, and I was meant to be her father, and she was meant to be my daughter.

A consistent theme among adoptive fathers like Ethan was that genetic ties do not determine family; rather it is the presence and the depth of emotional bonds that establish familial relationships. In their everyday interactions, gay adoptive fathers and their children are challenging hegemonic discourses that assume biology and heterosexuality to be a prerequisite for family. Thus, it should not be surprising that many of the adoptive fathers I spoke with reflected on the political implications of adoption. For many of these men, adoption was more than a personal decision; it was also a political act. For example C.J., a 39-year-old childless man living in Manhattan, vividly remembered what triggered him to want to become an adoptive father. He explained that he had read a story in *People* magazine in 1987 that told the story of a young girl in India who was going to be put to death in her village because she had a discoloration on her face and the villagers thought she was possessed by the devil. The story continued with a heartwarming account of how a gay man in San Francisco adopted her even though the villagers said that God was going to condemn him. Almost 20 years later, at the time of the interview, C.J. still had the article in his possession and referred to this story countless times throughout our conversation as "the most influential thing I had ever read." C.J.'s desire to one day adopt a child was not only a personal decision that would enrich his own life, but was conceptualized as an act with political ramifications that could contribute to global human betterment.

For other men, the political implications of adoption were closer to home. Spencer, the father of a mentally challenged 12-year-old boy, Joseph, explained:

> My son was 10, he was 8 when I met him, and he was 10 when he moved in, and 10 is deemed the point of no return because when a boy turns 10 he is not going to be adopted. You know I think it's funny that people who are opposed to gay parenting … I say, "Well, who's going to adopt these very-hard-to adopt kids? … It's the gay people because you folks certainly are not doing it."

By adopting Joseph, Spencer was not only satiating his fathering desires; he was to some extent doing activism. Spencer criticizes public and legal discourses that ban gays from adopting, asserting that without gay and lesbian adopters these children would languish endlessly in the foster care system—an assertion validated by reports of gay men fostering and adopting children with health challenges and typically deemed unadoptable by heterosexuals. Yet, many gay men are willing and determined to adopt those children considered to be undesirable along such medical, age, or racial criteria. In fact, Spencer continued to tell me how he wants his next child to be African-American because

> I was one of those people who was oblivious to their own racism 10 years ago until I joined the Unitarian Universalist Church and I have learned so much about racism and what it does.… I have developed a passion for being involved in anti-racism work.

He then asserts that he wants to adopt a third, Latino child because of the large Latino population in Boston. Spencer is engaging in and constructing his adoption as an activism of sorts that combines anti-racist motives and social responsibility. His fatherhood desires and plans were shaped by the effects of urban poverty, racism, and neglect in the city that was his home.

When I asked Craig why he and his partner decided to become foster parents in New York, he responded that he and his partner, an interracial couple, wanted to adopt a black child or at the very least a child of color. Craig was well-versed on the racial politics of adoption and explained that he was "very fascinated by institutionalized racism, and [I] believe that the foster care system is almost a precursor to what the prison system is for adults, and how that plays out for black culture." Perhaps because many of these men were from urban metropolises, such as Manhattan and Boston, where poverty and racism are ubiquitous to anyone who pays attention, the thought of pursuing international adoption was—to be cliché—a foreign, if not ridiculous, option. Craig explained:

> Some people go to Guatemala or you know Honduras or whatever to adopt babies and I think it kind of gives them a false sense of security about what kind of treatment the mother may have had or you know, make sure they're not somehow handicapped in some way or other. But they're much more reluctant to get an African-American or Latino-American child. I talked to some guys last week about their adoption in Ecuador. It took them six months to get their kid home. Six months. One of them had to live there for three months … and I'm thinking, people don't want to go through the public system because of the bureaucracy, but they're willing to go get a yellow child in Ecuador, give up six months of their lives.

Participants were aware of the history of gay men adopting or fostering children that were considered undesirable. Men considering adoption were forced to think about what level of undesirable or unadoptable they were prepared to deal with. Art and Rick told me that when they were considering adoption they

> were afraid that the only way for us to get a child would be a very special-needs child.… We didn't have the patience, we knew it was something we couldn't do.… It takes a very special person, God bless them, but it is not for us.

The adoption process gives parents the discursive space to decide if they are prepared for the possibility of a disabled child. Parker recalled his conversation with his partner:

> We did not want to deal with severe retardation or Down syndrome … because we're talking our first kid, and we were not prepared to deal with that.… But you have a choice … that's one of the great things about adoption.

Where most men were eager to father hard-to-place children, their eagerness did not extend to parenting special-needs children. The demands for caring for a child with disability or trauma are extraordinary and all of the men in my sample could not imagine themselves taking on this challenge—that is, all except for Spencer. Where Spencer claims he "does not have even the slightest little regret, even though it is a slow process," the overwhelming majority of men were completely unwilling to even consider adopting a child with disability or trauma. Nevertheless, the ability to have the discursive space to consider the possibility of parenting a child with special needs was viewed by these men as one of the built-in benefits of adoption.

Lawrence, too, remembered the conversations he had with his partner about what kind of child they were prepared to raise:

> We also had to think about, you know do I want a child who has disabilities, if so, what kind of disabilities, you know. What about race, you had to be really honest with yourself. Do I want a child who's black? You had to be completely honest about what you wanted. It couldn't be like, oh yes, wouldn't it be nice to adopt a black child and not really mean it, you know.... You had to really express to each other what you want, and what you could live with.

America is not a color-blind society. To be frank, race matters. It matters in housing and hiring practices, in life chances, in choices for a life partner, and in adoption. In the private adoption marketplace, there is a discernable pattern in which children are valued according to racial/ethnic heritage. Although black children are being adopted in greater numbers than ever before, the demand for children and babies of other racial/ethnic groups is greater. Given these data it shouldn't come as any surprise that of 12 white gay men, Craig, the only man in my sample in an interracial relationship, was also the only man currently raising a black child. Although five other men were raising children of color, these children were Latino, Asian-American, or mixed race, and thus would be categorized as part of the intermediary group of honorary whites.

Later in our conversation Lawrence further elaborated on the issue of thinking about and planning for the possibility of fathering a child of color:

> You can never transmit to the child that they are anything less than perfect. If you are saying I could love a black child but I would rather have a white child, you know that sense is always going to be transmitted to your children.... I felt most comfortable with a Latino child, being Italian, than with a blond-haired, blue-eyed ... we didn't necessarily want a white child.... I am from New York so I felt more connected to Latino cultures.

To be clear, I am not assuming that Lawrence and his partner would not have been perfectly happy if their child was black. In fact, they most likely would have been thrilled. However, I employ this narrative fragment to illustrate how his mental negotiations were constructed within a racial hierarchy that positions white at the top, black at the bottom, and many Asian groups, light-skinned Latinos, and biracial persons in the middle. Moreover, arguments such as Lawrence's that emphasize preferences for cultural or physical similarity consistently surface as reasons behind why some families prefer to adopt white (or honorary white) infants, in that adoptive parents suspect these children will blend better into their families, at least phenotypically.

The fact that adoptive parents with more financial means can try to control the health and the racial and ethnic heritage of their child is consistent with Western values that hinge on our ability to control our present and future experiences. As detailed earlier, adoption was a realm where these men had limited power. Thus, the ability to choose and plan for their future children was one dimension of the process that they could seemingly control. These men were concerned with their children's futures and with the discrimination their children would likely experience for having a gay father. Some of the ways they may have felt they could minimize this discrimination was through forgoing the burden of caring for a disabled child, eschewing the prejudice that accompanies black-white racism, and wanting to have a family that phenotypically resembles one another. Because the idea of control resonates well with American definitions of responsibility, the ability to plan for—and more frequently—avoid issues of racism and disability was simply discussed as good family planning. Yet, men's conversations about which children are most desired provide considerable insight into the class and race politics of adoption and the extent to which consumerism is intertwined with the adoption system.

DISCUSSION

When I began analysis of my interviews with gay adoptive fathers for this chapter, my intention was to describe the heteronormative challenges and barriers these men faced in their transition to adoption. However, what emerged instead is a story of how a select group of privileged gay men navigate a system saturated with race and class ideologies and hierarchies. In spite of our best efforts, consumerism dominates everything in American society. Nowhere is this more visible than in the field of adoption. The gay adoptive fathers in my sample did not just experience the transition to fatherhood through their marginalized sexual identities, though this did impede their pathway to parenthood. Their social location as white economically privileged men had as much to do with their adoption experience as their gay identity; and the ways by which these men were able to imagine and navigate their reproductive choices cannot be understood in isolation from any of their intersecting identities.

REFERENCES

Brodzinsky, D., Patterson, C., & Vaziri, M. (2002). Adoption agency perspectives on lesbian and gay prospective parents: A national study. *Adoption Quarterly*, 5, 5–23.

Maldonado, S. (2006). Discouraging racial preferences in adoptions. *Seton Hall Law School, Public Law, and Legal Theory, Research Paper 36*. Newark, NJ: Seton Hall Law School.

SECTION VII
Families without Children

INTRODUCTION

Over the last 50 years, the percentage of adults living without children—in myriad household configurations—has gone from 52.5 percent in 1967 to 71.3 percent in 2016 (Schondelmyer 2016). One reason for the increasing number of households without children is the reality that more people are remaining childless (or childfree)—by chance or by choice – a fact that contradicts social expectations. Among men between the ages of 40 and 50 years, approximately 17 percent in 2014 had never been married and 24 percent were childless. For women in the same age range, about 14 percent were never married and about 15 percent were childless in 2014 (Monte and Knop 2019). This represents a significant drop from 1980, when only 6 percent of men and women were unmarried (Elliott et al. 2012). This section looks at the experiences of individuals who do not have children to better understand their experiences, goals, and choices.

VOLUNTARY CHILDLESSNESS

Individuals who, as far as they know, are capable of having a child but opt not to are categorized as voluntarily childless—or childfree. In fact, an increasing number of adults are intentionally avoiding parenthood. Why individuals do not want children varies. Reasons include focus on career or education, a lack of resources, declining marriage rates, disliking the changes children bring, wanting flexibility and freedom, or feeling it is more socially or environmentally responsible to not have children. For those who do not want to become parents, remaining childless has become easier with the advent of more reliable forms of contraception, as Section V showed. Amy Blackstone's chapter in this section explores these dynamics in more detail.

In general, individuals without children face stigma, even as the reasons for not having children vary. One recent American study showed how people without children are seen as damaged and may be socially punished. Researchers found that the college students in the study evaluated those who were voluntarily childfree as significantly less psychologically fulfilled than those with children and felt greater moral outrage toward those without children (Ashburn-Nardo 2017). Those who choose to be childfree are perceived more negatively than those who have children and those who face infertility.

Illustrating how enduring these attitudes are, President Theodore Roosevelt gave a speech in 1905 "on American Motherhood." In it, he addressed those who were childless in particular, offering pity to those who face infertility, and contempt for those who choose it:

> There are many good people who are denied the supreme blessing of children, and for these we have the respect and sympathy always due to those who, from no fault of their own, are denied any of the other great blessings of life. But the man or woman who deliberately foregoes these blessings, whether from viciousness, coldness, shallow-heartedness, self-indulgence, or mere failure to appreciate aright the difference between the all-important and the unimportant,—why, such a creature merits contempt as hearty as any visited upon the soldier who runs away in battle, or upon the man who refuses to work for the support of those dependent upon him, and who tho able-bodied is yet content to eat in idleness the bread which others provide.
>
> (Roosevelt 1905)

The pressures to reproduce still remain, as do the negative views of adults who do not have children. As Carolyn Morrell's chapter shows, women who opt out of motherhood face particular scrutiny, as gender and motherhood are closely tied. They face assumptions that they are selfish or damaged, are told they will inevitably regret their decision, and endure others' assumptions that whatever they do is a way of compensating for not having children. As Morell suggests, even women who feel certain they do not want children have moments of questioning their choices or circumstances, which is not the same as regret.

Involuntary Childlessness

Some number of adults without children would have preferred to have children. Some face infertility and others find themselves in circumstances in which they feel childbearing is not a good option for them. Infertility is defined as a medical condition in which a sexually active couple not using contraception does not conceive a pregnancy within one year and can also include women who cannot carry a pregnancy to term. About 12–15 percent of couples experience infertility. About one-third of infertility cases are caused by problems in men and another one-third result from fertility problems in women. The remaining third result from a mixture of challenges on both sides or are simply unknown (DHHS 2019). The chapter by Tracey Loughran in this section (along with chapters in the prior section on reproduction) shows how women often struggle with the experience of infertility. Although fertility decreases with age, the chapter by Nicholas Raine-Fenning disputes the notion that women's fertility plunges suddenly with age, which is often used as a cautionary tale to encourage women to have children before it is too late.

The line between voluntary and involuntary is not always distinct. People who may not be medically infertile may nonetheless find themselves childless because of life circumstances. This can include not having a partner or adequate social support or lacking social or financial resources that would make parenting possible. Some have careers that are incompatible with child rearing and others find that they are fulfilled without children and never felt the need to make them a priority.

Patterns among Adults without Children

Although adults across all categories may not have children, some are more likely than others. Among women between the ages of 40 and 44, those with more years of education are more likely to be childless. Although 7 percent of women without a high school diploma are childless, this goes up to 13 percent for women who graduated high school or have some college experience. Among women who graduated from college, 19 percent of those with a bachelor's degree and 22 percent with a master's degree are childless (Livingston 2015a).

Some of the effects of education seem to be shifting. For example, for women in 2014 with an MD or PhD, 20 percent were childless, compared to 35 percent of women with an MD or PhD in 1994. The changes are smaller for women with lower levels of education (Livingston 2015a). As we saw in Section III, women with more education are more likely to marry. Thus, the patterns that show that higher educated women are less likely to have children cannot be entirely attributable to questions of whether they marry or have partners. Rates of childlessness vary by race and ethnicity. Hispanic women are far less likely to remain childless, with only 10 percent having no biological children, compared to white (17 percent), Black (15 percent), or Asian (13 percent) women. Data on childless men are much more limited.

Patterns along lines of education also exist for men, but reveal different dynamics. Men with more education are actually more likely to be fathers. In fact, 14 percent of fathers do not have a high school diploma, compared to almost 22 percent of childless men. About 12 percent of fathers hold a graduate or professional degree, compared to 7.6 percent of childless men (Monte and Knop 2019). Overall, men are more likely than women to remain childless. In particular, by the time men are 40–44 years of age, 24 percent are childless, compared with 15 percent of women in the same age range (Livingston 2015b). Men also may feel less pressure to have children. In a national survey of people ages 15–44 years, 29 percent of men without children said they would not be bothered at all if they never had children. In contrast, only 19 percent of childless women in that survey said the same (Livingston 2015b).

Men without children appear to have different occupational trajectories than men with children. Fathers are half as likely to be unemployed (3.3 percent in 2014) as are childless men (6.7 percent). Childless men are less likely to be in management positions as well (Monte and Knop 2019). Some of these differences may illustrate the "fatherhood bonus" in which presumptions that men need more money and opportunity to support children may lead to greater rewards.

LONG-TERM QUESTIONS

Adults without children may face fewer challenges relating to caregiving responsibilities early in life, but may face significant issues as they age. Because the United States relies heavily on family caregivers for social, medical, and financial support, adults without children will have to identify other sources of care. As childless adults age, their strategies may depend on the resources, whether they have a spouse, and the kinds of relationships they have around them. Estimates are that 15 percent of the elderly population in the United States is childless (Xu et al. 2018).

Childless seniors who are gay or lesbian and grew up without opportunities for same-sex marriage or assisted reproduction may face additional challenges, including discrimination in healthcare settings. They may also face challenges in obtaining care and rely on a wider array of informal caregiving relationships (Muraco and Fredriksen-Goldsen 2011). Some may identify paid caregivers, residential care facilities, and various friends who can act as caregivers, medical decision-makers, and advocates. Their experiences with aging may reflect greater planning efforts and what some scholars have called deferred reciprocity, in which their help with others' care may become a resource to them later in life.

Other differences between people with and without children may emerge as well. During their reproductive years, people without children are measurably happier on average than those with children. There appear to be few differences between the groups later in life, and studies suggest that marital status may matter more for happiness in old age may than having children, and more for men than women (Umberson, Pudrovska and Reczek 2010). Further, women without children tend to be more educated and better situated to invest in cultural resources, as Morrell's chapter suggests.

Taken together, the research on adults without children illustrates the powerful role of contextual factors in shaping experience. Women face more pressure to become mothers, and may in turn feel those expectations and the stigma of childlessness more acutely. Social structure, including access to education, financial resources, and social networks all affect how those without children live and age. Like all aspects of the family, inequality shapes the meanings of individual situations.

REFERENCES

Ashburn-Nardo, Leslie. 2017. "Parenthood as a Moral Imperative? Moral Outrage and the Stigmatization of Voluntarily Childfree Women and Men." *Sex Roles* 76(5–6): 393–401.

DHHS. 2019. "Male Infertility." Office of Population Affairs, U.S. Department of Health and Human Services. (https://www.hhs.gov/opa/reproductive-health/fact-sheets/male-infertility/index.html).

Elliott, Diana B, Kristy Krivickas, Matthew W Brault and Rose M Kreider. 2012. "Historical Marriage Trends from 1890–2010: A Focus on Race Differences." Pp. 012–12 in *Annual Meeting at the Population of America*. San Francisco, CA.

Livingston, Gretchen. 2015a. "Childlessness." (https://www.pewsocialtrends.org/2015/05/07/childlessness/).

Livingston, Gretchen. 2015b. "College-Educated Men Take their Time Becoming Dads." Pew Research Center. (https://www.pewresearch.org/fact-tank/2015/06/19/college-educated-men-take-their-time-becoming-dads/).

Monte, Lindsay M. and Brian Knop. 2019. "Men's Fertility and Fatherhood: 2014." *Current Population Reports* (June): P70–162.

Muraco, Anna and Karen Fredriksen-Goldsen. 2011. "'That's What Friends Do': Informal Caregiving for Chronically Ill Midlife and Older Lesbian, Gay, and Bisexual Adults." *Journal of Social and Personal Relationships* 28(8): 1073–1092.

Roosevelt, Theodore. 1905. "Address by President Roosevelt before the National Congress of Mothers." Theodore Roosevelt Collection. Houghton Library, Harvard University.

Schondelmyer, Emily. 2016. "No Kids in the House: A Historical Look at Adults Living without Children." U.S. Census Bureau. (https://www.census.gov/newsroom/blogs/random-samplings/2016/12/no_kids_in_the_house.html).

Umberson, Debra, Tetyana Pudrovska and Corinne Reczek. 2010. "Parenthood, Childlessness, and Well-Being: A Life Course Perspective." *Journal of Marriage and the Family* 72(3): 612–629. doi: 10.1111/j.1741-3737.2010.00721.x.

Xu, X., J. Liang, B. Kim, M. Ofstedal, J. Raymo and Q. Zheng. 2018. "Trajectories of Living Arrangements among Childless Older Americans." *Innovation in Aging* 2(suppl_1): 162–163.

34

Childless... Or Childfree?

Amy Blackstone

Consider the following comments, the first from Bob, a partnered, childfree man in his late 30s, "People who have decided not to have kids arguably have been more thoughtful than those who decided to have kids. It's deliberate, it's respectful, ethical, and it's a real honest, good, fair, and, for many people, right decision."

And Janet, a single childfree woman in her early 30s, remarks, "To get where we are has been a constant decision making process because every relationship you enter into, especially romantically, that's the expected thing. You're constantly making a decision about remaining childfree."

For Bob and Janet, not having children is neither fate nor accident. It is a deliberate choice they must re-articulate each time they enter new relationships, field questions about their family status, and when reminded by well-meaning folks that they need to provide grandchildren for their parents. Although much recent media and research attention has focused on the increase in child-raising trends among single women, lesbians, and gay men, more people than ever aren't raising children at all. Bob and Janet are 2 of the 45 interview participants in my study of childfree adults. They are among an increasing number of people in the United States who have opted out of parenthood.

STUDIES THAT DO NOT ASK ABOUT CHOICE BUT USE THE TERM "CHILDLESS" CONFLATE THOSE WHO WANT KIDS AND THOSE WHO DO NOT

In considering this "emerging childfree movement," as sociologist Kristin Park once described it, one question is whether people are making a conscious choice to opt out of parenthood (the childfree) or whether they want children but do not have them (the childless). Birthrates, often cited in news stories about the childfree, do not tell us whether those not bearing children intentionally chose this outcome nor do they take into account adoption patterns. The language in many research studies further confounds the issue. Studies that do not ask about choice but use the term "childless" conflate those who want kids and those who do not (perhaps indicative of the normative expectation that one *should* want children).

Researchers at the National Survey of Family Growth address this challenge by measuring birth desire, asking respondents if they want a baby at some point. Yet a problem with this approach is that desires do not always match outcomes. Other researchers sub-categorize nonparents as either "early articulators" who know from an early age that they do not want kids, or "postponers" who put off deciding until their childbearing years have passed. Of course, not all postponers are alike; some identify as childless, others as childfree. Despite these methodological challenges, we do know that fewer Americans are having children today than in the past.

CHILDFREE COUPLES ARE THE INCREASING FOCUS OF MEDIA ATTENTION
....

Who Doesn't Have Kids and Why

Whether by choice or by circumstance, birth rates have declined significantly over the last 40 years. In the United States, the percentage of women who have not given birth by their 40s has nearly doubled since 1976, when 10 percent of women had never given birth by their 40s. The technical term for this is "nulliparous." A 2013 Centers for Disease Control report notes the total US fertility rate has been below the population replacement rate of 2.1 children per woman since 1971.

Data from the 2010 Current Population Survey show that 19.1 percent of white women, 17.2 percent of black women, and 15.9 percent of Asian women ages 40–44 did not have children.

Much of what we know about non-parents comes from studies that, unfortunately, do not differentiate between the childless and the childfree. From these studies we know that nonparents (including childless *and* childfree) are more heavily concentrated in professional and managerial occupations. Also, non-parent couples are, on average, more highly educated, less religious, more likely to live in urban areas, and hold less traditional beliefs about gender roles than couples with kids.

Studies that focus on the childfree specifically, find several differences between women and men. For childfree women, the choice not to parent is often linked to the desire to develop meaningful careers. Men identifying as childfree cite the high cost of rearing children and a desire for financial flexibility as important to their decision. Childfree men and women also differ with regard to education; while higher education greatly increases women's likelihood of being childfree, it does not for men. In 2006, researchers at the National Center for Health Statistics found that about half of 35–44-year-old women without kids were childfree. That is, they were nulliparous by choice. Participants in this study were asked whether they expected to have children; those who did not expect to have children but were capable of having them were defined as "voluntarily childless," or childfree.

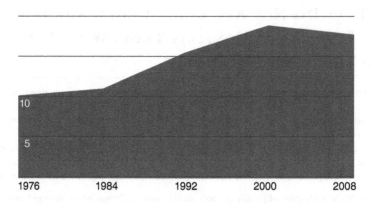

Figure 34.1 Percent of women who have never given birth, ages 40–44.
Source: Pew Resource Center.

The women and men I've interviewed say not wanting to give up valued activities is one reason they are childfree. Steve, an engineer in his early 30s, shared, "I want to be able to travel. I want to be able to do things that I would not be able to do if I had kids." Janet said simply, "I don't want to give up my healthy sex life."

Interview participants also describe not having kids as an ethically responsible choice. Kate, a student in her mid-30s, said, "I'm really just concerned about our world. At this time in our social structure right now it's not going to be a good thing to have children. We can't bring them up healthfully." April, a social worker in her late 30s, said not having children

> is responsible. Instead of this kind of blindly following the societal expectation, it means really taking a lot of factors into consideration. I think about all kinds of stuff. I camped over the weekend and I saw the trash that people with kids left and let build up from so much over use of a camp site. I think about stuff like acceptable population levels.

CHILDFREE IDENTITY

As concern over declining birth rates mounts, longstanding stereotypes and the accompanying cultural hostilities toward childfree people have emerged. Recognizing their choice as stigmatized, some childfree have mobilized around this identity. In 2013, childfree authors and activists resurrected Non-Parents Day, a celebration originally founded by the National Organization for Non-Parents in 1973. This "annual recognition of amazing childfree people and their lives" was renamed International Childfree Day and serves to foster acceptance of the childfree choice. Each year the International Childfree Man and Woman of the Year are named for their efforts to promote acceptance of the childfree choice in society.

Via blogs and social networking sites, the childfree find camaraderie and challenge cultural stereotypes and misperceptions. This online community is growing; a 2009 University of Oxford paper identified 18 Facebook groups focused on the childfree; today over 80 such groups exist. The role of online communities in childfree people's lives has not yet been systematically examined, but research shows online communities help other stigmatized groups unify, solidify identities, and provide support.

Whether the childfree identity is one around which people can effectively mobilize remains a question. Several studies note that the heterogeneity of the childfree as a group may hamper collective organization efforts. So far, that hasn't seemed to slow the proliferation of childfree-focused blogs, meet-up groups, or dating sites.

ENTERING THE PUBLIC CONSCIOUSNESS

Some businesses have heard the collective voice of the childfree, or at least taken note of their economic power. In the past year, airlines and restaurants made headlines as they added kid-free sections and hours. DeVries Global, a market research firm, published a 2014 "Shades of Otherhood" study noting that each woman who doesn't have children represents "enormous untapped potential as a consumer and influencer."

The media too has taken notice. "The Childfree Life" graced the cover of *Time* last summer, *Slate* and other news sources weighed in, and childfree guests made the talk show circuit on *Katie* last fall. Conservative commentator Harry Siegel in his 2013 *Newsweek* article laments the rise of "postfamilial America" and remarks that "the choice to be childless is bad for America." This fear has been echoed by others such as Pope Francis who commented that the childfree are doomed to a fate of "old age in solitude, with the bitterness of loneliness."

Despite changes that have paved the way for more than one possible answer to the question of whether to parent, cultural narratives have not yet caught up to this reality. The dominant narrative continues to be that, of the two options, parenthood is the more mature, selfless choice. Pop culture depictions of the childfree perpetuate the myth that not having kids is an unnatural choice made by deviant people who may eventually change their minds. Robin Scherbatsky of *How I Met Your Mother* and *Big Bang Theory's* Bernadette Rostenkowski Wolowitz are two of the few primetime childfree female characters. Robin, a gun-toting commitment-phobe, and Bernadette, a scientist with a PhD in microbiology, challenge our dominant cultural ideals of femininity. While this is laudable, it also contributes to the myth that the childfree choice is "unnatural." As one news piece put it last year, happily childfree women are viewed as "dangerous oddities."

In Robin and Bernadette's cases, both characters ultimately soften their childfree stance, reinforcing the myth that all childfree women eventually change their minds. Upon learning she can't have children, Robin breaks down, mourning the fertility she'd spent six seasons evading. Bernadette decides she would consider changing her mind if her partner agreed to stay home with the kids.

Despite negative popular narratives, sociological research indicates that the childfree may have more time and motivation to contribute to their communities through charitable and volunteer efforts. Recent studies also suggest that they help rear the next generation by serving as mentors, teachers, counselors, and friends to children, and that they lead fulfilling and happy lives; form "chosen families"; care about our collective future; and enjoy the benefits of diverse social networks as they age.

As these studies proliferate, they may widen awareness and understanding of the childfree choice and contribute to more realistic predictions of the implications of people choosing to remain childfree.

35

Unwomanly Conduct

The Challenges of Intentional Childlessness

Carolyn M. Morell

> You know, I still am Barb. I still can be a whole person without having to mother, having to carry an infant around full-term, you know. I *can* be somebody. And, in fact, I am.
>
> (Barb, age 43)

In popular consciousness, childlessness is regarded as an affliction. In a world where womanhood is synonymous with motherhood, and motherhood is seen as both moral obligation and ticket to fulfillment, this comes as no surprise. Historically, childless women (along with a variety of others who deviated from prescribed gender roles) have been subject to a "rhetoric of rejection," the use of stigmatizing labels that exclude them from the category of good woman. Since a good woman experiences fulfillment through nurturant activities, and the intentionally childless woman is presumed not to be nurturant, the labels are unpalatable: "selfish," "unfulfilled," "regretful."

HISTORICAL CONTEXT

The symbolic distinction between mothers and childless women we experience today is deeply tied to the extraction of women's unpaid household labor. Scientific support for the collapse of woman-into-mother was produced in the nineteenth century in Britain and the United States by primarily white, upper-class professional men who argued against the growth of women's higher education and participation in public life on the grounds that their reproductive powers would be diminished and their offspring damaged. As summarized by Jane M. Ussher, "the brain and the uterus were conceptualized as being in competition for vital resources and energy, so that to concentrate one's resources in one was to deprive the other." The natural "uterine" woman could be assured of a happy destiny while the "mental" woman, who developed her mind and shunned bearing children, could "only hope to be a freak, morally and medically."[1]

Toward the end of the nineteenth century, middle-class and wealthy women began openly challenging maternalist ideology, creating a crisis within Victorian society. Women who questioned their role as

Morell, Carolyn Mackelcan. *Unwomanly Conduct: The Challenges of Intentional Childlessness.* New York and London: Routledge, 1994.

childbearers and wished to assume the rights of men were labeled as "hysterics," as "petty tyrants," as "malingerers," who were attempting to avoid their womanly responsibilities. This group of women was, for the most part, non-procreative and sought independence and a career of some kind.

Today, when many women "do both" child-tending and participate in the paid labor force, women are still socialized into looking toward motherhood for identity and fulfillment. It is acceptable for a woman to "do both," but women who "do only" a vocation or an avocation that excludes motherhood are continually chastised and warned about distressing real or potential consequences of going against the grain. The updated version of the good woman/bad woman split defines the good woman as mother, whether or not she has a career. The bad woman, who deviates from the reproductive norm, becomes the unmotherly "career woman," who is portrayed as dangerous, unhappy, perhaps even deranged.

As I talked with the women in my sample (and later read and reread their words) I listened for their stories of childlessness. Together we discussed the ways in which childlessness is constructed in the dominant society and narrators provided alternative constructions. The "big picture" posits mothering as the primary and best role for women and childlessness as its vacant yet negative opposite. Three dubious discourses about childless women help paint this portrait. They are the discourses of *derogation* (these women are morally flawed), *compensation* (not-mothers' activities and attachments are simply efforts to make up for the absence of children), and *regret* (the only future for the childless).

DEROGATION

Maternalist thinking links motherhood with female moral virtue. Mother love is an extraordinarily powerful symbol for the most selfless kind of human practice. Indeed, motherhood, nurturance, and self-sacrifice are made synonymous through language; when women act in caring ways toward people other than their own children, they are often described—and describe themselves—as acting maternally. But this connection between mothering and concern for others has unfortunate consequences for women who intentionally remain childless: if women don't care for children, they care only for themselves. A moral boundary has been constructed between parents and not-parents. It is fictitious. It is constructed by what is emphasized about not-parents (selfishness) and what is not emphasized about parents (selfishness). The border distorts reality and it ignores class and societal issues. Yet it remains a cultural force to be reckoned with.

The association of childlessness with selfishness was well understood by the women I interviewed. All were familiar with the common stereotype of the married woman who acts against motherhood as a self-centered, ungiving person. One narrator explained that when others ask if she has children and she replies "no," she "wonders if they are thinking sterile or selfish?" This is the social construction of childlessness in a nutshell.

Not surprisingly, few participants saw themselves in this light. Most often, the link between childlessness and inappropriate self-centeredness provoked strong reactions. As one woman said, "there are ways to give other than motherhood." Some women felt that because of their childlessness they were able to reach out to others in ways that mothers might find difficult given their family responsibilities. In the examples below, women reclaim their right to be seen as ethically sound people and describe the nonfamilial forms their giving assumes:

> I think one of the interesting ironies is that sometimes people wall say "these must be selfish people because they don't have kids." And yet, when I look at the way we live, in many ways, we are not at all into what people would expect us to be like—heavy consumers, privatization, the couple together, being selfish whatever they are doing. But we have quite the opposite, I think, reaching out all the time which is identified with families but it's often not the way most families function right now where you have this turning inward.
>
> (Louise, age 45)

> I'll tell you, I think you are more thoughtful of your friends and are more concerned with other people and their problems because you don't have children. I think you are a more concerned person because somebody that has children has got their hands full right there taking care of problems.
>
> (Marge, age 76)

The only thing I care about is that I lead my life in a way that doesn't harm future generations. I am as worried about the planet as if I had children. I think for a lot of people, and you hear this in the rhetoric all the time, that people do things on behalf of their own children, that people's social conscience is derived from simply guilt from doing wrong to their children. My feelings are not oriented toward any specific child or person. It's more that all people should be able to enjoy life.

(Jo, age 43)

Certainly most narrators resented their exclusion from the high moral ground reserved for mothering women. One woman's comment summarizes for others the central reaction: "My capacity to love, I don't think, would be increased if I had kids."

As a social worker I have worked with poor mothers so over-whelmed by the demands of socially unsupported parenting they were unable to practice compassion toward their children. I have also met middle-class women who violated their children's bodily and emotional integrity in their efforts to guide and protect them. In my sample I found women who were socially active and women who weren't; some who viewed themselves as selfish, some who didn't; some identified as pacifists, some not. None, of course, are mothers. "I'm probably a little selfish but I think most of us are. But, I mean, are most people willing to admit it?" Rhonda related her reluctance to take on motherhood to her inability to maintain "a certain amount of unselfishness" that she believes is required.

Selflessness is connected to mothering. Yet in my sample it is clear that not-mothers engage in unselfish work and develop their life-affirming skills in social practices other than parenting. Indeed, peace-oriented social activists I spoke with saw the absence of children as a direct contributor to their ability to act on their social commitments:

Since I haven't had children and I haven't really had to put personal activities on hold because I was taking care of them and keeping things together for us as a little social unit, I've been able to develop myself as an individual and as a political person ... I have hopes that my political work could be something that is life-affirming in another sense than having children ... I think that if I'm very successful, I'll be able to do something for kids ... and to make it into a more human world.

(Margaret, age 41)

I would not argue that childless women are essentially socially oriented because they are childless. But the social practices of childlessness may reinforce caring behavior which simply takes a different shape from that practiced by mothers. Not-mothering women's caring may take a less privatized form, necessarily less intertwined with biological ties. This is illustrated by my participants' plans for their estates. The importance of social class will be obvious.

Parents leave their property to their children, almost universally and automatically. Childless women disrupt this reproduction of class patterns associated with inheritance. But the women are not busily and selfishly spending everything now, or writing wills leaving everything to their cats. Rather, without excluding relatives and friends, their plans emphasize cross-class giving primarily through commitments to public need.

Among the women I interviewed, the beneficiaries most often mentioned were charitable organizations or institutions of importance, such as churches and colleges. A number of women spoke of setting up special funds or scholarships to help others who had financial needs:

I've written a will ... Well, I have a scholarship fund for women. I mean, I think not being able to go to medical school myself ... I have some young women who I've known, they've gone to college and so forth and they are just trying to start careers and I'm leaving some to them. And then to some causes like Amnesty and things like that.

(Elizabeth, age 48)

We have charities that we feel very strongly about, and our estate is set up with the charities and groups that we particularly like. For example, I read a great deal. So, we designated money to our library association. My husband's active in the Animal Rescue League. He's been their treasurer and vice-president for years. So that's another charity ... We're very comfortable with the choices, the disbursal of the estate. And that gives its own pleasure. Like, "oh good, this will be good for them and that will be good for them." Items that are precious to us are designated in the will to friends.

(Lee Bishop, age 45)

The intentionally childless women I talked with knew others might think of them as selfish because of their not-mothering status. They also were aware that others often thought of their activities and interests as compensations for missing children. An additional attitude was especially threatening: you will regret your decision.

COMPENSATION

Somebody just recently asked about my grandchildren and I said it was not possible because I didn't have any children. And they said, "Oh, I'm so sorry." I wondered about what.

(Lee Henry, age 66)

Compensatory discourses make motherhood the natural condition for women by describing the activities and attachments of not-mothers as compensations for the original deficiency, *no child*. Every aspect of a childless woman's life may be interpreted through the lens of this deficiency. These discourses make central what one does not possess, what one has not done. *Whatever* a childless woman *does have* or *does* may be viewed as merely compensation for the missing real experience of motherhood. Motivations to achieve, active public commitments, avocations, and relationships with pets are commonly interpreted as evidence of the inevitable void left by a failure to mother. Of course, comparable activities and attachments among mothers are not viewed in this fashion.

One narrator alerted me to the fact that "the notion of compensatory means that there is a standard that you're not meeting." She spoke of the oppressive nature of such an assumption:

People talk about us as whatever we're doing is compensatory. The reason I'm working so hard is that I'm compensating for not having children—that's the oppression and being ostracized. And I do get a lot of that. "She works all the time, no wonder she publishes all that. I wouldn't like to be like that. I wouldn't want to be so single-minded because that's not a balanced personality."

(Elaine, age 48)

Many women I interviewed found that others saw their lives as simply making up for the lack of children. The following words of one of the participants points to this experience:

Most people are overwhelmed with the number of things I do. Now, of course, I guess you could say that, "Oh my God, of course she does all this as a way of compensating." Well, I mean, after a point, if the person wants to believe that that's the case, what can you do? But I don't think of it as compensatory. I like to do these things. I'm a real active person. I have certain values and I want to make those active in the community, so I get out of my doorstep. But it's not like a compensation for me. Maybe the cat is the compensation, I don't know, maybe the cat... (laughing).

(Louise, age 45)

Indeed. What about the cat? Women's relationships with animals provide a forceful example of how compensatory ideology works. A prevalent cultural view is that among the childless, attachments to animals signify a substitution for the missing child. One woman told about the "cute and sweet" way her husband's father inquired about their parenting plans: "Is this the best you can do, kitty cats? Roger's answer was 'yes' and that was that."

Given the common nature of the symbolism, it isn't surprising that some narrators who had deep bonds with four-legged creatures often defined their interspecies love as maternal. Even so, women were always clear that they enjoyed the unique relationship that develops with animals for its own sake. It had intrinsic merit. Pets were pets, not replacements. But narrators were conscious of compensatory thinking and did contrast pets with children. They spoke in good-natured, humorous ways, sometimes even announcing a preference for animal companions over child companions. One narrator's letter with photo that I received a week after our phone interview demonstrates the centrality that pets can assume on their own terms:

The only other thing I would like to add to our conversation of last Saturday is about my dog, Sally. She is so black that you can only see her brown eyes and her Christmas ribbon in the photo of the three of us. Sally is a very important part of my life, and Ed jokes that in the event of a fire I will save Sal before I will think of him. She is ten years old and very loving, playful, a big tease and she is obedient. If there is any shred of maternal needs within me, I lavish them all on Sally. Having a dog is so much better than having children—we don't have to hire a babysitter if we go to the movies, she doesn't play loud rock music, she doesn't bring her sloppy teenage friends over to mess up the house, and she is always in a good mood.

(Kay, age 46)

Another woman I interviewed is nicknamed "The Mother Theresa of the Animals" in her rural community where she engages in animal rescue work. When I asked Ruth if she could identify any ongoing theme in her life, she reflected briefly, then spoke: "Probably the love of animals. I just really love animals and I always have." She talked about the advantages living with animals has, given her strong commitment to her architectural business:

While the commitment [to animals] is very strong, it's a commitment that you can leave for the day and still come back and they love you just as much and you haven't lost anything by not being with them. They haven't lost anything. But I think a child needs to—especially when they are young—they need continuous attention and they need continuous development to be the people they need to be.

(Ruth, age 43)

Women I interviewed were familiar with the ideology that turned pets into replacements for missing progeny, and, for the most part, rejected it. Lee Bishop loves her cats, "they're fun to watch, they're fun creatures," and she often jokes about them being her children. But she doesn't think of them as substitutions for children. "They don't require as much care. I often laugh about the fact that my children can stay in the garage."

One effect of compensatory discourses is that childless women begin to feel that they *do* need to compensate for the fact that they are not mothers. In my sample, several women spoke of the need to achieve something special because, if all else fails, they could not fall back on motherhood to provide status and a sense of accomplishment. Some narrators felt that others are more understanding if you are doing (or have done) something outstanding with your life. This created internal pressures. One woman expressed it this way: "If you don't have kids, then hell, you'd *better* have achievements that compensate." Deena, a physician, facetiously said, "Oh I think they just think I made the decision (to be childless) because I'm a *doc*-tor. Being a *doc*-tor overrides all that. You have a *ca*-reer, *doc*-tor. That's obviously almost as good." Almost, but not quite.

In summary, the evaluation of childless women's activities and relationships as surrogates for motherhood enforces one life path for all women—a path where a child of one's own is the natural object of love and where the care of one's own children is the central activity. Women who do not meet this expectation are compared to those who do—and evaluated on those terms. Even to make the care of nonbiologically related others central, through various public activities that do not include childrearing, is seen as second rate. The privatized nuclear family is the privileged site for women's time and attention; a committed public life is an inferior substitute.

Perhaps if motherhood were not so massively privileged as the central source of gratification for women, a wide range of satisfactions equal to motherhood would be legitimated, making the option to forgo reproduction more thinkable. Compensatory thinking is a minor irritant compared to rhetoric that sentences childless women to a lifetime of regret.

REGRET

Certainly the thought of "will I regret it when I'm old?" is impossible to avoid, that sentence even, because it's just out there. So I think I've said, "Gee I wonder if I'll be sorry when I'm older." But it doesn't have any power for me right now.

(Beth, age 44)

We were married in 1969, and we made the decision right before we were married ... And in the first few years we were married we had strangers and friends actually stopping us and asking us, "When are you going to have children?" And when we said, "Never," they'd say, "What do you mean? You are going to regret it."

(Isabel, age 45)

I've always got a lot of satisfaction in my life from my friends and from all my activities and the teaching that I do, so all those kind of generative activities that I would suspect that most people get from raising their children, I get from other things. I don't know, I mean, people say, "Oh, you will wake up at seventy or something and you will regret this." Maybe this is the case, I don't know. But I certainly know women in their 60's, 70's, and 80's who didn't have children and have pretty happy lives.

(Louise, age 45)

The statements of not-mothers that appear above clearly demonstrate the fact that regret is an emotion assigned to the childless—an assignment impossible to escape. Motherhood, by contrast, is rarely associated with regret, a cruel word implying pain rooted in fruitless longing. Women considering motherhood do not have to reckon with discourses that threaten them with future regret if they become mothers. The notion that childless women, as they age, will look back and lament their decision acts as a powerful reproducer of the ideology and practice of motherhood. Indeed, threat of regret is one way that pronatalism is promoted.

The texts of intentionally childless women provide little evidence that women suffer from ongoing or serious feelings of regret. Most women who were adamant about remaining not-mothers described whatever regrets they did have as they aged as tied to their work lives. Women spoke regretfully about various facts, such as missing the opportunity to go to college right out of high school, of having to postpone graduate work or of giving up the dream of medical school due to lack of money, or of leaving academia for the corporate world. Most didn't regret not having children; many never desired to have children in any strong way. Rather, what many women did describe was ongoing comfort and reinforcement of their childlessness over time, along with occasional "rumblings"—times when childlessness erupted into consciousness for reconsideration or review. And a few women shared stories of emotional upheaval with the transition of childlessness from a temporary to a permanent status.

"Dead Forever"

At twenty-three and thirty and thirty-two (pause) I know there were points where I checked in on the decision. And at thirty-two it was dead forever. Even as a discussion in my own head.

(Sara, age 46)

For those women who had an aversion to or no interest in motherhood, their childless status remained comfortable. Carole, age 55, said, "I never had a coming-to-terms experience, I just knew I didn't want them." Helene, age 48, thought it is important for those going through reproductive decisions to know that they won't regret it later. "If it *feels* right, chances are you won't regret it."

Women talked about childlessness becoming more and more settled with passing time. External pressures to reproduce ceased as women aged. And their partnerships, creative work, careers, and activist commitments became strong centers in their lives. As one woman put it, "it has been a matter of constant reinforcement in a sense." Numerous women used the word "reinforcement" to describe their experience of childlessness over time. "It just gets more and more comfortable, like sinking into an old shoe."

I really don't share the experiences that women have who reconsider their decision at certain ages in their lives. It's like once I made it, it was forever made. And it never came back to haunt me in any way ... The struggle that goes on for so many years for some women, it baffles me sometimes because I am not a part of that and I haven't been a part of it.

(Susan, age 74)

One of the oldest women in the sample stated that her decision to remain childless was "one of the few things in my life where I absolutely have no regrets." And another woman in her 70s spoke of her reproductive choice as "the best choice I've ever made," since many of the things she valued about her life she saw as directly related to that decision.

Writing in *Off Our Backs*, Carole Anne Douglas repeats the non-regretful stance of narrators when she says:

> So how does it feel to be 45 and not be a mother? It feels much the same as not being a China scholar, another career option that I seriously considered. In other words, I feel that bearing and raising a child was one of the interesting possibilities that I decided against because I chose another focus... I thought it might be interesting to women who are making the decision to hear from someone who does not regret her choice.[2]

In short, regret is not an accurate descriptor. All but one narrator rejected the label "regretful." The designation seemed too pervasive, deep, and enduring to describe their experiences. Instead, women tended to relate specific occasions when they experienced "wistful" feelings, or unsettling "rumblings," or "twinges" of doubt, or "passing thoughts" about the road not taken.

Rumblings

Death or illness of a family member could be one such occasion for second thoughts. One woman's experience is illustrative. Her certainty about her decision was shaken with the premature death of her husband:

> If there was one time when I really had remorseful feelings it was after my husband died. And you see he was only 56 and I was 51. And honestly, we were so used to each other, gosh, when you think of it, from the time I was 16 and all, we were each other's world ... In those first few days when it was so darned hard, to be very honest, a few times I thought then that, gosh, it certainly would be nice if there had been a son or so to turn to, to feel that you weren't completely alone. But that comes of your weakness and loneliness of the moment. Eventually, naturally, you get back in stride and you're the master of your ship again, and things go on.
>
> (Marge, age 76)

Marge's feelings were temporary; she gathered strength and found needed solace in female friendships. She recovered from her loss by modeling herself after her favorite aunt who was widowed before her. And she thought beyond her aunt, to "all the millions of widows all over this world and forever backwards, and I thought, 'why, they all managed and you can too.'"

For women who were caring for an ill or aging parent at the time of the interview, they couldn't help but wonder, as Elaine said it, "and who will do this for me?" Another woman, Helene, quipped that although she has experienced nothing at all resembling regret, she might have regrets "if I'm alone in the nursing home and other people are getting visitors and I'm not."

Another time that rumblings occurred for women was during transition times in their own lives, times when work became stale, times when they were going through periods of dissatisfaction or boredom or loneliness—those fallow times when life becomes drained of meaning and purpose. Linda, a woman seriously committed to remaining childless, was sterilized at age 30. She had this to say:

> It really wasn't significant to me at all until probably, maybe a year ago. I think what happened is that I started to think about turning forty and about getting old and whatever that entails and about moving into a different part of my life. At that point I started wondering if I did the right thing and I thought in recent times it was the right thing because (pause)... I don't know what's going to happen with my consulting business, it's been a real upheaval for the last year or so and it's been real unpleasant for me. I've decided that maybe I'm going to walk away from it. I think it's time to focus on other things ... When you sit still long enough you start thinking: "Gee, what do I want to do now? Well, gee, I can't have kids now, that's not going to occupy my time." In that context it's come up now. But it's never come up as a real sadness or never come up as something I've regretted. It's really only been something I've mused about.
>
> (Linda, age 40)

And for Kay, second thoughts occurred when she felt lonely on a holiday that is associated with sociability and family gatherings:

> Once made, the decision, I didn't have to think about it anymore. And I didn't have any second thoughts. There was only one time when I—not regret—but I felt sad that (pause). It was our last July 4th in Kennebunkport, so that must have been about four years ago. We were alone and we didn't have any company and there was no one around to celebrate with and we both felt very lonesome. And I thought at that time, "if I had had children we would have children around here. The kids would be teenagers by that time, but they would be in and out and there would be some contact with people." But that was the only time, just one day in all these years when I've kind of felt nostalgic about it. And it wasn't even a regret or it wasn't a change of heart but just the thought, "how would it have been different if I had had kids on this July 4th?" But that was the only time. And I haven't had that feeling since then.

> (Kay, age 46)

Perhaps these thoughts and musings are not surprising when one considers the social meanings attached to children. For women especially, a child often represents an expectation of permanent security, a relationship that guarantees you will not be isolated or alone. In periods of transition then, or of difficulty or boredom, it was not uncommon for some women to wonder if a child would "fix" their lives. The culture tells women that if they are not a mother they are missing out. At those points in women's lives when they were missing something, it's not surprising that they sometimes wondered if a child would correct whatever problem they experienced. Of course, mothers have lonely times as well.

Lastly, some women experienced rumblings when they were around children. Most women realized that children are a source of unique pleasures as well as a lot of work and responsibility. One woman talked about having "twinges" sometimes when she's around her sister's children—they add fun to her life.

Ellen recognizes that

> there's a great deal of joy that can come from having wonderful children. When my best friend has her kid's Sweet Sixteen party, I can get a great deal of joy out of seeing this one little girl, who used to be ten and now is sixteen and is on her way to being a fully formed person. You can get some level of joy. It's not the same as having your own.

For Margaret, the feeling is not,

> Oh, we've passed this thing up. But you know, kids are kind of neat, it might have been fun. It's more like what would be really nice is to live in an extended situation with other people where we could be like an aunt and uncle, so we could do things with kids, you know.

Women recognized the pleasures that come with children but that did not mean they regretted being childless. They didn't. But some recognized that they incurred losses by remaining childless.

> Perhaps if you could just skip the middle step and go right to the grandchildren, I would have liked that … I mean, grandchildren seem to be the best part of the whole deal when you look at it objectively.

To summarize, it is not surprising that the majority of not-mothers I spoke with are challenged by moments or periods of internal questioning related to their childless state, no matter how committed they were to that state. Participants experienced rumblings and engaged in speculations about what might have been if they had had children. Rumblings were not considered problematic by most, but rather just temporary musings that happen from time to time depending on circumstances. Family transitions, age, and social context were related to consciousness of childless status. A settled issue becomes temporarily unsettling. For most, they just seemed to be a part of the experience of remaining a not-mothering woman. Those women who had greater discomfort with their status had to come to terms with their internalized beliefs about childless women and their idealized fantasies about motherhood.

FINAL THOUGHTS ON SYMBOLIC POLITICS

Maternalist ideology depends on the depreciation of not-mothers to discipline women's desires and behaviors in the direction of motherhood. Women who refuse this direction (or cannot achieve mothering status) are symbolically censured and may find themselves struggling with internalized negative images.

Even though the real boundaries of gender have changed, the symbolic boundaries remain. "Motherhood" remains a powerful signifier of women's normality and superior caring abilities. Negative representations of childlessness, combined with a largely implicit positive view of motherhood, disguise the fact that both not-mothers and mothers experience costs and benefits related to reproductive status. If mothers and not-mothers were equally privileged in the symbolic life of the culture, images of the nuclear family would become less seductive, and what are now fearful images of living outside the norm would become more attractive. Thus patriarchal power would lose an important reinforcer.

NOTES

1   Barbara Ehrenreich and D. English, *For Her Own Good: 150 Years of Experts' Advice to Women* (London: Pluto Press, 1979), p. 116. Quoted in Jane M. Ussher, *The Psychology of the Female Body* (London: Routledge, 1989), p. 2.
2   "Oh Dear, I Forgot to Have Children," in *Off Our Backs* (May 1992): 17.

36

Infertility through the Ages – and How IVF Changed the Way We Think about It

Tracey Loughran

To all outward appearances, Louise Brown looked exactly the same as thousands of other babies when her blinking, slightly quizzical gaze met newspaper readers on the morning of July 25, 1978. But as the first child born using the technique of in vitro fertilisation (IVF), she was utterly unique in the history of humankind.

Forty years later, the media is saturated with articles about people's experiences of infertility. There is frequent debate about the possible dangers of current and future reproductive technologies. These include intracytoplasmic sperm injection (the direct injection of sperm into eggs obtained via IVF), uterus transplants, artificial wombs and human cloning.

And there is good reason for news outlets to be concerned about infertility. It remains an immediate and painful problem for many people today. In 2010, an estimated 48.5 million couples worldwide were infertile. We will never know how many people suffered from infertility in past generations – the numbers were never counted – but there are fears that rates are now rising.

Today, declining fertility rates are often blamed on wider changes in Western women's lives in the early twenty-first century. The average age of first-time motherhood is rising in England and Wales and across most of Europe. The reasons behind this change are complex, but in Western Europe include increased educational and professional opportunities for women and changing models of family life. Childlessness is often perceived to be a direct result of these changes.

For these reasons, many people assume that infertility is a distinctively modern experience. Likewise, when they think about infertility, they think about modern medical approaches to its treatment. But the history of infertility goes back much further than 1978, and in the past people often did not think of it as a medical condition at all.

Men suffer from fertility problems too and there is increasing public debate on male infertility. But looking back over a longer time frame shows that for most of history, women have been blamed for childlessness. In some ways this has not changed since 1978. Because IVF is a technology that intervenes on women's bodies, it also reinforces the focus on how women's reproductive systems might "fail".

Loughran, Tracey. "Infertility through the Ages – And How IVF Changed the Way We Think About It." *The Conversation*, May 1, 2018.

On the 40th anniversary of Louise Brown's birth, it makes sense, then, to reflect on women's experiences of infertility in past and present societies. This is a good time to consider the longer history of infertility – and how the experience of involuntary childlessness has changed.

A Long History

It's easy to forget that only a few decades ago, the birth of one baby via IVF was widely perceived as a scientific miracle. But writings and stories about infertility stretch back to the medical texts of ancient Egypt, Greece and beyond.

The entire Judaeo-Christian tradition begins with the story of Sarah and Abraham's desperate desire for a child. In Icelandic sagas, Indian epic narratives and ancient Greek plays, we find stories of childlessness, miraculous births and adoptions that cross national boundaries.

In centuries past, couples sought all kinds of remedies for childlessness. They prayed and went on pilgrimages. In medieval England, men and women took remedies containing the sexual organs of animals in the belief that this would stimulate their reproductive organs. In eighteenth-century Europe, childless women were encouraged to "take the waters" in spa towns to ease their nerves and prevent spasms of the womb. More recently, in the mid-twentieth century, doctors who believed that female infertility was a psychosomatic condition recommended adoption as a "cure". They argued that becoming a mother to an adopted child made women relax and increased their chances of conception.

Behind the chant about the wives of Henry VIII that British schoolchildren learn in the playground – "divorced, beheaded, died; divorced, beheaded, survived" – there also lies a tale of the king's desperate and bloody quest for more children. In the modern era, Federico García Lorca's 1934 play, Yerma, recently reworked in a lauded production at London's Young Vic theatre, charted one woman's obsessive quest for motherhood – an issue that has featured in many TV soap opera storylines in recent decades.

Yet despite this historical evidence, many people persist in thinking about infertility as a product of the modern age. One reason is that IVF itself has made infertility socially visible to an extent unparalleled in earlier decades. Newspaper stories, government inquiries and oral histories show that in the 1950s and earlier, British couples often perceived the arrival of children as entirely down to chance. As one woman, born in 1943, told the oral historian Elizabeth Roberts: "Nature ... it tricks you doesn't it? I've always loved babies but you know I just never had any".

With the first live birth of a baby conceived via IVF in 1978, such fatalism became less common. The media storm following Brown's conception and birth (the Daily Mail reportedly paid the Browns £325,000 for exclusive rights to their story) put infertility in the public eye and encouraged other couples to proactively seek medical support and technological solutions to their childlessness. Some women about to undergo IVF now believe that the technology works for everyone. Many women are shocked to discover the relatively high rate of failure of a single cycle of IVF. The success rate for women under 35 to have a live birth is 32.2 percent, declining to just 1.9 percent for women over 44, according to the UK's National Health Service (NHS) data from 2010.

In only 40 years, a technology once perceived as equivalent to a miracle has come to be seen almost as a cure-all for fertility problems. The arrival of IVF brought infertility as an issue into the public domain – and led people to believe it was a modern problem that could be solved. But there are other reasons, apart from IVF, why infertility feels like a late twentieth-century phenomenon. It was part of a series of changes, which began nearly 20 years earlier, that altered the way women thought about their own bodies.

Choice and Control

In Britain, the oral contraceptive pill was made available in 1961 and abortion was legalised six years later. Dramatic changes in women's sexual, reproductive and family lives followed over the ensuing decades. As women were better able to plan and space out births, the birth rate plummeted and the average age of first pregnancy rose. At the same time, pre-marital sex, illegitimacy and divorce were on the rise. More married women now worked outside the home. The Women's Liberation Movement proclaimed that women should take their futures into their own hands.

Above all, these developments resulted in a new sense that at long last, people might be able to control their reproductive futures. In practice, not all women could easily access contraception or abortion. It wasn't until 1974 that the contraceptive pill was made available free on the NHS to all women, regardless of marital status or age. Nevertheless, throughout the 1960s and 1970s, public debates, social policy and political discourse emphasised choice and control. Because of this emphasis, infertility was often ignored.

For infertile couples, public ignorance around their plight was compounded by the fact that more effective family planning meant fewer newborn children were available for adoption. By the time Brown was born in 1978, a unique set of circumstances prevailed: social changes had encouraged women to believe they had power over their destinies, while technological advances had led to unprecedented faith in the power of women to control their fertility.

Yet at the same time, one of the traditional solutions to childlessness was being lost. While childless couples can still adopt today, they are likely to become parents to older children rather than babies. Child adoption is also now much more heavily regulated in England than it was in the early twentieth century. Some couples are not deemed suitable to adopt, while others decide not to continue with the process after making initial enquiries.

TECHNOLOGY HAS THE ANSWERS

It's possible to trace this focus on technology back even further in time. Since the 1930s, it has been possible to detect pregnancy very early on by measuring the level of progesterone in women's urine. Back then, the test was expensive to carry out, but in the late 1960s the home pregnancy testing kit was invented, and is now easily accessible in the West. In the 1950s, ultrasound was developed, and by the 1970s obstetricians were recommending use of the technique on all pregnant women.

This ability to visualise the foetus in the womb is taken for granted today, but it changed common perceptions of pregnancy beyond all recognition. But in previous centuries, this wasn't the case. Early modern medical authorities tell us that there was often much uncertainty about the diagnosis of pregnancy. Take, for example, Mary Tudor's phantom pregnancy in 1555. The queen of England fully believed that she was pregnant until long past her expected due date. She has sometimes been portrayed as delusional, driven mad with grief by her longing for a child. But her courtiers also believed that a royal birth was imminent, and the most up-to-date medical knowledge available at the time could not disprove them until the child failed to materialise.

In the mid-twentieth century, the march of technology seemed unstoppable. By the time IVF became available, as adoption became more difficult, couples were primed to pin their last hopes of raising a child from birth on a technological breakthrough. This is the vital context for understanding initial responses to IVF as a medical miracle. No one seemed to think it was genuinely possible until the late 1960s, yet previous advances such as the pill and ultrasound meant than when it arrived, people quickly trusted the new reproductive technology.

The belief in this miracle "cure" exerted considerable influence on the shape of public discussions of infertility in subsequent decades – not least in the unthinking confidence many couples have in IVF.

All this shows that to understand past experiences of infertility, we need to realise just how radically recent changes in medicine and technology have altered the way we think about the body. Infertile women now experience involuntary childlessness differently to their forebears. But the emotions women often go through when dealing with infertility remain remarkably similar, despite the advent of new technologies.

"Not a Proper Woman"

This argument is at the centre of a recent history of infertility I co-edited with medical historian Gayle Davis, which spans the ancient world to the present day, taking in Britain, Europe, Asia and North America.

My own research compares depictions of infertility in British mass-market women's magazines and in feminist publications in the 1960s and 1970s. Because of developments in contraceptive technology, the women featured in these publications often believed that they were now able to control their reproductive destinies. They were less prepared than women of previous generations for the possibility that they could be powerless to have a baby. But in a pre-IVF period, if they did experience difficulty in conceiving, there was no promise of an effective technological solution to the problem.

Desperation was the most constant theme in mass-market magazine coverage of infertility in this period. Women described infertility as a "tragedy", a feeling of "emptiness" and like being "dead inside". They told of their inability to come to terms with the diagnosis, and their perception of infertility as an irreparable loss. One woman begged an agony aunt: "Can a woman ever come to terms with this tragedy? If so, tell me how?"

These women had expected to become mothers. Infertility was a loss of this anticipated future. More than this, they felt that childlessness meant a loss of feminine identity. The victim of infertility often described herself as "not a proper woman". Above all, infertile women felt themselves separated from pregnant women and mothers.

One woman recounted standing "outside Mothercare, looking in the window with tears streaming down my face", while others dreaded visiting friends who had recently given birth. These descriptions of infertile women's emotions remained remarkably constant, despite the sweeping social changes of these two decades. And women reported similar emotions in feminist publications as in the mass-market magazines. Both before and after 1978, when Brown was born through IVF, infertile women expressed intense feelings of powerlessness and despair.

A History of Stigma

It seems infertility has been stigmatised in many different historical contexts. Noble women in medieval Japan were disdained if their marriages remained childless. In sixteenth-century England, childless women suffered because motherhood was perceived as the most important marker of femininity. And in nineteenth-century France, many doctors linked childlessness to abortion, venereal disease or promiscuity.

In widely different societies, women have borne the brunt of the blame for fertility problems. Yet in some circumstances, women have also been stigmatised for seeking help. In the mid-twentieth century, there was much debate over whether married women who conceived by use of artificial insemination by donor sperm had committed "adultery". For much of history, it seems, childless women literally couldn't win, no matter what they did.

Infertility is still often seen as a woman's problem today. In the media, childlessness is often blamed on women's "selfishness" in seeking to build careers or wait for the right partner before trying to become pregnant. A reality check is desperately needed to stop this cruel finger pointing. Men have fertility problems too. Not all women suffer fertility troubles because they start trying too late. But even when an age-related decline in fertility is the root of the problem – why should a woman be blamed for wanting to wait until she feels ready to be a good mother?

It might seem depressing to conclude that women have always been blamed for infertility. But maybe putting their own stories in historical perspective could help infertile women now. The ability to research and to understand the many different reasons for infertility, and the different options open to those who are unable to conceive, helps couples to exert control over a situation that makes them feel powerless.

This ability to exert increased control by making informed decisions about what path to take next has been identified as an important mechanism for coping with infertility. Understanding the history of infertility could have the same effect. Humans are historical creatures. The ability to place our own experiences in historical perspective could help those who cannot conceive to come to terms with their situation, and not to blame themselves.

We need to look beyond that famous photograph of Brown, a baby unaware of what she would come to represent for so many millions of people. Instead we should open our eyes and really look at the human face of infertility throughout history – to help people understand that in all ages, women and men have had to cope with this experience, and to learn from their struggles.

37

Hard Evidence

Does Fertility Really "Drop Off a Cliff" at 35?

Nicholas Raine-Fenning

Everyone's favourite property expert and house hunter extraordinaire, Kirstie Allsopp, raised some eyebrows when she recently suggested that women's fertility "falls off a cliff" when they hit 35. Her argument was that women should prioritise pregnancy and childbirth before careers. But does fertility really drop so quickly as women age – and specifically after 35?

Female fertility does fall with advancing age and, at the same time, the likelihood of losing a pregnancy increases. There are biological reasons for this. Women are born with a finite number of eggs, or oocytes, within the ovary. As women age both the number and quality of the remaining eggs decline. However, there is no "cliff" – rather a gradual decline.

WHAT IS FERTILITY?

Fertility is defined as the rate of childbearing in a population. It remains relatively stable up to the age of 30, with about 400 pregnancies for every 1,000 women (40 percent) not using contraception for one calendar year. It then begins to decrease until around the age of 45, when only 100 women will conceive for every 1,000 (10 percent) not using contraception. Miscarriage rates also steadily increase. About 10 percent of women will miscarry at the age of 20, compared to 90 percent or more at 45 years of age or older.

Studies have shown that 82 percent of couples will conceive within a year of trying and that this rises to 90 percent after two years where the woman is in the 35–39 age range. These figures are not that dissimilar to those seen in women aged 19–26 – 92 percent of whom conceive within one year and 98 percent within two years. These figures show that most couples fall pregnant in the first year and of those who do not conceive, about half will do so in the second year. This is why couples should seek assessment and referral to a fertility clinic after trying for 12 months. At this stage tests can be undertaken to exclude obvious problems and if reassuring, the couple can continue trying for that second year.

Raine-Fenning, Nicholas. "Hard Evidence: Does Fertility Really 'Drop Off a Cliff' at 35?" The Conversation, July 15, 2014.

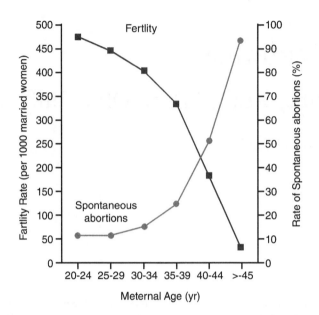

Figure 37.1 Fertility and miscarriage rates as a function of maternal age. Linda Heffner et al/Nejm.

OTHER RISKS

When we look at age it is not only fertility and pregnancy outcome that we must consider. The maternal risks associated with pregnancy also increase, especially in women aged 40 or more when there is an increased chance of death. One of the main risk factors is hypertensive disease (heart problems that occur because of high blood pressure) which is twice as common among women aged 40 or older compared to younger women.

The risk of delivering a low birth weight or preterm infant is also increased in women in their 40s and about 1 percent of babies are stillborn. However, most pregnancies proceed uneventfully and women should be reassured that even after 40 the majority will not have complications and will deliver healthy babies.

It is probably more important to understand is that each and every woman's fertility is different at the same age and, to some degree, impossible to predict.

AGE AND IVF

In developed countries about one in seven heterosexual couples are affected by infertility. Some will require assistance either because they have not conceived within two years or because there are identifiable problems such as blocked Fallopian tubes, endometriosis, polycystic ovaries, and/or low numbers of poorly motile sperm.

IVF was introduced to bypass tubal problems and ICSI, where a single sperm is injected into an egg to address fertility problems in men. Both ultimately involve the transfer of an embryo, or fertilised egg, back into the woman.

We cannot predict which couples will need IVF but the chances of successful treatment do fall with advancing female age and more so from 35. Pregnancy rates are fairly stable (30–35 percent) for each embryo transferred up to the age of 30, but then fall to 20 percent by 40 and are only 5 percent by 45. But women who elect to have an egg from a donor maintain the higher pregnancy rate seen in younger women (30–35 percent) and the much-reduced risk of miscarriage and foetal abnormalities. This is why to be an egg donor you must be younger than 36.

Taking referral, and the work-up required before IVF, a woman using her own egg ideally needs to start trying in her early 30s to ensure she is treated before she turns 35. In the UK, NICE recommend three cycles of IVF on the NHS, but only one between the ages of 40 and 42.

For IVF, then, a woman's age does start to become a consideration. Having a family is a very personal decision, and timing is just as important. Neither should be influenced by age but we cannot ignore biology or IVF statistics. But there are no guarantees – trying at an earlier age might increase your chances but it still won't work for everyone.

The best two tests to predict how a woman will respond to ovarian stimulation drugs appear to be one that measures a hormone known as AMH and an antral follicle count scan. Each follicle contains an egg and produces some AMH so a high measure of either indicates a better response to drugs and IVF success. People are increasingly using these tests to try to measure fertility and predict its end. But they weren't developed to assess a woman's fertility, and there are no robust studies to support such predictions.

EVEN THE MENOPAUSE ISN'T SUDDEN

The ultimate fertility "cliff" that all women face is the menopause – or final period – which, for most women, lasts many years. Most women enter the menopause in their late 40s or early 50s. Fecundity in the time leading up to the menopause, known medically as the peri-menopause, is low but women require contraception as pregnancies still occur.

So when should women try for a family? Taking everything into consideration, the best compromise would be the decade between 25 and 35, as Linda Heffner has suggested. Clearly this is neither appropriate nor opportune for all women but gives some guidance for those who have choice. An increasing number of women are having IVF and freezing their own eggs as a back-up. Social egg freezing is not only increasingly in popularity but has also become a much more successful process, with 80 percent of eggs now surviving the process.

So what does this all mean? The take home message is that yes, fertility does fall with advancing age but there is no "cliff" – most couples will conceive within one to two years of trying, even at 40.

SECTION VIII
Children and Teens in Families

INTRODUCTION

Children are seen as vulnerable and in need of protection, a role the US federal, state, and local governments have increasingly claimed. Regulation of the family often revolves around purported concerns about children and teens. At times, policymakers have called for greater investment in young people. At other times, they have identified and regulated possible threats that potentially could corrupt or harm young people. And sometimes, young people themselves are seen as a threat and policy aims to manage or control them.

As with other aspects of the family, the meanings of childhood and adolescence, and experiences of children and teens, are shaped by social forces and structures of inequality. Like adults, children and teens feel the effects of changes in the economy, experience shifts in the structure of family, and respond to political pressures. Young people actively engage in adult worlds, but also have social worlds that are uniquely theirs. Youth have their own peer cultures and perceptions, which are situated in time and place. What it meant, for example, to be an elementary school kid in 1960 in a Midwest farm town was likely quite different from what it was like to be a kid in an east coast city in the 1920s. This section provides a brief overview of some of the historic changes of childhood and adolescence and explores how inequality shapes young people's lives.

HISTORIC MEANINGS OF CHILDHOOD

Progressive era reformers heavily shaped contemporary social meanings of childhood. Many of these social reformers were single, white, college-educated women. They were among the first generation of women to attend college and they graduated with skills and ambitions but few opportunities. Many of them longed to use their education to help others, even as they did so in ways that reflected their privilege. Key among the wide array of social programs reformers launched in the late nineteenth and early twentieth centuries was the creation of settlement houses. Women reformers, like most famously Jane Addams, would often take possession of houses in poor urban and often immigrant neighborhoods so they could serve a range of functions. These houses operated as boarding houses, community centers, after-school clubs, childcare centers for children, and libraries, and volunteers there regularly offered English classes, citizenship classes, and places for meetings.

The Progressive era also marked a dramatic change in views of children. Having been a source of much-needed income through the 1800s, children rapidly became economically useless to their families as

Progressive reformers advocated for new laws to limit or ban child labor. Reformers successfully advocated for mandatory education for children, funding and allocation of urban spaces for playgrounds to keep children safe, redefinitions of power so charities could intervene in child maltreatment, and development of juvenile courts separate from adult systems. They also provided expert advice in hopes of encouraging parents to invest more heavily in each child. These changes all served to reshape cultural definitions of childhood (Zelizer 1985). The result of these efforts was the view—still with us today—that children are unique from adults, are precious, and require high levels of support and investment.

THE RISE OF THE TEEN

Adolescence is a distinct time between childhood and adulthood that has not always existed as a category. In 1904, the first president of the American Psychological Association, G. Stanley Hall, completed a study of adolescence, one of the first concerted efforts to describe this phase of life. He pointed to major social changes, including child labor laws and educational requirements, which had reshaped young people's teen years. Hall promoted the view of adolescence as a time of "storm and stress" in which young people experience emotional and behavioral upheaval before establishing a more stable existence in adulthood. He identified many issues that are associated with adolescence today: depression, fear of social exclusion, propensity toward crime, problems of gossip, and desire for excitement. He wrote that "youth must have excitement, and if this be not at hand in the form of moral and intellectual enthusiasms, it is more prone... to be sought for in sex or in drink" (quoted in Arnett 2006:188).

One of the most significant changes to the meanings and experiences of adolescence was the rise in high school attendance. In 1910, only 12 percent of those aged 14–17 were enrolled in school and 9 percent of American youth graduated from high school. By 1940, 70 percent of teens were enrolled and 56 percent graduated from high school (Schmidt 1996). Rates of school attendance differed greatly by race and region, but across the country, rates steadily increased. Despite facing high levels of racial discrimination, African American enrollment in high school increased to 80 percent by 1950. In short, by the mid-twentieth century, the education of teens had become the norm. Schools were no longer only available to the children of the elite. They also became places where teens could interact with limited adult supervision.

As adolescents, a group that was termed teenagers in the 1930s and 1940s, began to establish their own cultural norms and interests, companies began to recognize them as having significant purchasing power. Teens increasingly became the focus of movies, media, and advertisements, and an increasing number of products aimed to appeal to them and not their adult counterparts. The rise of dating culture, as detailed in Section II, also contributed to teens' growing influence as consumers. A key aspect of this was access to a car, which provided young people with relatively private space, as the chapter by Gary Cross describes.

THE IMPACT OF LEGAL AND STRUCTURAL INEQUALITY ON YOUNG PEOPLE

Cultural and social changes reconfigure families, thereby affecting young people. For example, economic downturns might force a family to relocate or to share housing with other families. Changing patterns in marriage have reconfigured children's lives in various ways, including how they spend time across multiple households, whether they have stepparents, and how they fare economically. Children conceived with the use of an ovum donor might face different questions than did children decades before that technology was created. Children born to women who are unmarried face less stigma today than a century ago when "bastard" was routinely stamped on birth certificates.

Lawmakers and political leaders often advocate for laws and policies to respond to cultural changes. The ways these policies are enacted almost always reflect systems of inequality. The result is that young people's lives are legally regulated in ways that are not always entirely visible. At times, children are explicitly the focal point of laws and regulations. Some laws aim to protect them, like those that dictate what online information children under age 13 can access without parental consent or those that require teachers, childcare providers, physicians, and others who work with children to report suspected abuse or neglect. At other times, the laws or policies aim to change young people's behaviors, like those that create curfews for minors or criminalize teens who stand together on sidewalks under the auspices of anti-gang efforts, or require teens to get parental consent for birth control or abortion. In these examples and many others, laws that sound relevant to all young people disproportionately affect brown and black young people. Other times, the goals of laws and effects are not entirely clear. As Tey Meadow's chapter shows, efforts to limit the kinds of treatment gender-nonconforming kids can receive may seem like an effort to protect them, but may actually cause harm.

Notably, many policies that do not target young people directly nonetheless affect them. For example, no-fault divorce legislation changed family configurations with broad impacts on children. Changes in immigration policy also affect children's households in significant ways. Changes to eligibility requirements for supplemental nutrition programs may alter children's overall long-term health. Changes in criminal justice may determine whether a young person grows up with an incarcerated parent—an issue Kate Luther explores in more detail in her chapter. Failures to regulate communities, including lax laws regulating gun ownership, affect young people too, as Kieran Healy reminds us in his chapter on the frequency of school shootings.

Laws and cultural changes inform each other. For example, laws passed in the 1990s and 2000s introduced graduated driver's license requirements for teens, which made getting a license harder. At the same time, changes in school funding and priorities made driver education a private, relatively expensive endeavor, rather than part of the school day, and thus free. The outcome has been that fewer teens get driver's licenses. Access to technology, changes in parents' work hours, and shifting expectations also change the circumstances of teens' lives, which in turn changes their behaviors, as Jean Twenge's chapter illustrates. For myriad reasons, teens today drink less alcohol and become sexually active later than did teens in prior generations.

Young people's lives are heavily shaped by broader systems that allocate resources and opportunities, including race, ethnicity, class, gender, sexuality, immigrant status, and disability. Although the US Supreme Court declared racial segregation to be unconstitutional in 1954, more than half of schools remain racially segregated, with at least 75 percent of students being either white or non-white (Meatto 2019). Only about one in eight white students (12.9 percent) attends a school where a majority of students are children of color. By comparison, nearly seven in ten black children (69.2 percent) attend such schools. These differences tend to map onto socioeconomic inequality as well. Fewer than one in three white students (31.3 percent) attend a high-poverty school, whereas more than seven in ten black students (72.4 percent) do (García 2020). These patterns reveal significant educational inequality that shapes future opportunities. As the chapters by Margaret Hagerman and Jessica Calarco show, how parents make choices about their children's schools and invest time and money in them often help to perpetuate unequal resources in schools. Children whose parents are economically insecure may have limited opportunities for educational success for other reasons. As Aggie Ebrahimi Bazaz shows, children of migrant farmworkers often miss school because of the migration patterns their families follow to obtain work. Which extracurricular activities young people join, how much support they can obtain from schools, whether they work for wages, and how much money their parents' associations are able to raise inevitably reflect broader patterns of inequality that shape long-term outcomes.

AGEISM AGAINST YOUNG PEOPLE

In spite of claims that children are sacred and in need of support, there is significant evidence of bias against young people. Although all young people experience bias against them based on age, those experiences are filtered through race, class, and gender. These experiences form how young people learn social rules of interaction with institutions, which in turn shapes their opportunities and expectations of the world. Children and teens from more privileged backgrounds often learn to see institutions as flexible and adaptable to their needs, while low-income children and teens are more likely to see institutions as rigid and inflexible (Lareau 2003). These perceptions come from observations of parents, as well as first-hand experiences of regulation each day in subtle or pronounced ways. Whether through the presence or absence of police in their neighborhoods to dress codes in their schools to the role of the city in maintaining their parks, young people develop a view of the state. In some cases, these experiences might be supportive, like when the mayor recognizes an elementary school for its academic performance or a winning sports team is invited to the Capitol to be honored. In other cases, state intervention might be demoralizing, like when young people have to walk through metal detectors or use clear backpacks to enter school, or when they see beloved teachers removed from their schools because of low student test scores. How public systems respond to requests for inclusive services for children with learning disabilities or respond to the bullying of or hate crimes against queer youth also shape perceptions of the state. Unsurprisingly, whether these experiences are supportive or undermining will affect whether young people trust the state and its regulatory functions, and over time, these views may be very hard to change.

Young people's social location as minors subjects them to particular kinds of regulations, about which they have notably few opportunities for input. Young people are often dismissed as undeveloped "citizens in the making" (Gordon 2009) or even as intellectually or neurologically undeveloped, as the arguments about the "teen brain" suggest.

The willingness to dismiss young people because of their youth can be seen in various places, but it is especially clearly articulated in arguments about whether voting rights should be extended to those younger than 18 years of age. Those who oppose lowering the voting age largely base their arguments on stereotypes of young people. As one newspaper editorial argued against a failed 2019 bill to lower the voting age to 16 years:

> Generally speaking, a 16-year-old has no significant life experience and, in the United States, has usually been a coddled dependent of his parents at home and the school system. Almost all of his real-life challenges have been countered by one proxy or another. With few exceptions, 16-year-olds have never managed a household, struggled to pay the bills, run a business or even filed their own taxes. For many, getting a driver's license is their first real interaction with any government agency at all.
>
> (Boston Herald Editorial Staff 2019)

These arguments posit one kind of childhood in which children are "coddled," given little opportunity to make decisions, and shielded from responsibility. This image ignores the reality that more than one-third of teenagers have jobs or spend several hours each day providing care to family members (Bauer et al. 2019). In contrast to such dismissive views of youth, adult allies of young people point to the growing number of teen activists who are speaking out about issues ranging from gun control to climate change as evidence that teens are prepared and qualified to vote. They note that women did not have the right to vote in federal elections until 1920, with many arguing that women lacked the expertise or mental capacity to offer a useful opinion about political issues. Notably, the voting age has only been 18 since 1971, when the 26th amendment lowered the age from 21 years old. Each change to voting rights has been controversial in its time and each has come to be broadly accepted.

Voting is just one place where claims of youth inferiority are visible. In countless places, children and teens face "adultism," that is, preference toward those who have achieved adult status. Young people face discrimination as consumers in retail locations and restaurants. They have limited abilities to participate in governance, even in their own schools. Yet, deciding not to hire someone because they are too young, irrespective of experience, is also legal and socially acceptable. Although discrimination based on old age is illegal, young people do not have similar protections.

Meanings of youth are historically contingent, socially contextual, and responsive to social change. They are refracted through larger structures of race, ethnicity, class, gender, sexuality, immigrant status, and disability. Yet, unlike other forms of inequality, young people, barring tragedy, always age out of the inequality they face because they are young. Many even grow up to join the chorus of adult voices who dismiss and discount those who are young. This transition illustrates how the meanings of youth will continue to shift over time, with different social and regulatory responses to follow, and these changes will shape different peer experiences of childhood and adolescence.

References

Arnett, Jeffrey Jensen. 2006. "G. Stanley Hall's Adolescence: Brilliance and Nonsense." *History of Psychology* 9(3):186.

Bauer, Lauren, Patrick Liu, Emily Moss, Ryan Nunn and Jay Shambaugh. 2019. "All School and No Work Becoming the Norm for American Teens." Brookings. (https://www.brookings.edu/blog/up-front/2019/07/02/all-school-and-no-work-becoming-the-norm-for-american-teens/).

Boston Herald Editorial Staff. 2019. "Editorial: Sixteen Is Perfect for the Prom, Not the Polls." *Boston Herald.*

García, Emma. 2020, "Schools Are Still Segregated, and Black Children Are Paying a Price." Economic Policy Institute. (https://www.epi.org/publication/schools-are-still-segregated-and-black-children-are-paying-a-price/).

Gordon, Hava R. 2009. *We Fight to Win: Inequality and the Politics of Youth Activism.* New Brunswick, NJ: Rutgers University Press.

Lareau, Annette. 2003. *Unequal Childhoods: Class, Race, and Family Life.* Berkeley: University of California.

Meatto, Keith. 2019. "Still Separate, Still Unequal: Teaching About School Segregation and Educational Inequality." *New York Times.* May 2, 2019.

Schmidt, Stefanie Rae. 1996. *School Quality, Compulsory Education Laws and the Growth of American High School Attendance, 1915–1935.* Cambridge: Massachusetts Institute of Technology.

Zelizer, Viviana A. 1985. *Pricing the Priceless Child: The Changing Social Value of Children.* New York: Basic Books.

38

Where Has Teen Car Culture Gone?

Gary Cross

For nearly a century, coming of age in America meant getting behind the wheel. A driver's license marked the transition from childhood and dependence to adult responsibility and freedom. To many, it was a far more important milestone than voting or legal drinking. It was the beginning of a new world—of cruising down Main Street to meet with friends and compete with rivals; the ritual of being picked up for a date and making out while "parking"; and of the pleasures and frustrations of repairing, souping up, customizing, or racing a car.

This world, familiar to anyone who has seen *American Graffiti*, the 1973 paean to teen driving, was unique to the United States. No teens in any other country in the world shared American teens' level of enthusiasm for all things automotive. This was in part because in the mid-twentieth century there was a wealth of available cars—cheap used ones from the late 1920s—as well as the fact that by 1940, American teenagers were more likely to be attending high school than working. Elsewhere, 16-year-olds rode bikes or buses and had jobs. Practically nowhere else on earth did teens have the means—and, as high-school students and not full-time workers, the time—to join the adult world of automobility. And they did so on their own terms, partially emulating their elders who had cars, but also by using cars to craft their own personal styles and escape their parents' control.

Some young car enthusiasts remain today, but American teens have as a whole moved on. According to the Federal Highway Administration, the percentage of American 16-year-olds with driver's licenses was roughly 25 percent in 2014—a steep drop from about 46 percent in 1983. Older Americans who gather at old hotrod and antique car shows lament how their offspring show no interest in their hobby, and car makers and dealers fret over how to sell to an increasingly elusive teen market. What's changed? The answers are technological, legal, and cultural.

One thing is clear: It is harder to get a car these days. Thanks to technological advances, the cars of the last few decades are better made and last longer—and thus cost more, even when they're used. And the old strategy of buying a "junker," a car in bad shape, and then replacing a faulty alternator with a cheap scrap-yard part is practically impossible to do on one's own; repairs in the digital age require more skill and equipment than most teens have. And rising costs meant that poorer teens—especially African American and Hispanic teens—have been more likely to do without. A half-dozen years ago, about a quarter of

---

Cross, Gary. "Where Has Teen Car Culture Gone?" *The Atlantic*, May 27, 2018.

16-to-18-year-olds from households earning less than $20,000 per year had driver's licenses, compared to the three-quarters of their counterparts in households earning over $100,000 who had licenses.

Vehicles aside, getting a license in the first place is harder than it used to be. Once, it was a rite of passage to turn 16 and become a full-fledged driver. But since the 1970s, psychologists, safety officials, and legal scholars have campaigned to raise the age requirement to 17 or 18, with more limited permits provided for younger ages. They've argued that younger age requirements are a holdover from a time when America was more rural and families needed their teen children, sometimes as young as 14, to drive vehicles on the family farm. These experts amassed great troves of data showing that 16-year-olds, especially boys, lacked the maturity to drive powerful machines on the public road, noting that 16- and 17-year-olds were responsible for far more crashes than were even their 18- or 19-year-old counterparts.

By the mid-1990s, most states were adopting the so-called Graduated Driver's License, a multi-step licensing process for young drivers that includes complicated rules about when and where 16-year-olds can drive. The requirement of adult-supervised behind-the-wheel training, prohibitions against night driving, and special penalties for infractions, as well as the rising costs of driver-education classes (which have been dropped from some high-school curricula in recent years) have all led many young people to delay learning to drive until they turned 18 and were free of these restrictions. This new legal regime brings America more in line with many other industrial nations, where the age of 18 has long been the norm.

But the decline of teen driving over the past few decades has roots beyond the practicalities of getting a car and a license: Local authorities have also become less willing to allow teens to play around with cars. By the 1980s, many politicians and local businesses demanded that police across the country restrict and ultimately ban the rites of "cruising" (driving around aimlessly) and "parking" (making out in parked cars). Cruising was considered a nuisance because it could interfere with people going about their daily errands and commutes. This inconvenience was tolerated for some time, but by the late 1970s, some local authorities and businesses were voicing concerns about an invasion of outsiders (often nonwhite ones) from different neighborhoods—in part a product of the expansion of freeway systems in areas such as suburban Los Angeles. Complaints like these prompted cruising bans across the country.

While cars themselves are losing their place in teen culture, the freedoms and pleasures that they once brought to young people now often seem to be won through other means. The smartphone is the most obvious replacement, offering a virtual liberation from the constraints of family that the car once provided physically. Additionally, with more parents—particularly more moms—away from home during the day, many teens can find privacy right in their own living rooms and bedrooms, with no need for a car to take them elsewhere or provide its own sanctuary.

Though these changes mean that teens still find the freedom and privacy that cars once afforded, one thing is gone: that magical age of 16, when suddenly a world opened up. Many teens have been using smartphones since they were kids; privacy in their homes has been granted to them gradually over time. The rite of passage is gone, along with the excitement and anticipation that preceded it for so many.

39

For the Parents of Gender-Nonconforming Kids, a New Approach to Care

Tey Meadow

Ari had a difficult time talking about his gender.

He had always been feminine, insisting on wearing only androgynous clothing, flowing pants in bright colors, patterned shirts and scarves. His hair was long and carefully arranged, and his nails were usually painted with a kaleidoscope of colors. By the time he was 12, he vacillated between using male and female names and pronouns. At school, he mostly socialized with female classmates while performing in school plays and making art.

When I met his mother, Sandy, at an event for parents of trans and gender-nonconforming children, she spoke anxiously about his experience of puberty, his struggles with depression and the daunting task of helping him cope with the changes in his body. Sandy read every parenting manual on gender nonconformity she could get her hands on. She wasn't sure whether Ari would grow up to be a gay man or a transgender woman, and she felt a tremendous amount of discomfort with that uncertainty.

Sandy was like many parents I met while doing research for my new book on families raising gender-nonconforming children. These parents often struggled with the question of how to tell if their child was really transgender, merely experimenting with gender or, instead, simply growing into an adolescent gay identity.

THE MEDIA TEACHES PARENTS TO DOUBT

The parents and clinicians with whom I spoke all wished that there was some foolproof method to determine whether kids were actually trans. They longed for a formula that would tell them, with certainty, that they could safely assist these kids with social and medical gender transition without fear of mistake or regret.

News articles and blog posts on the subject seem to appear weekly. In July, for example, *The Atlantic* published a cover story about Claire, a gender-nonconforming 14-year-old. After a period of consideration, Claire

Meadow, Tey. "For the Parents of Gender-Nonconforming Kids, a New Approach to Care." *The Conversation*, August 29, 2018.

decided that she didn't ultimately feel the need to transition. The author of that article, Jesse Singal, used Claire's experience to illustrate the complexities of parenting gender-diverse children.

I found the article troubling, however, because it was a prime example of two dangerous trends in public discussions of parenting gender-nonconforming youth.

First, Claire's experience is not at all typical. The American Psychological Association has found that children who "consistently, persistently and insistently" tell the adults who surround them that they are transgender almost never have a sudden and complete change of heart. Indeed, they say, gender identity is resistant – if not immutable – to environmental intervention. Children can and do learn to "cover," a term sociologists use for downplaying parts of one's identity to assimilate. But that's different from no longer feeling transgender.

Second – and perhaps more important – this chapter and others shift the focus from whether a child might be transgender to asking how it might be possible for them to not be.

This is called "cisnormativity" – the cultural belief that being gender-normative is inherently better than being trans. And the media is, at times, its biggest proponent.

Stories and false statistics that exaggerate the proportion of children who stop exhibiting gender nonconformity may offer comfort to anxious parents who long for an easy life for their kids. They also prompt those parents to interpret any signs of struggle or ambivalence as de facto evidence their child is not trans, to withhold information about transgender lives from interested children and to create an atmosphere in which children learn to hide the complexities of their experiences to garner the approval of adults.

Embracing Uncertainty

This is not a new story.

For decades, transgender adults have written about how, when seeking gender reassignment, they needed to seem authentically trans – and report a total identification with the other gender – to physicians and psychologists. This could entail an exclusive preference for clothing and activities consistent with the other gender, a heterosexual sexual orientation and an ability to pass as a member of that gender. Absent those criteria, trans people would be turned away from medical care and disbelieved by friends and family.

As a result, many learned to cover up their ambivalences, struggles and self-doubts. They learned to present a version of trans that seemed foolproof to cisgender people: a narrative in which gender is certain, impervious to the vicissitudes of actual emotional life.

This is not to say these trans people were uncertain about who they were. That's simply untrue. But self-knowledge rarely comes packaged in a single coherent narrative.

And yet, this is the expectation we have of the children in our lives.

It's possible to do better. Development is not a linear process. It can weave through joy and ambivalence, through pain and delight. Adult gender doesn't come easily to anyone. It's fertile ground for self-doubt and humiliation, experimentation and adaptation.

Think for a moment about your own adolescence, the time when you experienced rapid bodily changes, social maturity and emergent sexuality. Few of us remember this process as smooth and linear. Now imagine you had adults – perhaps even your parents – scrutinizing this process each step of the way and trying to nudge you to fit neatly into an identity or way of behaving that felt uncomfortable. This is a recipe for depression and anxiety in children. In anyone, really.

It doesn't have to be that way. Gender-nonconforming children who are supported by their parents in expressing their identities by and large thrive. In fact, recent studies show that trans youth who are affirmed and supported by their families to transition are psychologically healthier than children who are gender-nonconforming but receive no such encouragement.

Moving Toward an Affirmative Model

Dealing with uncertainty and ambivalence can be especially difficult for parents who fear their children will face discrimination in their communities. But the truth is, it's difficult for all parents.

As more families grapple with the complexities of gender development, we see stories of children and parents being offered guidance and support by clinicians who work from "an affirmative model of care."

This affirmative model doesn't push kids toward a transgender outcome or even a linear narrative. Instead, clinicians teach parents to pause, absorb the messages their children are sending and then articulate what they are seeing back to their children. Parents and psychologists help children express their genders in authentic ways, and then work to understand the significance of the things they are saying and doing. It takes time and practice.

Affirmative clinical work treats all gender variations as signs of health – not illness – and supports the unhurried unfolding of a child's emergent self. In this context, uncertainty and ambivalence are a part of transgender development, just as they are for all gender development.

After some time and discussion, Sandy, Ari and his therapist decided to put Ari on Lupon, one of a class of drugs used to suspend the body's production of the hormones that incite puberty. Sandy works hard to allow Ari to vacillate in his gender presentation and in his sense of self.

When we last spoke, she told me she didn't know where he would end up. She knew there was no foolproof way to tell, only a process to endure.

Whatever the conclusion, she told me, Ari knew that she was walking alongside him – but letting him lead the way.

40

White Families and Race

Colour-Blind and Colour-Conscious Approaches to White Racial Socialization

Margaret A. Hagerman

INTRODUCTION

How do white children come to understand race? And how does the context in which they are embedded shape that understanding? While psychologists have long recognized the content and impact of racial prejudices, little research has investigated how whites form ideas about race in the first place. Specifically, the role that social context plays in the process of white racial socialization remains unexplored. Because whites occupy dominant positions within social institutions and because racial ideologies 'justify or challenge the racial status quo' (Bonilla-Silva 2006, 11–12), understanding how young whites develop racial common sense is important in terms of transforming or cultivating these ideas in ways that lead to actions that promote racial equity.

Understanding how white youth today make sense of racial dynamics is of particular interest given the current sociopolitical moment in which we are experiencing many demographic and ideological transformations. These transformations include a growing 'minority' majority, contested notions in popular culture about how or when race matters, and widely divergent ideas among adults about whether racial inequality is even a problem in the USA anymore. For example, recent research on adults has found a growing predominance of colour-blind racial ideology, a racial common sense that 'explains contemporary racial inequality as the outcome of nonracial dynamics' (Bonilla-Silva 2006). This work tends to include a number of assertions about how white children develop racial ideas but such assertions remain largely untested.

Developmentally, ages 10–12, or middle childhood, is a period when children 'acquir[e] a social perspective of ethnicity' and begin to form an increased sense of social justice and the ability to think ideologically. While ideas about race undeniably form throughout the life course, middle childhood is an important developmental period to explore, one that has heretofore not received the attention that it deserves.

To fill these gaps in existing research, I present findings from an original ethnographic study of the racial contexts in which white, upper-middle-class parents and their white children live and interact. Focusing on the choices that parents make about schools and neighbourhoods as well as the everyday ways that they talk to their kids about race, I demonstrate that white parents approach racial socialization through the construction of different racial contexts of childhood. I show empirically that the outcomes of white racial socialization, as well as the process itself, depend in large part on the distinctive racial contexts in which white children live. I then draw connections between these racial contexts of childhood and the ideas about race that children form within them.

Racial Socialization

Historically, racial socialization has focused on how black parents prepare children for experiences of racial discrimination... Given the nature of racism, families of colour teach their children lessons about race with the goal of helping their children develop strategies for countering racism and to build resilience and empowerment. Although much is known about the content and mechanisms of racial socialization for children of colour, less research has focused on this process in white families.

As this chapter demonstrates, white upper-middle-class parents with access to nearly unlimited resources construct different racial contexts for their children, which are often informed by their own racial logic and parenting priorities. Children interact within these contexts, interpreting the social world around them and producing ideas about race as a result.

METHODS

I conducted ethnographic research in a US Midwestern metropolitan community. Between January 2011 and October 2012, I used a triangulated approach to collecting ethnographic data through conducting semi-structured in-depth interviews with 30 white families including 40 white parents and 35 middle-school-aged children, systematic observations of families and the communities in which they were embedded, and a content analysis of a range of sources of information about local dynamics including local newspapers, websites and blog posts. My role in the field included offering childcare duties, coaching a sports team and simply being a member of the local community.

Families were recruited through a snowball-sampling method. Emails were sent to parents introducing the study as 'research on how white kids learn about race'. In each of the 30 families, I interviewed at least one parent along with their child. Given still persistent gendered divisions in household labour, and similar to other studies, most of the parents who participated in interviews were mothers. I interviewed ten fathers. In seven families, I interviewed both parents. Here, parents generally shared similar views, which helped allay fears that interviewing only mothers would distort findings. I conducted observations of the families in everyday public spaces such as parks, community events and restaurants, and in private spaces such as within homes and country clubs, while driving children places and at birthday parties. I spent approximately four hours observing most families in their homes, although I spent significantly longer periods of time with some families. I also immersed myself in the community by working as an athletic coach. However, given my focus on families, I did not collect data in schools, but I did interview a few teachers as informants to explore emerging themes.

This chapter analyses data from families living in two distinct communities within the larger Petersfield metro area (Table 40.1). (Names are changed.) The first community I study, Evergreen, is a neighbourhood located within Petersfield; the second, Sheridan, is in a nearby affluent, white suburb. Property values in both neighbourhoods range from $400,000 to $3,700,000 and less than 1 percent of the residents are non-white.

Although Evergreen and Sheridan are predominantly white, the public schools in Evergreen are racially integrated. Sheridan schools are almost exclusively white (Table 40.2).

Families in my study identify as white and possess economic privilege, or what I call 'upper-class status', defined as families in which at least one parent: (1) holds a graduate/professional degree, (2) has a professional-managerial career and (3) owns a home. Families in Sheridan and Evergreen, from my assessment, have access to the same general array of upper-class choices and resources.

Table 40.1 Petersfield County race demographics.

Race	%
White	84
Black	6
Latino	5
Asian	4
Native American	<1

Table 40.2 School profile comparisons.

	Evergreen Middle	Sheridan Middle	Evergreen High	Sheridan High
% white	57	93	42.7	96
% black	25	1.9	26.8	1.2
% Latino	13.7	1.6	14.5	2
% Asian	14.2	3	10.5	1.3
% low income	49.2	3.5	56.5	4
Average scores	81% math-proficient eighth graders; 90% reading-proficient eighth graders	93% math-proficient eighth graders; 95% reading-proficient eighth graders	ACT: 22.6; SAT CR: 631, SAT Math: 628	ACT: 23.3; SAT CR: 629, SAT Math: 625

Note: The ACT and SAT are standardized tests taken by high school students. Scores on these tests are often an important component to the college admissions process. CR stands for the Critical Reading portion of the test, which is different than the Math portion.

FINDINGS AND DISCUSSION

Colour-Blind Approach: The Sheridan Context

NEIGHBOURHOOD AND SCHOOL CHOICES: THE SCHULTZ FAMILY

The Schultz's Tudor-style home is part of a new, sprawling housing development in Sheridan, a small suburb with a new public high school, a historic downtown and a strong sense of community. Ninety-nine percent of residents are white. The median annual household income is $90,000. While median property values in Sheridan are $350,000, the families in my study live in homes that well exceed this average.

The Schultz's home has seven bedrooms, a large yard and an equestrian trail at the back perimeter of the lot, weaving throughout the neighbourhood. Mrs Schultz, a petite blonde, has stylishly designed the interior of the family home. She is currently a stay-at-home mum, although previously involved in state politics. Mr Schultz is rarely home, as he is a well-renowned and busy surgeon. The 4 Schultz kids, Joelle (15), Erica (13), Natalie (11) and Danny (8), are blonde, outgoing, athletic children.

Like most parents interviewed, Mrs Schultz moved to Sheridan for the sake of her children's education:

> We initially chose Apple Hills [an affluent, white neighbourhood in Petersfield]… we wanted to be in a community where you had sidewalks…, where it was a small close-knit community… we were very, very happy there… it came time for our oldest to start high school, … so we looked for the best high school we could and decided that's where we would move. That was the only decision… We moved to benefit our children's education. We didn't need to leave… it was the high school that drove us… to Sheridan.

Apple Hills is an exclusive, predominantly white neighbourhood in the city of Petersfield. This community is 'close-knit' and has its own country club. Most of the kids who live there attend private elementary and middle schools in Petersfield. However, high school presents different challenges as the private schools in town do not offer as many sports, advanced placement (AP) courses or activities as the public schools. Mrs Schultz describes Evergreen High, the public high school that Joelle would have attended if they had remained in Apple Hills, in negative terms:

> We had some concerns about the school because we had heard negative things, but we wanted to go check it out... But there was no one who would make any arrangements for us to come and tour... Finally one day, I just called the principal, and said... 'We're just going to come'... and we just forced our way in. It wasn't a welcome mat.

Mrs Schultz specifically points to an African American student:

> We were out in a hallway talking to a... teacher. And an African American student came up to her and starts talking... We just mentioned that, 'We're going to this Mr Donald's class'... And this African American student says, 'You're going to that asshole's classroom? I can't stand that bastard.' Well, the teacher's mortified, right? I can see the look of shock on her face... And she's trying to shut this girl up, who's just talking and talking, really inappropriately, really loudly, to parents! Prospective parents!

When describing this experience, Mrs Schultz sits on the edge of her chair, clearly impassioned and astounded at the perceived lack of adult control in the school:

> What stunned us was that... the teacher did not have control of the situation. And that frightened us a little bit... Who's in charge? Who's running the ship here? So then we go to Biology, and we're sitting through [the] class, which we enjoyed thoroughly... after class, [the teacher] took us aside... he said, 'What other schools are you looking at?' And I said, '...I'll be touring Sheridan tomorrow.' And he said, 'I've been a summer school teacher in Sheridan for the past 17 years. ... I know those families, I know that community, I know those students, and I will tell you right now... if she were my granddaughter, she'd be going to Sheridan in a minute. That is an excellent school with excellent students and an excellent, excellent community. Get her out of Evergreen.' This is their number one teacher telling me this! I'm like, okay then.

Paradoxically, despite the schools' reputations, both have similar ACT (ACT is a standardized test used as a college readiness assessment measure) scores and AP offerings, and in fact, Evergreen High has higher average SAT scores than Sheridan High (see Table 40.2). However, the reputation of Evergreen High, especially in white, affluent circles, is that it is not a good school but rather a dangerous and unsafe environment:

> Maggie, there were policemen on every single floor... We were walking down halls and kids would physically hit our bodies, ...at Sheridan... kids moved out of our way. One boy even held the door for us. They'd say, 'excuse me,' It was a much more respectful environment... I just felt like at any moment, things could explode at Evergreen... and become an unsafe situation. I don't want my kids to worry about safety. I want them to concentrate, focus, and direct their energies at school, nothing else. So I went to Sheridan the next day and thought, 'This school would fit for all of our kids because all our kids are very mature, focused, children.'

Mrs Schultz's concerns about Evergreen High centre on safety, the behaviour of the children who attend the school and her perception that the teachers and administrators are unable to maintain control. While none of this discussion is overtly about race, Evergreen High's racial demographics are undeniably different to those of Sheridan: many more students of colour attend Evergreen. Prioritizing a particular type of school and community experience for their children, the Schultz family, like many others, moved to Sheridan. Erica, Natalie and Danny moved from their private elementary/middle school to the public Sheridan Middle

School, which is 96 percent white, while Joelle attends Sheridan High. I ask Mrs Schultz if she thinks about the lack of racial diversity in her children's lives:

> [Sheridan] is lily-white... [but] no, we don't talk about it. It's, you know, it's a non-issue for us. I would welcome more people of color, but I just want everyone who's here to be on the same page as all the parents like me. I want to be in a community that all feels the same as we do, which is, we value education. And that is what this community is – we've found a community that really supports education.

While the Schultz's choice reflects priorities of safety and quality education, the choice is also connected to racialized local understandings about who values education, what kinds of communities support education and how different groups of children behave. The biology teacher's comments about the 'excellent community' and 'those families' in Sheridan in contrast to the African American girl's words in the hallway, while subtle, reflect the local racial common sense shared by many members of the white community in the Petersfield area, as do Mrs Schultz's comments above about who values education. As a result of these choices, informed in part by local, shared, white racial common sense, the Schultz kids, like many of their peers, live and interact in a segregated, white context. They live in predominantly white neighbourhoods, attend predominantly white schools and have exclusively white friends. Living and interacting within this context of childhood, constructed by white parents through choices around schools and neighbourhoods, shapes the ideas that their children form about race.

(NOT) TALKING ABOUT RACE: THE AVERY FAMILY

When asked how they talk to their children about race, most Sheridan parents tell me that 'the conversation has never really come up' or 'we don't really talk about it because it isn't part of our life'. As Mrs Bentley, a mother of three, puts it: 'It's really cool that kids don't think race is a big deal... we as parents try not to say much of anything about it.' Similarly, Mrs Preston, an outgoing mother of two boys, explains to me: 'I tell [my kids], it doesn't matter what color you are, it's really just what your goals are and how hard you work.' Mrs Avery, a nurse, tells me: 'If you asked my daughter about Obama, she doesn't even see the big deal of it! Race just doesn't matter to her. I think that's really wonderful.' Like the Schultzs, the Averys moved to Sheridan for the schools: to 'escape the problems of Petersfield' and for 'the best education possible'. I ask Mrs Avery, while sitting in her large, modern kitchen, if she thinks about the diversity in her children's lives: 'They get *very* little racial diversity in Sheridan... we try to take different opportunities to expose them to different things. I look for those examples to teach them because they are not living it every single day.'

I encourage Mrs Avery to describe some of the opportunities that she has taken to engage with her children in discussions about human difference:

> I tell the kids stories about [how] depend[ing] on the color of your skin, well *The Help*, Alicia and I read the book... I have probably more of a knowledge base about that stuff than Alicia does, but both of us were reading the book, ...and you're just horrified. You're like, 'Oh my god! Seriously? That is what they dealt with?' ... We all went to see the movie... there are parts of it where your mouth is just hanging open because you just can't quite believe what you are seeing..., and [Alicia] will say, 'Oh my gosh, thank god I didn't live then! Thank god we live now where it doesn't really matter what the color of your skin is.'

Mrs Avery acknowledges that her children do not have exposure to much diversity in their daily lives, and she believes that racism has largely ended. I ask Mrs Avery if she ever thinks about being white. She tells me:

> I just think it's a box that I check on a form... I think that's what we have taught our kids too – it doesn't matter whether you are a girl or a boy, it doesn't matter if you are brown, black, blue, purple, um, it's what's inside that counts.

Mrs Avery talks to her kids about race, drawing on dominant colour-blind rhetoric.

Parents' decisions with respect to neighbourhoods, schools and what conversations to have (or not have) with their children reflect their approach to white racial socialization. While Sheridan parents, like Mrs Schultz or Mrs Avery, may not appear on the surface to be engaging in racial socialization with their white kids, the context that they have created shapes the racial common sense that their kids develop. In short, these parents construct a colour-blind racial context of childhood in which race is a 'non-issue' once the context is constructed. Ironically however, racial common sense has played a central role in how that context was initially designed.

Colour-Conscious Approach: The Evergreen Context

NEIGHBOURHOOD AND SCHOOL CHOICES: THE NORTON-SMITH FAMILY

Homes in Evergreen are expensive, eclectic and built very close to one another. Popular public parks are found every few blocks. A few family-run restaurants are within walking distance of these homes, as are yoga studios and a cooperative supermarket. Evergreen is located in close proximity to a neighbourhood that has four times the poverty rate than the rest of the city and is 17 percent black, in comparison with the 4 percent city-wide black population. Evergreen parents report that they value the existence of human difference and want their children to grow up in a diverse space.

The Norton-Smiths live in a large purple Victorian house surrounded by wild flowers; a compost pile and picnic table are in the backyard. Mrs Norton-Smith works as a civil rights attorney and her husband works as an immigration attorney and law professor. Mrs Norton-Smith explains why they chose to live in Evergreen:

> People are here because they want to be in a more open situation where there is an awareness that exposure to people who are not well-off and who come from very different racial backgrounds and who may make you uncomfortable is really important. I like to think that my son is in some kind of position to better negotiate that discomfort... I think that is a really useful sort of skill...

While they joke that they feel like outcasts wearing business suits in their 'earthy-crunchy' neighbourhood, these parents explain that they try to diversify and complicate the racial context in which their children live. Mrs Norton-Smith, like other Evergreen parents, wants her children to feel social discomfort at times, prioritizing diversity over reputation or status:

> I'm not really focused on someone being top of their class, or getting into the best college, or making the most money, or being the most famous, which I feel there is more of that [in Sheridan] and it makes me happy to be here... It is more important that my child knows how to interact with all kinds of people around him.

Similarly, Mr Norton-Smith tells me about the flourishing social activism of Evergreen:

> We liked the idea of what the neighborhood was and the people who lived here... there are a lot of people here who live what they believe. It's totally impressive. They live it in the community, they live it in their own families, they live it individually... that's what this neighborhood means. There is more racial diversity and sexual preference diversity too.

Mrs Norton-Smith describes how 'fortunate' she feels that Evergreen is located in close proximity to a more diverse neighbourhood as this leads to racially and economically integrated public schools – 'a rare occurrence in America', she tells me while we cook dinner together one evening.

While some worry about the cost of living in Evergreen and the relatively few people of colour living there, respondents still view this community as diverse. Janet McMillan, mother of one daughter and an environmentalist, tells me:

> I like that my daughter sees black people in our house and on our street. We have friends who are black, and we have friends who have adopted from Ethiopia and another neighbor from Guatemala.

And you know, in this area, there's a fair number of gay and lesbian couples so she's used to seeing that. It's just integrated into her life.

Almost all of the Evergreen families tell me that they choose to live here and to send their children to the affiliated public schools deliberately because they want more opportunities for their kids to engage with human diversity for purposes of social activism.

TALKING ABOUT RACE: THE NORTON-SMITH FAMILY

Mr and Mrs Norton-Smith explain their everyday approach to talking about race with their kids:

I think recognizing people's differences and backgrounds is really important... I want [our son] to be an empathetic human being as he goes through the world, and in order to do that, you have to appreciate what someone else's experience might be vis-à-vis yours. Conor is a white male from a privileged household and he needs to be very cognizant of that so we talk about race and gender a lot.

Conor, a superb trombone player, goes to an integrated, well-funded public middle school in Petersfield, has 'equal-status' friends who are black and Latino, and participates in interracial social activities and extracurriculars regularly. The Norton-Smiths also participate in the programme Big Brothers Big Sisters, through which they have been paired with a black child for over five years:

Mrs Norton-Smith: It's not always easy to talk about race... one of the things we did was... participate in the Big Brothers Big Sisters program. We have a partner in that and she is a part of our family. This brings up a lot of questions of inequality and race... we talk about that a lot with the kids.

Mrs Norton-Smith continues to describe how she talks about race with her son:

He's aware when certain arenas are dominated by certain people. That's not lost on him. So why try to be subtle? ... We will get questions from him like, 'Why are basketball teams predominantly black?' or 'Why are there so many black homeless guys on Main Street?' They are asking because they notice... you can't just be like, 'Huh, isn't that funny.' No. It's serious. So we talk about it.

Beyond talking openly about injustice, these parents push their kids towards social action. As Mr Norton-Smith tells me: 'You can't really be content until other people have the same opportunities you have and you gotta be somebody in that space. You can't just feel bad. You gotta *do* something.'

Other Evergreen parents 'call out' their children when they think the kids are 'dissing someone or a group of people'. As Celia Marshall, artist and mother of two, tells me: 'Of course my kid is racist! And I'm going to try to call him out when he needs it! Even if that makes him uncomfortable.'

These families also travel internationally to experience different cultures. They talk frequently about politics and 'help the kids understand the world'. As parents, their goal is to expose their children to human diversity as a means of encouraging their kids' critical thinking about and recognition of privilege. This colour-conscious racial context that they work to create also offers the potential for, but does not guarantee, implicit racial socialization, including lessons on how to operate in diverse spaces and what it feels like to experience social discomfort.

Part of constructing a colour-conscious racial context also includes continuous intervention. Mr Norton-Smith, on the sidelines of his son's football game, worries about the messages that his son is interpreting:

I remember him articulating confusion and asking questions like, 'Why is it that it's always the black kids that are getting in trouble?' And we had to talk through that. So I have an awareness that this is what he is learning. That black equals getting in trouble.

He goes on to tell me that he prompts open conversations with his son because 'it's better to have real conversations about difficult subjects than to avoid them altogether. That's how ignorance forms.' Other parents echo these concerns, worrying about the lack of black teachers and administrators as well as what associations between black families and poor families their children are forming at school. Overall, Evergreen parents construct a colour-conscious context through school and neighbourhood choices, although they also intervene on a daily basis when their children articulate ideas about race that parents perceive to be problematic.

Despite their commitment to equality, white Evergreen families continue to maintain an incredibly privileged status within their community as the result of individual behaviours as well as structural conditions. While some parents intentionally supplement gaps in public schooling, they all send their kids to integrated schools with students who have unequal lives, and kids likely play an active role in enacting privilege at school. These Evergreen observations parallel other school-based research findings that many white parents who are committed to integrated, urban public schools tend to 'rule the school', pushing their own agendas while ignoring the voices of minority parents (Lewis 2003; Noguera 2008; Posey 2012), as well as research on how private businesses and policymakers seek to retain middle-class families in urban schools, valuing them more highly than their working-class or poor peers (Cucchiara 2013).

The colour-conscious context that parents in Evergreen construct is thus distinct from, and in some ways more complex than, the colour-blind context constructed by parents in Sheridan. On the one hand, colour-conscious parents construct contexts that are more diverse, they speak openly to their children about privilege, they intervene constantly and they are socially active. On the other hand, many of these parents are faced with a structural conundrum of privilege – even when they want to teach their kids to recognize and fight against injustice, how much commitment is enough, especially when this commitment implicates their own children's futures or includes elements perceived to be beyond their control?

Parents living in Evergreen use a colour-conscious approach to white racial socialization, and they acknowledge that they do so. Evergreen parents have chosen to live in Evergreen and to send their kids to the local racially diverse public school, although they contemplate the politics of these choices regularly. They believe that it is important to teach their privileged kids about the existence of social hierarchies so these parents talk openly to their children about inequality.

Choices that parents make about neighbourhoods and schools influence not only the reproduction of various forms of inequality, but also the process of childhood racial socialization. My data show that living and interacting within these two different contexts leads white children to talk about and make sense of race differently. This is not to suggest that parents directly dictate the racial views of their children; rather, parents use their resources to construct different racial contexts of white childhood, and children ultimately form their own ideas based on their interpretations of these contexts and the experiences that they have within them. Thus, the social reproduction of ideas about race is an active, bidirectional socialization process. Still, growing up in these two different contexts produces differences in white children's ideas about race.

Kids' Voices

'IS RACISM A PROBLEM?'

Existing research demonstrates that white children who spend time in segregated, white spaces do not notice their whiteness (Lewis 2001; Perry 2001; Lewis 2003). I found the same for Sheridan children. For instance, this common experience occurred while interviewing an otherwise enthusiastic 12-year-old:

MAGGIE: Do you think racism is a problem in your school?
CHARLOTTE: No. Not at all.
MAGGIE: Do you think that racism is a problem in America?
CHARLOTTE: Nope.

When I ask 11-year-old Jacob Avery the same question, his response is: 'Well, I don't really know because, [it's] not where I live, but... I mean, isn't the KKK still around?' While Jacob does not entirely agree that the USA is racism-free, he identifies racism as existing only within certain communities, and certainly not his own. Charlotte, Jacob and many of their Sheridan peers do not see racism in their lives and have no reason to believe that racism exists. This is what they learn through subtle and implicit interactions within the racial context that their parents have constructed. Exceptions to this are found in the data, especially when Sheridan kids insist that they have observed acts of racism; however, this important discussion is beyond the scope of this chapter.

When I ask the same question to kids in Evergreen, I receive a much different response:

CONOR: I think [racism] is a *way* bigger problem than people realize. It's nowhere near what it used to be… it's just different and white people don't realize it… I think it's still there. It's just not as present and people want to hide it. Because they are scared to talk about it.

Conor not only speaks to the invisibility of racism to white people but recognizes that his peers are scared to talk about race for fear that they might 'mess up'. The complexity of his response is largely a result of the context of childhood that his parents have constructed. He attends a middle school that is racially and economically diverse, he speaks openly with his parents about inequality and he has meaningful relationships with people of colour.

Children growing up in colour-conscious contexts are better able to identify and discuss what they perceive to be acts of racism in their daily lives. Lindsay, for example, a football star and pianist, tells me a story about her teacher and her black friend Ronnie:

My third grade teacher was racist… she kept making fun of this one kid who was my friend Ronnie. He's my buddy… he didn't really do well in school… she would hold up his work and then make fun of it in front of the whole class… And she would yell at him… she only did that kind of thing to *that* race! … One time, he was late to school. It was in the middle of winter, and so him and his brother were getting yelled at. … I overheard… them say that the bus never came, so they had to walk to school… they didn't have any boots, so their shoes were all wet, and they didn't really have coats.

When Lindsay told her parents about what she was observing at school, her parents talked openly about what Lindsay perceived as 'racist' and took subsequent action.

Children growing up with colour-conscious racial socialization more frequently think about their own behaviour in racialized terms. Ten-year-old Sam, who loves debating current events, tells me:

[We] were at the beach and… there were a bunch of people who looked like they were Hispanic… they were wearing gangster-kind-of-looking clothes, they were drinking alcohol… [My friend] Brian was going, 'Sam, we have to leave *now*' and so we biked for while… eventually we were able to get away… afterwards we were saying, 'Oh my god, that was the scariest thing ever' and we were going into all these different things like [if they would] attack us…. Brian was like, 'Maybe they're just trying to see how racist we are.' I was like, 'Really?' He said, 'If you think about it, you're not going to be as threatened by people who are white wearing gangster outfits, drinking alcohol' … and I thought about that for awhile and I guess it kind of made sense but it just didn't really feel right to think that that made sense because it doesn't really make sense. But at the same time it does.

The conversation between the two white boys leads to Sam's recognition of what he believed to be racism within himself. He tells me that he discussed this incident with both his parents. Clearly, in Sam's world, talking openly about race with other white people and being aware of his own racial biases is part of his socialization experience.

Finally, I observed a marked difference in the way that children from these two contexts of childhood use immigration and the police as evidence for the non-existence or continued existence of racism, which reflects differences in how these children think about race. Eleven-year-old Ryan, who lives in Sheridan and loves snowboarding, explains:

I think we have moved beyond [racism]. But like, uh, but like down on the Mexican and American border, I think it is wrong to let illegal immigrants come in without having a green card and steal our money. We work hard in America. They can't just come here and be lazy and take it. But for racism, yes, I think as a country we have moved beyond it.

Ryan uses anti-immigration rhetoric in order to displace any possibility of continued racial conflict onto non-whites. When I ask Conor the same question, he also brings up immigration, but he attributes responsibility for racial conflict to policies drafted and enforced by whites:

In Arizona, I know they passed a law that you have to... carry around your photo ID or something and police, they're always stopping Latinos because they don't believe that they're Americans. They believe that they're illegal immigrants but really they're just picking on people that are a different race... I think it's really wrong and racist.

These statements come from two boys who are very similar but have been exposed to different racial contexts of childhood. And while these boys are both recipients of structural white privilege, they are constructing distinct ideological understandings of race and privilege. Similarly, other Evergreen children tell me that 'police are more aggressive toward black people' and that 'white kids... have more power... so disciplinary actions aren't brought down as hard upon them', while Sheridan children comment that 'people of all races get in trouble equally'.

'DOES BEING WHITE GIVE YOU ANY ADVANTAGES IN SOCIETY?'

Unlike colour-blind ideology that makes whiteness invisible and normalized, colour-conscious racial logic urges children to recognize their white privilege and connect it to other forms of privilege. For example, 12-year-old Ben, who lives in Evergreen and is a member of a debate team, compares white privilege to male privilege: '[Being white] gives you an advantage! Just like gender, you'll get an advantage just by being a white male rather than a black female.' Eleven-year-old Chris, while playing chess with me, explains: 'I think [white people] just kind of have the upside... much of society is run by white people... like, you know, if you look at the CEOs of oil companies, they're all white men.'

These boys recognize that systems of privilege intersect with one another, a strikingly distinct finding compared to responses from Sheridan children, whose answers to this question are uniform and straightforward: 'No.'

While many of the kids in Sheridan articulate the core beliefs of the American dream, associating hard work with upward social mobility, many kids in Evergreen are sceptical of the rags to riches story. As Sarah tells me: 'If you're black and your ancestors were slaves back then, you *never* really got a chance to like sit upon a large sum of money.... I would easily say 99.9999% of the upper class are probably white.' Chris also discusses the challenges to social mobility: 'Look at the oil tycoons, they don't even like do anything! They just sit there and be a face. So I don't think it's hard work as much as luck almost and just kind of... where you start out.' When I ask Chris what race he thinks most 'oil tycoons' are, he says, without hesitation, 'white'.

IMPLICATIONS AND FUTURE DIRECTIONS

Given the differences found in the racial logic of child participants, this study suggests that the reproduction of white privilege at the ideological level is connected to the racial context in which kids live and interact, especially in middle childhood. Parents design contexts that are racialized differently; kids produce multifarious ideas about race as a result of interacting within these contexts. While this study makes no claims about generalizability of findings, given the documented predominance of colour-blind ideology, as well as patterns of severe racial segregation in the USA, it would follow that the way that children in Sheridan are learning about race is more common than that of the Evergreen kids. Future studies ought to examine the prevalence of these approaches to racial socialization.

Findings from this research also challenge assertions made by the white racism literature that suggest that all white children, like sponges, adopt hegemonic ideological racial views. This study illustrates the variation in white children's racial common sense, demonstrating that kids participate in their own socialization through interactions within a racial context, a view on the social reproduction of ideology that includes children's agency. This agency is important when considering how ideological positions on race can be reworked rather than reproduced, which has significant implications for launching challenges against the racial status quo. Future research ought to evaluate the extent to which white children who adopt these counter-hegemonic ideological positions in middle childhood retain them as they grow throughout the life course.

While none of the Evergreen children are literally dismantling racism, their ideas suggest that a link can be found between how white children construct racial ideas and the racial context in which they interact. Racial ideologies are one 'mechanis[m] responsible for the reproduction of racial privilege in a society' (Bonilla-Silva 2006, 9). Thus, children with colour-conscious racial views possess the rhetorical tools and agency necessary to challenge and rework dominant racial ideology, demonstrating the participatory role that children play in social change and hopeful possibilities for future racial justice.

REFERENCES

Bonilla-Silva, Eduardo. 2006. *Racism without Racists: Color-Blind Racism and the Persistence of Racial Inequality in America.* Lanham, MD: Rowman & Littlefield.

Cucchiara, Maia. 2013. *Marketing Schools, Marketing Cities: Who Wins and Who Loses When Schools Become Urban Amenities.* Chicago, IL: University of Chicago Press.

Lewis, Amanda E. 2001. "There Is No 'Race' in the Schoolyard: Color-Blind Ideology in an (Almost) All-White School." *American Educational Research Journal* 38 (4): 781–811.

Lewis, Amanda E. 2003. *Race in the Schoolyard: Negotiating the Color Line in Classrooms and Communities.* New Brunswick, NJ: Rutgers University Press.

Noguera, Pedro. 2008. *The Trouble with Black Boys… and Other Reflections on Race, Equity and the Future of Public Education.* San Francisco, CA: Jossey-Bass.

Perry, Pamela. 2001. "'White Means Never Having to Say You're Ethnic': White Youth and the Construction of "Cultureless" Identities." *Journal of Contemporary Ethnography* 30 (1): 56–91. doi:10.1177/089124101030001002.

Posey, Linn. 2012. "Middle and Upper Middle Class Parent Action: Promise or Paradox?" *Teachers College Record* 114 (1): 1–43.

41

When "Helicopters" Go to School

Who Gets Rescued and Who Gets Left Behind?

Jessica Calarco

We've all read about – and maybe even known – the "helicopter" parents who sweep into K-12 schools, demanding special treatment for their children, second-guessing teachers' grades or comments, and insisting that schools adapt to their child's unique needs. Teachers complain that these parents are "always rescuing their kids," hovering over them and "making sure everything is done for them."

As one elementary school teacher wrote in an "open letter" to "helicopter" parents,

> I love you, I do. But some of the things you do drive me nuts and are really bad for your kid! …Please, let them do their own work. Let them make mistakes and learn from them. Teach them hard work, success and failure.

In an online magazine for teachers, fifth-grade teacher Abigail Courter warned that parents may be "educators' greatest assets" but they are also "at times, our biggest nemesis," especially when they set their children up for failure by not teaching them how to cope with setbacks.

Yet whatever the long-term risks may be, "helicopter" parenting can give kids an edge in the tight race for "elite" college admissions and "elite" professional jobs. Most "helicopter" parents are highly educated, affluent white mothers who intervene because they want their children to grow up to be highly educated and affluent as well. "Helicopter" parents send their children to "high-quality" schools – schools whose reputation for academic rigor will help their children get into an elite college. But they do not shrink from undermining that rigor when it comes to their own children. They lobby for their children's admittance to "gifted" programs and Advanced Placement (AP) courses even when they don't qualify. They resist their children being punished when they break the rules. They demand that their children be given higher grades even when they didn't earn them and press for letters of recommendation to elite colleges even when their children weren't offered those on their own merits.

Now, it's clear why "helicopter" parents have an interest in giving their children an edge in school. What's less clear, though, is why schools are willing to let those parents give their children that edge at the expense of other children in school. Most educators honestly believe in equal treatment – and equal consequences – for all their students. So why do so many schools end up catering to privileged "helicopter" parents and

Calarco, Jessica. "When 'Helicopters' Go to School: Who Gets Rescued and Who Gets Left Behind?" *CCF News*, March 1, 2020.

their children, even when it goes against what teachers believe is best for students and undermines a school's commitment to fair and equal treatment of students?

To answer this question, I spent three years observing and interviewing teachers, administrators, parents, and students at a socioeconomically diverse, public elementary school I call Maplewood (research-related regulations require that I protect the privacy and anonymity of my participants by not disclosing their names or the name of the school). In doing so, I found that:

To achieve or maintain a reputation as "high-quality," schools rely on privileged "helicopter" parents for tax dollars, donations, and volunteer hours. "Helicopter" parents (especially higher-SES, white, stay-at-home and part-time-employed mothers) are often the mainstay of the unpaid volunteer labor force that schools must rely on to provide quality instruction and activities. As a result, teachers use special favors and strategic rule exemptions to avoid conflict with such parents and keep on their good side.

- Teachers told me they want to enforce rules but worry that doing so will lead privileged "helicopter" parents to make trouble for them with higher-ups in the administration. As fourth-grade teacher Ms. Russo explained:

    Edward [a higher-SES white student] forgets his homework. And so I tell [Edward's mother] that Edward will have to stay in for recess. And she writes back, [including the principal in the email, saying]: "I really believe that recess is a time for them to run around. I don't believe in staying in." [And the principal conceded]. So Edward has no consequences. If something happens, he'll go home and tell mom, and she'll write an email to the principal. And she's threatening with words like "advocate," "lawyer," all these things. And because [Edward's mother is] saying that, because she's using the fear factor – has Edward stayed in for recess? No. He hasn't had to face those consequences.

- Even without pressure from school administrators, teachers recognize that failure to meet the demands of entitled "helicopter" parents will jeopardize the help they get from such parents. As third-grade teacher Ms. Filipelli explained:

    At Maplewood, I get lots of emails. Daily emails. A lot of emails. There's been one parent [a higher-SES, white mother], she's… oh my goodness. It's like I need a secretary to be dealing with all these emails. But I know those parents love their children. And those are the parents that help. So, if they have questions, I'm going to answer them. And you might find someone else complaining about it, but at [the lower-SES school where I used to teach], I never had any support. I would have, like, one parent helping. So, bring it on! I'm just happy to have the support.

In consequence, teachers tend to grant the special favors and rule exemptions that privileged "helicopter" parents desire, even when they believe those actions will be detrimental to students. Meanwhile, when less privileged students and students with less involved parents break the rules, teachers regularly keep them in for recess, reprimand them in front of their peers, take off points on their assignments, and evaluate them less favorably.

- Fifth-grade teacher Mr. Fischer, for example, knew that Ms. Becker, a higher-SES white mother, was doing her son Nate's homework for him, noting that she tended to *"over-manage"* everything Nate did, limiting Nate's ability to develop any *"independence."* But Mr. Fischer did not try to stop the practice. Nor did he subject Nate to any punishment or grade deductions for failing to do the homework on his own.

- When higher-SES white student Drew, whose mother was highly involved in the PTO, forgot to do a language arts project, his fifth-grade teacher Ms. Hudson told him: "Don't worry about it," adding "That's what responsibility gets you. There's a trust, okay?" Yet when Cody, a lower-SES, mixed-race student whose parents were not visibly involved in school, read the wrong section of the book for homework, Ms. Hudson kept him in for recess, cutting off his explanation and saying sharply: "Well, the first thing is to make sure you have the assignment right. That's responsibility."

POLICY IMPLICATIONS

Inadequate and unequal funding for public education makes schools dependent on higher-SES "helicopter" parents to achieve or maintain a reputation as "high-quality" schools. When schools can rely on those parents' tax dollars, donations, volunteer hours, and support for students at home, they can provide the kinds of school environments – high test scores, small class sizes, ample materials, experienced teachers, enrichment courses, extracurricular activities, and state-of-the-art facilities and technologies – that most parents (especially higher-SES white "helicopter" parents) desire.

Since such amenities are not standard educational entitlements, schools are dependent on privileged "helicopter" parents to attain them, and that dependence routinely leads schools to capitulate to those parents' demands. The result is a vicious cycle. The schools' reliance on "helicopter" parents sustains the enrichment activities that create a first-class learning environment, but it also allows such parents to game the system for their children, thereby reinforcing successes that may be the result of *special treatment* rather than *special merit*.

Adequate and equitably distributed school funding (particularly if coupled with redistribution of funds raised by Parent-Teacher Organizations) has the potential to reduce schools' dependence on higher-SES "helicopter" parents. Those resources would allow schools to offer high-quality opportunities and amenities for students without the need for support from privileged parents. They would also alleviate pressure on parents (especially mothers) to provide "helicopter"-like support for students both at home and in school.

42

Missing School Is a Given for Children of Migrant Farmworkers

Aggie Ebrahimi Bazaz

In the summer of his junior year, Luis Miguel was struggling to stay in high school. He and his family of four – who work various agricultural jobs from picking blueberries and cherries to pruning grapes and canning tomatoes – live in one of California's 24 migrant family housing centers.

As a documentary filmmaker, I have been studying these housing centers and the rhythms of life for families who reside in them since I first arrived in a center in 2014 during fieldwork for an oral history project with former *bracero* farmworkers.

Tucked in the shadows of county jails and water treatment plants, these centers provide tile-floored apartments at subsidized rents to migratory farmworkers and their families during peak harvest season. The centers house as many as 1,890 farmworking families, mostly from Mexico.

Given California's affordable housing shortage, these housing centers are a coveted option for farmworking families. Outside the housing centers, migrant farmworkers might reside in less favorable conditions – sleeping in cars, garages, old motels or under tarps in the fields.

But while the centers resolve the affordable housing problem, they create another: second-class citizenship.

STATE-MANDATED ANNUAL MOVE

A 2016 survey of the housing centers noted that more than half the families residing in centers across the state – 1,037 families to be exact – have school-aged children, many of whom, like Luis Miguel's sister, are natural-born US citizens.

In late fall or early winter when harvest season ends, families must vacate their apartments and move at least 50 miles away for three to six months. The rationale behind this rule is to ensure that the housing serves families who are truly migratory.

Most families cannot afford unsubsidized housing in California and thus spend the off-season months in their Mexican hometowns. While in Mexico, the youth either miss school or attend inconsistently. "It all

Bazaz, Aggie Ebrahimi. "Missing school is a given for children of migrant farmworkers" *The Conversation*, April 26, 2019.

depends where the students live," Migrant Education Program counselor Laura Aguayo says. "Some students don't have a chance because they live too far away from a school. Others can't go because the schools don't take them in." This is because they will only be enrolled for a couple of months before they return to the United States, she says.

This means that each year, school-aged children living with their families in California's migrant family housing centers, many of whom are U.S. citizens, miss between three and six months of schooling.

"Moving Makes Things Complicated"

Migrant education counselors, administrators and teachers try to help migrant students make up whatever academic credits they're missing. But "moving makes things complicated," says Luis Miguel. "We lose a lot of time, and it's hard to concentrate."

The summer of his junior year, Luis Miguel got so discouraged by the routine of moves and having to make up credits that he lost motivation and began to veer off the path to graduation. To help students like Luis Miguel make up credits, California has developed an online program called Cyber High.

But Cyber High has its own issues. "There are a lot of internet problems," Aguayo explains. "All the schools in California are using Cyber High so the system slows down. Students can be taking a test and it kicks them out."

Impact of Annual Migration on Student Achievement

The move also makes it hard for students to succeed in the kinds of extracurricular activities that can make students more attractive to colleges.

While in high school, Luis Miguel had joined cross-country to work with the coach, Rick Cuevas, who is himself Mexican-born and the child of a farmworker. Coach Cuevas understands the students better than almost anyone, calls them "mihija" or "mihijo," Spanish terms for "my daughter" or "my son," respectively.

"Running changed my life," Luis Miguel says. "Before running, I never thought about my future. And now that I run, I take things more seriously." But he ruminates on losing his conditioning. "I wanted to be the best, but moving makes it complicated because I can't go to all the practices," Luis Miguel adds.

It's not hard to see how missing a few months of school each year disadvantages students. The Modesto Bee reports 74 percent of migrant students "were not meeting English language standards and 80% were not up to par in math" in the 2016–2017 academic year.

Parent interviews across migrant family housing centers also speak to the impact of the moves. For instance, in a 2014 survey of migrant farmworkers conducted at Buena Vista, Ochoa, Parlier and Williams migrant housing centers by the advocacy group Human Agenda, 91.4 percent of farmworkers answered "yes" to "Does the 50-mile rule affect your children's education?"

"What gets farmworkers out of bed in the morning, six days a week at 5 a.m. to work in the fields for 10 hours a day is the dream that their children will have a better life," Ann López of the Center for Farmworker Families says. "But the 50-mile regulation impedes that possibility."

López is a leading member of Apoyo Campesino, a collective within Human Agenda comprised of researchers, lawyers and organizers who have for years advocated to end the 50-mile regulation.

This group's efforts got the ear of the California legislature, and in June 2018, then-Gov. Jerry Brown signed a provision in the state budget exempting up to 50 percent of the farmworking families living in each center from the 50-mile regulation.

Under this new provision, families must still vacate their apartments each year and search for short-term affordable housing. But "immediate family members of the migratory agricultural worker" are exempted from the 50-mile rule. This means that Luis Miguel and his family will continue to be required to move out of the housing center annually, but he and his sister can stay within their school districts with one parent, while the other parent must live at least 50 miles away for three months.

CRAFTING A SENSE OF BELONGING

In May 2018, driving Luis Miguel to graduation rehearsal, I asked him how he got out of that junior year funk. Without hesitation, he smiled and said, "Coach Cuevas."

Luis Miguel now studies at Modesto Community College, though he's had to stop running so he can focus on his studies. He continues to live at one of the housing centers with his family during the harvest season. This year, thanks to the new regulations, he and his sister are spending the off-season in an RV in the backyard of an extended family member.

Luis Miguel's story demonstrates that despite their many challenges, some students living in these housing centers are graduating from high schools and even colleges.

Such successes can be made easier when housing authorities foster partnerships with local schools. The high school that Luis Miguel attended, East Union in Manteca Unified School District, for example, accommodates the migration schedules of students by offering an earlier final exam in December. According to the school, in the 2016–2017 academic year, 100 percent of migrant students graduated. While such institutional supports have a positive impact, East Union President Raul Mora, who himself is Chicano, worries they might also send an unhealthy message to students that "they don't quite fit the mold."

For Mora, nurturing achievement among migrant students requires fostering a sense of belonging. Since starting as principal at East Union in 2015, Mora has placed at least one Spanish-speaking administrator in each of the school's three main offices. "It's about creating a belief system and a culture," Mora says. "It's making sure that when the students come back and see our registrar, that she welcomes them in their language."

Despite these efforts at cultural sensitivity and holistic education, students in migratory conditions are still called "camp kids" or terms even more derogatory by their peers – potentially fueling the belief that they don't belong.

But inside a two-bedroom apartment at the migrant family housing center, Luis Miguel and two friends craft their own sense of belonging. Together, they formed a hip-hop trio, 95231 Productions.

The group reflects on their experiences growing up as the children of farmworking parents, their struggles against racism and their work to craft an identity that reflects their heritage. In a page in his lyrics notebook, the front cover adorned with a colorful *calavera*, Luis Miguel writes: "Soy de piel moreno. Orgulloso Mexicano, y brown pride de corazon, y en el corazon llevo al inmigrante trabajador" – "I am Brown, proud Mexicano, brown pride of the heart, and in my heart I carry the immigrant laborer."

43

Stigma Management among Children of Incarcerated Parents

Kate Luther

Introduction

Incarceration is a stigmatizing experience. The stigma reflects societal ideas about who criminals are thought to be—whether that be unethical, untrustworthy, or dangerous—and follows felons post-incarceration in their transition to mainstream society. The stigma of a criminal record and/or incarceration extends beyond the criminal and can "spoil" (Goffman 1963) the identities of their family members. Children of incarcerated parents, who may not have committed any delinquent or criminal behaviors themselves, can still be stigmatized by parental law-breaking behavior and imprisonment.

Although researchers have documented the "courtesy stigma" (Goffman 1963) associated with parental incarceration, we know very little about how these children manage their spoiled identity. Framed by scholarship on courtesy stigma and stigma management, I explore the techniques used by adult children of incarcerated parents to manage the "mark" of parental incarceration. I seek to understand how children of incarcerated parents, who do not want to follow the criminal paths of their parents, manage the stigma to support an identity-in-contrast, which can also be called a prosocial or conventional identity.

To investigate these topics, I conducted in-depth interviews with 32 college students who experienced parental incarceration during childhood. Although many children of incarcerated parents may experience and manage stigma, I chose to only study those working toward educational goals because little is known about resilient populations of children with incarcerated parents. Furthermore, this sampling choice allowed me to investigate children of incarcerated parents whose current life trajectories are different from those of their parents and may necessitate stigma management techniques.

The Experience of Parental Incarceration

Over 1.7 million children under the age of 18 have a parent incarcerated in state or federal prison and this experience can disrupt children's lives in numerous ways. They may undergo changes with their primary caregivers and living situations. During parental incarceration children may face barriers, such as a lack

Luther, Kate. "Stigma Management among Children of Incarcerated Parents." *Deviant Behavior* 37, no. 11 (2016): 1264–1275.

of transportation to prison or support from caregivers, to maintaining a relationship with their parents. Children can encounter further problems during the post-release process of reuniting with their formerly incarcerated parents.

We know this population also experiences other forms of disadvantage. Adverse childhood experiences, which include, but are not limited to, living with individuals who commit crime, abuse substances, or suffer from mental illness, co-occur. Likewise, the families of these children of incarcerated parents commonly face economic disadvantage. Thus, it may not just be that parental incarceration relates to adverse outcomes; instead, additional challenges may intensify the experience of parental incarceration.

Consequently, there is an association between having an incarcerated parent and increased risk in multiple areas. Researchers find that parental incarceration is related to negative outcomes including aggression (Geller et al. 2009), behavioral difficulties in school (Hanlon et al. 2005), and antisocial behavior (Murray, Farrington, and Sekol 2012). One of the most concerning areas of research on this topic is the risk of future incarceration. Specifically, scholars identify a relationship between parental incarceration and subsequent delinquency (Kjellstrand and Eddy 2011) and contact with the criminal justice system (Huebner and Gustafson 2007). This increased risk of future law breaking behavior may contribute to the stigma associated with being a child of an incarcerated parent. In particular, their stigma may result from the assumption that they will become delinquent or criminal "just like their parents."

COURTESY STIGMA AND STIGMA MANAGEMENT

In addition to the aforementioned difficulties, children may be stigmatized by parental criminality and/or incarceration. Goffman (1963) argued that stigma is not contained only in the individual with the spoiled identity; instead, it can extend beyond to those around them. Using an example of a daughter of an incarcerated father, Goffman wrote that a type of "wise person"— his term for someone who is close to a stigmatized person and understands their situation to some degree—is one whose relationship to a stigmatized individual "leads the wider society to treat both individuals in some respects as one" (p. 30). In particular, he used the term "courtesy stigma" to refer to the stigma that is placed on individuals who are not deviant themselves.

Supporting the concept of courtesy stigma, qualitative researchers have found that parental incarceration can stigmatize children. For children of incarcerated parents, they may become "guilty by association" and "fear being identified as 'just like your Dad/Mom' by both family and outsiders" (Adalist-Estrin 2006:7). These findings are supported by other scholars and illustrate how the stigma of criminality and/or incarceration can move beyond the individual who committed the law-breaking acts to their family members.

Existing research on courtesy stigma management has primarily concentrated on parents, caregivers, and service providers of stigmatized individuals who are viewed as being responsible to some degree for the source of the stigma or the care of the stigmatized person. Barton (1991) found that parents engaged in impression management and information control in response to the courtesy stigma associated with their children's drug abuse. Likewise, Koro-Ljungberg and Bussing (2009) found that parents of children with attention deficit hyperactivity disorder (ADHD) managed their courtesy stigma by minimizing and normalizing ADHD, avoiding interaction with certain groups, and even politicizing the stigma to make change in the school system. In contrast to these populations, children of incarcerated parents are not thought to be responsible for parental criminality or care. Therefore, they may engage in stigma management techniques that are distinct from other populations with a courtesy stigma.

METHODS

To study stigma management among children of incarcerated parents, I chose to interview college students whose parents had been incarcerated during their childhoods. Although all children of incarcerated parents may engage in identity work associated with the stigma of parental incarceration, it is especially interesting to consider this process for those on a path at odds with a criminal future[1] because it may be especially necessary for them to distance themselves from their parents. By examining college students with incarcerated parents, which is only one of many prosocial populations of children of incarcerated parents (e.g., technical school students, military members, employees), I was able to explore how they managed their stigma to sustain a prosocial identity.

To be eligible for the study, participants needed to be college students who experienced parental (biological, step, or adoptive) incarceration for a period of at least six months prior to the age of 18. Although having an incarcerated stepparent may be a different experience than a biological/adoptive parent, I allowed for stepparents because they could still alter the stability of the family and cause the child to be stigmatized. I also chose a minimal period of six months of incarceration[2] to ensure that the parental absence was long enough to potentially disrupt the family's functioning. Finally, all participants had to be over the age of 18 at the time of the interview.

I interviewed 32 adult children of incarcerated parents. Ninety-one percent of participants experienced the incarceration of a biological parent. Most (72 percent) incarcerated parents were fathers or stepfathers; only three participants had an incarcerated mother and six participants had both their mother and father incarcerated. Of the sample, 13 attended community college, 15 attended four-year universities, and four were graduate students. The majority (81 percent) went to colleges in the Pacific Northwest. Participants ranged in age from 18 to 39 with a mean age of 23.38 years. Furthermore, my sample consisted of 20 females and 12 males. Of this sample, 14 participants were white, 12 were black, four were Latino, and two were biracial.

During the interview, I asked participants what they knew and felt comfortable sharing about their parent's incarceration. Although there was great variability in the type of crimes (e.g., wire fraud, assault, domestic violence, theft, and attempted murder) their parents committed, almost half ($n = 15$) indicated their parent was incarcerated for drug-related reasons. Participants also estimated the length of their parent's incarceration. This was difficult for some participants to do, as they were children at the time, but their estimates ranged from 6 months to 13 years of incarceration prior to their 18th birthdays. On average, parents were incarcerated for three years during their childhood.[3] Four participants, who knew their parents were incarcerated for more than six months at a time, were not included in this calculation; they indicated that the constant "in- and-out" of jail/prison made it difficult for them to determine the specific length of incarceration.

FINDINGS

This sample of children of incarcerated parents understood they had been marked by their parents' criminal behavior and/or incarceration. Their awareness of the stigma associated with parental incarceration was especially apparent when almost every participant indicated they did not readily share this information in their social circles. When asked why, participants responded with answers such as: "I didn't really tell very many people why my father was gone or what he was gone for because I felt like I would be judged because I'm related to him" (Autumn; father incarcerated for second-degree murder[4]) and "I just kind of keep it to myself so I don't have that extra judgment towards me" (Gabriella; father incarcerated for drug-related charges). These quotes highlight the stigma management technique of passing, which was common among participants. Furthermore, Malcolm (father incarcerated for robbery) articulated the significance of this courtesy stigma: "you'll be the apple off the tree." Thus, participants felt parental incarceration reflected negatively on them.

When discussing who would stigmatize them, participants' answers ranged from their peers and community members during childhood, to their current college classmates or someone they encountered in a professional environment... In general, parental incarceration was viewed as a stigmatizing experience and participants believed they could be negatively perceived based on the behavior of their parents.

These adult children of incarcerated parents found ways to overcome their spoiled identity. In particular, they managed stigma and sustained a prosocial identity in three ways: (1) by separating themselves from their incarcerated parent, (2) by viewing their incarcerated parent as a role model, and (3) by framing their parent's incarceration positively.

Separating from Incarcerated Parents

The first technique used by participants was to separate themselves from their incarcerated parents. In these cases, this commonly included physical separation (e.g., not having contact with them) and/or emotional separation (e.g., not being emotionally connected with them). This idea of separation followed the associational distancing Snow and Anderson (1987) observed in their research on homeless individuals. They wrote: "since one's claim to a particular self is partly contingent on the imputed social identities of one's associates, one way to substantiate that claim, in the event that one's associates are negatively evaluated, is to distance oneself from them" (p. 1349). In the present study, some participants worked to fully distance themselves from their incarcerated parent. Other participants selected to only distance themselves from their parents' criminal behavior, which still allowed them to be viewed as a good parent. The majority of participants who used this technique were elementary school aged or younger when their parents were first incarcerated. This might be the result of participants experiencing parental incarceration at a young age when: (1) they lacked control over staying in contact with their parents; and (2) in some cases, stepparents replaced their biological parents.

The first category of participants separated themselves from their parents completely. They did not view their incarcerated parents as good parents and through the interviews it was clear they had worked to fully distance themselves from their parents. Hannah shared that her father (incarcerated for a drug-related offense) was "kind of like a stranger" and Maya (mother currently incarcerated for attempted murder, kidnapping, and assault) explained that she tells people: "I'm over my mom and they don't understand. They're like 'when do you go see your mom? Why don't you go?' and I'm like 'cuz [sic] I'm over it." By viewing their incarcerated parent as someone they were not connected with, they were able to support a distinct identity from their law-breaking parent.

Many of these participants made purposeful language choices to highlight their distance from this parent. In one case, Dominic expressed these concerns:

> as of now it's not gonna be a father-son relationship. It's just gonna be a, you know, conversation on the phone. … I would say he's a father, not a dad. Like, I don't know, I don't know if he's gonna be a dad ever.

He understood his biological ties to his father, who is currently incarcerated for arson, but their connection did not extend into the "dad" category. Dominic also recounted how his mother and older brother filled the absence of his father. Similarly, Serena remarked that she would not call her biological mother "mom." Although this made her biological mother upset, Serena viewed her grandmother as her mother because she raised her while her biological mother was committing drug-related offenses. Another participant, Julian, commonly referred to his father (incarcerated for domestic violence, driving under the influence and detained for immigration-related issues) as "the drunk" and with much emotion shared:

> I don't like my dad. I don't like him at all. I actually used to hate him, but now I go to that point where I say, I shouldn't hate him for what he is. He is what he is, that doesn't involve me. I just feel sorry for him … so I don't consider my dad my father or anything. So I pretty much discarded him.

A couple of participants, Autumn and Hannah, chose to legally change their last names to their noncriminal stepfathers' last names. For these participants, they did not see their parents as good parents who made bad choices, but instead as poor parents and criminals.

This distance between participants and their incarcerated parents resulted for numerous reasons. For instance, some, like Autumn and Hannah, had stepparents who took over the role of their incarcerated parents, some were young when their parents were incarcerated and never got to know them, some had primary caregivers who made it challenging to stay close to their incarcerated parents, while others cut ties with their parents due to the nature of the crime (e.g., family violence) or just needing to move on with their lives. Regardless of the particular reason, these participants provided examples of how they distanced themselves from their incarcerated parent.

Other participants chose to only separate themselves from the criminality of their parents. These participants viewed their parents as good parents, while simultaneously not condoning their law-breaking behavior. When asked about her father (incarcerated for drug- and fraud-related offenses), Susan stated: "It's hard to explain—he's good [as a father], he's just a criminal." Based on Susan's positive relationship with her father, she was able to think about his criminal behavior as something distinct from his parenting behavior. Likewise, in almost the exact phrases, Debbie (stepfather incarcerated for assault), Elizabeth (father incarcerated for wire fraud), and Malcolm all remarked that children could love a parent despite their criminal behavior. Their ability to separate the crime from the person was not only related to their positive relationships with their formerly incarcerated parents, but it was connected to the type of crime. In the cases mentioned above, their parents did not commit crimes against them or family members.

Being able to separate from their parents and/or their criminality allowed participants to manage their courtesy stigma and support a prosocial identity. This idea was articulated by Natalie (stepfather incarcerated for manslaughter):

> because I was able to separate myself from that part of my mother's relationship [with my incarcerated stepfather] or my part in that, that I just realized I'm my own person, and I can, I have control, complete control over my life.

Natalie's quote showed the result of being able to distance oneself: she has an identity that is her own and she has control over her life.

Viewing Incarcerated Parents As Role Models

For some of the participants, another aspect of their stigma management was to view their parent as a role model. Although role models are commonly assumed to be positive, a negative role model is "an individual who has experienced some kind of failure or misfortune, [and] can motivate others to avoid similar distress" (Lockwood, Marshall, and Sadler 2005:379). Incarcerated individuals are not commonly thought of as role models, yet many participants described their incarcerated parents as a negative role model: someone whose criminality and incarceration modeled a path they did not want to follow. By doing this, they were able to address the potential negative influence of criminal parents on children, but frame this influence as something that contributed to their prosocial identity.

Some participants used the term role model to describe their parents. Their use of the term highlighted the negative role model and was clearly recounted by Serena:

> It sounds weird, but I'd say my role model at that time would be my mother because when I looked at her, I always say, "hey, I will never touch a drug. … I don't want to be in jail, I don't want to do none of that, I want to get my college done, I wanna [sic] stay in high school." Like she was my role model because she was everything I did not want to be.

Similarly, in response to my question of role models during the time that his father was incarcerated for domestic violence, Ethan replied:

> no, I didn't have one … all the people [father and two older brothers] that I had, they weren't role models. People that I was like 'okay, I'm not going to do that,' you know? It has always been kinda like this inverse sort of like dynamic.

Ethan's quote mirrored Serena's understanding of her mother as her role model. These quotes highlighted their ability to turn parental criminality into an example of what they did not want to be.

Not every participant used the term role model to describe their parent like Serena, yet many still discussed their incarcerated parent as meeting the definition of a negative role model. For example, Maria (father incarcerated for domestic violence) recounted:

> we [her and her siblings] don't want to be in his footsteps, in my dad's footsteps. We don't want to end up incarcerated. … It kind of goes back to being an example of something we don't want to be.

Martin, whose mother and father had both been incarcerated for drug-related offenses, extended this idea beyond their criminal choices to their parenting. He shared: "I'm going to be a better person than my father. ... I will be a better father than he was." Like Maria, Martin's criminal father gave him a model of what he did not want to be and he was working toward his own prosocial goals.

For some, it was not just their parents who acted like negative role models; instead, their entire neighborhood acted as negative role models. Malcolm illustrated this point by stating:

> I kinda got to the point where, I never really had anyone positive in my life to tell me to go in this direction or go in that direction, but I saw everyone dying or going to prison and I don't want to do that.

For Malcolm, in addition to his father's and older brothers' criminal behavior and incarceration, his neighborhood modeled the kind of behavior that he did not want to follow.

In contrast, one participant viewed his incarcerated parent as a more conventional role model. Andre, who had a positive relationship with his father pre-incarceration, during incarceration and over the past year since his release, explained:

> I did consider my dad as a role model because of the sense that I felt that he would always go out of his comfort zone. He would always go out of his limits to accomplish what he wanted and what he needed for his family. Not necessarily for the actions [drug trafficking] he took, but for the way he took them.

Unlike the other participants, Andre saw his father's crime as motivated by providing for his family, which allowed him to view his father as a more traditional role model.

Framing of Parental Incarceration

The last technique participants used to manage the stigma of parental incarceration and support a prosocial identity was to frame parental incarceration in a positive way. Participants knew parental incarceration was not viewed favorably by society and they worked to construct this experience as something that positively contributed to their identity. Their technique followed the idea of retrospective interpretation, which "reconstitutes the deviant's central identity through a searching and reorganizing of past behavior and indicators" (Rossol 2001:331). My participants framed their parents' incarceration as something that benefited their identity. This framing of parental incarceration was clearly articulated by Martin: "we can't change that our parents were in prison, but we can change how we look at it and how we move forward."

Participants positively interpreted incarceration as something that "made me who I am." Dominic explained:

> I'm way more comfortable now, because I realize it made me who I am. So I mean, back in the day it was like, I put it off but like, now I realize, it's my story, it makes me who I am.

Carter (mother incarcerated for drugs, prostitution and assault; father incarcerated for drugs) illustrated a similar sentiment:

> It has made me who I am, but I really do love every part about me. ... I'm grateful that I went through some of those things. In my own way, I really am. I wish I could say I hate it, I'm upset, I'm angry, but I've learned so much, you know, about not giving up and you know just finding a silver lining.

Both Carter's and Dominic's quotes indicated that they now view the incarceration of their parents as something that contributed to who they are; it positively shaped their identity. Scott (father incarcerated for drug dealing) expanded on this idea:

> I wouldn't trade it [incarceration] for the world. I know that probably isn't what you would hear from other people, but everything brought me to be here [college]. ... I don't regret it. It kinda sounds weird, but I'm kinda thankful I had to go through it.

Scott's quote suggested that he understood parental incarceration was viewed negatively, but he acknowledged that it could be interpreted positively. Unlike most participants, Scott considered himself to be highly religious and he shared that his faith contributed to him being able to be "thankful" for his father's incarceration.

In addition to participants framing parental incarceration as what led to where they are in life, other participants discussed more specific positive outcomes. Renee (parents incarcerated on drug-related charges; father currently incarcerated) described: "they [incarcerated parents] didn't affect my grades at all. They actually, if anything, they improved my grades. They made me more motivated to get my school work done." Likewise, Marcus (father currently incarcerated for robbery) responded: "How has it impacted me? ... It's made me be more independent. ... The biggest way it impacted me, it made me more ambitious." In these examples, participants' framing of incarceration allowed them to understand it as something that favorably contributed to their identity.

Still other participants used retrospective interpretation to discuss broader benefits they received from the incarceration of their parent. Elizabeth explained: "I feel like a lot doesn't really faze us kids anymore. ... This really is nothing compared to *that* experience. So, it just kinda helped shape life now and puts things in perspective." By framing parental incarceration positively, participants were able to distance themselves from the stigma. They knew society viewed them as having the potential to follow the criminality of their parents; instead, many participants found ways to understand their childhood experiences that contradicted this stigma and contributed to their prosocial identity.

Conclusion

Participants managed the courtesy stigma of parental incarceration to support an identity-in-contrast to their parents. Although there is a stigma attached to being a child of an incarcerated parent, these college students found ways to manage the stigma and sustain a prosocial identity that was conducive to educational goals.

Three key stigma management techniques emerged. First, participants separated themselves from their incarcerated parents. This technique followed previous research on deviants creating distance from other deviants as they exit their deviant careers (e.g., Farrall 2011; Hedin and Mansson 2003). For my participants, though, the process of separation was complicated by their familial connections to criminals. Next, participants viewed their parents as role models. Paradoxically, this connection to their parents contradicted the previous theme of separation from their parents. It appeared that they wanted to be different from their parents, yet they created this difference through the criminal identity of their parents. In the majority of cases, participants saw their parents as negative role models who showed them what *not* to do. Last, following ideas of retrospective interpretation, participants framed parental incarceration in a positive manner. Their responses indicated that they knew society viewed parental incarceration as a negative experience and they were able to reflect on the ways this challenging experience contributed positively to their identity.

Through these stigma management techniques, participants were able to sustain a prosocial identity in opposition to the criminal identity of their parents. Furthermore, as rates of incarceration have climbed in the United States, it is necessary for researchers to explore resilience among this population. These findings shed light on how children and young adults can understand and frame parental incarceration to support conventional life trajectories.

Notes

1 Two participants were incarcerated as adults; three were arrested, but not incarcerated, as juveniles. These five participants all described turning points that put them back on prosocial life trajectories.

2 Although six months is not a prison sentence, this minimum length was chosen to include parental time in jail or prison, and to also avoid participants whose parents had just spent the weekend in jail.

3 If a participant's parent had been incarcerated multiple times or both parents had been incarcerated, I used the longest incarceration for this average.

4 The descriptions of parental crimes are based on participant's understanding and knowledge of their parent's crimes and incarceration. Additionally, in the four cases where parents were incarcerated during the time of the interview, they are referred to as currently incarcerated.

REFERENCES

Adalist-Estrin, Ann. 2006. "Providing Support to Adolescent Children with Incarcerated Parents." *The Prevention Researcher* 13:7–10.

Barton, Judith. 1991. "Parental Adaptation to Adolescent Drug Abuse: An Ethnographic Study of Role Formulation in Response to Courtesy Stigma." *Public Health Nursing* 8:39–45.

Farrall, Stephen. 2011. "Exiting Deviance: Cessation and Desistance." Pp. 590–596 in *Routledge Handbook of Deviant Behavior*, edited by C. Bryant. London: Routledge.

Geller, Amanda, Irwin Garfinkel, Carey Cooper, and Ronald Mincy. 2009. "Parental Incarceration and Child Well-Being: Implications for Urban Families." *Social Science Quarterly* 90:1186–1202.

Goffman, Erving. 1963. *Stigma.* New York: Simon & Schuster.

Hanlon, Thomas, Robert Blatchley, Terry Bennett-Sears, Kevin O'Grady, Marc Rose, and Jason Callaman. 2005. "Vulnerability of Children of Incarcerated Addict Mothers: Implications for Preventative Intervention." *Children and Youth Services Review* 27:67–84.

Hedin, Ulla-Carin and Sven Mansson. 2003. "The Importance of Supportive Relationships Among Women Leaving Prostitution." *Journal of Trauma Practice* 2:223–237.

Huebner, Beth and Regan Gustafson. 2007. "The Effect of Maternal Incarceration on Adult Offspring Involvement in the Criminal Justice System." *Journal of Criminal Justice* 35:283–296.

Kjellstrand, Jean and J. Mark Eddy. 2011. "Parental Incarceration During Childhood, Family Context, and Youth Problem Behavior Across Adolescence." *Journal of Offender Rehabilitation* 50:18–36.

Koro-Ljungberg, Mirka and Regina Bussing. 2009. "The Management of Courtesy Stigma in the Lives of Families with Teenagers with ADHD." *Journal of Family Issues* 30:1175–1200.

Lockwood, Penelope, Tara Marshall, and Pamela Sadler. 2005. "Promoting Success or Preventing Failure: Cultural Differences in Motivation by Positive and Negative Role Models." *Personality and Social Psychology Bulletin* 31:379–392.

Murray, Joseph, David Farrington, and Ivana Sekol. 2012. "Children's Antisocial Behavior, Mental Health, Drug Use, and Educational Performance after Parental Incarceration." *Psychological Bulletin* 138:175–210.

Rossol, Josh. 2001. "The Medicalization of Deviance as an Interactive Achievement: The Construction of Compulsive Gambling." *Symbolic Interaction* 24:315–341.

Snow, David and Leon Anderson. 1987. "Identity Work among the Homeless: The Verbal Construction and Avowal of Personal Identities." *American Journal of Sociology* 92:1336–1371.

44

Why Today's Teens Aren't in Any Hurry to Grow Up

Jean Twenge

TEENS AREN'T WHAT THEY USED TO BE

The teen pregnancy rate has reached an all-time low. Fewer teens are drinking alcohol, having sex or working part-time jobs. And as I found in a newly released analysis of seven large surveys, teens are also now less likely to drive, date or go out without their parents than their counterparts 10 or 20 years ago.

Some have tried to explain certain aspects of these trends. Today's teens are more virtuous and responsible, sociologist David Finkelhor has argued. No, says journalist Jess Williams, they're just more boring. Others have suggested that teens aren't working because they are simply lazy.

However, none of these researchers and writers has been able to tie everything together. Not drinking or having sex might be considered "virtuous," but not driving or working is unrelated to virtue – and might actually be seen as less responsible. A lower teen pregnancy rate isn't "boring" or "lazy"; it's fantastic.

These trends continued even as the economy improved after 2011, suggesting the Great Recession isn't the primary cause. Nor is more schoolwork: The average teen today spends less time on homework than his or her counterparts did in the 1990s, with time spent on extracurricular activities staying about the same.

To figure out what's really going on, it's worth taking a broader look at today's teens – a generation of kids I call "iGen" – and the environment they're living in.

A DIFFERENT CULTURE, A SLOWER PATH

Working, driving, drinking alcohol, having sex and dating have one thing in common: They are all activities adults do. This generation of teens, then, is delaying the responsibilities and pleasures of adulthood.

Adolescence – once the beginning of adulthood – now seems to be an extension of childhood. It's not that teens are more virtuous or lazier. They could simply be taking longer to grow up.

Twenge, Jean. "Why Today's Teens Aren't in Any Hurry to Grow Up." *The Conversation*, September 19, 2017.

Looking at these trends through the lens of "life history theory" might be useful. According to this model, whether development is "slow" (with teens taking longer to get to adulthood) or "fast" (getting to adulthood sooner) depends on cultural context.

A "slow life strategy" is more common in times and places where families have fewer children and spend more time cultivating each child's growth and development. This is a good description of our current culture in the United States – when the average family has two children, kids can start playing organized sports as preschoolers and preparing for college can begin as early as elementary school. This isn't a class phenomenon; I found in my analysis that the trend of growing up more slowly doesn't discriminate between teens from less advantaged backgrounds and those from wealthier families.

A "fast life strategy," however, was the more common parenting approach in the mid-twentieth century, when fewer labor-saving devices were available and the average woman had four children. As a result, kids needed to fend for themselves sooner. When my uncle told me he went skinny-dipping with his friends when he was eight, I wondered why his parents gave him permission.

Then I remembered: His parents had six other children (with one more to come), ran a farm and it was 1947. The parents needed to focus on day-to-day survival, not making sure their kids had violin lessons by age five.

Is Growing Up Slowly Good or Bad?

Life history theory explicitly notes that slow and fast life strategies are adaptations to a particular environment, so each isn't inherently "good" or "bad." Likewise, viewing the trends in teen behavior as "good" or "bad" (or as teens being more "mature" or "immature," or more "responsible" or "lazy") misses the big picture: slower development toward adulthood. And it's not just teens – children are less likely to walk to and from school and are more closely supervised, while young adults are taking longer to settle into careers, marry and have children.

"Adulting" – which refers to young adults performing adult responsibilities as if this were remarkable – has now entered the lexicon. The entire developmental path from infancy to full adulthood has slowed.

But like any adaptation, the slow life strategy has trade-offs. It's definitely a good thing that fewer teens are having sex and drinking alcohol. But what about when they go to college and suddenly enter an environment where sex and alcohol are rampant? For example, although fewer 18-year-olds now binge-drink, 21- to 22-year-olds still binge-drink at roughly the same rate as they have since the 1980s. One study found that teens who rapidly increased their binge-drinking were more at risk of alcohol dependence and adjustment issues than those who learned to drink over a longer period of time. Delaying exposure to alcohol, then, could make young adults less prepared to deal with drinking in college.

The same might be true of teens who don't work, drive or go out much in high school. Yes, they're probably less likely to get into an accident, but they may also arrive at college or the workplace less prepared to make decisions on their own.

College administrators describe students who can't do anything without calling their parents. Employers worry that more young employees lack the ability to work independently. Although I found in my analyses that iGen evinces a stronger work ethic than millennials, they'll probably also require more guidance as they transition into adulthood.

Even with the downsides in mind, it's likely beneficial that teens are spending more time developing socially and emotionally before they date, have sex, drink alcohol and work for pay. The key is to make sure that teens eventually get the opportunity to develop the skills they will need as adults: independence, along with social and decision-making skills.

For parents, this might mean making a concerted effort to push your teenagers out of the house more. Otherwise, they might just want to live with you forever.

45
Rituals of Childhood

Kieran Healy

Back in April, in Ireland, my nephew Luke made his first communion alongside his school classmates. I did much the same thing myself in much the same place about 40 years ago. My brother tells me that the preparation nowadays is a little more humane than the version we enjoyed. But there is as much anticipation beforehand, and no less excitement on the day. Luke's little suit lacked the stylish navy-blue velvet panels mine sported in 1980, but in essence the event was the same in its purpose, in its form, and in most of its details. A first communion inducts a child into one of the sacraments of the Church, having them take a step toward adulthood in expectation of the regular re-enactment of the event throughout the rest of their lives.

Sociologists like me often highlight these rituals of childhood in our writing and teaching. One of the founders of our field, Émile Durkheim, made them the centerpiece of his work. Institutions, he argued, are rituals that bind people to one another as a group. In a ritual, each person finds their place and does their part, and expects everyone else to do the same. Crucially, those involved all see one another participating in the event. By doing so, they enact their collective life in view of one another, demonstrating its reality, expressing its meaning, and feeling its pulse in their veins. That, Durkheim thought, is at root what a society is.

In any given week in America, you can watch as a different ritual of childhood plays itself out. Perhaps it will be in El Paso, at a shopping mall; or in Gilroy, at a food festival; or in Denver, at a school. Having heard gunshots, and been lucky enough to survive, children emerge to be shepherded to safety by their parents, their teachers, or heavily armed police officers. They are always frightened. Some will be crying. But almost all of them know what is happening to them, and what to do. Mass shootings are by now a standard part of American life. Preparing for them has become a ritual of childhood. It's as American as Monday Night Football, and very nearly as frequent.

The United States has institutionalized the mass shooting in a way that Durkheim would immediately recognize. As I discovered to my shock when my own children started school in North Carolina some years ago, preparation for a shooting is a part of our children's lives as soon as they enter kindergarten. The ritual of a Killing Day is known to all adults. It is taught to children first in outline only, and then gradually in more detail as they get older. The lockdown drill is its Mass. The language of "Active shooters", "Safe corners", and "Shelter in place" is its liturgy. "Run, Hide, Fight" is its creed. Security consultants and credential-dispensing experts are its clergy. My son and daughter have been institutionally readied to be shot

Healy, Kieran. "Rituals of Childhood." https://kieranhealy.org/blog/archives/2019/08/03/rituals-of-childhood

dead as surely as I, at their age, was readied by my school to receive my first communion. They practice their movements. They are taught how to hold themselves; who to defer to; what to say to their parents; how to hold their hands. The only real difference is that there is a lottery for participation. Most will only prepare. But each week, a chosen few will fully consummate the process, and be killed.

A fundamental lesson of Sociology is that, in the course of making everyday life seem orderly and sensible, arbitrary things are made to seem natural and inevitable. Rituals, especially the rituals of childhood, are a powerful way to naturalize arbitrary things. As a child in Ireland, I thought it natural to take the very body of Christ in the form of a wafer of bread on my tongue. My own boy and girl, in America, think it natural that a school is a place where you must know what to do when someone comes there to kill the children.

Social science also teaches us something about how rituals end, although not enough. The most important step is to kindle a belief that there are other ways to live, other forms that collective life can take. That can be surprisingly hard to do, because a side effect of ritual life is that participation in it powerfully reinforces its seeming inescapability, even when people are uncertain or disbelieving of the sense or meaning of what is happening. That is why change, when it comes, often comes suddenly and unexpectedly, as people finally acknowledge not just privately in ones and twos but publicly to one another that what they have been doing amounts to an empty parody that no one really believes. A further difficulty is that this sort of sudden, collective collapse is in many ways the good outcome. A worse one is when solidarity is replaced with its bitter sibling, schism. Instead of competition or conflict within some framework that opponents are nevertheless bound to, real schism yields much of the febrile, effervescent energy of collective solidarity, but delivers few of its stabilizing benefits.

It's traditional to say that there are "no easy answers", but this is not really true. Everywhere groups face the problem of holding themselves together. Every society has its enormous complex of institutions and weight of rituals that, through the sheer force of mutual expectation and daily habit, bring that society to life. But not every society has successfully institutionalized the mass shooting. Only one place has done that, deliberately and effectively. The United States has chosen, and continues to choose, to enact ritual compliance to an ideal of freedom in a way that results in a steady flow of blood sacrifice. This ritual of childhood is not a betrayal of "who we are" as a country. It is what America has made of itself, how it worships itself, and how it makes itself real.

SECTION IX
Experiences and Expectations of Motherhood

INTRODUCTION

Mothering and the cultural expectations of motherhood are powerful in thinking about the family. The expectations that girls will eventually become mothers is ubiquitous and reinforced early in life, through toys, media, and social interactions. In 2016, 86 percent of women in their 40s had ever given birth (Livingston 2018). As Section VII shows, women who reject motherhood have been the focus of scorn or concern for some time. In fact, out of concern for women's roles as mothers, many physicians in the nineteenth century argued that women should not be allowed to attend universities, insisting that "too much intellectual strain went again women's nature, damaging the nervous system and compromising female sexuality and fertility" (Kennaway 2011:26). Although women now outnumber men in college attendance, many women today still face warnings that pursuing careers, enrolling in graduate programs, or delaying childbearing to pursue other opportunities will harm their capacity to become mothers. This image of the biological clock counting down reminds women that they are running out of time to fulfill their "true" potential as women to become mothers.

In examining these expectations, it is helpful to think about the differences between maternity, that is the capacity to become pregnant and give birth, and maternalism, the desire and capacity to nurture. We frequently conflate the two and treat them interchangeably, but, in fact, their differences are useful for thinking about motherhood. Maternity is a biological experience, but it is not the same as being nurturing. By treating them as the same, we assume that motherhood is natural, that the ability to become pregnant and give birth makes a woman nurturing, or that being nurturing means women can and will become pregnant and give birth. One result is that when we hear about women who abandon or abuse their children, we are often more shocked than when we hear about other forms of violence. How, we ask, could a mother do that? We are also surprised when seemingly nurturing women forego motherhood.

The connection between maternalism and maternity is historically relatively new. Before the invention of infant formula around 1865, wet nursing, in which a woman would breastfeed other women's offspring, was common. In some cases, hiring a wet nurse was an elite practice in which the wealthy would hire a woman to nurse their children. In other cases, wet nursing was a way to sustain infants whose mothers were sick, unavailable, or had died, as was relatively common. In fact, at the end of the nineteenth and beginning of the twentieth century, for every 1,000 live births, about 6–9 women and 100 infants died (CDC 1999). The result was that many women nurtured children to whom they did not give birth, and might have even been called mother, irrespective of their lack of legal or biological relationship. Women also gave birth to children they did not nurture.

THE RISE OF THE MOTHERHOOD MYSTIQUE

The social role of the child changed in the late nineteenth century and so did the institution of motherhood. Economic and political transformations that occurred at the end of the nineteenth and beginning of the twentieth century were integral for shaping family life. Among them were industrialization, legal reforms, including laws that limited child labor, and an influx of immigrant labor. One outcome of these changes was that children became less economically useful as a source of income to the family, and instead became sentimentally important (Zelizer 1985). As children became priceless, the role of women as caretakers also changed. For middle- and upper-class women, becoming full-time mothers and supporting a peaceful home as an escape from the seemingly corrupt world of urban capital became the ideal of womanhood in the late nineteenth century. This ideal gradually spread to working-class women too (Zelizer 1985). Single, childless, and poor women continued to work in factories, as domestic servants, or even as teachers, but were seen as falling short of this ideal, even as they worked in other women's homes or on behalf of other women's children.

By the early twentieth century, a range of experts—physicians, social reformers, educators, and government agencies—began providing advice on how mothers should care for their children. What became known as "scientific motherhood" was the widely promoted belief that mothers needed expert scientific and medical advice to raise their children to be healthy and successful. Rather than listening to their own mothers, friends, and other women in the community, women were told that good mothers followed expert advice. Experts advised, for example, against breastfeeding and erroneously suggested that bottle-feeding was nutritionally superior. As historian Rima Apple explains,

> Women increasingly were told that they continued to be responsible for the well-being of their families, but needed to follow the directions of their physicians. Such instruction positioned mothers as both responsible for their families and incapable of that responsibility.
>
> (Apple 1995)

As the chapter by Sarah Bowen, Sinikka Elliott, and Joslyn Brenton on contemporary feeding advice and the chapter by Kate Cairns, Norah MacKendrick, and Josée Johnston on the impossibility of sustained organic consumption show, advice to mothers has only intensified, often in ways that create unrealistic expectations.

The result of these powerful cultural forces has been the development of what many scholars have called the "motherhood mystique." This mystique has several interlocking components. It encompasses the cultural belief that women's ultimate fulfillment is achieved by being a mother; that to be a good mother, a woman must like being a mother and all the work that goes with it; that the work of mothering (like cooking and taking care of the house, while also actively engaging with her children and supporting her husband) fits together in non-contradictory ways; and that a woman's intense exclusive devotion to mothering is good for children (Hoffnung 1989, 1995). These expectations have resulted in "intensive mothering" practices, which expect women to follow expert advice and expend considerable time, money, and energy to successfully raise their children (Hays 1996). As was true a century ago, women with the most resources are most able to appear to be satisfying these labor-intensive and consumerist standards of motherhood. Notably, no similar expectations exist for fathers.

MOTHERHOOD AND MOTHERWORK

The institution of motherhood, with its cultural expectations, is separate from the experience of mothering. Yet, both are shaped by historical contexts, as Maxine Baca Zinn's chapter in the first section illustrated. In fact, mothering occurs within and is "framed by interlocking structures of race, class, and gender" (Collins 1999:197). Women's relative ability to meet the standards of motherhood reflects access to resources and social location, including region, religion, sexual identity, citizenship, ethnicity, income, and, as Angela Frederick's chapter shows us, disability.

Within systems of inequality, mothers in general and mothers of color specifically must strategize their work on behalf of their own children, a process sociologist Patricia Hill Collins terms "motherwork." Rejecting the separate spheres of home and work that have inaccurately characterized motherhood for many mothers, Collins highlights three aspects that "form the bedrock of women of color's motherwork" on behalf of their children: physical survival, power, and identity. Physical survival is often taken for granted for infants in white families, whose infant mortality rates of 4.9 per 1,000 births are significantly lower than those for babies who are Black (11.9 per 1,000 births) or Native American (9.4) (CDC 2019). Mothers of color work hard to support the physical survival of their children by facing threats their children face—from infant mortality, poverty, environmental harms, violence, and, as the chapter by Dawn Marie Dow shows, harm from police or community members. Mothers of color must also claim power, which may include making decisions of whether to become a mother, avoiding being sterilized without consent, or retaining custody of one's children, a significant issue insofar as children of color are overrepresented in the child welfare system. Power may also entail challenging schools that may devalue children's culture, language, or heritage. Motherwork also requires women of color to protect their children's sense of self. As Collins writes, "women's motherwork reflects the tensions inherent in trying to foster a meaningful racial identity in children within a society that denigrates people of color" (Collins 1999: 208). This work may encompass efforts to support children's sense of self, equip them to resist dominant culture, and avoid racist ideology from schools, media, and other social institutions.

Survival, power, and identity shape motherwork for all mothers, but the stakes for ethnic and racial minority mothers who face racist systems each day are different than for white mothers and may take an even greater toll on them. Illustrating the significance of motherwork, poet Audre Lorde writes, "Raising Black children—female and male—in the mouth of a racist, sexist, suicidal dragon is perilous and chancy. If they cannot love and resist at the same time, they will probably not survive" (Lorde 1992: 254).

THE COSTS OF MOTHERHOOD

Despite strong social pressures to become a mother, there is little done to support mothers in the United States, a reality that can be seen in the challenges faced by mothers who are in the paid workforce. In 1970, 48 percent of minor children had a mother who stayed at home; by 2012, only 28 percent of children had a mother who stayed home. This reflects the reality that American wages have declined over time, making two incomes a necessity for most families as well as the increase in woman-headed households. Among mothers who stay home, about 6 percent in 2012 indicated they would like to work but could not find a job. For many mothers who do not work for wages outside the home, they face circumstances in which the high cost of childcare might negate or exceed the financial benefits of working (Cohn, Livingston and Wang 2014).

The US is the only industrialized nation that provides no paid leave at the time of the birth or adoption of a child. Since 1993, Americans have had access to the Family Medical Leave Act—a federal law that provides up to 12 weeks of unpaid leave to care for a family member (defined in fairly restrictive ways), to manage one's own illness, or for the birth or adoption of a child. In order to be eligible, employees must have worked 1,250 hours during the 12 months prior to the start of leave for a company that has at least 50 employees within 75 miles. Notably, workers in smaller companies, part-time employees, and contract workers are not likely to be eligible. Many who are eligible find it challenging to take unpaid leave. As a result, as of 2020, eight states and the District of Columbia have passed state laws to create funds to subsidize workers so they may take paid family leave (KFF 2020). Such leave programs will likely make an important difference to new parents and also apply to individuals with health challenges and certain caregiving responsibilities that they might not otherwise be able to afford to address.

Research also shows that women face a "motherhood penalty," a series of systematic disadvantages because they have children. These include discrimination in hiring, reduced pay and benefits, fewer opportunities for promotion, and perceptions that they are less competent or less committed to their jobs than childless women and all men in the workplace. This penalty increases with each child and is still measurable even when studies control for time out of workforce, loss of experience, and job formats (Budig and England 2001, Correll, Benard and Paik 2007). Social support within the family also matters in women's career trajectories as Jessica Valenti's chapter shows.

Mothers face a great deal of pressure and as a large body of research shows, they are not happy. Said succinctly by journalist Jennifer Senior (2014), American parenting is "all joy and no fun." Parents in general and mothers in particular pay what has been called "the happiness penalty" by having children, in which American parents are less happy than their childless counterparts. However, the lack of public policy to support parents exacerbates this penalty. One study showed that when comparing American parents to those in 22 other countries, American parents were significantly less happy and that difference was explained by the presence or absence of family policies, including paid time off and childcare subsidies (Glass, Simon and Andersson 2016).

American mothers also face significant pressures to follow advice, intensively invest in their children, support their children's personal and emotional growth and safety, and guard against myriad perceived threats. Women in particular spend time worrying about decisions, feeling guilty about their parenting, and evaluating their choices in an ever-increasing landscape of expert advice that has significantly increased since the early days of scientific motherhood. My chapter on how parents come to reject vaccines illustrates these dynamics. These issues are even more complex for mothers who provide care to children with developmental or health challenges, as Eva Kittay Feder shows in her chapter on caring for her daughter Sesha. As Feder's chapter illuminates, women's abilities to meet the multiple demands of working, parenting, and emotionally supporting family members often depend on a complicated web of caregivers who themselves often have their own family responsibilities.

REFERENCES

Apple, Rima D. 1995. "Constructing Mothers: Scientific Motherhood in the Nineteenth and Twentieth Centuries." *Social History of Medicine* 8(2):161–178. doi: 10.1093/shm/8.2.161.

Budig, Michelle J. and Paula England. 2001. "The Wage Penalty for Motherhood." *American Sociological Review* 66(2): 204–225. doi: 10.2307/2657415.

CDC. 1999. "Achievements in Public Health, 1900–1999: Healthier Mothers and Babies." *MMWR Weekly* 48(38): 849–858.

CDC. 2019. "Infant Mortality." Centers for Disease Control and Prevention. (https://www.cdc.gov/reproductivehealth/maternalinfanthealth/infantmortality.htm).

Cohn, D'Vera, Gretchen Livingston and Wendy Wang. 2014, "After Decades of Decline, a Rise in Stay-at-Home Mothers." Pew Research Center. (https://www.pewsocialtrends.org/2014/04/08/after-decades-of-decline-a-rise-in-stay-at-home-mothers/).

Collins, Patricia Hill. 1999. "Shifting the Center: Race, Class, and Feminist Theorizing About Motherhood." Pp. 197 in *American Families: A Multicultural Reader*, edited by S. Coontz, M. Parson and G. Raley. New York: Routledge.

Correll, Shelley J, Stephen Benard and In Paik. 2007. "Getting a Job: Is There a Motherhood Penalty?" *American Journal of Sociology* 112(5): 1297–1338.

Glass, Jennifer, Robin W. Simon and Matthew A. Andersson. 2016. "Parenthood and Happiness: Effects of Work-Family Reconciliation Policies in 22 OECD Countries." *American Journal of Sociology* 122(3): 886–929.

Hays, Sharon. 1996. *Cultural Contradictions of Motherhood*. New Haven: Yale University Press.

Hoffnung, Michele. 1989. "Motherhood: Contemporary Conflict for Women." Pp. 157–75 in *Women: A Feminist Perspective*, edited by J. Freeman. Mountain View, CA: Mayfield.

Hoffnung, Michele. 1995. "Motherhood: Contemporary Conflict for Women." *Women: A Feminist Perspective* 5: 162–181.

Kennaway, James. 2011. "The Piano Plague: The Nineteenth-Century Medical Critique of Female Musical Education." *Gesnerus* 68(1): 26–40.

KFF. 2020. "State Policies on Paid Family and Sick Leave." Kaiser Family Foundation. (https://www.kff. org/other/state-indicator/paid-family-and-sick-leave).

Livingston, Gretchen. 2018. "They're Waiting Longer, but U.S. Women Today More Likely to Have Children than a Decade Ago." Pew Research Center. (https://www.pewsocialtrends.org/2018/01/ 18/theyre-waiting-longer-but-u-s-women-today-more-likely-to-have-children-than-a-decade- ago/).

Lorde, Audre. 1992. "'Man Child: A Black Lesbian Feminist's Response' I." in *Race, Class, and Gender*, edited by M. Andersen and P. H. Collins. Belmont: Wadsworth Press.

Senior, Jennifer. 2014. *All Joy and No Fun: The Paradox of Modern Parenthood*. London: Hachette UK.

Zelizer, Viviana A. 1985. *Pricing the Priceless Child: The Changing Social Value of Children*. New York: Basic Books.

46
Mothering While Disabled

Angela Frederick

When she was just two days old, Mikaela Sinnett of Kansas City, Missouri, became a ward of the foster care system. The local social services agency took her away from her parents before the family left the hospital. What horrible crime, one might ask, did Mikaela's parents commit to result in the loss of custody of their newborn daughter? Mikaela's parents were not guilty of abuse or neglect. Rather, they were blind.

Responding to Mikaela's mother's difficulty breastfeeding, a nurse reported the parents to a hospital social worker, setting in motion the bureaucratic machinery of the state's protective services.

Mikaela's parents cooperated with the social worker, answering questions about the care they would provide for their newborn. They could take their daughter's temperature with a talking thermometer; they had access to transportation; and they could take Mikaela to the hospital if she needed immediate medical attention. The one response the social worker wanted, which the parents could not provide, was that someone with sight would be with the child at all times.

According to Erika, Mikaela's mother, the social worker declared "I can't in good conscience send this baby home with blind parents." Erika and her partner were not even allowed to hold their daughter before she was taken into foster care.

It took Mikaela's parents 57 days to get their daughter back. During this time, Erika and her partner were only allowed to spend two to three hours with their daughter each week, and only with supervision. After two months of court hearings and legal action, child protective services closed the case.

Mikaela is now four years old, but the incident, and the associated trauma, will always be a part of her family history.

I too am a mother—of a two-year-old girl. And I am blind. I followed this story closely as it unfolded. What agony this mother must have endured, I thought, as I read the reportage. From the moment I contemplated becoming a mother, I began collecting resources and advice on how I would care for my child without sight. As I spoke to other blind mothers, I learned the tricks of the trade: how to track toddlers by pinning bells to their clothes; how to wear babies and pull rather than push strollers to accommodate white canes and guide dogs; how to place tactile markings on syringes to measure medicine.

Frederick, Angela. "Mothering While Disabled." *Contexts* 13, no. 4 (2014): 30–35.

And I learned much more: that as a mother with a disability, the chance of being investigated by social services is ominously high. "Be prepared," these women warned me, "You will be visited by a hospital social worker after childbirth." As a mother, these warnings made me anxious. But as a sociologist I was curious. How much training do social workers and medical professionals receive about disability? What measures are in place to protect mothers with disabilities from discrimination?

People with disabilities must frequently confront stigmatizing attitudes challenging their right to be in the world, which can have devastating consequences for them and their families.

LEGACIES OF EXCLUSION

We tend to think of disability as an issue facing a very small segment of the population. In actuality one in five Americans lives with some kind of disability, and one in ten has a severe disability that limits one or more major life activities. Approximately 2.3 million US mothers caring for children have a disability, and almost 10 percent of American children are currently being cared for by a parent with a disability. As historian Kim Nielsen argues, "Disability is not the story of someone else. It is our story, the story of someone we love, the story of who we are or may become, and it is undoubtedly the story of our nation."

Impairments come in many forms, from physical limitations that limit mobility or stamina, to sensory impairments like blindness or deafness, to cognitive and social disabilities. Some disabilities are easy to identify through one's appearance or the tools and technology one uses. Other impairments, such as learning or psychiatric disabilities, are invisible, and are not immediately noticeable. Some disabilities involve significant pain or illness. Others do not. Individuals can experience the same impairment in very different ways.

In the 1960s, Americans with disabilities began to cultivate a shared political identity as members of an oppressed group. Activists in the disability rights movement demanded recognition as full citizens with rights to live independently outside of institutions, to access quality education and employment, and to participate fully in their communities free from structural and attitudinal barriers. They argued that disabled people, not professionals or charity organizations, should speak on behalf of their communities.

Armed with new political identities and with the civil rights protections guaranteed by the 1990 Americans with Disabilities Act, disabled Americans are more fully participating in their communities than ever before. Yet, despite this progress, public recognition of the right of people with disabilities to parent has yet to be realized. In fact, Through the Looking Glass, an advocacy organization for parents with disabilities, claims that securing the rights of disabled Americans to parent without unreasonable interference is "the last frontier in disability rights."

This form of prejudice has been particularly insidious for women with disabilities. During the twentieth-century eugenics movement, the state subjected disabled people to forced institutionalization, marriage restriction laws, and compulsory sterilization. Eugenicists primarily targeted women in their efforts to purify the genetic make-up of the population. Justifying their work as necessary to eliminate the danger posed by the "feebleminded," the state authorized the forced sterilization of women with a range of disabilities, women believed to be sexually impure, and Black, Native-American, and immigrant women.

The legacy of the eugenics movement persists today. Women with disabilities still encounter the widely held belief that they cannot perform motherhood competently and that they will spread "defective genes" by passing their impairments to their children. New cultural values about motherhood pose particular dilemmas for disabled mothers. Women are now expected to create child-centered homes that shield children from responsibility and hardship.

Mothers are expected to devote ample amounts of money, time, and energy to nurturing and overseeing their children's development. Disabled women pose a threat to the intensive mothering ethos as they can make visible the realities of imperfection, risk, and even pain and suffering—the very hardships from which mothers are now expected to shield their children.

The Child Welfare System and Disability

Safety is the word most often used to question the rights of disabled mothers. After all, how can the human rights of people with disabilities stack up against the public concern for children's safety? Mothers with disabilities come from all walks of life. They have the same wide range of parenting skills and personal strengths and weaknesses found in the broader community. They experience the same wide range of privileges and hardships as the general population. Some are model parents. Some are not. And, yes, some do abuse and neglect their children.

In cases in which the mother has a disability, however, her status is often used as a proxy for real evidence that she cannot adequately care for her children. Disability communities and advocacy organizations like Through the Looking Glass have a wealth of knowledge about the strategies parents with various disabilities employ to successfully care for children. Frequently, however, the state launches investigations and makes custody determinations without considering these options.

Parents with disabilities often do face barriers, including higher rates of unemployment and poverty, lack of access to transportation, and diminished access to quality healthcare.

Yet, despite these challenges, research shows that these parents are still no more likely to harm their children than parents without disabilities. In other words, parents' disability status is a poor predictor of child maltreatment. According to Paul Preston, anthropologist and director of the National Center for Parents with Disabilities and Their Families, "The vast majority of children of disabled parents have been shown to have typical development and functioning and often enhanced life perspectives and skills."

While we can be deeply moved by media accounts of extreme cases of child abuse and child welfare system's failure to protect children from harm, it is important to remember that these severe cases of abuse actually represent only a small proportion of child welfare cases. Most parents who are involved with child protective services are accused of neglect rather than abuse, and decisions about their cases often entail highly subjective assessments.

Misunderstanding Disabled Mothers

The subjective determinations that must be made about children's welfare create moments of misunderstanding that place the rights of disabled mothers in jeopardy. Social workers, judges, and other professionals have considerable authority to claim expertise about parents and children, and are in fact required to do so. The state asks social workers and medical professionals to make judgments about parental fitness, even though these professionals don't often know much about disability and are likely to hold the same negative attitudes, which pervade the broader culture. Many mothers with disabilities report living with a sense of fear that they will be scrutinized by medical authorities. At times, when members of the public see a disabled woman out with her children and become concerned, they report the family to child protective services. Mothers with disabilities are at particular risk, as cultural beliefs suggest that mothers rather than fathers are still primarily responsible for their children.

Disability becomes even more daunting for families who have an open case with child protective services. In 37 states, a disability can be legal grounds for termination of parental rights. The focus of child welfare and custody cases in these states easily shifts from considering the actual signs of neglect or abuse, to speculating about potential parenting deficiencies the mother's disability might pose. In fact, disability is one of the few instances in which parental rights can be terminated on the basis of parents' identity status rather than their actions. According to advocates from Through the Looking Glass, words such as "obviously" and "clearly" are often used to draw conclusions about disabled individuals' capacity to parent, and negative language such as "wheelchair-bound" or "afflicted with a disability" often shore up negative assumptions about parents' capacity to care for their children.

When child welfare agencies remove children from their homes, parents with disabilities have fewer opportunities to reunify their families. These agencies offer disabled parents few supports to ease the effects of structural barriers such as lack of access to transportation and quality housing, and they rarely offer parents the opportunity to acquire the adaptive training and equipment that might help them care for their children.

The Adoption and Safe Families Act, signed into law in 1997, marked a dramatic shift in focus for the child welfare system, as the law now requires agencies to prioritize "permanency" for children over reunification with their parents. The new time limits for reunification, as well as emphasis upon adoption, have created even steeper barriers for parents with disabilities seeking to reunify with their children.

Finally, custody decisions in family courts are often particularly difficult for parents with disabilities, as the "best interest of the child" standard for custody determinations in family court leaves even greater room for judges to make decisions based on negative attitudes about disability. Three years ago, a Durham, North Carolina judge awarded full custody of Alaina Giordano's two children to Giordano's ex-husband, acknowledging that Giordano's stage IV breast cancer was a determining factor in her decision. The judge cited the testimony of forensic psychiatrist Helen Brantley, who argued, "Children want a normal childhood, and it is not normal with an ill parent." Giordano died the following year. She was able to spend the last few weeks of her life with her children only after her lawyer filed an emergency motion in family court.

Protecting the Rights Of Mothers with Disabilities

Disabled mothers are more likely to experience unwarranted investigations from social service agencies. They are more likely to have their parental rights terminated, and when children are removed these families receive fewer supports for reunification.

A handful of states have passed legislation to address these problems. In 2011, partly in response to the Mikaela Sinnett case, Missouri passed legislation that prohibits the child welfare system from discriminating against parents with disabilities. Several states now require that courts consider testimony from disability communities, and include information about adaptive equipment and alternative skills that parents with disabilities employ. Other states now mandate that courts must establish a clear causal relationship between a parent's disability and child maltreatment before disability can be used as grounds for termination of parental rights. Idaho has passed the most comprehensive legislation protecting the rights of disabled parents.

The National Association of Social Workers now recommends that the federal government establish a national fellowship program to train a "disability specialist" from every local and state child welfare agency, who would then participate in investigations and decisions made in cases involving parents with disabilities. A similar model has been used to improve the handling of cases of domestic violence. Other states, including Tennessee, are implementing training programs to educate state workers about disability and parenting, and offer them information about how they can best support struggling parents.

Mikaela Sinnett's story illuminates the devastating consequences families can endure when stigmatizing attitudes about disability influence child welfare decisions. Despite the gains of the disability rights movement, disabled women's still receive undue scrutiny about their right to mother. Instead of asking whether or not disabled mothers should have children, we should be asking how we can help their families to thrive.

47

I've Talked to Dozens of Parents about Why They Don't Vaccinate. Here's What They Told Me

Jennifer A. Reich

"You know when you pick your child up from preschool and the teacher tells you he had a really good day? I have never had that day."

This is how one mother who I'll call Katie described what it's like parenting her son, who is now six years old. She visited 15 preschools before she found one she thought would work for him, a place where teachers would understand his passion for space but also his difficulties reading social cues or transitioning between activities. She meticulously manages his diet due to his extensive food allergies and eczema. She also rejects vaccines, which she fears could impair his seemingly challenged immune system or worsen his autism spectrum disorder traits.

Katie is just one mother I spoke to while studying parents who reject some or all vaccines for their children. I'm a sociologist who aims to understand how parents make choices for their families and children, and compiled almost a decade of research into my book *Calling the Shots: Why Parents Reject Vaccines*.

Katie, like many of the mothers I spoke with, agonizes over how to make sure her kids are healthy, happy, and able to succeed in what seems an increasingly dangerous, competitive, and uncertain world.

Their reasons for rejecting vaccines vary widely. Vaccines, these parents tell me, do not always protect children. Some insist their children's immune systems would benefit from contracting the illness. Some don't trust the government agencies that approve vaccines because they are "too close" with pharmaceutical companies. Many believe their healthy lifestyle or prolonged breastfeeding ensures that their children will not experience the worst outcomes of a vaccine-preventable disease.

All insist that each parent must gather her own information and make an informed decision without feeling pressured by expert recommendations. And all insist that whatever happens to their children, they will ultimately be responsible.

Right now, the country is watching the number of measles cases increase each day, hitting a new high of 764 cases across 23 states since it was eradicated from the United States in 2000. With 60 new cases in the past week, we can expect the outbreak will continue to spread.

Reich, Jennifer. "I've Talked to Dozens of Parents about Why They Don't Vaccinate. Here's What They Told Me." *Vox.com*, June 13, 2019.

There is no disagreement that vaccine refusal is the cause of outbreaks. More than 70 percent of measles cases this year were in people who had received no vaccines, and in all, 88 percent of cases were associated with under-immunized, close-knit communities. Yet parents' decisions have effects that can reach far beyond these networks and neighborhoods.

It's easy to question why any parent would choose not to vaccinate, and to look at mothers like Katie with suspicion, confusion, or disgust. As a mother of three vaccinated children and the granddaughter of a woman who lived her life with a limp that resulted from polio, I too wonder this. And while it is easy to dismiss these parents as anti-science, selfish, ignorant, or delusional, the answer is much more complicated.

PARENTS WHO DON'T VACCINATE ARE PRIORITIZING THEIR CHILDREN OVER OTHER PEOPLE'S CHILDREN

First, a few points of clarification. Although I spoke with fathers and mothers in my research, it became clear that healthcare decisions tend to be maternal terrain. Mothers are most likely to take their kids to doctor appointments and make decisions about food and daily care. They also face scrutiny for their children's behaviors, performances, and abilities, which makes every decision—including whether to vaccinate—feel high-stakes.

Second, there's a small number of people who will never believe vaccines work and will never be persuaded to accept them, and I spoke to some of them. This is the group we tend to conflate with the entire world of people who don't vaccinate.

But the larger and more interesting group to discuss is the significant portion of American parents who say they believe in vaccines but just don't want them for their children—or don't want all the vaccines that experts insist are safest and most efficacious. As much as 20–25 percent of American parents fall into this latter group, and they arguably pose the greatest threat to herd immunity. They are also the most likely to be persuaded as long as we don't call them ignorant and selfish.

Finally, parents who refuse vaccines are most likely to be white and college-educated, and to have a higher-than-average family income. I believe their decisions are less about how informed they are and more about the culture of what I term individualist parenting—one that insists parents are personally responsible for their own children, but not other children. Individualist parenting has encouraged mothers to trust their own judgment more than that of experts and believe they can manage their way out of disease risk, even as their choices present risk to others.

For the past two decades, we have increasingly prioritized individual behaviors and choices as the key to good health. Experts recommend people count their calories, steps, pounds, or servings of vegetables as a path to disease prevention. When we hear someone is sick, our first question is often, "What did they do, or fail to do, that led to illness?" These questions ignore how the majority of illness is beyond individual control and reduce health promotion to a series of consumption decisions.

For mothers, the pressure to manage their children's nutrition, body size, learning styles, peer interactions, or physical activity is boundless and reinforced by schools, doctors, peers, and parenting magazines. Beyond health, we see demands that mothers individually manage their children's lives and optimize opportunities for their success. Choosing schools, traveling soccer teams, or SAT tutors promises to increase some children's opportunities for success. Yet when parents choose to send their kids to private schools or competitive public schools, they implicitly accept that it is fine that other children don't have safe or adequately resourced schools—as long as it's not their own kids. The culture of individualist parenting makes clear: Parents have a duty to exercise choice to the bounds of their resources, even at the expense of others.

Mothers often tell me how hard they work to do "research" about raising their children. They don't mean systematic research in the way scientists do. Rather, they conduct research the way we all do before making a consumption decision like going to a new restaurant or buying an appliance: They gather information, read advice from experts, talk to friends and family, peruse reviews and comments, weigh risks and benefits, and, in the end, trust their instincts. On a range of topics—from cooking to finding a pediatrician to requesting the best teacher to deciding whether to consent to vaccines—mothers routinely share information and advice to support their efforts to make good decisions for their families.

We know that parents who refuse vaccines tend to cluster and that living near a high number of other unvaccinated people significantly increases risk of infection. After all, most people are more likely to trust those who are like them. It is therefore not surprising that many of the outbreaks we are seeing are in tightly woven ethnic and religious communities with shared values and practices.

Although public health campaigns aim to convince parents to vaccinate because they love their children, the reality is that vaccines work best when used at a population level. In fact, many vaccines provide more protection to others than the child who receives them.

For example, rubella, which is the third component of the measles-mumps-rubella (MMR) vaccine, is a mild disease in childhood but can cause blindness, deafness, mental disabilities, and a range of birth defects in fetuses, or miscarriage, when pregnant women are infected. Measles can kill about one or two of every 1,000 people infected at any age but is most dangerous to infants and adults. The mothers I studied would often weigh each of these facts to decide if and how it would benefit their own children to get vaccinated. They would not consider that those too young, too old, or too immune-compromised to be vaccinated might benefit most from the herd immunity caused by mass vaccination.

I am not suggesting that parents should no longer advocate for their own children or prioritize their family's values in making choices for their children. Rather, I am suggesting that we should consider how we can begin to reject the logic that we are only responsible for our own children.

Parents' rejection of vaccine recommendations often emerges from fear of the uncertainties that surround children in a world that feels increasingly risky. I understand and admittedly sometimes even share these anxieties. I also recognize the pressures on parents to anticipate all possible outcomes and aim to control for them.

When thinking about her son's struggles, Katie, like many mothers, made clear that she feels alone. Feeling unsupported by schools, healthcare providers, insurance companies, and her extended family, Katie insists she alone must take responsibility for her child and become his advocate.

Like high-quality education, safe drinking water, food inspection, or any number of resources children need to thrive, infectious diseases cannot be controlled with individual hard work, and thus cannot remain a private concern. In the end, we must find ways to protect each other's children and support everyone's family. And perhaps then, mothers who don't think their children need vaccines will consent anyway.

48

The Joy of Cooking

Sarah Bowen, Sinikka Elliott, and Joslyn Brenton

It's a hot, sticky Fourth of July in North Carolina, and Leanne, a married working-class black mother of three, is in her cramped kitchen. She's been cooking for several hours, lovingly preparing potato salad, beef ribs, chicken legs, and collards for her family. Abruptly, her mother decides to leave before eating anything. "But you haven't eaten," Leanne says. "You know I prefer my own potato salad," says her mom. She takes a plateful to go anyway.

Her seven-year-old son takes medication for ADHD and often isn't hungry until it wears off, usually right before bedtime. Leanne's one-year-old daughter gets fussy when her mom cooks, and looks for attention. Her husband doesn't offer much help; his contribution involves pouring barbecue sauce on the ribs, which Leanne calls "working his magic." Leanne wipes her brow and mutters to herself about the $80 she spent on ingredients. By the time she's finished cooking, she says, "I don't want to eat!"

In the fight to combat rising obesity rates, modern-day food gurus advocate a return to the kitchen. Michael Pollan, author of *Cooked*, and America's most influential "foodie-intellectual," tells us that the path to reforming the food system "passes right through the kitchen." *New York Times'* food columnist Mark Bittman agrees, saying the goal should be "to get people to see cooking as a joy rather than a burden." Magazines such as *Good Housekeeping* and television personalities like Rachael Ray offer practical cooking advice to get Americans into the kitchen, publishing recipes for 30-minute meals and meals that can be made in the slow cooker. First lady Michelle Obama has also been influential in popularizing public health messages that emphasize the role that mothers play when it comes to helping children make healthy choices.

The message that good parents—and in particular, good mothers—cook for their families dovetails with increasingly intensive and unrealistic standards of "good" mothering. One could say that home-cooked meals have become the hallmark of good mothering, stable families, and the ideal of the healthy, productive citizen.

Yet in reality, home-cooked meals rarely look this good. Leanne, for example, who held down a minimum-wage job while taking classes for an associate's degree, often spent her valuable time preparing meals, only to be rewarded with family members' complaints—or disinterest. Our extensive

Bowen, Sarah, Sinikka Elliott, and Joslyn Brenton. "The Joy of Cooking?" *Contexts* 13, no. 3 (2014): 20–25.

observations and interviews with mothers like Leanne reveal something that often gets overlooked: cooking is fraught.

FEEDING THE FAMILY

Over the past year and a half, our research team conducted in-depth interviews with 150 black, white, and Latina mothers from all walks of life. We also spent over 250 hours conducting ethnographic observations with 12 working-class and poor families. We observed them in their homes as they prepared and ate meals, and tagged along on trips to the grocery store and to their children's check-ups. Sitting around the kitchen table and getting a feel for these women's lives, we came to appreciate the complexities involved in feeding a family.

While Pollan and others wax nostalgic about a time when people grew their own food and sat around the dinner table eating it, they fail to see all of the invisible labor that goes into planning, making, and coordinating family meals. Cooking is at times joyful, but it is also filled with time pressures, tradeoffs designed to save money, and the burden of pleasing others.

Wanda and her husband Marquan, working-class black parents of two young girls, were constantly pressed for time. Both were employed by the same fast food chain, but in different rural locations 45 minutes apart. They depended on Wanda's mother, who lived 30 minutes away, for childcare. During the five weeks we spent with them, their car was broken down and since they did not have enough money to repair it, they relied on a complex network of friends and family members for rides. Their lives were further complicated by the fact that they didn't know their weekly schedules—what hours, shifts, or even days they would be working—until they were posted, sometimes only the night before. Once they learned their shifts, they scrambled to figure out transportation and childcare arrangements.

Wanda liked her job, but her unpredictable schedule made it difficult to cook regular meals the way she wanted to. This time dilemma was also hard for Leanne, who worked for the same fast food corporation as Wanda and Marquan, but in an urban area that lacked reliable public transportation. Sometimes, Leanne would take a taxi to work only to find out that business was slow and she was not needed. At other times, she was asked to work late. Because of this, Leanne and her family had no set meal time: cooking and eating were often catch-as-catch-can.

Wanda and Leanne's situation is increasingly common. As real wages have stagnated, many households depend on every adult family member working, sometimes in multiple jobs and jobs with nonstandard and unpredictable hours, to make ends meet. Since the 1960s, working women have cut back on household tasks, including cooking and cleaning, according to sociologist Liana Sayer. Even so, balancing paid work and unpaid work at home, women today have less free time than they did a generation ago; and, in line with heightened expectations of motherhood, they now report spending more time engaged in childcare than did mothers in the 1960s. It's not surprising that they struggle to find time to cook.

And, of course, cooking isn't just about the time it takes to prepare the meal. It also involves planning ahead to be sure the ingredients are on hand, and it means cleaning up afterward. Samantha, a single white mother of three, was blunt when we asked her if she liked cooking. "Not really," she said.

> I just hate the kitchen…having to come up with a meal and put it together. I know I can cook but it's the planning of the meal, and seeing if they're going to like it, and the mess that you make. And then the mess afterwards…If it was up to me, I wouldn't cook.

Though the mothers we met were squeezed for time, they were still expected to produce elaborate meals cooked from scratch. Even the middle-class women we talked with, who enjoyed regular work hours and typically shared the household work with a partner, said they lacked the time to cook the way they felt they should. Most got home from work around six o'clock, and then attempted to cook meals from scratch (as the experts advise) while their children clamored for their attention.

Between Time and Money

Greely, a married middle-class white mother of one child, had recently started her own catering company. She was working long hours during the week to get her business off the ground, and reasoned that taking time on the weekend to prep vegetables and lunches would help her create ideal meals. She explained,

> I feel [that] when I have the time I enjoy cooking. And when it's so compressed and after a stressful day, it's kind of horrible. I feel like, because I'm not able to spend as much time with Adelle now, I don't want to spend an hour cooking after I pick her up from school every day. You know, like it's fine sometimes, but I want to be able to sit down and help her with her homework or help her finish her Valentines for her classmates or whatever that may be. I was supposed to soak black-eyed peas last night and I forgot.

The mothers we met who were barely paying the bills routinely cooked—contrary to the stereotype that poor families mainly eat fast food—because it was more economical. Isis, a poor single black mother, told us that she got tired of cooking, but continued to do so to save money. "If I don't cook then they'll go get something out to eat," she said. "But then that's wasting money."

Yet being poor makes it nearly impossible to enact the foodie version of a home-cooked meal. The ingredients that go into meals considered to be healthy—fresh fruits and vegetables, whole grains, and lean meats—are expensive. A recent study of food prices around the globe found that it costs $1.50 more per day—or about $550 a year per person—to eat a healthier diet than a less healthy diet.

The cost of healthy ingredients is not the only barrier. Many of the poor mothers we met also lacked reliable transportation, and therefore typically shopped just once a month. As a result, they avoided buying fresh produce, which spoiled quickly. Mothers also struggled to prepare meals in small trailers or apartments with minimal space. We observed homes without kitchen tables or functional appliances, infested by bugs and rats, and lacking basic kitchen tools like sharp knives, cutting boards, pots and pans.

The idea that home cooking is inherently ideal reflects an elite foodie standpoint. Romantic depictions of cooking assume that everyone has a home, that family members are home eating at the same time, and that kitchens and dining spaces are equipped and safe. This is not necessarily the case for the families we met.

During the month we spent with Flora, a poor black mother who was currently separated from her husband, she was living with her daughter and two grandchildren in a cockroach- and flea-infested hotel room with two double beds. They prepared all of their food in a small microwave, rinsing their utensils in the bathroom sink. Many of the families we met lived in trailers or homes with thin walls that provided little protection from the outside elements. Some homes had holes in the floor or walls, making it nearly impossible to keep pests out. Claudia, a married Latina mother of four, was battling a serious ant invasion in her home. She watched in horror as the ant poison her 12-year-old son was scattering around the trailer's perimeter drifted through an open window and settled on the food she was preparing at the kitchen counter.

Still mothers felt responsible for preparing healthy meals for their children and keenly experienced the gap between the romanticized version of cooking and the realities of their lives. When asked what an "ideal world" would look like for her, Ruth, a widowed black mother of two, said she would like to have a bigger house that included a "bigger stove, and kitchen, and refrigerator so I can cook a little more and do what I need to do to cook healthier. Give me the money to provide for them a little healthier." With more money and space, Ruth could cook the elaborate meals she loves.

To our surprise, many of the middle-class mothers we met also told us that money was a barrier to preparing healthy meals. Even though they often had household incomes of more than $100,000 a year, their membership in the middle class was costly. While they did not experience food shortages, they were forced to make tradeoffs in order to save money—like buying less healthy processed food, or fewer organic items than they would like. For low-income mothers, the tradeoffs are starker: they skipped meals, or spent long hours in line at food pantries or applying for assistance, to make sure their children had enough to eat.

Food Fights

"I don't need it. I don't want it. I never had it," exclaimed four-year-old Rashan when his mom served him an unfamiliar side dish. Rashan's reaction was not uncommon. We rarely observed a meal in which at least one family member didn't complain about the food they were served. Some mothers coaxed their children to eat by playing elaborate games or by hand-feeding them. One middle-class mother even set a timer, telling her son that he had to eat as much of what was on his plate as he could before the time ran out. Feeding others involves taking multiple preferences into consideration, and balancing time and money constraints.

Rather than risk trying new and expensive foods that might prove unpopular, many low-income mothers opted to cook the same foods again and again. They reasoned that it was better to stick with foods (often processed) that they knew their families would eat, rather than risk wasting money and food.

Giselle, a single black mother of two, worked two part-time jobs to make ends meet. There was little room in the food budget to experiment with new or expensive foods. When it came to decide what to make for supper, Giselle played it safe. She explained, "Because I don't want to cook something [they won't like] because I'll like waste the food. Right? Waste the food."

Low-income mothers tended to avoid using recipes, because the ingredients were expensive and they weren't sure if their families would like the new dishes. Instead, they continued to make what was tried and true, even if they didn't like the food themselves. Sandy, a white mother of two, tried hard to cook around her boyfriend's preferences. She liked fish, but her boyfriend didn't. So she ignored her food interests in order to "do something for my whole house." Sociologist Marjorie DeVault also found in her book *Feeding the Family* that women considered men's needs, sometimes above all others, when it came to preparing meals.

For middle-class mothers, cooking was about more than negotiating preferences for certain foods. They felt that offering new foods was crucial for developing their kids' palates—even if the process sometimes led to food fights. Their stories suggest that cooking like Pollan and other experts prescribe is time-consuming and stressful. Some spent significant amounts of time reading the literature on the latest and best healthy foods, seeking out and trading new healthy recipes, and reworking the food budget to include more organic food—leading to greater anxiety about cooking and serving food.

For Elaine, a married white mother of one child, cooking involved high stakes. She and her husband worked full-time, and Elaine's efforts to make meals from scratch rarely ended happily. She spent time prepping food on the weekends in order to cook ideal meals during the week. She explained,

> When we get home it's such a rush. I just don't know what happens to the time. I am so frustrated. That's why I get so angry! I get frustrated 'cause I'm like, I wanna make this good meal that's really healthy and I like to cook 'cause it's kind of my way to show them that I love them, 'This is my love for you guys!' And then I wind up at the end just, you know, grrr! Mad at the food because it takes me so long. It's like, how can it take an hour for me to do this when I've already cut up the carrots and the celery and all I'm doing is shoving it into a bowl?

Even the extensive prep work that Elaine did on the weekends didn't translate into a relaxing meal during the weekday Instead, like so many mothers, Elaine felt frustrated and inadequate about not living up to the ideal home-cooked meal. Their stories suggest that utopian family meals are nearly impossible to create, no matter how hard mothers try.

Thinking Outside the Kitchen

The vision of the family meal that today's food experts are whipping up is alluring. Most people would agree that it would be nice to slow down, eat healthfully, and enjoy a home-cooked meal. However, our research leads us to question why the frontline in reforming the food system has to be in someone's kitchen. The emphasis on home cooking ignores the time pressures, financial constraints, and feeding challenges that shape the family meal. Yet this is the widely promoted standard to which all mothers are held. Our conversations with mothers of young children show us that this emerging standard is a tasty illusion, one that is moralistic, and rather elitist, instead of a realistic vision of cooking today. Intentionally or not, it places the burden of a healthy home-cooked meal on women.

So let's move this conversation out of the kitchen, and brainstorm more creative solutions for sharing the work of feeding families. How about a revival of monthly town suppers, or healthy food trucks? Or perhaps we should rethink how we do meals in schools and workplaces, making lunch an opportunity for savoring and sharing food. Could schools offer to-go meals that families could easily heat up on busy weeknights? Without creative solutions like these, suggesting that we return to the kitchen en masse will do little more than increase the burden so many women already bear.

49

The Deadly Challenges of Raising African American Boys

Navigating the Controlling Image of the "Thug"

Dawn Marie Dow

I interviewed Karin, a married mother, in her apartment while she nursed her only child. Karin let out a deep sigh before describing how she felt when she learned the baby's gender:

> I was thrilled [the baby] wasn't a boy. I think it is hard to be a black girl and a black woman in America, but I think it is dangerous and sometimes deadly to be a black boy and black man. Oscar Grant[1] and beyond, there are lots of dangerous interactions with police in urban areas for black men ... so I was very nervous because we thought she was a boy.... I was relieved when she wasn't. It is terrible, but it is true.

Karin's relief upon learning her child was not a boy underscores how intersections of racial identity, class, and gender influence African American middle- and upper-middle-class mothers' parenting concerns. They are aware their children will likely confront racism, often start addressing racism during their children's infant and toddler years, and attempt to protect their children from racially charged experiences. Responding to these potential experiences of racism, parents believe giving their children the skills to address racism is an essential parenting duty. Although the participants in this research were middle and upper-middle class, and thus had more resources than their lower-income counterparts, they felt limited in their abilities to protect their sons from the harsh realities of being African American boys and men in America.

This chapter examines how African American middle- and upper-middle-class mothers raising young children conceptualize the challenges their sons will face and how they parent them in light of these challenges. I focus on mothers because they are often primarily responsible for socializing young children, and specifically on middle- and upper-middle-class African American mothers because they typically have more resources to address discrimination than do lower-income mothers. Indeed, one might assume that these mothers' resources would enable them to protect their sons from certain challenges. African American mothers are more likely to engage in the racial socialization of younger children and to prepare children to address experiences of racism than are African American fathers. They are also more likely to be single and, thus, principally responsible for decisions related to their children's educational, social, and cultural resources and experiences.

Although masculinity is associated with strength, participants' accounts of their parenting practices revealed their belief that the thug image made their sons vulnerable in many social interactions. Participants feared

Dow, Dawn Marie. "The Deadly Challenges of Raising African American Boys: Navigating the Controlling Image of the 'Thug'." *Gender & Society* 30, no. 2 (2016): 161–188.

for their sons' physical safety and believed their sons would face harsher treatment and be criminalized by teachers, police officers, and the public because of their racial identity and gender. Their accounts revealed four strategies used to navigate these challenges, which I term *experience, environment, emotion,* and *image management.*

RACED, CLASSED, AND GENDERED PARENTING CHALLENGES

Gendered Racism and Controlling Images

African American boys and girls experience different levels of social integration within suburban schools. Boys are viewed as "cool" and "athletic" by classmates and are provided more opportunities to participate in high-value institutional activities, while girls are viewed as aggressive and unfeminine, and are provided with fewer similar opportunities. Despite having somewhat positive experiences with peers, boys' encounters with teachers and administrators are fraught, as educators often perceive them as aggressive, violent, and potential criminals. Compared to whites and African American girls, African American boys are disciplined more severely in school, and their in-school discipline is more likely to lead to criminal charges.

African American boys are also more likely to have encounters with law enforcement than are whites or African American girls, and these interactions are more likely to have negative outcomes. The news provides numerous examples of fatal shootings of unarmed African American teenage boys, often by white police officers and private citizens.

Collins (2009) theorizes how controlling images function as racialized and gendered stereotypes that justify the oppression of certain groups and naturalize existing power relations, while forcing oppressed populations to police their own behavior. Scholars studying controlling images examine how these inaccurate depictions of black sexuality, lawfulness, temperament, and financial well-being are used to justify policies that disempower women of color (Collins 2004, 2009; Gilliam 1999; Hancock 2003; Harris-Perry 2011) and impact African Americans' experiences in their workplaces, school settings, and other social contexts (Beauboeuf-Lafontant 2009; Dow 2015; Ong 2005; Wingfield 2007, 2009). These images depict African American men as hypermasculine: revering them as superhuman or reviling them as threats to be contained. Scholars suggest that African American men enact the thug, a version of subordinate masculinity associated with violence, criminality, and toughness, because they are not permitted to attain hegemonic masculinity (Schrock and Schwalbe 2009). Indeed, African American men who enact alternative versions of manhood that are associated with being educated or middle class confront challenges to their masculinity and racial authenticity.

Expanding on this scholarship, I examine how the thug image influences African American middle- and upper-middle-class mothers' parenting concerns and practices when raising sons. Building on Ford's view that "black manhood refers to imagined constructions of self that allow for more fluid interactions in Black and nonblack, public and private social spaces" (Ford 2011, 42), I argue that this fluidity is not just permitted but required to protect black male bodies and manage their vulnerability in different contexts. Black manhood and double consciousness are complementary concepts because each requires individuals to see themselves through the broader society's eyes. These concepts also illuminate how individuals who are associated with privileged identities, such as "man" or "American," confront obstacles that prevent them from benefiting from those identities' privileges.

METHODS

This chapter is based on data from a larger project that examined how African American middle- and upper-middle-class mothers approach work, family, parenting, and child care: 60 participants were recruited to the study, of which 40 were raising sons only or sons and daughters. Aside from the opening quote describing a mother's relief upon learning she was not having a son, this analysis focuses on participants raising sons.

All participants lived in the San Francisco Bay Area and were middle or upper-middle class as determined by their education and total family income. Participants attended college for at least two years, and their total annual family incomes ranged from $50,000 to $300,000. The majority of participants (63 percent) earned advanced degrees such as MD, JD, PhD, or MA, with 27 percent earning college degrees and 10 percent attending some college. Three-fourths of the participants were married or in a domestic partnership, and one-fourth were divorced, never married, or widowed. All participants were raising at least one child who was ten years old or younger, as this research focused on mothers who are raising young children. Participants' employment status included working full-time or part-time, or not working outside of the home (i.e., stay-at-home mothers).

As a middle-class African American mother, I shared traits with my participants. These characteristics, in some ways, positioned me as an insider with participants and facilitated building rapport and their willingness to share information about their lives. This status also required that I refrain from assuming I understood a participant's meanings. I balanced building rapport with guarding against making assumptions by probing for additional clarification when a participant suggested I understood something based on our shared background.

PROTECTING SONS FROM BABY RACISM AND CRIMINALIZATION

Although participants described parenting concerns that transcended gender and related to fostering other aspects of their children's identity, this chapter examines their specific concerns about raising sons. Participants' concerns included ensuring the physical safety of their sons in interactions with police officers, educators, and the public, and preventing their sons from being criminalized by these same groups.

Gender, Racial Identity, and Parenting

Generally, middle-class children are thought to live in realms of safety, characterized by good schools, an abundance of educational resources, and protection from harsh treatment from police, teachers, and the public. However, numerous scholars have demonstrated that despite the expansion of the African American middle class, its members face economic, social, residential, and educational opportunities that are substantively different from those of middle-class whites. Middle-class African Americans continue to face discrimination in lending, housing, and employment. African American middle-class children often attend schools that are poorly funded, lack adequate infrastructure, and are characterized by lower academic achievement than their white counterparts. These children are also more likely to grow up in neighborhoods with higher levels of crime and inferior community services as compared to their white counterparts. Although participants recognized that their middle-class status afforded them additional resources, they believed that their sons' access to middle-class realms of safety was destabilized and diminished because of their racial identity and gender.

Charlotte, a married mother of four sons, who lived in an elite and predominately white neighborhood, held back tears as she described her fears about how others would respond to them:

> I look at the president. I see how he is treated and it scares me. I want people to look at my sons and see them for the beautiful, intelligent, gifted, wonderful creatures that they are and nothing else. I do not want them to look at my sons and say, "There goes that Black guy," or hold onto their purse.

Similarly, Nia, a married mother of two sons, who lived in an economically diverse, predominantly African American neighborhood, described interactions with other families at local children's activities that she called "baby racism":

> From the time our first son was a baby and we would go [to different children's activities]. Our son would go and hug a kid and a parent would grab their child and be like, "Oh, he's going to attack

him!" And it was just, like, "Really? Are you serious?" He was actually going to hug him. You see, like little "baby racism." ... I have even written to local parents' listservs to ask, "Am I imagining this ...?" And the response was interesting. Almost all the black mothers wrote in, "You're not imagining this, this is real. You're going to have to spend the rest of your life fighting for your child." And all the white mothers said, "You're imagining it. It's not like that. You're misinterpreting it." And it was like, okay, so I'm not imagining this.

Charlotte and Nia, like other participants, believed that when African American boys participated in activities that were engaged in by predominantly white and middle-class families, their behavior faced greater scrutiny. Race and gender trumped class; poverty and crime were associated with being an African American boy. Participants believed the process of criminalizing their sons' behaviors began at an early age, and was not confined to educational settings but was pervasive. Although participants had no way of knowing how others were thinking about their sons, numerous studies support their belief that African American boys' actions are interpreted differently in a range of settings.

Participants also saw teachers and educators as potential threats to their sons' development. Karlyn, a single mother of a son and daughter, described her son's experience of being harshly disciplined at school:

A teacher was yelling at my son because some girls reported that he cheated in Four Square. ... I had to let her know "don't ever pull my son out of class for a Four Square game again. ... And don't ever yell at my child unless he has done something horrible." ... I told the principal, "You know, she may not think she is racist but what would make her yell at a little black boy over a stupid Four Square game?" ... He said, "Oh my God, I am just so glad that you have the amount of restraint that you did because I would have been really upset." I said, "As the mother of a black son, I am always concerned about how he is treated by people."

Like Karlyn, others relayed stories of educators having disproportionately negative responses to their sons' behavior, describing them as aggressive or scary, when similar behavior in white boys was described as more benign. Karlyn, and others, continuously monitored their sons' schools to ensure they received fair treatment. Participants' middle-class status did not protect their sons from these experiences.

Mary, a married mother of a son and daughter, also believed her son faced distinct challenges related to his racial identity, class, and gender and sought out an African American middle- and upper-middle-class mothers' group to get support from mothers who were negotiating similar challenges. Mary described a conversation that regularly occurred in her mothers' group, revealing her worries about adequately preparing her son to navigate interactions with teachers and police officers:

With our sons, we talk about how can we prepare them or teach them about how to deal with a society, especially in a community like Oakland, where black men are held to a different standard than others, and not necessarily a better one. ... When you are a black man and you get stopped by the policeman, you can't do the same things a white person would do because they might already have some preconceived notions, and that might get you into a heap more trouble. ... We talk about our sons who are a little younger and starting kindergarten. What do we have to do to make sure teachers don't have preconceived ideas that stop our sons from learning because they believe little brown boys are rambunctious, or little brown boys are hitting more than Caucasian boys?

It is worth emphasizing that although these participants were middle- and upper-middle-class African American mothers with more resources than lower-income mothers, these resources did not protect their sons from gendered racism. Also, middle-class mothers are depicted as viewing educators as resources, but these participants viewed educators as potential threats. They believed their sons' racial identity marked them as poor, uneducated, violent, and criminal, and they would have to actively and continuously challenge that marking and assert their middle-class status in mainstream white society—a version of the politics of respectability. Some participants attended workshops aimed at helping them teach their sons to safely engage with teachers, police officers, and the public.

Although most participants believed their sons faced challenges related to the thug, a few did not. These participants attributed their lack of concern to their sons' racially ambiguous appearance. Kera, a married mother of two sons, said,

> The way they look, they're like me. They could be damn near anything depending on how they put their hair. ... I don't think they'll have the full repercussions of being a black man like my brothers or my husband.

Kera's comments echo research suggesting that skin color differences impact African Americans' experiences in employment, school, and relationships.

Participants also believed their sons faced pressure to perform specific versions of African American masculinity that conformed to existing raced, classed, and gendered hierarchies. Nora, a married mother of a son and daughter, said,

> There is a lot of pressure for black boys to assume a more 'thuggish' identity. There aren't enough different identity spaces for black boys in schools ... and so I want my kids to have choices. And if that's the choice, I might cringe ... but I would want it to be among a menu of choices.

Elements of the thug, such as criminality, aggression, and low academic performance, recurred in participants' accounts as something they and their sons navigated. Nora's comments underscore that these negotiations begin at a young age.

Given these pressures to perform specific versions of African American masculinity associated with poverty and criminality, participants tried to protect their sons from early experiences of subtle and explicit racism because of the potential impact on their identity formation. Sharon, a married mother of a son and daughter, captured a sentiment shared by many participants when she stated,

> Each time a black boy has a racially charged interaction with a police officer, a teacher, or a shop owner, those experiences will gradually start to eat at his self-worth and damage his spirit. He might become so damaged that he starts to believe and enact the person he is expected to be, rather than who he truly is as a person.

Participants believed their sons were bombarded by negative messages about African American manhood from the broader white society and, at times, the African American community. Participants worried about the toll these messages might take on their sons' self-perception as they transitioned to manhood. They steered their sons away from enacting the thug, but also observed an absence of other viable expressions of racially authentic middle-class masculinity.

Strategies to Navigate the Thug

Participants walked a tightrope between preparing their sons to overcome the gendered racism they might confront and ensuring they did not internalize these views or use them as excuses to fail. Christine, who was engaged to be married and the mother of a son, explained that in teaching her son what it means to be an African American man, she wanted to ensure that he did not grow up "with that black man chip on the shoulder. Feeling we are weak. Whites have done something to us and we can't do something because of white people." Christine wanted her son to understand how some viewed him, but she tried to foster a version of double consciousness that emphasized his agency and discouraged him from feeling bitter toward whites, disempowered, or constrained by others' views.

Next, I outline the strategies participants used to navigate the thug image and teach their sons how to modulate their expression of masculinity, race, and class. Participants often preferred one strategy but they may have used other strategies, or a combination of strategies, during different periods of their sons' lives.

Experience and Environment Management

Participants used two explicitly race-, class-, and gender-conscious strategies to manage their sons' regular social interactions: *experience* and *environment management*. *Experience management* focused on seeking out opportunities for sons to engage in activities to gain fluency in different experiences—both empowering and challenging—of being African American boys and men. *Environment management* focused on monitoring their sons' regular social environment, such as their school or neighborhood, with the aim of excluding sources of discrimination. These environments were often primarily middle class but diverse in terms of racial identity, religion, and sexual orientation. Participants often used environment management when children were preschool age to avoid early experiences of discrimination. Despite having additional resources, participants navigated a landscape of institutionalized child care, which they believed included racially insensitive providers.

Participants using experience management tried to help their sons acquire what they viewed as an essential life skill: the ability to seamlessly shift from communities that differed by race, class, and gender. Experience management involved shuttling sons to activities, such as Little League baseball, basketball, or music lessons, in a variety of neighborhoods comprising African Americans from different economic backgrounds. Participants also exposed sons to African American culture and history and African American men, including fathers, uncles, cousins, coaches, or friends, whom they believed expressed healthy versions of masculinity. Karlyn said, "I worry about my son because he is not growing up with the kind of 'hood' mentality that me and his father had, but he will have to interact with those people." Karlyn's son was not completely ensconced within the safety of a middle-class community. She believed as her son traveled through his day—to school, riding on buses, walking down the street, going in and out of stores, and interacting with police officers and the public—he would be perceived in a range of different and primarily negative ways. Karlyn believed her son would have to adjust the expression of his masculinity, racial identity, and class to successfully interact with people from that "hood mentality"—a version of subordinate masculinity and people from other racial and class backgrounds. She believed that lacking regular experiences in settings like the one she grew up in put her son at a disadvantage in these situations. Karlyn sought out experiences to help her son learn to navigate a world that she believed viewed him primarily as an African American boy and potential troublemaker, rather than a good middle-class kid. She ensured that her son had regular contact with his father and other African American men. She also regularly discussed examples of clashes between African American men and the police with her son.

Maya, a married mother of four, also used experience management. She described how she and her husband exposed their son to alternative and, in her view, more positive ideals of masculinity:

> With our son, we definitely have a heightened level of concern, especially around public schools, about what it means to be a black male in this society. …[My] husband does stuff with him that is very much male socializing stuff. …But, it is worrisome to think about sending him into the world where he is such a potential target. … I know how to make a kid that does well in school and can navigate academic environments. My husband knows how to help young people—black young people—understand their position, how the world sees them and how they might see themselves in a different and much more positive way.

Through these experiences, out of necessity, participants aimed to help their sons develop a double consciousness—"a sense of always looking at one's self through the eyes of others" (Du Bois [1903] 1994, 5). Maya and her husband did this by teaching their son how others might perceive him while rejecting prevailing images of African American masculinity and crafting alternatives.

Environment management involved managing sons' daily social interactions by excluding specific kinds of exposures. Rachel, a married mother of a son and daughter, said,

> My son thinks he is street-smart but he is used to being in an environment in which he is known. No one thinks of my son as a black boy, they think of him as my son, but when he goes out into the real world people will make assumptions about him.

Rachel lived in a predominately white neighborhood with few other African American families. She believed her neighbors did not view her family as "the African American family," but simply as a family, and this protected her son from challenges associated with being an African American male in the broader society where he might be assumed to be part of the urban underclass. Charlotte, mentioned earlier, described her efforts to find a neighborhood with the right kind of community:

> When we lived in [a different predominately white suburb], none of the mothers spoke to me. Maybe they would wave but I was really taken aback by how shunned I felt. We were the only black family in the school and no one spoke [to us]. …Here [another predominately white area], over the summer, people knew my name and I didn't know their name. …There was a feeling of welcome and friendliness from the group. … You know, I just worry so much for them. I want them to be accepted, and not judged, and not looked at like a black kid. I want people to look at them as "that is a good young man or a good boy." … Maybe if they know my sons and me and my husband, it won't be "Oh, there are the black kids"; it will be "There is us."

Charlotte wanted her sons to have access to better resources and schools, and that translated to living in primarily white neighborhoods. Nonetheless, revealing the diversity in white settings, she looked for white neighborhoods where she believed her sons would not face discrimination. Charlotte hoped to transform her sons from "anonymous" African American boys, assumed to be up to no good, to "the kid next door." Being African American was accompanied by assumptions about lower-class status and criminality that participants sought to overcome. Charlotte's experience underscores how intersections of race, gender, and class are used to value individuals and the challenges her sons confronted to be seen as both African American and "good middle-class kids."

Participants living in economically diverse predominantly African American communities with higher crime rates faced particular challenges when using environment management. Jameela, a single mother of a son, explained,

> I live in Richmond because it is more affordable, but I don't see a lot of parents like me. I keep a tight leash on my son because of where we live. I don't want him to get involved with the wrong element.

Jameela, and participants living in similar environments, often did not let their sons play with neighborhood children. Her experiences highlight class divisions within African American communities and the intensive peer group monitoring parents engaged in when their residential choices were limited. These children's regular environment did not include their immediate neighborhood but was confined to controlled spaces, including their school, church, or other settings that were diverse, free of racial discrimination, and often primarily middle class.

Experience and environment management both focus on social interactions but with different aims. Experience management aims to inform sons through regular controlled activities about the challenges they may face as African American boys and men and teach them how to modify the expression of their masculinity, class, and racial identity. Environment management aims to reduce or eliminate the challenges of being an African American male so they are not the defining features of their sons' lives. These mothers tried to find or create bias-free environments that would not limit their sons' expression of their masculinity but worried about their sons' treatment outside of these "safe havens."

Image and Emotion Management

Participants also used *image* and *emotion management* to reduce the vulnerability they believed their sons experienced related to the thug image and to prevent them from being associated with poor urban African Americans. These strategies were also explicitly race, gender, and class conscious and focused on their sons' emotional expressions and physical appearance. Sons were encouraged to restrain their expressions of anger, frustration, or excitement lest others view them as aggressive or violent. Participants also counseled their sons to strictly monitor their dress and appearance so they would be viewed not as criminals but as middle-class kids.

Karlyn engaged in something she called "prepping for life" with her son. She said,

> I talk to [my son] constantly. We do scenarios and we talk about stuff. I'll pose a situation, like say, if you are ever kidnapped, what do you do? If the police ever pull you over, how do you need to react? So we do scenarios for all of that, it's just prepping for life.

It would not be unreasonable for a parent to instruct their child to view police officers as sources of help. What is striking about Karlyn's examples is that she viewed child predators and police officers as equally dangerous to her son. She used emotion management with the hope that preparing her son for these scenarios would give him some agency in his response in the moment.

Some participants looked for places where their sons could safely express "normal boy" behaviors while gaining control over those behaviors. Heather, a divorced mother of a son and two daughters, described her plan to help her son control his emotions at school:

> I'm hoping to get [my son] into enough relaxation-type yoga classes so he is a little bit calmer when he does go to school. I want to make sure he lets it all out in the play yard and activities after school.

Through activities like yoga, karate, and meditation, these participants hoped their sons would learn to restrain their emotions, and that this ability would translate to their interactions with teachers, police officers, peers, and the public. Participants emphasized that there were appropriate times to express feelings and advised their sons to refrain from responding to discrimination in the moment, instead taking their time to determine the best approach. This often meant reframing race-related grievances in nonracial terms so they would be better received by white teachers and administrators. Although masculinity is associated with strength, participants believed their sons were vulnerable and did not have the freedom to exhibit certain feelings or behaviors.

Participants also encouraged their sons to engage in image management to avoid being viewed as thugs. Rebecca, a widow with one son who also raised her nephew in his teenage years, recounted discussions during which she counseled her nephew about how people interpreted his clothing:

> Things like him wearing his hoodie and the assumption that he is up to no good. I tried to explain that to him because he didn't understand. He said, "I am just wearing my hoodie." "But baby, I understand what you are doing, and there is nothing wrong with that, but if you walk through the [poor, primarily African American and high-crime] neighborhood near my school, we see something different." You know, just having to protect him and trying to shelter him from unnecessary stress and trauma. ... You know, the sagging pants and all the things that teenage boys do that don't necessarily mean they are doing anything wrong. ... Is it fair? No. Is it reality? Yes.

Rebecca's comments illustrate a parenting paradox. Even as Rebecca challenged the double standards that she believed were used to evaluate her nephew's and son's behavior and appearance, as a practical matter, she felt compelled to educate them about these different standards. At times, she counseled them to adhere to those standards for their own safety. Given the recurring news stories of unarmed African American boys shot by police officers and private citizens, Rebecca's approach seems reasonable. Participants believed their sons might be labeled thugs because of their attire, thus leaving them vulnerable to attacks from others. Participants could not prevent these interactions from happening, but wanted their sons to survive them.

Conclusion

This research was bookended by two shooting deaths of unarmed African American males. The first, Oscar Grant, was shot in the back by Officer Johannes Mehserle while lying face-down on a Bay Area Rapid Transit platform. The second, Trayvon Martin, was pursued, shot, and killed by George Zimmerman, a neighborhood watch coordinator, while walking home in his father's "safe," middle-class, gated community. Despite being a child from that community, it was not safe for Mr. Martin. He was not viewed as a good middle-class kid, but was instead interpreted as a threat. Since these incidents, African American parents are increasingly sharing the concerns they have for their sons' safety. Incidents like these reminded participants that their sons have different experiences with the public than do white boys and men.

Existing research suggests that having a male body and access to masculinity confers privileges and protections that serve as a symbolic asset in social interactions. However, my research demonstrates that depending on its racialization, the male body can be a "symbolic liability." The thug image derives its power and strength from intimidation and is used to justify attacks on African American boys' and men's bodies and minds. Participants' additional labor to protect their sons and its raced, classed, and gendered nature is largely invisible to the people it is meant to make more comfortable. Despite having additional resources, participants and their sons were not immune to a social system that required them to police their behaviors, emotions, and appearance to signal to others that they were respectable and safe middle-class African American males. Ironically, by feeling compelled to engage in strategies that encouraged their sons to conform to stricter standards and engage in acts of deference, participants contributed to reproducing a social structure that subordinates African Americans. Their accounts show a continuing need for African Americans to have a double consciousness through which they understand how society views them. Their actions also suggest a tension between individual strategies of survival and strategies that challenge and transform existing gendered, classed, and raced hierarchies.

NOTE

1 On New Year's Day 2010, Johannes Mehserle, a white Bay Area Rapid Transit police officer, fatally shot Oscar Grant, an African American teenager, in Oakland. During the incident, Grant was unarmed, lying face-down on the train platform, and had been subdued by several other officers. On July 8, 2010, Mehserle was found guilty of involuntary manslaughter, not the higher charges of second-degree murder or voluntary manslaughter.

REFERENCES

Beauboeuf-Lafontant, Tamara. 2009. Behind the mask of the strong black woman: Voice and the embodiment of a costly performance. Philadelphia: Temple University Press.

Collins, Patricia Hill. 2004. Black sexual politics: African Americans, gender, and the new racism. New York: Routledge.

Collins, Patricia Hill. 2009. Black feminist thought: Knowledge, consciousness, and the politics of empowerment, 2nd ed., Routledge classics. New York: Routledge.

Dow, Dawn. 2015. Negotiating "The Welfare Queen" and "The Strong Black Woman": African American middle-class mothers' work and family perspectives. Sociological Perspectives 58:36–55.

Du Bois, William Edward Burghardt. (1903) 1994. The souls of black folks. New York: Gramercy Books.

Ford, Kristie A. 2011. Doing fake masculinity, being real men: Present and future constructions of self among black college men. Symbolic Interaction 34:38–62.

Gilliam, Franklin D., Jr. 1999. The "Welfare Queen" experiment. Nieman Reports 53:49–52.

Hancock, Ange-Marie. 2003. Contemporary welfare reform and the public identity of the "Welfare Queen." Race, Gender & Class 10:31–59.

Harris-Perry, Melissa V. 2011. Sister citizen: Shame, stereotypes, and black women in America. New Haven, CT: Yale University Press.

Ong, Maria. 2005. Body projects of young women of color in physics: Intersections of gender, race, and science. Social Problems 52:593–617.

Schrock, Douglas, and Michael Schwalbe. 2009. Men, masculinity, and manhood acts. Annual Review of Sociology 35:277–295.

Wingfield, Adia Harvey. 2007. The modern mammy and the angry black man: African American professionals' experiences with gendered racism in the workplace. Race, Gender & Class 14:196–212.

Wingfield, Adia Harvey. 2009. Racializing the glass escalator: Reconsidering men's experiences with women's work. Gender & Society 23:5–26.

50

The 'Organic Child' Ideal Holds Mothers to an Impossible Standard

Kate Cairns, Norah MacKendrick, and Josée Johnston

Last year, a widely publicised study found that eating an exclusively organic diet drastically reduces a family's exposure to pesticides. Paired with warnings from reputable voices such as the American Academy of Pediatrics, popular coverage would lead you to believe it's a no-brainer: yes, you really *do* need to shell out for higher-end organic options to protect your family. And the 'you' in this story is often presumed to be the mother.

As sociologists who study the work of feeding children – and two of us are mothers ourselves – we know many parents read this coverage with a sense of alarm or guilt. The message is nothing new. Today's caregivers are expected not only to make sure kids eat their vegetables, but also to read labels, research omega-three to omega-six ratios, and think about the plastic packaging of Organic Cheddar Bunnies.

The ideal of providing an organic diet has become a kind of gold standard of healthy child-raising practice. Over the past decade, we have conducted extensive research on food and mothering that included interviews with more than 100 mothers in Toronto and New York City. We can tell you: mothers are feeling the pressure. Even prosperous parents with an ample grocery budget feel like they are failing to live up to this ideal. Each new health story about arsenic in baby food, the impact of plastic packaging on IQ, or tips for feeding picky children can encourage mothers to wonder if they're doing enough by their children.

We do not question the science that toxic chemicals in our food are dangerous and can do real damage to our children. We are also certain that the answer to this real problem is not expert, attentive mothering. The star of this story is the 'organic child': an imagined pure child who is shielded from risk through careful feeding practices. The organic child ideal suggests that children are best protected through the (conscientious and expensive) practices of parents, and especially mothers. It's a bad ideal, impossible to fully attain.

In our research, we've spoken with many mothers who prioritise organic milk and vegetables, those who focus on minimising food waste, and others who seek to protect kids from fast food. Priorities vary, but the message emerges that mothers are responsible for making carefully considered, often costly food purchases to protect children from the pervasive risks of an industrial food system. The news media and public health initiatives consistently target women as primary caregivers responsible for grocery shopping and home cooking. When it comes to protecting children's health, mothers are held to a much higher standard than

Cairns, Kate, Norah MacKendrick, and Josée Johnston. "The 'Organic Child' Ideal Holds Mothers to an Impossible Standard." *Aeon*, February 19, 2020.

fathers. Even when fathers care about environmental issues, they are less likely to take on the work of managing toxins and family health through food choices.

The ideal of the organic child places a load of care-work on mothers' shoulders. In practical terms, it means keeping up with the growing list of harmful chemicals lurking in seemingly nutritious snacks, developing new strategies for sneaking vegetables into kid-friendly meals, and preventing children from clamouring for the newest sugary temptation. Feeding an organic child requires shopping at speciality grocers and making baby food from scratch, and also the labour of researching options, planning shopping routines, and factoring in family food preferences. It all leaves many women feeling like they've fallen short. One mother we interviewed in New York City joked that she gave up on sleep to find time to make meals from scratch and pack healthy lunches for her children. We also learned that even parents with ample time, money, privilege, and access to farmers' markets struggle to reach the elusive ideal of the organic child.

The organic child ideal has taken hold at a time when an increasing proportion of families struggle to make ends meet. In Canada and the United States, one in six children experiences food insecurity. In an age of tremendous inequality, promoting an ideal of artisanal, chemical-free food is not only unrealistic but downright absurd.

Most time- and resource-strapped mothers simply cannot keep up with the demands of the organic child. The constant struggle of feeding children in the context of poverty is vividly depicted in the book *Pressure Cooker* (2019) by the sociologists Sarah Bowen, Joslyn Brenton, and Sinikka Elliott. They tell the stories of mothers and grandmothers in North Carolina who care deeply about cooking and eating but don't have the means to enact the 'perfect' family meal, sometimes forgoing their own dinner to ensure their children have something to eat. While the strain of poverty is pervasive, women of colour face the added challenge of defending their feeding practices against racist judgments. Black and Latinx mothers in particular are more likely to face the scrutiny of authorities – doctors, social workers, teachers – who might judge a child's body weight as a reflection of 'bad' mothering practices, with potentially severe consequences.

Many low-income consumers tell us they dream of healthy, organic meals, but their daily food realities look quite different. In research with families in California, sociologist Priya Fielding-Singh found that junk food was one of few indulgences poor parents could offer their kids. In a context of material deprivation, saying yes to a request for chips or chocolate can be an expression of care. In addition, some mothers might be sceptical of food recommendations and body standards perceived as white, top-down, and elitist. The material realities of our stratified food system are seldom visible in the glossy pages of food and parenting magazines expounding on the virtues of an organic diet.

The organic child ideal weighs on hearts and minds because it resonates with a common notion: that caregivers and especially mothers, rather than state regulation of industry practices, are the best way to protect children. This presumption leads to impossible demands. And as long as the persistent toxic compounds circulate in our air, water, and soil, even the most privileged mothers cannot safeguard their children within an organic bubble.

Striving for an organic child distracts from working for a more democratic, just, and sustainable food system. It reinforces a system of protection for the most elite shoppers, while inequalities abound. It is low-income communities and communities of colour who are more likely to live near polluting highways, waste incinerators, and factories. They are at greater risk of having high levels of lead in their household and school water supplies. These are problems of racism, corporate exploitation, and government neglect.

Adopting a shopping list of organic food staples appears easier (and more achievable) than the challenging, collective work of ensuring that all children have access to safe and nutritious foods. Yet other countries do manage to address the problem as a nation. In 2015, Sweden devised dietary guidelines that make sustainability a national concern, rather than an individual choice. The country, like all members of the European Union, also benefits from stronger protections from toxic substances; regulators require chemical safety to be evaluated *before* a substance is allowed on the market. Meanwhile, in the United States, chemicals are allowed on the market with very little preliminary testing or review.

We have a long way to go to protect children in the United States from harmful foods and toxic chemicals, but there is growing support for a universal school lunch programme that would feed all our children a nutritious midday meal for free. In October 2019, the senators Bernie Sanders and Ilhan Omar introduced a bill that would do just that. In her book, *The Labor of Lunch* (2019), the social scientist Jennifer Gaddis argues that a truly universal school lunch programme must prioritise children's health alongside environmental sustainability and worker rights, to build a world where school cafeteria workers are empowered to cook nutritious, ethically sourced meals that are free for all children.

We'll secure real justice only if we move beyond our own carefully screened shopping lists, and take up joint food projects dedicated to the well-being of *all* children – not just the organic ones.

51

"Not My Way, Sesha. Your Way. Slowly"

A Personal Narrative on Raising a Child with Profound Intellectual Disabilities

Eva Feder Kittay

A CHILD IS BORN

> The most important thing that happens when a child with disabilities is born is that a child is born.
>
> (Ferguson and Asch 1989, 108)

The most important thing that happens when a woman becomes the mother of a child with disabilities is that she becomes the mother of a new child. When Sesha was born, I, along with Jeffrey, her father and my life partner, fell madly in love with our baby. It was 1969. I was 23, my husband 25, and we were pioneers in the natural childbirth movement. Exhilarated by the vigorous labor of propelling my baby into the world, and amazed by the success of my own body's heaving, I now gazed into a little face emerging from me, a face wearing a pout that slowly became the heralding cry of the newborn infant. The nurses cleaned her off, handed her to me, and my Sesha melted into my arms. With her full head of black hair, her sweet funny infant's face, and her delicious temperament, this baby was the fulfillment of our dreams. We saw in her the perennial "perfect baby": the exquisite miracle of a birth. This birth, and each birth, unique and universal—common, even ordinary, and yet each time miraculous. Such were my reflections as I lay in a New York City hospital room watching the snow fall while bathing in the glory of a wanted, welcomed baby. Only the hospital wasn't conforming to my mood or my expectations. I had anticipated seeing my baby shortly after she had been wheeled out of the delivery room, and thought she would soon thereafter join me in my room. I was to have my baby in my room after a 24-hour observation period. But more than 24 hours had passed and no one had brought her in. Why? Could something be wrong? The nurses evaded my questions, and the doctors were nowhere to be found. Finally someone provided an explanation. Sesha had some jaundice ("common, nothing to worry about") and a cyanotic episode of no known origin (that is, she had briefly stopped breathing). She had been examined by a pediatrician, and she seemed fine. I could start nursing her and we could leave the hospital according to schedule. It was four months before anyone thought again about that episode.

As the months wore on, I slowly adjusted to motherhood, and Sesha helped make the adjustment easy. Jeffrey and I shared all aspects of parenting, except that I did the nursing. One wise nursing book, I no longer recall who wrote it, advised against a baby nurse for the nursing mother. Instead it urged that the

Kittay, Eva Feder. "Not My Way, Sesha, Your Way, Slowly" from *Love's labor: Essays on Women, Equality and Dependency*. New York and London: Routledge, 2019.

father (grandmothers, friends, and paid help, if affordable) should help care for the mother and take over all tasks except the care and feeding of the nursing baby. This would allow her to regain her strength, and to nurse the baby in a rested condition and peaceful frame of mind. I was fortunate enough to be able to follow that advice. In fact, I recognized then and have come to believe still more deeply that this advice contained a profound principle: that to nurture a dependent being well, and without damaging the nurturer, requires that the nurturer herself be nurtured. This advice embodied the egalitarian ideals of marriage and parenthood that I shared with my spouse.

So the two of us embraced our parenthood and were blissful with our new baby. Sesha didn't cry much, fell asleep at my breast at night, and by day slept and munched (though with less vigor than I had expected). While she slept a great deal, when awake Sesha had a wonderful wide-eyed questioning look that made us feel that she was very alert and taking in everything around her. At four months she was developing into a beautiful little baby, very cooperative and oh so sweet. Only she wasn't doing new "tricks." When friends and relatives would ask us what the little prodigy was up to, we'd have curiously little to report. But then, I wasn't interested in foolish competitions of how early my child did such and such. All potential sources of anxiety were water off a duck's back: I was the happy mama, content to be gliding through this new period of my life with duckling and mate in tow. Yet it was precisely at this fourth month that a swell of extraordinary proportions engulfed us and interrupted my blissful journey into motherhood.

At this time, friends with a baby approximately Sesha's age visited us, and we were disturbed by the significant difference in the development of these two infants. A physician friend indicated that I ought to visit a pediatric neurologist. (Our own pediatrician responded to my query of why Sesha, at four months, was still not picking up her head, by saying that she must have a heavier head than the average baby and that such a trait is generally inherited from one of the parents. He advised me to go home and measure my husband's head to see if he, too, had a large head. Like fools, my husband and I pulled out the tape measure and determined that, yes, my husband's head was somewhat large. What cowardice propelled this pediatrician to evade his responsibility to be forthright and refer us to a specialist?!) The neurologist we visited must have known then that Sesha was severely impaired, but he was breaking the news to us gradually—over a period that lasted nearly two years. In contrast to my pediatrician, this physician was being kind, not evasive. He did not try to falsely reassure us. His efforts to gently ease us into the realization of the extensive damage Sesha had sustained were nonetheless thwarted when, on his recommendation, we visited the star pediatric neurologist on the West Coast while on holiday.

Sesha was six months old, still as lovely and sweet and pliant as one might wish any baby to be. The handsome, well-tanned doctor examined our daughter briefly, and told us without any hesitation that she was and would always be profoundly retarded—at best severely and not profoundly retarded. His credentials as a physician who can correctly predict an outcome remain secure, but his understanding of how to approach parents with such harsh news, also an important skill for a physician, is quite another matter. The swell that had been threatening to engulf us for two months now crested, and we were smashed onto a rocky shore with all the force that nature could muster against us. Never will I forget how ill I was in that San Francisco hotel room—how my body convulsed against this indigestible morsel. My husband had to care for Sesha and me, even as he ached. This brutal, insensitive manner in confronting parents with such devastating news is one that I have heard recounted again and again. The stories differ. The pain of the prognosis is matched only by the anger at obtuse and insensitive doctors. In our own case, we had a near repeat performance when, just to be certain of his suspicions, our first and humane physician wanted still one more consultation. We thought that we had now visited the Inferno, and we were prepared to begin the arduous climb back up—to find some equilibrium, some way to live with this verdict. But on our encounter with the third pediatric neurologist we were again told outright—after a five-minute exam—that our daughter was severely to profoundly retarded and that we should consider having other children because "one rotten apple doesn't spoil the barrel." As I type these words nearly 27 years later, I still wonder at the utter failure of human empathy in a physician—one whose specialty, no less, is neurological impairment.

Sesha would never live a normal life. It would be another year before we completed the tests, the evaluations, the questionings that confirmed those first predictions. We couldn't know or fully accept the extent of her impairment, but some things were clear. We knew it wasn't a degenerative disability and for that, we were grateful. But the worst fear was that her handicap involved her intellectual faculties. We, her parents, were intellectuals. I was committed to a life of the mind. Nothing mattered to me as much as to be able to reason, to reflect, to understand. This was the air I breathed. How was I to raise a daughter that would have no part of this? If my life took its meaning from thought, what kind of meaning would her life have? Yet throughout this time, it never even occurred to me to give Sesha up, to institutionalize her, to think of her in any other terms than my own beloved child. She was my daughter. I was her mother. That was fundamental. Her impairment in no way mitigated my love for her. If it had any impact on that love it was only to intensify it. She was so vulnerable. She would need so much protection and love from us to shelter her from the scorn of the world, from its dangers, from its indifference, from its failure to understand her and her humanity. We didn't yet realize how much she would teach us, but we already knew that we had learned something. That which we believed we valued, what we—I—thought was at the center of humanity, the capacity for thought, for reason, was not it, not it at all.

PORTRAIT OF SESHA AT 27

I am awakening and her babbling-brook giggles penetrate my semiconscious state. Hands clapping. Sesha is listening to "The Sound of Music." Peggy, her caregiver of 23 years, has just walked in and Sesha can hardly contain her desire to throw her arms around Peggy and give Peggy her distinctive kiss—mouth open, top teeth lightly (and sometimes not so lightly) pressing on your cheek, her breath full of excitement and happiness, her arms around your neck (if you're lucky; if not, arms up, hands on hair, which caveman-like, she uses to pull your face to her mouth). Sesha's kisses are legendary (and if you're not on your toes, somewhat painful).

Sesha was almost 12 before she learned to kiss or to hug. These were major achievements. Sesha is now a young woman in chronological age. She has the physical aspect of a young teen. She's tall, slender, long-legged, with dark beautiful brown eyes, brown short wavy luxuriant hair, a shy smile, which she delivers with a lowered head, and a radiant laugh that will make her throw her head back in delight. Sesha has been beautiful from the day of her birth, through all her girlhood and now into her young adulthood. Her loveliness shines through a somewhat twisted body, the bridge that substitutes for her natural front teeth (lost in a fall at school), and her profound cognitive deficits. The first thing people remark when they meet Sesha, or see her photo, is how beautiful she is. I've always admired (without worshipping) physical beauty and so I delight in Sesha's loveliness. The smoothness of her skin, the brilliant light in her eyes, the softness of her breath, the tenderness of her spirit. Her spirit.

No, Sesha's loveliness is not skin deep. How to speak of it? How to describe it? Joy. The capacity for joy. The babbling-brook laughter at a musical joke. The starry-eyed far away look as she listens to Elvis crooning "Love Me Tender," the excitement of her entire soul as the voices blare out "Alle Menschen werden Brüder" in the choral ode of Beethoven's Ninth Symphony, and the pleasure of bestowing her kisses and receiving the caresses in turn. All variations and gradations of joy. Spinoza characterized joy as the increase in our power of self-preservation and by that standard, Sesha's is a very well-preserved self. Yet she is so limited. She cannot speak. She cannot even say "Mama"—though sometimes we think she says "Aylu" (our translation, "I love you"). She can only finger feed herself, despite the many efforts at teaching her to use utensils. She'll sometimes drink from a cup (and sometimes spill it all). She is "time trained" at toileting, which means that she is still in diapers. Although she began to walk at five, she no longer can walk independently—her scoliosis and seizures and we do not know what else have robbed her of this capacity—and is in a wheelchair. Her cerebral palsy is not severe, but it is there.

She has no measurable I.Q. As she was growing up she was called "developmentally delayed." But delay implies that she will one day develop the capacities that are slow in developing. The jury is no longer out. Most capacities she will not develop at all. Is she then a "vegetable?" The term is ludicrous when applied to Sesha because there is nothing vegetative about her. She is fully a human, not a vegetable. Given the scope and breadth of human possibilities and capacities, she occupies a limited spectrum, but she inhabits it fully because she has the most important faculties of all. The capacities for love and for happiness. These allow those of us who care for her, who love her, who have been entrusted with her well-being to form deep and abiding attachments to her. Sesha's coin and currency is love. That is what she wishes to receive and that is what she reciprocates in spades.

On the Very Possibility of Mothering and the Challenge of the Severely Disabled Child

My mother would help in the early days and months of Sesha's life. My mother is a warm affectionate woman. She miraculously survived the Holocaust, and survived it emotionally intact. She loves children and especially loves babies. As an only child, I alone could provide her with grandchildren, and Sesha was the first and only grandchild on both sides of the family. All the grandparents were thrilled with Sesha's birth, and deeply saddened at the news that there were suspicions of retardation. We thought that we would slowly introduce them to the idea that the prognosis was as dire as we knew it to be. In the meanwhile, my mother would baby-sit Sesha when both Jeffrey and I were busy and would take her for the night when I had a paper to write for graduate school. We never brought the grandparents to the doctor's visits, hoping to spare them some of the pain we experienced at each visit, but once it could not be helped. It was on that fateful visit that my mother grasped the full extent of the trauma to Sesha's brain. (There is still no etiology of her impairments—the cyanotic incident may have been a cause or an effect of some other injury or underlying congenital problem.) Upon our return, my mother, in her inimitable and insistent fashion, urged me to place Sesha in an institution.

Of all the traumatic encounters in that first year and a half of Sesha's life, none, perhaps not even the realization that Sesha was retarded, was as painful as these words from the woman that I loved most in my life: The woman who had taught me what it was to be a mother, to love a child, to anticipate the joys of nursing, of holding and caring for another, of sacrificing for a child. My model of maternal love asking me to discard my child? Would she have banished me to an institution had I been "damaged?" Surely, she couldn't mean this. But, no, she *insisted*, with conviction, with surefooted rightness that I *had to* put this child out of my life. It made me crazy. I couldn't comprehend it. Only the images and stories of the Holocaust could reclaim for me my mother and her love. Only the knowledge that in those bitter times, a limp was a death warrant (to merely be associated with disability was a death warrant), could redeem my mother at this time in my life. Of course she was acting like a mother, as someone whose interest was my well-being. I see now that she thought this child would ruin my life, but she was unable to transcend her own maternity and project that quality onto me: To realize that the maternal love and concern she had for me, I had for Sesha. I remained in her eyes a child, a daughter and not a mother with her own daughter. She who had taught me that "she, too, was a mother's child" could not see that her child was also a mother. This was her failure to engage in analogical thinking.

But my fury and disappointment in her was also my own inability to understand her feelings. Now I think back and wonder how much of my mother's response was attributable to fear of the unknown (and what was known but in different circumstances), how much was the result of the stigma attached to disability, and how much was resistance to the reality of my maternity? In time, my mother came to understand that we could build a good life with Sesha. She allowed herself to love Sesha with the fullness of a grandmother's love. And in time, I forgave my mother and came to appreciate how her intense, if misdirected, love for me fueled her stubborn insistence that we "put Sesha away."

This was 1970, and parents did institutionalize retarded children. I cannot say what I might have thought if we did not have, as we did (through the good fortunes of family), ample resources to care for Sesha. The image I had of public institutions was that they were merely dumping grounds. No one whose material resources gave them a choice would opt for such putative "care." Private institutions were perhaps less dismal, but nonetheless sad affairs for families who for a variety of reasons, some financial, some psychological and emotional, could not see themselves facing the challenge of raising a mentally retarded child at home. But nowhere in my heart and mind did I find room for that alternative, and in this my husband and I were in complete accord.

It was simply impossible for me to part with my child. This is what I knew of mothering, mothering, at least, that is chosen. A child is born to you. This child is your charge—it is your sacred responsibility to love, nurture, and care for this child throughout your life. Is this "maternal instinct"? I don't know what those words mean. Do all women who become mothers believe thus? Clearly not. Is it then a cultural construct? If so, it is a belief constructed in many cultures, in many historical periods. Perhaps this commitment is rather the condition for the possibility of motherhood—realized differently in different cultures, under different conditions, and differently realized even by women within a single culture, or a single historical period. It may not be inspired by birth, but by adoption, but once a child is "your" child, at that moment you become its mother and the duty emerging from that bond is one of the most compelling of all duties. At that point you commit yourself to the well-being of one who is dependent upon you, whose survival, growth, and development as a social being is principally (if never solely) your responsibility.

The birth of a child with very significant impairments may test the limit of the commitment that I take to be the very condition for the possibility of mothering. It may do so for some women, under some—adverse—circumstances. In my own understanding this felt conviction is so fundamental that it serves as a benchmark. The extent to which a woman cannot realize it (in the idiom appropriate to her own culture) because of adverse social, political, or economic conditions, to that extent she faces an injustice. I take it then that the requirement to be able to mother, that is, to realize the condition for the possibility to mother, constitutes one of the "circumstances of justice." So many women worldwide face daunting obstacles in choosing to mother a significantly impaired child. I would not judge another woman who makes a choice not to mother a disabled child. I had the moral luck to make a lucid moral choice. It was to abide by what was both a principled and a heartfelt conviction that I and her father would not leave her fate to a hoped-for kindness of strangers.

MOTHERING DISTRIBUTED: THE WORK OF DEPENDENCY CARE

I never wanted to hire help to care for my child. I believed that with shared parenting it should be possible to care for a child and still pursue an additional life's work. I soon found that I was wrong. All families where each parent takes on work additional to childcare and domestic duties require help with childcare. The scandal of an affluent nation such as the United States is that such help is not provided for, and the scandal of American feminism is that for all its efforts in advancing the cause of women, and in spite of the precipitous rise in the number of women in the labor force, it has not fought sufficiently long and hard for this most basic of women's rights.

Had Sesha been the normal toddler, I would have tried to hunt out the few daycare programs that were being established in the 1970s to meet the new demand of women like me who, while not driven by economic necessity, were nonetheless committed to both motherhood and some other life's work. But Sesha could not play in the easy way other young children could play. She needed intense stimulation. She mouthed (and continues to mouth) everything. Her attention faded quickly; if left to her own devices, she'd simply stare off in space. Keeping Sesha stimulated was, and remains, hard work.

For a while Sesha was enrolled in one of the pilot projects in early intervention for the developmentally delayed. She made wonderful progress in the first five months of the program. But Sesha's story, unlike so many I have read about, was not one of continuing development. After several years in that same program the improvements became more and more minimal. The notion of mainstreaming was taking hold at this time for many disabled children, but it seemed too far from Sesha's condition and Sesha's needs.

While needing childcare was something I shared with other mothers, my daughter's profound disability was the reason I was dependent on house-bound help. Finding good care would be a challenge. Certainly someone could give Sesha perfunctory custodial "care," that is, attend to her bodily needs but without ever seeing the person whose body it is, without tapping into her desires, without engaging her potential, without responding to and returning her affection—her affection which is her most effective means of connecting with others, in the absence of speech and most other capacities required for interpersonal activities.

Some wonderful and some less than wonderful help supplemented our own caring for Sesha. From one young woman, I learned that to enter a child's world, especially one as attenuated as Sesha's, required a talent as precious as an artist's. Childcare work has been viewed as one of the least skillful occupations, second only to janitorial work. To see an exceptional childcare worker engage a child dispels, in an instant, such devaluation of this oldest and most universal of women's work. But to commit to care for Sesha required an ability to give your heart to a child, who, because she would never outgrow the need for your continual care, would not release you from an abiding bond and obligation. While we found a number of talented caregivers, few were willing to yield to the demands of caring for Sesha for an extended time. When done well, caring for Sesha is intensive labor and the relationship enabling such care must also already be intensive.

It is my hope this set of reflections will encourage more discussion about the relation between dependency work and mothering a disabled child; between dependency work and disability; between the dependency worker and the disabled person.

She Came to Stay

As the commitment to egalitarian parenting gave way to professional time demands, my spouse and I moved to a model which, for want of any other adequate term, I'll call "distributed mothering." I am Sesha's one mother. In truth, however, her mothering has been distributed across a number of individuals: her father, various caregivers, and Peggy.

Sesha was four when a woman walked into our lives who came and stayed. How and where we acquired the instincts I don't know, but we knew immediately that Peggy was right. She was scarcely interested in us. Her interview was with Sesha. But she wouldn't take the job. Peggy feared the intensity of the involvement she knew was inevitable. We pleaded and increased the salary. She told me later she would never have taken the job if the agency hadn't urged her to do a trial week. At the end of the week, it was already too late to quit. Sesha had worked her way into Peggy's heart. Twenty-three years later, Peggy told me the following story:

> I had been with Sesha in Central Park and I was working on some walking exercises that the folks at Rusk [Rusk Institute at New York University Medical Center, Sesha's early intervention program] had assigned. I was working terribly hard trying to get Sesha to cooperate and do what I was supposed to get her to do. I sat her down in her stroller and sat down on a park bench. I realized that I was simply exhausted from the effort. I thought, how am I going to do this? How can I possibly do this job, when I looked down at Sesha and saw her little head pushed back against her stroller moving first to one side and then to another. I couldn't figure out what she was doing. Until I traced what her eyes were fixed on. She had spotted a leave falling, and she was following its descent. I said "Thank you for being my teacher, Sesha. I see now. Not my way. Your way. Slowly" After that, I fully gave myself over to Sesha. That forged the bond.

Forging the relationship, through this insight into who Sesha is and how she sees the world, made possible the caring labor itself. This caring labor so infused with the relationship has enhanced the relationship and has made it as solid as the bonds of motherhood.

As I write this essay, a much older Peggy still cares for a much older Sesha in many of the same ways. But as Peggy and Sesha age, we reach the limits of the laboring aspect of caring. This is a difficult and troubling state of affairs—for us as parents, for Peggy, and, if Sesha understands it, for her. Sesha's possible future without Peggy troubles me profoundly—not simply because we have come to so rely on her, but because I cannot bear the thought that such a central relationship in Sesha's life could be sundered.

What is this relationship? "A relationship with no name" as my son so aptly said once. Why has no one spoken of such a relationship? Could our family be so privileged as to be unique? Privileged first in having the resources? Privileged above all in having found such a steadfast companion and caregiver for our daughter? What has this daughter and this relationship taught me about mothering? Can anything be generalized and learned from such a perspective of privilege, on the one hand, and anomaly, on the other? For I have come to understand, especially from the exposure to the literature on disability, how extreme my daughter's condition is, how profound is her retardation and her limitations. To us, she is simply Sesha, that unique individual whom we call our daughter.

In time, neither Peggy nor Sesha's father or mother has sufficed for the total care she requires, and we have had to call in others—part-time and mostly weekend help—most of whom have stayed with Sesha for years, until their lives called them to move on. With Sesha it takes more than a village. As Sesha has grown older, we have felt the need for more and more help so that we could pursue our roles as professionals and as parents of our son and as folks entitled to some leisure. We need such gratification and fulfillment not only for their own sake but so that we can love Sesha without resentment that her overwhelming needs rob us of the satisfactions we might otherwise enjoy.

There is something very profound in this expectation because it is part of the expectation of becoming a parent. That expectation does not alter with the birth of a child with disabilities. It is perhaps a fear that this expectation cannot be met when a child is severely disabled that will influence some parents to institutionalize a child and will influence potential parents to choose to receive prenatal testing and abort if the results indicate a significant impairment.

The move to distributed mothering, in the absence of socially provided means of caring for Sesha, has served to inoculate us from the sense of being cheated, and so also has inoculated Sesha against resentment or bitterness that we could not lead lives approximating the lives of those with only "normal" children. Of course, there have been compromises and sacrifices. There are limitations placed on our mobility and the considerable financial cost of Sesha's care. When Sesha is ill (her disabilities make her medically vulnerable) our lives stop. Distributing the mothering no doubt eases the burden. But distributed mothering itself has costs that go far beyond any material ones which I gladly, and with gratitude, pay. To *share* in the intimacy of caring for a profoundly needy child is to engage in an intricate and delicate dance—fraught with stubbed toes and broken hearts, but also yielding its own joys and rewards.

Peggy and I

Peggy and I are like two metals of not very dissimilar composition, each tempered under very different circumstances. Ten years and one month my senior, Peggy was born before the war and lived her youth in wartorn Ireland and Britain. I was born after the war, and grew to maturity in the booming economies of Sweden and the United States. Both of us are immigrants—she traveled here willingly as a young woman accompanied only by her sister; I came as a reluctant young girl brought by my parents. Peggy was one of thirteen children raised lovingly, but in poverty, in wartime with her father off to battle. I was an only child, the precious projection of hope by two survivors of Hitler's murderous rage against the Jews. She was raised to be fiercely independent; I was over-protected. She was raised to be self-reliant and hardy; I was looked over as a fragile flower. She had to make her own way early, I never *had* to make my own way at all. Peggy and I are not easily compatible. She is always punctual and I am always late. She is a doer while I am a thinker. She insists on routine and I'm incapable of following routine. We come together on politics, on compassion, on a love of books, and most important of all on our passion for Sesha.

Peggy and I respect each other. There may even be love there, but we never speak of it. The worst times are when Sesha gets ill. Sesha's disabilities are multiple, which means her illnesses easily compound. An elevated temperature, a small infection, a bit of nausea will lower her threshold for seizures. When the seizures start up, she becomes sleep deprived and that aggravates her condition. Things can snowball quickly. When Sesha is ill, we don't know what bothers her, what hurts her, what the pain feels like. We are deprived of a vital avenue for diagnosis. This makes her so vulnerable, and makes us crazy. Peggy in her frustration vents her fear and anger on me. I feel guilty: I am not doing enough; why do I not care for her myself? But I also question why I have to cope with Peggy's anger. How long can I continue to live with this tension? This anger? This pain? Can we continue to care for Sesha in our home? What happens when Peggy leaves? Is Sesha's illness life-threatening? What happens when we die?

The threat that Sesha might die, the expectation that we will die—these are always the terminal points for all our questionings concerning Sesha. What is Peggy's terminus? "What happens when I am not here? Why do I stay? Sesha is not my daughter, I am not her mother. If I don't care for Sesha, will she die?" Peggy has often said to me, "You can get away from concerns about Sesha with your work. But Sesha is my work." Peggy can think of leaving. I cannot. But really, can Peggy?

Sometimes I feel that my relationship to Peggy vis-à-vis Sesha is like the patriarchal relation of husband to wife vis-à-vis their children. Peggy accompanies me to doctors' visits with Sesha. Actually it seems more as if it is I who accompany her and Sesha. I deal with the authorities (much as the father does), she undresses Sesha (much as the mother does), although since it is distasteful to me to stand idly by, I "help" (much as an involved father might). I pay the bills, Peggy wheels Sesha out. Some roles we can reverse, others we can't—they are set in the larger practices in which we participate. Each time I see the analogies, it makes my feminist and egalitarian flesh creep. And yet, I can't see my way out of this. I cannot function without this privilege, and yet I despise it. I cannot see how to live my convictions. Of course, even this dilemma is a great luxury. So many other mothers with children like Sesha have to make much more difficult choices.

My choices and my dilemmas are shaped by my personal circumstances and ambitions as they can be realized within the constraints of the social world I inhabit. Distributed mothering as I live it is a privatized model. Many of its discomforts and difficulties are, I believe, attributable to lack of social services, services provided in other nations more attuned to dependency concerns. While the disability community in the United States has significantly improved the lives of disabled citizens in the years since Sesha's birth—the same years that have marked the emergence of this movement for the rights of the disabled—the United States remains shamefully behind other, less wealthy industrialized nations in providing a good system of services for the disabled and their families. In a nation with a better social welfare system, would I find myself in this same bind? I believe the answer is no, but I can't honestly say. What I do know is that were services freely and widely available, more mothers would be able to share the dependency responsibilities, not only with a spouse, but with caring others. There would be more places to turn to for help, for relief, and also for sharing the joys of loving a person as special as Sesha.

52

Kids Don't Damage Women's Careers—Men Do

Jessica Valenti

One of the most pernicious modern myths about motherhood is that having kids will damage your career. Women are told that we need to choose between our jobs and our children, or that we'll spend our most productive work years "juggling" or performing a "balancing act."

For those of us uninterested in circus tricks, a bit of perspective: It's not actually motherhood or kids that derail women's careers and personal ambitions—it's men who refuse to do their fair share.

If fathers did the same kind of work at home that mothers have always done, women's careers could flourish in ways we haven't yet imagined. But to get there, we need to stop framing mothers' workplace woes as an issue of "balance," and start talking about how men's domestic negligence makes it so hard for us to succeed.

Yes, we know American men are doing more than they have in past years: Fathers report spending about eight hours a week on child care, or three times as much as fathers in 1965. (Though keep in mind that the data are self-reported, and men tend to overestimate how much domestic work and child care they do.)

Men doing *more*, however, is not the same thing as men doing *enough*. Despite progress made, mothers are still spending almost twice the amount of time that men do, 14 hours a week, on child care. And not all parenting is tangible, quantifiable work—it's the mental labor of having kids that's often the most taxing. It's easy to split, for example, who packs a school lunch or dresses a child in the morning. But someone also needs to keep track of those days when lunch needs to be bagged for a field trip, or when it's time to buy new underwear or sneakers. How many dads do you know who could tell you their child's correct shoe size?

This kind of invisible work almost always falls on women, and we rarely talk about the impact it has on our professional lives. Imagine if instead of our mind being filled with to-do lists about grocery shopping and dentist appointments, we had available head space for creative thinking around our work and passions. For mothers, the freedom to just think is a privilege.

Studies also show that fathers continue to have significantly more leisure time than mothers and that mothers use their off time to do chores and child care while fathers use time off for hobbies and relaxing. This, too, is about careers: We know that people who have more leisure time and time for creative activities tend to perform better at work.

Valenti, Jessica. "Kids Don't Damage Women's Careers – Men Do." *Medium.com*, September 13, 2018.

To be sure, there are also "motherhood penalties" in workplaces that have nothing to do with men. (At least, not the ones we share beds with.) Mothers are much less likely to be hired than non-mothers, and when they have children, their wages fall off a cliff. Studies from 2017 led some analysts to come to the conclusion that the wage gap was almost entirely attributable to motherhood. Men, however, tend to see more money once they have children. Individual and structural discrimination against mothers remains, and that takes a tremendous toll on women's abilities to achieve in the public sphere.

But the answers to workplace discrimination are straightforward, and more importantly, they're finally being recognized as necessary. That men do less child care is widely known, but it's not widely condemned. We hear again and again, for example, that women just "care" more.

I promise you, there is nothing fulfilling about remembering that your daughter needs hair ties, or that she's about to grow out of that pair of sandals. There's no joy in changing a diaper or clipping tiny toenails. If women in relationships with men seem to be more concerned with these tasks, perhaps it's because we know it's not our husbands who will be looked at askance if our kid goes to school sporting inch-long fingernails or ill-fitting shoes.

Americans need to stop believing that women do the majority of care work because we want to. It's because we're expected to, because we're judged if we don't, and most of all, because it's incredibly difficult to find male partners willing to do an equal share of the work.

So let's stop saying that it's motherhood that holds up women's careers; it's not the institution of parenthood that makes advancing at work difficult. It's not our kids. It's that there's no chance of equality at work while there's inequality at home. It's not that women can't "have it all," it's that men won't stop taking it.

SECTION X
Defining Fatherhood

INTRODUCTION

Fathers as Good Providers

Fatherhood, as a role, experience, and institution, has changed over time. Prior to the nineteenth century, fathers were actively involved in nurturing and educating their children. As discussed in prior sections, industrialization transformed the family. Through the separation of home and work, fatherhood over time came to be defined in economic terms: working hard, paying the bills, providing food, paying for his children's education, and other financial responsibilities. At the same time, men were not necessarily expected to be emotionally expressive or supportive. As Jessie Bernard defines men's role, "He might have many other qualities, good or bad, but if a man was a good provider, everything else was either gravy or the price one had to pay for a good provider" (Bernard 1981, 3). Men gained status through financial success.

The "good provider role" ascribed to men also shaped women's opportunities and experiences. Assumptions that men had families to support justified pay inequality between men, while women's labor force participation was seen as unnecessary in many sectors. Many twentieth-century women, in turn, turned their energies away from investing in their independence. Bernard (1981, 2) explains the impact of the good provider role on women's opportunities, goals, and ambitions:

> By discouraging labor force participation, it deprived many women, especially affluent ones, of opportunities to achieve strength and competence. It deterred young women from acquiring productive skills. They dedicated themselves instead to winning a good provider who would "take care of" them.

The good provider role emerged from and naturalized the nuclear heterosexual family. Those who did not fit these roles, including men who could not advance professionally or earn enough to support their families as well as single women who required a livable wage, but who were assumed to be taken care of by a husband, suffered socially and financially. In fact, the image of the good father is inextricably linked to the ability to be perceived as a good provider, even as men in different social locations have different access to earnings and status.

Emotionally Available Fathers

Expectations that men will be good providers continue today. Yet, men also now face new expectations that they will be socially and emotionally involved with their children. The result is that men today spend more time interacting with their children than did their counterparts a generation ago. In 1965, married fathers with children under the age of 18 spent an average of 2.6 hours per week caring for their children. Over the subsequent two decades, fathers' time spent caring for their children increased to three hours per week in 1985 and then doubled to 6.5 hours in 2000. However, even with increased care from fathers, married mothers' time caring for children also increased. From 1965 to 2000, married mothers went from 10.6 hours per week to 12.9 (Livingston and Parker 2011).

How men spend time with their children is also different from the past and different from the time women spend caring for children. For example, fathers' childcare activities are more likely to be recreational, to take place on evenings or weekends, and to include a partner. Mothers' childcare activities are more likely to be managerial and to take place in the middle of the day or on a weekday. Time-use studies show that although mothers' childcare activities are typically shorter than fathers' activities, mothers tend to spend more cumulative time in childcare each day (McDonnell, Luke and Short 2019). As the chapter by Dawn Trussell and Susan Shaw shows, men may also gain some status for their involvement in children's extracurricular activities, even as women facilitate their involvement.

Time spent with children does not look the same for all men. Although men who live with their children provide more care than did fathers in the 1960s and 1970s, many more fathers do not live with their children, which reconfigures their time with their children. About one in four fathers of children 17 or younger (24 percent) live apart from at least one of their children, and 17 percent live apart from all of them (Livingston 2018). In contrast, in 1960, only about 11 percent of children lived away from their fathers (Livingston and Parker 2011). There are racial differences among fathers who live away from their children. About half of black fathers (47 percent) live apart from at least one of their minor children, and 36 percent live apart from all of their children. Among Hispanic fathers, about 26 percent live away from one or more of their children. For white fathers, this rate is about 17 percent. Education seems to matter. Among men with a bachelor's degree or more education, about 8 percent do not live with one or more of their children, compared to 28 percent of men with lower levels of education. A majority of all men say they spend too little time with their children (Livingston 2018).

In fact, as men increasingly face cultural expectations that good fathers are involved with their children, there are signs men want to meet those expectations. On a personal note, the chapter by Shailen Singh describes the challenges and experiences of being the father of a child with disabilities. Looking more broadly, other studies show how men view and even aspire to be involved fathers. One study by Sarah Thébaud and David Pedulla (2016) shows that men's perceptions of peers matter in their goals as fathers. They find that men who believe that their male peers want gender-egalitarian relationships are themselves more likely to prefer a progressive relationship structure and that the presence of supportive work-family policies, such as those allowing men to take leave or have flexibility around work time to accommodate parenting, further these aspirations. These new expectations do not supplant those of being a good provider. In fact, the role of breadwinner remains associated with respect, maturity, masculinity, and status. The role of father now encompasses even more. The chapter by Gayle Kaufman examines the challenges men face in "having it all."

Defining Fathers through Marriage

As family life has become more complex, definitions of who should be legally recognized as a father have as well. Historically, social and legal arrangements have defined men as fathers, not genetic ones. In particular, fatherhood has come through marriage, with a man automatically the father of children born to his wife. In this way, children were the product of marriage, a history outlined in the chapter by historian Nara Milanich. Although technologies for genetic testing now provide new routes to defining fathers, legal systems generally still see marriage as a key aspect of legal fatherhood.

A pivotal 1989 US Supreme Court case illustrates this. In the case of *Gerald D. vs Michael H.*, Carole (an international model) and Gerald (a businessman in a French oil company) were married and lived together in California, except when one of them was traveling for business. In 1978, Carole began an affair with a neighbor, Michael. Two years later, Carole gave birth to a daughter, Victoria. Gerald held out the baby as his own and listed his name on Victoria's birth certificate as the father. Shortly after Victoria's birth, Carole told

Michael she believed he might be the biological father and a subsequent blood test revealed that with 98.07 percent probability Michael was indeed Victoria's genetic father. Over the subsequent year, Carole and her daughter moved between Michael, Gerald, and a third man, Scott. In November 1982, after Carole refused to allow Michael to visit with Victoria, Michael filed a lawsuit in California Superior Court to establish his paternity and right to visitation. By June 1984, Carole was again with Gerald and they continued to live together with Victoria for the following years leading up to this Supreme Court case over whether or not Michael could establish paternity.

In this case, the US Supreme Court confirmed that legal claims to fatherhood come through marriage, not genetics. They sided with Gerald who insisted that California state law (Cal.Evid.Code § 621), passed in 1872 and amended in 1955, makes clear that the offspring of "a wife cohabiting with her husband, who is not impotent or sterile, is conclusively presumed to be a child of the marriage." The law specifies that the husband or wife can challenge this presumption within two years of the child's birth, but that others cannot. The attorney (guardian ad litem) appointed to protect Victoria's interests argued with Michael that Victoria should have the ability to have a paternal relationship with both men. In addition to clarifying that children do not have the right to challenge presumptions of paternity, the Court made clear that children cannot legally have more than one father. The decision explained that while the guardian ad litem might believe that filial relationships with both men "can be of great psychological benefit to a child, the claim that a State must recognize multiple fatherhood has no support in the history or traditions of this country."

In this decision, the Supreme Court protected formal definitions of family, including the requirement that there can only be two parents recognized in law, explaining, "California law, like nature itself, makes no provision for dual fatherhood." The decision also made clear that if they were to grant Michael visitations, he would also have access to other parental rights, noting,

> Michael was seeking to be declared the father of Victoria. The immediate benefit he evidently sought to obtain from that status was visitation rights… But if Michael were successful in being declared the father, other rights would follow – most importantly, the right to be considered as the parent who should have custody.

This status, the decision elaborated, would inevitably include

> the sum of parental rights with respect to the rearing of a child, including the child's care; the right to the child's services and earnings; the right to direct the child's activities; the right to make decisions regarding the control, education, and health of the child; and the right, as well as the duty, to prepare the child for additional obligations, which includes the teaching of moral standards, religious beliefs, and elements of good citizenship.

Throughout, the decision protects the nuclear family. The law, the decision insisted, excludes "inquiries into the child's paternity that would be destructive of family integrity and privacy." In this decision and others, courts make clear that marriage is the gateway to parental rights and that protecting marriage is a goal of excluding biological fathers who are not part of the marriage. Notably, women whose husbands father children outside of marriage are never presumed to be legal parents, as the legal mother is more clearly defined by birth, not marriage.

In recent years, about a dozen states, including California, have allowed judges to recognize more than two parents if the legal parent(s) have agreed to and fostered the relationship between the third party and the child, doing so is in the child's best interests, and it reflects a sincere relationship between parent and child. This is not yet common.

When a married father divorces, the divorce decree will include orders relating to custody and visitation. This is a significant benefit from formal recognition. In cases when divorcing fathers discover they are not genetically related to their legally recognized children, they are seldom able to reject those rights and responsibilities, including the obligation to pay child support. Fathers who can prove they accepted their role as father as a result of fraud have been at times able to denounce their child and paternal obligations. Doing so almost always means giving up all rights, including visitation, to a child they may have helped raise for many years. Men have aimed in many court cases to use genetic tests to prove they are not a child's biological father to avoid child support, while still wanting to maintain a physical and emotional relationship with their children. Unless they can show fraud and deception and also accept that rights and responsibilities are a package deal—that obligations for child support and rights to visitation and decision-making are linked—they virtually always lose.

Unmarried Parental Rights and Responsibilities

Today about 40 percent of babies are born to unmarried parents (CDC 2017), raising new questions about how to define fatherhood. To address this change in the family, the Uniform Parentage Act (UPA), a form of model legislation drafted by a panel of experts, created a legal framework by which courts could determine parental rights and responsibilities, irrespective of marriage. First drafted in 1973, the UPA has been updated multiple times. Every state has adopted at least some of its provisions into state law.

Prior to UPA, most states did not hold a father of a child born out of wedlock to any legal or financial obligations and did not grant him any rights. Children born to unmarried mothers had no right to child support and biological fathers had no right to custody. Since 1973, the UPA has been amended multiple times to add or clarify provisions. Revisions have addressed parentage of children conceived in ways other than through sexual contact, when genetic tests should be used to refute fatherhood, how parentage as it relates to reproductive technologies should be assigned, and, in 2017, following the legalization of same sex marriage, to make the language of parentage gender-neutral.

In terms of defining fatherhood, the UPA defines a father as someone who is the presumed father through marriage or because he resided in the same household with the mother of the child at the time of conception or during the child's first two years of life and openly claimed the child to be his. Men can become legal fathers through adoption, based on court order, by consenting to assisted reproduction (which might include using donor sperm), or by entering into a gestational surrogacy agreement. Men who donate sperm through a medical intermediary, like a doctor or sperm bank, may not claim fatherhood. More recently, courts have also interpreted same-sex marriage as providing presumptive parentage. In other words, children born within marriage to a same-sex couple who likely are not both genetically related to the child can both receive parental rights. The result is that men who donate sperm directly to a married lesbian couple or who impregnate a woman who is married to someone else will have a difficult time claiming parental rights, consistent with the precedent set in the case of *Gerald D. vs Michael H.*

An unmarried man who thinks he might be a father can enter himself in a state-run registry for unknown or putative (presumed but not confirmed) fathers. Doing so will lead the state to notify him if there is a legal proceeding for adoption or termination of parental rights. In many states, men who do not enter the registry within 30 days of the birth of a child are not entitled to block an adoption or claim rights, and typically, once the child reaches the age of one year, the registry no longer has any effect. About 25 states also allow a man to voluntarily sign a legal document known as a declaration of paternity at the birth of a child. Some states treat a birth certificate as a legal claim to fatherhood. All but two states allow fathers to revoke their claims of paternity, but how long a man has to do so varies (Child Welfare Information Gateway 2018).

The UPA also clarifies when genetic testing can and should be used to define fatherhood. Courts can order genetic testing if there is a reasonable probability of sexual contact between the mother of the child in question and the man assumed to be the father. Courts can also order genetic testing of relatives if the man is unavailable. If a custodial parent applies for public assistance, she will be required to name the father so that agency can collect child support, much of which will likely be used to reimburse the government for welfare payments. Because of this financial goal, agencies can also request genetic testing to establish a man is the legal father. State and local welfare agencies' ability order paternity tests can complicate social relationships. For example, agencies have asked women to identify men who gave them sperm for the purposes of impregnation, but who never intended to parent, as a condition of public assistance.

The ability to claim—or be compelled to test to establish—fatherhood is time-limited, unless no other man has been identified as a father. If there is no legal second parent, a man can be identified at any time. Unmarried men may hesitate to request parental rights due to the relatively inevitable connection of rights to child support. However, by waiting, they may lose the ability to establish those rights in ways that are automatic for married men. In some cases, men—particularly those who are perceived to be poor providers or as a liability to children—may be discouraged from seeking parental rights by courts and social service agencies, as my chapter on men's experiences in the child welfare system shows.

Throughout, the legal rights of biological mothers and fathers are different, as are the rights of married and unmarried fathers. For example, children of unmarried parents born outside the United States have different claims to citizenship, depending on whether their mothers or fathers are US citizens, with citizenship coming from an American mother much more easily than from an American father. These laws often do not reflect the reality of family life. For example, several same-sex married couples are suing the US State Department for refusing the grant citizenship to their children, born outside the United States using reproductive technologies. Other cases of adults born out of wedlock who face deportation are challenging the government claims that they are not protected by the citizenship of their American fathers, but would be if it had been their mothers who were citizens.

Beyond legal claims, how families function is often not entirely encompassed in formal definitions. The chapter by Joshua Gold examines many of the myths about being a stepfather, and recommends ways to support meaningful relationships. Although children are still only allowed to have two legal parents, in reality, many children have many more adults who function as parents. Parentage is one place where the disconnect between formal and functional families is most apparent. In a multitude of ways, fatherhood is a powerful institution, representing a significant role, and has been subjected to multiple forms of regulation in response to its evolution.

References

Bernard, Jessie. 1981. "The Good Provider Role: Its Rise and Fall." pp. 235–254 in *Diversity and Change in Families: Patterns, Prospects, and Policies*, edited by M. R. Rank and E. Kain. Englewood Cliffs, NJ: Prentice Hall.

CDC. 2017, "Unmarried Childbearing." (https://www.cdc.gov/nchs/fastats/unmarried-childbearing.htm).

Child Welfare Information Gateway. 2018. *The Rights of Unmarried Fathers*. Washington, DC: U.S. Department of Health and Human Services, Children's Bureau.

Livingston, Gretchen. 2018, "Most Dads Say They Spend Too Little Time with Their Children; About a Quarter Live Apart from Them." Pew Research Center. (https://www.pewresearch.org/fact-tank/2018/01/08/most-dads-say-they-spend-too-little-time-with-their-children-about-a-quarter-live-apart-from-them/).

Livingston, Gretchen and Kim Parker. 2011, "A Tale of Two Fathers: More Are Active, but More Are Absent." Pew Research Center. (https://www.pewsocialtrends.org/2011/06/15/a-tale-of-two-fathers/).

McDonnell, Cadhla, Nancy Luke and Susan E. Short. 2019. "Happy Moms, Happier Dads: Gendered Caregiving and Parents' Affect." *Journal of Family Issues* 40(17):2553–2581. doi: 10.1177/0192513X19860179.

Thébaud, Sarah and David S. Pedulla. 2016. "Masculinity and the Stalled Revolution: How Gender Ideologies and Norms Shape Young Men's Responses to Work–Family Policies." *Gender & Society* 30(4):590–617. doi: 10.1177/0891243216649946.

53

Organized Youth Sport and Parenting in Public and Private Spaces

Dawn E. Trussell and Susan M. Shaw

INTRODUCTION

The emergence of youth sport organizations during the past half century in North America resulted in new forms of socialization of children and the nature of their leisure. Further, with each new generation, the popularity of organized youth sport has continued to grow, becoming a significant aspect of children's and parents' lives. This may reflect important generational ideological shifts and changing cultural and structural factors. Grounded in a middle-upper class value system of postindustrial societies, a culture of *involved fathering* and *intensive mothering* parenting ideologies has emerged and may have important connections to organized youth sport. That is, a parent's *moral worth* may be evaluated by their children's successful participation in sport.

On the surface the cultural expectations, beliefs and practices of involved fathering and intensive mothering ideologies seem to evoke notions of gender equity; however, these practices may also hide underlying inequality. Organized youth sport may provide a setting where fathers can be actively involved in their children's lives, while feeling comfortable, knowledgeable and able to share their sport expertise with their children. For fathers, children's organized sport programs may also provide a context in which they can successfully avoid the dilemma of feminizing the fathering role.

The purpose of this exploratory study is to understand the connection of organized youth sport to cultural beliefs, values and practices of contemporary parenting ideologies. More specifically, we wanted to explore if parents perceived that organized youth sport was important to their own parenting roles and responsibilities related to childrearing.

SOCIAL CONSTRUCTION OF INVOLVED FATHERING AND ORGANIZED YOUTH SPORT

From Breadwinner to Involved Fathering

The definition of fatherhood is changing. For most of the twentieth century, a father's employment status and ability to provide financially for his family underpinned strong ideological assumptions about masculinity

Trussell, Dawn E., and Susan M. Shaw. "Organized Youth Sport and Parenting in Public and Private Spaces."
Leisure Sciences 34, no. 5 (2012): 377–394.

and the fatherhood role. Unlike previous generations, the emergence of new fatherhood ideologies means that the current generation of fathers' moral worth is evaluated based upon the meaningful time spent with their children.

In response to the fatherhood ideological shift, many fathers have expressed difficulty in attaining the involved ideal. This difficulty seems to stem from the expectation of having a greater involvement in their children's lives, while at the same time continuing to be the primary breadwinner for their families...
In that, fathers are expected to contribute primarily in the public sphere of paid work, but they are also increasingly expected to contribute to what is often seen as the private sphere of family and home life. Nonetheless, most fathers have the desire to provide an enriched childhood for their own children and leisure often provides an important context to do this.

Leisure-Based Fathering as the Primary Context for Involvement

Compared to mothers, fathers devote less time to the emotional and physical care work of their children; rather, fathers spend time with their children in play and companionship activities outside the home such as sports, outdoor activities and hobbies. For many fathers, the opportunity to share the sport experience with their children brings warm and nostalgic memories from their own childhood, of time they spent with their father. Many fathers want to ensure that they pass on what they have learned to their children, who will in turn do the same for future generations. Yet some fathers intentionally do things differently and in opposition to the memories that they have of their fathers. For example, men who had fathers who were overbearing, competitive and demanding of their sport excellence may be determined to provide a more positive sporting experience for their children. Also, fathers who feel they were not encouraged to participate in youth sport may be highly motivated to support their children's sport participation.

A father's (in)ability to support his children's sport participation may also lead to feelings of inadequacy. Fathers have expressed feeling judged by their children for the amount of time they are able to share with them in the sport context. Fathers have also expressed self-criticism and guilt related to the amount of emotional and physical support they can provide their children and the feeling that they can never meet their own expectations.

Different sets of issues also arise when considering fathers' involvement in their children's sport participation. The cultural expectation for fathers to increase the amount of time they spend with their children challenges hegemonic forms of masculinity, and some fathers may use youth sport as a vehicle to fulfill new involved fatherhood cultural expectations without challenging the dominant masculine discourse. That is, children's organized sport programs may provide a context in which they can successfully avoid the dilemma of feminizing the fathering role.

SOCIAL CONSTRUCTION OF INTENSIVE MOTHERING AND ORGANIZED YOUTH SPORT

The Idealization of Intensive Mothering

As the ideology of involved fathering has emerged, so has a culture of intensive mothering. For women, "the character of mothering has intensified. Contemporary mothering arguably entails more involved and deliberate practices" (Arendell, 2001, p. 168). Mothers are expected to be child-centered and direct their children's lives. Motherhood is also generally entwined with notions of femininity, nurturing and caring. In fact, in most cultures, "feminine and mother are combined to form a single representation of WOMAN – and for most women in the world this is still their only self-representation" (Lax, 2006, p. 1). Moreover, unlike men's expected contributions to the public sphere of paid work, women's primary contributions to home and family may be traditionally thought of within the private or domestic sphere of life.

What is considered the dominant ideology of intensive mothering is actually one that is rooted in a white, middle-class value system based on the nuclear family model that promotes women who can afford and/or desire to stay at home with their children. Yet the ideal of motherhood is universalized and does not embrace the diversity of mothers' lived-experiences structured by the status of employment, marital, (dis)-ability, race and ethnicity. Despite the diversity of women's lives, all mothers are subject to judgment and censure by society if they are not able to live up to the universalized ideal.

The Centrality of Organized Youth Sport to Intensive Mothering Practices

The ideology of intensive mothering embodies motherhood as child-centered, emotionally absorbing, self-sacrificing, labor intensive, with mothers as active managers of their children's time and activities (Hays, 1996). Compared with previous generations, mothering now extends beyond the provision of children's safety and well-being and involves an enrichment process to ensure the children's time is well managed and highly productive in terms of their ongoing growth and development.

The enrichment aspect of intensive mothering is similar to Lareau's (2002) concept of "concerted cultivation" (p. 748). Mothers seek out opportunities to foster their children's talents, skills and abilities through organized leisure activities. This ideology is rooted in middle-class values that expect parents to "enroll their children in numerous age-specific organized activities that dominate family life and create enormous labor, particularly for mothers. The parents view these activities as transmitting important life skills to children" (p. 748). Other research has also supported the purposive and all-encompassing nature of mothers' labor in the organization of children's activities and often at the expense of the mothers' own leisure experiences. As mothers seek out organized activities to meet the cultural expectations of being a good mother, children's organized sport participation may become an important context in the provision of such opportunities. Moreover, as noted earlier, leisure-based activities may be important to the development and growth of the father-child relationship.

This begs the question of whether the framework and philosophy of children's sport has contributed to and/or perpetuated the dominant ideologies of intensive mothering as well as involved fathering. Although children's sport participation may be for the benefit of the child, it may have important implications (both positive and negative) in terms of the parents' lives and family life in general.

PROJECT DESIGN

Methods

The data draw on a purposive sample of 13 participants (seven sets of parents; seven mothers and six fathers, with one father who declined participation). To ensure elements of homogeneity, all families had at least one child in the 12–15-year-old age group who was currently participating in organized sport. Participants were recruited through contacting several volunteer organizations in a small community in Ontario, Canada, who helped identify potential participants in their community. Separate interviews were conducted with each parent in the belief that it would provide a composite story of family life that would be richer than joint interviews which may privilege one dominant voice over another.

FINDINGS

The analysis of the data revealed the high value and significance of children's participation in organized sport opportunities as it related to being a *good parent*. Moreover, the analysis of the parental discourse discovered that parenting went beyond the home environment and became a public act that was observed by other parents, with these observations creating the basis of what was deemed to be a good parent. Three main themes that best reflected the parents' perspectives emerged: (a) paying a high price to play, (b) judging other parents and (c) maintaining the gendered ideal. From these three subthemes a core theme emerged: parenting in private and public spaces. The three subthemes and core theme are discussed in the following sections.

Paying a High Price to Play

The first theme revealed the significance of facilitating children's participation in organized sport, and parents clearly believed that these activities would help prepare children for their adult years. For example, one father talked about the value of organized youth sport to a child's life:

> Whether it's organized sports or an organized club, I feel every child should be involved. Sports builds up not only your own inner self-esteem, but it teaches you how to play as a teammate and it prepares you for the real world so to speak.
>
> (Father, family #2)

This sentiment was echoed by many of the parents; however, what stood out in this study were the comments that indirectly *critiqued* other parents in the community. For example, these two fathers explained:

> I see some of the kids in the neighborhood that have parents … the kids aren't involved in sports at all. And I think it's something the kids should have a chance at.
>
> (Father, family #1)

> There are still a lot of kids out there that don't play. Maybe they can't afford it. I know some that can afford it and they're just not involved. Maybe, it's the kid's choice too but I think a lot of times it's the parents.
>
> (Father, family #6)

Children's participation in organized sport was deemed necessary, and for some parents this necessity extended to the provision of additional opportunities to enhance their basic skill development. As best illustrated by one mother: "Everybody thinks your kid's a superstar but they don't want to give them the tools that they need to be a good player. They don't want to spend any extra to have them take power skating lessons" (Mother, family #4).

Another issue was the need for parents to provide opportunities, so that their children would not feel resentment in later years. As one father explained:

> And you know, a friend of ours just lives outside of town here and he was an awesome hockey player and he was invited to the junior camp [try-outs for a higher level hockey league] and his mom never told him about it until it was over. And he's still bitter about it and he's almost 50 years old now. So, you know, we don't want our kids to look at us, you know 20 years from now and say you never gave me the opportunity.
>
> (Father, family #2)

The parents in this study also talked about their hectic schedules and feeling like their family was always "on the go." Some parents explained how their children's sport controlled their lives. As one mother explained, all aspects of family life would be scheduled around the games and practices: "Well it takes over right. I would say it just becomes what you do. It becomes your life. You fit everything else around the games or practices" (Mother, family #3). A father who talked about the loss of couple time with his wife echoed this sentiment:

> The biggest one is time we spend one on one with your spouse. Or you know, if we are together it's usually one or two kids with us. Yeah, I keep telling [wife], it will come back. We'll have the time again.
>
> (Father, family #2)

The consumption of family finances and the economic strain on the family were also prevalent, with some parents reporting exorbitant fees for even one child's participation. As these two parents explained, the extra costs related to equipment and transportation also consumed the family resources:

> Registration is $1,800. That's just registration, that's not equipment, that's not tournaments, that's not $100 a week in gas. And that's not hotels if you are in a tournament. Like [child] did four tournaments and they're all sleepovers.
>
> (Mother, family #3)

Definitely, the registration which is dear. And then it's all the equipment which is expensive and then there is the gas running around all over. Like all winter long, I don't think the car ever cooled down. You drive home and you want to just leave it idling in your driveway because you know you'll be going somewhere again shortly.

(Father, family #5)

Yet the centrality of providing these opportunities was significant to the idea of being a good parent. This may be one reason that families were willing to make significant sacrifices to other aspects of family life. Thus, in part, a good parent was defined by the very provision of opportunities for their children, even though these opportunities were seen to constrain their lives.

Judging Other Parents

As the second theme highlights, underlying much of the parental discourse about the notion of good parenting were evaluative statements about the *other* parents' level of involvement as it related to their children's sport participation. Most of the parents were highly critical of absent parents, who were seen as parents who dropped their children off at the door, and did not actively support their children at the sport venue. For example,

It's sad. You can see it in the kid's face if they [the child's parents] are not there … or if they are there and they're an ass it's even worse. It just destroys the kid. Why would you sign your kid up if you don't want to be involved?

(Mother, family #3)

Another parent, her son plays goalie, but his dad's never there. And you know, you see him there once in a blue moon to watch his [son's] games and it's like, I just couldn't handle that. I just feel bad. I mean, it's not that he's not there in other ways, it's just hockey isn't his thing. But I couldn't imagine not being at the hockey game! I mean we try to get to all the boys' games, but for him not to come if he could be there…

(Mother, family #1)

As the above quotes illustrate, a good parent was seen to provide emotional and physical support to their child—although not all parents shared similar views on the right type of support. For some, it meant a positive and supportive attitude; for others, it meant harsh and honest criticism. As best exemplified by one mother: "Praise is always a good thing. It doesn't matter if you win or lose, just be supportive" (Mother, family #4). In contrast, another parent explained that harsh honesty was more important as he described his own feedback to his sons: "I'll say, 'Remember back when you couldn't even skate? Remember how long it's taken to get half-ass good at it? Cause you're still not a pro, you know'" (Father, family #3). These personal perspectives related to parenting practices would then become the basis in which other parents were judged.

It was clear that judgments were often made of other parents who were forcing their children to play at a higher competitive level. Similarly, parents who pushed their children too hard at a game/practice were deemed to be behaving inappropriately:

Like, I'd never force my boys into anything. They've all always had their own decision. Because I'm not gonna force them. It's their decision. I've seen too many parents wreck a kid's career, drop out of hockey altogether because they're just forced into it too much.

(Father, family #1)

I am the least competitive parent there is. It actually drives me insane when I go to the arena and kids aren't really enjoying [figure] skating or whatever and they're coming off and they're like: "I want my skates off!" or "I want to go home!" or whatever, and their parents are like "Get out there!" It always infuriates me. I know some parents think the competitive aspect. I just don't understand that and it just sends me overboard. That's the part of the sport that just about drives me the most crazy. The other parents who are just too overboard – too much.

(Mother, family #5)

Moreover, a good parent was seen as someone who volunteered and helped out with his or her child's sport organization. Active involvement in their children's lives was deemed to be important, to both the children and sport organization:

> A parent who volunteers. One that doesn't just send their kid out on the ice or send their kid out on the diamond and just sits there and watches. You know – be involved. You know the kids see it and they know it.
>
> (Mother, family #6)

> And you get some [parents] that just have no idea – just bringing little Johnny out and never volunteer. You know, you get that crowd that never help out. Bitching and complaining but never helping out.
>
> (Father, family #3)

Judgment of absent parents was also revealed to be directed at spouses as well. That is, family conflict was evident when one spouse was seen to be unsupportive and did not attend games and/or was not involved with the sport organization. For example, two mothers explained:

> Like it kind of bugged me about [husband], he knows so much about hockey ...but he would never go out because he didn't want parents grumbling at him kind of thing.
>
> (Mother, family #1)

> Like [son] had rugby yesterday and it took a lot of ... I dropped a lot of hints saying "you know, this will probably be the only time you'll get a chance to see [son]." And [husband's] like "oh no, I'm busy, I've got to go pick rocks." [They are farmers.] And I said, "God it'd be nice if you'd go to see his game because it's the only chance you'll get. Pick rocks tomorrow!!! When you look back, are you going to be glad you picked those rocks or be glad you got to see your son play rugby?" I don't know...
>
> (Mother, family #6)

Perceptions of a good parent were also framed by reflecting upon their own childhood and their parents' level of involvement: "I do it because I want my kids to see that I am involved. My mom never was involved in anything and why wouldn't I be involved? Why would I expect somebody else to do it for my kids?" (Mother, family #6).

Many of the parents talked in great detail about misbehaving parents and what they saw as inappropriate spectator behavior, particularly at children's hockey and baseball games. Narratives of parents yelling and screaming while watching their children play were cited in almost all of the parental interviews. For example, one of the fathers described some of these incidents:

> If you're sitting beside her [another parent], she just yells the whole time, hanging over the glass just screaming at her kids. You know, "get down there!" or "Hurry up!" or "Get the hell off the ice if you're tired!" and that kind of thing. You know? You see it all and again is that a good parent? I don't know. Sometimes, some of the things they say, you maybe kind of wonder, "geeze!"
>
> (Father, family #5)

Another father talked about physically separating himself from his wife and the other parents: "Sometimes it gets so bad that if I'm up in the bleachers I'll go stand in the lower part behind the glass. I just can't take it" (Father, family #1).

Maintaining the Gendered Ideal

It was clear, too, that the mothers were responsible for the orchestration and scheduling of the children's activities. For example: "At the beginning of the year, I write the schedule down. I kind of color coordinate. [Daughter]'s schedule is in red, [son]'s in blue, and my work is in black" (Mother, family #2). Some of the mothers talked about equal responsibility, yet it was the mothers who were primarily responsible for the hidden work, the emotional labor and the coordination of the family activities. Husbands also re-affirmed this, by talking about helping out, while their wives coordinated the family schedules. As this couple revealed:

> I would say that it's pretty equally involved. Like maybe … I would have to say overall it would have to be equal.
>
> (Mother, family #1)

> Well, she'll write down on the board what's happening, like on the calendar. And she'll say "well do you want to take [child #1] or [child #2] or [child #3]?" And I'll say, "well I haven't seen [child #2]'s game for a while, so I'll take [child #2]." That's how we do it, but she'll kind of look after the scheduling.
>
> (Father, family #1)

Because of the hectic schedules and the husbands' inability to help out at all times due to their perceived work demands, some of the mothers expressed sentiments of time stress and fatigue as they tried to balance their employment and domestic responsibilities with their children's sport schedule. As one mother explained:

> It's very hard! It's hard on family life. It can be very stressful. You know, you come home and if they haven't … I get upset and you're expecting something to be done and it's not done. I get frustrated sometimes. Or if you've asked the kids to do stuff and they haven't done it, it's like "Listen, I'm running you here and there, you guys need to step up and help!" Especially now that I'm full-time [employment].
>
> (Mother, family #1)

In contrast, these sentiments of time stress and fatigue were not prevalent in the fathers' interviews.

It also appeared that women's traditional responsibilities for planning and organization within the family unit were extended into the public domain and the organization of the children's sport leagues. Underlying much of the talk about the organizational demands and responsibilities was a sense of the gendered politics related to the respective roles that the mothers and fathers held within the sport organization. When asked the open-ended question – "What are the expectations for mothers and fathers in the sport organization?" – many of the parents initially talked about a sense of equality related to the leadership roles. For example: "I would say it's probably about 50/50. Where I think a few years ago it was more dads" (Mother, family #4). Some parents even revealed that women predominantly held leadership roles for the local leagues' board of directors.

Yet it was also clear that the type of sport appeared to influence the gendered nature of the volunteer work. Fathers were still typically involved with administration roles in sports traditionally considered as masculine (i.e., hockey and, in particular, the more competitive leagues). However, mothers were principally responsible for the facilitation and leadership roles for feminine sports such as figure skating, while fathers provided very little leadership support in this area. For example, one couple revealed:

> There isn't a dad involved with the skating club. We have not had a dad anywhere in sight.
>
> (Mother, family #5)

> Don't get me wrong, like a male could do that. It would be no different than the bookwork I did for the snowmobiling club, but I haven't been asked and I probably won't volunteer. Can we leave it at that? [Laughter to ease the discomfort.] I probably could but it just seems … it is a little different I guess. I don't know. It shouldn't be. I don't think there's any males who've done it in the past.
>
> (Father, family #5)

These sentiments were echoed by another mother who explained that the absence of fathers might be because of their lack of knowledge in a particular sport: "The figure skating executive would be mostly moms. You would never – very seldom see a dad. I don't know if dads understand figure skating so …" (Mother, family #4). Yet at the same time, many of the women who were involved in leadership roles for the hockey's board of directors did not have any previous experience with hockey.

In visible leadership roles such as coach or trainer there was also a sense of change with more women becoming involved, particularly with the onset of girl's hockey and its league rules. As a mother explained: "Hockey is men [referring to coaches] but there are definitely women trainers sitting on the bench. Actually with girls' hockey there has to be. That's a league rule for the girls' team because of going into the dressing room" (Mother, family #5). However, beyond the initial few examples given, it became evident that the fathers were still primarily involved in visible leadership roles such as the coach, with only an emerging sense of the mothers' involvement in this form of volunteer work.

Moreover, when families that typically embodied egalitarian principles in their household were confronted with what they perceived to be inequity in the sport organization, they would simply avoid confrontation. For example, the mother quoted above used to compete in the sport her children were currently participating in. As she explained: "I allow it to carry on [mothers fulfilling secondary roles] even though I might feel differently, unless it's a really big heart tug for me, I'm okay with it" (Mother, family #2).

It was also clear that the gendered affairs of sport organizations were also revealed in the fundraising responsibilities of mothers and fathers. Although both mothers and fathers talked about the importance of fundraising and the high costs of children's sport participation, it tended to be the mothers who talked about the work (planning and organizing) of fundraising activities. As illustrated by one mother: "Like we had the year end tournament for the Pee Wee girls at our center. We got that so I did all the fundraising. I organized and got that all together. That was a big job" (Mother, family #6).

Core Theme: Parenting in Private and Public Spaces

Throughout the interviews, there was an overall sense that parenting went beyond the home environment and became a public act that was observed by other parents, and it was the basis of these observations that reinforced the meaning of a good parent. That is, not only did parents talk about their own children's sport participation, but they also talked in great detail about their observations of other families.

The analysis of the data revealed the high value parents place on children's participation in organized sport opportunities. The parents emphasized that the very provision of opportunities was a central aspect of being a good parent. Moreover, parents made numerous judgments of other parents (including spouses and their own parents) who did not provide appropriate opportunities. The analysis also illustrated the contradictions inherent in the parents' discourse as they criticized both under-involved and overinvolved parenting. That is, parents were highly critical of other parents who were absent from the children's games/practice, and they were also highly critical if they thought other parents were forcing their children to play and/or were too hard on them. In addition, diverse opinions were also evident related to the type of feedback and support parents should give their child (e.g., positive and encouraging versus highly critical and harsh). However, regardless of diverse opinions and critiques, the essence of judging other parents' actions in the community was consistent throughout all of the interviews.

Interestingly, there was an overall sense of lack of empathy and recognition of differences that was missing from the parental discourse on judging other parents. Although many parents shared stories of their difficulties in supporting their own children (e.g., work schedules, finances), their view of other parents and the difficulties that they might encounter was absent in the discussion. One mother expressed this lack of understanding from other parents. She said:

> In the past years there's been times when we've struggled [financially]. It's been more difficult or whatever. I'm working a little more too which helps. But it can be … people don't understand what other people do, what their issues are.

> (Mother, family #1)

Applying a gendered analysis to parents' organizational responsibilities revealed a sense of change with women's increasingly public roles. Yet this analysis also demonstrated the reproduction of sport as a traditionally masculine domain with men in the visible center roles and women in the hidden periphery roles. It appeared that women's traditional responsibilities for the planning and organization within the family unit were extended into the public domain and the organization of the children's sport leagues. This was particularly evident in the local leagues and traditionally feminine sports. Thus, expectations and practices that formed around appropriate parenting practices and behaviors were constructed in not only the private context of the family unit but also extended into the broader community; organized youth sport played a central role in this discourse.

DISCUSSION

This study revealed the parents' perspectives on the high cost of youth sport for the family unit (emotional, physical and financial), the judgment of other parents' behaviors and the gendered nature of fulfilling parental responsibilities related to youth sport. Embedded throughout all of the interviews and the parental discourse was the meaning and significance of *being a good parent*. When considering the parents' emotional and physical work and the consumption of family resources, why was children's participation in organized sport such a valued and important aspect of family life? In part, it may be due to their moral worth as a parent evaluated by their children's successful participation in youth sport, and the parents' visible investment in this pursuit. This may be why parents are so willing to alter family budgets, accommodate the financial resources required to support their children's sport participation and reproduce traditional gender relations.

The power of the ideology of intensive mothering was reflected in the passion and commitment to facilitate children's organized sport involvement. The narratives spoke of the mothers' lives as child-centered, self-sacrificing and active managers of their children's lives. Compared to previous generations, a central aspect of being a good mother today involves the provision and facilitation of enrichment activities and the willingness to make personal sacrifices in order to do this. Organized youth sport appeared to reflect and further strengthen this ideology of self-sacrificing motherhood not only in the private context of the home (e.g., scheduling, food and equipment preparation) but also in the public context of the community with the gendered work of the sport organizations (e.g., filling the hidden roles such as fundraiser, board of directors).

The ideological shift of fathering from monetary support to a more involved style of fathering was exemplified in this study. The value of supporting their children's sport participation through the provision of opportunities and attendance at games was central for the attainment of this ideological imperative. Through children's organized sport participation, the fathers were able to publicly display a sense of their physical and emotional support for their children and meet cultural expectations for the new fathering ideal. In doing so, they were also able to successfully avoid the dilemma of feminizing the fathering role while reproducing and strengthening the preservation of hegemonic masculinity through sport. Thus, organized youth sport facilitated both the reproduction and resistance of traditional gender relations related to motherhood and fatherhood ideologies.

REFERENCES

Arendell, T. (2001). The new care work of middle class mothers: Managing childrearing, employment, and time. In K. Daly (Ed.), *Minding the time in family experience: Emerging perspectives and issues* (pp. 163–204). London, England: Elsevier Science Press.

Hays, S. (1996). *The cultural' contradictions of motherhood*. London, England: Yale University Press.

Lax, R. (2006). Motherhood is unending. In A. Alizade (Ed.), *Motherhood in the twenty-first century* (pp. 1–21). London, England: Karnac.

Lareau, A. (2002). Invisible inequality: Social class and childrearing in black families and white families. *American Sociological Review, 67*(5), 747–776.

54

Who's Your Daddy? Don't Ask a DNA Test

Nara Milanich

"Man Ordered to Pay $65K in Child Support for Kid Who Isn't His." "Father Hopes to Change State Paternity Law" after losing custody of his biological daughter to another man. The headlines are lurid and seemingly nonsensical. How can a man bear financial responsibility for a child that is not "his"? How can he be denied legal paternity of a child whom he conceived?

The gist of these stories is that such outcomes are not only ludicrous but unjust. Such tales not only appear in the mainstream media but provide fodder for men's rights websites and have even inspired bills to make DNA testing mandatory at birth, though none has actually become law.

But history suggests such cases are not so strange. In fact, they follow from a long tradition in which paternity was a social and legal relationship, not a biological one.

After all, it was only in the 1980s that DNA testing emerged, with its promise to reveal the identity of the biological father. For most of human history, no such technology existed – nor was it missed. Paternity was based on presumption, deduced from social behaviors and legal conventions.

FATHER, BY TRADITION

Historically, the father was defined by marriage. Pater est quem nuptiae, in the Roman formulation: The father is he whom marriage indicates, even in circumstances when, well, he could not be. The tradition carried forward over the centuries. According to seventeenth-century English common law, for example, if a husband was located anywhere within the "Four Seas" of the King of England at the time of his wife's conception, he was legally presumed the father of her child.

As for children born out of wedlock, courts, especially those operating in the civil law tradition, deduced paternity from a man's actions or public reputation. The father was he who cohabited with the mother or kissed the baby in public, the man whom a neighbor saw paying the wet nurse. Paternity was performative.

Such definitions of fatherhood did not mean it was less certain or less true: It was simply that the truth of paternity was social, not physical.

Milanich, Nara. "Who's Your Daddy? Don't Ask a DNA Test." *The Conversation*, June 13, 2019.

This situation contrasted with the logic of maternity. Mater certissima est – the mother is always certain, in the Roman formulation. Maternal identity could presumably be known by the physical facts of pregnancy and birth.

A More Muddled Modern Landscape

Today, according to some observers, reproductive technologies like surrogacy and egg donation have disrupted the certainty of the Roman dictum on maternity. After all, maternal identity is not so obvious when the gestational mother who births the child and the genetic one whose egg creates it can be two different people.

By contrast, DNA was supposed to make biological paternity certain. And yet the older reasoning that long defined paternity as a social relationship endures.

Today, family law in the United States and elsewhere continues to recognize nonbiological lines of reasoning. A man's behavior, intent, the nature of his relationship with the mother, stability in a preexisting parent-child relationship – all these criteria, rather than biology, may define the father. If anything, reproductive technologies like sperm donation and new family forms, like those born of the frequency of divorce, have only multiplied the scenarios in which biology may take a backseat to social criteria.

But in some contexts, the biological continues to prevail. This is often the case in immigration and citizenship law. Kin relations play a central role in immigration proceedings in the United States and other countries because citizens can sponsor close relatives to immigrate, and under certain circumstances refugees have a right to join family members in their adoptive country.

Increasingly, countries that are migration destinations use DNA to verify family relationships. In May 2019, the US Department of Homeland Security began a pilot program to test Central American migrant families at the southern border.

As critics have noted, this practice imposes a narrow, biological definition of family. Kinship practices like adoption, stepparenthood and relationships based on a social understanding of parentage are considered perfectly legitimate when practiced by natives but are vilified as fraudulent and criminal when practiced by foreigners.

These apparently contradictory definitions of parentage reflect the fact that paternity's definition varies depending on whose parentage is at stake – and how much power they hold.

Law and custom have always purposefully obfuscated the fatherhood of certain categories of men: the slave owner, the priest, the colonizer, the soldier. Thomas Jefferson's paternity of Sally Hemings' children was publicly obscured for two centuries. In an entirely different historical context, German women after World War II found it impossible to bring paternity suits against American soldiers who had fathered their children.

The fact that some fathers, like Jefferson and the GIs, have remained strategically uncertain suggests the very notion of paternal uncertainty is not a biological axiom but a political idea.

Life's Too Complicated to Rely on DNA

Over the last century, the distinction between legitimate and illegitimate children has lost much of its social and legal significance in the West. The once markedly different criteria for proving maternity versus paternity have largely, though not entirely, disappeared. Under US law, children born abroad to unmarried citizen fathers still do not enjoy the same rights to citizenship as those born to citizen mothers, for example.

At the same time, stratification has been reinforced in other contexts, as in the contrasting definitions of parentage among citizens and foreigners. New dynamics of discrimination have also arisen as assisted reproductive technologies and same-sex couples produce new permutations of family.

Take the recent conundrum faced by two dads and their young daughter. Both are US citizens and are legally married; their daughter was born abroad to a surrogate. Drawing on a tortured combination of both biological considerations – the fact that child was not genetically related to both parents – and social ones – nonrecognition of the couple's marriage – the State Department denied their child US citizenship. What such a case shows is not that old laws have failed to keep pace with new family forms, but how the state can generate new forms of stratification even as older ones fade.

With the dawn of the DNA era, many observers predicted that, by revealing the truth of paternity, genetic science would one day abolish ambiguity and deliver equality and justice. Today science can indeed find a father, but its impact has been rather more complex than once anticipated. Rather than sweeping away older social and legal definitions with a new biogenetic one, it has actually heightened the tensions between different ways of defining paternity.

Who's your daddy? Perhaps science isn't best positioned to answer, because this question arises from society, not nature. It might not be the right question anyway. A better one is, what does society want a father to be?

55

Biology and Conformity

Expectations of Fathers in Reunification in the Child Welfare System

Jennifer A. Reich

Dusty Benjamin saunters to the table and pulls out the metal-framed chair. He is wearing a dirty baseball-style jacket with a hole in the sleeve. Sam Richman, a man he has never met before but who will now, as his court-appointed attorney, represent him, sits down across the table without looking up. I walk in behind them, aware that I can smell Dusty's stench from several feet away. Dusty slouches in his seat, with his long thin legs straight out in front of him.

Sam begins working through his standard questions for new clients: does Dusty have any Native American ancestry? Although Dusty doesn't know why he is asked, Sam needs to find out if the provisions of the Indian Child Welfare Act might apply to his case. Dusty shrugs and says he doesn't know, explaining, "I have seizures and lose my memory sometimes."

Sam pages through the initial report, trying to understand the case. Dusty explains that his wife, Marla Chue, says that someone else—her boyfriend Dirk Haigenberger—is the baby's father. I recalled seeing Marla, a young Laotian woman with some kind of cognitive impairment, standing in the lobby with a heavier set white man with a shaved head. I had also seen Dusty, a lanky white man, slide his hand around Marla's waist and call her "Hun." Sam asks if he and Marla are married and whether he lived with her ten months prior, at the time of conception of the now one-month-old baby in protective custody. Upon hearing Dusty say "Yes," Sam begins explaining how being legally married to her makes him the legal father of the infant, Todd.

"Grab a cigar. Congratulations, you're a dad," Sam declares, with some sarcasm. Dusty, who doesn't understand the reference, explains that he likes cigars.

Sam more slowly explains that being married and having lived with Marla makes him the legal father, no matter what Marla says. He asks Dusty whether he wants to pursue custody of the baby, if the court decides Marla cannot take care of him.

Dusty appears to ponder the issue seriously. After a few moments, he explains that he wants to help Marla, but that he doesn't know if he wants custody of the baby, since that would hurt Marla. He also mentions that his own mother, with whom he lives, does not know about the baby. Sam tells him that he needs to call his mother and tell her about Todd. He tries to explain that this is not a matter of "helping" Marla; this is a question of whether he wants to pursue becoming a full-time parent.

Reich, Jennifer. "Biology and Conformity: Expectations of Fathers in Reunification." In *Fixing Families: Parents, Power, and the Child Welfare System.* New York and London: Routledge, 2005.

Dusty considers the question aloud, following different thoughts as they arise. He has a new girlfriend now. He moved out four months ago, after he found out Marla was cheating on him with Dirk. "She is supposed to be faithful. We're married." He wishes he could get her back, but then again isn't sure. He again mentions that he has a new girlfriend. When I ask him later, he says he would pick Marla over his new girlfriend.

After these ruminations, he appears uncertain of whether he wants the baby and explains that he has never seen Todd. Sam tells Dusty to think of Todd as his son, and himself as Todd's father. As such, he has the right to visit Todd and participate in his life. Sam suggests that Dusty act like he wants the kid. Dusty says he does. Sam explains that there are responsibilities that come with fatherhood, "like paying child support, and if Todd goes into foster care and gets adopted out, it will have repercussions for future children you may have."

Dusty seems excited about the possibility of being a father. He explains that he has always wanted to have a kid when he was 25 years old. Now he is 25, almost 26. He smiles to himself, and for a moment it appears he believes that this is all part of an adolescent plan coming to fruition. He recalls, "I thought about it when I was eighteen, but I decided I needed to calm down." I ask him what he means and he explains that he wanted to get his seizures under control—with medications, the last three months have been seizure-free— and "be more mature." He takes out a small heart-shaped box and shows us his medications, then stuffs it back in his pocket.

Sam explains that they will go into court shortly to see the judge and provides a brief overview of what will be decided that day. Dusty says that he does not have any other questions, and Sam leaves to see his next client.

★★★

The child welfare system (CPS), with policies that appear to be gender neutral, holds unique expectations for men who wish to gain custody of their children—who wish to be full-time fathers. The institution of fatherhood carries its own social significance. Permitted to stay emotionally distant, good fathers have in the last century been the ones who financially supported their wives and children through paid employment (if not through inheritance). In the last two decades, a more modern interpretation of ideal fatherhood has grown to include expectations that men should be emotionally involved with their children and participate in caregiving. However, even with these new expectations, it is primarily through financial support that fathers are evaluated, with other qualities viewed as additional assets. As Kjersti Ericsson notes of assessments of parental capability in the Norwegian child welfare system, "The minimal standard for being a good mother is the ideal, for each shortcoming she slides into the negative. The minimal standard for the father is the detached, old-fashioned model. For each 'modern' achievement, he climbs into the positive."[1] For men who do not (or are not able to) provide financially, particularly those who also do not live with their children, achievement of ideal fatherhood remains elusive. Men who fail to be good providers are labeled in public rhetoric and policy as "dead-beat dads." Although this term reflects the reality that child support payments to single mothers are often low and frequently unpaid, it also symbolically binds financial competence with capable fathering.

Hegemonic masculinity requires men to have claims to authority, positions of responsibility, and self-control. For the fathers whose children are in CPS custody, these requisite characteristics, often facilitated by professional or financial success, remain out of reach. CPS fathers are disproportionately men of color, frequently have histories of criminal convictions, and have had only limited success in employment, education, intimate relationships, or property ownership. Instead, some of these fathers have defined their manhood through their participation in crime, violence, illegal sources of income, or the "siring" of children outside of committed relationships. Although these activities may have provided a source of masculine competence in their own social worlds, they are devalued and even present a liability in the CPS system.

Men are constrained by legal requirements that exclude fathers never married to the mothers of their children. They are also limited by CPS professionals' presumptions about their lack of caregiving abilities, exacerbated by their failure to meet cultural definitions of competent fatherhood. To be perceived as capable of reformation by CPS—the agency responsible for protecting children by resocializing bad parents—fathers in CPS must subordinate themselves to culturally legitimated definitions of fatherhood (and their accompanying meanings of manhood).

Becoming a CPS Father

Many fathers enter CPS because of the actions of the mothers of their children, with whom they often do not live. One common route is when a baby is born positive for illegal drugs and enters CPS at birth. Another common route into CPS for nonoffending fathers is when CPS intervenes because a half- or step-sibling has been abused or molested, in which case protective custody of the child's siblings is automatic. In many of these cases, the men have not directly caused the risk or harm that led the family into CPS and may not have even known about it. Yet once the children are placed in protective custody, the court will notify fathers of the proceedings and assess them for possible placement. Despite their lack of offense, many fathers are ruled unsuitable for placement because of their social or criminal history or current living situation. Legally children must be in imminent danger to be removed from their homes by CPS. Once in protective custody, their well-being is the responsibility of the county. Consequently a higher standard exists for returning or placing children than for removing them. After children have become dependents of the court, nonoffending fathers—that is, fathers who are not directly responsible for the harm that led their children into the system—are scrutinized against this higher standard.

The case of Leonard King, a 28-year-old African American man, provides a useful example. Leonard's six-month-old daughter Leonisha was removed from his girlfriend Traci Mays' custody when she left the six-month-old with her five half-siblings, the oldest of whom was 15. Traci's other children had been in CPS custody before Leonisha's birth, following their molestation by their father and the death of one child from what Leonard described as a vitamin overdose—most likely iron poisoning. The current case, in which Leonisha and her five half-siblings were placed in protective custody, began when the social worker responsible for monitoring Traci's children after they were reunited with her conducted an unannounced visit and chose to remove them from what was described as a filthy house. Although Leonard did not live there, he was denied placement of his infant daughter, likely because of a past conviction for drug dealing. Voicing his frustration, he explains,

> When they took my daughter, they should have notified me ahead of time and gave me my daughter. They shouldn't have just popped up and taken my daughter and then try to make me out to be someone I'm not. To me, they messed up…They shouldn't, they shouldn't make the mom or the father suffer because of what the other parent does.

The vocabulary of "reunification" does not really apply to men like Leonard who have never had custody of—or been unified with—their children. Nonetheless, the only mechanism that exists for fathers who are deemed unsuitable but who wish to gain custody of their children is the totality of the reunification services system. For example, Scott Hughes, an African American man in his late 30s, came to court to gain custody of his newborn daughter who tested positive for cocaine at birth, the fourth "pos-tox" baby born to Scott's girlfriend, Chantelle Carter. In keeping with federal legislation that does not require the county to attempt reunification in situations where parents have not benefited from prior services, Chantelle was not given an opportunity to reunify with her newborn daughter. Although Scott did not have any other children, Tess Bachmeier, a white attorney in her mid-30s representing the baby, argued in court that Scott should also be denied services. Citing a four-year-old conviction for driving under the influence of alcohol and his failure to complete court-ordered services for that felony, as well as a conviction for driving without a license one year ago, Tess contended that "the father has quite a history of alcohol…and not a lot of respect for court orders." Here Scott, who was not suspected of drug use and had never received family reunification services before, had to fight to establish his right to vie for custody of his daughter.

In addition to his criminal record, Scott's romantic involvement with a woman who was drug addicted was offered as proof that he was not capable of adequately parenting. Pointing to his inability to adequately protect the fetus from drug exposure, Tess continued to outline her position: "Perhaps most concerning is his ambivalence about taking care of his own child…He had knowledge of the mother's substance abuse problem and use during her pregnancy." In his own defense, Scott, who had never lived with Chantelle, said that he had tried to get her to stop using. However, Isabel Guzman, a Latina county attorney—joining with Tess—argued that the fact "that he involved himself with the mother in a fashion that led to the conception of this child" was itself cause for concern. Although he was offered services and visitation with his daughter, his unwillingness to abandon Chantelle eventually led to the termination of his parental rights.

A father who refuses to abandon an abusive or drug-addicted girlfriend, wife, or partner will fail to reunify with his children. When a father has a girlfriend without a prior CPS or criminal history, she is often perceived as an asset to his case, especially when she attends visits and services. He may have been living with her and her children without incident, which can provide some promise of a stable home life. However, men who remain in relationships with "bad women" are seen as poor choice makers. For example, Juan Reyes, a Latino truck driver, wanted to reunify with his two daughters and stepdaughter. To do so, he needed to abandon Leigh, his drug-addicted wife, who was neither participating in court-ordered services nor drug treatment, and who attended court hearings while self-declaredly under the influence of drugs and alcohol. (As an example of her lack of desire to present herself as attempting reform, her attorney asked her before a court hearing when she last used drugs and alcohol, to which she responded, "What time is it?") Although Juan did eventually separate from Leigh, his hesitance to do so worked against him and nearly cost him his parental rights.

The quality of the partners men choose represents their ability to make responsible decisions—a key aspect of competent masculinity. By having children with women to whom they are not married, men are already suspect, particularly when those women behave in ways that lead to state intervention. Chris Vaughn's case provides an example of this. Chris, a 37-year-old white man, had a brief relationship with Erica Finola, a woman he met at a Narcotics Anonymous meeting. After their affair ended, Erica disappeared and was presumed to have relapsed both in her drug addiction and schizophrenia, for which she refused to take her prescribed medications. Approximately one year later, Chris ran into Erica. She informed him that she had given birth to a baby girl that had been taken into CPS custody and that the baby was probably his. Fearful that he would owe child support, Chris hesitated to contact the county and identify himself as the likely father. By the time he did come forward to claim custody of his daughter Shelby—a few months later—the county fought him, insisting that he had come forward too late to qualify for reunification services. The judge eventually awarded Chris a case plan, which included services and scheduled visits with Shelby, that he would have to complete to gain custody of her. Despite Chris's initial victory, he felt it was unjust that he was required to complete services. In an argument with his attorney, Chris bemoaned the cumbersome nature of reunification services. His attorney, Rebecca Channing, retorted, "You went and got a woman pregnant who went and got herself in CPS." In essence, Chris—like Scott, Juan, and other men who impregnate drug-addicted women—was seen as a poor decision maker, and, by association, incapable of adequate fathering.

MEN'S RELATIVE RIGHT TO SERVICES

Men who are married to the mothers of their children are assumed to be the children's father, unless there is legal documentation to the contrary. Once a man who is not married to the mother of his child at the time of conception or birth comes forward and is identified as someone who is most likely the child's father, he becomes, as far as the court is concerned, the "alleged father." In some cases, there may be multiple alleged fathers. To be entitled to reunification services, an alleged father must become a "presumed father" (or "putative father"), of which there can only be one. The ways a man can establish presumed father status vary slightly from state to state. In California, establishing presumed father status typically requires that men provide the court with some combination of the following documentation:

- A copy of a declaration of paternity, signed at the child's birth (this is a form voluntarily claiming parentage);

- A child support order from the district attorney's office;

- The mother's testimony that he is the biological father, that they lived together at the time of conception, and that she does not believe any one else could be the father; or

- A copy of the birth certificate with the man's name on it. (On its own, the birth certificate does not establish paternity, but does serve as evidence of who the mother believed was the father at the time of birth. However, implementation of the Personal Responsibility and Work Opportunity Reconciliation Act of 1996 requires that unmarried fathers cannot be listed on birth certificates unless they sign a declaration of paternity.)

Alternatively, the court can order a paternity test. This genetic test compares the DNA of the alleged father to that of the child in question and determines with 99.9 percent certainty whether the child was conceived from sperm from the alleged father.

Although it would seem simple for an alleged father to provide one of these forms of proof, it is often quite difficult. The case at the beginning of this chapter provides such an example. In that case, a 26-year-old Laotian woman named Marla Chue, who suffers from mental retardation and mild cerebral palsy, was legally married to Dusty Benjamin, a 25-year-old white man who is also cognitively impaired, most likely as a result of a lifetime of severe grand mal seizures. Marla became pregnant and announced that the baby was not Dusty's, but instead belonged to Dirk Haigenberger, a 23-year-old white man who is also impaired, but is the highest functioning of the three. At the time of conception, all three adults were sharing an apartment, but upon learning of the sexual relationship between Marla and Dirk, Dusty moved out.

Jeff Roper, an independent living specialist employed by the county, was assigned to assist Marla and Dirk with the baby. His work included coming to their residence and teaching them appropriate care of the baby, housekeeping, and basic infant safety. Dusty also came over every morning to his former dwelling to "help," though he was told by Jeff that all social services (including those that Jeff provided) were exclusively for Marla and Dirk. Jeff was concerned that Marla and Dirk were unable to keep the infant safe and lacked interest in learning to do so. Within days of the baby's birth, he reported them to CPS. An investigating social worker determined the infant was in imminent danger and placed him in protective custody. The case then went to court.

One of the first tasks for the court was to determine which adults should be eligible to reunify with the infant. Like many states, California presumes that men who are legally married to the mother of their children are the legal fathers. Based on his legal marriage to Marla and their shared residence at the time of conception, Dusty was given the status of presumed father. However, Dirk's appointed attorney, Murray Liebman, a white man in his early 50s, contended that his client, who had signed a declaration of paternity at the hospital at the time of the baby's birth, was legally the father. He argued that according to the statute, that declaration held the same legal power as a court order finding him the father. Unfortunately Dirk could not produce a copy of the document he claimed to have signed. Marla insisted that Dirk was the father and that he too had shared a residence with her at the time of conception. Capturing the murkiness of the competing legal claims, Dusty's attorney explained during a prehearing conference, "The legal term for this is a mess."

As the judge saw it, the obvious solution was to order a paternity test to establish who was actually the biological father. Dirk's attorney argued that the law did not allow the court to order a paternity test when a presumption of paternity existed. Thwarted, the judge explained that he was unsure how to proceed since there were two competing legal presumptions of paternity in this case. Each presumption stemmed from statutes that are meant to be complementary, but were in this instance contradictory. Ending the stalemate, Marla's attorney finally said that his client was willing to request the paternity test, though Marla, who only minimally comprehended the proceedings, never actually voiced the requisite uncertainty, and thus never actually made the request. Nonetheless, once entered on the record, this request overrode all legal presumptions and the paternity test determined that Dirk was in fact the biological father. Dusty became a nonparty to the proceedings.

Most parents in CPS are not legally married. Thus paternity almost always hinges on biology. A father who is not genetically related to the child will find it difficult to remain involved in the case. For example, I observed a case in which a man requested reunification services, only to discover that the six-year-old girl he had lived with and raised as his daughter since her birth was not biologically—therefore not legally—his. He was instantly excluded from the process. His parents, who had requested to be considered as relatives for foster placement, were no longer eligible for expedited kinship placement and had to undergo foster care licensing to gain placement of the little girl that they considered their granddaughter. Men in this situation can petition for de facto parent status—that is, recognition that they are parents in fact, even if not in law—but they must demonstrate to the court that their continued involvement is in the best interest of the child. If they were part of the allegation that brought the family into CPS, or if they have a criminal history, there is little to no chance they can demonstrate that their continued involvement is in the child's best interest.

Encouraging Absentee Fatherhood

The CPS system advises fathers who come forward to establish paternity that doing so may not be in their best interest. First, parents in CPS may be billed for some portion of the costs of foster care, regardless of whether they succeed in gaining custody of their children.

While attempting to gain custody of their children, parents also absorb some or all of the costs of services, in addition to the costs of foster care and legal representation, if they are deemed capable of paying. Parents often perceive these costs as an added hurdle to reunification. Mateo Estes, a Latino father in his early 20s, was accused of breaking the leg of his four-year-old stepdaughter, Leanna. He denied causing the spiral fracture and insisted that it was broken when it became lodged between her bed frame and the wall while she was jumping on the bed as he tucked her two-year-old half-brother into his bed in the same room. One proposed solution was for Leanna to undergo an interview at the multidisciplinary interviewing center (MDIC). These centers are staffed by psychologists, social workers, law enforcement officers, and representatives from the district attorney's office who are all present at one location and view a single interview. These centers have grown in popularity nationally, since this "one-stop shop" approach allows for the child to be interviewed only one time (following the initial interviews at the hospital and by social workers) and because the interviewers are considered to be professional and impartial. Though the interview might support his claim that his daughter's leg was broken while jumping on the bed, Mateo felt the costs of the interview would add considerable financial stress.

> They want to do an MDIC on my Lee-Lee, which costs like, which costs like three grand, I was told. And we have to pick that up. And I've borrowed enough from my father. I have to pay my father back five grand (borrowed to hire a private attorney). I can't be tacking on more money on that. I wouldn't ask my family to do that.

Fathers who are not yet identified as legal fathers can avoid these costs by deciding not to participate in reunification. Without establishing legal paternity, they will not be billed. Needless to say, this is an option almost entirely unavailable to mothers.

Also, fathers who come forward assume the risk of failing to reunify, which carries potentially far-reaching consequences. Many counties have adopted federal provisions that allow them to automatically remove other children from parents who have a history of failing to reunify with a child. In such cases, the burden is on the parent to prove that his or her life is substantively different from when the prior CPS case was decided. Although this is a gender-neutral issue, fathers who have not yet established their presumed father status are cautioned that they will need to commit themselves to the process, since failing to reunify can affect their ability to retain legal custody of future children they may have. Mothers, who are easily identified as legal parents, are seldom offered this caution or escape route.

Working to Reunify

Once a man has established his legal status as the presumed father, he will be assessed for placement of his child. Placement is based on some assessment of risk, drawing on a medley of variables, including employment history, criminal history, history of alcohol or drug use, current housing arrangement, and ongoing social support. During my research, I saw only two cases in which a father gained immediate custody of his children with the court dismissing dependency, meaning they would not even monitor the children in the father's home. Neither man had a criminal history and both were middle-class and employed. Both men had been married to the mothers of their children.

The court gives outright custody to few fathers, so most men are subjected to the machinations of the reunification process, whether or not they are directly involved in the harm or risk that led their children into the system. As previously mentioned, once a nonoffending father enters the reunification process, he is treated virtually identically to men who committed an offense against a child. Tim Ross, a white man in his early 20s, confronted this expectation. Tim came to court in a bid for his infant son, a child his ex-girlfriend, Lisa Flynn, a white woman in her early twenties, denied was his. Their infant son James became a dependent shortly after birth because Lisa's five-year-old daughter, James's half-sister, had been in protective custody for more than a year after being molested by a male friend of Lisa's. Tim came to court insisting he was James's father and demanded consideration. Although Lisa identified another man as James's father, she indicated that she was not certain. (The other man who received notice from the juvenile court never came forward.) A judge ordered paternity testing, but Lisa's failure to make James available for the test delayed Tim's ability to establish his claim. He became frustrated, an emotion he made known to those with whom he came in contact.

At the next hearing, the family reunification social worker assigned to James's case reported to the court that Tim had been "hostile and aggressive." As the judge asked him about his behavior, Tim stated defensively that he was "just being assertive." The judge informed Tim that should he actually be James's father, the county agency and the court would be in his life for a long time and would make his life more complicated. The judge sternly advised Tim to be cordial. One might recognize Tim's behavior as consistent with hegemonic masculinity's requirements for aggression, dominance, and self-control. In other situations—including those of his own social world—his behavior might have been rewarded. However, in the context of the system, deference is necessary to succeed.

EMPLOYMENT VERSUS COMPLIANCE

Once fathers establish their legal right to participate in reunification, they must prove they can act as children's primary caregivers and be good fathers. Many men understand this to mean that they must first and foremost be good economic providers. For many CPS fathers whose earning potentials are limited by lack of formal education, discontinuous work histories, or prior convictions, appearing to be competent breadwinners is challenging. However, the desire of many men to appear to be good providers distracts them from completing services, which on its own can prevent them from successfully gaining custody of their children.

Parents who try to maintain paid employment often find it difficult to comply with reunification services. Robert Davis, a construction worker, described his difficulties: "I just lost a lot of jobs. I'm always on probation [at a new job]. If I were part of the union, they would not have been able to fire me." Yet CPS also made it difficult for Robert to join a union. He explained,

> I would be on probation also. And that's one of the things I've been hesitating about, going all the way for the union job, because I would also be on probation when I first started and I don't want to lose that opportunity because I start out on probation and then I get kicked out.

When asked if CPS was the reason that he was having difficulty remaining employed, he answered tentatively:

> I'm not going to point any fingers. I had to go to parenting classes, I had to go to anger management classes, I have to go to court, I have to go to counseling of some type—that was part of my case file. And each and every one of those things I had in between job hours so I'll let you label that.

Complying with services is even more difficult for parents who work outside of the geographic area. Juan is a Latino man in his late 30s. His two daughters and stepdaughter were placed in foster care because of general neglect stemming in large part from his wife's addiction to methamphetamine. During the timeframe for reunification, Juan decided he needed a stable job to support his children. Approximately ten months after his case began, he enrolled in a vocational training program to become a truck driver. While in trucking school, his court-ordered visits with his daughters became irregular. When he completed his three-month truck-driver training program, he began driving interstate routes, which also interrupted his visits. When his spotty visitation record was brought up in court, he argued that he often called his social worker and attempted to arrange alternative times for visits or would ask his estranged wife Leigh to arrange the visits for him. In his mind he was making a sincere effort to comply, not realizing that both were poor strategies in light of Leigh's total lack of compliance with her own reunification case plan and his social worker's overwhelming caseload.

Although parents identify their own ways of demonstrating competent parenting—including the ability to provide financially for their children—the court holds them accountable for completing the services as laid out by the social worker. The high volume of cases social workers handle translates into practice where case plans are neither flexible, nor negotiable. Although the fathers described above were largely perceived as noncompliant, they were attempting, in a way that made sense to them, to reunify with their children. But in defining their own schedule or priorities, such as prioritizing a job over counseling or drug testing, they allow the state to view them as uncommitted to their rehabilitation.

PROVING THE CAPACITY TO PARENT

In addition to proving—or performing—commitment to self-improvement, men who want custody of their children must also show that they can provide day-to-day care. To gain custody of their children, fathers must convince social workers and court officers that they cannot only keep their children free from harm, but can adequately meet their daily needs.

In addition to the gendered assumptions about them, many men of color, most frequently African American men, felt that racial stereotypes further hindered their attempts to assert their right to parent. They faced images of African American men as dangerous, irresponsible, and predatory, in addition to visions of them as incapable of parenting. Sensing these prejudices, Robert articulated how he felt these stereotypes reinforced perceptions of him as unable to father: "I've had stereotype. Black man been convicted once before. Black man believed to be hostile. Black man that's not wealthy. Black man that's been involved with a mother who's a controlled substance abuser, sexually. Man does not raise children."

Some men of color articulated their belief that these racialized assumptions actually led to their entrance into the system. Frank Ramirez, a 44-year-old man of Cuban and African American descent, entered CPS when his 37-year-old white live-in girlfriend Shelly gave birth to their son Francisco, who tested positive for methamphetamine. Although Shelly had eight other children from her prior marriage, Francisco was Frank's only child. Shelly's six blonde-haired, fair-skinned daughters who had been living with Shelly and Frank also became dependents of the state, while her 16-year-old son, who was attending a residential school out of state, did not (nor did her 19-year-old daughter). In discussing their entrance into CPS, Frank identifies race as a factor:

> They look at it from another standpoint. They look at it like here we got this black man with six white girls… I can read people pretty good and before I had this attorney here they were really infringing on seeing me with this woman and these kids. Ya know you could see it. They really wanted to get at me because I'm black and I'm with all of these little white girls. You can see it on people's faces, their attitudes, and stuff.

For many fathers, race, class, and gender come together to form a presumption that they are unfit to father. Their experiences of inequality and of presumed incompetence inform each other. While these intersections of inequality shape men's experiences in CPS, they also construct men's experiences in other institutions, including the criminal justice system. This is of particular relevance as criminal histories—affected by the disparate treatment of poor men and men of color in the criminal justice system—interfere with the ability of men to reunify with their children.

BAD MEN AS GOOD FATHERS?

To have their children immediately placed with them, fathers must have little or no criminal history or history of substance use or abuse. In fact, a criminal history for violent or drug-related crimes is one of the most significant hindrances to reunification… As a result, the inequalities in treatment of poor men and men of color in the criminal justice system are reproduced in CPS where criminal history is a significant litmus test for reunification.

Many men in this study were committed to being parents, despite their lengthy criminal records. Yet when entering CPS, they found that their criminal records weighed heavily on assessments of their parenting abilities. In Richie's case, a lengthy criminal history interfered with his ability to gain custody of his daughter. He explained, "Yeah, and I went to court and they thought I was crazy, especially because I have a record that probably stands higher than this table." Richie claims that his criminal history included "rape, robbery, violence with guns, assaulting police officers—everything, everything" but explained that "the main thing they were concerned about was that I had two possessions of marijuana on my record."

Men's criminal history may not bear directly on their ability to father. Richie raised five children with three different women between bouts of incarceration; several of his children went on to college. At the time Richie learned about nine-month-old Christina, who had been born in jail to Richie's drug-addicted ex-girlfriend, he had sole custody of his three-year-old daughter Laquanda, whose drug-addicted mother, according to Richie, voluntarily gave her to him. Although his criminal behavior predated the births of both girls by at least six years, he argued that the social workers "were treating me like shit at first, I think more because of my record." An unsuitable father on paper, Richie explained why he was not necessarily a bad placement for Christina.

> I haven't done anything to my kids, so there was no reason for that [removal]. Ya know, like I told them, they were worried about my record and like I told them, you shouldn't worry about my record. You should look at what I learned from what I done.

Despite Richie's struggle with his reunification and his initial battles with his social worker, he was successful. His attorney explained to me that his case changed direction after the social worker went by his house for an unannounced visit, a strategy that often reveals the proverbial "smoking gun" in an unsuccessful bid for reunification. What she found was a loving, affectionate father at home playing with Laquanda and a few of his grandchildren who were visiting. Upon seeing Richie, an "inappropriate man" engaged in actively appropriate fathering, she began to advocate for him. Christina was returned to Richie shortly thereafter. In addition to the specifics of this case, this story also reveals how easy it was for Richie, as a black man, to exceed the very low expectations his social worker had of him. We can imagine that had a social worker discovered a mother playing with her children, it would not likely have so dramatically swayed her case. However, because unmarried men—especially men of color—are imagined to be incapable of caring for children, Richie was exceptional.

The centrality of drugs and criminal convictions to definitions of adequate parenting also complicate caregivers' abilities to strategize on their children's behalf. For example, Miguel's criminal conviction created confusion for Audrey who, having reunified with her five-month-old daughter after she and Miguel were arrested for drug dealing, was still monitored by social workers. Unlike Audrey, whose criminal charges were dropped, Miguel was convicted of drug dealing. Lacking American citizenship, he will be deported to Mexico upon his release. Because he and Audrey were not legally married, he will have no grounds to challenge his deportation. Nonetheless, Audrey hoped she could sustain a relationship between her daughter and boyfriend, who she regarded as a good father. Audrey agonized over whether she should bring her infant daughter to see Miguel in prison. In fact, she had not been advised against it, but knowing that she was under CPS surveillance, she feared reprisal. Although she was confused about whether she could take the baby to visit, she was most clear about the assumptions of the system:

> I don't know if it's okay for me to take her or, I just—they just don't want us to be a family. In their eyes they don't think we're a healthy family...That's really disturbing because I know how much he loves his daughter. How he lived his life and how he made money didn't affect how he treated her, and the way he treated me.

For other caregivers—including relatives who have foster placement—who understand how social workers perceive their charges' parents, deciding and mediating contact and visitation can be risky, particularly if allowing parental visits permits CPS to view these foster parents as also failing to adequately defer to state definitions. Yet care providers or custodial parents like Audrey may quite reasonably believe that allowing their children to maintain a relationship with their fathers is in the children's best interest, even as the state defines their fathers as failures.

RESOCIALIZING BAD MEN

The CPS system—with its overburdened workers and generic solutions— grants only limited time and ways for men to demonstrate their ability to be caretakers to their own children. Many fathers attempt to demonstrate their allegiance to hegemonic masculinity, which they interpret as synonymous with good fathering, by attempting to maintain paid employment or by challenging the frustrating and seemingly irrelevant requirements of the system. In these ways, they could demonstrate how they were autonomous, self-sufficient, and authoritative. However, without demonstrating their deference to system processes and meanings, CPS fathers cannot succeed.

NOTE

1 Kjersti, Ericsson. "Gender, Delinquency and Child Welfare," Theoretical Criminology2, no. 4 (1998), 455.

56

Navigating the Tricky Waters of Being a Stepdad

Joshua Gold

Joining a family can be awkward: Are you supposed to act like a father? Should you discipline the kids?

The American family is evolving. Fifty years ago, a nuclear family of two biological parents and children was the norm. But divorce rates and growing numbers of single parents have opened up more opportunities for the formation of stepfamilies (one biological parent, one nonbiological parent plus children of the biological parent).

Today, over 50 percent of families include partners who have remarried or recoupled, and 1,300 stepfamilies are being formed every day. Some predict that the number of stepfamilies will eventually exceed nuclear families.

Stepfamilies that consist of a father, stepmother and his biological children make up only about 15 percent of all stepfamilies. The most common composition of stepfamilies – about 85 percent – consists of a mother, her biological children and a stepfather.

Families with a stepfather, then, constitute a disproportionate number of stepfamilies. But stepfathers seem to have a particularly difficult time becoming integrated into the family unit. As a family counselor who has researched stepfamilies for over 25 years, I've found that many stepfathers have misguided expectations about the role they're supposed to play.

THREE PRIMARY MISCONCEPTIONS

Practitioners of cognitive therapy believe that people often act or behave based on previously held assumptions.

Unless someone understands their own underlying assumptions, it's unlikely they'll change their behavior. So a key aspect of cognitive therapy is getting people to explore and understand their assumptions. It's the first step toward changing destructive or self-defeating behaviors, and this approach forms the foundation of my latest book, *Stepping In, Stepping Out: Creating Stepfamily Rhythm*.

Gold, Joshua. "Navigating the Tricky Waters of Being a Stepdad." *The Conversation*, June 15, 2017.

So what misconceptions do stepfathers seem to possess? I've found that three social myths seem to undergird their assumptions.

1. Being a stepfather is just like being a biological father.

Being a stepfather is nothing like being a father, even if the stepfather is also a biological father. Because the stepchildren did not "pick" their stepfather – and might simultaneously feel conflicted about their attachments to their biological father – they will likely be wary about affection toward and receiving discipline from the stepfather.

In the end, a stepfather has no history or legacy with these children. So it's pretty normal for a stepfather to experience feelings of being unwanted, dismissed or peripheral; but it's also important for the stepfather to recognize that this isn't a reflection of his capacity as a man or father.

2. A stepfather needs to establish authority, and discipline the children if necessary.

Stepfathers might wish to assume the "hard hand" in the family. Their wives might even want them to. But this is almost impossible to effectively do. The foundation for effective authority and discipline is trust, but because stepfathers lack prior experience with the stepchildren, they haven't developed the trust necessary to mete out discipline.

Instead, in stepfamilies, it's the responsibility of the biological parent – with the stepparent providing input – to create, relate and enforce family expectations. A united parenting approach can be helpful, but the mother should be the base of authority.

3. Stepfathers need to compensate for the absent biological father.

I've found that most attempts at coming between children and an absent father will backfire – and result only in acrimony toward the stepfather.

Stepfathers cannot define themselves by what another man did (or didn't do). In addition, any overt comparison with the absent father will generate more ill will than gratitude. In instances when the biological father plays a prominent co-parenting role, it's wise to step aside to allow the father and children the special time that each needs – and to respect the role that that absent father still holds in the affections of the children.

There's Still an Important Role to Play

While it's critical for stepfathers to understand they aren't a replacement for the biological father, they can play a supportive role in the home by being a patient and caring presence. By simply maintaining a healthier marriage than the one demonstrated by the kids' biological parents, stepfathers can be a positive role model.

In the end, it's a challenge and an opportunity. The challenge comes in rejecting previously held beliefs about what it means to be a father. Stepfathers – and I count myself as one – must avoid outmoded notions of compensating for the absent biological father or paternal dominance.

The opportunity comes in devising a parenting role that expresses the best and fullest aspects of being a man and a father figure. Done consciously and deliberately, the role and function of the stepfather can be tremendously fulfilling for all, and a source of lifelong joy and pride.

57

I Am Who I Need to Be

Reflections on Parental Identity Development from a Father of a Child with Disabilities

Shailen Singh

Five years ago, my son was diagnosed with a form of cerebral palsy. I vividly remember sitting in a doctor's office while a neurologist explained that his brain damage was extensive, affecting three-quarters of my son's brain, resulting in both physical and cognitive delays. My partner asked a lot of questions, but I sat in stunned silence having difficulty processing the information I had just received. These first few moments were among the few where a doctor sat in front of us attempting to explain what brain damage means, and how it occurs and how it might impact our child, but I was too stunned to hear the information.

The next few weeks were filled with even more uncertainty as we attempted to figure out who we needed to be as parents to care for our precious child. We mourned the loss of predictability – of the confidence in what we were doing as parents. Erikson's (1963) formative model of identity development includes a dimension where an individual has an unconscious sense of the timeline he/she will travel through. We had that prior to my son being born. We lost it when he was diagnosed.

Quickly, my partner and I realized that the only sense of loss was one that we were feeling. Our son's life did not change, he was who he had always been. Ours, however, had changed significantly, but we did not want to let our process of understanding and internalizing disability as a component of his identity impact him negatively. We realized that we needed to stop mourning the loss of predictability, and start charting new paths.

Borrowing from Gloria Anzaldúa's (2012) work *Borderlands: The New Mestiza = La Frontera*, parents of children with disabilities straddle invisible borders between abled and disabled. These invisible borders are emotional and spiritual, and call for the creation of a third consciousness, focused on the creation of a new unique identity from the need to straddle the border. Anzaldúa describes the borderland as an 'open wound' and an 'unwelcome homeland', which can aptly describe the contradictory emotions associated with the early stages of parenting a child with a disability. The border came unexpected through a diagnosis – and now that border would define our lives moving forward.

As my son got older, and he fell further and further behind the neurotypical developmental curve, disability became a (not the) defining characteristic of our family and a significant component of our individual and collective identity as parents. From structuralized discrimination demonstrated through the lack of available

Singh, Shailen. "I Am Who I Need To Be: Reflections on Parental Identity Development from a Father of a Child with Disabilities." *Disability & Society* 34, no. 5 (2019): 837–841.

childcare for children with disabilities, to micro-aggressions associated with doctors' and therapists' offices not being designed with accessibility in mind, we straddled the world between abled and disabled and did our best to take care of our son.

When my son was diagnosed, a number of colleagues and acquaintances provided us with the platitudes of 'special children only go to special parents', which was simply infuriating and reaffirmed a sense of isolation that we were somehow 'set apart' from the start and therefore different than other parents. I am not a special parent because of my son's disability. I am a good father to all of my children. Being a father is central to my identity, and therefore my life choices are centered on who I need to be in order to be the best father I can be to my children. Being a good father, in this case, meant not only doing what I did for my other children, but also developing competencies to ensure I could be what he needed me to be – an advocate, a bully when needed and an expert in everything about his disability.

We became fluent in medical terminology in an effort to develop a level of cultural capital to communicate well with our team of doctors. We developed the self-efficacy associated with self-advocacy and knowing which battles to fight and how to fight them. We began to understand the challenges we would face as parents, both in the short term and in the long term, and started the gentle process of struggling with them to determine sustainable structures and plans.

Who Do I Need to Be?

Parental identity has long been defined as a reflexive process. Galinsky (1987) described it as a process where child development creates the need for new parenting skills, thus resulting in parents constantly evolving to meet the needs of their evolving child. Fracasso (2017) describes the period of adolescence as one where parents figure out how to balance the child's need for independence with their own need for connectedness – another concurrent reflexive process that involves stimulus/response between child and parent.

But neither one of those models accurately reflects my identity development. My son is very much the same child he was when he was born, leaving little room for reflexive growth. He is slightly more independent, but still 100 percent reliant on his parents for self-care-related needs. As it stands right now, it appears as if he has no higher order needs resulting in me needing to develop new parenting skills. However, I have developed significantly as a parent, not as a result of my son's development, but rather from a reflexive process of attempting to manage the borders between disability and ability. We have failed over and over again, but each of those failures has taught us something new about who we need to be as parents to best care for our son.

The metaphorical borders defined by Anzaldúa have become practical borders that we navigate on a daily basis between home and work. Attempting to balance fulfilling careers with the time demands associated with therapy appointments, lack of reliable childcare and unpredictable health concerns has resulted in a reflexive shift in how we manage work/life conflict. The borders between work and home need to be flexible and permeable in order for us to effectively care for our son, leading to career changes. Corporate daycare systems are not designed for children with disabilities, and public school only runs nine months out of the year, which led us to relocating to be closer to family.

Managing the Border

The challenges associated with parenting children with disabilities largely go unnoticed, despite one out of every six children having some kind of developmental disability, ranging from attention deficit hyperactivity disorder to cerebral palsy to other developmental disorders. Parents of children with disabilities (predominantly mothers) have lower employment rates due to the lack of affordable and adequate childcare. Caregiving demands have been defined as the most common reason for unemployment by mothers of adults with disabilities. The unpredictability associated with medically fragile children leads to higher levels of work stress for parents of children with disabilities because parents are physically at work, but are always emotionally on call to pick up their child from school.

Indeed, my view of disability is limited by my own lived experience. I cannot begin to grasp the full depth of the identity my son is going to develop as a disabled person living in an ableist world. However, I echo Ryan and Runswick-Cole (2008) who say that parents of children with disabilities cannot simply be defined as allies when we ourselves experience marginalization and disablism. We are more than allies because our child's success depends on our ability to be fluent in medical terminology, educational law, insurance policies and procedures, among other things. For better or for worse, our failures are directly tied to the developmental ceiling for our children.

Parents of children with disabilities should be recognized as border-crossers and gatekeepers to their child's welfare. Therefore, improving the lives of children with disabilities involves strengthening and empowering parents to effectively manage borders. Furthermore, the process of creation and maintenance of these borders rarely includes the input of parents. For example, meetings to discuss Individualized Educational Plans are scheduled only between the hours of 08:00 and 17:00, without any consideration for parents with little to no flexibility in their work schedules. The success of our children is based on our ability to navigate a system created by people who rarely have practical experience with parenting in our world.

As my partner and I learned quickly, there is no 'how to' associated with raising a child with disabilities, but perhaps there should be – and that 'how to' should be developed in conjunction with parents and caregivers in an effort to create meaningful systems and borders that are permeable, flexible and easily navigated. Enhancing the capacity of parents to effectively both navigate and influence borders in service of their children can directly impact the developmental trajectory of children with disabilities.

Parents of children with disabilities are not a homogeneous group. Identity development of parents of children with disabilities, therefore, should not be looked at from a linear, homogeneous lens. The level to which a person identifies parenting as a key role in their life will directly impact the manner in which they navigate the borders associated with parenting a child with a disability. Preconceived ideas regarding disability will directly impact the manner in which a parent takes on the challenges and opportunities associated with children with disabilities. Educational level, socioeconomic status, race and ethnicity all play a role in how well a parent of a child with a disability is effectively able to navigate the boundaries associated with raising a child with disabilities.

A New Form of Identity

Fundamentally, there needs to be a shift in how we conceptualize the role (and resulting responsibilities) of a parent of a child with disabilities. Instead of simply focusing on the day-to-day tasks associated with the care and development of children with disabilities, more focus should be given to the process by which parents actualize disability as a component of their identity, and develop the necessary skills associated with being an able-bodied person navigating systems associated with disability.

My partner and I have had at least two occasions where we perceived someone utilizing their expertise to undermine our efforts to support our child. Both times we were able to rely on our educational capital and do research to get our points across productively, despite what others were telling us. At the end of the meeting we cordially shook hands with the administrators who we had disagreed with, as if to say that the disagreement was all business – but it was not. My goals for my children are deeply personal, and I am fortunate to have the ability (based on experience and access to resources) to advocate for my son through bureaucratic structures.

Through that experience, I could not help but wonder about the other parents who did not have the cultural capital that I do. The ones who love their child just as much as I love mine, but have never had access to the knowledge necessary to effectively advocate for the services their child needs, because advocating involves the ability to successfully navigate from one side of a border to the other.

The conversation regarding identity development for parents of children with disabilities should not be focused solely on disability, and nor should it be solely focused on parenting. Rather, it should be focused on the complex set of skills necessary for parents to understand and operate within the context of multiple systems – all of which ask parents to straddle the border between ability and disability. It should be focused on the practical decisions parents make in order to reorganize their lives around the needs of their child. The paradigmatic framework by which parents make decisions for their children, and for themselves, is in and of itself a form of identity.

REFERENCES

Anzaldúa, G. 2012. Borderlands: The New Mestiza = La Frontera. San Francisco: Aunt Lute Books.

Erikson, E. H. 1963. Childhood and Society. New York: Norton.

Fracasso, M. P. 2017. "The Concurrent Paths of Parental Identity and Child Development." In Identity Flexibility during Adulthood, edited by J. Sinnott. Cham, Switzerland: Springer.

Galinsky, E. 1987. The Six Stages of Parenthood. Boston: Addison-Wesley.

Ryan, S., and R. Runswick-Cole. 2008. "Repositioning Mothers: Mothers, Disabled Children and Disability Studies." Disability & Society 23 (3): 199–210.

58

Fathers Also Want to "Have It All"

Gayle Kaufman

Have you seen the T-shirt slogan: Dads don't babysit (it's called "parenting")?

This slogan calls out the gendered language we often still use to talk about fathers. Babysitters are temporary caregivers who step in to help out the parents. But the fact is that fathers are spending more time with their children than ever before. In fact, American fathers today spend 65 percent more time with their children during the workday than they did 30 years ago.

According to the 2016 National Study of the Changing Workforce, almost half of fathers in heterosexual relationships say they share caregiving responsibilities equally or take on a greater share of caregiving than their partner.

Recently, we witnessed the release of the first *State of America's Fathers*, a report that draws on numerous social science research studies as well as new analysis of the 2016 National Study of the Changing Workforce.

As a sociologist who studies fatherhood worldwide, I think the most important message of this report is a simple one: Fathers are parents, too.

But dads' desire to "have it all," as we once talked about in relation to working mothers, means that they are also having difficulties successfully combining work and family. The report, among other things, suggests that we need to pass paid, non-transferable, job-protected leave. I agree.

WORK-LIFE BALANCE IS IMPORTANT TO MEN, TOO

The *State of America's Fathers* report highlights that a majority of fathers experience work-life conflict, and that this has increased over time. For example, 60 percent of fathers in dual-earner families say they have problems balancing work and family, compared to 35 percent of such fathers in 1977.

This is likely due to the fact that a majority of fathers feel they don't spend enough time with their children. This situation may be due to the continued pressures on men to earn a good income. According to the 2016 National Study of the Changing Workforce, 64 percent of Americans feel that fathers should contribute

Kaufman, Gayle. "Fathers Also Want to 'Have It All,' Study Says." *The Conversation*, June 15, 2016.

financially even if taking care of the home and children. Millennials are just as likely to agree with this statement as baby boomers.

In my own research published in my book *Superdads*, fathers continually expressed frustration at not being able to balance work and family. It's no longer a question of whether fathers want to be more active in their children's lives, but how they will do so when workplace and government policies do not offer the support necessary.

MEN NEED WORK-LIFE POLICIES AS MUCH AS WOMEN

A big part of the problem is that the workplace has not really adjusted to working women and caregiving men.

Instead the idea of the ideal worker, someone (usually a man) who can focus entirely on work while a partner (usually a woman) takes care of everything else, still holds power among employers. But the *State of America's Fathers* report reveals that most workers have some family responsibilities, and only a minority of families fit the "traditional" breadwinner father, homemaker mother model. Only 20 percent of couples live off of one income. This means that most fathers have partners, female or male, who also work, and more single fathers have shared or primary custody of their children. These men do not have the choice to push off caregiving onto someone else.

Like working mothers, working fathers face stigma when they seek greater flexibility in the workplace. A very similar number of fathers (43 percent) and mothers (41 percent) think asking for flexibility could have a negative impact on their careers.

In addition, there is evidence that leave-taking negatively impacts chances of promotion, frequency of raises, and performance evaluations, and these penalties are stronger for men than women. Men who seek flexibility are even seen as less masculine.

THE BENEFITS OF FATHER INVOLVEMENT

Why should we be so concerned about men's ability to balance work and family?

The simple answer is that fathers who take leave and spend more time with their children are really good for their families. Their children benefit from better cognitive, behavioral, psychological, and social outcomes.

According to the *State of America's Fathers* report, these fathers also pave a path toward greater gender equality as their sons are more accepting of gender equality while their daughters feel more empowered. Their partners benefit because they are more likely to be satisfied with their relationships and less likely to experience postpartum depression. They are also more able to focus on their own careers, which has the potential to benefit the larger economy as well, with one estimate showing an increase of 5 percent in GDP if women's labor force participation rate equaled men's rate. Fathers themselves benefit by engaging in healthier behaviors and creating more ties to family and community.

And in the end, men are just as capable of caring for children as women. It is the act of providing direct care for a child that increases one's capacity for caregiving. Men's body chemistry reacts the same way as women's to close physical contact with infants. In other words, fathers show similar hormonal changes, and this means they can experience similar levels of bonding with their children.

PAID PARENTAL LEAVE COULD HELP

In an analysis of policies in 185 countries, the International Labour Organization finds that the United States is only one of two countries that does not guarantee paid parental leave. In fact, the US ranks dead last among 38 OECD nations in government-supported time off for new parents.

Our only national policy, the Family and Medical Leave Act (FMLA) of 1993, offers up to 12 weeks of leave, but in addition to being unpaid, it only covers about three-fifths of workers due to a number of restrictions. The act only applies to employers with 50 or more employees and only covers employees who have worked for that employer for at least one year. Additionally, 20 percent of employers that are required to comply with the FMLA offer fewer than 12 weeks of leave to employees who are spouses/partners of new mothers (mainly fathers), in direct violation of the law. Amazingly, only 12 percent of US workers in the private sector have access to paid family leave, and this applies to a paltry 5 percent for low-income workers.

Worldwide paternity leave is becoming more prevalent, with 71 countries now offering it. Fathers are most likely to take leave when it is specifically designated for them. Around 90 percent of fathers in Nordic countries take leave.

These programs may seem out of reach, but we have seen successful paid leave in the US Funded by a very small payroll tax of 0.9 percent, California's groundbreaking Paid Family Leave program helped new parents spend more time caring for their children. At the same time most employers have seen no cost increases or abuse and in fact witness less turnover as employees are able to care for their new children and return to work.

We are also starting to see more models of paid leave among companies such as Ernst & Young, Facebook, and Twitter, but I would argue we need something more far-reaching. The FAMILY Act, for example, proposed by US Senator Kirsten Gillibrand of New York to provide up to 12 weeks of paid leave, is a start.

This will help fathers to have it all, and be the parents they want to be.

SECTION XI
Poverty and Family Policy

INTRODUCTION

Welfare programs are one of the most visible ways the state regulates families. The role of the government in providing direct relief and assistance to people only began in the twentieth century. Prior to that, local churches and charities sometimes provided assistance to those deemed worthy of support—those they perceived to be poor through no fault of their own. Using discretion, which resulted in widespread discrimination, private charities helped many but remained suspicious of claims for help. Until the twentieth century, private charity was entirely responsible for managing poverty, in whatever ways church and community leaders felt were appropriate.

The first major legislative initiative was the mothers' pension, which provided cash payments to support women with dependent children who did not have a man in the house who could financially support them. Progressive reformers argued that women's work raising children was a public service and should be supported in the same way soldiers received pensions for serving their country. This program reflected social reformers' frustrations that many children were placed in foster care institutions by parents who could not afford to raise them. Illustrating this, in 1894, more than 33,500 children in New York State lived in institutions. An 1890 study of institutions for children found that many of those children had been committed by responsible parents who could not afford to raise them at home (Sribnick and Johnsen 2012).

The movement to create mothers' pensions received support when President Theodore Roosevelt convened the first White House Conference on the Care of Dependent Children in 1909. The goal of this conference was to raise public awareness of issues facing children, including the negative effects of institutionalization. The conference emphasized the importance of home and family and advocated several reforms, including the creation of a federal Children's Bureau, systems of safe foster care with regular inspections, and a mothers' pension program. Illinois was the first state to pass a statewide mothers' pension law in 1911. By 1913, 18 states had enacted a similar law, and by 1919, 39 states had. These laws signaled acknowledgement that private local charities alone could not solve poverty. Notably, these funds were targeted at those mothers deemed most worthy of support: widows. As a result, many programs, which were administered locally, excluded mothers who were never married, were divorced, or had been abandoned by their husbands. There was also widespread discrimination and women of color were often excluded from benefits.

THE GREAT DEPRESSION AND THE NEW DEAL

The Great Depression led to widespread poverty, which would inevitably overwhelm the resources of local mothers' pension programs. It also became increasingly hard to differentiate the "worthy" and "unworthy" poor when so many were affected. The solution came when President Franklin D. Roosevelt offered federal support for the mothers' pension program by including it in the Social Security Act of 1935 as the new program, Aid to Dependent Children (ADC). At the time, ADC was the first and only federal program to address poverty in families. ADC received support as an inexpensive way to keep children with their mothers, as compared to more costly institutionalized care. The federal government's commitment to pay one-third of the costs of the program (which eventually rose to half) helped sustain it.

The Social Security Act created other social programs too. It included the federal school lunch program, for example, which allowed the federal government to buy surplus crops from farmers suffering from price collapses during the Great Depression to feed children who might otherwise be malnourished with meals prepared by thousands of women who needed jobs. (In 1946, Congress would strengthen the school lunch program, justifying it by noting that supporting healthy children who could grow into strong soldiers was a matter of national interest.) The Social Security Act also created the food stamps program, which subsidized nutrition to poor families, workers compensation insurance, health insurance for those who were poor, unemployment, and financial support for those who were poor and disabled. The Social Security Act also created what was termed "old age insurance," now known colloquially as social security, which would financially support retirees based on lifetime payroll deductions. In short, the Social Security Act of 1935 created a social safety net to support those who needed help.

The ADC program, along with the other provisions of the Social Security Act, carved out a new role for the federal government. It also confirmed the view that mothers' work in raising children was of public importance. However, questions of worthiness never entirely went away and given that state and local governments administered the program without federal oversight, discrimination continued to be widespread. Women were routinely subjected to home visits to determine if their home was suitable for children. Evidence that a man was living there, even as a boarder who rented a room, could cost a woman her benefits. The "man-in-the-house rule," in which a child otherwise eligible for welfare benefits could be disqualified if his or her mother was living with or having relations with an able-bodied man, continued until 1968 when the US Supreme Court declared the practice unconstitutional (*King v. Smith*, 1968).

THE WAR ON POVERTY AND THE EXPANDING ROLE OF THE STATE

The 1960s and President Lyndon Johnson's Great Society plans created several additional social programs, which were proposed under the umbrella of the "War on Poverty." In 1964, Johnson introduced the Office of Economic Opportunity and called on Congress to pass the Economic Opportunity Act. This bill created local community agencies that could provide opportunities for job skills, education, and training that could "break the cycle of poverty." This effort included the creation of a job corps that created more than 100,000 jobs for low-income young people between the ages of 16–21 years. These jobs included work on conservation projects and community investment, as well as participation in programs at newly created education and training centers. The law funded federal work-study programs, which have helped hundreds of thousands of Americans attend college who could otherwise not have afforded to go. Johnson's plans also created a service corps that could help poor communities, loan forgiveness programs, incentives to employers who offered jobs to those who were unemployed, money for farmers to buy land and create co-ops, and childcare support. Additionally, Head Start programs provided preschool for low-income children, and libraries and special education programs received funding.

The federal Housing and Urban Development Act of 1965 offered funds to support city revitalization efforts, contingent on those cities also creating minimum housing standards for low-income housing. This act also created rental subsidies for those who qualified for public housing as well as mortgage programs to help people buy homes. At the same time, Congress passed laws to create safety standards for drinking water, laws to control air pollution, emission standards for cars, and wildlife protection. Some of this funding supported the creation of trails in parks and protection of rivers. Laws in this era also created product safety protections for consumers in general and for children in particular.

In 1965, Congress passed and Johnson signed the National Foundation on the Arts and Humanities Act, which created the National Endowment for the Humanities and the National Endowment for the Arts. These groups continue to support research in the humanities, fund cultural organizations, including museums, libraries, public television and radio, and public archives. Noting the important role of culture in a great society, the law stated that "the arts and humanities belong to all the people of the United States" and that culture is a concern of the government, not just private citizens (Phelan 2014). Also in 1965, Congress passed the Immigration and Naturalization Act, which ended quotas based on nationality and prioritized reuniting families, even as limits on immigration remained.

Among the most significant reforms presented during Johnson's War on Poverty were the creation of health insurance programs for those in need. In 1965, Johnson oversaw the passage into law of Medicare, which covered those older than 65 years of age and with particular diseases, and Medicaid, which covered the poor.

CONTROVERSIES OVER THE UNWORTHY POOR

Increases in ADC enrollment, which in the 1960s would become Aid to Families with Dependent Children (AFDC), made the program increasingly controversial. Questions of whether recipients were responsible for their situation and arguments about whether able-bodied mothers could and should work grew louder. Some argued cash assistance programs decrease motivation to work and create dependence. As Ricki Solinger's chapter in Section VI showed, resentment toward welfare recipients reflected racial hostilities, even as whites were the majority of recipients—a trend that continues to this day. Illustrating the declining support for public welfare programs, one 1977 poll found that more than half of Americans believed that "most people who receive money from welfare could get along without it if they tried" (Sribnick and Johnsen 2012).

Racism has been a backdrop of assistance programs since the very beginning, as Alma Carten describes in her chapter in this section. Yet, resentment of recipients and perceived abuses of public support became more explicit in the 1970s. At a campaign event in 1976, would-be president Ronald Reagan blamed welfare programs for societal problems, and introduced a symbol of welfare abuse: the welfare queen. Reagan described this imagined abuser of programs: "She used 80 names, 30 addresses, 15 telephone numbers to collect food stamps, Social Security, veterans' benefits for four nonexistent deceased veteran husbands, as well as welfare. Her tax-free cash income alone has been running $150,000 a year" (Black and Sprague 2016). In reality, the greatest levels of welfare fraud come from vendors who bill agencies for food and services, not participants (Kim and Maroulis 2015). Nonetheless, states began to require increasing levels of documentation from recipients in an effort to ferret out individual abuse. Still, resentment of government and its programs grew through the 1980s.

When Bill Clinton ran for president in 1992, he vowed to "end welfare as we know it" if elected. Making good on that campaign promise, Clinton signed the Personal Responsibility and Work Opportunity Reconciliation Act (PRWORA), known as "welfare reform". Built around the assumptions of malfeasance embodied in the image of the welfare queen, this sweeping legislation ended AFDC as a federal program, reconfigured programs, and created new requirements for those receiving benefits.

Welfare reform imposed several significant changes. First, the legislation ended the AFDC program and replaced it with Temporary Assistance to Needy Families (TANF). Rather than sending federal funds to cover half the costs of public assistance as it had for AFDC, the federal government funds TANF through block grants to states, which gives states flexibility on how to allocate funds, so long as they meet certain requirements. Unlike AFDC, which adjusted the payment to the state depending on the number of enrollees, block grants provide a fixed payment that is not easily adjustable, even during a recession, pandemic, or natural disaster, which might rapidly increase need.

TANF has many more requirements than did AFDC. Among them are time limits. Recipients now face a five-year cumulative lifetime maximum for receipt of support. As the chapter by Mark Rank shows, most low-income workers cycle on and off welfare, depending on changes in the economy, family, region, or workforce. Under PRWORA, each month counts toward a 60-month cumulative eligibility for benefits, even if those months are years apart. Although five years is the federal maximum, states may shorten this time limit even further.

Welfare reform also created new work requirements for recipients. Those receiving TANF must work at least 20 hours per week (and a two-parent family must work a combined 37 hours) to maintain eligibility. The law allows states to subsidize jobs, which includes the ability to give welfare funds to employers and exempt recipients from some labor law protections. It also crafts new requirements for job placement, requires personal employability plans, allows workers to be paid less than minimum wage if they receive food assistance, and specifies how job searching or job training are calculated as part of work effort and time. PRWORA excluded immigrants—both documented and undocumented—from receiving benefits.

Many of the changes written into PRWORA were not fiscal, but designed to support particular views of the family or in reaction to the most cynical assumptions about recipients. The law gave states the power to enact a family cap, in which families receiving public assistance cannot receive any additional money for babies born while receiving public assistance. The chapter by Diana Romero and Madina Agénor explains why this provision has been overly punitive and ineffective in changing recipients' reproduction.

The law also required mothers who apply for public assistance to name the fathers of their children as a condition of benefit enrollment. This information, as discussed in Section X on fatherhood, is used by agencies to collect child support, which can be used to reimburse agencies for the costs of public assistance. Women who refuse to name a father risk having their benefits cut by a minimum of 25 percent.

The myth that teenagers intentionally become pregnant to gain welfare payments or that teen pregnancy causes teens to drop out of school (rather than the reality that most have left school before becoming pregnant) led Congress to include provisions targeting teens specifically. To remain eligible for benefits, unmarried teen parents who apply for public assistance are required to live at home and stay in school. If a teen mother cannot live at home, she must live with "a responsible adult or in an adult-supervised setting" and participate in educational and training activities in order to receive assistance. The law expects states to offer teen pregnancy prevention programs in at least 25 percent of communities. The bill also ordered the US Attorney General to examine the links between teen pregnancy and statutory rape (where a minor who is legally incapable of consent has sex with someone over 18 years of age), and to increase prosecutions. PRWORA also included funding to promote abstinence-only education and to fund programs that increase non-custodial fathers' involvement.

Policy makers assume the worst about welfare recipients, which informs welfare legislation, and with the flexibility block grants provide, states often add additional requirements. For example, at least 15 states require recipients to take a drug test before receiving aid, an expensive program that has turned up very few positive results (Black and Sprague 2016, NCSL 2017). The result of a system built on suspicion is that interactions between recipients and the caseworkers who are supposed to help them are often strained. The chapter by Vicki Lens and Colleen Cary demonstrates how these interactions undermine programs intended to meet families' needs.

The long-term result of welfare reform is that many fewer families are receiving aid. The Center for Budget Policy and Priorities estimates that in 2017, TANF helped 1.7 million families. However, if it had the same reach as it did in 1996, TANF could have helped 3.8 million families in need. Said differently, TANF served 68 out of every 100 families with children in poverty in 1996, but by 2017, TANF only helped 23 of every 100 children living in poverty (Burnside 2019). If declining rates indicated that more families lived above the poverty line, this would be excellent news. Unfortunately, the declining reach of TANF suggests that a higher portion of families living in poverty lack the support a social safety net would provide.

Many suggest the United States no longer has a welfare system. Under current law, recipients have few rights to assistance and states under the block grant system are incentivized to limit the numbers of families who receive help, since they can reallocate unused block grant funds for other expenses. For example, Ohio uses some of their unspent funds on childcare for those in low wage jobs or work programs, Wisconsin funds tax credits for the working poor, Michigan funds college scholarships for young adults without children, and Texas spends funds on the child welfare system (Edin and Shaefer 2016). Although these programs may benefit low-income families, the reallocation of welfare funds to pay for these programs reduces the total amount that could help families meet their most basic needs.

SOCIAL SAFETY NET PROGRAMS FOR BASIC NEEDS

Cash assistance is only one way states and federal agencies help low income families. The Supplemental Nutrition Assistance Program (SNAP), formerly known as food stamps, is another such federal program. Individuals and families are eligible for SNAP so long as their gross monthly income is at or below 130 percent of the federal poverty line. In 2020, the poverty line for a family of three was $1,778 a month, so 130 percent would allow a family to earn up to $2,311 a month and still be eligible. Any income, including TANF funds, social security, or unemployment, counts in that calculation. Non-disabled adults without children can receive SNAP for up to three months and are required to prove that they have worked at least 80 hours a month for more than three months to receive food assistance. States may request a waiver from this requirement if they have areas with high unemployment rates. Immigrants are generally not eligible for SNAP benefits, though children irrespective of documentation usually are. SNAP benefits provide access to food, but do not allow purchases of other necessities, including diapers, which Jennifer Randles examines in her chapter in this section.

The Special Supplemental Nutrition Program for Women, Infants, and Children (WIC) is another public investment in low-income families. Started as a pilot in 1972 to address malnutrition among pregnant women, babies, and children, this federal program became permanent in 1975. Pregnant, postpartum, and breastfeeding women, infants, and children up to the age of five years are eligible for WIC. To access benefits, families must have a gross income of 185 percent of the federal poverty line and be screened and determined to be at "nutritional risk." Unlike SNAP, which allocates a certain amount in funds to be used with some discretion on food, WIC benefits typically come in the form of vouchers in specified nutritional categories. Rather than choosing their own food, WIC recipients often have limited options of foods that meet WIC specifications.

Medicaid and Medicare remain important components of the safety net. Since their creation in 1965, these programs have provided health insurance for low-income, disabled, and older Americans. In 2010, Congress passed and President Barack Obama signed the Patient Protection and Affordable Care Act (ACA). This law expanded access to Medicaid for low-income adults who had not previously been eligible for health insurance. States are not required to participate in efforts to expand Medicaid. In 2020, 36 states and the District of Columbia chose to do so.

People who live in states that expanded Medicaid under ACA are eligible for insurance if they have incomes at or below 138 percent of the poverty line ($17,236 for an individual in 2019). In contrast, people in the 14 states that did not expand their Medicaid programs are limited to 40 percent of the federal poverty line, which was an annual income of $8,532 for a family of three in 2019. Additionally, childless adults are ineligible for enrollment in those states (Garfield, Orgera and Damico 2020).

Public assistance programs reveal how states regulate family life. Throughout the history of poor assistance, tensions have existed between helping those in need and refusing aid to those deemed unworthy. Those who are sympathetic, including families with children, often fare better in programs, despite the reality that many others, including lesbian and gay people, those in rural communities, and many with health challenges, have high rates of poverty. The chapter by M.V. Lee Badgett, Soon Kyu Choi, and Bianca D.M. Wilson discusses some of these patterns.

As agencies work to distinguish between the deserving and undeserving poor, people who have needed help face increased surveillance and sacrifices of privacy. From the man in the house rule to drug testing, adults who request help face levels of institutional scrutiny that those with private resources usually escape. Notably, existing programs aim to varying degrees to address basic material needs for survival—food, shelter, healthcare. They do not equalize opportunities, as Vikki Katz's chapter shows. Nonetheless, the worthiness of public assistance continues to be politically contentious, as states and many in the federal government continue to strive to tighten eligibility requirements for SNAP and TANF, eliminate the ACA, and promote ideals of self-sufficiency that remain unattainable for a large number of families.

REFERENCES

Black, Rachel and Aleta Sprague. 2016. *The Rise and Reign of the Welfare Queen*. Washington, DC: New America. (https://www.newamerica.org/weekly/rise-and-reign-welfare-queen/).

Burnside, Ashley. 2019. "Tanf at 23: Over 2.5 Million More Families Could Be Getting Cash Assistance, Work Supports." Center for Budget and Policy Priorities. (https://www.cbpp.org/blog/tanf-at-23-over-25-million-more-families-could-be-getting-cash-assistance-work-supports).

Edin, Kathryn and Luke Shaefer. 2016. "20 Years since Welfare 'Reform': America's Poorest Are Still Dealing with the Consequences of the Legislation that Bill Clinton Signed into Law Two Decades Ago Today." *The Atlantic*, August 22.

Garfield, Rachel, Kendal Orgera and Anthony Damico. 2020. "The Coverage Gap: Uninsured Poor Adults in States That Do Not Expand Medicaid." Kaiser Family Foundation. (https://www.kff.org/medicaid/issue-brief/the-coverage-gap-uninsured-poor-adults-in-states-that-do-not-expand-medicaid/).

Kim, Yushim and Spiro Maroulis. 2015. "Rethinking Social Welfare Fraud from a Complex Adaptive Systems Perspective." *Administration & Society* 50(1):78–100. doi: 10.1177/0095399715587520.

NCSL. 2017. "Drug Testing for Welfare Recipients and Public Assistance." National Conference of State Legislators. (https://www.ncsl.org/research/human-services/drug-testing-and-public-assistance.aspx).

Phelan, Marilyn E. 2014. *Museum Law: A Guide for Officers, Directors, and Counsel*. Rowman & Littlefield.

Sribnick, Ethan G. and Sara Johnsen. 2012. "Mothers" Pensions." *Institute for Children, Poverty, and Homelessness* (Fall):28–32.

59

As American As Apple Pie

Poverty and Welfare

Mark R. Rank

For many Americans, the words poverty and welfare conjure images of people on the fringes of society: unwed mothers raising several children, inner-city black men, high school dropouts, the homeless, and so on. The media, political rhetoric, and often even the research of social scientists depict the poor as alien and often undeserving of help. In short, being poor and using welfare are perceived as outside the American mainstream.

Yet, poverty and welfare use are as American as apple pie. Most of us will experience poverty during our lives. Even more surprising, most Americans will turn to public assistance at least once during adulthood. Rather than poverty and welfare use being an issue of *them*, it is more an issue of *us*.

THE RISK OF POVERTY AND DRAWING ON WELFARE

Our understanding about the extent of poverty comes mostly from annual surveys conducted by the Census Bureau. Over the past three decades, between 11 and 15 percent of Americans have lived below the poverty line in any given year. Some people are at greater risk than others, depending on age, race, gender, family structure, community of residence, education, work skills, and physical disabilities.

Studies that follow particular families over time—in particular, the Panel Study of Income Dynamics (PSID), the National Longitudinal Survey (NLS), and the Survey of Income and Program Participation (SIPP)—have given us a further understanding of year-to-year changes in poverty. They show that most people are poor for only a short time. Typically, households are impoverished for one, two, or three years, then manage to get above the poverty line. They may stay above the line for a while, only to fall into poverty again later. Events triggering these spells of poverty frequently involve the loss of a job and its pay, family changes such as divorce, or both.

There is, however, an alternative way to estimate the scope of poverty. Specifically, how many Americans experience poverty at some point during adulthood? Counting the number of people who are ever touched by poverty, rather than those who are poor in any given year, gives us a better sense of the scope of the problem. Put another way, to what extent is poverty a "normal" part of the life cycle?

Rank, Mark R. "As American as Apple Pie: Poverty and Welfare." *Contexts* 2, no. 3 (2003): 41–49.

My colleague Tom Hirschl and I have constructed a series of "life tables" built from PSID data following families for over 25 years. The life table is a technique for counting how often specific events occur in specific periods of time, and is frequently used by demographers and medical researchers to assess risk, say, the risk of contracting breast cancer after menopause. It allows us to estimate the percentage of the American population that will experience poverty at some point during adulthood. We also calculated the percentage of the population that will use a social safety net program—programs such as food stamps or Aid to Families with Dependent Children (AFDC, now replaced by the Temporary Assistance for Needy Families [TANF] program)—sometime during adulthood. Our results suggest that a serious reconsideration of who experiences poverty is in order.

Figure 59.1 shows the percentage of Americans spending at least one year living below the official poverty line during adulthood. It also graphs the percentage who have lived between the poverty line and just 25 percent above it—what scholars consider "near poverty."

By the age of 30, 27 percent of Americans will have experienced at least one year in poverty and 34 percent will have fallen below the near-poverty line. By the age of 50, the percentages will have risen to 42 and 50 percent, respectively. And finally by the time Americans have reached the age of 75, 59 percent will have spent at least a year below the poverty line during their adulthood, while 68 percent will have faced at least a year in near poverty.

If we included experiences of poverty in childhood, these percentages would be even higher. Rather than an isolated event that occurs only among the so-called "underclass," poverty is a reality that a clear majority of Americans will experience during their lifetimes.

Measuring impoverishment as the use of social safety net programs produces even more startling results. Figure 59.2 draws on the same PSID survey to show the proportion of people between the ages of 20 and 65 who will use one of the major need-based welfare programs in the United States, including food stamps, Medicaid, AFDC, Supplemental Security Income, and other cash subsidies such as general assistance. By the time Americans reach the age of 65, approximately two-thirds will have, as adults, received assistance for at least a year, while 40 percent will have used a welfare program in at least five separate years. (Again, adding

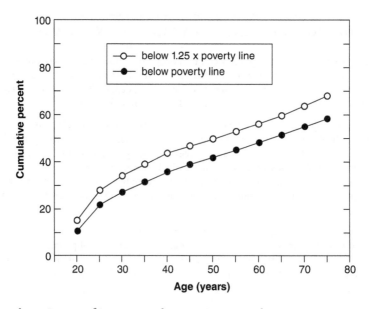

Figure 59.1 Cumulative Percent of Americans Who Have Experienced Poverty.
Source: Panel Study of Income Dynamics.

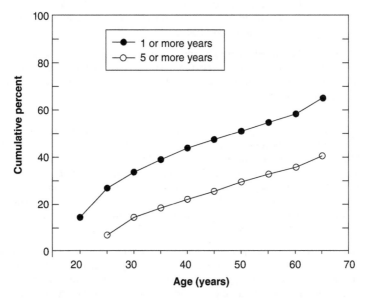

Figure 59.2 Cumulative Percent of Americans Who Have Received Welfare.
Source: Panel Study of Income Dynamics.

childhood experiences would only raise the rates.) Contrary to stereotypes, relying on America's social safety net is widespread and far-reaching.

Of course, people with disadvantages such as single parents or those with fewer skills will have even higher cumulative rates of poverty and welfare use than those shown in Figures 59.1 and 59.2. Yet to portray poverty as an issue affecting only marginalized groups is clearly a mistake.

WHY IS THE RISK OF POVERTY SO HIGH?

Time. First, most discussions of poverty look at single years, or five or ten years at a stretch. The life table techniques employed in Figures 59.1 and 59.2 are based upon assessing the risk of poverty across a lifetime, more than 50 years. Over so many years, individuals face many unanticipated events—households split up, workers lose their jobs, family members become sick, and so on—that become financial emergencies. The familiar saying of being "one paycheck away from poverty" is particularly apt. For example, it is estimated that families with average incomes have enough assets to maintain their standards of living for just over one month.

The Safety Net. A second reason poverty rates are so high is that there is little government help to tide households over during financial emergencies. Although most Americans will eventually rely on need-based government aid (as shown in Figure 59.2), that assistance often fails to save them from poverty. Contrary to the rhetoric about vast sums being spent on public assistance, the American welfare system can be more accurately described as minimal. Compared to other Western industrialized countries, the United States devotes far fewer resources to assisting the economically vulnerable.

Most European countries provide a wide range of social and insurance programs that effectively keep families from falling into poverty. These include substantial cash payments to families with children. Unemployment assistance is far more generous in these countries than in the United States, often providing support for more than a year following the loss of a job. Furthermore, universal health coverage is routinely provided along with considerable support for child care.

These social policies substantially reduce the risk of poverty in Europe and Canada, while US social policies—aside from programs specifically directed to aid the elderly—have reduced poverty modestly at best. As economist Rebecca Blank notes in It Takes a Nation,

> the national choice in the United States to provide relatively less generous transfers to low-income families has meant higher relative poverty rates in the country. While low-income families in the United States work more than in many other countries, they are not able to make up for lower governmental income support relative to their European counterparts.

(pp. 141–142)

Scholars who have used the Luxembourg Income Study (LIS), an international collection of economic surveys, have documented the inability of the American safety net to reduce the risk of poverty. For example, Finnish social scientist VeliMatti Ritakallio has examined the extent to which cash assistance reduces poverty across eight European countries, Canada, and the United States. European and Canadian programs reduce rates of poverty by an average of 79 percent from what they would have been absent the assistance. Finland, for instance, reduced the percentage of its residents who would have been poor from 33 percent down to 4 percent. In contrast, the United States was only able to reduce its percentage in poverty at any given time from 29 percent to 18 percent. As a result, the current rates of US poverty are among the highest in the industrialized world.

The Labor Market. A third factor elevating the risk of American poverty across the life course is the failure of the labor market to provide enough jobs that pay well enough. During the past 30 years, the US economy has produced increasing numbers of low-paying jobs, part-time jobs, and jobs without benefits. For example, the Census Bureau estimated that the median earnings of workers who were paid hourly wages in 2000 was $9.91. At the same time, approximately three million Americans were working part-time because of a shortage of full-time jobs. As journalist Barbara Ehrenreich and others have shown, these jobs simply do not support a family.

A higher percentage of the US workforce falls into this low-wage sector than is true in comparable developed countries. For example, economist Timothy Smeeding and his colleagues have found that 25 percent of all American full-time workers could be classified as being in low-wage work (defined as earning less than 65 percent of the national median for full-time jobs). This was by far the highest percentage of the countries analyzed, with the overall average of non-US countries falling at 12 percent.

In addition, there are simply not enough jobs to go around. Labor economist Timothy Bartik used several different approaches to estimate the number of jobs that would be needed to significantly reduce poverty in the United States. Even in the booming economy of the late 1990s, between five and nine million more jobs were needed in order to meet the needs of the poor and disadvantaged.

To use an analogy, the demand for labor versus the supply of decent paying jobs might be thought of as an ongoing game of musical chairs. That is, the number of workers in the labor market is far greater than the number of jobs that pay a living wage. Using SIPP data for 1999, I estimated this imbalance as ranging between 9 percent and 33 percent, depending upon how poverty and labor market participation were defined. Consequently, between 9 and 33 percent of American household heads were either in non-living-wage jobs or looking for work. The very structure of the labor market ensures that some families will lose out at this musical chairs game and consequently will run a significant risk of poverty.

Some may point out that US rates of unemployment are fairly low when compared to European levels. Yet Bruce Western and Katherine Beckett demonstrate that these lower rates are largely a result of extremely high rates of incarceration. By removing large numbers of American men from the labor force and placing them into the penal system (thus out of our musical chairs analogy altogether), unemployment rates are kept artificially low. When this factor is taken into account and adjusted for, US unemployment rates fall more into line with those of Europe.

CHANGING THE POVERTY PARADIGM

A life course perspective shows us that Americans are highly susceptible to experiencing poverty first-hand. Understanding the normality of poverty requires us to rethink several of our most enduring myths.

Assuming that most Americans would rather avoid such an experience, it becomes in our enlightened self-interest to ensure that we reduce poverty and establish an effective safety net. This risk-sharing argument has been articulated most notably by the philosopher John Rawls. As well as being charitable, improving the plight of those in poverty is an issue of common concern.

We are also beginning to recognize that, as a nation, we pay a high price for our excessive rates of poverty. Research shows that poverty impairs the nation's health, the quality of its workforce, race relations, and, of course, its future generations. Understanding the commonality of poverty shifts how we choose to think about the issue—from a distant concept of them, to an active reality of us. In addition, much of the public's resistance to assisting the poor and particularly those on welfare is the perception that the poor are often undeserving of assistance, that their poverty arises from a lack of motivation, questionable morals, and so on. Yet my analysis suggests that, given its pervasiveness, poverty appears systemic to our economic structure. In short, we have met the enemy, and they are us. C. Wright Mills made a similar point about unemployment:

> When, in a city of 100,000, only one man is unemployed, that is his personal trouble, and for its relief we properly look to the character of the man, his skills, and his immediate opportunities. But when in a nation of 50 million employees, 15 million men are unemployed, that is an issue, and we may not hope to find its solution within the range of opportunities open to any one individual. The very structure of opportunities has collapsed. Both the correct statement of the problem and the range of possible solutions require us to consider the economic and political institutions of the society, and not merely the personal situation and character of a scatter of individuals.

So too with poverty. That America has the highest poverty rates in the Western industrialized world and that most Americans will experience poverty during their lifetimes has little to do with individual motivation or attitudes. Rather, it has much to do with a labor market that fails to produce enough decent paying jobs, and social policies that are unable to pull individuals and families out of poverty when unforeseen events occur. The United States has the means to alleviate poverty, and a range of models from other countries to borrow from. Allowing our policies to be mired in self-righteous moralism while millions of citizens suffer is unconscionable. It is time to shift the debate from one of blame, to one of justice and common concern.

60

How Racism Has Shaped Welfare Policy in America Since 1935

Alma Carten

A recent UNICEF report found that the US ranked 34th on the list of 35 developed countries surveyed on the well-being of children. According to the Pew Institute, children under the age of 18 are the most impoverished age population of Americans, and African-American children are almost four times as likely as white children to be in poverty.

These findings are alarming, not least because they come on the 20th anniversary of President Clinton's promise to "end welfare as we know it" with his signing into law, on August 23, 1996, the Personal Responsibility and Work Opportunity Reconciliation Act (P.L. 104–193).

It is true that the data show the number of families receiving cash assistance fell from 12.3 million in 1996 to current levels of 4.1 million as reported by *The New York Times*. But it is also true that child poverty rates for black children remain stubbornly high in the United States.

My research indicates that this didn't happen by chance. In a recent book, I examine social welfare policy developments in the US over a 50-year period from the New Deal to the 1996 reforms. Findings reveal that US welfare policies have, from their very inception, been discriminatory.

Blemished by a History of Discrimination

It was the 1935 Social Security Act, introduced by the Franklin Roosevelt administration, that first committed the US to the safety net philosophy.

From the beginning, the policy had two tiers that intended to protect families from loss of income.

On one level were the contributory social insurance programs that provided income support to the surviving dependents of workers in the event of their death or incapacitation and Social Security for retired older Americans.

The second tier was made up of means-tested public assistance programs that included what was originally called the "Aid to Dependent Children" program and was subsequently renamed the Aid to Families with Dependent Children in the 1962 Public Welfare Amendments to the SSA under the Kennedy administration.

Carten, Alma. "How Racism Has Shaped Welfare Policy in America since 1935." *The Conversation*, August 21, 2016.

The optimistic vision of the architects of the ADC program was that it would die "a natural death" with the rising quality of life in the country as a whole, resulting in more families becoming eligible for the work-related social insurance programs.

But this scenario was problematic for black Americans because of pervasive racial discrimination in employment in the decades of the 1930s and 1940s. During these decades, blacks typically worked in menial jobs. Not tied to the formal workforce, they were paid in cash and "off the books," making them ineligible for social insurance programs that called for contributions through payroll taxes from both employers and employees.

Nor did blacks fare much better under ADC during these years.

The ADC was an extension of the state-operated mothers' pension programs, where white widows were the primary beneficiaries. The criteria for eligibility and need were state-determined, so blacks continued to be barred from full participation because the country operated under the "separate but equal" doctrine adopted by the Supreme Court in 1896.

Jim Crow Laws and the separate but equal doctrine resulted in the creation of a two-track service delivery system in both law and custom, one for whites and one for blacks that were anything but equal.

Developments in the 1950s and 1960s further disadvantaged black families.

This happened when states stepped up efforts to reduce ADC enrollment and costs. As I examined in my book, residency requirements were proposed so as to bar blacks migrating from the South to qualify for the program. New York City's "man in the house rule" required welfare workers to make unannounced visits to determine if fathers were living in the home – if evidence of a male presence was found, cases were closed and welfare checks discontinued.

Always an Unpopular Program

Because of the strong American work ethic, and preference for a "hand-up" versus a "hand-out," the means-tested, cash assistance programs for poor families – and especially ADC renamed AFDC – have never been popular among Americans. As FDR himself said in his 1935 State of the Union address to Congress, "the government must and shall quit this business of relief."

As the quality of life did indeed improve for whites, the number of white widows and their children on the AFDC rolls declined. At the same time, the easing of racial discrimination widened eligibility to more blacks, increasing the number of never-married women of color and their children who were born out of wedlock.

One point, however, to note here is that there has always been a public misconception about race and welfare. It is true that over the years blacks became disproportionately represented. But given that whites constitute a majority of the population, numerically they have always been the largest users of the AFDC program.

Holes in the Safety Net

The retreat from the safety net philosophy can be dated to the presidencies of Richard Nixon and Ronald Reagan.

On the one hand, politicians wanted to reduce the cost of welfare. Under Reagan policies of New Federalism, social welfare expenditures were capped and responsibility for programs for poor families was given back to states.

On the other hand, the demographic shift in the welfare rolls exacerbated the politics around welfare and racialized the debate.

Ronald Reagan's "Welfare Queen" narrative only reinforced existing white stereotypes about blacks:

> There's a woman in Chicago. She has 80 names, 30 addressees, 12 Social Security cards and is collecting veterans' benefits on four nonexistent deceased husbands. She's got Medicaid, is getting food stamps and welfare under each of her names. Her tax-free cash income alone is over $150,000.

Reagan's assertions that the homeless were living on the streets by choice played to conventional wisdom about the causes of poverty, blamed poor people for their own misfortune and helped disparage government programs to help the poor.

The 1990s Gear Change

By the late 1990s efforts of reforms targeting the AFDC program shifted to more nuanced forms of racism with claims that the program encouraged out-of-wedlock births, irresponsible fatherhood and intergenerational dependency.

The political context for the 1996 reforms, then, was fueled by racist undertones that played into public angst about rising taxes and the national debt that were attributed to the high payout of welfare checks to people who were not carrying their own weight.

This emotionally charged environment distorted the poverty debate, and paved the way for a reform bill that many saw as excessively punitive in its harsh treatment of poor families.

Although credited to the Clinton administration, the blueprint for the 1996 welfare reform bill was crafted by a caucus of conservative Republicans led by Newt Gingrich as part of the Contract with America during the 1994 congressional election campaign.

Twice President Clinton vetoed the welfare reform bill sent to him by the GOP-dominated Congress. The third time he signed, creating much controversy, including the resignation of his own adviser on welfare reform, the leading scholar on poverty David Ellwood.

The new bill replaced the AFDC program with Temporary Assistance to Needy Families (TANF). Stricter work requirements required single mothers to find work within two years of receiving benefits. A five-year lifetime limit was imposed for receiving benefits. To reinforce traditional family values, a core principle of the Republican Party, teenage mothers were to be prohibited benefits, and fathers who were delinquent in child support payments were threatened with imprisonment. States were banned from using federally funded TANF for certain groups of immigrants and restrictions were placed on their eligibility to Medicaid, food stamps and Supplementary Social Security Income (SSI).

The Impact

Despite many bleak predictions, favorable outcomes were reported on the tenth anniversary of the bill's signing. Welfare rolls had declined. Mothers had moved from welfare to work and children had benefited psychologically from having an employed parent.

However, the volume of research generated at the ten-year benchmark has not been matched, in my observation, by that produced in years leading up to the 20-year anniversary.

More research in particular is needed to understand what is happening with families who have left welfare rolls because of passing the five-year lifetime limit for receiving benefits but have not sustained a foothold in an ever-increasing specialized workforce.

DISENTANGLING INTERTWINED EFFECTS OF RACISM AND POVERTY

US welfare policy is, arguably, as much a reflection of its economic policies as it is of the nation's troublesome history of racism.

In the words of President Obama, racism is a part of America's DNA and history. Similarly, the notion that anyone who is willing to work hard can be rich is just as much a part of that DNA. Both have played an equal role in constraining adequate policy development for poor families and have been especially harmful to poor black families.

Racism has left an indelible mark on American institutions. In particular, it influences how we understand the causes of poverty and how we develop solutions for ending it.

Indeed, with the continual unraveling of the safety net, the 20th anniversary of welfare reforms can be an impetus for taking a closer look at how racism has shaped welfare policy in the United States and to what extent it accounts for the persistently high poverty rates for black children.

61

The Diaper Dilemma

Jennifer M. Randles

Just before he left office, Barack Obama proposed a $10 million federal initiative to test potential projects aimed at increasing low-income families' access to diapers. The funding was never administered. States have tried, too: in September 2016, by a vote of 54-12, the California Assembly passed the first state-level diaper assistance bill. It would have provided $50 monthly diaper vouchers to cover the 120,000 children receiving state welfare aid, but the governor, Jerry Brown, vetoed it, citing the bill's $120 million price tag. He subsequently vetoed another bill, one that would have eliminated state sales taxes on diapers, which the California Assembly had deemed "medically necessary" and therefore qualified for a tax exemption.

The problem these bills aimed to remedy, diaper need, is a common and often hidden consequence of American poverty. One in three mothers in the United States experiences diaper need—the lack of sufficient diapers to keep an infant dry, comfortable, and healthy—and 45 percent of infants and toddlers under the age of three live in low-income families whose budgets are impossibly tight. All together, diaper need affects over five million US children, and disproportionately those who are Black and Latinx, those from immigrant families, and those whose parents lack a high school diploma or experience unemployment.

Diaper need can lead to several problems for children, including infections and rashes, irritability, and trouble securing childcare. Severe cases of diaper dermatitis ("diaper rash") can require emergency room visits and hospitalization. For parents, diaper need creates stress, guilt, and anxiety. Diaper need can also interfere with children's educational opportunities and parents' abilities to work, as most childcare centers require parents to bring at least a week's worth of diapers at a time. If they cannot fully provide diapers, alongside other needs including milk and medicine, parents are left feeling inadequate. As one mother studied by psychologist C. Cybele Raver and colleagues explained, "It's the same thing as not being able to put food in their mouth. It's more of a need than a want." Yet diapers are still not conceptualized as a need in US social policy.

DIAPER GAPS

The average cost of disposable diapers is $18 a week or $936 annually per child. This is over 6 percent of a year-round, full-time federal minimum wage salary ($15,080). Though existing federal and state policies do not cover all eligible families, there are currently public programs to address every other essential need young children have, including food, housing, healthcare, and education. But diapers are not an "allowable expense" for Women, Infant, Children (WIC) or the Supplemental Nutrition Assistance Program (SNAP). California's food stamp program categorizes diapers as "invalid purchases" alongside cigarettes and alcohol. Parents can use Temporary Assistance for Needy Families (TANF) or welfare cash aid for this expense, but if they do, the benefits do not usually stretch enough to cover other basic needs. In 2016, the average monthly TANF benefit for a single-parent family of three ranged from $170 in Mississippi to $923 in Alaska. The average monthly diaper bill would use up between 8 and over 40 percent of a family's cash aid check—and only one in four US families in poverty receives any TANF benefits at all. Early Head Start programs provide diapers and formula, but here, too, only a fraction of low-income children are enrolled, and the program does not offer diapers for evenings and weekends.

Cloth diapers are not a viable alternative for most low-income families because they cannot afford in-home washers and dryers (assuming they have homes), it is illegal to wash reusable diapers in most public laundry facilities, and daycare centers require disposables. This leaves many parents struggling to devise "diaper stretching" strategies, including borrowing from friends and family, creating makeshift diapers from plastic bags and paper towels, reusing diapers by hanging wet ones to dry or scraping feces from dirty diapers, or toilet training children much earlier than recommended. Poor parents also lack access to diaper cost-cutting strategies that more affluent parents take for granted, such as subscription services and bulk purchasing. Diapers can cost up to twice as much at the local markets and drug stores that are closer to where low-income parents live, and parents in poverty rarely have access to transportation to get to big box stores or the space needed to store diapers even if they could purchase in bulk. All this means that poor parents often end up spending more on diapers than higher-income families.

Diaper need is a huge need, and it has negative health, social, and economic consequences for low-income families. So why are policymakers willing to ignore this issue? They seem willing to assume that, contrary to readily available data, all parents can make childbearing and diapering choices unconstrained by economic need.

NEEDS, WANTS, AND PUBLIC POLICY

In addition to the efforts noted earlier, in November 2015, federal lawmakers introduced the "Hygiene Assistance for Families of Infants and Toddlers Act." If passed, the law would have funded state-based pilot programs to test innovative approaches to providing diapers or diaper vouchers, such as integrating diaper distribution programs with other need-based government services. The bill would have amended the federal Social Security Act to recognize that "Access to a reliable supply of clean diapers is a medical necessity for the health and welfare of infants and toddlers, their families, and child care and health care providers." The bill explicitly acknowledged that diapers are necessary for children's access to safe, quality childcare, and parents' abilities to work and fully care for their children. It further recognized that parents need diapers in order to comply with the requirements of other means-tested programs. For example, parents need to supply diapers to childcare providers so that they can work in order to meet the requirements of receiving TANF cash aid. The Hygiene Act bill never got past the Subcommittee on Human Resources.

What about the California diaper bill that Governor Brown vetoed? California Assemblyperson Lorena Gonzalez Fletcher's persistence paid off. She reintroduced a revised bill that passed both the State Assembly and Senate by a wide margin in October 2017. Brown immediately signed the bill, AB480: Diaper Assistance for CalWORKS Families, which provides a $30 monthly diaper voucher for the state's welfare-to-work program participants. As the country's first statewide public diaper program, it will perhaps be a model for other states considering diaper legislation. Not all families who experience diaper need will be eligible for the vouchers, nor will it cover eligible families' full needs, but it is a start.

Families across the country are also able to reach out for help from non-profit diaper banks, which work much like food banks and often partner with family agencies. Founded in 2011, the National Diaper Bank Network (NDBN) consists of over 300 diaper banks and is the largest national organization advocating on behalf of policy solutions for diaper need. The NDBN has contracted with national diaper manufacturers to allow community organizations to purchase their products for distribution at a substantial discount. Though non-profit and market-based solutions—such as founding diaper banks and creating more efficient packaging and diapers without licensed cartoons that drive up production expenses—have significantly reduced the costs of diapers, community organizations still struggle to meet families' full needs.

Together, diaper need and the policy vacuum surrounding it represent a distinct cultural and economic problem. It is also an important case in how some services and resources get framed as "needs" while others are conceptualized as "wants," unworthy of a policy remedy. The notion that diaper need is not worthy of political intervention rests on the assumptions that disposable diapers are a luxury and that poor parents can simply choose reusable options that presumably cost less, last longer, and have a smaller environmental impact. Many policymakers have ignored this issue because they erroneously assume that disadvantaged parents make choices about diapering within middle-class circumstances—or that they should have never chosen to have children at all. Some lawmakers object to diaper legislation because they believe it supports low-income parents' choices to have children they cannot afford. This critique echoes racist and classist "welfare queen" stereotypes and exhortations that people in poverty should simply choose not to have babies. This misguided political culture of choice harms poor families by discounting how access to an array of diapering options is a form of privilege and how access to any diapers at all is, in fact, a crucial family need.

62

Why Policies Meant to Discourage Poor Women from Having Children Are Ineffective and Punitive

Diana Romero and Madina Agénor

Over two decades have gone by since Congress enacted the 1996 Personal Responsibility and Work Opportunity Reconciliation Act intended to reform the US welfare system. With tenets that endure to this day, this act imposed lifetime limits and stringent work requirements on recipients of Temporary Assistance to Needy Families (TANF). In some states, controversial family-cap provisions also sought to discourage poor women from childbearing by refusing to give additional cash assistance for a newborn child – a dramatic departure from historical criteria in US welfare programs. But after early debates, the ensuing decades have seen very little discussion of the ineffectiveness and injustice of such provisions.

We conducted key-informant interviews with officials from all 24 states with family caps in their welfare programs, to learn more about the policy's status and implementation and about opinions regarding its effectiveness, advantages, and disadvantages. The results from our interviews suggest that this provision of welfare reform has been more symbolic and punitive than substantive. We have empirical findings about how states have informed clients of this provision, as well as about their limited efforts to support pregnancy prevention and collect data to enable relevant policy evaluations. We have also learned that, despite little proof of effectiveness, states have gone to considerable lengths to extend the "reach" of family caps in their welfare programs.

LITTLE EVIDENCE THAT FAMILY CAPS WORK

Twenty-four states implemented a family-cap policy in the early years of post-1996 welfare reform. Few states bothered to evaluate these policies, but findings from almost all large-scale analyses assessing the impact of these family caps indicate they have had no effect on child bearing – that is, there was no demonstrable decline in births among women receiving welfare. The first family-cap evaluations were conducted in New Jersey and Arkansas, two states that implemented a family-cap policy in the early 1990s, prior to the 1996 legislation. The evaluations found no difference in births among those subject and not subject to the family cap; but a significant increase in abortions was reported in New Jersey. Several other studies were carried out using data from the early 1990s through the mid-2000s to compare fertility-related

Romero, Diana and Madina Agénor. "Why Policies Meant to Discourage Poor Women from Having Children are Ineffective and Punitive." *Scholars Strategy Network*, July 13, 2018.

behaviors among women in states with and without the family-cap policy. Most failed to find that these caps had the desired effect of discouraging births among aid recipients.

STATE WELFARE AGENCY OFFICIALS REVEAL ON-THE-GROUND REALITIES

In our interviews, we collected information regarding experiences with and evaluations of family caps in order to better understand implementation across the states. Most welfare administrators told us that the administrative burdens and negative economic impacts on poor families outweighed any potential benefits. Some states implemented related policies that further undermined family well-being or refused to adopt policies that would extend Medicaid coverage of family planning services. Family caps seemed to be maintained as a punitive social policy. Different states implemented and evaluated caps in various ways, and officials offered varying opinions as to their efficacy and purpose.

- Just three quarters of the states with caps reported that case workers told recipients about this policy. Eighteen provided written information (and 13 also offered verbal explanations). As one example, South Carolina said that family-cap information was not "routinely provided [to clients] as part of initial screening."

- Most of the surveyed officials did not believe the policy reduced births to low-income mothers, but some said that the cap addressed public worries about people on welfare. In fact, a North Dakota official described the family cap as a "feel good policy [that] makes the State Legislature and general population feel that at least some attempt is being made to alter … participants' reproductive behaviors."

- An Alaska official candidly opined that the cap hinders "families from adequately providing for their child because [they] lack the funds that are needed."

- In the seven states whose officials indicated that evaluations had been conducted, respondents had little knowledge about what became of those findings. Notably, none of the 24 states had plans for future evaluation of the effectiveness of family caps.

OVERDUE COURSE CORRECTIONS

What should be done with a policy of dubious effectiveness still in force after two decades? We propose a series of steps to reconcile stated goals and actual implementation at the state level.

- States should discontinue the objectionable practices of garnishing child support payments made to "capped" children and applying the family cap to teen mothers who were previously in their mothers' capped household. Such steps hurt members of already impoverished families and in need of support.

- Welfare officials in states that do not have a Medicaid family planning waiver should advocate for it, given that the services it funds align with the goals of the family cap and help all poor women in the state better control their fertility.

- If states really want fewer births among recipients of TANF, they should better inform their clients of the policy and track whether women receiving cash assistance get access to contraception and other reproductive services, as well as have babies that do well by standard measures of infant well-being.

Unless the US Congress decides to eliminate the state option to impose family caps, only states can make changes. Both national and state policymakers should take account of research on the ineffectiveness and adverse impact of these caps and either eliminate them or find ways to improve implementation. It makes no sense to simply continue the mistakes of the past.

63

Negotiating the Discourse of Race within the United States Welfare System

Vicki Lens and Colleen Cary

Policies within welfare offices are also implemented in ways that further disadvantage people of colour. In the United States, case-worker discretion has increased under welfare reform, inviting differential treatment among workers who can now choose between what Mead (1997, p. 24) calls "help or hassle". There is some evidence that people of colour are more likely than their white counterparts to receive the latter. Several studies have found that African-American recipients are more likely to be sanctioned for violating work rules. They are also more likely to be offered less support, including educational support.

An under-explored aspect of the worker-client relationship is how recipients of colour, including African-Americans and Latinos, navigate the racial undercurrents that permeate welfare and may result in such differential treatment. Drawing from qualitative interviews with 24 recipients of colour in a large urban city in the United States, this study seeks to understand the ways in which they negotiate their relationships with workers in the context of race and racial stereotyping.

RACE AND WELFARE IN AN ADMINISTRATIVE CONTEXT

For welfare participants, welfare means the web of relationships, rules and bureaucratic pathways they must navigate to secure its benefits and avoid its penalties. That pathway is often strewn with hurdles. Welfare bureaucracies in the United States have a long history of bureaucratic disentitlement, or the denial of aid to eligible people through excessive and obstructive procedural demands. Unlike more consumer-friendly government bureaucracies that serve primarily the middle class, welfare bureaucracies function in an environment of suspicion and distrust. While rules and regulations provide guidance and structure, workers also rely on their own practical and moral judgments when dispensing or denying benefits. Thus, based on their assessments of people, workers may choose to be helpful, arbitrary or punitive, and may oscillate between all three. Tangible help may be withheld for intangible reasons, as when workers punish recipients for a poor attitude towards work or a lack of gratitude, or deflect recipients to whom they don't relate or whose behaviour they don't like.

Lens, Vicki, and Colleen Cary. "Negotiating the Discourse of Race within the United States Welfare System." *Ethnic and Racial Studies* 33, no. 6 (2010): 1032–1048.

For participants, this means not only knowing the rules but also being able to read and understand their workers. They must learn to simultaneously engage and resist workers, and contain and control them. In the United States, a dependence on welfare echoes African-American subservience as slaves. Being silent and nonassertive, or loud and angry, has different implications for the recipient of colour. As Elijah Anderson (1999, 2002) describes in his study of African-American culture in inner city Philadelphia, to survive in a white world, African-Americans will refrain from acting too angry or "street" when dealing with white institutions, believing it "will somehow lead to social and economic salvation for themselves and for their loved ones" (Anderson 2002, p. 1541). Other people of colour, such as Latinos, must adopt similar tactics, as they are also viewed as outsiders and more likely to rely on welfare than others. Thus, while their historical legacy is different to African-Americans', they also encounter a form of welfare racializing within the welfare system that whites do not.

This study explores how people of colour, both male and female, navigate welfare racism when interacting with welfare workers. It examines how the racial discourse that hangs implicitly, if not explicitly, over welfare relationships affects the ability of recipients to ask for and get what they need.

DATA AND METHODS

Face-to-face qualitative interviews were conducted with participants who had been receiving public assistance and had received notices discontinuing or reducing their aid. They were asked a series of open-ended questions that explored their general experiences of applying for and receiving welfare, their relationships with their case-workers, incidents involving the reduction and discontinuance of aid, and the strategies and tactics they used to maintain their benefits, including the use of formal procedures such as fair hearings, and other informal processes. This study draws from the 24 recipients from the urban area (New York City) who were members of minority groups. They included 19 African-Americans, four Latinos and one who was both African-American and Latino. Consistent with the composition of public assistance caseloads, and especially the Temporary Assistance for Needy Families programme, where women compose 90 percent of adult recipients, 21 out of the 24 participants were female. The average age was 45. Eighty-four percent (22 recipients) had received welfare for more than three years. Thirty percent (eight recipients) had less than a high school education; 26 percent (seven recipients) had a high school or equivalency diploma and 42 percent (11 recipients) had some college.

PLEADING NEED AND WORTHINESS

Welfare dependency is considered a degraded state in our society. The PRWORA (Personal Responsibility and Work Opportunity Reconciliation Act passed in 1996) represented the culmination of a neoliberalism discourse that emphasizes free and private markets and "personal rather than public responsibility for economic well being" (Smith 2005, p. 216). Welfare is the help of last resort, and considered, both in political discourse and among ordinary citizens, a personal, not a market, failure. Welfare discourse is laced with stereotypes that depict a plea for help as an admission of failure in the realms of work and home. In short, welfare recipients are considered failed citizens, if citizens at all, who cheat the system and live unfairly and freely off the labours of other citizens.

Because racial stereotyping often underlies many welfare interactions, recipients who are both poor and people of colour bring additional baggage. Workers assume recipients, and especially people of colour, are unworthy of aid. They are more apt to say no rather than yes, often in arbitrary and unjust ways. Recipients must respond without further alienating their workers, while also asserting their deservingness. Sometimes this means becoming complicit in the racial stereotypes that structure social relations within the welfare centre. It means not acting in ways they think will reinforce such stereotypes, thus implicitly accepting their power and validity.

As Elijah Anderson (1999, 2002) describes in his study of African-American culture in inner city Philadelphia, people devise strategies for surviving in a hostile world, often divided among black and white. This includes dividing themselves into

> two opposing status groups – "decent" and "street"… Decent is most often associated with the wider, conventional "white" society, whereas "street" or its own descriptive analogue, "ghetto" – is often used as an epithet (especially by those identifying themselves as decent) and strongly associated with the most troublesome aspects of ghetto life.

Other groups have their own version of this split; for example, Latinos may use the epithet "project chicks", which is comparable to "ghetto". (The analogue in the lingo of social scientists is the terms "normative" and "deviant".)

To survive in a white world and especially within white institutional settings, people of colour often code switch, altering their public behaviour between "decent" and "street" depending on the setting. They will also "at times overcompensate by trying to be more decent than others of their race" (Anderson 2002, p. 1541). As Anderson explains, people draw these distinctions with others of their group in the hopes of securing better treatment.

Within the welfare centre, all recipients – and especially recipients of colour – are "street" in the eyes of workers. This "street" label parallels welfare discourse in general, which, as noted above, is framed around an ideology that separates the deserving from the undeserving. Decent people do not ask for welfare; they are self-reliant and self-sufficient. They rely on the private markets, not government "hand-outs" to survive. Asking for welfare is a mark of personal failure. For people of colour, asking for help is doubly injurious. Already grappling with the stigma of race, they must also contend with the stigma of welfare, in a setting that equates the two. Uma, a 57-year-old Latina woman, explicitly makes this connection as she describes her experience applying for welfare: "I [was treated] like I was a low-life, like a minority. I'm asking for a handout."[1] Participants like Uma, who have held steady jobs and whose welfare use is episodic or crisis related, are confronted with a conundrum in the welfare centre: how do they prove their decent bona fides?

Stanley, a 43-year-old African-American man with a wife and four children, is an example of this problematic. Stanley began his adult life in the military, an institution he "loved" and which showed him "you are more than you think". He worked his entire adult life, either in security or construction, eventually reaching his version of the American dream – owning his own floor-care subcontracting business. About five years ago, he became disabled after a truck hit him. The family lived off their savings for four years, and then spiralled into homelessness when their savings ran out. Seeking emergency shelter, he and his wife applied for public assistance.

Stanley is not treated as the victim of misfortune he thinks he is, but as a potential swindler. He describes how the workers treated him and his wife: "drilled us, they questioned us, they separated us, they questioned us, asked, trying to catch one in a lie and it was like you're being interrogated". His sense of independence and agency is shattered; welfare, as he puts it, "has full control over you, full control over your children, you know, the whole nine-yards". He is humiliated and defeated, as the system makes him "feel like I ain't trying to do nothing, like I'm a drug addict".

To counter his feelings of disgrace, Stanley activates the welfare discourse, and tries to claim the mantle of deservingness. He describes welfare as something he is owed: "I'm a worker, I worked all my life. I pay my tax… I'm a taxpayer; I'm a veteran as well. So I've spent my time." He briefly deviates from this discourse to express solidarity with his fellow recipients who are also homeless: "They are not here and homeless on the streets because they want to be… we've been stereotyped and I can say, we, why, because I've lived it." But then he immediately follows this with the reminder that "I have a good background". Later he explains how the welfare system is "a totally different society because it's not like you are dealing with all the regular class people that are out there that already have a foundation".

Thus, the welfare discourse provides Stanley with a way to salvage his worth; he, unlike other recipients, is "regular", "decent", a worker and a veteran to boot. He flirts briefly with breaking this discourse – "we've been stereotyped" – but then reverts back to a narrative of "us" versus "them" as he describes those not receiving welfare as "regular class people" and the welfare reliant as without a "foundation". He, now welfare reliant himself, buys into a discourse that emphasizes the personal defects of the poor. It allows him to express his anger at the system, but channels it in a certain way. He should be treated well, not because he is poor, but because he was once not poor. Left unquestioned or obscured are the reasons why Stanley and his fellow recipients are poor, and the ways in which they are more alike than different.

While Stanley could fall back on his decent credentials, long-term welfare users cannot. Nonetheless, they employ similar discourses to shield themselves from welfare's judgmental sting. To salvage their self-respect, they, like Stanley, differentiate themselves from other recipients; they try to prove they are not "street". Simone, a 43-year-old African-American woman with five children ranging in age from three months to 20 years, has been on public assistance for 21 years, virtually her entire adult life. To "decent" people she is the archetypical "welfare queen". That is not how she sees herself: "I know some people abuse it [welfare] but I think, I'm not one of them. I just do what I have to do to – I mean, to survive with the children." She presents welfare not as a choice but as a necessity for a good mother like herself concerned with her children's welfare. So that she can justify her use of welfare, she borrows from the "mothering discourse", which places mothering on a pedestal and emphasizes its centrality. Like Stanley, Simone also employs the welfare discourse, by first judging her fellow recipients as undeserving – "I know some people abuse it" – and then claiming "I am not one of them".

The finding that welfare recipients, black and white, view themselves as atypical has persisted through decades of welfare changes and reforms. Disassociating from one's fellow recipients serves both a personal and political purpose. On a personal level, it is a way of coping with stigma. By proclaiming their difference from other recipients, recipients can salvage their self-worth. On a political level, such beliefs reinforce the view that dependency is a problem of individuals, not the system. It keeps welfare recipients divided from one another and blind to the commonality of their cause. For recipients of colour, who often serve as the public symbol of welfare excess, the bar is higher. A double dose of disassociation is required. They must refrain from acting both too "welfare-like" and too "street". Because of the visibility of race, "passing" is harder and requires, as described next, a highly tuned monitoring system and the constant restraint of emotions.

SMILING ON THE OUTSIDE

Welfare systems are purposely designed to make proving and maintaining eligibility difficult. Documents are continuously demanded and work habits routinely evaluated. Bureaucratic snafus – the ubiquitous red tape bureaucracies are known for – can occur often. A failure to provide the correct document or demonstrate sufficient work commitment can result in the cut-off of aid. Even when participants have satisfied the bureaucracy's demands, glitches and errors can result in random and arbitrary reductions or denial of aid. Clearing up such mistakes takes time, persistence and patience. It requires participants to maintain a "decent" persona in the face of often arbitrary and frustrating bureaucratic demands.

To stay within the system's good graces, participants must carefully and delicately manage their relationships with front-line workers. They must figure out how to respond to workers who are often stressed out, overwhelmed and angry. As Laurel explains, workers "always have on this shield of protection… they always in that type of mood. Their face is angry." Delilah's description of her worker's greeting after a long wait – she "sticks her teeth at me" – captures the tension and annoyance that characterize welfare relationships.

Recipients' powerlessness, however, constrains their options. Expressions of anger about system slip-ups or their treatment – however justified – put them at risk of even poorer treatment and of being judged street rather than decent. Stella, a 46-year-old African-American woman with two children, learned how to restrain her anger and act the conciliator rather than antagonizer. Like most recipients, Stella had continuing difficulties with what she called the "maze" of welfare that "will take your spirit". Workers, she explained, "come with their biases" and do not want to help you and/or are ignorant of ways in which they can (in her case an exemption to the work rules because of domestic violence). But as Stella explained, if you "ruffle his or her feathers" you can end up sitting and waiting for hours. Stella thus put on a veneer of politeness no matter how angry she was. As she explained, while she may be thinking "what a jerk", she "was always courteous" and would say "thank you very much".

Stella's experience was typical of many other recipients. Anger was to be avoided because it antagonized workers. As Sharlene, a 47-year-old African-American woman receiving welfare for the last ten years, explained,

> there are times when you are so angry and frustrated that you want to lash out. But if you do anything disrespectful, they'll do anything they can to… oh… there's an error in the system, or the computer's fault, or the case got closed by mistake.

Masking one's thoughts and personality is necessary. As Audrey, a 40-year-old Latina woman who has cycled off and on welfare most of her adult life, explains:

> I felt a little intimidated because if I felt I expressed my feelings even in a genuine and proper way, I felt like she [her worker] would have a way of mismanaging my food or my food stamps, cash and I had babies to deal with.

Uma, a Latina woman, explains "a lot of times I had to hold my tongue and just grin and bear it even though I was hurting inside".

Anger on the inside was transformed to a smile on the outside. This was true among those long-versed in the system's ways, like Simone and Audrey, and those new to it. Laurel was 61 years old when she applied for welfare for the first time, after leaving a long and troublesome marriage marred by domestic violence. Like Simone and Audrey, she gingerly handled her workers, suppressing her anger over how she was treated:

> I went with a smiling face and started talking to her and she was just you know like a snake, And I leave there with a smile on my face; I didn't let her get to me because I really wanted to get this help.

Disrespect, a common complaint among recipients, was better met with its opposite – respect. As Sally explained, "Be calm and respectful. Answer their questions. And then just wait and see."

Participants not only put a smile on their faces but try to put one on their workers' faces as well. In an inversion of roles, participants sought to take care of workers. Tamsin, a 49-year-old African-American and a long-term recipient, describes how she metaphorically switched roles when her worker treated her poorly:

> I told her look, I don't know what kind of day you're having, but take a pill, I'll bring you some Anacin. You know, Tylenol, or whatever it is but don't take it out on me. I'm just here to do whatever I gotta do, whatever you tell me to bring, I'll bring.

Nathan, a 49-year-old African-American man with a teenage daughter who has been receiving welfare for about a year, also initially plays the helper rather than the helped. He first diagnosis the problem: "They see cases like mine every day so a lot of them are burnt." He then administers the cure: "I'm a very mannerable individual… I try to get people to relax… I'm going to make it easy on you. I'm not going to be one of your headaches today." After receiving conflicting information about his eligibility for rent arrears payments, he explains to his worker that "this is my first time… If you talk slowly to me and tell me why, then I can understand." By casting himself as the meek and obedient ingénue, he makes himself less threatening, less of a "headache" to his worker. He will not lash out or be too noisily demanding, thus making her job easier.

Aggressiveness is especially to be avoided. An in-your-face bravado that signals one is not to be messed with was viewed as out of place in the predominantly white-run public institution of the welfare centre. Recipients who demanded help were looked down upon by other recipients. They had too much "attitude" or were "acting out" or "acting crazy".

As Stella explained, such behaviour made things worse, not better. As she put it "profanity, loud speaking or physical gyrations" had no place in the welfare centre. Such participants might get what they needed "temporarily", but workers would make a "mental note" of it, causing problems later. Stella emphasized that she "never went in there acting like other clients', it wasn't 'who I am'". She did not "give workers a hard time", but instead "killed them with kindness".

Sally, an African-American woman in her early 40s with two grown children, similarly observed that "some people go in there and start acting crazy, but it doesn't work, you can't do that". Nathan echoed her assessment of his fellow recipients: "A lot of people get caught up in the moment. They let their emotions rule their good sense." Laurel, an older woman, criticized the "attitude" of some of the younger women: "If they don't get what they want and they just make matters worse when they confront them and they talk out." In contrast, she explained

> I always try and present myself in a decent manner…I don't like the attitude thing. I would say it very peacefully what I have to say or I may say two words… say thank you and walk and go home and may cry.

"Attitude" could also get you in more serious trouble. Security was omnipresent at the welfare centre, signalling that recipients must be watched and were untrustworthy. The security guards, serving as a message to other recipients not to behave similarly, often escorted out recipients who "acted out". As Uma explained,

> I see how they treat people when they fight or argue or even say curse words. They will just hold you back or ignore you… but other times they take the security and escort you outside. I didn't want to be put through all of that.

Lacy, a 45-year-old African-American woman with two children who has been receiving welfare on and off for 15 years, was one of the rare recipients who refused to smile. Her description of her behaviour in the welfare centre was more "street" than "decent": "A lot of times I had to scream on 'em, holla at 'em." Instead of backing down when she is told "I can't come in here and act like that", she adopts the discourse of a citizen and responds "why not, because you're a public servant, ok, and that's your job to service the client".

Lacy did not start out behaving this way. At first, she explains:

> I'm coming in and I'm being hospitable to you and you just are being nasty and ignorant towards me for no reason. And I'm wondering I'm putting all the blame on myself but then I'm looking at the fact that it's not my fault, that's just the way you are really. You don't treat me like I treat you, then I'm gonna say something about it.

In response to the harsh treatment she receives, Lacy begins to redefine her experience:

> They tell me I can't do it and I say I have every right to do it because the customer is always right. Because I worked retail, so I know the customer is always right just like here. You're getting a paycheck – you supposed to work certain hours, you supposed to service your client. Customer service is job one, so come on.

Thus, instead of adopting the welfare discourse, Lacy draws on the language of citizenship –

"you're a public servant" – and the language of consumerism – "the customer is always right". In so doing, she constructs herself as powerful, rather than powerless. She, not the worker, is the one to be soothed and serviced. In her language and her behaviour, she tries to dispel the sting of subordination. She tries to make the welfare centre into something she thinks it should be, in contrast to what it is.

Like Lacy, other recipients were aware that the welfare office, unlike other government offices, treated them differently. Delilah, a long-term recipient, describes the difference:

> It is so much more calm [in other government offices], you know, in a public assistance office, you feel that you're being attacked all of the time. And when you go to a government office it's like come on in sit down, have a cup of coffee [laughs]. You know it's a very very very different experience there. It's definitely different.

However, most recipients, unlike Lacy, did not try and assert their status as citizens in the welfare centre. Justifiable indignation at rude workers and red tape– the expected response from a poorly treated citizen – was not reasonable in the welfare centre. While participants found other ways to challenge workers, including speaking to supervisors, requesting fair hearings and complaining to the Commissioner, none of these strategies altered the basic nature of their interactions with workers. Their welfare relationships remained antagonistic, harsh and distant. In their day-to-day interactions, participants focused on the personal rather than the institutional, believing that if they just got along the bureaucracy could be tamed. The enigmatic smile of the powerless remained, as did the need to suppress anger and restrain emotions. In this way, participants refrained from claiming the mantel of citizenship and the power it implies, instead maintaining their subordination and perpetuating the dominant discourse of undeservingness.

DISCUSSION AND IMPLICATIONS

While all welfare participants carry the burden of welfare stigma, people of colour confront a double bind. Because welfare often serves as a proxy for race, recipients of colour must do more than others to demonstrate their deservingness. They must prove not only their social worth but racial worth as well. To deflect racial stereotypes, participants monitor their behaviour for traces of anger that could be construed as "street" rather than "decent", and divorce themselves from those that don't. Preoccupied with proving they are unlike others of their kind, they mimic the discourse of the powerless, seeking to placate and sooth workers, who ostensibly exist to serve them. Instead of expressing anger when government ties them up in red tape, they quietly and discreetly unravel it. Rather than demanding respect from officials, they give it. In place of asserting a right to government benefits, they gently plead. And instead of asserting their citizenship status, recipients humbled themselves before workers, marking themselves as supplicants rather than citizens, unequal and inferior to the government official who serves them.

While all recipients use such tactics, the need to beseech rather than insist resonates louder for certain groups. For African-Americans, this discourse replicates historical patterns of powerlessness where they were first not citizens, and then second-class citizens. For other people of colour, such as Latinos, it echoes the discourse over immigration, which often lumps Latino citizens with undocumented immigrants, and hence tainting their very right to citizenship.

Thus for such groups, the social relations and discourse that characterize welfare relationships threaten their hard-won and precarious sense of citizenship. Few discourses in our democracy are more powerful than our notion of citizenship. Citizenship bestows belonging and signifies inclusion. It is the antidote to "otherness", which negates citizenship and consigns certain groups or individuals to outsider or inferior status. It is within government institutions like the welfare centre that people evaluate their status as citizens. Respect and civility are especially important, and citizens will evaluate the fairness of government authorities by these markers. Treating people respectfully acknowledges their citizenship; treating people poorly implies a disregard for it. For the poor, the civic lesson gleaned from the welfare centre is one of exclusion and second class status. For people of colour, the message is double-barrelled and amplified; it echoes and repeats exclusionary messages from elsewhere in the body politic.

To be sure, the strategy employed by recipients has its advantages. By acting "decent", they align themselves with their workers, thus facilitating a more expedient, effective exchange. It is a strategic, proactive choice, not a passive one, which helps them survive within the welfare system. But it also pits recipients of colour against each other, as they disown and distance themselves from others of their group. Participants thus unwittingly reinforce their own subordination and racial stigmatizing by acting in ways that emphasize rather than challenge their inferior status.

NOTE

1 To protect the confidentiality of the participants, all names are pseudonyms.

REFERENCES

Anderson, Elijah. 1999. Code of the Street: Decency, Violence, and the Moral Life of the Inner City, New York: W W Norton.

———— 2002 'The ideologically driven critique', The American Journey of Sociology, vol. 107, pp. 1533–50.

Mead, Lawrence. 1997. The New Paternalism: Supervisory Approaches to Poverty, Washington, DC: Brookings Institution Press.

Smith, Dorothy. 2005. Institutional Ethnography: A Sociology for People, Oxford, UK: Altamira Press.

64

LGBT Poverty in the United States

M.V. Lee Badgett, Soon Kyu Choi, and Bianca D.M. Wilson

Although prior research has documented rates of poverty among lesbian, gay, bisexual, and transgender (LGBT) people and shown evidence of economic disparities for LGBT people, most studies on the topic have not been able to fully describe the entire LGBT community across the United States. Many past studies used data that do not allow for identification of transgender people or people not living in same-sex couples. This study addresses earlier shortcomings of the research on poverty to provide a new lens on one of the most important measures of economic security—living on very low incomes. In particular, this new research on LGBT poverty comes from the Behavioral Risk Factor Surveillance System (BRFSS) survey, which has asked questions about sexual orientation and gender identity (SOGI) since 2014. This report covers self-identified lesbians, gay men, bisexual people, and transgender people (of various sexual orientations) in 35 states from 2014 to 2017. The focus of the full report is on answering the following questions about LGBT poverty:

1 Do poverty rates differ by SOGI? How do these differences look across various demographic characteristics?

2 Do LGBT and cisgender (cis) straight people differ in ways that affect poverty?

3 Accounting for other known factors related to poverty, do LGBT people still experience higher rates of poverty compared to cisgender straight people?

MAIN FINDINGS

- Poverty rates differ by SOGI. We examined poverty rates separately for cisgender straight men and women, cisgender gay men and lesbian women, cisgender bisexual men and women, and transgender people. (Figure 64.1).

    - LGBT people collectively have a poverty rate of 21.6 percent, which is much higher than the rate for cisgender straight people of 15.7 percent.

    - Among LGBT people, transgender people have especially high rates of poverty—29.4 percent.

Badgett, M.V. Lee, Soon Kyu Choi, Bianca D.M. Wilson. "LGBT Poverty in the United States: A Study of Differences between Sexual Orientation and Gender Identity Groups." Williams Institute, UCLA School of Law.

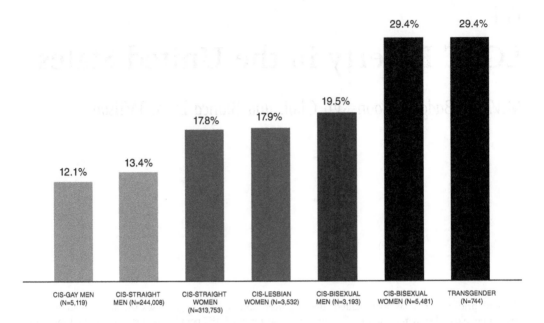

Figure 64.1 Poverty rates for cisgender straight men and women, cisgender gay men and lesbian women, cisgender bisexual men and women, and transgender people.

- Lesbian (17.9 percent) and straight (17.8 percent) cisgender women have higher poverty rates than gay (12.1 percent) and straight (13.4 percent) cisgender men. But cisgender lesbian women do not have significantly different poverty rates than cisgender straight women.

- Bisexual cisgender women (29.4 percent) and men (19.5 percent) had higher poverty rates than cisgender straight women and men, respectively.

Poverty was also particularly high at the intersection of racial and SOGI minority statuses.

- Black, White, Asian, and other-race LGBT people have statistically significant higher poverty rates than their same-race cisgender straight counterparts. For example, 30.8 percent of Black LGBT people live in poverty, whereas 25.3 percent of Black cisgender straight people live in poverty.

- The patterns of racial disparities in poverty rates were similar for both LGBT and cisgender straight people. That is, for nearly all SOGI groups, people of color had significantly higher poverty rates than White people.

- LGBT people in rural areas (26.1 percent) have the highest poverty rates, compared to LGBT people in urban areas (21.0 percent) and cisgender straight people in either rural (15.9 percent) or urban (15.5 percent) areas.

- LGBT and cisgender straight people differ in ways that affect the likelihood of poverty.

- Several characteristics known to be related to poverty are more common among LGBT people. LGBT people, particularly bisexual and transgender people, are more likely to be:

  - people of color,

  - young, and

  - experiencing a disability.

- However, some LGBT groups have higher levels of education, live in urban areas, and have fewer children (namely, gay cisgender men), all factors that protect them from poverty.

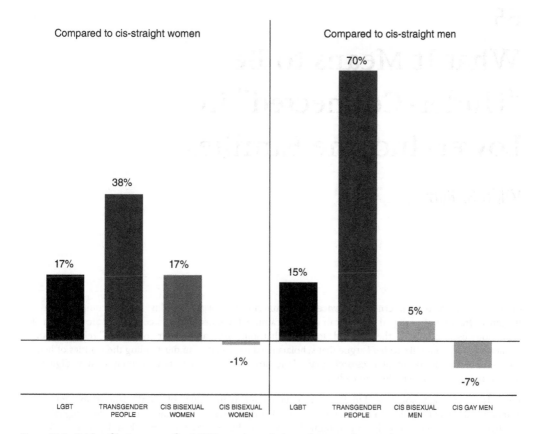

Figure 64.2 Odds of being poor for LGBT people and cisgender straight people.

- Once factors such as race, age, location, education, disability, language marital status, employment, health, and children are taken into account, we find that LGBT people are still more likely to experience poverty than their cisgender straight counterparts.(Figure 64.2).

  - Beyond the poverty-related factors that are more common among LGBT people such as those previously listed, LGBT people as a group had higher odds of being poor than cisgender straight people—17 percent higher odds compared to cisgender straight women and 15 percent higher compared to cisgender straight men. The chart below shows these differences, but the bars in light blue show differences that are not statistically significant.

    - However, compared to cisgender straight women, bisexual cisgender women and transgender people drove this economic disparity. Lesbians were neither more nor less likely to be poor than cisgender straight women.

    - Once accounting for the effect of other factors, bisexual cisgender men no longer had significantly lower poverty rates compared to cisgender straight men, but transgender people remained more likely to experience poverty. Gay cisgender men were just as likely to be poor as cisgender straight men (the difference in likelihood was not significantly different for gay and straight cisgender men).

Taken together, this report extends our knowledge of LGBT poverty. Using a new dataset with more detailed measures of SOGI and a much larger sample size than previous studies reveals important differences in the collective group of LGBT people.

65

What It Means to Be "Under-Connected" in Lower-Income Families

Vikki S. Katz

Constrained access to the internet and devices that connect to it, or *digital inequality*, is more complex than the binary framing of a "digital divide" can possibly capture. If connectivity is a continuum along which all technology users are placed, then it stands to reason that some users are "under-connected," relative to how connected they would like to be. I argue that scholars need to prioritize understanding the realities of being under-connected, adjusting their research methods accordingly, if we are to fully account for how digital inequality impacts both children and adults.

I will also argue that scholars need to consider digital inequality in context of social relationships, not as individualized experiences. In the case of children, family context is especially crucial to how digital inequality is experienced. Children's constrained access to technology is never entirely independent; after all, they rely on parents to purchase devices, prioritize monthly payments for internet access, or get them to libraries if the family doesn't have internet at home. Less obviously, children depend on parents and siblings as sources of support for learning with technology. As a result, family interactions are fundamental to understanding digital inequalities among children, and to identifying potential pathways for resolving these social disparities.

I primarily base my comments on a study I led between 2013 and 2016 to investigate how low-income US parents and their school-age children make decisions about adopting the internet and related devices, and how they integrate those technologies into everyday routines. I was particularly interested in how families responded to national, state, and local policy initiatives that target them with subsidized technology offers to empirically assess how well those digital equity programs are addressing families' needs.

My team and I began by conducting in-depth, qualitative interviews with 170 Mexican-heritage parents and their focal child in grades K to 8 ($N = 336$) who qualified for reduced-cost school meals[1] in three school districts in Arizona, California, and Colorado. In early 2015, we deployed a nationally representative telephone survey of 1,191 lower-income US parents with a child in the same grades. Our study is unusual for two key reasons: First, the robust quality of our formative qualitative research strengthens our ability to triangulate and interpret survey findings. Second, by limiting our samples to lower-income parents and children, we were able to focus directly on the specific contours of digital inequality and how they impact families' technology experiences.

Katz, Vikki S. "What It Means To Be "Under-Connected" in Lower-Income Families." *Journal of Children and Media* 11, no. 2 (2017): 241–244.

Beyond Access: Conceptualizing "Under-Connectedness"

Carmen Gonzalez and I have defined *meaningful digital connectivity* as possessing "the requisite technical skills to engage new communication technologies and mobilize information resources to address a broad range of everyday goals and concerns" (Katz & Gonzalez, 2016, p. 238). Fundamental to that definition is having meaningful access to the internet and devices that enable connection to it.

We found that researchers can no longer rely on simple yes/no questions to assess whether families have access; the quality and consistency of connectivity are critical to interpreting what access can actually offer. Almost all (94 percent) parents who took the survey reported that their families had some kind of internet access (e.g., via a computer at home or a mobile device with a data plan). The same was true for families who participated in the qualitative interviews; only eight of 170 families were going online for the first time through the subsidized internet offers introduced in their district.

Had we stopped at basic access questions, we would have missed that the majority of interviewed and surveyed families are under-connected in one or more ways. Among surveyed parents with internet access through a computer (i.e., *home access*), 52 percent said their internet was too slow, 26 percent said that too many people share the computer to have enough time on it, and 20 percent had had their service disconnected in the last year due to non-payment. And among the one-quarter (23 percent) of surveyed parents who only access the internet through a smartphone or tablet (i.e., *mobile-only access*), 29 percent had hit their plan data limits in the past year, 24 percent had had their service disconnected in the last year due to non-payment, and 21 percent said that too many people share the device to have enough time on it.

Identifying who is under-connected (and how) also requires differentiating between the affordances of devices that they have available to get online. Our findings demonstrate that mobile-only connectivity should also be treated as a form of under-connectedness. Families who only have access via a smartphone or tablet use the internet less frequently, and for a narrower set of activities, than families who go online via a computer at home.

These differences are not trivial. Mobile-only parents were significantly less likely to shop online (36 percent vs. 66 percent with home access), use online banking or bill-paying (49 percent vs. 74 percent), and apply for jobs or services online (42 percent vs. 56 percent). Online shopping can save parents money, online banking can save them time, and applications for many services and jobs are now exclusively online. As such, mobile-only parents and children are likely less connected to opportunities that help families to get by and to get ahead. Likewise, children in mobile-only families were significantly less likely to use the internet daily (31 percent vs. 51 percent with home access) or to seek information online about things they are interested in (35 percent vs. 52 percent). Daily use is positively associated with digital skill development, and "interest-driven learning" experiences are associated with greater motivation and learning confidence in children. Our findings therefore suggest that even relative to their lower-income peers, children with mobile-only access are experiencing more acute digital inequality.

Family Learning Environments and Children's Digital Inequality

Parents and children can be under-connected due to inconsistent and low-quality internet connectivity, limited functionality of devices or opportunities to use them, or by having mobile-only access. All of these dimensions of under-connectedness affect how meaningful digital connectivity is to children's and parents' everyday lives and access to social resources. Children's interactive exchanges with parents and siblings as they use technology together are at the core of what makes their digital connectivity meaningful because they frequently scaffold each other's digital skills development. The relational context of technology use is therefore critical to explaining variations in under-connectedness among lower-income children – and can be a resource for efforts to resolve such challenges.

Our survey results reinforced our interview findings with regard to how intergenerational collaborations around technology enable both parents and children to gain confidence and new skills, and to accomplish goals online. Among surveyed families where the parent and focal child both use the internet, 77 percent of parents have helped their children use technology; 53 percent say their children have helped them to do the same. Among families with more than one 6- to 13-year-old and a computer in the home, 81 percent of siblings help each other learn about computers or mobile devices either "sometimes" or "often." These family dynamics are related. We find that the nature of parent-child interactions around technology predicts the activities that school-age siblings do together. Parental mediation is therefore only one part of the family technology story; children are guided by parents, but they are also actively brokering their parents' and siblings' technology experiences. Fluid exchanges of expert and learner roles during joint technology engagement can facilitate powerful learning experiences for all family members.

For families often defined by their deficits – in income, parental education, and so forth – their frequent and intense technology engagement should be treated as an asset for efforts to reduce digital inequality. For example, local organizations can expand on families' existing technology practices by providing relevant opportunities for technical support or further skill development. These sorts of possibilities for addressing under-connectedness emerge by moving beyond a binary framing of the digital divide to a spectrum of possible connectivity. By researching digital inequality in ways that more closely match the lived experiences of children and families, scholars are also better positioned to contribute to policy and program initiatives that support families in developing meaningful digital connectivity.

NOTE

1 The income threshold to qualify for digital equity initiatives is often tied to eligibility for subsidized school meals; e.g., www.everyoneon.org/about/c2c/.

REFERENCE

Katz, V. S., & Gonzalez, C. (2016). Toward meaningful connectivity: Using multilevel communication research to reframe digital inequality. *Journal of Communication, 66*, 236–249.

SECTION XII
Aging

INTRODUCTION

The number of Americans who are over 65 years of age is large and growing, expanding from 3.1 million in 1900 to 52 million in 2018 and expected to reach 95 million by 2060 (Population Reference Bureau 2020). This means that right now about 16 percent of the population is over the age of 65, but that that proportion will grow to 23 percent over the next 40 years. By 2035, the Census Bureau estimates that seniors, mostly baby boomers born between 1945 and 1964, will outnumber children (McPhillips 2019). They are a numerically large generation, though not as big as millennials, and in many ways are changing how people age.

People over 65 years of age today look and act differently than people in that same age group did a generation ago. In many ways, there are positives to how we think about aging that this generation brings, but there are also new challenges. They are healthier on average than were prior generations and as a result, the average life expectancy has increased from 68 years in 1950 to 78.6 years in 2017. Today's seniors are continuing to work for much longer than did seniors in the past. In 2018, 29 percent of baby boomers between the ages of 65 and 72 were working (or looking for work), which is about 8–10 percent higher than in prior generations (Fry 2019). Baby Boomers control about 70 percent of all disposable income in the United States, making them a dominant force in the economy. One study found that almost half of baby boomers planned to spend between $1,000 and $5,000 toward an upcoming vacation (US News and World Report 2015). The result is that companies continue to cater to them and they in many ways drive product marketing and development.

Baby boomers also changed norms about family as they led the "divorce revolution," which included no-fault divorces becoming law—a process described in Section IV. Older couples today are more likely to divorce than they were in the past. In 2015, for every 1,000 married people who were 50 and older, 10 divorced. This was a notable increase from five per 1,000 in 1990. Among those ages 65 and older, the divorce rate has roughly tripled since 1990, reaching six people per 1,000 married persons in 2015 (Stepler 2017). Some of this trend reflects generationally different views of marriage, which shifted toward a greater emphasis on personal fulfillment. Having divorced in record numbers in midlife, baby boomers also face more marital instability later. Adults older than 50 who have remarried divorce at twice the rate of those in their first marriages. Of all divorces among those over age 50, almost half were in their second or higher marriage (Stepler 2017). These patterns mean that an increasing number of seniors may be single and live alone in their later years.

Baby boomers were the first generation to be educated in high numbers, which they owe to policies that expanded funding and aimed to increase educational opportunity. After World War II, the Servicemen's Readjustment Act of 1944, also known as the GI Bill of Rights, provided support to veterans to attend college. In the 1960s, as part of his Great Society programs, Lyndon Johnson signed the Higher Education Act, which provided federal support for college through tuition grants, guaranteed student loans, and work-study funding. The Civil Rights Act of 1964 outlawed segregation in public places and banned discrimination on the basis of race, color, religion, sex, or national origin. These policy innovations facilitated many more Americans getting a college education than would otherwise have been able. The impacts were particularly notable for white women who were best situated to benefit from these new legal protections.

These programs tripled higher education enrollments. It is important to note that these programs and public investment in education, which have notably shrunk in recent decades, made educational affordable. Between 1980 and 2014, the average cost of college tuition went up by nearly 260 percent, which was much higher than the rate of increase of all other consumer items, which by comparison increased almost 120 percent (Jackson 2015). Students with need were offered grants then, rather than loans as they are now, making this a generation who never experienced the debt that many recent college graduates endure today. In 1989, just 17 percent of 20-somethings had student debt; today, 42 percent do. This debt will inevitably alter wealth accumulation for younger generations as they age.

AGING AND INEQUALITY

Just as the composition of the country is increasingly racially and ethnically diverse, the older population is also increasingly diverse. Estimates are that although 77 percent of the older population is white, that number will drop to 55 percent in the coming decades. This diversity reflects the reality that not all seniors age the same way. The forces that shape childhood and adult life also affect old age. Just like with other parts of the life course, inequality affects how someone ages. Among adults over 65 years of age, 17 percent of Latinos and 19 percent of African Americans lived in poverty in 2017. This is twice the rate of white older adults, which is about 7 percent. Poverty shapes whether seniors continue to work, how they access healthcare and medication, whether they have adequate nutrition, what kinds of housing are available to them, and whether their care needs are met. Estimates are that 5.3 million seniors, or 7.3 percent of the senior population, were food insecure in 2018 (Feeding America 2020).

Environment also matters in aging. Living in poor neighborhoods affects health, irrespective of individual income. Living in low-income neighborhoods can accelerate the aging process as residents tend to have high rates of chronic illnesses, more mobility challenges, and more cognitive impairment than those in wealthier neighborhoods. Neighborhoods that provide social connection can help to mitigate these issues (Ailshire and García 2018). However, as Stacy Torres shows in her chapter, processes of gentrification often compromise neighborhood connections for seniors in urban places.

Women in general and women of color specifically may face greater inequality in old age. In 2017, 4.3 percent of women aged 65 and older had total incomes below the poverty line. This rate was higher for widows (13.9 percent), divorced women (15.8 percent), and never-married women (21.5 percent) (Li and Dalaker 2019). Older women typically receive about $4,000 less annually in social security payments than older men, largely a result of pay inequities over their lifetimes, time taken off for caregiving, and occupational segregation into lower wage work. Older women of color fare even worse. In 2013, African American single women between ages 65 and 84 had a median wealth of $55,700, compared to $187,000 for white single women in the same age category (Sullivan and Meschede 2016). Even with a college degree, older single African American women still had lower levels of wealth accumulation, averaging about $11,000, compared to white college-educated women whose median wealth was about $384,400 (Lincoln 2018). In myriad ways, the effects of inequality accumulate over the life course and shape life in old age.

HOUSING AND AGING IN PLACE

People over 65 years are not evenly distributed across the country, raising different issues in different places. In 2018, more than 20 percent of residents who lived in Maine and Florida were over 65 years. Some seniors relocate to places like Florida in retirement, but states like Maine and much of the Midwest are seeing the average age of residents go up in large part because younger people are moving away. In contrast, Utah and Alaska have the lowest share of seniors, with just over 11 percent of the state's population over 65 years of age (McPhillips 2019). The kinds of services, transportation options, hospitals and medical facilities, or cultural venues that exist that are accessible to seniors vary dramatically by region.

As people age, their needs in terms of housing and care change. Many seniors want to stay in their homes as they get older, rather than downsizing or moving into a retirement community or assisted living facility, a practice known as aging in place. One survey found that 76 percent of Americans age 50 and older prefer to remain in their current residence as they age, but only about half believed they would be able to do so.

There are many challenges to aging in place. Residents may have declining mobility over time or other health challenges and may find their homes increasingly difficult to navigate safely. This is not a minor issue as falling down presents one of the leading cause of senior injuries and death from injury. Estimates are that one in four adults aged 65 and older will fall. This represents 29 million falls, three million emergency department (ED) visits, 800,000 hospitalizations, and 28,000 deaths. This results in an estimated $31 billion in annual Medicare costs (CDC 2017).

Costs of housing present another challenge to aging in place, since many cannot afford to keep their homes as their income declines in later life. In 2009, 48 percent of homeowners with a mortgage and almost 59 percent of renters aged 65 and older spent 30 percent or more of their income on housing and utilities (HUD 2013). Among low-income renters, 72 percent pay more than 30 percent of their income toward housing and nearly half pay more than 50 percent (HUD 2013). A lifetime of racial disparities in income and wealth accumulation also matters. Estimates are that 76 percent of African American and 85 percent of Latino seniors do not have sufficient financial resources to meet projected lifetime expenses (HUD 2013). Public programs to subsidize housing, fund housing adaptations, and provide long-term care help to fill these gaps, but as need for help is expected to increase without increases in funding, they are unlikely to be adequate.

RESIDENTIAL CARE

Older adults with health challenges who are aging in place often find in-home caregivers to help them. Some may need higher levels of care and support, which require them to enter residential care facilities. The two major forms of residential care and support are assisted living and nursing homes. Both are forms of housing in which staff provide help with many of the activities of daily living, including bathing, dressing, and personal care, and can also help residents keep track of medications, do laundry, and provide housecleaning. Both usually offer social support and activities to keep residents socially engaged and provide meal service. Nursing homes provide higher levels of medical support and monitoring and often appear more institutional. Assisted living often looks more like apartments, but has the ability to support individuals with mobility or memory challenges.

Only about 3 percent of people over the age of 65 years lived in institutional settings in 2016, but this percentage increases with age. About 1 percent of people between the ages of 65 and 74 live in institutional care settings, which increases to 3 percent of people age 75–84 years and to 9 percent for those who are 85 years and older (ACL-DHHS 2018). Expectations are that the baby boom generation will increase demand for nursing care in the United States by 50 percent, from 1.2 million in 2017 to 1.9 in 2030 (Population Reference Bureau 2020). Although this remains a small percentage of residential arrangements, there are still serious questions of whether there will be adequate supply of housing options, since nursing care facilities are already near capacity. Additionally, costs are significant. In 2018, the median annual cost across the country for assisted living was $48,000 (Guzman 2019). This is out of reach for most people. Some programs provide financial support for low-income seniors or seniors with disabilities, but these costs remain a significant barrier to access.

SOCIAL ISOLATION AND ENGAGEMENT

Even as seniors aim to age in place, many find that as they do, they become socially isolated. One survey suggests that about three in ten adults report lacking companionship, feeling left out, or feeling isolated from others (Binette and Vasold 2018). About 20 million seniors age 65 and older are single. Women may be at higher risk of isolation. In 2018, 26 percent of women between the ages of 65 and 74 lived alone. Among women between the ages of 75 and 84, 39 percent lived alone. About 55 percent of women over 85 years of age lived alone (Population Reference Bureau 2020). Many older people are finding innovative ways to use technology to stay safe and connected, as the chapter by Meika Loe shows, but not all are equally able.

Not all seniors are socially isolated. Many are more socially engaged than were seniors in past generations. About 30 percent of baby boomers volunteer (Americorps & Senior Corps 2020), and many still work. Almost half of seniors over age 65 years use Facebook (Gramlich 2019) and other social media. As Sheila Cotton's chapter suggests, younger people can do a great deal to support technology and social media use among seniors to increase their social engagement. Seniors are also using technology to connect in other ways. At least 13 percent of seniors over the age of 65 years have used dating apps (compared with one-third of all adults and 48 percent of 18–29 year-olds) (Vogels 2020).

More than half of adults between the ages of 65 and 74 are sexually active, which drops to about 26 percent for adults between 75 and 85 years (Lindau et al. 2007). For women who are more likely to be widowed, this figure was lower. At least one in seven men uses Viagra or similar medications to support sexual performance (Lindau et al. 2007). As the chapter by Lisa Miller shows, sexuality changes throughout the life course, but remains an important aspect of life.

Seniors' intimacy and autonomy varies by their caregiving relationships and housing circumstances. Gay and lesbian couples, whose relationships may predate the legalization of same-sex marriage, may face facility policies or staff attitudes that challenge their ability to remain together or receive recognition as a family. In residential care facilities, older adults often have less privacy, and staff may monitor them—issues explored in the chapter by Elisabeth O. Burgess, Alexis A. Bender, and Christina Barmon. In one particularly complicated recent case, a 78-year-old man was charged with sexual abuse of his wife who suffered from severe dementia. By all accounts, this was a loving couple, the wife was happy to see her husband when he visited, she did not seem to resist having sex with him, and there were no signs of abuse. However, the couple's adult daughter notified the nursing home staff that she was concerned about her mother and after consulting with her mother's doctor, the nursing home decided the woman was unable to provide consent and told the husband he could not have sex with his wife. When he ignored this directive, he was arrested and charged with sexual assault.

This case and an increasing number of others like it raise important questions about the basis of sexual consent, particularly as people's cognition declines in old age. However, adding to the complexity of the situation is the reality that physical intimacy and touch are important in old age. As a director of a residential care facility advocating for a sexual rights policy for seniors explained,

> Touch is one of the last pleasures we lose. So much of aging and so much of being in a long-term care facility is about loss, loss of independence, loss of friends, loss of being able to use your body. Why would we want to diminish that?
>
> (Belluck 2015)

Though in this particular case, the husband was found not guilty, questions like these are likely to continue to arise as the population ages. In 2014, Alzheimer's disease and related dementias affected five million people, which is 1.6 percent of the US population. This figure is expected to increase to about 14 million by 2060, which will affect almost 3.3 percent of the population. Among people ages 65 and older, African

Americans have the highest prevalence of Alzheimer's disease and related dementias (13.8 percent), followed by Hispanics (12.2 percent), whites (10.3 percent), American Indian and Alaska Natives (9.1 percent), and Asian and Pacific Islanders (8.4 percent) (CDC 2018). The chapter by Richard Gunderman and Lily Wolf provides an important reminder that diseases like dementia have very different meanings across cultures. These important differences will nonetheless be mediated by law and regulation.

AGING AND CRIMINAL JUSTICE SYSTEMS

Prisons were not built with those who are aging in mind, but the prison population in the United States is aging, which creates new challenges. Incarcerated adults over the age of 50 years now make up about 16 percent of the state and federal prison population and this number is expected to increase (Skarupski et al. 2018). Among the reasons for this are trends toward longer sentences and fewer opportunities for parole or early release because of "tough on crime" legislation over the past few decades. The conditions of incarceration, including poor access to healthcare, poor nutrition, and lack of opportunities for health promotion activities, appear to speed up the aging process for many. The limited data that exist show that half of all incarcerated adults have at least one chronic health condition, including cancer, high blood pressure or history of stroke, diabetes, heart disease, kidney disease, arthritis, asthma, or cirrhosis. Almost 38 percent of incarcerated adults in one 2004 study reported physical and cognitive impairments, including vision (17.4 percent), learning (13.3 percent), hearing (11.4 percent), mobility (6.1 percent), mental (5.0 percent), and/or speech (3.5 percent) (Skarupski et al. 2018). The result is that this system, which was not set up to manage complex healthcare needs, is increasingly providing nursing home-like care as well as end-of-life care.

Criminal justice policy is also driving the increase in the number of seniors who are raising their grandchildren. More than 2.5 million grandparents report they are responsible for their grandchildren. Of those, 41 percent are older than 60 years, and approximately 57 percent are in the workforce. About 69 percent are married and almost two-thirds are female. Almost 20 percent of these grandparent caregivers live in poverty and more than 25 percent have a disability. About 53 percent are white, about 20 percent are Black, 20 percent Latino, 3 percent are Asian, and around 2 percent are American Indian or Alaska Native (Lent and Otto 2018).

Although there are many reasons why grandparents take over parenting responsibilities for their grandchildren, among the most common is drug addiction. One recent analysis showed that states with the highest rates of opioid prescribing also had the highest rates of children living with grandparents (Anderson 2019). Deportations are increasingly playing a role as well. These caregiving relationships in many cases bring added financial and social stress to seniors who may not have adequate savings or earnings to provide for themselves and their grandchildren, may struggle to find childcare or healthcare resources for their grandchildren, and may find this new role complicates their relationships with immediate and extended family (Lent and Otto 2018). In some cases, foster care and social service agencies can provide support. In many other cases, seniors may find themselves on their own, navigating this new role.

AGEISM

Not all challenges facing seniors are material. There is significant bias against people as they age. The term "ageism" was first used in 1969 to describe "a form of bigotry we now tend to overlook." Age discrimination or ageism represents "prejudice by one age group toward other age groups" and is "a personal revulsion to and distaste for growing old, disease, disability; and fear of powerlessness, 'uselessness,' and death" (quoted in Levy and Macdonald 2016:5).

Federal law protects against age discrimination for those who are 40 years or older. The law does not protect younger people and does not forbid an employer from preferring an older person to a younger person. Although complaints of age discrimination are rising, many are hard to demonstrate. For example, in a workplace, an older employee might not be identified as a priority for a training program or continuing education funding based on the belief that younger people learn better or need the opportunities more. Excluding older people from interesting assignments, meetings, or opportunities to socialize outside of work are all subtle ways age discrimination persists. Enduring jokes about one's age or being asked about retirement plans constitutes workplace harassment.

Age discrimination can be subtle. Assumptions about a person's competence or presumption they suffer impairment are examples. Beauty norms are one place where ageism—especially against women—is easily visible. Although the industry of anti-aging products continues to grow for men and women, women face greater pressure to avoid signs of aging. Men's lined faces and gray hair might point to maturity, but for women, they are seen as a liability.

Healthcare is another place where ageism emerges. Whether seniors are offered a full range of treatment options, including access to clinical trials, are empowered to manage their own care, or are taken seriously may be manifestations of ageism. In routines ways, physicians often dismiss many treatable complaints as just a symptom of old age or ignore requests for help around sexual or mental health. Physicians often speak overly slowly or patronize older patients in ways that reflect stereotypes about older age.

There are multiple opportunities to address ageism and to engage in dialog about stereotypes about seniors. As writer Ashton Applewhite argues, "Ageism is the perfect target for collective advocacy because it affects everyone. That very attribute, its universal nature, means that we undermine ageism when people of all ages show up for stuff" (Applewhite 2017:online). More generally, many manifestations of inequality in old age could be addressed through public investment in programs, neighborhoods, and health. Looking ahead, the millennial generation is even larger than baby boomers. Millennials are more diverse than the generations before them with 44.2 percent from an underrepresented racial or ethnic group (US Census Bureau 2015). Given that all generations will eventually age, the return on these investments would be enormous.

REFERENCES

ACL-DHHS. 2018. "2017 Profile of Older Americans." Administration for Community Living, U.S. Department of Health and Human Services. (https://acl.gov/sites/default/files/Aging%20and%20 Disability%20in%20America/2017OlderAmericansProfile.pdf).

Ailshire, Jennifer and Catherine García. 2018. "Unequal Places: The Impacts of Socioeconomic and Race/Ethnic Differences in Neighborhoods." *Generations* 42(2):20–27.

Americorps & Senior Corps. 2020. "Demographics." Corporation for National and Community Service. (https://www.nationalservice.gov/serve/via/demographics).

Anderson, Lydia. 2019. "The Opioid Prescribing Rate and Grandparents Raising Grandchildren: State and County Level Analysis." U.S. Census Bureau.

Applewhite, Ashton. 2017. "Building an Anti-Ageism Movement: The Time Is Now." Next Avenue. (https://www.nextavenue.org/whats-ageism-got-to-do-with-it/).

Belluck, Pam. 2015. "Sex, Dementia and a Husband on Trial at Age 78." *New York Times.*

Binette, Joanne and Kerri Vasold. 2018. *Home and Community Preferences: A National Survey of Adults Age 18-Plus.* Washington, DC: AARP Research. (https://doi.org/10.26419/res.00231.001).

CDC. 2017. "Take a Stand on Falls." Centers for Disease Control and Prevention. (https://www.cdc. gov/features/older-adult-falls/index.html).

CDC. 2018. *U.S. Burden of Alzheimer's Disease, Related Dementias to Double by 2060.* Atlanta: Centers for Disease Control and Prevention. (https://www.cdc.gov/media/releases/2018/p0920-alzheimers-burden-double-2060.html).

Feeding America. 2020. "Senior Food Insecurity Studies." Feeding America. (https://www.feedinga merica.org/research/senior-hunger-research/senior).

Fry, Richard. 2019. "Baby Boomers Are Staying in the Labor Force at Rates Not Seen in Generations for People Their Age." (https://www.pewresearch.org/fact-tank/2019/07/24/baby-boomers-us-labor-force/).

Gramlich, John. 2019. "10 Facts about Americans and Facebook." Pew Research Center. (https://www.pewresearch.org/fact-tank/2019/05/16/facts-about-americans-and-facebook/).

Guzman, Shannon. 2019. "Affordable Supportive Housing Fills Gap for Older Adults and People with Disabilities." AARP Public Policy Institute. (https://www.aarp.org/content/dam/aarp/ppi/2019/06/affordable-supportive-housing.doi.10.26419-2Fppi.00069.001.pdf).

HUD. 2013. "Aging in Place: Facilitating Choice and Independence." Housing and Urban Development Office of Policy Development and Research. (https://www.huduser.gov/portal/periodicals/em/fall13/highlight1.html).

Jackson, Abby. 2015. "This Chart Shows How Quickly College Tuition Has Skyrocketed since 1980." *Business Insider*. July 20, 2015.

Lent, Jaia Peterson and Adam Otto. 2018. "Grandparents, Grandchildren, and Caregiving: The Impacts of America's Substance Use Crisis." *Generations*, Fall 2018.

Levy, Sheri R. and Jamie L. Macdonald. 2016. "Progress on Understanding Ageism." *Journal of Social Issues* 72(1):5–25.

Li, Zhe and Joseph Dalaker. 2019. "Poverty among Americans Aged 65 and Older." Congressional Research Service.

Lincoln, Karen D. 2018. "Economic Inequality in Later Life." *Generations* 42(2):6–12.

Lindau, Stacy Tessler, L. Philip Schumm, Edward O. Laumann, Wendy Levinson, Colm A. O'Muircheartaigh and Linda J. Waite. 2007. "A Study of Sexuality and Health among Older Adults in the United States." *The New England Journal of Medicine* 357(8):762–74. doi: 10.1056/NEJMoa067423.

McPhillips, Deidre. 2019. "Aging in America." U.S. News and World Report. (https://www.usnews.com/news/best-states/articles/2019-09-30/aging-in-america-in-5-charts).

Population Reference Bureau. 2020. "Fact Sheet: Aging in the United States." Washington, DC: Population Reference Bureau. (https://www.prb.org/aging-unitedstates-fact-sheet/).

Skarupski, Kimberly A., Alden Gross, Jennifer A. Schrack, Jennifer A. Deal and Gabriel B. Eber. 2018. "The Health of America's Aging Prison Population." *Epidemiologic Reviews* 40(1):157–165.

Stepler, Renee. 2017. "Led by Baby Boomers, Divorce Rates Climb for America's 50+ Population." Pew Research Center. (https://www.pewresearch.org/fact-tank/2017/03/09/led-by-baby-boomers-divorce-rates-climb-for-americas-50-population/).

Sullivan, Laura and Tatjana Meschede. 2016. "Race, Gender, and Senior Economic Well-Being: How Financial Vulnerability over the Life Course Shapes Retirement for Older Women of Color." *Public Policy & Aging Report* 26(2):58–62.

US Census Bureau. 2015. "Millennials Outnumber Baby Boomers and Are Far More Diverse, Census Bureau Reports." US Census Bureau. (https://www.census.gov/newsroom/press-releases/2015/cb15-113.html).

US News and World Report. 2015. "Baby Boomer Report." US News and World Report.

Vogels, Emily A. 2020. "10 Facts about Americans and Online Dating." Pew Research. (https://www.pewresearch.org/fact-tank/2020/02/06/10-facts-about-americans-and-online-dating/).

66
Aging in Places

Stacy Torres

Today a new generation of poor and moderate-income urban elders struggles to grow old in gentrifying cities like New York, Los Angeles, San Francisco, and other urban areas around the country whose residents are graying as the municipalities where they live absorb affluent new arrivals in search of urban amenities.

They face the traditional challenges associated with old age, such as declining physical mobility; difficulties performing activities of daily living; and the loss of friends, relatives, and other social connections, sometimes in the absence of strong or nearby familial support, in an urban context that offers many advantages for older people who wished to stay independent but also special hurdles for those who remain in some of the most valuable, coveted, and increasingly expensive real estate in the country. Unlike previous generations, as these older people enter their later years, they are not retreating into the family homestead or moving to a far-away retirement community but staying put in their present neighborhoods and living spaces for as long as possible.

While elderly poverty rates have dropped over the past half century, older adults remain vulnerable economically, especially as they move further away from the traditional retirement age. With their entrance into deep old age, they must also cobble together a means of supporting themselves financially on dwindling savings, if any, and fixed incomes. Even those elders who had enjoyed comfortable middle-class incomes in their younger years are not immune to the fallout of economic shocks, such as the most recent Great Recession.

While overall poverty rates for older adults have declined from 35 percent in 1959 to 8.7 percent in 2011, this picture worsens when using alternate poverty measures such the Census Bureau's Supplemental Poverty Measure, which factors in regional cost-of-living differences and medical expenses.

Securing affordable housing also poses a steep hurdle for seniors living on fixed incomes and a growing concern even for older adults with more resources, who in another era likely would have experienced greater housing support. But across the country, elders face the continued effects of the Great Recession and high housing costs. Since 2004, the number of elderly households that spent more than 30 percent of their income on housing has increased. Housing costs in expensive urban areas take an even greater bite out of many seniors' household budgets. For example, in Los Angeles, rent accounts for more than half the

---

Torres, Stacy. "Aging in Places." In *Critical Gerontology Comes of Age*, pp. 151–162. New York: Routledge, 2018.

expenses of an older person living on her own, and 70 percent of these older California renters struggle to make ends meet (Wallace and Smith 2009).

"I'd rather die than go to a nursing home" became a common refrain among the older adults with whom I spent five years conducting participant observations in New York City. Their outspokenness about wanting to die before entering a nursing home was more than hyperbolic natter, and in most cases, they passed away before ever having to move to an institutional setting. But some faced a longer period of illness, a few weeks to a few months, and spent time in a nursing facility before dying.

Their aversion to institutional care reflects a broader desire among older Americans to age in place despite rising economic vulnerability. In 2005, 89 percent of adults aged 50 and above surveyed by the American Association of Retired Persons (AARP) wished to remain in their homes (Klinenberg, Torres, & Portacolone, 2012). The number of people living alone has risen significantly over the past half century and when people can afford solo living they choose this arrangement whenever possible, especially when the alternative is moving in with family at older ages (Klinenberg 2012). Yet, the design and infrastructure of most cities and towns cater to families with young children and are ill equipped to meet the needs of an aging population. Despite the vast need and desire for home-based care, we lack sufficient funding for non-medical supportive services to aid aging in place. Proposed cuts to Medicaid and Medicare seem perpetually on the horizon, posing threats first to services that help elders remain in their homes. Our social policies reflect this institutional bias and incorrectly assume family can and will step in when elders' needs exceed available resources.

With growing numbers of elders, scholars, policymakers, and ordinary people have an interest in understanding the conditions that enable older people to thrive in their communities. Aging in place is popular among older people who want to remain in their communities and with policymakers, who see aging in place as a less costly and popular alternative to institutional options. At the same time, elders living alone in the community may face a sense of precariousness due to their difficulty or inability to access necessary resources and bewilderment in navigating a tangled web of social services. My longitudinal observations over five years of ethnographic study offer a glimpse into how elders navigated their neighborhoods in the face of aging-related challenges, such as health declines, mobility concerns, and gentrification, pointing to a more fundamental question of what home and place means for older adults growing old in their communities.

AGING IN PLACE IN NEW YORK CITY TODAY

The research participants in my study of aging in place in New York City represent several key demographic trends that will shape the experience of growing old for generations to come, and thus offer another glimpse into the future of urban aging in twenty-first-century America. Most of them lived alone by choice and were single, due to a combination of widowhood, divorce, and having never married. Many never had children. The majority were women, who continued to face significant economic disadvantages in old age and higher poverty rates than their same-aged male counterparts. While elders in New York City may not be representative of older people in other parts of the country, they stand on the cusp of future trends that subsequent baby boom cohorts will further, such as having fewer children and multiple committed relationships during their lifetimes, along with rising economic pressures and higher retirement ages. In this context, it is even more crucial that we understand how elders forge supports and grapple with the blessings and burdens of increased longevity.

Rather than offer a prescription for how to age "well" or framing aging in America as a "crisis," my study provides an in-depth ethnographic account of how people attempted to age meaningfully and with dignity in communities where they had lived for decades or their entire lives. Many found social support in "third places" in the absence of kin yet struggled to balance the need for connection with the desire for autonomy. And growing discrepancies between people's constricted mobility and the neighborhood's changing retail landscape threatened their social ties and the larger possibilities for belonging to a community.

Like many in old age, my research participants have had to act as unwitting pioneers, forging alternate communities as they embarked on an uncertain process that tested people's strength, resilience, and creativity. Inline with the fluid nature of time and daily routine after retirement, the older adults I encountered during the course of my study often eschewed institutionalized spaces such as senior centers. Thus, their choices provide one possible blueprint for reimagining late life in this time of unprecedented demographic change with the aging of baby boomers. For example, despite the critical role centers play in the lives of elders, especially for low-income, vulnerable older adults, research has revealed baby boomers' reluctance about this option and dislike of the centers in their current incarnation, which suffer from an image problem (i.e., "not sexy"). Given the flurry of late-life opportunities and constraints, my ethnographic research suggests that aging scholarship across a range of disciplines should devote greater attention to the neighborhood contexts where these informal bonds blossom. They are more important than ever for older people living in urban areas and perhaps of growing importance in suburban and rural areas, where people may know their neighbors and live closer to family but still crave intergenerational ties with people beyond the home and less formalized bonds that allow for more privacy and lower obligation. Alternative social ties stand alongside, and in some cases rival, other structures critical to well-being in old age, such as family and home.

I began observing social life at La Marjolaine Patisserie,[1] a mom-and-pop bakery in a gentrified Manhattan neighborhood. Over time, I noticed that this nondescript establishment not only evoked an earlier era in New York City history but also attracted its fair share of old New Yorkers, men and women predominately in their 70s and 80s, who were the bakery's most loyal customers and spent the most time there. For retirees on fixed incomes with plenty of time but who often could not walk more than a few city blocks, La Marjolaine served as a convenient gathering spot with reasonable prices and few restrictions on how long customers could linger. Most had lived in the neighborhood for multiple decades, and several had lived there for their entire lives.

Unlike the fictional bar in the television show *Cheers*, at La Marjolaine, everyone may not have known your name but usually offered a friendly hello. People checked on each other, asked about a neighbor's whereabouts, and waved to passersby. This place served as a clearing house of neighborhood information, and older customers caught up on news both good and somber, sharing pictures of grandchildren, updates on neighbors in nursing homes, and notices of wakes.

This remnant of a pre-gentrified neighborhood sat nestled among three main residential swathes—a union-built, low-equity co-op; public housing projects; and a large rental complex. These buildings housed many long-time tenants, a number of whom frequented the bakery. The rental protections afforded to them in the housing projects and co-op, or through rent control and stabilization programs in the rental buildings, meant that many long-time, lower-to-middle income residents had remained in a neighborhood now home to upscale restaurants and million-dollar condominiums. Many co-op and project residents had aged in place and lived independently in buildings classified as Naturally Occurring Retirement Community (NORCs), which Federal law defines as "a community with a concentrated population of older individuals" (Niesz 2007). New York City has 27 NORCs in four boroughs. The concentration of older adults in these residential settings often facilitates a more cost-effective and efficient delivery of services to residents with multiple needs in late life.

As a customer at La Marjolaine, I came to know the bakery regulars—a fluid group of women and men older than 60 years, which skewed female, Puerto Rican, Jewish, ethnic white (Italian, Greek, Irish descent), and low-to-middle income, reflecting neighborhood demographics prior to gentrification. After the bakery closed, I followed former customers as they scattered across the neighborhood and gathered in other places within the surrounding blocks, including a McDonald's and Pete's Delicatessen. I also visited participants in their homes, hospitals, and nursing homes; attended wakes and funerals; and accompanied them to other neighborhood places such as park benches.

During the course of my study, I discovered how a nondescript mom-and-pop bakery on Manhattan's West Side satisfied much more than its older customers' craving for sweets and helped meet their desire for company in the face of loneliness, support when struggling, and perhaps most importantly a sympathetic ear to bear witness to the greater and more mundane struggles of late life. What may have appeared to the outsider a shabby bakery with worn tablecloths and hamantaschen was a bubbling hub of neighborhood life, the center of an invisible world of older people hiding in plain sight. The local McDonald's served not just burgers and fries but as a refuge when this group became displaced from their neighborhood gathering spot.

Neighborhood places not only allowed old people to socialize together but also offered a mix of companions in these intergenerational and diverse public spaces. They offered the possibility of alternate caretaking opportunities that differed from the more typical position of older adults in their families, where contact often involves receiving care and crisis management when a problem arises. Even when older adults take on roles as involved grandparents who provide significant financial and childcare assistance, this bond is a complicated family relationship overlaid with obligation and responsibility.

Public and neighborhood places in my study proved as important as home. Outside ties cultivated in nearby gathering spots helped enable many of my research participants to remain in their homes more comfortably as people formed ties with those who could help with smaller tasks, such as assistance with fixing a remote control or computer, which could otherwise feel overwhelming. In more extreme situations, such as a health crisis, connections to others saved lives, such as when someone had fallen or collapsed in their home and a neighborhood acquaintance went to check on them after noticing their absence. Outside help, usually unpaid and informal, freed people from over-reliance on family and healthcare institutions. But this form of assistance could also prove less reliable, not bound by pay or the obligation that more unconditional family ties impose.

Discovering this vital type of urban place for elders in my study raises the question of the meaning and contour of home to my research participants: what was the home that they wanted to return to after a bout with illness, a hospitalization, even a visit of a few days with relatives, and never leave? Their apartment residences of several decades formed a central component of their aging in place experience, but they aged in *places*. And the neighborhood places that ringed their residences in a radius of walkability served as crucial venues to develop connections with others, effectively serving as extensions of their living rooms.

For example, Dottie's circumstances toward the end of her life reflect many challenges my older research participants faced as they struggled to remain independent and dealt with health declines that threatened their ability to live on their own. After suffering a heart attack, Dottie, 83, landed in the hospital indefinitely. She and her family, along with an extended network of friends and neighborhood acquaintances, wrestled with tough medical questions about her future treatment and living arrangements. Faced with this crossroads, Dottie confronted major, life-altering losses of physical ability. Her feeble condition worsened in the following weeks, in the hospital, and later a nursing home. In this rarer case of a permanent move to institutional care, Dottie and her family had to confront three searing realities while grappling with great uncertainty along the way. Physical consequences of the health crisis and the specter of death loomed first, followed by adjustment to institutional living with its concurrent loss of privacy and control, and finally the loss of home and neighborhood.

Months before she entered the nursing home, Dottie had great difficulty accessing the neighborhood places where friends and other familiar faces gathered daily. During an arduous walk with her one day from McDonald's to her home, a distance of approximately three and a half city blocks, I saw the difficulty she faced walking as she hunched over her metal shopping cart for support, sweating and breathing hard. The walk lasted 45 minutes. Her heartache and distress at the prospect of losing her apartment while in the nursing home stood as the final step in a more protracted process of loss that had started in earnest with the disappearance of the bakery. Once that gathering spot, affordable and less than a block from her building, shuttered, she fell further away from the group of regulars that had anchored her. In the months that followed the closing, she admitted feeling depressed about losing contact with people she used to see there. In the nursing home, her daughter Liz taped a picture to the armoire I had taken of Dottie and the bakery crowd alongside a treasured World Series photo of Yankees baseball player Derek Jeter clipped from the local newspaper. "I always knew where I could find Mom," Liz said, referring to the bakery.

The affection that Dottie developed for the bakery is representative of many former patrons' feelings for that establishment and other places where they gathered throughout the neighborhood. They often joked about the bakery's shabby, outdated décor; the worn table cloths; and the wobbly chairs, but the older adults who frequented this space daily revealed great sadness when the store closed after losing its lease. In the years after its shuttering, former customers spoke of this business as fondly and vividly as people in their lives whom they had also lost. Their attachment to this place reveals how much the bakery had for many become the center of their daily rounds and routines, echoing the observations of urban scholars such as Lyn Lofland (1998) on the transformation of public spaces into "home territories" that anchor people in neighborhoods and provide opportunities for repeated interactions over time (p. 70). For example, one older man who ate dinner alone every evening at a nearby diner never lacked for company. He sat by himself at the same booth near the kitchen, beneath a flat-screen television ideal for viewing the baseball and basketball games he enjoyed. He chatted with the waiters as they dashed past to pick up orders, and they honored his nightly "reservation" by setting out a placard that read RESERVED to save his booth. For urban-dwelling older adults facing multiple vulnerabilities, the accessibility of these public venues and the ability to make them their own provided crucial opportunities to connect. My research participants cultivated genuine affinity for the staff and other regulars at these establishments, reflected in their continual "sightings" of former bakery patrons they spotted in the neighborhood and reflections about how much they missed the characters who went there.

Sweeping demographic change will shape society and institutions for decades to come, bringing forth new challenges and new ways of living in old age. With this societal aging comes new vulnerabilities for older adults, due to our lack of preparedness and growing precariousness in many realms of social life. We no longer live in a society where we can count on one lifelong employer, intimate partner, or place of residence to sustain our needs. But the erosion of these traditional arrangements does not necessarily mean cause for alarm, if we take a proactive approach to shaping and implementing policies grounded in lessons learned from a wealth of existing scholarship. Previous qualitative studies provide a core foundation for understanding the array of changes and needs in late life and new challenges leave room for expansion of our knowledge and updating for a new century. The refashioning of old age will continue with new generations of elders, and as my research suggests, subsequent cohorts will adapt to their newfound freedoms and the necessity of forging new social bonds based less around family and formal community institutions.

My participants, the majority of them single and living alone while aging in place, represent larger demographic trends which will grow with future elderly cohorts. Higher rates of divorce and lifelong singlehood, coupled with increased longevity and the lengthening period that elders can expect to live independently, will compel greater numbers of older adults to construct support networks that enable them to thrive in their communities. Accordingly, more will draw these connections from unconventional venues such as informal public places and develop ties with people such as neighbors and acquaintances, which become more central in their lives over time and may prove hard to define but important nonetheless. For example, my participants managed to supplement their own living spaces by using a private business's openness to fit their needs.

Urban areas are ideal places for people to grow old due to their greater walkability, public transportation options, and a denser infrastructure of social services. With growing constraints on finances and mobility, coupled with an increase in surplus time, the rising importance of neighborhood for elders aging in place complicates a simpler narrative of aging at home. The advantages that make them attractive for older adults often draw younger, more affluent professionals who can afford to pay higher rents and desire upscale amenities and businesses. In burgeoning downtowns across America, vulnerable elders in the poorest stretches now face the added threat of gentrification, risk of wrongful evictions, and danger of ending up on the street. The buildings where my research participants lived represent some of the last large-tract affordable housing left in New York City, a great urban center that once had sufficient protections to enable the current generation to age in place but no longer provides a solid base for many future elders to grow old comfortably. They will face housing insecurity and dwindling access to the neighborhood spaces that transform a collection of buildings, sidewalks, and storefronts into home.

NOTE

1 For confidentiality reasons, I have changed the names of most sites and people.

REFERENCES

Klinenberg, E. 2012. *Going Solo: The Extraordinary Rise and Surprising Appeal of Living Alone*. New York: Penguin Press.

Klinenberg, E., Torres, S., and Portacolone, E. 2012, May. *Aging Alone in America*. New York: Council on Contemporary Families Briefing Paper.

Lofland, L. H. 1998. *The Public Realm: Exploring the City's Quintessential Social Territory*. New York: Aldine de Gruyter.

Niesz, H. 2007. *Naturally Occurring Retirement Communities*. Federal Grant Opportunities. Connecticut General Assembly, Office of Legislative Research. Hartford, CT.

Wallace, S. P. and Smith, S. E. 2009. *Half a Million Older Californians Living Alone Unable to Make Ends Meet*. Los Angeles, CA: UCLA Center for Health Policy Research.

67

Doing It My Way

Old Women, Technology, and Wellbeing

Meika Loe

INTRODUCTION

Understanding how old women create support for themselves near the end of life is an important topic, and particularly pressing as the population ages, becomes feminised, and remains largely home-centred. In 2000, 4.2 million people in the United States were aged 85 and older; this number is projected to increase to almost 10 million by 2030 and to 21 million by 2050. The ratio of women to men in this category is roughly 2:1.

Currently 83 percent of Americans aged 65 and over own their own homes, in comparison with 4 percent who reside in long-term care facilities. Given the growing population of elders likely to "age in place" – or in their homes – in future generations, scholars of ageing (as well as commercial entities) have focused on the role of assistive technologies and design in home care. This chapter focuses on women in their 90s (nonagenarians) who are ageing in place in upstate New York. I analyse these old women's use of everyday technological tools to care for themselves in old age and construct meaning. I argue that despite what we may expect, nonagenarian women can be and are technogenarians in their active use of everyday technologies to create meaningful lives and maintain health. Specifically, old women use and negotiate old and new technologies in the context of gendered repertoires to achieve goals such as self-efficacy, wellbeing, and connectedness.

This chapter explores how old women take responsibility for their own health and care through adapting everyday technologies – from slow cookers to gardening tools to televisions – to fit their needs and to age comfortably. I argue that health for elders includes being able to maintain social networks, intellectual growth and participation, and physical wellbeing; much of this is accomplished with the help of everyday technologies. Policymakers must take this into account, and address the cost of monthly telephone, television, and internet bills in ageing initiatives.

METHODS

Because all informants for this study were born before 1930, their gendered scripts as well as approaches to ageing, health, and technology probably differ from those women born in later birth cohorts. For

Loe, Meika. "Doing It My Way: Old Women, Technology and Wellbeing." *Sociology of Health & Illness* 32, no. 2 (2010): 319–334.

example, many nonagenarians have learned to live in moderation, and to appreciate and use technologies as they became available, including radios, sewing machines, kettles, and slow cookers. Today, few own or regularly use microwaves, dishwashers, or computers. Some are ambivalent about new biotechnologies like prescription drugs and medical devices (especially those not utilised by their parents), but may also defer to their doctors when it comes to unfamiliar health issues.

Data were collected through interviews and participant observation with ten women aged 90–96 who are actively ageing in place in upstate New York. Initial contacts were made through connections with senior services centres, senior activities programs, social clubs, and local newspaper coverage. All took part in at least one in-depth semi-structured digitally recorded interview during this period. Interviews included open-ended questions across the lifecourse, focusing on each woman's family, educational and work backgrounds as well as current daily routines and approaches to ageing and self-care.

In addition, I employed ethnographic methods to collect data about lived day-to-day experiences. Beyond regular visits to homes, between 2006 and 2009 I participated in informants' lives and daily routines outside their homes, including intermittent doctor visits, grocery shopping trips, social club meetings, exercise classes, neighbourhood meals, funeral services, and religious rituals. In addition, I logged approximately 150 hours observing a combination of regional ageing-related meetings and conferences, touring institutions dedicated to elder care, and conducting interviews with professionals in elder support and care.

The sample of ten women is largely representative of the national population in the 85 and over age group. According to the US Census (2005) category of the "oldest old" (85+), 70 percent lived in non-family one-person households and 79 percent of the women in this category were widows. In terms of racial demographics, over 90 percent of those over 85 years of age were White; 6 percent were Black. Likewise, this sample includes eight widows and two married couples. Nine identify as White (with Polish, Danish, Irish, Italian, or Jewish ethnic backgrounds) and one as Black. Of the ten nonagenarians, eight live independently and two live with and care for spouses. In terms of housing, two rent apartments, two own condos, and six own houses.

Notably, none of the women in the sample are wheelchair-bound; all are ambulatory in some way and this dramatically shapes their self-care regimens. Two women, Florence and Lillian, employ a home healthcare aid for a few hours each day. The rest of the sample depends on informal caregivers. Four have family members living within a 20-mile radius of their homes who help with transport and care on an intermittent basis. In general, most nonagenarians in this sample prefer to be totally independent, or to go beyond family assistance to utilise social networks, formal transport services (including paid drivers and public transport), or delivery services for day-to-day needs.

FINDINGS

From Tea Bags to Automobiles: Nonagenarians Get Moving

Mobility is a central component of creating and maintaining wellbeing. The spectrum of technologies that enable mobility for elders is much broader than walking sticks, walkers, wheelchairs, and stair lifts – typically classified as "assistive devices" – and can include everything from automobiles, to public transport, to rock salt, security systems, special shoes, clothing, medication, heaters, and caffeinated beverages. Some elders prefer to be sedentary or home bound, and technologies like reclining chairs and walkers (used mostly as tables) can be used to support this goal as well. Most importantly, nonagenarians creatively utilise a broad range of mobility tools (not always as designers imagine they would be used) to achieve a variety of goals.

For example, Ruth has a self-designed mobility system that includes a variety of technologies, including walkers, a scooter, countertops, rock salt, and a home security system, each with a particular purpose. Her electric scooter is for use outside on the sidewalks, in nice weather. However, Ruth needs someone to bring it outside (down a few stairs) for her to use it, so it typically sits in her dark sitting room, covered. Her indoor walker moves with her, but not everywhere. Because she inhabits a compact area on the ground floor of her home, she relies on counters and walls for leverage when navigating halls and the kitchen. However, when she needs to leave the house, she must walk a distance to the back door, and relies on walker #1 to get there. She leaves one walker at the top of the back staircase, and at the bottom stands her walker #2, waiting for her. Walker #2 goes with Ruth when she must leave the house for doctor's appointments. In the winter, Ruth keeps a bucket of rock salt near her back door and scatters the salt on the icy concrete before stepping outside. A few steps (on the salt) with the help of the walker and she can reach the door of the car waiting to drive her to her appointment. Together her walkers are "absolutely necessary" as "another pair of legs" without which Ruth believes she would fall. Finally, Ruth says she would never leave the house without operating her home security system, including a variety of locks and a security alarm; these assuage her fears and assure her that everything will be the same when she returns.

Walkers can serve a variety of purposes. After losing her balance while walking in her neighbourhood this past year, Alice relies on her walker to navigate her home and beyond. She calls her red walker her "saviour" because it allows her to continue to "get out and around". This device is primarily used for mobility assurance, balance, and movement, but it also doubles as a key piece of furniture and storage space. Whether the walker is being actively used or not, it is always nearby and Alice's purse is always draped over the side. Florence is even better prepared, storing her flashlight, a chequebook, and pocketbook on the walker shelf. She also hangs her life support remote health monitoring device over the side. Since Florence spends most of the day in her recliner resting her sore back with the walker at her side, the walker is more table space than mobility device. In this way the walker ironically enables Florence to (primarily) avoid ambulatory discomfort, and support her sedentary lifestyle.

Mary lives with her husband on the second floor of a "walkup" (an apartment building with no elevator) downtown. They use walking canes to steady themselves on the outside stairs and then once inside, her husband uses a stair lift to get up to the floor they inhabit. Together these assistive devices enable them to continue to live downtown, in the same building where Mary's husband housed his dental practice 40 years ago. Mary says she dislikes anything that makes her dependent, but she uses a walking cane to prevent falls. "It gives me the feeling that maybe I'll be okay". Likewise, she says she uses the stair lift when she has morning stiffness and when she has to carry groceries up, but prefers to walk most of the time. Mary is able to approach these mobility technologies as an option for comfort, security, and health. Interestingly, when grandchildren and neighbours visit, these technologies take on new meanings: the stair lift becomes a fun ride for all ages and the cane becomes a toy walking stick.

Mary, Shana, and Julia drive their own cars, mostly during the day and on short familiar routes. For Julia the car is a crucial component in her life that allows her to remain engaged in activities; a way to "get with people" at church, with her book group, and over meals. It is a way to access the social networks that sustain her. However, she fears driving at night, admitting that she gets scared, and lost, and "driveways get confused with streets". Shana, a committed gardener, says she must continue to drive her station wagon to pick up new plants at the nursery. Alice, who does not drive, keeps her 1970s era car in the garage, available to anyone who will drive it, including a driver she hires to take her shopping, on picnics, and to medical appointments. She holds out hope that someday, when her vision improves, she will be back driving. For her and Mary access to a car symbolises years of independence and self-sufficiency. This can still be achieved, in part, with a hired driver who operates the women's cars on their terms.

Anna and Dorothy depend on walking to get to most places they need to visit. Each highly values her active lifestyle, and depends on various technologies to stay consistent with her exercise routines. Neither is interested in elder-specific mobility devices, nor do they need them. Instead, they depend on transport options, hot beverages, and special fabrics and materials to stay warm, comfortable, and confident. Taking the bus and then walking to the community swimming pool enables Anna to "see sides of my city I have never seen before". Anna then relies on her swimsuit and shower cap for regular exercise in the indoor pool (in all seasons). Similarly, Dorothy swears by her "beloved Yaktrax", special shoes that grip the ice, as well as a full-length insulated coat, to feel secure on a winter day's walk.

Several nonagenarians mentioned the importance of heaters, medication, and hot caffeinated beverages to help them to get moving and participate in healthy activities. For Anna, a hot cup of coffee warms and energises her before her pool exercise class. Similarly, Ruth depends on a routine that combines strong hot tea, over-the-counter pain relievers, and a heated bathroom to loosen her joints and get moving in the mornings. These technologies then facilitate their mobility as they intend it.

"My Collection of Handy Gadgets": Staying in Touch, Feeling Alive

The telephone is the top technology that elders rely on, particularly women who are taught to value social connection. For the nonagenarians with whom I spoke, the telephone holds instrumental and symbolic meanings associated with mortality, overcoming loneliness, coordinating care, and staying in touch with family and friends. Everyone agrees about the importance of this technology. Nonagenarians talked about the telephone being a primary tool in case of a personal emergency; yet they also referred to it as a reminder of one's own mortality as well as that of one's friends and loved ones. Many associate a ringing phone with the possibility of news of another friend or family member who is gone. All of these women come from an era when telephone use was rare; it was utilised primarily to convey important news. After receiving a call about the death of a dear friend, Alice commented that when it comes to her "collection of handy gadgets", including calculators, timers, a CD player, a walker, a television, and a computer, "[T]he telephone… is probably the most important thing because it means life and death".

At the same time, elders actively use the telephone as a tool for staying connected, to feel part of something larger than oneself, to feel needed, and to maintain friendships particularly in the context of limited mobility. Without the ability to interact with others, all these women would experience isolation in their own homes in magnified ways. Alice points out that social relationships and health motivations tend to underlie technology use. She says, "The only real necessity beyond food, drink and shelter is friendship, and if technology can enable this, it can be important". She goes on to say that many of her friends are either deceased or unable to leave their homes. Staying in touch with friends who are housebound requires regular use of the telephone.

Alice and others find that cordless phones can be crucial for maintaining social networks as well as for coordinating self-care. Having a telephone nearby provides assurance that emergency service providers can be reached. Doctors' offices, pharmacies, care providers, and drivers can be reached by phone. Alice jokes that if the phone rings a long time, this means she has left it in the bathroom again. Dorothy has a strategy to avoid this; she never lets her cordless telephone leave her side. Dorothy has a special purse for her telephone that she carries with her throughout the day. She developed this strategy after she learned the hard way, having fallen during the night far from the telephone.

Communications technologies are a key tool for those ageing in place, serving as medical assistive technology as well as a familiar communication tool. Old women's uses of technologies are in part informed by fears of being injured and left helpless. In addition to phones, remote communication tools may be purchased by elders, and these can be associated with very different social meanings. Alice tells of how she begins and ends her day by pressing the button on her Lifeline communication device "to let them know I'm OK". This detached health monitoring is perfect for Alice, who prefers to keep most medical technology at bay, but also feels reassured that if she needed help, this device would dispatch it. The machine also helps to order her day. However, this technology can become intrusive. When Alice had to leave town unexpectedly, she left a note on her door explaining the situation in case anyone checked on her. When she returned she realised that an emergency unit had been dispatched, and had ransacked her home in the process of trying to locate her.

While Alice and Florence pay for a phone-based health monitoring program called Lifeline Medical Alert in their urban area, the majority of nonagenarians create their own grassroots health monitoring networks and avoid the monthly bills associated with remote monitoring. For example, every morning several neighbours in a rural village check in on one another. Joanne calls Carol at 8 am. Carol then calls Dorothy. If for some reason someone does not answer, the next step is to make a visit. Dorothy admits that this calling network has saved her life several times. Recently, a friend helped her to install an amplified phone ringer to ensure that she hears the phone. Rose relies on an evening phone check-in with a friend who always asks if she needs anything. For Ruth, who is almost completely home-bound (with many days spent in bed), a ringing telephone is a reminder that she is alive. When a friend calls, she frequently tells him or her, "Your call reminds me that I am alive, that I am not forgotten".

Phone communication offers a sense of continuity across the lifecourse for women like Ruth and Rose for whom friendship and motherhood have become synonymous with quality of life, and even life itself. Regular telephone calls offer countless benefits beyond this: a reminder that someone cares; a routine that helps to order a day; a sense of participation in the outside world; and a feeling of security. Most importantly, perhaps, communication technologies including amplifiers, cordless phones, and lifeline devices, in combination with nonagenarians' creative approaches to monitoring and staying in touch (e.g. phone trees and phone purses), have enabled ageing in place for most study participants.

"Have You Seen My Apparatus?" Using Machines to Foster Intellectual Growth

While the telephone is crucial for health, elders incorporate a range of other communications technologies, including computers, televisions, and radios, into self-care routines and meaning making. These tools not only help them stay connected and in control, but also help to foster intellectual growth and, by association, the health benefits that scientists now associate with brain stimulation.

Despite her daily reliance on the telephone, Dorothy says the computer is the one machine she could not live without. She uses the computer not only for email correspondence, but also for typing and storing her memoirs, engaging in translation work (as a favour to academic friends), and monitoring her finances. She explains:

> I even write my checks on the computer. Nobody else in the village does this, I don't think. They may not know about it. I think it is wonderful. It helps me because sometimes I don't know if 2 and 2 is 4 or 22! So this way I can see what I'm working with (Dorothy).

Not only does the computer provide Dorothy with a steady hand and a clear budget, but it also reinforces her reputation as a technogenarian in her community, a reputation of which she is proud.

Ruth stares at a screen every day, but it is not a computer. Because her eyes are poor, she relies on a machine that helps her read. It magnifies the text of each book page and projects it onto a large screen, from which she reads. Ruth explains that she has been reading since age five, but now she cannot read normally. She lost a retina in the concentration camp, and so she has only one good eye. "Have you seen my apparatus?" she asks. She walks me into her reading room, pointing out a small television-like machine on a desk. She points to the power cord, plugged into the wall, then carefully turns on the monitor and the mouse-like "reader", and moves it on the page of a Jewish community newsletter to show me how she reads with the help of the machine. Nearby on the twin bed is a stack of reading material, including holiday cards, business cards, newspapers, and hardbound books. Ruth's reading machine helps her to be both involved in her community and in control of her life, as well as to escape. She uses this technology to keep up with a broad range of personal business. At the same time, she uses the machine to enable her to escape from her immediate life and pain, into her favourite fiction books. "I would be dead without the apparatus," she says.

All the nonagenarians in my sample incorporate televisions and radios into their lives in various ways. For many, watching or listening to the news is a way to feel connected to community and history; many associate this technology with family tradition. Some emphasised particular programming that they choose to consume. Alice never misses listening to the city mayor discuss local issues on a weekly radio program. Ruth has always listened to music to lighten her mood. Others watch the local news to stay in touch with the world around them.

For Lillian and her husband, television (movie) time represents something they can look forward to in the evenings. Lillian associates this time and technology with romance and companionship. She says:

> I am so in love with this man... Every night Bernie picks out something for us to watch. So we see a movie or something else – we have full cable. So that is great fun. We like the romances, they are so wonderful (Lillian).

Alice and Shana utilise public television programming to learn new things. Alice commented, "I saw the poet laureate on Charlie Rose [interview show] so I got this book out to get more information on her. Very interesting poetry!" Similarly, Shana recalled, "I watched Julia Child on public television – she lived to age 93! She reinforced my love of cooking". In these examples, we see how technology creates a sense of social engagement, ranging from a romantic evening to exposure to new written works or ways of ageing.

Similarly, Anna is always looking for a new project and television helps her with this. Because she has a particular interest in successful women in society, Anna has incorporated the evening news with Katie Couric into her routine:

> I'm following the career of Katie Couric. She got the interview with the pilot, I saw. You know, the Hudson River landing – just a few weeks ago. A big triumph for Katie! And I appreciate her salary – five million a year. That's a sizeable salary (Anna).

Florence's recliner faces the television and a flashing photo frame with family pictures. She says she is content to watch television to pass the time. But she has grown tired of the repetition both on television and in her photo frame, commenting "I've seen it all on TV. They are all repeats. And the pictures, I've memorised them all". In contrast to the others, the imaging technologies that Florence depends upon for stimulation have failed to deliver what she desires.

In nonagenarians' daily lives, communication technologies can provide a respite from loneliness and boredom, and/or or intensify these emotions. They can symbolise mortality and life, stimulation or stasis, isolation or connection, and continuity and change. Elders like Ruth, Dorothy, Anna, Alice, and Lillian use technologies like the radio, the computer, the reading machine, and the television to maintain lifelong continuity, control and connectedness, mental health and wellbeing. As with the telephone, each uses these devices to extend their participation with the outside world, particularly in the context of compromised health and mobility.

Fun with Sauté Pans and Slow Cookers: Creatively Nourishing Oneself

For many nonagenarians, kitchen technologies such as kettles, slow cookers, stoves, and ovens are ey instruments for self-care. They are also tools that can elicit creativity, connection, expression, health, and even exciting new challenges. Such tools, many of which existed in the kitchens they inhabited as children or newlyweds, provide continuity over the course of a day and a life.

Shana, who was deboning a chicken just as I arrived for an interview, pointed to her kitchen as one of her favourite spaces in her home, and the place in which she starts her day. Ruth also begins her day in the kitchen, and described how turning the kettle on in the morning helps to "psych [herself] up" and face the day. She explains, "First thing I do is turn on the kettle and get two tea bags – I need a hot strong tea to start the day. Then I go and wash myself". For both of these women, preparing food and drink was akin to preparing oneself for what lay ahead. Kitchens and kitchen technologies can be extensions of self, family, and lifelong routines.

For Anna, a self-described "diet freak" in response to being "robust" as a child, a specific food preparation routine (involving a slow cooker) allows her to maintain her weight and figure. Dorothy, someone who is always looking for a new challenge, has recently discovered that stovetop food preparation can be a creative process that can be novel, suspenseful, and rewarding:

> Cooking is a completely creative thing. With fresh vegetables and chicken and fish, and there's so much you can do with those things! In the summer I go to the farmers market and in the winter I go on Fridays with a friend to the store. And I always get too much! But it is the process, the fun, and looking forward to eating it. Sometimes [what I sauté; in the pan] it turns out great, sometimes not (Dorothy).

Julia describes how kitchen technologies enable her and a homeless friend to eat together; each warming up frozen or canned foods in the microwave for dinner:

> She brings food – she's one of those who goes to the dumpster – you know that grocery stores have to throw out out-of-date things, so she gets good quality frozen meals and brings that with her. She eats

with me and offers it, but I don't take it. I just warm up canned soup or something. But I enjoy her company! (Julia).

Several nonagenarians mentioned the electric slow cooker as their favourite kitchen technology, perhaps because of its ease of use; it is difficult to burn a meal or make a mistake using this technology. When I first met Alice she talked about the importance of her slow cooker in terms of ease when it comes to making hot healthy meals for herself. She had just replaced her "tired" 35-year-old model with a new "beautiful" one. With changes in economic markets as well as her energy level and eyesight, Alice now attaches slightly different meanings to this technology:

> My new fun project is to create meals that are as cheap as possible, and healthy. Like rice and beans. I'd like to make large portions that I can freeze for the future as well. That way I can save money and time and work on other things, like taxes (Alice).

This section reveals how lifelong gender roles and expectations continue to organise elders' lives and technology use in old age. Social scripts that nonagenarians attach to kitchen technologies go well beyond health and food preparation. Kitchen technologies are used here to aid in achieving a wide range of goals including saving money, building connections, achieving a particular diet, waking up, carrying on family traditions, and expressing and nourishing oneself. This list of daily goals conveys the multidimensionality of self-care and health in old age. Ironically, while kitchen, mobility, and communication technologies are central to daily meaning making for women nonagenarians focused on health and autonomy, medical technologies rarely enter into discussions about self-care.

"Newfangled Medical Things": Monitoring One's Body and Opting Out

Pharmaceuticals and over-the-counter medications are generally associated with health and wellbeing. However, paying attention to the meanings nonagenarians attach to medical use and non-use can illuminate how these biotechnologies are positioned as an array of techniques elders use to practice self-care. When asked about their medications, nonagenarians tend to say very little, suggesting that biotechnology has limited symbolic importance in their daily routines. Lillian remarked on the sheer number of pills that she takes on a daily basis. Julia commented on the pretty colours, saying,

> I take a mass of pills. Eight pills a day. I have four in the morning and they are yellow, white, blue and pink. So pretty! And I take the ones that make me lightheaded at night. I guess I have a bad heart.

Others were not aware of exactly how many pills they took in a typical day, and what they were for.

Ruth and Lillian spoke of medications that are meaningful to them in large part because they are tied to their own history or family tradition. They spoke of these biomedical technologies as a way to neutralise the body, to balance things out. Interestingly, both utilised biomedical products that were widely available (over-the-counter and by prescription) with long histories of use in the United States:

> In the morning, to get going I take two tea bags – very hot strong tea… I take my daily laxative – I have a weak stomach from the war, we all do, from not eating. And I take my extra strength Tylenol. I use this [Velcro wrist support] so that I will not move my wrist. I did not want the surgery. So I use these instead (Ruth).
>
> Nitro… it is such a nothing pill, and I've been taking it forever. But [when I asked for it in the hospital] the doctor didn't give it to me, and that's when I had my heart attack. Why wouldn't he do this? My grandmother took this. I still remember her sticking it under her tongue, and I'd ask what it was and she gave me the sign with her finger like "wait" and then tell me, "That's Nitroglycerin". It makes me feel better. I always keep it by my bed at night (Lillian).

Pharmaceutical technologies that are linked to family and personal history, like Ruth's laxatives, which she has taken since leaving the concentration camp at the end of WWII, and Lillian's nitroglycerin tablets, which she witnessed being taken by her grandmother, can be added to the list of tools that help to provide continuity across the lifecourse. However, aspects of medical technology that are unfamiliar can be unwelcome. Lillian, Alice, and Mary spoke critically about the medical profession and over-use of medical technologies in their own lives:

> I talk with [a friend] about old age and what they do to old people – medically I mean – these newfangled medical things. She told me she saw someone in the hospital, 83, and she was in pain, and they were giving her something so she could live five months. We both agree, we don't want any part of that. We'd rather be comfortable. To me, the eye [injections] are worth doing. I can try that again, and see if it works. So far not. But that other stuff – I won't take it. It is for the doctors, not for us. Their pride. That's why I'm not going to a nursing home. I need to be in control – that's the big thing (Alice).

> Recently I have been having TIAs [transient ischemic attacks]… they come on quickly and then disappear. Even though I feel fine afterwards, I go to the emergency room to be checked. Each time I am subjected to a full day of tests, and sometimes they keep me overnight to observe. This is frustrating, because I know I am fine and really I just want to be home. Then last week my gynecologist suggested a precautionary measure – a biopsy –to make sure I didn't have ovarian cancer. Was this really necessary? I don't know. I didn't really want to go, but [my daughter] wouldn't let me pass on it. Afterwards I was very uncomfortable and had heavy bleeding for weeks. It reminded me of the surgery I had –that created more stress on my body, in new places. I just don't know about all of this (Mary).

In this section, nonagenarians are negotiating medicine in their daily lives, making decisions about both use and non-use of medical technology, revealing a spectrum of meaning making around biotechnology. For these women it comes down to self-determination and control – are they able to make decisions about their own care, or is their care determined by others? For Alice, having a choice about a medical procedure for her eyes fits with her self-care ethic. In contrast, being "subjected" to medical surveillance and care can be akin to being in a nursing home where a patient retains very little self-determination, a fate Alice and Mary both describe as "worse than death".

CONCLUSION

This study contributes to research that explores how old women creatively utilise and adapt everyday technologies to construct meaningful lives. Nonagenarians can teach us how everyday technologies can become technologies of ageing; instruments of continuity, control, and health; or just the opposite. As we have seen, creative use of technology underscores self-determination and nonagenarians' ability to do self-care mostly on their own, even as some are thwarted by techno-solutions.

This research contributes to our understanding of health, ageing, and gender as agentic; as actively "done" in day-to-day life in combination with technology use. When Alice is engaged in her daily slow-cooker food preparation routine, she is accomplishing womanhood and wellbeing in her active use of technology, and in the context of a life of women's work nourishing others. Nonagenarians in this sample push on scholarship in gender studies and science and technology studies to reveal how the active accomplishment of gender is technology-based just as it is age- and health-focused.

Many women nonagenarians have developed creative approaches to technology use and self-care, and utilise these daily in their final years of life. These techniques include designing purses for phones, staging walkers at key places, using reading machines to connect and escape, creating telephone monitoring networks among friends, sewing items to enable comfort at home, using computers to keep track of household finances, and utilising simple kitchen technologies to create affordable healthy meals. In these ways, nonagenerians further their lifelong expertise in using technologies that assist with care work and the co-ordination of routine mundane tasks. This expertise, now taken for granted after years of practice, comes in handy when it comes to food preparation, health monitoring, connecting with others, and creating and maintaining a home over many years.

As communities include more individuals ageing in place, all elders must be able to meet their own health needs through access to care *and* technology. While much political rhetoric focuses on access to care issues, key technologies like telephone and television services, as well as other communications technologies, kitchen technologies, and mobility technologies can be "the difference between life and death". And they can also be costly. Age-based technology discounts and coverage are crucial to ensuring access to these "health" technologies. Policies aimed at assisting elders as they pursue health, community, and changing forms of independence need to address the escalating costs of communication technologies in the home.

These old women's lives reveal that perhaps the answer to the question about an ageing populace, home support, and health is not simply new biotechnologies, assistive technologies, or design strategies, but a renewed emphasis on elder agency and an awareness of existing technology repertoires and daily strategies to emphasise continuity and autonomy. After all, despite all the emphasis on successful ageing, elders in this project ultimately aim to achieve something more akin to comfortable ageing that emphasises ease.

For these nonagenarians, a self-care ethic is about accomplishing and maintaining a broad sense of health that involves comfort, confidence, continuity, autonomy, *and* social capital in the context of old age. The real power of technology, as many of these nonagenarian women reveal, is in the implicit social relationships and other manifestations of humanity that underlie our use of tools and devices. As we have seen, self-efficacy and ageing in place are realistic goals when technology can be used to reveal and reinforce social networks, ensure continuity across the lifecourse (when it comes to everyday routines and roles), and enable intellectual participation and physical wellbeing.

68

Could Different Cultures Teach Us Something about Dementia?

Richard Gunderman and Lily Wolf

Picture two different families, each dealing with a diagnosis of dementia in one of its members. In one case, the patient is a retired executive, whose family tries as long as possible to keep the diagnosis secret, relying primarily on professional caregivers and eventually a nursing home. In another case, the patient is a grandmother. As soon as the diagnosis is suspected, her family pulls together, bringing her into their home and surrounding her with affection.

These two approaches to dementia reflect very different attitudes toward the disease. One regards it as an irreversible neurologic condition associated with considerable stigma, a problem best left to health professionals and kept out of public view. While not denying that dementia is a medical condition, the other seizes on it as an opportunity to draw together around a loved one in need, giving family members not a secret to keep but an opportunity to care.

A DISEASE OF PATIENTS AND THEIR FAMILIES

Dementias touch many lives. For example, the most common dementia, Alzheimer's disease, currently afflicts 5.7 million Americans and is expected to afflict 14 million by 2050. This increase partly mirrors population growth. But because risk increases with age, the rise also reflects our success in battling other causes of death, such as heart disease and stroke, enabling people to live longer. And the effects of the disease are not confined to patients; 16.1 million Americans now provide uncompensated care to dementia patients.

If you asked a physician to define dementia, most of us would probably describe it as a neurodegenerative disorder marked by declining cognitive abilities and memory. While this account is true as far as it goes, there is a problem: attacking most types of dementia as strictly biological entities has largely failed to advance our ability to diagnose and treat it. In the case of Alzheimer's disease, definitive diagnosis still requires a biopsy, and new drugs to prevent, retard, or reverse it have proved disappointing.

Gunderman, Richard and Lily Wolf. "Could Different Cultures Teach Us Something about Dementia?" *The Conversation*, August 17, 2018.

A Cultural Perspective

Perhaps the time has come to expand our thinking about dementia to encompass not only cellular but cultural perspectives. Our society needs to recognize that dementia is not only a brain disorder of the person suffering from it but also a social disorder that can be understood in a variety of different ways. In other contexts, such disorders tend to be viewed in light of a larger circle of social relationships and cultural traditions. All generalizations must be qualified, but we have much to learn from other cultures.

In Japan, for example, to age well is not only to avoid contracting diseases but also to maintain a circle of family and friends right up to the moment when we breathe our last. Being of sound mind and body means continuing to exert ourselves both mentally and physically, remaining deeply invested in our personal relationships and receiving help from and helping others. So long as we continue to enrich others' lives, we can remain "whole" in ways that exceed the mere absence of a medical diagnosis.

A large segment of traditional Chinese culture tends to see such matters similarly. Confucianism places a premium on family, and the decline of cognitive capacities of those who have led long and full lives can be seen not as the onset of a disease but as an opportunity for friends and family to express how much they care. Assuming increasing responsibility for an aging loved one represents an opportunity to show how strong the family really is.

The Hindu culture of India also prizes the opportunity to care for parents. What Americans tend to regard as a lamentable medical condition can be seen as a part of life's natural cycle and the passage into a second childhood. The emphasis is not on the stigma of dementia, but rather on a withdrawal from worldly affairs to focus on other more essential matters. When an older person begins to show such signs, it is time for a natural transfer of authority to younger members of the family.

Seeing Dementia Anew

Viewing dementia from the standpoint of other cultures can help Americans see it with fresh eyes and re-pose fundamental questions that lie at its heart. What, for example, is a person, and how is personhood situated in the larger context of family and community? How does such a condition relate to what it means to be a good person and lead a good life? To what degree does dementia fracture us and what are the possibilities that it could bring us closer together?

The point of such a cultural approach is not to argue that biomedical accounts of dementia are fundamentally wrong. In virtually any disease state, but especially with a condition such as dementia, the experience of patients and families involves social, moral, and even spiritual perspectives, no less than biological ones. Perhaps because of our high regard for self-sufficiency and independence, dementia in the United States tends to be relatively stigmatized.

Conceiving of dementia in different terms could offer new opportunities for prevention and treatment. Suppose, for example, that we Americans viewed it in terms similar to physical fitness. If we do not utilize our mental, physical, and social capacities, they will tend to dwindle – use it or lose it. However, if we remain active and challenged in each of these spheres, contributing where we can to enrich the lives of others, we can ease the strain of dementia in our lives.

To be sure, healthy neurons require adequate rest, nutrition, and even medical care. But the health of a person is more than the functioning of cells. People also need opportunities to put abilities to the test, connect with others, and lead lives that make a real contribution. If we tend not only to our neurons but also to our intellects, characters, and relationships, there is good reason to think that we can lighten dementia's burden and make the most of the opportunities to care for those living with it.

69

The Perils and Pleasures of Aging

How Women's Sexualities Change across the Life Course

Lisa R. Miller

Aging is constructed as negative in US society, but hostile attitudes toward older adults are fairly recent. Ageism is now rampant insofar as older adults are viewed with pity, fear, disgust, and condescension. However, it was not until the late nineteenth century that American society began to view late adulthood as a period characterized by decline, dependence, weakness, and illness. Following the institutionalization of retirement around the age of 65, older adults began to be viewed as sick, useless, unattractive, and incompetent. A tendency to view late adulthood as a period of decline, thus, does not universally exist across varying historical contexts. Further, epidemiological and demographic transitions occurred during the nineteenth century, as improvements in medicine, hygiene, and nutrition contributed to a decrease in mortality rates and longer life expectancy. A natural outcome of longer life expectancy is that older adults began to experience decline, chronic illness, and disease. Consequently, medical practitioners and gerontologists alike became preoccupied with overcoming negative effects of aging, such as decline and loss.

Until recently, researchers were almost exclusively preoccupied with documenting negative effects of aging, including diminished physical and mental health, chronic illness and disability, retirement, and poverty. Consequently, little attention has been given to whether women's lives also improve as they age. Thus, in this chapter, I offer women a voice on how their romantic and sexual lives improve as they age.

SEX, RELATIONSHIPS, AND PARTNERING ACROSS THE LIFE COURSE

Aging and life course perspectives are used to explain how people's sexual experiences unfold over time. Biological evidence suggests that people's sex lives change as they age. Prior research documents that people experience a decline in their frequency of sexual activity, due to hormonal changes (DeLamater 2012). Erectile dysfunction may impede the occurrence of vaginal-penile penetration, leading to a decrease in sexual intercourse among both women and men. Following menopause, women experience lubrication problems, thinning of the vaginal walls, and pain during sex, which also impact the frequency of

Miller, Lisa R. "The Perils and Pleasures of Aging: How Women's Sexualities Change across the Life Course." *The Sociological Quarterly* 60, no. 3 (2019): 371–396.

vaginal-penile intercourse. However, studies also show that menopause causes women to view sex as an issue of pleasure instead of reproduction (Dillaway 2012; Gott and Hinchliff 2003).

WOMEN'S SEXUALITIES AND CHANGE OVER TIME

There is a growing body of scholarship on women's sexualities, although most of this research focuses on adolescent and emerging adult women. Adolescent girls have difficulty expressing sexual desire, in part, because they experience shame and guilt for doing so. Moreover, peer culture plays a large role in the regulation of gendered and sexual norms in adolescence and emerging adulthood, potentially constraining women's sexual choices. It is possible that women have more positive sexual experiences by midlife, namely increased sexual agency, sexual assertiveness, and sexual pleasure. Women are less likely to experience peer pressure in midlife and late adulthood, suggesting that they are able to make less constrained choices about dating and sexuality. Women potentially relinquish some of the shame and guilt associated with sex, which may result in sex becoming more pleasurable in midlife and late adulthood. Further, aging offers people opportunities for self-reflection, which may help women better understand their sexual desires and what most pleases them. Sexual experiences are cumulative insofar as earlier positive and negative sexual experiences shape future sexual behaviors.

METHODS

Data come from 39 life story interviews with single, heterosexual women ages 35–91. I only interviewed single participants because I was interested in examining *current* experiences with finding new romantic and sexual partners. Additionally, I intentionally include women from a wide range of ages in this chapter. Participants were grouped with either middle-aged (35–54 years) or older adult (55–91 years) women. Further, I confine my analysis to heterosexual women because their experiences with dating and sex are likely gendered and distinct from queer women's experiences. Indeed, prior research finds that heterosexual relationships and sexual interactions are rife with gender inequality and difference.

The mean age for the sample is 56. In addition, 56 percent of participants are between the ages of 35 and 54, while 44 percent of participants are over the age of 55. All participants reside in the Midwest. The sample is predominantly (95 percent) white; 2 percent are Asian, and 3 percent multiracial. The sample is also highly educated: 69 percent hold at least a bachelor degree. Twenty-six percent are never married, 53 percent are divorced/separated, and 21 percent are widowed. Sixty-nine percent of participants are parents. Sixty-two percent consider themselves religious, while 38 percent consider themselves non-religious.

FINDINGS

Women highlight several changes in their romantic and sexual lives, including lower odds of partnering as they age. Unique barriers arise in midlife and late adulthood, including a small dating pool and caregiving responsibilities that impede their ability to romantically and sexually partner. Thus, the number of recent partners that middle-aged and older adult women report having is small. Another change reported is that women feel more disadvantaged in the dating and sexual marketplace compared with men, as the latter are able to date down in age. Finally, the last major change reported is higher quality of sex as a consequence of aging. Women, specifically, note that aging increases comfort with and openness to sex, sexual assertiveness, and sexual satisfaction.

Small Dating Pool

Consistent with prior research, women report that the dating pool shrinks as they age. Indeed, few women have recently gone on a date or had a sexual encounter. This idea is especially salient when Jane (43, never married) remarks:

> It's like, it's been an abyss is what it's been. I haven't met anyone in ages … and, so, I'm always hoping that whenever I go to a party, or I go to a talk, or I go wherever, I'm always looking, like, "Oh," – looking at the hands – "is that person wearing a ring? Is that person wearing a ring?" It's been abysmal. It's like a desert. I'm like a cartoon and the person crawling in tattered clothes towards water. It's abysmal.

Jane is painfully aware of how small the dating pool is, not unlike other women. Relatedly, heterosexual women report that the dating pool is small because there are few eligible bachelors, and most men their age are already married. Other middle-aged women highlight a lack of places to meet potential romantic and sexual partners.

> Because of this difficulty meeting partners, middle-aged women often reveal that online dating was commonly used and perhaps required; older adult women, however, rarely reported online dating experiences. Middle-aged women remarked that online dating made it easier to meet people, but that the nature of online dating does not facilitate successful romantic relationships. A common complaint was that they already knew too much about the person before meeting them, which tended to stifle conversation on the first date. For example, Mikala (39, never married) expresses:
> Because you have to go through so much to get those dates, especially eHarmony … By the time you actually meet the person, first off, all of your small talk is gone because you've already emailed it back and forth to each other. And secondly, it's like six weeks down the road, and you're like, "Who are you again, and what? Oh, right." And then when it doesn't work, you're like, 'Oh my God, we spent six weeks setting this up, and in five minutes we're like, "Eh?"

Thus, investments in online dating rarely yielded successful returns or paid off.

Women over the age of 55 similarly reveal that they did not know where to meet men at their age; in their view, this was due to men passing away earlier in life and a sex-ratio imbalance in retirement communities. Consistent with prior literature, middle-aged and older adult women alike attributed their singlehood to exclusionary beauty standards and men's ability to date down in age (Calasanti and Slevin 2001). Francine (51, divorced) notes: "for men, the dating pool is much bigger. You can be a 55-year-old that can conceivably date a 30- or 35-year-old. Women, not so much. We have a shorter shelf life." Similarly, Ida (56, divorced) remarks that men her age are looking for "arm candy" and women "20 years younger." In sum, middle-aged and older adult women face exclusion.

Caregiving Responsibilities

One major life transition faced by women is the inheritance of caregiving responsibilities, which often impeded women's ability to date. Single motherhood, specifically, surfaced in the 30s and 40s, resulting in the prioritization of childcare over dating. Janet (38, divorced, parent) remarks,

> Finding childcare to go out on a date is … weird. What if it [the date] wants to go longer than a couple hours? … You have to plan so far in advance that it's a job. Dating becomes … a full-time job itself.

Middle-aged participants, thus, believe they have little energy and time to date. Likewise, women reported facing another major life transition in their 50s and 60s: the inheritance of responsibilities to care for an ill or dying family member. Due to these responsibilities, women again emphasize a lack of time to date.

Further, caregiving is at odds with middle-aged women's ability to date and sexually partner because it is viewed as incompatible with mothering. In this way, women express role conflict. Indeed, women express resistance to their children seeing them as sexual beings and thus often forbade their partners in the early stages of dating from staying the night with them. Shelly (48, divorced, parent) expresses:

> When that husband left … My son was entering puberty, and we were both dealing with this huge loss. He was my number one priority. [I] was helping him get through all this. There's a guy I met a

year later. I remember him asking, he said, "I'm coming to town. I'm coming with a friend" – he lives an hour away – and he said, "Can we stay at your house?" I remember telling him, "Absolutely not. Are you kidding? I have a 15-year-old son. This is his place. I can't bring a man in here." That's been a tension, too.

Similar to Shelly, other women note that sexual activity is off-limits if their children are home. Women express reservations about having their children and partners interact with one another, due to an internal desire to set a "good example" for their children. Barbara (46, divorced) remarks,

> I would kind of make it as a joke that my children aren't going to grow up with a series of uncles or Mommy's friends … Plus, my daughter was 14. So, personally, I thought I was really setting a precedent, really showing her by example. I tried to set a good example.

Implicit here is an expectation that mothers model "good" sexual behavior for teen daughters, as a way to avoid normalizing sexual behavior. Additionally, women often reduce interaction between potential partners and children to protect their children; some fear that children will get hurt if a break-up occurs, while others want to ensure that men are responsible and have good character before introducing them to their children.

Increased Comfort and Openness with Sex

Despite reporting negative consequences of aging, women also indicate that their sex lives improve as they age. For example, a major change reported is that women become more comfortable with sex as they age. Carol (58, divorced) remarks, "We're more in tune with our sexuality as we get older." She elaborates that she is more open to having sex now than she was as a younger woman. Here, we see that Carol understands her sexual self better with age. Other participants attribute this increased comfort with sex to growing confidence with age. Amanda (35, never married) offers the following explanation for changes experienced:

> Well, yeah, I think in the same vein that I'm confident and probably enjoying it more. And I really think there are things that I'm good at and know how to do. … Definitely remember times in my 20s, even when I wasn't with someone for a while – like in that 7-year relationship – I remember points where doing certain things, like being on top during sex, being very nervous during that: "How am I supposed to do this, and where am I supposed to put my hands?" Really overthinking it. Whereas now I'm much more like, I haven't done everything, but I feel fine about it…

Amanda's remarks reveal that the accumulation of sexual experience results in increased sexual confidence. She later also attributes her growing sexual confidence to becoming more comfortable with her body and knowing herself better.

Although penetrative sex was the predominant form of sexual activity for women when they were younger, women find themselves open to trying new sexual activities with age. Dora (56, divorced) describes this increased openness:

> I think, too, as I've gotten older, I think I've let myself become more open to things, doing things, let's put it that way. Then it became more pleasurable. Like I said, becoming more open to doing things in different ways. Not being stuck in one type of intercourse. … Oral sex and different positions and foreplay, games, toys, all kinds of things.

Dora emphasizes that that her openness led to increased sexual pleasure. In addition, women experience important turning points that alter their sexual trajectories, consistent with the life course premise that some major life events are influential enough to alter people's life paths. For example, Dorothy (71, separated) describes a sexual relationship she had following divorce. In these encounters, her partner helped her understand that sex can be "fun and enjoyable and pleasurable," primarily because he respected her wishes and desires. Other women similarly report a yearning for sexual exploration after divorce and relationship dissolution. Karen (54, separated) describes how a new partner offered her a sexual exploration opportunity:

> … I only like asked for what I wanted, and I had a willing person to explore that with me. And I can honestly say I – I love that person for that, because it really opened my mind … He had several (sex toys) that he bought … And he showed me how to use them … And I hadn't really investigated that before. And I also had not engaged in anal sex before. I did engage in that with him, but not with his penis. He used a toy. It was a butt plug … And I didn't know what it was before either, and I know what it is now … So, that was something that intensified my pleasure. Yeah, and interestingly enough, in that relationship, I had the most open, honest, true-bone conversations I've ever had about sex and my needs.

The introduction of new sexual partners in midlife and late adulthood offers women an opportunity to explore what pleases them and to try new sexual activities. Because previous marital relationships were typically monogamous, they prevented women from having access to new partners. Thus, divorce and relationship dissolution are turning points because they offer women access to new sexual partners who alter their sexual trajectories.

Women below the age of 35 rarely reported that relationship dissolution altered how they viewed sex, suggesting that this turning point is unique to the experience of middle-aged and older adult women. The acquisition of new partners also suggests that the accumulation of sexual experiences drives women's increased comfort and openness with sex.

Increased Sexual Assertiveness

Analyses of the data also revealed that women, particularly non-parents, became more sexually assertive by their mid-30s and early 40s. Allison (46, never married) remarks,

> As I get older, I'm not shy about asking for what I want. When I was younger, that was certainly, you know, a lot more difficult for me … I still wasn't quite clear what I wanted. And I hit a point where, I mean, the hot guy I just told you about, I'm the one that initiated. Because I knew I wanted it, and I knew it – he made indications that he was receptive, and so I made the first move.

Not only does Allison find herself more likely to initiate sex when older, but she is also less afraid to ask for what she wants sexually. Jackie (59, divorced) echoes this point, asserting that aging and experiencing divorce taught her to stand up for her needs more. Here, women reveal that they find their sexual voice more as they age. Women's narratives again reveal that divorce is a key turning point that alters sexual trajectories because it facilitates greater sexual assertiveness.

Another major change in women's sexualities is that they are more at ease with making decisions regarding sexual activity as they age, including when to give or deny consent. Women note that they are now more likely to say no to sex when it is undesired, and also enforce that answer, compared with when they were younger. Prior scholars argue that adolescent girls are always expected to abstain from sex, placing them in a position where they are unable to make their own decisions regarding sexual matters. Middle-aged women's narratives reveal that they become embodied sexual subjects who now better understand and voice their sexual wants and needs. This embodiment of sexuality suggests that middle-aged women are now able to more freely and enthusiastically consent, a sign that they are engaging in healthier and more consensual sexual encounters at older ages.

Women's ability to voice what they want sexually also offers some evidence that women have more sexual agency in midlife. Some women feel that their sexual choices are less constrained now compared to when they were younger. Karen (54, separated) remarks:

> I don't see anything as taboo anymore. If two people are consensual and they're involved in an intellectual, open, honest relationship, I think that there's nothing to be frightened of in that

situation ... There's nothing to hold you back in your mind, like parents or church or anything, cause it's between you two ... It's just that there's a just a different mindset there for me ... I think I was pretty, pretty hung-up for a long time. And I'm not – I don't feel that way anymore.

Here, Karen's remarks reveal that parents and church are not as likely to constrain the decisions that women make about sex when they get older. Women's ability to relinquish sexual shame provides additional support for the idea that they experience increased sexual agency in midlife.

Increased Sexual Pleasure

Some participants remark that sex is more pleasurable for them at older ages, primarily because reciprocity and mutual pleasure are prioritized. Jane (43, never married) notes,

Sex has changed pretty dramatically for me in that I'm much more comfortable in understanding that it's about my pleasure as well. And I certainly wasn't when I was young ... Sort of when entering into sexual activity, I expect it to be pretty mutually beneficial as opposed to just doing it because somebody else wants it done.

Jane emphasizes that she stood up more for her right to sexual pleasure as she aged.

In addition, some participants suggest that the accumulation of sexual experience helps women shift their focus in sexual interactions from male pleasure to mutual pleasure. Vicky (51, divorced) highlights this shift:

I think it's just, we think, when we're in the bedroom, it's all about us serving men and pleasing them; so, we have to fake it. But as you get older, and you've discovered what does and doesn't work for you, and maybe even had through masturbation, stuff you've learned, things about your body. And when you get older, you just don't feel as inhibited ... The feedback I've gotten is that actually turns them on; they actually like that.

Vicky reveals that the accumulation of sexual experience helps her figure out what most pleases her, lessons she carries with her into future sexual interactions.

Another turning point in women's sexual trajectories is menopause, which typically occurs in their 40s and 50s. Specifically, menopause is one of the mechanisms responsible for increased sexual pleasure. Karen (54, separated) remarks:

I was already all the way through menopause. I went through it very quickly. And so there was this first time outside my marriage in a relationship where I realized ... I can't get pregnant anymore. I don't have to worry about that. And that really gave me a sense of relaxation and freedom, and also to ask more for what I wanted ... I didn't have to worry anymore about, you know, it wasn't about procreation any more; at my age, it's about pleasure.

Karen highlights a shift from procreation to pleasure, as a consequence of menopause. Other postmenopausal women also remark that pregnancy fears no longer serve as barriers to sexual activity and pleasure. Nevertheless, the findings provide mixed evidence for whether menopause causes a higher sex drive, as some women report decreased desires to have sex after menopause.

Cohort and Period Effects

Multiple generations of women are included in the sample, and thus cohort differences in their experiences were detected. A major generational difference is that older adult women are generally less receptive to casual sex than middle-aged women. The sexual experiences that older adult women reported having later in life often occurred within the confines of a monogamous relationship. Women over the age of 65 were especially more likely to oppose premarital and casual sex on moral and religious grounds.

Consistent with earlier studies, older adult women also typically expressed that they desired a companion, but were less willing than middle-aged women to enter a cohabiting, long-term marital relationship. Dorothy (71, separated) eloquently voices a concern raised by many older women:

> I don't know. The biggest part… goes back to my independence. They're not moving into my house. … Just men my age wants to be taken cared of. I believe that's the generation that I'm from where women were taught to take care of them. I don't care to take care of them.

Dorothy's disavowal of cohabiting, long-term relationships is explained by a desire for independence and can be read as a rejection of gender roles in late adulthood. This theme likely represents a generational difference – as many older adult women came of age during a period where marriage, economic dependence on men, and caregiving were generally expected. Thus, many older adult women are experiencing independence outside of marital relationships for the first time in their lives.

A period effect may be responsible for some of the sexual changes that women report – that is, changing sexual cultures may have broadened the array of sexual choices available to women. A period effect may especially help explain why women report increased openness and willingness to try new sexual activities at older ages. Indeed, oral and anal sex are more prevalent today than in decades past. Thus, the prevalence of non-penetrative forms of sex may impact not only the sexual repertoires of younger people, but also those of middle-aged and older people. For example, Jackie (59, divorced) discusses BDSM desires that emerged later in life. She notes,

> There's more possibilities in the culture, maybe, not to have to go by old models … It's possible seeing that in the culture. That's why I say 50 *Shades* was a great thing because there's no other way I would've been able to accept that part of myself and explore it, even to the small extent I have without that.

Recent US popular cultural depictions of BDSM offer Jackie an opportunity to explore sadomasochist desires. Here, we see that Jackie is not attributing the process of aging to these changes, but rather a transformation in the broader culture that opened up new possibilities for sexual exploration.

Likewise, women from varying generations acknowledge that they have more sexual opportunities today. Changing attitudes and beliefs toward women's sexualities may uniformly impact the experiences of women from varying generations. Thus, a period effect may potentially explain why women report more positive sexual experiences at older ages. Although women are much more likely to address aging and the accumulation of life experience as factors responsible for why they experienced changes, changing sexual cultures may also play a role.

DISCUSSION

This chapter used retrospective life story interview data to investigate the positive and negative changes that women experience with dating and sex as they age. Based on empirical evidence, I argue that women's romantic and sexual lives both worsen and improve as they age. Finally, I offer middle-aged and older adult women a much-needed voice in research on dating and sexuality, providing an examination of whether gender expression in the sexual arena looks different in midlife and late adulthood.

Compared with their younger selves, heterosexual women report lower odds of partnering, due to having a smaller pool of available partners. In addition, caregiving responsibilities impact women's ability to partner, a marked difference from earlier life experiences. Middle-aged women note that motherhood is at odds with finding new romantic and sexual partners. Caregiving also limits the amount of time that middle-aged and older adult women have available to date.

Countering these stories of decline, women report positive changes in their sex lives, including increased comfort with sex, sexual assertiveness, and sexual satisfaction as they age. Although the quantity of partnering declines as women age, sex is higher quality when it occurs; this finding has been documented among married women, as well (Lodge and Umberson 2012). Notably, many of the turning points that altered women's sexualities occurred during midlife and the early years of late adulthood.

Importantly, these data reveal that aging has positive consequences on women's sexualities (i.e., increased comfort with sex, sexual assertiveness, and sexual satisfaction with age). Thus, aging is not simply a story of peril; rather, there are pleasures of aging, as well. Accordingly, scholars must examine a wider range of outcomes and measures to further document the ways in which aging positively impacts people's lives.

REFERENCES

Calasanti, Toni M. and Kathleen F. Slevin. 2001. *Gender, Social Inequalities, and Aging*. New York: Altamira Press.

DeLamater, John. 2012. "Sexual Expression in Later Life: A Review and Synthesis." *Journal of Sex Research* 49:125–141. doi:10.1080/00224499.2011.603168.

Dillaway, Heather E. 2012. "Reproductive History as Social Context: Exploring How Women Talk about Menopause and Sexuality at Midlife." In *Sex for Life: From Virginity to Viagra, How Sexuality Changes throughout Our Lives*, edited by Laura M Carpenter and DeLamater John, pp. 217–235. New York, NY: New York University Press.

Gott, Merryn and Sharon Hinchliff. 2003. "How Important Is Sex in Later Life? The Views of Older People." *Social Science and Medicine* 56:1617–1628.

Lodge, Amy C and Debra Umberson. 2012. "All Shook Up: Sexuality of Mid-To-Later Life Married Couples." *Journal of Marriage & Family* 74:428–443.

70

Think You're Not Having Enough Sex? Try Being a Senior in Assisted Living

Elisabeth O. Burgess, Alexis A. Bender, and Christina Barmon

Love is in the air for millions today, but probably not so much for seniors in assisted living facilities. And it may not be for lack of desire.

Over two million American adults are in this position, living in assisted living or in skilled nursing facilities. Need for long-term care services increases with age, and recent estimates suggest that the majority of older Americans will utilize long-term care services at some point in their lives.

Interested in the sexual lives of older adults, we studied life in assisted living facilities and found their rules and practices make it difficult for seniors to develop romantic relationships. Fixing that will require changes in how we view seniors' sexual desires and how these facilities are run.

Adults of all ages have the capacity for and interest in romance, intimacy and sexuality. It might appear that older adults, especially the oldest old, are less interested in sex and less sexually active than younger adults, but sexual behavior and desire involve more than how often people have sex. Multiple social and health barriers can limit opportunities to pursue sexual relationships. For example, limited access to healthy partners because of living arrangements and imbalanced sex ratio diminishes opportunities as we age.

Although assisted living aims to be an environment in which older adults maintain autonomy, independence and control, these goals do not necessarily extend to sexuality. As the baby boomer generation – a generation that came of age during the sexual revolution – ages and more older adults utilize assisted living, it will be important to create specific policies and training regarding sexuality. This holds true for following generations, too.

As researchers who study gerontology, we wanted to examine whether seniors' sex lives were being respected and protected.

We wanted to know more about opportunities for and barriers to sexual expression in this emerging environment. In order to do this, we conducted interviews and focus groups with staff and administrators in six assisted living facilities in a large southeastern city. Although limited to one city, our findings provide insight into the challenges of resident sexuality for assisted living facilities across the country.

Burgess, Elisabeth O., Alexis A. Bender and Christina Barmon. "Think You're Not Having Enough Sex? It Could Be Worse…." *The Conversation*, February 17, 2017.

A KNOCK AT THE DOOR, BUT NO DELAY

The term "older adult" is broad. It includes people 65 and beyond. Living status, health concerns, desire and other factors vary widely across this spectrum. Younger groups of older adults are more likely to be married or partnered, live independently and have more active lifestyles than older cohorts, which facilitates access to sex and intimacy.

At one end of the spectrum is the lonely, frail, cognitively impaired older adult who has no interest in or capacity for pursuing a relationship. On the other end are the frisky, swinging singles who are at risk of STDs. But in reality, sexuality in later life is much more complicated than stereotypes.

As people age, factors change. Older adults may experience their own or their partner's health conditions, a need for assistance with activities of daily living or the loss of a spouse. Because of these and other changes, an increasing number of older adults are choosing intermediate care settings, such as assisted living, which is the fastest growing segment of long-term care for older adults.

Assisted living differs from skilled nursing facilities because they are intended to provide minimal to moderate levels of help with everyday tasks in a homelike environment that emphasizes choice and control for the residents.

Most of our respondents recognized the need for sexual expression and the desire of residents to have intimate relationships. Yet the day-to-day reality restricted opportunities for intimacy. This happened in two broad ways – surveillance of resident behavior and justification for limiting sexual freedom. Surveillance was subtle and nuanced in ways that limited sexual expression.

For example, staff needing access to resident rooms to provide housekeeping or care would frequently engage in what we term "the knock and walk," whereby staff would give a cursory knock and then enter the room without waiting for a response. This act sometimes resulted in staff walking in on residents in the middle of a different act in what should have been a private space. Thus residents, even in the privacy of their rooms, had limited opportunity to engage in sexual behavior.

THE RETURN OF HALL MONITORS?

Another way that staff controlled behavior was more overt and purposeful. We found that in public spaces, such as dining and activity rooms, staff felt they had a responsibility to maintain decorum and keep the peace. As a result they actively discouraged and limited contact between people who might appear interested in pursuing a relationship.

Staff and administrators in this study cited various reasons why they limited sexual freedoms in assisted living, including safety, family concern and consent. Policies exist at the state level that hold facilities accountable for resident safety. Yet there was incredible variability in how these policies were interpreted and applied within and across facilities.

People who work in assisted living have to think about the needs of all residents in the facility and justify limitations as for the good of the whole. Because family members were frequently the ones selecting and paying for the care, staff and administrators were also concerned about family perceptions of residents' sexual behaviors.

Also of concern to administrators and staff was the health and cognitive ability of residents and how to assess the ability of residents to fully consent to sexual activity. Ethics around sexuality and dementia are still emerging and facilities tend to err on the side of protection.

At least one nursing home has been successful at creating and implementing a policy that supports sexual freedom, which could serve as a model for assisted living and other long-term care settings. The "sexual expression policy" at this facility allows residents the opportunity to be sexual and even facilitates romance through happy hours and a dating service. Some fixes are as simple as creating a "do-not-disturb" hang tag for residents' rooms.

Policies and training should address and accommodate the diversity of sexual needs and desires or older adults. Additionally, as the number of older adults with dementia in assisted living increases, staff and administrators will need to prepare for the ethical dilemmas regarding sex and dementia.

Policies and trainings on sexuality, aging and dementia have the potential to both protect the autonomy and independence of older adults in assisted living and prevent staff and administrators from acting according to stereotypes rather than the true needs of older adults. While more research is needed, we believe that all adults, regardless of age or living arrangements, should be able pursue love and intimacy.

71

Skip Fights about Digital Devices over the Holidays – Instead, Let Them Bring Your Family Together

Shelia R. Cotten

Holidays are a time for family and friends to come together, to celebrate and to enjoy each other's company. Older adults, who are often *lonely and socially isolated*, can particularly *look forward* to reconnecting with family and friends. However, when technology enters the picture, gatherings may not be quite so positive.

All across the United States, people of all ages are *increasingly using technology* – including *adults 65 and older*. My research, and that of others, has found that using computers, smartphones and the internet can help seniors *fight depression and loneliness*, and *enhance their sense of well-being and self-worth*. Technology use can also help older adults *feel like they matter to others* and help them stay connected with loved ones.

However, my research, with colleagues, has also found that older adults still *prefer in-person social interactions*. This can cause problems during holiday-season family gatherings, when younger relatives are likely to want to spend lots of time on their smartphones and other devices, often ignoring others in the same physical location. It's a conflict one of my Ph.D. students, *Christopher Ball*, has called the *"physical-digital divide."* Fortunately, our work both offers explanations for these difficulties and suggests ways to turn holiday disagreement and disappointment into increased family connection that can last all year long.

CONFLICTING FEELINGS

When they're away on family visits that can last several days, it's common for young people – tweens, teens and those in their 20s – to want to stay connected to their friends. However, older adults nearby may feel frustrated, disrespected, isolated and even offended.

In our study, older adults told us they often attempt to limit this and other negative effects of digital devices by *declaring tech-free "bubbles" at particular times or places*. They ask their friends and relatives to put devices aside during mealtimes and other key activities, to better focus on engaging with others face to face.

But that's not the only way to create a balance between using technology and interacting directly.

Cotten, Shelia. "Skip Fights about Digital Devices over the Holidays – Instead, Let Them Bring Your Family Together." *The Conversation*, December 17, 2017.

FINDING OPPORTUNITIES

Certainly there can be times when devices should be put down and in-person interaction comes first. Yet all generations can benefit when older family members see how *they can use technology to improve their own lives.*

Our work suggests that situations with potential for intergenerational conflict can be shifted to bring relatives together: Younger generations can show their older family members about technological devices.

Grandchildren, for example, can demonstrate to their grandparents how they use mobile phones, tablets and social media, explaining what they like about the technologies. It might even turn into a teaching opportunity, helping older family members learn to entertain themselves online. They might even want to find out how to text – or even video chat – with geographically distant relatives. Using these technologies can help people stay connected to friends and family once the holidays are over.

That will likely require some additional patience on the part of the younger technology coach. Older adults *learn at slower rates than younger generations.* And it may be harder for them to *remember instructions*, so they might need to be shown how to use the device or app several times. A key factor is making sure the relatives know they *can ask for help* when technical difficulties inevitably strike.

If older family members see how excited their descendants are about using digital devices, they may decide to cross the generational digital divide – which can help them live more enjoyable, connected lives not just during the holidays, but all throughout the year.

Epilogue

Future Families

The family, in its many diverse forms, will continue to matter in our lives, even as family life shifts and changes over time. How individuals function in families, how families work as units, and how the state defines and recognizes families will continue to transform. As the readings in this book show, the family is a critical place where political, economic, and social transformations land in dynamic ways.

It is hard to predict the exact changes families will undergo, or the political battles about the family that are to come. However, it is easy to expect the changes to come will reflect existing inequalities and illustrate the ways the family adapts to context. Some changes will demand legal solutions. Others may not. Examining current shifts, as this book does, offers some clues to what lies ahead for the future of the family.

MULTIGENERATIONAL HOUSEHOLDS

The number of households with members of at least two adult generations living together continues to grow in the United States. In 2016, a record 64 million people, or 20 percent of the US population, lived with multiple generations under the same roof. This growth is occurring among all US racial and ethnic groups and most age groups (Cohn and Passel 2018). This growth is notable since the population living in multigenerational households declined from 21 percent in 1950 to 12 percent in 1980 and has now risen again to almost 20 percent, and appears to be increasing. This increase is due to a range of social forces, including recessions and economic changes, limited career opportunities for young adults without a college degree, increasing costs of attending college, growth in immigrant families, and complex caregiving needs for both seniors and children (Cohn and Passel 2018). Extended life expectancy will also make these households more common.

MULTIFAMILY HOUSEHOLDS

In the coming decades, we can expect an increasing number of households consisting of people who are not legally recognized as families, but operate in familial ways. For example, economic and social conditions, including declining marriage rates and rising housing costs, may lead to increases in the number of single parent families who share households and caregiving responsibilities.

Cohousing and intentional communities are also increasing in popularity. Though they take different forms, most cohousing communities provide limited private spaces in favor of collective space oriented toward multifamily interaction. Areas that were once seen as central to the normative American home—kitchens, dining spaces, yards, and gardens—are, in these new cohousing formations, the sites for community meals and collaborative decision-making processes. Cohousing often provides some low-income units and often intentionally includes seniors. Some are built for seniors while a large number aim to accommodate multigenerational residents. This alternative housing model, which is much more popular in parts of Europe, is becoming more common in the United States. They often provide solutions to social isolation seniors experience, offer connection in a way that traditional neighborhoods and residences where seniors are aging in place do not, and provide a vision of community and family that many desire.

POLYAMOROUS AND POLYGAMOUS FAMILIES

Polyamory refers to the practice or acceptance of having multiple emotionally close relationships that may or may not be sexual in nature, with the consent of everyone involved (Balzarini et al. 2019). About 4–5 percent of individuals identify themselves as part of committed non-monogamous relationships, and about 20 percent of Americans say they have at some time been a part of an open relationship (Moors et al. 2015). Committed non-monogamy overlaps with polyamory, but also includes casual sexual relationships, whereas polyamory tends to emphasize emotional connection in relationships, even in those that are not sexual. In polyamorous relationships, individuals agree to have intimate, romantic, or sexual relationships with people outside of their existing relationships, but with disclosure and permission. Although more research is needed on how widespread committed non-monogamous and polyamorous relationships are, there are indications that the number of people entering these relationships is increasing and that they may be more common among millennials. Some research suggests that those in polyamorous relationships are more likely to identify as bisexual or pansexual and may be more gender fluid (Balzarini et al. 2019).

Polygamous families involve marriage between more than two people. People participating in polygamy may be motivated by factors that are different from those of people in polyamorous relationships, including religious or ethnic tradition. Polygamists notably want formal recognition of their relationships, including access to legal marriage. Given some small victories for polygamous families, including the decriminalization of non-legal marriage in Utah, their efforts to gain rights and recognition may succeed in coming years. We may eventually see legal recognition of plural marriage. Additionally, new state laws in about a dozen states that allow judges to recognize "tri-parents" suggest poly families are gaining legal rights, responsibilities, and recognition. More generally, we are likely to see greater social acceptance of and familiarity with polyamorous and non-monogamous relationships.

GENDER-FLUID FAMILIES

Through much of *State of Families*, we have used terms like same-sex marriage to denote how the law frames changes in marriage. As individuals increasingly reject gender binaries, we should expect to see more families that reflect gender fluidity. Laws like the Uniform Parentage Act, which was originally written for unwed fathers, have in the past decade been revised to be gender neutral and courts are already showing a willingness to open once narrow definitions of gender in the family. Children too are finding greater support for self-expressions that are gender fluid and schools are increasingly adopting gender-affirming practices. In myriad ways, the family is already becoming more flexible, more adaptive, and more gender-queer. Given that young adults are driving many challenges to the gender binary, we can anticipate that the family will also shift to reflect their views and values.

MULTIPARENT FAMILIES

As we have seen through the readings, formal definitions of families as related by blood, marriage, or adoption may be outdated. Reproductive technologies, open adoption, remarriage, childbearing outside of marriage, and non-monogamous relationships can yield more than two adults who want rights and are also willing to assume responsibility for children. To date, legal systems—even with greater flexibility in some places—have with few exceptions continued to insist that only two parents can be legally recognized. As families become increasingly complex, lawmakers and judges are beginning to recognize "tri-parenting" or grant parental rights to additional adults. Although these cases still appear to be rare, they will likely become more common as families and households continue to change. Additionally, lawmakers may eventually opt to locate new legal spaces for additional adults who want relationships with children, even if not full parental rights. This could mean developing legal categories for tiered parental rights and responsibilities, creating processes that could grant visitation rights to those who are not primary parents, such as estranged stepparents or long-term care providers, or systems to evaluate the best interests of children that consider the value of multiple adult relationships. Doing so could do a great deal to ensure children's emotional and physical needs are satisfied.

RACIALLY DIVERSE FAMILIES

Families are increasingly racially diverse. Between 2000 and 2017, the percentage of 5- to 17-year-olds who were white decreased from 62 to 51. The greatest increases have been among Hispanic and Latino-identified youth, whose percentage increased from 16 to 25 (Brey et al. 2019). In the 1980s, African Americans were the largest racial group after whites. Today, fewer than 14 percent of children under 17 are Black (Frey 2019).

Interracial and interethnic marriage is also increasing. In 2000, 7 percent of married couples were interracial or interethnic. From 2012 to 2016, that number grew to 10 percent. By 2015, about 17 percent of spouses identified as from different racial or ethnic groups (Mather and Lee 2020). By 2060, about 6 percent of the population and 11 percent of children under the age of 18 years will likely be multiracial (Mather and Lee 2020). In general, kids born after 1997 are more racially diverse than millennials (Frey 2019).

These rapid changes in the racial and ethnic composition of young people underscore transformations in the family. Despite increasing diversity, racial inequality continues to present a significant challenge. In 2017, about 17 percent of children under age 18 lived in poverty. Children of color are more likely to live in poverty and rates of poverty for children of color have increased. In 1976, just over half of children in poverty were Black or Hispanic. By 2016, Black and Hispanic children represented about 63 percent of children in poverty (Wilson and Schieder 2018). Moving forward, ensuring equal access to power and resources, including equity in education and opportunity, will be essential to strengthening and supporting all families.

TECHNOLOGICALLY CONNECTED FAMILIES

Technology has changed the way families interact and connect. Whether it is a divorced father Skyping with his daughter, enlisted military personnel stationed overseas speaking to her spouse stateside, a recent immigrant sending remittances via Venmo, or a family having a birthday party or memorial over Zoom because of a pandemic, families are using technology to meet a wide variety of needs in novel and evolving ways.

One in five children has a cell phone by the time they are eight years old, and more than half of all children have a cell phone by the time they turn 11 (Kamanetz 2019). In some ways, mobile devices can cause conflict and undermine sleep for people of all ages. Yet, there are signs that parents and children are having less conflict about cell phones than in the past (Robb 2019). In fact, young people connect with their parents via their smartphones at increasing rates. As young people today age, technological communication will be even more routine for them, which will inevitably play a sizeable role in their family relationships.

The United States still has a significant digital divide. People in low-income neighborhoods and rural communities have less access to broadband internet. About 29 percent of adults with household incomes below $30,000 a year don't own a smartphone, 44 percent don't have broadband internet services, and 46 percent don't own a laptop or desktop computer. These technologies are nearly ubiquitous among adults in households earning $100,000 or more a year (Anderson 2017). Those in rural communities are about 12 percent less likely to have home broadband than the country as a whole, which is a notable improvement from 2007 when the gap was closer to 16 percent, but still represents a significant limitation. People with disabilities are also less likely be online (Anderson and Perrin 2017). Whether the digital divide persists or narrows will have significant effects on communities in terms of their engagement with economics, politics, education, and social life. These forces will inevitably affect family life.

QUESTIONING CLAIMS ABOUT THE FAMILY

Family change is not without controversy. As families change in response to economic, social, cultural, and political shifts, there will most certainly be calls for laws and policies to change, control, or redefine the family. Some will likely draw on nostalgia for a version of the past in which there was less diversity or more traditional gender roles. These calls for a return to the past typically ignore the ways inequality was common and romanticize a past that was not as tranquil as imagined. Others will argue that family should be changed to recognize anyone who functions as a family or to make boundaries of family increasingly permeable.

As educated community members, each of us has a responsibility to question claims about the family and to examine proposals about the family. Campaigns to broaden formal recognition of families should make clear the ways rights and responsibilities are bound together. Individuals should not gain privileges in a family without also accepting the obligations that accompany family life. Claims or proposals that further inequality should also be met with suspicion. We will each bring our own perspectives, values, and experiences to the process of evaluating claims about the family. Nonetheless, we can each weigh in on supporting policies that allow everyone's families to thrive.

References

Anderson, Monica. 2017. "Digital Divide Persists Even as Lower-Income Americans Make Gains in Tech Adoption." Pew Research Center.

Anderson, Monica and Andrew Perrin. 2017. "Disabled Americans Are Less Likely to Use Technology." Pew Research Center. (https://www.pewresearch.org/fact-tank/2017/04/07/disabled-americans-are-less-likely-to-use-technology/).

Balzarini, R. N., C. Dharma, T. Kohut, B. M. Holmes, L. Campbell, J. J. Lehmiller and J. J. Harman. 2019. "Demographic Comparison of American Individuals in Polyamorous and Monogamous Relationships." *Journal of Sex Research* 56(6):681–694. doi: 10.1080/00224499.2018.1474333.

Brey, Cristobal de, Lauren Musu, Joel McFarland, Sidney Wilkinson-Flicker, Melissa Diliberti, Anlan Zhang, Claire Branstetter and Xiaolei Wang. 2019. "Status and Trends in the Education of Racial and Ethnic Groups 2018." NCES 2019038. National Center for Education Statistics.

Cohn, D'Vera and Jeffrey S. Passel. 2018. "A Record 64 Million Americans Live in Multigenerational Households." Pew Research Center. (https://www.pewresearch.org/fact-tank/2018/04/05/a-record-64-million-americans-live-in-multigenerational-households/).

Frey, William H. 2019. "Less Than Half of Us Children under 15 Are White, Census Shows." Brookings Institute. (https://www.brookings.edu/research/less-than-half-of-us-children-under-15-are-white-census-shows/).

Kamanetz, Anya. 2019. "It's a Smartphone Life: More than Half of U.S. Children Now Have One." NPR. (https://www.npr.org/2019/10/31/774838891/its-a-smartphone-life-more-than-half-of-u-s-children-now-have-one#:~:text=Just%20over%20half%20of%20children, lot%20of%20decoding%20to%20understand).

Mather, Mark and Amanda Lee. 2020. "Children Are at the Forefront of U.S. Racial and Ethnic Change." (https://www.prb.org/children-are-at-the-forefront-of-u-s-racial-and-ethnic-change/).

Moors, Amy C., Terri D. Conley, Robin S. Edelstein and William J. Chopik. 2015. "Attached to Monogamy? Avoidance Predicts Willingness to Engage (but Not Actual Engagement) in Consensual Non-Monogamy." *Journal of Social and Personal Relationships* 32(2):222–240.

Robb, Michael B. 2019. "The New Normal: Parents, Teens, Screens, and Sleep." Common Sense Media. (https://www.commonsensemedia.org/sites/default/files/uploads/research/2019-new-normal-parents-teens-screens-and-sleep-united-states-report.pdf).

Wilson, Valerie and Jessica Schieder. 2018. "The Rise in Child Poverty Reveals Racial Inequality, More than a Failed War on Poverty." Economic Policy Institute. (https://www.epi.org/publication/the-rise-in-child-poverty-reveals-racial-inequality-more-than-a-failed-war-on-poverty/).

Original Citations for Selections

Acosta, Katie L. "The Language of (In) Visibility: Using in-between Spaces as a Vehicle for Empowerment in the Family." *Journal of Homosexuality* 58, no. 6–7 (2011): 883–900.

Ault, Michael K. and Bobbi Van Gilder. "Polygamy in the United States: How Marginalized Religious Communities Cope with Stigmatizing Discourses Surrounding Plural Marriage." *Journal of Intercultural Communication Research* 44, no. 4 (2015): 307–328.

Badgett, M.V. Lee, Soon Kyu Choi and Bianca D.M. Wilson. "LGBT Poverty in the United States: A Study of Differences between Sexual Orientation and Gender Identity Groups." Williams Institute, UCLA School of Law.

Batabyal, Amitrajeet A. "What Meeting Your Spouse Online Has in Common with Arranged Marriage." April 4, 2018.

Bailey, Beth. "From Front Porch to Back Seat: A History of the Date." *OAH Magazine of History* 18, no. 4 (2004): 23–26.

Bazaz, Aggie Ebrahimi. "Missing School Is a Given for Children of Migrant Farmworkers." *The Conversation* April 26, 2019.

Berkowitz, Dana. "'It Was the Cadillac of Adoption Agencies': Intersections of Social Class, Race, and Sexuality in Gay Men's Adoption Narratives." *Journal of GLBT Family Studies* 7, no. 1–2 (2011): 109–131.

Blackstone, Amy. "Childless… or Childfree?" *Contexts* 13, no. 4 (2014): 68–70.

Bowen, Sarah, Sinikka Elliott, and Joslyn Brenton. "The Joy of Cooking?" *Contexts* 13, no. 3 (2014): 20–25.

Budnick, Jamie. "Straight Girls Do Kiss on Campus, But What about Those Who Don't Go To College?" October 13, 2016.

Burgess, Elisabeth O., Alexis A. Bender and Christina Barmon. "Think You're Not Having Enough Sex? It Could Be Worse…." *The Conversation* February 17, 2017.

Cairns, Kate, Norah MacKendrick and Josée Johnston. "The 'Organic Child' Ideal Holds Mothers to an Impossible Standard." *Aeon* February 19, 2020.

Calarco, Jessica. "When 'Helicopters' Go to School: Who Gets Rescued and Who Gets Left Behind?" *CCF News* March 1, 2020.

Carten, Alma. "How Racism Has Shaped Welfare Policy in America since 1935." *The Conversation* August 21, 2016.

Cooney, Teresa M., Christine M. Proulx, Linley A. Snyder-Rivas, and Jacquelyn J. Benson. "Role Ambiguity among Women Providing Care for Ex-husbands." *Journal of Women & Aging* 26, no. 1 (2014): 84–104.

Cotten, Shelia. "Skip Fights about Digital Devices over the Holidays – Instead, Let them Bring Your Family Together." *The Conversation* December 17, 2017.

Cross, Gary. "Where Has Teen Car Culture Gone?" *The Atlantic* May 27, 2018.

Czarnecki, Danielle. "Moral Women, Immoral Technologies: How Devout Women Negotiate Gender, Religion, and Assisted Reproductive Technologies." *Gender & Society* 29, no. 5 (2015): 716–742.

DePaulo, Bella. "More People than Ever before Are Single – And that's a Good Thing." *The Conversation* April 23, 2017.

Dow, Dawn Marie. "The Deadly Challenges of Raising African American Boys: Navigating the Controlling Image of the 'Thug'." *Gender & Society* 30, no. 2 (2016): 161–188.

Elliott, Sinikka. "'If I Could Really Say that and Get Away with It!' Accountability and Ambivalence in American Parents' Sexuality Lessons in the Age of Abstinence." *Sex Education* 10, no. 3 (2010): 239–250.

Frederick, Angela. "Mothering while Disabled." *Contexts* 13, no. 4 (2014): 30–35.

Gold, Joshua. "Navigating the Tricky Waters of Being a Stepdad." *The Conversation* June 15, 2017.

Goltz, Heather Honoré and Matthew Lee Smith. "Think Teens Need the Sex Talk? Older Adults May Need It Even More." *The Conversation* December 13, 2018.

Gunderman, Richard and Lily Wolf. "Could Different Cultures Teach Us Something about Dementia?" *The Conversation* August 17, 2018.

Foster, Diana Greene, Rana E. Barar, and Heather Gould. "New Evidence about Women's Experience with Abortion." *Scholars Strategy Network* May 25, 2016.

Haeder, Simon. "Born in the USA: Having a Baby Is Costly and Confusing, Even for a Health Policy Expert." *The Conversation* July 16, 2018.

Hagerman, Margaret Ann. "White Families and Race: Colour-blind and Colour-conscious Approaches to White Racial Socialization." *Ethnic and Racial Studies* 37, no. 14 (2014): 2598–2614.

Healy, Kieran. "Rituals of Childhood." https://kieranhealy.org/blog/archives/2019/08/03/rituals-of-childhood

Johnson, Matthew. "Have Children? Here's How Kids Ruin Your Romantic Relationship." *The Conversation* May 5, 2016.

Jordan, Tara. "Why Fewer and Fewer Americans Are Getting Divorced." *The Conversation* May 30, 2019.

Katz, Vikki S. "What It Means to be 'under-connected' in Lower-Income Families." *Journal of Children and Media* 11, no. 2 (2017): 241–244.

Kaufman, Gayle. "Fathers Also Want to 'Have It All,' Study Says." *The Conversation* June 15, 2016.

Kittay, Eva Feder. "Not My Way, Sesha, Your Way, Slowly." In *Love's Labor: Essays on Women, Equality and Dependency.* Routledge, 1999.

Lens, Vicki, and Colleen Cary. "Negotiating the Discourse of Race within the United States Welfare System." *Ethnic and Racial Studies* 33, no. 6 (2010): 1032–1048.

Littlejohn, Krystale. "Why Coverage of Prescription Contraception Matters for Men as Well as Women." *Scholars Strategy Network* August 21, 2017

Loe, Meika. "Doing It My Way: Old Women, Technology and Wellbeing." *Sociology of Health & Illness* 32, no. 2 (2010): 319–334.

Longo, Gina Marie. "Mothers and Moneymakers: How Gender Norms Shape US Marriage Migration Politics." *Gender & Society Blog.* August 3, 2018

Loughran, Tracey. "Infertility through the Ages – and How IVF Changed the Way We Think about It." *The Conversation* May 1, 2018

Luther, Kate. "Stigma Management among Children of Incarcerated Parents." *Deviant Behavior* 37, no. 11 (2016): 1264–1275.

Meadow, Tey. "For the Parents of Gender-nonconforming Kids, a New Approach to Care." *The Conversation* August 29, 2018.

Milanich, Nara. "Who's Your Daddy? Don't Ask a DNA Test." *The Conversation* June 13, 2019.

Miller, Lisa R. "The Perils and Pleasures of Aging: How Women's Sexualities Change across the Life Course." *The Sociological Quarterly* 60, no. 3 (2019): 371–396.

Minow, Martha. "Redefining Families: Who's In and Who's Out." *University of Colorado Law Review* 62 (1991): 269.

Montgomery, Mark and Irene Powell. "International Adoptions Have Dropped 72 Percent since 2005 – Here's Why." *The Conversation* February 28, 2018.

Morell, Carolyn Mackelcan. *Unwomanly Conduct: The Challenges of Intentional Childlessness.* New York: Routledge, 1994.

Natalier, Kristin. "What Type of Relationship Should I Have with My Co-parent Now We're Divorced?" *The Conversation* August 29, 2018.

Pfeffer, Carla A. "'Women's Work'? Women Partners of Transgender Men doing Housework and Emotion Work." *Journal of Marriage and Family* 72, no. 1 (2010): 165–183.

Raine-Fenning, Nicholas. "Hard Evidence: Does Fertility Really 'Drop Off a Cliff' at 35?" *The Conversation* July 15, 2014.

Randles, Jennifer. "The Diaper Dilemma." *Contexts* 16, no. 4 (2017): 66–68.

Rank, Mark R. "As American as Apple Pie: Poverty and Welfare." *Contexts* 2, no. 3 (2003): 41–49.

Reich, Jennifer. "Biology and Conformity: Expectations of Fathers in Reunification." In *Fixing Families: Parents, Power, and the Child Welfare System.* New York, NY: Routledge, 2005.

Reich, Jennifer. "I've Talked to Dozens of Parents about Why They Don't Vaccinate. Here's What They Told Me." Vox. com June 13, 2019.

Rodriguez, Maria and Jens Hainmuelle. "Immigration Policies Can Make the Difference between Life and Death for Newborn US Children." *The Conversation* April 25, 2018.

Romero, Diana and Madina Agénor. "Why Policies Meant to Discourage Poor Women from Having Children are Ineffective and Punitive." *Scholars Strategy Network* July 13, 2018.

Rothman, Barbara Katz. "Beyond Mothers and Fathers: Ideology in a Patriarchal Society." In *Mothering,* pp. 139–157. New York, NY: Routledge, 2016.

Ryan, Maura, and Amanda Moras. "Race Matters in Lesbian Donor Insemination: Whiteness and Heteronormativity as Co-constituted Narratives." *Ethnic and Racial Studies* 40, no. 4 (2017): 579–596.

Singh, Shailen. "I Am Who I Need to Be: Reflections on Parental Identity Development from a Father of a Child with Disabilities." *Disability & Society* 34, no. 5 (2019): 837–841.

Solinger, Rickie. *Wake up Little Susie: Single Pregnancy and Race before Roe v. Wade.* New York: NY: Routledge, 2013.

Syrett, Nicholas. "Child Marriage Is Still Legal in the US." *The Conversation* December 11, 2017.

Tesler, Pauline H. "Can This Relationship Be Saved? The Legal Profession and Families in Transition." *Family Court Review* 55, no. 1 (2017): 38–58.

Torres, Stacy. "Aging in Places." In *Critical Gerontology Comes of Age,* Chris Wellin (ed), pp. 151–162. New York, NY: Routledge, 2018.

Trussell, Dawn E., and Susan M. Shaw. "Organized Youth Sport and Parenting in Public and Private Spaces." *Leisure Sciences* 34, no. 5 (2012): 377–394.

Turner, Lynn H., and Richard West. "The Challenge of Defining 'family.'" In *The SAGE Handbook of Family Communication,* Lynn H. Turner and Richard West (eds), 10–25. Thousand Oaks, CA: Sage Publishing, 2015.

Twenge, Jean. "Why Today's Teens Aren't in Any Hurry to Grow Up." *The Conversation* September 19, 2017.

Valenti, Jessica. "Kids Don't Damage Women's Careers—Men Do." *Medium.com* September 13, 2018.

Wade, Lisa. "What's So Cultural about Hookup Culture?" *Contexts* 16, no. 1 (2017): 66–68.

Walters, Suzanna Danuta. "The Trouble with Tolerance." *Contexts* 13, no. 2 (2014): 87–90.

Wang, Leslie Kim, Iris Chin Ponte, and Elizabeth Weber Ollen. "Letting Her Go: Western Adoptive Families' Search and Reunion with Chinese Birth Parents." *Adoption Quarterly* 18, no. 1 (2015): 45–66.

Weber, Shannon. "What It's Like to Get a Queer Divorce after Fighting for Marriage Equality." *The Body Is Not an Apology* February 17, 2018.

Zinn, Maxine Baca. "Family, Feminism, and Race in America." *Gender & Society* 4, no. 1 (1990): 68–82.

Index